# THE ECONOMIC HISTORY
## OF ENGLAND

*BY E. LIPSON*

THE ECONOMIC HISTORY OF ENGLAND
VOL. I. THE MIDDLE AGES  *Tenth edition*
VOLS. II. AND III.  THE AGE OF MERCANTILISM
*Fifth edition*

THE HISTORY OF THE
WOOLLEN AND WORSTED INDUSTRIES

EUROPE IN THE XIXTH CENTURY: 1815–1914 *
*Ninth edition*

EUROPE 1914–1939 *
*Fifth edition*

A PLANNED ECONOMY OR FREE ENTERPRISE
THE LESSONS OF HISTORY
*Second edition*

\* These two also in one volume, *Europe in the
Nineteenth and Twentieth Centuries*

*ADAM & CHARLES BLACK: LONDON*

*Australia and New Zealand*
THE OXFORD UNIVERSITY PRESS, MELBOURNE
*Canada*
THE MACMILLAN COMPANY OF CANADA, TORONTO
*South Africa*
THE OXFORD UNIVERSITY PRESS, CAPE TOWN
*India and Burma*
MACMILLAN AND COMPANY LIMITED
BOMBAY     CALCUTTA     MADRAS

# THE ECONOMIC HISTORY
# OF ENGLAND

BY

## E. LIPSON

VOLUME III

## THE AGE OF MERCANTILISM

Fifth edition

ῥεῖ τὰ πάντα

ADAM AND CHARLES BLACK
4, 5 & 6 SOHO SQUARE LONDON W.1
1948

FIRST EDITION 1931     SECOND EDITION 1934
THIRD EDITION, ENLARGED, 1943
FOURTH EDITION 1947
FIFTH EDITION 1948

MADE IN GREAT BRITAIN
PRINTED BY R. & R. CLARK LTD EDINBURGH

# CONTENTS

## VOLUME III

### CHAPTER IV

### CHAPTER V

### CHAPTER VI

# ECONOMIC HISTORY

## CHAPTER IV

### THE MERCANTILE SYSTEM

THE term ' Mercantile System ' is generally employed to *Definition* indicate the commercial policy of the State in the sixteenth, *of the Mercantile* seventeenth and eighteenth centuries [1]. The use of the term *System.* is apt to be misleading : it suggests the systematic working out of a national economic system based on precise and definite principles. In reality the policy of the State was primarily dictated by the needs of an ever-changing environment. The fact that the term was not used by sixteenth or seventeenth-century writers [2] warns us against the attempt to give formal shape and substance to what was largely nebulous and opportunist. Nevertheless the Mercantile System serves as a convenient phrase to express a trend of thought. Broadly speaking, Mercantilism denoted the pursuit of economic power in the sense of economic self-sufficiency [3]. Its underlying idea was to establish the power or strength of a State by making it independent of other States in the economic sphere. This implied that a community must normally produce its own requirements in the shape of food and manufactured goods, and in so far as it exchanged its commodities for those of other countries it must keep the carrying trade in its own hands. The Corn Laws, the Protection of Industry and the Navigation Acts

[1] For the relation of Mercantilism to mediaeval urban economy, see *supra*, vol. i. 264-265, 307 (note 9), 455 ; vol. ii. Introduction, pp. lxxxvi-lxxxvii.

[2] I have not noticed any use of the term in sixteenth or seventeenth-century literature, and if not unknown it was at least extremely rare.

[3] For the term ' power ', see *infra*, p. 2, note 4 ; and for ' economic self-sufficiency ', see *infra*, Appendix, p. 489, No. 1.

thus constitute the three pillars of the Mercantile System, which in this respect may be considered an organic whole The prominence often assigned to discussions on treasure has tended to foster a distorted view of Mercantilism as though its basic principle was grounded upon a confusion of money with wealth [1]. We shall endeavour to show that the Mercantilists did not mistake the real nature of wealth [2]; and the stress laid upon the accumulation of treasure, not unintelligible in the circumstances of the period [3], must not be allowed to obscure the more permanent and fundamental aspects of mercantilist thought.

*Contact between politics and economics.* We have said that economic self-sufficiency was the kernel of Mercantilism. The end in view was primarily defence rather than aggression, though in the carrying out of the system it tended inevitably to assume the appearance of an aggressive economic nationalism. The development of the national resources was intended to promote national security, and ' consideration of power ' took precedence over ' consideration of plenty ' [4]. The most noteworthy example of the contact between politics and economics was the protection afforded to agriculture, where a definite attempt was made by artificial expedients such as bounties to check the diversion of capital into other and more lucrative channels [5]. In like manner the argument for fostering a native iron industry was a political one : " If there should be occasion for great quantities of guns and bullet and other sorts of iron commodities for a present unexpected war, and the Sound happen to be locked up and so prevent iron coming to us, truly we should then be in a fine case ! " [6]. In its pursuit of economic self-sufficiency Mercantilism was the antithesis of Free Trade, which rests upon the conception of an international division of labour. And critics were not

---

[1] *The Oxford English Dictionary, s.v.* Mercantile, gives the following definition : " *Mercantile System* : a term used by Adam Smith and later Political Economists for the system of economic doctrine and legislative policy based on the principle that money alone constituted wealth. Hence *mercantile school* : those who upheld this system ".

[2] *Infra*, p. 65.                    [3] *Infra*, p. 67.

[4] This antithesis between ' power ' and ' plenty ' is Bacon's : *supra*, vol. i. 592.         [5] *Supra*, vol. ii. 453.

[6] Yarranton, *England's Improvement* (1677), 63.

wanting, even in the seventeenth century, to condemn the doctrine. " To say, as many are apt to do, that England can live of itself without the assistance of any foreign nation is to give it not the least commendation beyond any other country. But to say, and that truly, that England by the industry of its inhabitants employed in shipping, plantations, mines, manufactures, pastures and tillage, doth not only abound in all sorts of commodities as native meat, drink, clothes, houses and coaches, fit for the necessities, ease and ornaments of life, but can outvy most nations of the world for the vast plenty in varieties of wines, spices, drugs, fruits, silks, pictures, music, silver, gold, precious stones and all other supports of grandeur and delight, that is to speak it a truly civilized and glorious nation indeed "[1]. The mercantilist school did not, of course, object to international trade although there was a tendency to measure its value by the test of a favourable balance, which was sometimes considered the only true source of a country's wealth [2]. None of the mercantilist writers, however, worked out their theories to a logical conclusion, and their *obiter dicta* must not be pressed too hard [3].

The Mercantile System lends itself to criticism on three grounds [3a]. In the first place, it involved the pursuit of aims which were mutually contradictory. The Navigation Acts were intended to foster seamanship but they hampered industry and trade [4]. The protection given to one branch of manufacture often reacted injuriously upon other branches ; the product of one industry was the raw material of another ; and a further complication was introduced when the prohibition of a foreign article reduced the demand abroad for the English wares sent in exchange [5]. Trade was expected to follow the flag [6] ; yet, instead of trusting to the operation

*Criticisms of the Mercantile System.*

---

[1] Thomas, *An Historical Account of the Rise and Growth of the West India Colonies* (1690), in *Harleian Miscellany* (ed. Malham), ix. 410.

[2] Davenant, *Works* (ed. 1771), i. 13, 386. See *infra*, p. 88.

[3] Their terminology may sometimes be a source of confusion, *e.g.* their use of the word ' wealth ', etc.—*infra*, Appendix, p. 490, No. 1.

[3a] For an estimate of the Mercantile System, see *supra*, vol. ii. Introduction, pp. xciii-c.

[4] *Infra*, p. 132.      [5] *Infra*, pp. 17, 19-20.

[6] " Trade has been ever observed to follow power " : Davenant, *Works* (ed. 1771), v. 457. The converse (' The flag follows trade ') was stated by Barbon, *A discourse of Trade* (1690), 40, in the words : " Trade may be assistant to the enlarging of Empire ".

of economic forces to achieve this, restrictions were imposed upon the colonies, which served to limit rather than to extend their capacity to consume the products of the mother country [1]. In the second place, Mercantilism established false standards. It taught men to look with jealousy upon the economic prosperity of their neighbours, to measure their own riches by comparison with those of other nations, and to believe that whatever weakened or depopulated other countries enriched and strengthened our own [2]. It failed to recognize that a trading nation benefits by having wealthy customers, and that the impoverishment even of a competitor breaks the circle of commerce and affects adversely every part of it. Even Petty went astray when he propounded a view of international trade analogous to the work-fund theory : " There is but a certain proportion of trade in the world " [3]. The conception of a fixed volume of trade implied that the economic progress of one nation was achieved at the expense of the rest, and that its elimination would automatically enable its rivals to grasp a larger share for themselves. The elastic nature of trade warns us against such facile assumptions. In the third place, the mercantilist school regarded the strict regimentation of economic life as the province of the State at a time when the machinery of government was primitive and a civil service hardly existed, and when the spirit of corruption (especially in the eighteenth century) pervaded the legislature and the executive. The ambitious economic programmes which are enshrined in the pages of the statute-book remained largely paper programmes, because the State lacked adequate resources to give them substance [4]. Yet the fact that they proved unworkable must not lead us to infer that the principles which they embodied were devoid of justification. The system of State control had behind it the weight of a

[1] *Infra*, pp. 172 *seq.*

[2] Coke, *Treatise* (1675), iii. 45 ; *Britannia Languens* (1680), 140 (in sect. ix.) ; *A Treatise wherein is demonstrated that the East India Trade is the most national of all Foreign Trades. By* Φιλοπάτρις (1681), 7 ; Hume, *Essays* (ed. Green and Grose), i. 345 ; *Annals of Agriculture*, iv. 17.

[3] Petty, *Economic Writings*, ii. 354. A similar view is implied in Davenant, *Works* (ed. 1771), ii. 12. See also *infra*, Appendix, p. 490, No. 2.

[4] *Supra*, vol. ii. 441 ; *infra*, pp. 319, 445, and Appendix, p. 491, No. 1.

powerful tradition, which did not consider public and private *Antithesis* interests as identical[1a], and declared that "private advantages *of public and private* are often impediments of public profit "[1]. It was urged, in *interests.* particular, that certain forms of trade may be beneficial to the merchant but hurtful to the nation [2]. " What does the merchant care, so that he be rich, how poor the public is ? Let the commonwealth sink, so that he gets his profit "[3]. This antithesis between public and private interests was a commonplace of mercantilist literature—and it was admitted by Adam Smith himself [4]. Those who did not share the traditional view were in a minority. Sir Dudley North, for example, claimed that there could be no trade unprofitable to the public, " for if any prove so men leave it off, and wherever the traders thrive the public of which they are a part thrives also ". He opposed State control on the ground that public regulations issued for the good of trade in general seldom proved other than prejudicial. In a striking passage, the most signal expression of the revolt against Mercantilism, he remarked : " Thus we may labour to hedge in the cuckoo but in vain, for no people ever yet grew rich by policies ; but it is peace, industry and freedom that brings trade and wealth, and nothing else "[5]. And North was only one of a group of early writers who, a century before the classical economists, pressed for the removal of the obstructions to trade such as the privileges of the trading companies, the rights of freemen in boroughs, the restrictions imposed by the Statute of Apprentices, and the disabilities laid upon Dissenters [6].

None the less, when due weight has been given to the *Other* foregoing considerations, the critic of Mercantilism must *considerations.* take into account two things. Throughout the sixteenth,

---

[1a] On this point, see *supra*, vol. ii. Introduction, pp. lxxiv-lxxv.

[1] Fortrey, *England's Interest and Improvement* (1663), 3.

[2] *Britannia Languens* (1680), 11 ; *The British Merchant* (ed. 1721), i. 1. For ' hurtful ' forms of trade, see *infra*, p. 14.

[3] *State Papers Domestic*, 1651–1652, p. 263. Similarly : Coke, *Treatise* (1671), i. 84-85 ; Child, *A New Discourse of Trade* (4th ed.), pp. xl-xli.

[4] This is sometimes overlooked. Cf. his attack on manufacturers in *The Wealth of Nations* (ed. Cannan), ii. 159-160.

[5] North, *Discourses upon Trade* (1691), pp. viii (Preface), v (Postscript). See also *infra*, Appendix, p. 491, No. 2.

[6] *E.g. Britannia Languens* (1680), sect. vi. and vii. ; Coke, *Treatise* (1675), iii. 46.

seventeenth and eighteenth centuries, as indeed before and since, statesmen were confronted with practical problems which they could only handle within the limitations set by the circumstances of their age. They could not lightly free themselves from the trammels of tradition. We are apt to judge earlier centuries by the standard of our own, and to overlook the fact that the change of outlook on which we pride ourselves has been largely the necessary consequence of a change of conditions. The advance of economic thought proceeds, as a rule, in close relation to the requirements of the existing economic system. Moreover the Government in its economic administration often showed a more liberal spirit than might be inferred from a literal reading of the sentiments expressed by contemporary writers. Of this some important examples will be given below [1].

*Criteria of prosperity.*   The intervention of the State in the affairs of economic life made it necessary to establish a standard whereby to measure national progress. Hence arose a question of fundamental importance : what constituted the ' criteria of the riches or poverty of a country ' ? [2]   On this subject mercantilist writers voiced the most divergent opinions. Some laid stress upon ' the plenty or scarcity of money '. " It is a true rule ", declared Sir Thomas Roe (1641), that " if money increase the kingdom doth gain by trade ; if it be scarce it loseth " [3]. " The barometer of the general trade of a nation ", observed Decker, " is its mint " [4]. Others applied the test of the balance of trade : it was held that a country was enriched or impoverished accordingly as exports exceeded imports or the converse [5]. A third indication was the rise and fall of the customs, though Roger Coke pointed out that if the ' greatness of the customs ' arose not from the ' greatness of the trade ' but from the ' greatness of the impositions ', then ' the higher the customs the worse the trade ' [6]. Child thought that " the increase and diminution

---

[1] *Infra*, pp. 71, 73, 125, 195, 354.   [2] Tucker, *Instructions* (ed. 1757), 58.
[3] *Sir Thomas Roe's Speech* (1641) in *Harleian Miscellany* (ed. Malham), iv. 456. Similarly : Gee, *The Trade and Navigation of Great Britain* (ed. 1730), 118.
[4] Decker, *Essay on the Causes of the Decline of the Foreign Trade* (ed. 1744), 2.    [5] *Infra*, pp. 85 *seq.*    [6] Coke, *Treatise* (1671), i. 85.

of our trade and shipping in general " furnished the best index to the condition of foreign trade ; yet his main criterion ' whether any country be rich or poor ' was the rate of interest [1]. Locke, again, believed that " an infallible sign of your decay of wealth is the falling of rents " [2]. Davenant coupled together interest and land as the standard of measurement : " In all rising nations in the world the price of land is high and interest is low " [3]. A gauge seldom applied was the level of wages : " Wherever wages are high . . . it is an infallible evidence of the riches of that country " [4].

The prosperity of England was judged not only by the criteria already mentioned—the balance of trade, the rate of interest, and the rise or fall in rents—but above all by comparison with the progress of other countries. In the sixteenth century Englishmen measured themselves with Spain, in the seventeenth with Holland, in the eighteenth with France, and in the nineteenth with Germany. They scrutinized carefully the condition of their rivals in the light of their own advantages and shortcomings : and the example of other nations was constantly held up to them as a pattern on which to model their own economic activities. As a consequence the Continent exercised in various ways a profound influence on English economic development [5]. *Comparison with other countries.*

Our natural advantages figured prominently in the comparisons made with other countries [5a]. " No kingdom so happy as ours ", said a member of Parliament in 1621, " by situation, by seas, rivers, staple commodities " [6]. England possessed a multitude of safe and convenient harbours ; an abundance of natural products—corn, wool, lead, tin, copper, coal, leather, and timber for shipping ' the best in *England's advantages.*

[1] Child, *A New Discourse of Trade* (4th ed.), 12, 176, 179. See *infra*, p. 226.

[2] Locke, *Works* (ed. 1801), v. 69.

[3] Davenant, *Works* (ed. 1771), i. 358-359. Similarly : Tucker, *Instructions* (ed. 1757), 58 *seq.*

[4] Child, *A New Discourse of Trade* (4th ed.), p. xi. Cf. *infra*, pp. 204 (note 3), 273 (note 3), 491 (No. 3).

[5] Cf. *infra*, p. 11.

[5a] See also *supra*, vol. ii. Introduction, p. xcvii.

[6] *House of Commons Journals*, i. 636. See also *Hist. MSS. Comm.* iii. 68 (? 1626) ; Mun, *England's Treasure by Forraign Trade* (ed. 1664), 176 ; J. B., *An Account of the French Usurpation upon the Trade of England* (1679), 21 ; *The British Merchant* (ed. 1721), i. p. xxxiii.

the world '; a coast enriched with fisheries ' more worth than the King of Spain's West Indies '; inhabitants ' stout and valiant, accompanied with a lively wit and healthful constitution'[1]; merchants' the most generous and honourable in trade'[2], whose profession was deemed 'full as honourable as that of an officer '[3]; manufacturers distinguished for their skill and ingenuity, whose fabrics clothed ' half of Europe '[4], and whose 'locks, chains, clockwork, mathematical instruments and all sorts of cutlery ware far exceed all others '[5]; sailors famed for their dexterity; adventurous pioneers filled with an enterprising spirit which ' compassed all the globe to make discoveries and obtain settlements in the New World '[6]. And she enjoyed inestimable benefits of another kind—the reign of law secured the liberty and property of the individual; the stability of the political institutions maintained the public credit [7]; freedom from foreign invasion, violent turmoil, industrial restrictions [8] and internal tariffs [8a], promoted the increase of wealth ; the fiscal system enabled the national revenue to expand automatically with the growth of trade ; the rise of a banking system afforded opportunities for the accumulation and employment of capital. Hence the conclusion drawn by a seventeenth-century writer that " no nation in the world is naturally so adapted for a mighty trade of all sorts as England " [9].

*Spain.* Spain, in spite of her possession of silver mines in the New World, was considered even in the sixteenth century inferior to England ' in people, in victual, in munition, in shipping '[10]. She served primarily to afford a warning of the

---

[1] Coke, *Treatise* (1671), ii. Preface.
[2] Decker, *Essay on the Causes of the Decline of the Foreign Trade* (ed. 1744), 42.          [3] Tucker, *An Essay on Trade* (ed. 1753), 34.
[4] *Supra*, vol. ii. 187.          [5] Tucker, *op. cit.* 34.
[6] Davenant, *Works* (ed. 1771), v. 393.
[7] *Hist. MSS. Comm. Various*, viii. 298.
[8] The degree of freedom here varied in different localities : *infra*, pp. 344 *seq.*          [8a] See *infra*, Appendix, p. 491, No. 4.
[9] *Britannia Languens* (1680), 45, 287. On the other hand, a correspondent wrote in 1670—" Strangers I find far more thrifty than we are ; they can work cheaper than we, and they have many pleasing inventions which we are not addicted to. . . . There are able heads in England to consult on matters in trade, but I fear we are not so diligent as our neighbours " : *State Papers Domestic*, 1670, p. 601.
[10] *Hist. MSS. Comm. Salisbury*, viii. 210 (1598).

dangers which attended a nation whose economic existence *Causes of* depended upon the importation of precious metals [1]. The *Holland's commercial greatness of Holland, on the other hand, aroused *greatness.* the envy of her contemporaries who debated the causes of the incomparable riches, multitude of shipping, and acknowledged supremacy in trade enjoyed by a country which was but ' a handful of the world ' and possessed ' neither wool, nor cloth, nor few other commodities ' [2]. The Dutch shared none of the advantages of England—who produced most of the raw materials for her manufactures and raised her own food supply—yet they made their country a ' magazine ' of the commodities of all other countries [3], and Amsterdam the storehouse of the world in place of Antwerp ' the late packhouse of Europe ' [4]. " Their country is a granary for all Christendom, and yet they have not corn of their own growth to feed the hundredth man in their dominions. They also outstrip all nations in their number of ships and seamen, and yet they have not wood of their own to warm themselves in winter. They abound in quality and quantity of all manufactures, and yet they fetch the materials thereof from all other parts of the world. . . . Their fishing trade upon our coast brings them not only food but infinite advantage in trade with other nations " [5]. The position held by the Dutch as ' the common carriers of the world ' was attributed to a variety of factors—their situation on the sea at the mouths of great rivers, which passed through rich countries and gave them ' the keys of trade ' of those countries ; their system of internal communication based on water carriage, which was much less expensive than land carriage ; their concentration on commerce in preference to husbandry ; the profit of their fishing trade ; their cheap freights due to building ships which cost less, sailed with fewer hands, and were adapted to the requirements of particular trades, whereas England built ' but one sort and that the most chargeable ' [6] ; the

[1] *Infra*, p. 66 ; and Appendix, p. 492, No. 1.
[2] *House of Commons Journals*, i. 672, 717 (1624). Similarly : Mun, *England's Treasure by Forraign Trade* (ed. 1664), 185 ; *Hist. MSS. Comm. Verulam*, 227 ; Coke, *Treatise* (1671), i. 65.
[3] Misselden, *The Circle of Commerce* (1623), 135.
[4] Wheeler's phrase : *A Treatise of Commerce* (1601), 17.
[5] *State Papers Domestic*, 1650, p. 180.     [6] See *infra*, p. 130.

varied character of their cargoes; the light customs which made their ports the centre of the world's traffic; their low rates of interest which facilitated the conduct of business on the most advantageous lines; their banking system which served 'to make a small sum equivalent in trade to a greater'; their registers of real securities, lands and houses, to serve as a basis for credit; the transference of bills for debt, which enabled their traders to turn over capital quickly; the absence of restrictions in their internal trade; their education of children, daughters as well as sons; their practice of equal inheritance; their thrift; their toleration in religion; their encouragement of immigration and inventions; their swift determination of suits in which mercantile interests were involved; and lastly, the presence of experienced merchants in their councils of state [1].

*Rivalry between England and Holland.* The interests of England and Holland clashed at many points. They were rivals in India, in Africa, in the Baltic, and in the Levant [2]: the wealth derived by the Dutch from fishing off the English coasts was a perpetual irritant [3]: and the impositions which they laid on English cloth in order to develop their own woollen manufacture added fuel to the flames [4]. The jealousy was already acute in the early part of the seventeenth century—" the Dutch eat us out in our navigation " [5], complained a member of Parliament in 1621 —and it came to a head when the Civil War in England afforded Holland an opportunity of extending and consolidating her commercial empire [6]. " The season cries aloud to us to be up and doing ", said one writer, " before the Dutch get too much the whip-hand of us " [7]. The House of Commons resolved in 1664 that " the damages, affronts and

---

[1] For these points, see—Raleigh, *Works* (ed. 1829), viii. 356 *seq.*; De Witt, *The True Interest of Holland* (ed. 1746), 28; *Hist. MSS. Comm. Rutland*, i. 470; Petty, *Economic Writings*, i. 59, 255-268; Coke, *Treatise* (1671), i. 87; ii. 106-107, 113-123; *Britannia Languens* (1680), 51-54; Child, *A New Discourse of Trade* (4th ed.), 2; Barbon, *A Discourse of Trade* (1690), 79 *seq.*; Puckle, *England's Path to Wealth and Honour* (1700), 20-21; Gee, *The Trade and Navigation of Great Britain* (ed. 1730), 129. Also *infra*, p. 492 (No. 2).     [2] *Supra*, vol. ii. 275, 320, 346, 355.
[3] *Infra*, p. 148.          [4] *Infra*, p. 295.
[5] *House of Commons Journals*, i. 642. Similarly: Mun, *England's Treasure by Forraign Trade* (ed. 1664), 205.
[6] *Supra*, vol. ii. 331, and *infra*, pp. 129, 173, 317, 526 (No. 1).
[7] Child, *A New Discourse of Trade* (4th ed.), p. xliv.

injuries " done by the Dutch were " the greatest obstruction of our foreign trade " [1]. Yet the fact that Holland was England's chief customer reinforced the argument that war is not the instrument of commerce, and that Dutch competition should be met by imitating its methods [2]. Holland thus became the model on which England in the seventeenth century was counselled to mould her economic policy : ' A precedent worth the looking on ' was the opinion expressed in the House of Commons (1624) [3]. Misselden wrote : " For policy and industry " the Low Countries " may read a lecture to all the other people of the world " [4]. Their influence made itself felt in many directions : in the art of husbandry, in the system of taxation, in shipbuilding, in engineering, in the construction of canals, in the advocacy of banks, negotiable bills and lower rates of interest, and in other spheres of economic activity [5].

In the eighteenth century the French supplanted the Dutch in public estimation as ' our greatest and most dangerous rivals in trade ' [6]. At one period there seemed every likelihood that France would outstrip England in the race for industrial supremacy. Endowed with a genial climate and a kindly soil which furnished the utmost variety of natural products—corn, fruits and the vine—possessed of extensive territories in North America and India to serve as the basis for a far-flung commercial empire, enjoying a good system of communications, and bearing a population—estimated at three or four times the size of that of England—which yielded abundant indications of artistic gifts and inventive talent, she gave greater promise of rapid industrialization than did her rival. But although France made

*Comparison between England and France.*

---

[1] *House of Commons Journals*, viii. 548.

[2] " The greatest of all our foreign markets " : *The British Merchant* (ed. 1721), i. 25-26, 32, 170 ; Coke, *Treatise* (1671), ii. Preface ; Yarranton, *England's Improvement* (1677), 61 ; *Britannia Languens* (1680), 61.

[3] *House of Commons Journals*, i. 717.

[4] Misselden, *The Circle of Commerce* (1623), 134.

[5] *Supra*, vol. ii. 373, 375, 445 ; and *infra*, pp. 57, 132, 143, 145, 149, 221, 226, 239. The ' neatness and elegance ' of the buildings at Yarmouth were attributed to intercourse with the Dutch : *Hist. MSS. Comm. Portland*, vi. 154 (1732).

[6] Wood, *A Survey of Trade* (1718), 113 ; *The British Merchant* (ed. 1721), i. p. xxviii. Contrast Davenant, *Works* (ed. 1771), v. 461.

great commercial strides in the eighteenth century [1], her advantages were offset by grave disabilities. The system of arbitrary government afforded no security of person or property : religious intolerance drove into exile the most industrious of her children, and made a gift of inestimable value to the countries now in the forefront of industrial progress : military ambitions involved a great drain of men and money, and were injurious alike to the accumulation of capital, the provision of skilled labour, and the supply of raw material : a vicious method of taxation imposed its burden upon the poorest section of the community, and took infinitely more from the taxpayer than ever reached the exchequer : antiquated gild restrictions handicapped industry, and internal customs barriers checked trade [2]. In another respect there was a marked contrast between England and France. The English traveller, accustomed in his own country to numerous gradations of wealth and rank, was struck by the extremes of poverty and riches which he found in France where he seemed to pass at once from beggary to profusion [3]. The gulf between rich and poor appeared absolute, while in England it was bridged over by intermediate classes. These differences in the distribution of wealth were reflected in the sphere of production. Seventeenth-century writers contrasted " the flimsy but tasteful French goods with the strong serviceable English " [4]. The former were designed for a wealthy clientele whose cultivated taste called for the best skill of craftsmanship. The latter were intended for a population among whom property was widely diffused, and whose standard of comfort was relatively high without being luxurious. The French market demanded wares graced with the beauty of form and

[1] See the statistics of French trade in Young, *Travels in France* (ed. Maxwell), 318.

[2] Tucker also notes the contempt of the nobility for trade : *An Essay on Trade* (ed. 1753), 25-26.

[3] Young, *Travels in France* (ed. Maxwell), 115 (also p. 24). A century earlier Petty may have had *England* in mind when he spoke of wealth concentrated in ' too few men's hands ' : *Economic Writings*, i. 23.

[4] Marshall, *Industry and Trade* (ed. 1920), 113, note 1. Tucker estimated the possessions of an English ' peasant or mechanic ' at thrice the value of those of a French peasant or mechanic : *Instructions* (ed. 1757), 26.

colour :  the English market wider in extent required, in the main, commodities which were sound and useful.

In the following sections we shall treat of mercantilist policy in respect of (i.) the protection of industry; (ii.) money and the balance of trade; (iii.) the navigation system; (iv.) the Colonies ; and (v.) Ireland.  Of the Corn Laws we have already spoken [1].

## (I)

### THE PROTECTION OF INDUSTRY

The principal method of protecting industry under the Mercantile System was to discourage imports [2].  All the nations of Europe, wrote *The British Merchant* (1713), " concur in this maxim that the less they consume of foreign commodities the better it is for them " [3].  The mercantilist attitude towards imports is explained by mediaeval precedents [3a] ;  by the fear of unemployment [3b] ;  by the fact that the use of foreign products ran counter to the national ideal of self-sufficiency [3c] ;  and by the cruder form of the mercantilist theory of trade, which assumed that in a commercial transaction one party always gained at the expense of the other [4], and was apt to ignore the possibility of reciprocal benefits.  Nevertheless the Mercantilists did not condemn all trade nor visit their disapproval on all imports. They drew a distinction between different branches of trade—a distinction which was expressed in a series of ' general maxims ' [5].  Trade was considered advantageous to a nation when it exported manufactured articles and ' superfluities ' such as tin, coal and leather ;  or when it imported raw materials to be worked up at home.  The exchange of our finished products for those of other countries was ' generally an advantage '.  Imports, bought partly for money and partly for goods, might be of national benefit provided they were mostly re-exported, ' as in the case of

*' General Maxims' of Trade.*

[1] *Supra*, vol. ii. chapter iii. sect. iv. and vol. ii. Introduction, p. lxxxix.
[2] Other methods are noticed *infra*, pp. 21 (note 6), 45, 118.
[3] *The British Merchant* (ed. 1721), i. 16-17 ; ii. 318.
[3a] *Supra*, vol. i. 363, 448, 454-5, 542 ; vol. ii. Introduction, pp. lxxxix-xc.
[3b] *Infra*, p. 15, note 2 ; also *supra*, vol. i. 363; vol. ii. Introduction, p. xc.
[3c] *Supra*, p. 1.
[4] " They do not imagine that either can gain what the other does not lose " : *Hist. MSS. Comm. Charlemont*, ii. 173.
[5] In a pamphlet by Sir Theodore Janssen.  Reprinted in *The British Merchant* (ed. 1721), i. 1-6.

East India goods', since in general all imports which were re-exported were beneficial. Imports with which a nation could not dispense, even though purchased with money, could not be esteemed bad, for example, naval stores and materials for building. A trade was disadvantageous to a nation which brought in " things of mere luxury and pleasure, which are entirely or for the most part consumed among us ", particularly wine. " Much worse is that trade which brings in a commodity that is not only consumed amongst us but hinders the consumption of the like quantity of ours " [1]; while " that trade is eminently bad which supplies the same goods as we manufacture ourselves ". The conclusion drawn from these maxims was that the profit of the trader was not the true measure of trade [2]: the nature of the imports and exports alone furnished the criterion whether a branch of commerce was beneficial or prejudicial.

*Prohibitions and tariffs.* The mercantilist theory of trade involved the corollary that some branches of commerce should be encouraged by fiscal immunities, and others discouraged by high tariffs or prohibitions. One of the main functions of the Commissioners for Trade and Plantations, appointed in 1696, was to investigate the means by which beneficial trades might be improved and prejudicial ones restrained [3]. In the case of some foreign commodities an absolute prohibition was enjoined. Early in the reign of Elizabeth an ' Act for the avoiding of divers foreign wares ' forbade the importation of girdles, rapiers, daggers, knives, saddles, stirrups, gloves, leather, laces or pins, ' being ready wrought ' [4]. The list of prohibited articles was extended at different times to include hats, wool-cards, silks, bonelace, cambrics and the rest [5]. The alternative to

[1] The example given is brandy, " which hinders the spending of our extracts of malt and molasses " : *ibid.* 4.
[2] Pollexfen, *England and East India inconsistent in their Manufactures* (1697), 15.
[3] *House of Commons Journals*, xiii. 298. Cf. *infra*, p. 310, note 3.
[4] 1563 : *Statutes*, iv. part i. 428-429. The Act was foreshadowed in 1559 : *Hist. MSS. Comm. Salisbury*, i. 163. A similar Act had been made by Richard III. : *Statutes*, ii. 495 (1484).
[5] Hats and caps : *Tudor and Stuart Proclamations* (ed. Steele), i. No. 1139 (1613) ; *Acts and Ordinances of the Interregnum*, ii. 242 (1649) Whale-oil and whale-bone (unless brought by English subjects in English ships) : *ibid.* i. 679-680 (1645). Wool-cards : *Statutes*, iv. part ii. 914 (1598). Silks : *State Papers Domestic*, Addenda, 1625–1649, p. 313
[contd.]

prohibition was the levying of heavy duties : thus at the Restoration a duty was placed on foreign cloth which amounted to a prohibition [1]. The mercantilist argument in defence of this policy is clearly stated in the preface to James I.'s Book of Rates : " If it be agreeable to the rule of nature to prefer our own people before strangers, then is it much more reasonable that the manufactures of other nations should be charged with impositions than that the people of our own kingdom should not be set on work " [2].

The progress of economic thought disclosed, however, *International division of labour.* another aspect of the problem, and seventeenth-century economists were already feeling their way towards a more enlightened view of commerce. It came to be recognized that international trade was not one-sided but conferred benefits upon both the parties to a contract. The doctrine was taught by Sir Dudley North (1691) that trade is nothing but ' a commutation of superfluities ' in which each gave what he could spare in exchange for what he needed [3]—this implied the international division of labour on which the argument for free trade was subsequently based. Petty remarked that countries were adapted for different economic pursuits ; and Davenant declared that Providence intended they should mutually supply the necessities of one another [4]. At times the aspiration of national self-sufficiency was discountenanced even officially, as when the commissioners, appointed by James I. to negotiate with the Dutch over the East Indies, claimed that nature had " so ordained that, having use one of another, we might keep and continue intercourse and society " [5]. From this conception of the world as an economic whole, of which the different parts were interdependent,

---

(Petition against wrought silks, ? 1628) ; *Statutes*, vi. 173, 443 (Act of 1690 prohibiting the importation of thrown silk except Italian) ; *Statutes at Large*, vii. 441, 559, 588 (Acts of 1762, 1765 and 1766 prohibiting foreign-wrought silks) ; *House of Commons Journals*, xxx. 210, 725-726, 758 ; xxxiv. 241. Bonelace : see *infra*, p. 19. Cambrics : *Statutes at Large*, vi. 290 (1745). Buttons : *Statutes*, vi. 392 (1693). Gold and silver thread : *Statutes at Large*, vi. 179 (1742). Leather gloves : *ibid.* vii. 578 (1766).

[1] *Statutes*, v. 186 (1660) ; *State Papers Domestic*, 1661–1662, p. 80.
[2] *The Rates of Marchandizes as they are set downe in the Booke of Rates*, 4 (Letters Patents, 8 James I.). See also *infra*, Appendix, p. 492, No. 3.
[3] North, *Discourses upon Trade* (1691), 2.
[4] Petty, *Economic Writings*, i. 258 ; Davenant, *Works* (ed. 1771), i. 104.
[5] *Hist. MSS. Comm. Buccleuch*, i. 169 (1615). See *supra*, vol. ii. 275.

it was only a single step to condemn the policy of discrimination between different branches of trade.

To illustrate the advance of economic thought, we may contrast Child's criticism of the Canary wine trade—a typical example of mercantilist reasoning—and Davenant's defence of the French trade. " The trade for Canary wines I take to be a most pernicious trade to England, because those Islands consume very little of our manufactures, fish or other English commodities; neither do they furnish us with any commodities to be further manufactured here or to be re-exported, the wines we bring from thence being for the most part purchased with ready money "[1]. This attempt to distinguish between different branches of commerce failed to take account of the interactions of commerce ; and Davenant pointed out the error in an illustration drawn from the French trade—" We lost in the balance with France, but perhaps if we had not dealt with the French, the French could not have traded with Spain and Italy ; and but for the traffic between France and Spain and Italy peradventure we could not have enjoyed the commerce so gainful to us with the Italians and the Spaniards. It is hard to trace all the circuits of trade . . . and to show what mutual dependence all traffics have one upon the other "[2]. Sir Dudley North formulated a correct theory of international trade, when he remarked that "the whole world as to trade is but as one nation or people, and therein nations are as persons " ; and that the loss of a trade with one nation is " so much of the trade of the world rescinded and lost "[3]. Yet even North was anticipated by an earlier writer (1644) who observed : " It may be said of the Body of Trade, one part hath such a dependency upon another that if any one fail in any remarkable manner the rest will in time suffer thereby "[4].

A more potent argument drove home the dangers of giving reins to the prejudice against imports. The gist of it was that in order to sell we must be ready to buy [5]. The

[1] Child, *A New Discourse of Trade* (4th ed.), 189.

[2] Davenant, *Works* (ed. 1771), i. 388 ; v. 380.

[3] North, *Discourses upon Trade* (1691), Preface, p. viii. See *infra*, Appendix, p. 493, No. 1.

[4] J. B., *The Merchants' Remonstrance* (1644), 9.

[5] Davenant, *Works* (ed. 1771), v. 388. Cf. *supra*, vol. ii. 462 ; and *infra*, Appendix, p. 493, No. 2.

countries which took our commodities would expect that we *Exports* should receive a due proportion of theirs : otherwise they *pay for imports*. would be forced to set up their own industries.  Mun asked the question :  " If we . . . use few or no foreign wares, how shall we then vent our own commodities ? " [1]   Robinson in 1641 pointed out that foreign wares were largely bartered for native commodities, " and we should not have vented ours in so great quantity without taking theirs " ; he therefore recommended that tariffs should be imposed with discretion " lest it become countermined " [2].  Thus Barbon advanced no novel argument, as is sometimes supposed, when half a century later (1690) he reiterated the contention that exports paid for imports, " so that the prohibiting of any foreign commodity doth hinder the making and exportation of so much of the native as used to be made and exchanged for it " [3].

One of the most cogent statements of the free trade [4] *Arguments* position is found in Roger Coke, whose place in economic *for free trade.* literature has not received the recognition it deserves.  It may seem reasonable, he wrote, to prohibit trades which hindered the employment of our people, yet on closer investigation such prohibition will prove dangerous to our trade abroad and at home.  Abroad it will provoke retaliation and so diminish our exports.  At home the absence of competition will cause a falling off in the efficiency of native manufacturers, who will take advantage of their monopoly to " make the English pay more for worse work than they did before, and make them so dear and bad " that we shall lose the foreign trade to our rivals ; whereas the importation of foreign goods will be " an awe upon the English to make ours so good and cheap as to supply us and the world better,

[1] Mun, *England's Treasure by Forraign Trade* (ed. 1664), 148.

[2] Robinson, *England's Safety in Trades Encrease* (1641), 8-9.  Cf. *infra*, p. 312, note 1.

[3] Barbon, *A Discourse of Trade* (1690), 71 *seq.*

[4] The term ' free trade ', as used in the seventeenth and eighteenth centuries, meant either (1) a trade free from the monopoly of a privileged company ; or (2) a trade free from prohibitions and high tariffs.  It did not normally mean (3) a trade free from all customs duties except those levied for revenue purposes only.  In the present chapter the term is used, as contemporaries used it in this connexion, to mean moderate tariffs and no prohibitions.  This was a stage in the evolution of free trade as the term is now understood.

or they will lose their employment "[1]. This argument
was used in the debate over the French trade, for when
the silk weavers petitioned Parliament in 1671 to prohibit
French silks, it was urged in opposition that new fashions
stimulated production, and that free trade alone prompted
ingenuity and industry[2]. Coke further maintained that
" by this free importation of goods into the ports of England,
we may infinitely improve the benefits which will accrue to
all sorts of artificers by the plenty and cheapness of all
things they need, and to the foreign trades of our woollen
and other manufactures by their returns "; and the English
carrying trade would also be increased. Moreover free trade
" would establish an interest with all those nations which
hold trade and traffic with us "; while prohibitions caused
" hatred and heart-burning between princes, whereby oftentimes wars ensue though under other pretences "[3]. In
short, freedom of trade was the means to stimulate exports,
extend the carrying trade, reduce the cost of living, lower
the price of materials, and promote friendship between
nations. Barbon added to the discussion when he contested
the common view that foreign goods ' hinder the consumption of our own '[4], on the ground that the prohibition of the
former did not necessarily promote the use of the latter,
since the desire for novelties played an important part in
stimulating consumption[5]. Davenant demonstrated the
injurious effects of high tariffs on foreign trade, by pointing
out that the " variety of additional customs which have
brought such a miserable load upon trade " yielded only a
low produce, which was " a sign but too visible how much
our foreign traffic is diminished ". He summed up the
general standpoint of this group of ' free trade ' economists
as follows : " Trade is in its nature free, finds its own channel,
and best directeth its own course ; and all laws to give it
rules and directions, and to limit and circumscribe it, may

[1] Coke, _Treatise_ (1675), iii. 47-48.
[2] _Hist. MSS. Comm._ ix. part ii. 14.
[3] Coke, _Treatise_ (1675), iii. 48 ; iv. 114.
[4] This view is expressed (_e.g._) in the report of the Commissioners for
Trade and Plantations : _House of Commons Journals_, xiii. 723 (1702).
[5] Barbon, _A Discourse of Trade_ (1690), 71 _seq._

serve the particular ends of private men but are seldom advantageous to the public. . . . Considering all the links and chains by which they hang together, peradventure it may be affirmed that in the main all traffics whatsoever are beneficial to a country ". He counselled his countrymen to lay aside the narrow notions of those who thought to advance the sale of our products by prohibiting goods from other countries, since " England never throve by trade but while she was an universal merchant " [1].

One argument against prohibition or high tariffs, as we *Retalia-* have seen [2], was the danger of retaliation. Other nations *tion.* would enact similar laws, and the result would be ' to ruin all foreign trade ' [3]. The history of Mercantilism affords many examples of retaliation. The Act of 1563 was one of the causes which led the Low Countries to break off trading relations with England [4]; and the Dutch forced James I. to remove the embargo on foreign steel and pins [5]. When bone-lace was prohibited [6], the Spanish Low Countries retorted (1699) by excluding English woollen manufactures. The value of the Flemish bonelace imported into England did not exceed £30,000, whereas our exports to the Spanish Low Countries amounted in 1681 to £400,000, of which the woollen manufactures accounted for £160,000 [7]. Parliament, therefore, undertook to repeal the prohibition of bonelace, if the Flemings removed their embargo on English cloth : eventually in 1707 the prohibition of foreign bonelace was withdrawn [8]. In other cases, also, it was found that the protection given to one branch of industry was detrimental to other

[1] Davenant, *Works* (ed. 1771), i. 98–99 ; v. 387, 391, 432, 452. See *infra*, Appendix, p. 493, No. 3.

[2] *Supra*, p. 17.

[3] Barbon, *A Discourse of Trade* (1690), 78.

[4] *Supra*, p. 14, and vol. ii. 198.

[5] *Acts of the Privy Council*, 1619–1621, p. 3 ; *Hist. MSS. Comm. Salisbury*, vii. 545 ; Price, *The English Patents of Monopoly*, 30, note 1.

[6] In 1662 and 1698 : *Statutes*, v. 405 ; vii. 304. On lace-making, see *Victoria County History, Bedfordshire*, ii. 122 *seq.* ; *ibid. Buckinghamshire*, ii. 106 *seq.*

[7] According to the report of the Commissioners for Trade and Plantations : *House of Commons Journals*, xv. 237 ; *House of Lords MSS.* 1706–1708, p. 243.

[8] *Statutes*, vii. 600 (1699) ; viii. 591 (1707). *House of Commons Journals*, xii. 584, 599 ; xiii. 269, 271, 299 ; xv. 237, 249. The repeal did not extend to France.

branches.  The following examples [1] illustrate the practical
difficulties raised by a protective system, and show the
soundness of Sir Dudley North's observation that " all
favour to one trade or interest against another is an abuse,
and cuts so much of profit from the public " [2].  A Bill was
introduced in 1727 to prohibit the importation of foreign
thrown silk.  It was supported by one section of the silk
workers, those engaged in the throwing, twisting and winding
of raw silk ;  and opposed by another, the silk weavers, who
declared that foreign thrown silk was necessary for carrying
on the industry.  The cloth manufacturers intervened in the
controversy but they also were divided.  The market of
the western clothiers was Turkey, the market of the eastern
clothiers was Italy.  The former asserted that the importation
of Italian thrown silk diminished the consumption of raw
silk imported from Turkey in return for cloth.  The latter
affirmed that their trade would be injured by any restrictions
on Italian imports [3].  The conflict of industrial interests was
again manifested when the linen manufacturers demanded
an additional duty on foreign linens.  The proposal was
resisted by the manufacturers of cloth, silk, cutlery, iron
and tin, all of whom expressed apprehension that the additional duty might provoke retaliation in foreign countries ;
in any case it would lessen the demand for English goods if
they were unable to send their linens here in return [4].  The
cloth made at Exeter, for instance, was " chiefly sent into
the Circle of Westphalia and that neighbourhood ", and
" paid for by bills on London out of the produce of [their]
linens ", since they had " nothing else by which they can
make returns to any considerable value " [5].  In view of the
argument against prohibition or high tariffs, based on the
mutual dependency of markets, it may appear surprising
that the protective system survived so long, but it must be

---

[1] For an example from the cotton industry, see *infra*, p. 44.
[2] North, *Discourses upon Trade* (1691), Preface, p. ix.
[3] *House of Commons Journals*, xx. 784, 808, 812, 817-818, 821, 823,
826.  Yarmouth pointed out that the returns for fish to Italy were generally
thrown silk :  *ibid*. xx. 826.  See also *The British Merchant* (ed. 1721),
ii. 315.
[4] 1744 :  *House of Commons Journals*, xxiv. 622, 637, 642, 646-647, 818,
825-826, 847.                                    [5] *Ibid*. xxiv. 819.

remembered that Governments were not entirely free agents. The pressure of vested interests, manufacturers and artisans alike, was often too strong ; and clamour sometimes extorted concessions which on economic grounds might seem indefensible [1]. Moreover the anxiety to conserve and enlarge the national stock of bullion intensified the desire to avoid the importation of ' vain and unprofitable ' commodities [2].

Apart from the method of prohibitions and high tariffs on foreign manufactured articles, the fiscal system was manipulated in other ways to afford encouragement or discouragement to different branches of trade. The general trend of policy was, first, to remove duties on foreign raw materials [3]—a principle foreshadowed in the Book of Rates issued by James I. in 1611, which expressed the intention to " exempt and forbear all such merchandises inwards . . . as serve for the setting the people of our kingdom on work (as cotton wool, cotton yarn, raw silk and rough hemp) " [4]. Secondly : to abolish or reduce the duties on native products exported abroad [5], and to provide a further stimulus by the payment of bounties [6], although the export of certain raw materials was prohibited [7]. Where these methods of pro-

*Manipulation of the fiscal system.*

---

[1] *State Papers Domestic*, 1660–1661, p. 363 ; 1661–1662, p. 80. *Hist. MSS. Comm. Eglinton*, 388.

[2] Stowe MSS. 554, f. 45 ; Rymer, *Foedera*, xvii. 414.

[3] *E.g.* Dyeing materials : *Statutes at Large*, v. 262 (1722). Flax ; *ibid.* v. 576 (1731). Cotton : *ibid.* vii. 622 (1766). Cf. Coke, *Treatise* (1675), iii. 49 ; *House of Commons Journals*, xix. 692 (1721).

[4] *The Rates of Merchandizes as they are set downe in the Booke of Rates*, 2 (Letters Patents, 8 James I.).

[5] In 1700 the export duty on woollen manufactures was abolished : *House of Commons Journals*, xiii. 208 ; *Statutes*, vii. 610 ; Davenant, *Works* (ed. 1771), v. 443, 446. (But in 1707 a duty of 5s. was imposed on every white woollen (broad) cloth exported abroad : *Statutes*, viii. 751.) Victuals were exempted in 1692 (*ibid.* vi. 311) ; sail cloth in 1696 (*ibid.* vii. 156) ; copper and brass wire in 1709 (*ibid.* ix. 134) ; and all commodities in 1722 with certain exceptions—lead, tin, tanned leather, coal, skins, white woollen cloth (*Statutes at Large*, v. 262).

[6] Sail cloth : *Statutes*, ix. 781 (1713). Silks : *Statutes at Large*, v. 261 (1722). Whale-fishery : *ibid.* v. 638 (1733). Linen : *ibid.* vi. 186, 274 (1743). White-herring fishery : *ibid.* vi. 474 (1750). Cordage : *ibid.* vii. 606 (1766). For corn bounties, see *supra*, vol. ii. 453. For bounties on colonial products, see *infra*, p. 185. Elizabeth granted 5s. a ton for every ship built of over 100 tons, and Charles I. 5s. per ton on ships of over 200 tons : *Tudor and Stuart Proclamations* (ed. Steele), i. No. 1472. Also see *infra*, Appendix, p. 493, No. 4.

[7] Wool and undressed cloth : *infra*, pp. 22, 376. Leather : *Statutes*, v. 378 (1662), 640 (repealed 1668). Iron : *ibid.* vi. 480 (repealed 1694). Cf. *Britannia Languens* (1680), 24, 170. Gun metal : *Statutes*, vi. 481 (1694). Certain kinds of skins : *Statutes at Large*, ix. 384 (1784).

moting native industries failed, there remained the compulsory wearing of home manufactures [1].

We shall now consider in detail some practical applications of the system of protection.

*Import-
ance of
English
wool.*

The most signal example of protection is seen in the attitude adopted in respect of the raw materials produced at home, especially wool. This commodity formerly occupied the place in our economic system now held by coal. It was England's chief raw material, the indispensable basis of her greatest industry, and the most highly prized of her products in other countries. Every class in the community, whether landlord, farmer, manufacturer or artisan, had a direct interest in wool ; and it provided a fertile ground for economic controversy.

*Prohibi-
tion of the
export of
wool.*

In the Middle Ages wool, ' the goddess of merchants ' [2] and ' England's golden fleece ' [3], was the staple article of export and the main source of royal revenue. Occasionally an embargo was placed by English rulers on its export [4]— a member of Parliament declared in 1621 that ' at least ' thirty Statutes had been enacted against the export of wool [5]—but the prohibition was usually short-lived ; and even when nominally in force it was easily evaded by the purchase of licences, granted for revenue purposes, allowing wool to be sent abroad. The growth of the woollen industry, however, enlarged the home market for English wool and caused a natural shrinkage of the export trade, which Wheeler in 1601 described as ' almost wholly decayed ' [6]. After the loss of Calais the Merchant Staplers still carried on operations [7], but they no longer enjoyed ' an assured place of residence ' abroad [8] ; and the system of licences and heavy duties handicapped legitimate exporters, while it

---

[1] See *infra*, p. 45.

[2] *Des marchantz la duesse* : Gower, *Mirour de l'Omme*, l. 25,370 (ed. Macaulay, i. 280).

[3] *A Discourse consisting of Motives for the Enlargement and Freedom of Trade* (1645), 3.

[4] *Supra*, vol. i. 453-455.        [5] *House of Commons Journals*, i. 653.

[6] Wheeler, *A Treatise of Commerce* (1601), 64.

[7] *Hist. MSS. Comm. Salisbury*, ii. 296 (1579) ; *Acts of the Privy Council*, 1586–1587, p. 207.

[8] *State Papers Foreign*, 1585–1586, p. 59. See *supra*, vol. ii. 20.

encouraged an illicit trade [1] which brought in no revenue. The fact that the normal and revenue-producing channels of the trade were thus drying up, facilitated an orientation of policy ; and in the seventeenth century the transport of wool beyond the sea was forbidden, not as a temporary expedient, but as a permanent feature of the new commercial system. James I.—" upon information of the setting up of clothing and drapery in the United Provinces, and the exportation of great quantities of wool into those parts " [2]— issued proclamations in 1614, 1617 and 1621 for the ' restraining of the wool of this realm from exportation '. They were repeated by Charles I. and Cromwell, and embodied in an Act of Parliament at the Restoration [3]. The changed situation had been foreshadowed in a change of name when the Merchants of the Staple of Calais were incorporated as the Merchants of the Staple of England [4].

In spite of all its efforts to check the export of wool, *Smuggling of wool.* reinforced by naval and military support [5], the Government was unable to repress an illicit trade which sprang up immediately. Among other places the people of Faversham are said to have grown ' monstrous rich ' by ' that wicked trade ' [6] ; and Kent and Sussex seemed at one period a smugglers' paradise [7]. The smugglers brought back with

[1] *Hist. MSS. Comm. Salisbury,* ii. 202 ; *Acts of the Privy Council,* 1592, p. 350.

[2] *Acts of the Privy Council,* 1618–1619, p. 122. See *infra,* p. 382.

[3] *Tudor and Stuart Proclamations* (ed. Steele), i. Nos. 1150 (1614), 1197 (1617), 1314 (1621), 1334 (1622), 3075 (1656), 3256 (1660). *Acts and Ordinances of the Interregnum,* i. 1059 (1648). *Statutes,* v. 293 (1660), 410 (1662), Rymer, *Foedera,* xvii. 412 (1622) ; xix. 155 (1630), 388 (1632) ; xx. 342 (1639). *House of Commons Journals,* ii. 162 (1642) ; iii. 44 (1643). Smith represents the proclamations of James I. and Charles I. as devices to raise money by licences granting exemptions : *Chronicon Rusticum-Commerciale* (ed. 1747), i. 171. But the Merchant Adventurers of Newcastle lost their trade in wool despite their complaints : *Newcastle Merchant Adventurers,* i. 8, 115-116, 119 ; ii. 13.

[4] In 1561 : Jenckes, *The Origin, the Organization and the Location of the Staple of England,* 66 ; *State Papers Domestic,* 1651-1652, p. 472. For the Merchant Staplers, see *supra,* vol. i. 565, 577 ; ii. 20-25 ; and *infra,* Appendix, p. 494, No. 1.

[5] *House of Commons Journals,* xi. 594 ; *State Papers Domestic,* 1668–1669, p. 556.

[6] Defoe, *Tour of Great Britain* (ed. 1724), i. Letter ii. 32.

[7] See *infra,* p. 24. In 1787 it was said that " larger quantities are smuggled from other parts of the kingdom " than from Kent and Sussex : Anstie, *A General View of the Bill . . . for preventing the Illicit Exportation of British Wool* (1787), 31. Wool was also exported through Scotland : *House of Commons Journals,* xii. 434.

them cargoes of silk, lace and liquors. Their methods are
described in a number of pamphlets written by William
Carter, for over a quarter of a century their indefatigable
adversary. " First, in Romney Marsh in Kent, where the
greatest part of rough wool is exported from England, put
aboard French shallops by night, ten or twenty men well
armed to guard it : some other parts there are, as in Sussex,
Hampshire and Essex, the same methods may be used but
not so conveniently. The same for combed wool from
Canterbury : they will carry it ten or fifteen miles at night
towards the sea with the like guard as before "[1]. As a
measure of precaution while the wool was afloat, it was
pressed into barrels with screws, and then the barrels were
' washed over with brine-water ' in order that they might
pass for beef or herrings. " These barrels are not put on board
in ports where they are liable to be examined, but conveyed
into creeks from whence they are shipped off "[2]. According
to one statement (1703), wool in its raw state (fleece wool)
was worth in Ireland fourpence per pound and combed wool
tenpence : in France the first was sold for half-a-crown a
pound, the second for five and sixpence or six shillings—
" so that the temptation is really almost too great to be
withstood, especially by such who only measure their
consciences by their gain "[3]. This estimate of the profits
made in the smuggling trade, if not exaggerated, points to
exceptional circumstances[4], though in time of war the risks
of the enterprise were always enhanced. A more moderate
calculation represented the profit at threepence a pound on
English wool, which amounted to 50 or 60 per cent. in regard
to the capital employed ' in that illicit trade '[5]. The wool
smugglers were called *owlers* ; and their desperate character
was shown in the hardihood with which they attacked the

[1] [Carter], *England's Interest asserted in the Improvement of its Native
Commodities* (1669), 17.
[2] *House of Lords MSS.* 1704–1706, p. 211 ; *A Brief Account of the
Woollen Manufactory of England* (1708), 28. Another device was to
manufacture woollen goods fraudulently, so that the wool was easily
unravelled : *House of Commons Journals*, xxi. 692.
[3] *House of Lords MSS.* 1704–1706, p. 211.
[4] Another ship commander stated (1704) that ' a glut of wool' brought
down the price of combed wool in St. Malo from 5s. 4d. to 3s. 9d. per lb. :
*ibid.* 219.    [5] Smith, *Chronicon Rusticum-Commerciale* (ed. 1747), ii. 536.

coast-guard men, who were often " obliged as it were to stand still and see the wool carried off before their faces, not daring to meddle " [1]. " None dare meddle with them without five files of soldiers " [2]. The severity of the punishments did nothing to discourage the smugglers and they " readily risked their necks for twelvepence a day " [3]. The sympathies of the local population, who in some places were almost all engaged in the owling-trade [4], were never in doubt; and the municipal authorities refused to assist the officers appointed to prevent the export of wool [5], while the latter—for the payment of whose salaries, and even expenses, no provision was apparently made other than the fines inflicted on offenders—became negligent and corrupt [6]. On one occasion William Carter arrested a smuggler at Folkestone, " but the women of the town . . . came out of their houses and gathered up stones upon the beach, which they flung about my ears so violently that having no help I was forced to quit my prisoner, hardly escaping myself " [7].

The evils of smuggling attracted considerable attention ; *Efforts to suppress smuggling* and a proclamation issued by James II. denounced those who ' by open force and violence with armed companies of men ' conveyed wool beyond the seas [8]. After the Revolution fresh legislation was enacted [9]. The severity of the penalty was

[1] Defoe, *Tour of Great Britain* (ed. 1724), 1. Letter ii. 50.
[2] *State Papers Domestic*, 1663–1664, p. 531.
[3] Cooper, " Smuggling in Sussex " in *Sussex Archæological Collections*, x. 73.  [4] *House of Commons Journals*, xii. 212.
[5] The duty of preventing the export of wool was first laid on the Commissioners of the Customs, but in 1689 special ' Commissioners for wool ' were appointed for the purpose  For a list of their surveyors in the different counties, the seizures of wool made by them, and their annual charges, see Smith, *Chronicon Rusticum-Commerciale* (ed. 1747), ii. 166-167.
[6] *House of Commons Journals*, xiii. 783 ; *State Papers Domestic*, 1664–1665, p. 153 ; *Hist. MSS. Comm. Downshire*, i. part ii. 678 ; *ibid. Le Fleming*, 89 ; *The Deplorable Case of the Chief and other Agents or Officers . . . concerned in the Preventing . . . the Exportation of the Wool* ; Woodford, *A Representation of Great Evils arising by the Exportation of Wool*; Trevers, *An Essay to the Restoring of our Decayed Trade* (1675), 18.
[7] Carter, *An Abstract of the Proceedings to prevent Exportation of Wool Unmanufactured* (1689), 3, 22-23. See also his *A Brief Advertisement to the Merchant and Clothier* (1672), and his petition in *State Papers Domestic*, 1671–1672, p. 171.
[8] 1688 : Bodleian Library—Ashmole, H. 23, ccclxiii.
[9] *Statutes*, vi. 96 (1689) ; vii. 118 (1696—repeal of Act of 1662 making the export of wool an act of felony) ; vii. 527 (1698). Cruising vessels
[contd.]

modified (1696) in order not to deter the prosecution of
offenders ; and ships were appointed (1698) 'constantly to
cruise on the coasts of England and Ireland' to seize
vessels exporting wool, though two years later the Admiralty reported that they had not taken a single vessel,
while they had lost two of their own and expected to
lose others, and the cost involved amounted to £2400 a
month [1]. The clothiers complained in 1701 that " notwithstanding this kingdom is at great charges in maintaining
vessels and men to prevent the exportation of wool, yet
within these two years many thousand packs of wool have
been exported into France and other foreign parts " [2]. The
Government, unable to devise any remedy, transferred the
responsibility to Parliament, and the speech from the throne
(1702) recommended the legislature to " find time to consider of some better and more effectual method to prevent the
exportation of wool, and to improve that manufacture which
is of great consequence to the whole kingdom " [3]. Many
schemes were propounded for preventing the export of wool [4].
The favourite expedient, which was mooted early in the
seventeenth century, and was widely canvassed in the next
century, was to establish official registers to " keep sight of
all wool from its being shorn till it was completely manufactured " [5]. A local scheme was put into operation by the
Act of 1698 which instituted a registry in Kent and Sussex.
It provided that all owners of wool in these counties within
ten miles of the sea " shall be obliged to give an exact account
in writing, within three days after the shearing thereof ", of

---

had been appointed in 1669 : *State Papers Domestic*, 1668–1669,
p. 556.                              [1] *House of Lords Journals*, xvi. 569.
  [2] *House of Commons Journals*, xiii. 426, 464.
  [3] *House of Lords Journals*, xvii. 156.
  [4] See *The Gentleman's Magazine*, xii. 83 *seq.*, 147 *seq.* ; *Some Impartial
Thoughts on the Woollen Manufacturies* (1742). One suggestion was to fine
the Hundred if the offenders were not apprehended or had no estate :
Manley, *A Discourse shewing that the Exportation of Wool is Destructive to
this Kingdom* (1677), 10. This was criticized by Pownall, *Live and Let Live*
(1787), 95, when the idea was revived a century later.
  [5] It is mentioned in *State Papers Domestic*, 1625–1626, p. 523 ; *House
of Commons Journals*, xiii. 784 (1702) ; Whitelocke, *A Proposal for preventing effectually the Exportation of Wool* (1695) ; Haynes, *A View of the
Present State of the Clothing Trade in England* (1706), 68 ; Cary, *An Essay
towards Regulating the Trade* (ed. 1719), 35.

the number and the weight of the fleeces, and the name of the person to whom it is disposed, and the place to which it is carried [1]. A proposal for a national scheme was rejected by the Commissioners for Trade and Plantations in 1732, on the ground that it would be very expensive and involve a 'multiplicity of accounts'[2]. Nevertheless a few years later the idea was revived [3] ; and in response to a petition from ' the lord mayor, aldermen and commons ' of London expressing ' unspeakable grief' at ' so great and crying an evil ', the House of Commons passed a resolution (1741) declaring that " a public register of the wool grown in Great Britain and Ireland is the most effectual method for preventing the exportation thereof to foreign parts " [4]. No machinery, however, was instituted for the purpose [5], and smuggling went on unchecked. The severity of the penalties did not deter those who boasted that " if a gallows was set up every quarter of a mile, yet they would carry the wool off " [6] ; and the efforts of the officials, as we have seen [7], were discouraged by the expenses involved in seizing and prosecuting offenders. " In effect ", it was said in 1677, " Calais is still no less your staple than while it was formerly under the English dominion " [8]. " Long experience hath demonstrated ", observed another writer (1680), " that the mere prohibiting of the exportation

[1] *Statutes*, vii. 422. " The registry of Essex (*sic.* ? Sussex) and Kent alone costs the Government £6000" a year to maintain : *Hist. MSS. Comm. Egmont (Diary)*, i. 162 (1731). The Commissioners for Trade and Plantations claimed in 1702 that by the active enforcement of the law " this unlawful trade is almost destroyed in those counties " : *House of Lords MSS.*, 1702 1704, p. 72. But later (1793) it was stated that " smuggling is carried on very successfully throughout this line of country from Eastbourne hither (Rye) " : *Annals of Agriculture*, xxii. 292-294.

[2] *House of Commons Journals*, xxi. 833.

[3] By Webber in *A Short Account of the State of our Woollen Manufacturies* (1739) ; *House of Commons Journals*, xxiv. 145, 158. It was criticized in *Remarks upon Mr. Webber's Scheme* (1741). See also *Some Observations on the Petitions now before the House of Commons ;* and *Considerations on Several Proposals for Preventing the Exportation of Wool* (1741), 8 *seq.*

[4] *House of Commons Journals*, xxiii. 647, 673.

[5] A register scheme of the Board of Trade (1742) was thrown out because it resembled an excise : Young, *The Question of Wool Truly Stated* (1788), 22.

[6] *House of Commons Journals*, xii. 212.     [7] *Supra*, p. 25.

[8] *A Letter from a Gentleman in Ireland to his Brother in England* (1677), in Smith, *Chronicon Rusticum-Commerciale* (ed. 1747), i. 309.

of wool is but a cobweb " [1]. Adam Smith, a century later, remarked : " It is exported, it is well known, in great quantities " [2].

It is a striking testimony to the importance of the woollen industry that the Act forbidding the export of wool remained on the statute-book more than a hundred and fifty years. One result was to create that rivalry of interests between agriculture and industry, which in one form or another has ever since been a feature of our economic system [2a]. The manufacturer demanded cheap raw material and cheap food ; and he came into conflict with the farmer over the first in the eighteenth century and over the second in the nineteenth century. Hence the woollen manufacturers found it necessary to exercise the utmost vigilance in warding off attacks upon a privilege, which had been wrested from the rulers of the State in the teeth of bitter opposition on the part of the landed interest. The graziers raised a violent agitation against their confinement to the home market, and an interminable argument was carried on in an unceasing stream of pamphlets and broadsheets.

The embargo on wool originated in the desire to secure an abundant supply of cheap raw material for the native manufacturer [3], who claimed a natural right to monopolize the use of native products [4]. But jealousy of continental rivals, rather than any apprehension of a scarcity, became the dominating motive. James I.'s proclamation of 1614, which marked the beginning of the change in commercial policy as regards wool [5], was intended to check the growth of the Dutch woollen industry, " so that we may not be killed with arrows from our own quiver " [6]: and later, French competition came to be greatly dreaded owing to the cheapness of French labour. Two propositions were accepted as axiomatic. One was that trade depressions were caused, or aggravated, by the export of wool—" whereby the stranger's wheel

---

[1] *Britannia Languens* (1680), 60. Similarly : Child, *A New Discourse of Trade* (4th ed.), 156.   [2] *The Wealth of Nations* (ed. Cannan), ii. 153. [2a] Cf. *infra*, Appendix, p. 494, No. 2.   [3] See *supra*, vol. i. 454-455. [4] *State Papers Domestic*, 1675-1676, p. 373 ; Davenant, *Works* (ed. 1771), ii. 148.   [5] *Supra*, p. 23. [6] *State Papers Domestic*, 1661-1662, p. 449 ; *Acts of the Privy Council* 1618-1619, p. 122 ; *Newcastle Merchant Adventurers*, i. 119 (1618).

is set going " [1]. The other was that foreign competition could
be extinguished by refusing to supply other countries with
raw material. Accordingly the discussion centred on the
question whether English wool was indispensable for the continental textile industries. It was sometimes maintained that
" there is not a piece of broad cloth or new drapery made in
France without the help of our wool " [2], one pack of the latter
being worked up with two of their own [3]. Spanish wool,
though fine, was short and required an admixture of English
or Irish wool to make fine thin cloth : other kinds of wool,
German or French, were so coarse that the cloth was not
' merchandisable ' unless mixed with British wool [4]. The
long staple or ' combing ' wool, in particular, was claimed to
be ' absolutely necessary in some of the French manufactures ' [5]. The prohibition of wool was therefore defended on
economic and political grounds alike. If we manufactured
all our wool, ran the economic argument, " we should have
the markets of the known world to ourselves and at our own
price " [6]. If we cut off France from supplies of English and
Irish wool, ran the political argument, our national enemy
would be unable to carry on her manufactures since bricks
cannot be made without straw, and we should be saved from
" falling a sacrifice to universal monarchy and arbitrary
power " [7]. " Our Fathers bravely pulled down the exorbitant
power of France at the expense of their blood and their
treasure, but never thought of the way to give her a more

[1] 1622 : Stowe MSS., 354. f. 65.   1630 : State Papers Domestic, 1629–
1631, p. 447.   1640 : Hist. MSS. Comm. Portland, viii. 2.   1647 : ibid.
Various, i. 115.   1649 : State Papers Domestic, 1649–1650, p. 64.   1677 :
ibid. 1677–1678, p. 241.

[2] Cary, A Reply to a Paper entituled The Linnen Drapers' Answer.
Similarly : A Proposal Humbly Offered to the King and Parliament for
raising a Considerable Sum of Money yearly to his Majesty.

[3] The Consequences of Trade as to the Wealth and Strength of any Nation.
By a Draper of London (1740), 15.

[4] State Papers Domestic, 1675–1676, pp. 374-375 ; 1677–1678, p. 69.
House of Commons Journals, i. 552 ; xxi. 691 ; xxiii. 647.   Britannia
Languens (1680), 59.   Also see infra, Appendix, p. 494, No. 3.

[5] Anstie, A General View of the Bill . . . for preventing the Illicit
Exportation of British Wool (1787), 41.

[6] The Case of the British Woollen Manufacturies ; Britannia Languens
(1680), 60.

[7] An Essay on the Improvement of the Woollen Manufacture.   By a
Merchant (1741), 5.

deadly wound than she could receive by the loss of ten battles and twice as many towns "[1]. The export of wool, protested the manufacturers, would be an unparalleled disaster : it would " change the current of their wealth, destroy their industry and enterprise, deprive the poor of their employment, add to the poor rates, and diminish the rental of the land "[2]. " Ere the next generation ", cried a panic-stricken ' Cheshire Weaver ' after recounting the fatal consequences attending the smuggling of wool, " England will be no more "[3].

*Arguments against the embargo on wool.* The advocates of free trade, on their part, endeavoured to show the folly of a system in which wool, the ' coveted vineyard '[4], was " watched with as much care and jealousy as the Golden Apples of the Hesperides "[5]. The policy of protection was denounced as an evil legacy of the Great Rebellion : it was the work of the Commonwealth party, which had " been assisted in the Civil Wars by great numbers of the wool-workmen, who liked much better to rob and plunder for half-a-crown a day than toil at a melancholy work for sixpence a day ", and which prohibited the export of wool in order " to encourage and reward them, and to weaken the gentry "[6]. The embargo on wool was condemned by the wool growers on three grounds—it was unnecessary ; it served to defeat its own ends ; and it was injurious to the landed interest.

*(i.) It was unnecessary.* The leading exponent of the argument that free trade in wool would not harm the English manufacturers was John Smith, whose book [7], though written with a polemical pur-

---

[1] *Some Impartial Thoughts on the Woollen Manufacturies* (1742), 53.

[2] *An Account of the Proceedings of the Merchants, Manufacturers and Others concerned in the Wool and Woollen Trade of Great Britain* (1800), 30.

[3] *Excidium Anglicae, or a View of the Fatal Consequences attending the Smuggling of Wool. By a Cheshire Weaver* (1727) in Bischoff, *History of the Woollen and Worsted Manufactures*, i. 123. Fantastical estimates were made as to the depreciation in the value of our woollen manufactures due to smuggling. One ' very moderate computation ' was that " the nation loses no less than 42 millions sterling yearly " : *The Consequences of Trade as to the Wealth and Strength of any Nation. By a Draper of London* (1740), 15.

[4] *A Brief Account of the Woollen Manufactory of England* (1708), 1.

[5] *Considerations on the East-India Trade* (1701), 79.

[6] *Reasons for a limited exportation of Wool* (1677), 8. Actually the policy had been that of the Early Stuarts : see *supra*, p. 23.

[7] *Chronicon Rusticum-Commerciale Or Memoirs of Wool* (1747).

pose, is a valuable storehouse of historical material. Of this work, it was said by an agriculturist that it "ought to be printed in letters of gold " [1]. The author sought to combat the notion that foreign nations could not carry on their textile manufactures without English or Irish wool. England and Ireland, he affirmed, did not possess the vaunted superiority in wool over all other countries [2] : we therefore gained no benefit from prohibiting its export. Smith was not the first to employ this argument—more than a century earlier Misselden had denied that foreign manufacturers could not make cloth without English wool [3]. It was difficult, however, to induce Englishmen to abandon the tradition, which had acquired almost the sanctity of a dogma, that English wool was the best in the world. The tradition went back to early times when the wool produced in this country enjoyed great repute. Thus Dionysius Periegetes, a geographer of antiquity, stated that the fleece of the sheep was ' so soft and fine ' that it was spun until it was ' comparable to a spider's web ' [4]. As late as the sixteenth century the Venetian envoy remarked (1551) that among England's chief endowments was her ' very fine and most excellent wool ' [5] ; while Lambard's boast (1576) that ' the exceeding fineness of the fleece passeth all other in Europe at this day ' [6] seemed borne out by the opinion of an Italian that ' Spanish wools cannot be compared to it ' [7]. In the seventeenth century the position was reversed, and English writers were now constrained to admit that " we must submit to Spain in the utmost curiosity of fineness " [8]. The reasons for the

[1] Quoted in Luccock, *Wool* (1805), 358. He merited, said Tucker, " the universal thanks and applause of his country " : *An Essay on Trade* (ed. 1753), 65. The work was attacked by Temple, *A Refutation of Mr. Smith's Memoirs of Wool* (1750).
[2] Smith, *Chronicon Rusticum-Commerciale* (ed. 1747), ii. 497.
[3] Misselden, *The Circle of Commerce* (1623), 51.
[4] Dionysius Periegetes, *The Survey of the World* (ed. 1572).
[5] *State Papers Venetian*, 1534–1554, pp. 354, 542.
[6] Lambard, *A Perambulation of Kent* (1576), 198-199.
[7] *State Papers Venetian*, 1557–1558, p. 1672 (1557).
[8] *The Interest of England considered in an Essay upon Wool* (1694), 4. D. Coffler, *Dissertatio juridica de Lana et Lanificis* (cited in *Notes and Queries*, 3rd ser. v. 95), wrote in 1682 : ' *Post Hispanicam praecipua bonitas est lanae Anglicanae* '. Similarly : W. S., Gent., *The Golden Fleece* (1656) ; *The British Merchant* (ed. 1721), ii. 246, 430. Cf. *infra*, Appendix, p. 494, No. 4.

deterioration in the quality of English wool were disputed. The graziers contended that it was due to the wool laws, which made it less profitable to concentrate on the fleece [1], but it was more commonly attributed to enclosures and the breeding of larger sheep [2] in place of the ' ancient small breed of English sheep '. " So long as Englishmen are fond of fat mutton ", it was said, " they must not expect to grow fine wool ". The best English cloth now contained a large admixture of Spanish wool [3] ; and our dependence on Spain deprived us of our former monopoly, and placed us on the same footing as other manufacturing countries [4]. The only kind of wool, which was sometimes admitted by the advocates of free trade in wool to be peculiar to England, was combing wool :

' The soft, the snow-white and the long-grown flake ' [5].

(ii.) *It defeated its own ends.* In the next place, the embargo on wool depressed its price in this country, and the low price encouraged illicit trading since the ' unnatural artificial cheapness ' [6] of the material at home made it worth while to smuggle it abroad.

[1] Anderson, *Report . . . on Shetland Wool* (1790), Appendix, iv. 45-46. Adam Smith's opinion was that though the wool laws depressed the price of wool, they had not much reduced the quantity grown nor the quality : *The Wealth of Nations* (ed. Cannan), ii. 152.

[2] *Annals of Agriculture*, ix. 526-527 ; *Wool Encouraged without Exportation. By a Wiltshire Clothier* (1791), 8, 31, 56 ; [Anstie], *A Letter to the Secretary of the Bath Agriculture Society* (1791), 14, 18-19 ; Bischoff, *History of the Woollen and Worsted Manufactures*, i. 255-256, 334-336. Parry ridiculed the suggestion that enclosures made sheep bear coarse wool, and thought that farmers ceased to " prefer the fine-woolled sheep, but seduced by fashion selected for breeding those of a larger mould " : *The Practicability of producing in the British Isles Clothing Wool equal to that of Spain* (1800), 11, 15.

[3] It was termed ' Spanish cloth '. Chamberlayne (*Angliæ Notitia*, ed. 1700, p. 41) asserted that it mostly contained English wool ; but Haynes (*A View of the Present State of the Clothing Trade in England*, 1706, p. 15) stated that it was made of a warp of English wool and a weft of Spanish. Smith, *Chronicon Rusticum-Commerciale* (ed. 1747), ii. 407 (note), 499, wrote : " It is certain that the best Spanish cloths, called superfine, have no English wool at all in them ".

[4] For statistics of the foreign wool imported into England at different periods, see Baines, *Yorkshire Past and Present*, i. 636-637 ; *Report of the Earl of Sheffield to the Meeting at Lewes Wool Fair* (1816) ; *Parliamentary Papers* (1821), xvii. 223 ; *ibid.* (1826-1827) xviii. 385.

[5] Dyer, *The Fleece*, bk. ii. 69. According to Pownall, *Live and Let Live* (1787), 73, English combing wool was chiefly used at Abbeville.

[6] In 1675 it was represented that the price of some wool had fallen from £12 to about £4 the pack : *State Papers Domestic*, 1675-1676, p. 376.

The fact that wool in England was kept below its ' natural value ' served as " an advantage, in the nature of a premium, to the exporter of woollen goods ; yet at the same time it affords equally a premium for the runnage of wool " [1]. " This in a word ", said Smith, " is the mainspring of the owling trade " [2]. As Child pointed out: "They that can give the best price for a commodity shall never fail to have it" [3].

There remained the final plea that it was the duty of the nation to preserve the landed classes, the ' masters and proprietors of the foundation of all the wealth in this nation ', who maintained great families, bore the burden of taxes, and filled all the magistracies and public offices [4]. The spoliation of the landed interest was deemed the more indefensible because it was ' the most considerable national interest ', and wool was its ' principal' support [5]. It was therefore on the ground of injustice that the wool growers denounced " the oppression which the grazier suffers under this iniquitous system of monopoly " [6]. They asked : " If he that combs, dyes, weaves, works, or exports wool, thrives—why should he that grows it be impoverished ? Why must the grazier be the only sufferer, where all other dealers in wool are gainers by it ? " [7] The manufacturers replied that the welfare of the landed and industrial interests ' mutually depend on each other'. The value of land depended on trade [8] inasmuch as a prosperous trade increased the demand for agricultural produce such as corn, beef, mutton, etc. ; hence the farmers were compensated in other directions, if their wool sold at a lower price at home than it would fetch abroad. [9] Smith retorted that the embargo on the export trade in wool might benefit the export trade in

*(iii.) It was injurious to the landed interest.*

---

[1] Smith, *Chronicon Rusticum-Commerciale* (ed. 1747), i. 225-226, 277 ; ii. 292, 516-517, 564.          [2] *Ibid.* i. 339.

[3] Child, *A New Discourse of Trade* (4th ed.), 157. Similarly : *Proposals and Reasons for Constituting a Council of Trade* (1701), 113.

[4] *Reasons for a limited exportation of Wool* (1677), 5. W. Carter replied to this pamphlet in *The Proverb Crossed* (1677).          [5] Smith, *op. cit.* ii. 554-555.

[6] Pownall, *Live and Let Live* (1787), 79.

[7] *The Grasier's Complaint. By a Lincolnshire Grasier* (1726), 33.

[8] Coke, *Treatise* (1675), iii. 68 ; Davenant, *Works* (ed. 1771), i. 16 ; Wood, *A Survey of Trade* (1718), 8, 21, 58.

[9] Defoe, *A Plan of the English Commerce* (ed. 1728), 18 ; Hustler, *Observations upon the Bill for preventing the Exportation of Wool* (1787), 7.

cloth, but it certainly created 'a monopoly against the grower ' : and " whether thus robbing Peter to enrich Paul is of any real public benefit ? that is the point to be considered " [1]. Arthur Young was conspicuous for the vigour with which he repudiated the alleged indentity of interests between agriculture and industry: " Let us hear no more from woolmen of the prosperity of land and manufactures being the same " [2]. He bitterly deplored that " the gentlemen of the landed interest have quietly laid themselves down to be fleeced by the woolmen, like their sheep " [3] ; and he roundly declared that ' the sweets of a monopoly of their raw materials ' had made the woollen manufacturers indolent and devoid of the ' ardour of enterprise ' or the ' spirit of invention ' [4]. That a Parliament dominated by landlords should have made the sacrifice, which the wool laws entailed, indicates that it was not incapable at times of subordinating class interests to what it considered to be the national interest. For, in spite of their arguments, the efforts of the wool growers to secure a limited exportation of wool proved unsuccessful ; and in 1788 the penalties on the export of sheep or wool were made even more stringent than before [5], amidst great rejoicings in the manufacturing districts where the bells were set ringing [6]. The severity of the penalties imposed at one period or another called forth Adam Smith's bitter reflection that the laws, " which the clamour of our merchants and manufacturers has extorted from the legislature for the support of their own absurd and oppressing monopolies ", may be said " like the laws of Draco to be all written in blood " [7].

*Export of leather.*  The controversy over the export of leather affords a fresh illustration of the conflict of economic interests between the producers and consumers of raw materials. The Act of 1559

[1] Smith, *Chronicon Rusticum-Commerciale* (ed. 1747), ii. 553.
[2] *Annals of Agriculture*, vii. 165 ; x. 240, 244.
[3] *Ibid.* vii. 171.     [4] *Ibid.* vii. 162-164.
[5] *Statutes at Large*, xi. 455 ; *Reports from Committees of the House of Commons*, xi. 300, 303 *seq.* Arthur Young strenuously opposed the Wool Bill : *Annals of Agriculture*, x. 1 *seq.* ; *The Question of Wool Truly Stated* (1788).
[6] *Letters to the Lincolnshire Graziers* in Bischoff, *History of the Woollen and Worsted Manufactures*, i. 244-245.
[7] *The Wealth of Nations* (ed. Cannan), ii. 146.

attributed the ' excessive price ' of tanned leather and hides to their transportation abroad, and ordered that it should cease [1]. The law was evaded, and a petition to the Long Parliament characterized the export of leather as ' a grievance beyond the insupportable burthen of ship-money '. " It is against the rule of trade and of policy ", declared the complainants, " to transport any native material unwrought : thereby the subject loses the benefit of manufacture and puts it into the hands of strangers " [2]. After the Restoration the prohibition was renewed (1662), but in 1668 the export of leather was permitted [3]. When the Act lapsed (1675), the London Cordwainers' Company attempted to prevent its renewal. Their arguments had a familiar ring. Transportation of the raw material " must ruin many thousand families that convert it into wares, there being a hundred to one more manufacturers than tanners and transporters " : it would enable foreign countries to develop their own leather manufactures, and " it is most certain, if they can get our leather, they will prohibit our leather wares in all places beyond the seas " [4]. The merchants and tanners, on the other hand, depicted the ' ill consequences ' of the embargo on leather— the glutting of the home market, the sinking of the value of raw hides, bark and calf skins, and the fall of rents and customs duties. They claimed that, owing to the neglect of Lent and the ' Fish Days ' [5], ' a third part more beasts ' were slaughtered ; this had increased the supply of leather, while at the same time the great use of stage coaches had diminished the consumption of leather in riding furniture for horse and man. They represented that leather was in a different category from wool : " for many thousands will be employed in making leather, and the bark of the kingdom expended, before it is exported " [6]. The producers of leather

---

[1] Statutes, iv. part i. 370, 435, 590.
[2] An Humble Petition and Remonstrance concerning the insupportable grievance of the Transportation of Leather (1641), 2, 9. See also Leather : A Discourse tendered to the High Court of Parliament (1629).
[3] Statutes, v. 378 (1662), 640 (1668).
[4] State Papers Domestic, 1675–1676, p. 371. It was said in 1657 that " leather is excellent in England and of great esteem abroad " : Hist. MSS. Comm. Various, ii. 200. [5] Infra, p. 117.
[6] State Papers Domestic, 1675–1676, pp. 369-373.

were more successful than the wool growers in gaining the
ear of the legislature ; and in 1685 the Act of 1668 permitting
the export of leather was revived [1].

*Protection
of woollen
cloth.*    The most conspicuous instance of protection given to the
manufactured article, as distinct from the raw material, is
that of woollen cloth.   The makers of cloth considered the
home market as their natural preserve, and sought to exclude
not only foreign woollen cloth but all foreign textiles which
competed with their own industry.   The pursuit of this principle gave rise to an agitation against the East India Company, which imported textile fabrics from the East as a
substitute for woollen goods.

> " When first the Indian Trade began,
> And Ships beyond the Tropicks ran,
> In quest of various Drugs and Spices,
> And sundry other strange Devices,
> Saltpetre, Drugs, Spice, and like Trading,
> Compos'd the bulk of all their Lading :
> Bengals and Silks of Indians making,
> Our Merchants then refus'd to take in,
> Knowing it wou'd their Country ruin."

But when men's ' chiefest Aim ' became ' private Gain ',
Indian silks were imported and—

> " Our Ladies all were set a gadding,
> After these Toys they ran a madding . . .
> And like gay Peacocks proudly strut it,
> When in our Streets along they foot it " [2].

The introduction of Eastern textiles into England is older
than this account represents. In the reign of James I. Mun
spoke of " the trade of calicoes of many sorts into which the
English lately made an entrance " [3].   They served ' both for
our own use and to carry into other countries ' [4]; and it was

---

[1] *Statutes*, vi. 14; *House of Lords MSS.* 1678–1688, pp. 312 *seq.*;
1689–1690, p. 115.
[2] *Prince Butler's Tale : Representing the State of the Wool-Case, or the
East-India Case truly Stated* (1699).
[3] Mun, *A Discourse of Trade from England unto the East Indies* (1621),
7-8. See also Foster, *The English Factories in India*, 1618–1621, pp. 46,
127, 137 ; and *supra*, vol. ii. 288, note 4.
[4] *Hist. MSS. Comm. Cowper*, i. 155 (*c.* 1623).

claimed that they "greatly abated the excessive prices of cambrics, Holland and other sorts of linen cloth which daily are brought into this kingdom "[1]. In the next reign ' great quantities of silk stuffs ' were brought from China and ' sold at very low rates '[2]. After the Restoration the East India Company is said to have sent out to India artisans to instruct the Indians in Western fashions, "after which began the great trade in manufactured goods from the Indies "[3]. A vigorous attack was made on the East India Company in the Parliament of 1680. " By the best computation that can be made," said one speaker, "we now spend in this kingdom per annum to the value of two or three hundred thousand pounds worth of goods manufactured in the East India: what part thereof are spent instead of our stuff, serges, cheneys and other goods, I leave to every man's judgment that hath observed how their Persian silks, Bengals, printed and painted calicoes, and other sorts are used for beds, hanging of rooms, and vestments of all sorts. And those goods from India do not only hinder the expense of our woollen goods by serving instead of them here, but also by hindering the consumption of them in other parts too, to which we export them "[4].

After the Revolution the agitation came to a head owing *Agitation against Indian textiles.* to circumstances which have never been explained, but which seem to have been as follows. On account of the war and the depreciation of the currency, the foreign exchanges turned against this country[5], and this stimulated the demand abroad for English woollen goods. The woollen manufacturers, however, attributed their prosperity to a shortage in the supply of Indian textiles occasioned by the losses of ships at sea[6]; and they pressed for the prohibition of the trade,

[1] Mun, *op. cit.* 8.          [2] *State Papers Domestic*, 1639–1640, p. 38.
[3] About 1672 according to *A True Relation of the Rise and Progress of the East India Company*, 1. Only " one or two dyers " to Bengal, was the Company's rejoinder : Macpherson, *Annals of Commerce*, ii. 605. Two or three years later the clothiers ' began to complain ' : *A Treatise wherein is demonstrated that the East India Trade is the most national of all Foreign Trades. By* Φιλοπάτρις (1681), 19-20. Cf. Wood, *A Survey of Trade* (1718), 271.
[4] Smith, *Chronicon Rusticum-Commerciale* (ed. 1747), i. 352.
[5] *Infra*, p. 78.
[6] Davenant, *Works* (ed. 1771), i. 95. The losses were very heavy in 1695 : *House of Lords MSS.* 1695-1697, p. 64.

in order to prevent the revival which proposals for the reorganization of the East India Company seemed to foreshadow[1]. Their efforts were seconded by the silk manufacturers, who in some instances combined both branches of the textile industry, for example, Norwich worsted stuffs were sometimes a mixture of silk and wool[2]. In 1696 the woollen and silk manufacturers gave evidence before a parliamentary committee, which resolved that the wearing of Indian and Persian silks and printed calicoes was ' very destructive to the woollen manufacture '[3]. A Bill was introduced into the House of Commons in 1696, when a multitude of weavers and their wives thronged the precincts of the House to press for its enactment[4] : but a divergence of opinion arose between the two Chambers. The House of Lords wished to extend the scope of the Act to include all foreign silks, and to prohibit under penalties the wearing as well as the sale of imported silks ; the House of Commons rejected these proposals and the Bill dropped[5]. The popular excitement, however, was not allayed. There was great alarm lest Indian silks and muslins should become ' the general ware ' and ' eat up our manufactures '[6]. " I question not ", said one writer, " but we shall have cotton cloth, and knaves to make it a fashion, and fools enough to wear it "[7]. The wearing of cotton, it was complained, put " all degrees and orders of woman-kind into disorder and confusion " since the lady " cannot well be known from her chambermaid "[8]. " The general fancy of the people ", wrote Defoe, " runs upon East India goods to that degree that the chints and painted calicoes, which before were only made use of for carpets,

---

[1] *Supra*, vol. ii. 309. For the quantity imported, 1697–1699, see *House of Commons Journals*, xiii. 176 *seq.*

[2] *House of Commons Journals*, xi. 437, 456, 474.    [3] *Ibid.* xi. 496-497.

[4] *Ibid.* xi. 497, 633, 682-684 ; *Hist. MSS. Comm. Le Fleming*, 346.

[5] The House of Commons objected that foreign silks were bought with English manufactures. The other House rejoined that so were Indian silks : *House of Commons Journals*, xi. 755-756 ; *House of Lords MSS.*, 1695–1697, pp. 238 *seq.*, 509-510.

[6] *Hist. MSS. Comm. Portland*, iii. 614.

[7] W. C., *An Alarum to England to prevent its Destruction by the loss of Trade and Navigation* (1700), 32.

[8] Rey, *The Weavers' True Case, Or the Wearing of Printed Callicoes and Linen destructive to the Woollen and Silk Manufactures* (1719), 30. Cf. *infra*, Appendix, p. 494, No. 5.

quilts, etc., and to clothe children and ordinary people, became now the dress of our ladies ; and such is the power of a mode as we saw our persons of quality dressed in Indian carpets, which but a few years before their chambermaids would have thought too ordinary for them ; the chints were advanced from lying upon their floors to their backs, from the footcloth to the petticoat ; and even the Queen herself at this time was pleased to appear in China and Japan, I mean China silks and calico. Nor was this all, but it crept into our houses and bedchambers ; curtains, cushions, chairs and at last beds themselves were nothing but calicoes or Indian stuffs ; and in short, almost everything that used to be made of wool or silk, relating either to the dress of the women or the furniture of our houses, was supplied by the Indian trade "[1]. The English workman, it was said, could not compete with Eastern labour, because "the people in India are such slaves as to work for less than a penny a day, whereas ours here will not work under a shilling "[2].

An array of arguments marshalled the case for Indian *The case for Indian textiles.* textiles. The plea that they were in a different category from foreign silks and linens, since the latter were ' purchased by the products of our manufactures '[3], was countered by the claim that we had begun to export to India large quantities of woollen goods in exchange for her silks[4]. Again London merchants, who exported woollen goods to the Continent, declared that the prohibition of calicoes would be attended ' with an immediate advance on wool', which would raise the price of woollen manufactures to the ' decay of the foreign trade '[5]. Thus the domestic consumption of English cloth would be stimulated at the expense of its consumption abroad, and the foreign demand would decline still more if the continental market were glutted with

[1] *Weekly Review* (1708), cited Baines, *History of the Cotton Manufacture*, 79.
[2] Smith, *Chronicon Rusticum-Commerciale* (ed. 1747), i. 351. Similarly : *Reasons Humbly Offered for Restraining the Wearing of Wrought Silks* (etc.).
[3] Pollexfen, *England and East India inconsistent in their Manufactures* (1697), 12. *House of Commons Journals*, xiii. 42, 66 ; xix. 169, 194.
[4] *House of Lords MSS.*, 1695–1697, p. 510 ; *House of Commons Journals*, xi. 623 (Petition of West Country clothiers).
[5] *House of Commons Journal*, xix. 236.

textiles excluded from the English market [1]. It was also represented that Indian textiles served in place of the more costly fabrics imported from France, Germany and Holland, so that the English consumer would either purchase more of the latter as a substitute, or obtain the former through Dutch channels. In each case the home demand for woollen goods would remain stationary, and the sole benefit would accrue to foreign linen manufacturers or the Dutch East India Company [2]. Moreover there was the danger that prohibition might undermine the whole fabric of our Indian trade, and react injuriously upon the carrying trade. It was further urged that to wear the cheaper Indian textiles, and reserve the more expensive native products for the export trade, was more profitable to the nation than the reverse. We should imitate the frugality of Holland, counselled Davenant, in " consuming at home what is cheap or comes cheaply, and carrying abroad what is rich and will yield most money " [3]. His critic, Pollexfen, demanded to know in what places our exports could be increased ; and he suggested that East India merchants might be tempted to increase their trade, until they had displaced English cloth from the foreign as well as the home market [4]. One final argument is worth attention in that it appears to anticipate the law of comparative costs. When " the people employed to make manufactures here " are more " than are necessary to procure the like from India", they are not employed to the kingdom's profit, for " if one man procures as much value by his labour from India as three produced before in England . . . he possesses as much as all the three before ". It were better, therefore, for the men employed in such manufactures to betake themselves to other industries, for

[1] *House of Commons Journal*, xix. 231 ; Davenant, *Works* (ed. 1771), i. 104. The prohibition affected adversely the demand abroad for Norwich stuffs : *Serious considerations on the several High Duties* (1743), 23.

[2] *House of Commons Journals*, xiv. 338 ; *Hist. MSS. Comm. Kenyon*, 401 ; Davenant, *Works* (ed. 1771), i. 114 ; *Five Queries Humbly Tender'd Relating to the Bill for the Prohibiting the Consumption of the East-India Silks* (etc.).

[3] Davenant, *Works* (ed. 1771), i. 102-103. Similarly : *The Linen Drapers' Answer to . . . Mr. Cary his Essay on Trade*.

[4] Pollexfen, *England and East India inconsistent in their Manufactures* (1697), 21, 24.

which this country was more suited. To crown the argument
there was the consideration that the East India trade, in
supplying commodities " with less and cheaper labour than
would be necessary to make the like in England, is therefore
very likely to be the cause of the invention of arts and mills
and engines ", in order to meet foreign competition [1].

The duel between the woollen manufacturers and the *Calico*
East India Company ended in the triumph of the former. *printing in England.*
Yielding to the outcry, the Government in 1700 forbade the
use of wrought silks made in India, Persia or China, and
of calicoes ' painted, dyed, printed or stained there ' [2]. The
exclusion of Indian silks and printed calicoes had an unexpected result, for the English calico printers seized their
opportunity to capture the market from which their Indian
rivals had been expelled. " As if this nation was never to
want a set of men to undo her ", complained the indignant
weavers, " no sooner were the East India chints and printed
calicoes prohibited from abroad, but some of Britain's unnatural children, whom we call Drapers, set all their arts to
work to evade the law of prohibition, to employ people to
mimic the more ingenious Indians, and to legitimate the
grievance by making it a manufacture " [3]. The Commissioners for Trade and Plantations reported in 1702 that
" the prohibiting of painted calicoes from India to be consumed in England has not had the desired success, for . . .
allowing calicoes unstained to be brought in has occasioned
such an increase of the printing and staining calicoes here,
and the printers and painters have brought that art to
such perfection, that it is more prejudicial to us than " the
importation of printed calicoes " was before the passing
that Act. For whereas then the calicoes painted in India
were most used by the better sort of people . . . the calicoes
now painted in England are so very cheap, and so much in
fashion, that persons of all qualities and degrees clothe themselves and furnish their houses in a great measure with

---

[1] *Considerations on the East-India Trade* (1701), 34-35, 51-52, 66-67.
[2] *Statutes*, vii. 598 ; *House of Commons Journals*, xiii. 176.
[3] *The Just Complaints of the Poor Weavers Truly Represented* (1719) in
Smith, *Chronicon Rusticum-Commerciale* (ed. 1747), ii. 192. Similarly: *The
Case of the Printing of Linen in Great Britain.*

them " [1]. Actually the art of calico printing in England was
older than some of the disputants in this controversy alleged [2].
Charles I. granted a patent for ornamenting calicoes and
other fabrics in 1634 [3] : calicoes were being printed in London
' about the year 1676 ' [4] : and a witness informed a committee of the House of Lords in 1696 that there were printers
who employed " two or three hundred persons a man. If
there come 10,000 pieces of calico white, 9,500 are stained
or printed here " [5]. Nevertheless the assertion that the art
was not much practised in England, before the prohibition of
foreign printed calicoes [6], may have been substantially correct.
The effect of the Act of 1700 was to give a stimulus to the
native printing of foreign calicoes as well as to the native
cotton and linen industries : nor was it easy to raise any
valid objections to these developments. The raw material
of the English cotton industry came partly from our colonies :
linen was largely manufactured in Great Britain and Ireland,
and its raw material was in part home-grown : foreign
calicoes brought in considerable revenue [7] : and the printing
of calicoes in this country gave employment to many
workers [8]. On these grounds it was held that calicoes
printed in England, whether foreign or native, were entitled
to be encouraged and protected as much as silk [9].

None the less voices were soon heard in protest at the

---

[1] *House of Lords MSS.*, 1702–1704, p. 71 ; 1706–1708, p. 250.

[2] *E.g.* Defoe, *A Plan of the English Commerce* (ed. 1728), 296.

[3] *Victoria County History, Surrey*, ii. 369.

[4] Macpherson, *Annals of Commerce*, ii. 578. " About 40 years since "
was the date assigned for the trade of printing calicoes here in *A Further
Examination of the Weavers' Pretences* (1719), 12. A patent was issued in
1690 to Rene Grillet for an invention for printing calico : *State Papers
Domestic*, 1689–1690, pp. 512, 541. On early calico-printing, see Thomas,
*Mercantilism and the East India Trade*, 122 ; Wadsworth and Mann, *The
Cotton Trade*, 130 seq., 307-308.

[5] *House of Lords MSS.* 1695–1697, p. 241. A petition against the Bill
of 1696 was signed by 50 calico printers : *ibid.* 243.

[6] *The Case of the Weavers of the City of London* ; *A Brief State of
the Question between the Printed and Painted Calicoes and the Woollen and
Silk Manufacture* (1719), 23.

[7] Asgill, *A Brief Answer to A Brief State of the Question* (1719), 8-11 ;
Rey, *Observations on Mr. Asgill's Brief Answer* (1719), 5, 12.

[8] *Reasons against the Prohibiting the Wearing of East India and Persia
Wrought Silks ; The Case of the Printers of Callicoes and Linens.*

[9] It was also denied that calicoes competed with woollen manufactures
to any great extent : *House of Commons Journals*, xiv. 334 ; *The Stuff
Weavers' Case against Printing Callicoes Examined ; A Further Examination
of the Weavers' Pretences* (1719), 31.

'unspeakable damage' to the woollen industry [1]. Appeals *The use of printed calicoes prohibited.* were made to women to discard the new fashions [2]; and the weavers raised a great clamour, created disturbances, and attacked in the open street the wearers of cotton stuffs, the ' Calico-madams ' or ' Calico Picts ' [3] as they were called, even tearing the clothes off their backs—proceedings which their enemies declared did ' rankly savour of Jacobitism ' [4]. Both sides published newsheets. In one, *The Manufacturer*, calicoes were denounced as " a worthless, scandalous, unprofitable sort of goods embraced by a luxuriant humour among the women, prompted by the art and fraud of the drapers and the [East India] Company, to which alone they are profitable " ; and it urged the House of Commons " to brand the very name of calico with a mark of infamy " [5]. Its rival, *The British Merchant*, met these effusions with the rejoinder that trade required other talents than " the ringing in a mob with the chimes of a Billingsgate Ballad, in order to animate them to demolish the calico-madams " ; and it declared that laws, prohibiting the wear of one manufacture to enforce the consumption of a dearer one, would " stifle it with too much care " [6]. Innumerable petitions poured in on Parliament [7], which was forced to pass another Act (1721)

[1] *House of Commons Journals,* xiv 280-283 (1704) ; xvi. 336 ; *The Case of Several Thousand Poor of the Wool Manufacture.* The weavers attributed the falling-off in their trade to the competition of calicoes, but it may have been partially due to the dearness of wool, which was complained of in 1719 : *House of Commons Journals,* xix. 204. This would help to account for the revival of the agitation at this period.

[2] *A Second Humble Address from the Poor Weavers and Manufacturers to the Ladies.*

[3] Steele, *The Spinster : In defence of the Woollen Manufactures* (1719), No. 1, p. 13.

[4] *The London Journal* (1719), No. 23 ; *Hist. MSS. Comm. Westmorland,* 351 ; *The Case of the Linen Drapers and other Dealers in Printed Calicoes and Linens.* It was also hinted that the fashion of wearing calicoes was fostered by political malcontents—Jacobites—to bring odium upon the Government : Rey, *The Weavers' True Case, Or the Wearing of Printed Callicoes and Linen destructive to the Woollen and Silk Manufactures* (1719), 15.

[5] *The Manufacturer* (1720), No. 21. Another newsheet published against calicoes was *The Weaver.*

[6] *The British Merchant* (1719-1720), Nos. 6, 10.

[7] Their number may be gauged from the following references : *House of Commons Journals,* xix. 168-169, 176-182, 184-187, 189-200, 204, 206-218, 224-226, 229-231, 234, 236-237, 240, 245, 253-254, 263, 295, 407-408, 413, 415-418. Petitions in favour of calicoes were presented from various
[*contd.*]

prohibiting the use of any 'printed, painted, stained or dyed' calicoes [1].

*The 'Manchester Act' (1736).*   A controversy soon sprang up as to whether printed fustians, made of linen and cotton, were definitely exempted from the Act of 1721. Manchester petitioned Parliament to confirm the right to make printed fustians [2]; and it received the support of the woollen manufacturers of Halifax, Wakefield and other places. The fustian manufacture was seemingly against their interests, but they argued that great quantities of woollen goods were exported to Africa and the West Indies, and in return 'very large quantities' of cotton wool were brought back : hence a reduced consumption of cotton would " prejudice and prevent the exportation of woollen goods to those places ". The argument was significant in its recognition that national industries are complementary to each other, and that the prosperity of one is bound up with that of all the rest. As a result of these representations the 'Manchester Act' (1736) expressly permitted the use of printed stuffs made of linen yarn and cotton wool, provided the warp was entirely linen yarn [3]. There was said to be 'so much likeness' between English cotton goods and Indian printed calicoes that the latter continued to be 'no very uncommon wear' in this country [4]. Moreover the Indian textiles, which were excluded from the English market, were now shipped off in 'great quantities' to the West Indies, so that the consumption of English woollen goods in the plantations was proportionately diminished [5]. On the whole, therefore, it appeared that the woollen industry gained little advantage from a policy which curtailed its markets abroad and nourished a rival at home [6].

---

quarters, including baymakers in Essex : *ibid.* 231, 236, 254, 295-298, 416, 418.      [1] *Statutes at Large,* v. 229.

[2] *House of Commons Journals,* xxii. 551, 592-595, 598. Counterpetitions came from London (589), Norwich (592), etc.

[3] *Statutes at Large,* vi. 2.

[4] Smith, *Chronicon Rusticum-Commerciale* (ed. 1747), ii. 277.

[5] *House of Lords MSS.* 1702–1704, p. 71 ; 1706–1708, p. 250. Smith, *Chronicon Rusticum-Commerciale* (ed. 1747), ii. 327.

[6] For protection in the silk industry, see *supra,* vol. ii. 101. Also Hertz, " The English Silk Industry in the Eighteenth Century " in *The English Historical Review,* xxiv. 713 *seq.*

The system of protection had its counterpart in the efforts to promote by direct means the domestic consumption of native manufactures. The use of English cloth, in particular, was enjoined on all as a patriotic duty. As far back as the thirteenth century Englishmen were bidden not to ' seek over-precious garments ', but to content themselves with native cloth [1]. A strong agitation in favour of the compulsory wearing of English cloth sprang up in the seventeenth century. Just as Queen Elizabeth enforced the consumption of fish on several days in the week in order to foster the fishing trade [2], so her successor endeavoured to compel his subjects to wear native instead of foreign textiles. The Commission of 1622 was instructed to consider by what means native cloth ' may be more frequently worn by our own subjects ' [3]. The previous year a Bill ' for the better venting of the cloth of this kingdom ' had been introduced into Parliament, but met with some opposition. " It is hard ", said a member, " to make a law whereby we shall not know our wives from our chambermaids ". Others, however, approved the Bill, and suggested the addition of a clause " that none under the degree of a baron should mourn in anything but cloth " [4]. Under Charles II. the agitation was renewed. In 1667 it was enacted that the dead must be buried in woollen cloth [5], " forcing the dead ", as Arthur Young said, " to consume what the living were inadequate to purchase " [6].

    " Since the Living would not bear it,
      They should, when dead, be forc'd to wear it " [7].

*Compulsory wearing of English cloth.*

[1] 1258 : *Historiæ Anglicanæ Scriptores Quinque* (ed. 1687), ii. 580; *Chronicon Walteri de Hemingburgh* (ed. 1848), i. 306.   [2] *Infra*, p. 117.

[3] Rymer, *Foedera*, xvii. 415. For this Commission, see *infra*, p. 307.

[4] *House of Commons Journals*, i. 584. A proclamation for English cloth to be worn at funerals was issued in 1622 : *Tudor and Stuart Proclamations* (ed. Steele), i. No. 1334. The Commission of 1622 recommended that the ' nobility and gentry ' should set the example of wearing English cloth in winter : Stowe MSS. 554 f. 45.

[5] *Statutes*, v. 598 (1667), 885 (1678), 940 (1680). It was calculated that about 20,000 died in London every year, and 140,000 in England: *State Papers Domestic*, 1677–1678, p. 70. For a criticism of the ' Flannel Act ', see *Hist. MSS. Comm. Egmont*, ii. 75.

[6] Young, *The Question of Wool Truly Stated* (1788), 21. In *The Trade of England Revived* (1681), 17, it is implied that the Act was not executed, but affidavits were made late in the eighteenth century.

[7] *Prince Butler's Tale : Representing the State of the Wool-Case, or the East-India Case truly Stated* (1699).

Later (1668) both Houses of Parliament urged the King to encourage the wearing of English manufactures ' by his own example and his Queen's '. Recognizing that practice is better than precept, they also resolved " that the House begin themselves to show a good example herein to the nation " [1]. A subsequent resolution (1678) required " all persons whatsoever to wear no garment, stockings or other sort of apparel, but what is made of sheep's wool only, from the Feast of All Saints to the Feast of the Annunciation of Our Lady inclusive " [2]. These efforts to enforce the use of English cloth were revived after the Revolution. In 1689 a Bill was sent up by the Commons to the House of Lords, enjoining the wearing of woollen manufactures during six months in the year, but it was rejected by the Lords [3]. In 1698 the Commons ordered the insertion of a clause in a Bill " that all magistrates, judges, students of the Universities, and all professors of the common and civil law do wear gowns made of the woollen manufacture " [4]. In short, as a pamphleteer wrote at the beginning of the eighteenth century, " both the Living and the Dead must be wrapt in woollen; indeed no other law is wanted to complete the business but only one, that our perukes should be made of wool " [5]

The policy of enforced consumption did not escape criticism. The 'natural' method of promoting the woollen manufacture, said Davenant, is not to force a trade at home by prohibitions and unnatural contrivances, but to find out ways which will enable us to 'command the markets abroad' [6]. One objection to the system was that it conflicted with the interests of other branches of the textile industry ; and silk manufactures, especially, suffered detriment from the compulsory wearing of woollen cloth [7]. Difficulties of this

[1] *House of Commons Journals*, ix. 80 ; *House of Lords Journals*, xii. 228.
[2] Except garments made of leather : *House of Commons Journals*, ix. 444.
[3] *House of Lords MSS.*, 1689–1690, pp. 261-263 ; *House of Lords Journals*, xiv. 311, 316.
[4] *House of Commons Journals*, xii. 67. Also see *infra*, Appendix, p. 494, No. 6.
[5] *Considerations on the East-India Trade* (1701), 79. The policy was also condemned by Wood, *A Survey of Trade* (1718), 250.
[6] Davenant, *Works* (ed. 1771), i. 99 ; ii. 148.
[7] For complaints of the silk-workers, see *Hist. MSS. Comm.* ix. part ii. 124 (1678) ; *House of Lords MSS.* 1689–1690, p. 264 ; *House of Commons Journals*, xii. 87 (1698).

kind were bound to arise, when the State endeavoured to *Other ex-*
regulate both the diet [1] and the apparel of its subjects by *amples of enforced*
creating a category of prohibited articles. Thus in 1566 it *consump-tion.*
was forbidden to make caps of felt, or to wear a cap or hat of
velvet if the wearer were under the degree of a knight [2]. A
few years later (1571), when the cappers complained that
men had left off wearing caps, Parliament ordered everyone
above six years old, ' except ladies and gentlemen ', to wear
a ' cap of wool ' on Sundays and holidays since the wearing
of caps was ' very decent and comely for all estates and
degrees ' [3]. Then at the end of the seventeenth century a
motion for a Bill to compel all women servants in England
and the colonies, whose wages did not exceed five pounds a
year, to wear felt hats made in England, was only narrowly
defeated [4]. Another application of the same policy may be
noticed : in 1736 it was enacted that every vessel built in
Great Britain or the colonies must, at her first sailing, be
furnished with a complete set of new sails made of sail cloth
manufactured in Great Britain [5].

The safeguarding of industry was only one link in the *Emigra-*
chain of protection [6]. " The next care to that of confining *tion of artificers*
the English people to our English product and manufactures",
declared *The British Merchant* (1713), " will be that of confining them to England " [7]. To prevent other countries
using English technical skill to build up their own industries,
an embargo was placed on the emigration of skilled artisans.
In the troubled reign of Charles I. textile workers in Norfolk
and Suffolk sought refuge in Holland from religious persecution [8], and more emigrated during the Civil War probably

[1] *Infra*, p. 117.           [2] *Statutes*, iv. part i. 494.
[3] The Act was repealed in 1598 : *ibid.* iv. part i. 555 (1571) ; part ii.
918 (1598).
[4] *House of Commons Journals*, xii. 613 (1699).
[5] *Statutes at Large*, vi. 32. Great opposition was aroused by the proposal, made in the interests of Macclesfield, to suppress the making of
horn buttons : *Hist. MSS. Comm. Cowper*, iii. 51 (1704).
[6] The other links were : the restraints on the emigration of artisans,
the embargo on the export of money and tools, the Corn Laws, the
Navigation Acts, the restrictions on Colonial and Irish manufactures.
[7] *The British Merchant* (ed. 1721), i. 170.
[8] *State Papers Domestic*, 1639, p. 357. Coke, *Treatise* (1671), ii. 109-
110 ; iii. 13. Coke even declared that " the fourth part of the inhabitants
[*contd.*]

owing to want of employment [1]. While some left the country under compulsion, others were enticed abroad. As early as 1591 a certain Field bound himself not to give advice on making cloth in any foreign country, nor help subjects of the realm to leave the kingdom, and " to procure those two English weavers and all other Englishmen that now are in Pomerland, and have any skill in cloth-making, to return home again into England with all convenient speed " [2]. Holland, Germany, France, Portugal and Spain are cited among the countries which encouraged the settlement of English artisans [3]. A letter of the secretary of state (1678), alluding to " the late Portugal ambassador's spiriting our men from hence to teach weaving and making bays and other stuffs there ", stated that " the practice still continues and men of that trade are every passage sent over, so that one Condé pretends to the setting up of one hundred and fifty looms himself, which if he succeed in it will set up a trade there, that will not only lose us our Portugal trade but in all probability our Spanish too " [4]. Yarranton (1677) spoke of clothiers who had emigrated to Germany where they established a woollen industry, " which hath already quite spoiled our coarse cloth trade eastward and the trade at Hamburg too " [5]. Another writer (1679) affirmed that " for want of employment many of our weavers go over into France " [6]. Of Holland, it was said in 1713 that " there was an English congregation in almost every one of their great

---

of Rotterdam, Middelburg and Flushing . . . are English and of English extraction ". See also Moens, *The Walloons and their Church at Norwich*, 86 *seq*.

[1] *State Papers Domestic*, 1649–1650, p. 64. Also see *infra*, p. 317.

[2] *Acts of the Privy Council*, 1591, p. 301.

[3] *Infra*, Appendix, p. 495, No. 1 ; *State Papers Domestic*, 1659–1660, p. 284 ; *Britannia Languens* (1680), 135 (in sect. viii.). See also following notes.

[4] *State Papers Domestic*, 1678, p. 394 ; *Britannia Languens* (1680), 162. According to *The British Merchant* (ed. 1721), iii. 82, an Irishman in the service of Charles II.'s Queen carried over ' several clothiers and bay-makers ' to Portugal in 1681, and three years later the King of Portugal excluded foreign cloth ' upon the Condé d'Ereicera's project ' to develop a Portuguese woollen industry. For Spain : *infra*, Appendix, p. 495, No. 2.

[5] Yarranton, *England's Improvement* (1677), 112. Some settled in the Palatinate : Coke, *Treatise* (1671), ii. 110.

[6] J. B., *An Account of the French Usurpation upon the Trade of England* (1679), 12.

towns. . . . I could not but reflect what a loss this was to Great Britain, and what a gain to those provinces "[1]. Besides woollen workers, efforts were made to entice abroad ship-wrights, gun-founders, frame-work knitters, paper manufacturers and watch-makers[2]. In particular, apprehensions were aroused by the action of English tobacco merchants, who contracted with the Tsar to send over to Russia "persons skilled in the spinning and rolling of tobacco . . . together with the instruments, engines, materials and liquors commonly used in that work . . . proceedings of most pernicious consequence "[3].

As a result of the outcry against the emigration of arti-ficers, an Act of 1719 imposed heavy penalties on those who induced English workmen to leave the country[4]. It recited that " divers ill-disposed persons, as well foreigners as sub-jects of this kingdom, by confederacy with foreigners have of late drawn away and transported . . . several artificers and manufacturers of and in wool, iron, steel, brass and other metals, clock-makers, watch-makers and divers other manufacturers of Great Britain, out of his majesty's dominions into foreign countries, by entering into contracts with them to give them greater wages and advantages than they have or can reasonably expect within this kingdom " ; thereby creating the danger that " many great and profitable branches of the trades and manufactures of this kingdom may be transplanted into foreign countries ". Accordingly, any one contracting with or enticing artisans to go into a foreign country was to be punished with a fine not exceeding one hundred pounds and three months' imprisonment ; an on the second occasion with a fine imposed at the discretion of the court and twelve months in prison. These penalties

*Embargo on the emigration of workmen, and on the export of tools.*

[1] *The British Merchant* (ed. 1721), i. 171.
[2] *State Papers Domestic*, 1634–1635, pp. 20, 69 (shipwrights and gun-founders) ; *Tudor and Stuart Proclamations* (ed. Steele), i. No. 3844 (paper-makers) ; *House of Commons Journals*, xix. 89 (watch-makers). For frame-work knitters, see *supra*, vol. ii. 106. Runaway English apprentices improved the art of the pewterer in France and Flanders : Lewis, *The Stannaries*, 47.
[3] *Hist. MSS. Comm. Portland*, iv. 191-192 (1705) ; *House of Lords MSS.* 1706–1708, pp. 277-278 ; *Acts of the Privy Council*, Colonial Series, 1680–1720, No. 971.
[4] *Statutes at Large*, v. 157 ; *House of Commons Journals*, xix. 83.

did not prevent the emigration of English workmen, and complaints were still made that " foreigners decoy our manufacturers from hence " [1]. The embargo placed by the Act of 1719 on emigration was supplemented by an embargo on the export of tools used in certain industries [2].

*England under-populated.* Apprehension of foreign competition [3] was the main reason for the restraints on emigration, but the argument in their favour was fortified by the belief that England was under-populated. Hence the negative policy of checking the drain of population abroad had a positive side in the attempts to make good the deficiency of population. This could be done in two ways—by inventions for the ' abridgement ' of labour, and by the settlement of aliens. Though both were minor factors in the general mercantilist scheme, they exercised a far more beneficial influence upon the development of English industry than did the elaborate network of restrictions imposed by the legislature. Indeed they were destined to undermine the whole protective system, by substituting the natural protection afforded by superior economic efficiency for the artificial protection attempted by legal expedients. In this manner they furnished an argument for the adoption of a free trade policy, which proved more potent than any of the theoretical considerations advanced by the early economists or even by Adam Smith himself [4]. They can therefore be most appropriately considered in the present section.

*Inventions.* " It is a kind of proverb attending the character of Englishmen ", wrote Defoe, " that they are better to improve than to invent " [5]. One important discovery, the knitting

---

[1] *House of Commons Journals*, xxv. 976 (1750) ; xxviii. 496 (1759). *Home Office Papers*, 1760–1765, pp. 414, 417, 620.

[2] *Statutes at Large*, vi. 467 (woollen and silk : 1750) ; viii. 364 (cotton and linen : 1774) ; ix. 243 (calico printing and linen printing : 1782) ; ix. 599 (iron and steel : 1785). In 1701 joiners, cabinet-makers, fan-makers and ' japanners ' complained of the export of models or patterns by which their arts were disclosed : *House of Commons Journals*, xiii. 553. For the embargo on knitting frames, see *supra*, vol. ii. 106.

[3] Attempts to establish a woollen manufacture in other parts of the world were jealously watched, and diplomatic pressure was brought to bear to discourage the promotion of such undertakings : see examples in *House of Commons Journals*, xiii. 298.

[4] See *infra*, p. 116.

[5] Defoe, *A Plan of the English Commerce* (ed. 1728), 299. Cf. Hume, *Essays* (ed. Green and Grose), i. 345-346.

frame of William Lee [1], showed that inventive genius was
not altogether lacking even in earlier ages ; and if, with this
conspicuous exception, the sixteenth and seventeenth
centuries were barren of great technical achievements, their
infertility was not due to want of ideas or energy [1a]. In
a single year (1691) the applications for patents included
refining of copper ore, smelting of iron ore, a new mill for
grinding corn, diving engines, dyeing, dressing of leather,
water engines and pumps, improved methods of making
pitch and tar, tanning skins, manufacture of saltpetre,
' water-works ', waterproof cloth, linen manufacture and the
rest [2]. But success in vital things eluded the grasp of the
seventeenth century ; and there was left, as Fuller observed,
" a new world of experiments to the discovery of posterity " [3].

The antagonism of labour towards inventions doubtless
helped to retard the progress of the movement. From the
earliest times the introduction of machinery proved a fruitful
source of dissension. In the thirteenth century there was an
agitation against the use of water mills by fullers [4] : in the
fifteenth century shearmen were forbidden to employ any
instrument other than ' the broad shears ' [5] : in the sixteenth
century Parliament condemned the use of ' engines ' for
stretching or straining cloth, and of ' gig mills ' for raising
the nap [6]. The latter prohibition does not appear to have
taken effect, for in the reign of Charles I. the London cloth-
workers, ' being about a thousand housekeepers ', complained
against the use of gig mills which enabled one man and a
boy to tow as many cloths as eight or ten could do by hand [7].

*Antagonism of labour towards inventions.*

[1] *Supra*, vol. ii. 104. For railways, see *supra*, vol. ii. 152 ; and *infra*,
Appendix, p. 495, No. 3.
[1a] For the Royal Society, see *supra*, vol. ii. Introduction, p. xlii.
[2] *State Papers Domestic*, 1690–1691 *passim*. Among other seventeenth-
century patents were : (1) an engine for raising water from pits by fire :
*supra*, vol. ii. 123 ; (2) an engine for slitting iron bars into rods : *State
Papers Domestic*, 1628–1629, p. 535 ; (3) an engine for spinning whereby
many spinners may be employed ' by the strength of one or two persons ' :
*ibid.* 1658–1659, p. 229 ; 1678, pp. 19-20, 41 ; (4) an invention for printing
calicoes : *supra*, p. 42. See also the Marquess of Worcester, *A Century
of Inventions* (1663).
[3] Fuller, *The History of the Worthies of England* (ed. 1840), iii. 53.
[4] *Supra*, vol. i. 484.                              [5] *Ibid.*
[6] *Statutes*, iv. part i. 156 (1552). On this process, see Lipson, *The
History of the Woollen and Worsted Industries*, 141, 144, 188-189.
[7] They were called ' mozing [*i.e.* brushing] mills ' to avoid penalties.
It was alleged that they over-stretched the cloth, which may have been
                                                              [*contd.*]

The King issued a proclamation against them in 1633[1], but they still continued to be used[2]. The Stuart Government also frowned upon other labour-saving devices in order ' to maintain the multitude of poor artisans '. It condemned the use of brass buckles—since a brass caster could make more buckles in one day than ten forgers of iron buckles— as well as a machine for making needles[3]. After the Restoration the Luddite riots were foreshadowed in 1675, when ' a great company ' of London weavers attacked the French ribbon weavers for using ribbon looms called ' Dutch loom engines ', which enabled a workman to weave as many as sixteen or more ribbons at the same time. These ribbon looms are said to have been invented on the Continent near the end of the sixteenth or early in the seventeenth century[4]. They met with great opposition abroad, and their use was prohibited in several countries. An attempt was made to introduce them into England as early as the reign of James I., for in 1616 it was urged that alien weavers " should entertain English apprentices and servants to learn these trades, the neglect whereof giveth them advantage to keep their misteries to themselves, which hath made them bold of late to devise engines for working of tape, lace, ribbon and such, wherein one man doth more among them than seven English men can do, so as their cheap sale of those commodities

---

the reason for their prohibition. The Gloucestershire clothiers denied that their mills were illegal since they were used only with small teasels, whereas gig mills were used with card wires : State Papers Domestic, 1633–1634, pp. 108, 164, 166, 362-363 ; Hist. MSS. Comm. Portland, viii. 2 (Report of the Commissioners for Trade, 1640).

[1] Rymer, Foedera, xix. 446.

[2] They are referred to in a report of 1707 : House of Commons Journals, xv. 459. In 1633 a Dutchman erected a saw-mill for sawing timber on the River Thames, when one man and a boy did as much work as twenty men, but it was suppressed : Macpherson, Annals of Commerce, ii. 377. In 1702 Parliament rejected a petition of the ' twisters ' of silk, silver and gold, against engines for spinning, one of which, with one pair of hands, was " able to work above twelve quills of plate, when the petitioners cannot work one single quill without employing five pairs of hands " : House of Commons Journals, xiii. 776.

[3] Needles : Tudor and Stuart Proclamations (ed. Steele), i. No. 1368 (1624). Buckles : ibid. i. No. 1653 (1633).

[4] The place of origin has been assigned to the Netherlands, Germany and Switzerland : Beckmann, A History of Inventions (ed. 1846), ii. 527 seq.

beggareth all our English artificers of that trade and enricheth them "[1]. There was a renewed protest in 1621 against "that devilish invention of looms brought in by strangers, which, by working twelve to twenty-four shuttles at once, are the destruction of many poor "[2]. A few years later we meet with another allusion to "tapes, ferret ribbons, silk ribbon and Norwich gartering made by strangers and some English, with looms of twelve to twenty-four shuttles, worked by one man's hands, which takes away the work of a dozen men "[3]. These references carry back the history of the ribbon loom sixty years earlier than the date generally assigned for its introduction into this country. In the reign of Charles II. their use here had become sufficiently common to provoke a great riot in 1675, when weavers in London and Middlesex broke into houses and destroyed the ribbon looms which they found there—one house contained no less than ten. The disorder continued for three days and the military forces were at last obliged to intervene [4].

In the interpretation of the past we must not isolate the different phases of economic growth into water-tight compartments [5]. There is no hiatus in economic development, but always a constant tide of progress and change in which the old is blended almost imperceptibly with the new. The inventions of the late eighteenth century were the outcome of a long series of industrial experiments, and to view them in their proper perspective the efforts of earlier pioneers must not be overlooked. The 'Industrial Revolution' constituted no sudden breach with the existing order, but was part of a continuous movement which had already made marked advance [6]. Already in 1695 Cary described an industrial society in which "new projections are every day set on foot". "Silk stockings are woven: tobacco is cut by engines . . . deal boards are sawn with mills : lead is smelted by wind

*Antecedents of the Industrial Revolution.*

---

[1] State Papers Domestic, James I., vol. lxxxviii. 112.
[2] *State Papers Domestic*, 1619–1623, p. 271.
[3] *Ibid.* Addenda, 1625–1649, p. 314 (? 1628).
[4] *State Papers Domestic*, 1675–1676, pp. 253, 257, 259, 475 ; *House of Commons Journals*, ix. 375 ; *Hist. MSS. Comm.* vii. 465-6 ; *ibid. Le Fleming*, 124 ; *ibid. Eglinton*, 80-81. For the indictment of the weavers, see *Middlesex County Records*, iv. pp. xxvii-xxxiii, 60-65.
[5] See *supra*, vol. i. 264.
[6] For the 'Industrial Revolution', see *supra*, vol. ii. Introduction, pp. cxxxvii-cxliv.

furnaces : all which save the labour of many hands, so the wages of those employed need not be fallen. Besides which, there is a cunning crept into trades. The clock-maker hath improved his art to such a degree that labour and materials are the least part the buyer pays for. The variety of our woollen manufactures is so pretty that fashion makes a thing worth twice the price it is sold for after—the humour of the buyer carrying a great sway in its value. . . . The same art is crept into navigation. . . . Cranes and blocks help to draw up more for one shilling than men's labour without them would do for five. New projections are every day set on foot to render the making our woollen manufactures easy. . . . The same for our product—mines and pits are drained by engines and aqueducts instead of hands "[1].

*The 'new world' dawns.* A generation before the accession of George III. the ' new world ', which Fuller predicted, had dawned. In the first decade of the eighteenth century Abraham Darby smelted iron ore with coke [2] : in the second Newcomen invented the steam engine to drain mines [3] : in the fourth Kay invented the fly shuttle [4] and Paul invented spinning by rollers : in the fifth Paul invented a carding machine [5], and Huntsman produced steel by the crucible process [6]. The following is a picture of the industrial state of England in the middle of the eighteenth century as drawn by Dean Tucker [7] : " Few countries are equal, perhaps none excel the English in the numbers and contrivance of their machines to abridge labour. Indeed the Dutch are superior to them in the use and appli-

---

[1] Cary, *An Essay towards Regulating the Trade* (ed. 1719), 98-99. There are some slight verbal differences in the original edition, published under the title, *An Essay on the State of England in relation to its Trade* (1695), 146 *seq.* Houghton mentioned in 1682 that he had seen " an engine to wind eight skeins of silk at a time, and it may do eight score with a small labour " : *Husbandry and Trade Improv'd* (ed. 1728), iv. 121. For Miege, see *supra*, vol. ii. Introduction, p. cxxxviii.

[2] *Supra*, vol. ii. 160.     [3] *Supra*, vol. ii. 123.

[4] A letter of Kay's has survived in which he stated that he had ' a great many more inventions ', but had been discouraged by bad treatment from putting them forward : Woodcroft, *Brief Biographies of Inventors*, 4. For Kay, see Lipson, *The History of the Woollen and Worsted Industries*, 142-145.

[5] Lipson, *op. cit.* 145-148, 155.

[6] Ashton, *Iron and Steel in the Industrial Revolution*, 55. These inventions are not noticed by Adam Smith, *The Wealth of Nations* (ed. Cannan), i. 245.

[7] Tucker, *Instructions* (ed. 1757), 20-21.

cation of windmills for sawing timber, expressing oil, making paper, and the like. But in regard to mines and metals of all sorts the English are uncommonly dexterous in their contrivance of the mechanic powers—some being calculated for landing the ores out of the pits, such as cranes and horse engines ; others for draining off superfluous water, such as water wheels and steam engines ; others, again, for easing the expense of carriage, such as machines to run on inclined planes or roads down hill with wooden frames in order to carry many tons of materials at a time. And to these must be added the various sorts of levers used in different processes. Also the brass battery works, the slitting mills, plate and flatting mills, and those for making wire of different fineness. . . . At Birmingham, Wolverhampton, Sheffield and other manufacturing places almost every master manufacturer hath a new invention of his own, and is daily improving on those of others. . . . As to machines in the woollen and stuff way nothing very considerable hath been of late attempted— owing in a great measure to the mistaken notions of the infatuated populace who, not being able to see farther than the first link of the chain, consider all such inventions as taking the bread out of their mouths ; and therefore never fail to break out into riots and insurrections whenever such things are proposed. In regard to the silk manufacture the throwsting mills, especially the grand one at Derby, are eminent proofs of the abridgement of that species of labour. And some attempts have been lately made towards helping forward the cotton and linen manufactures by means of certain engines ".

To disarm opposition to improvements, we find writers *Inventions and the* anticipating the arguments afterwards employed during the *employ-* ' Industrial Revolution ' by the apologists for machinery. *ment of labour.* They contended that " cheapness creates expense [spending], and expense gives fresh employments whereby the poor will be still kept at work " [1]. Tucker explained how machinery, by greatly reducing the cost of labour, ' prodigiously lowered ' the price of goods and so enabled ' the generality of a people ' to become purchasers. This increased " consumption must

[1] Cary, *An Essay towards Regulating the Trade* (ed. 1719), 99.

necessarily employ a vast variety of hands, whether the
original material is considered, or the number and repair of
machines, or the materials out of which those machines are
made, or the persons necessarily employed in tending upon
and conducting them. Not to mention those branches of
the manufacture—package, porterage, stationery articles and
book-keeping, etc.—which must inevitably be performed by
human labour"[1]. Similarly Dyer, speaking of Paul's invention of spinning by rollers, bade the spinners not to lose heart:

" Nor hence, ye nymphs, let anger cloud your brows ;
　　The more is wrought, the more is still requir'd "[2].

*Immigra-*
*tion of*
*aliens.*
　　Contemporary opinion in the seventeenth century saw
the remedy for under-population, not in devices to econo-
mize labour, but in alien immigration. " Because great
trades cannot be managed ", said a writer in 1679, " without
multitude of people, it would be prudence to invite foreigners
into this nation "[3]. The settlement of aliens must be
assigned a prominent place among the factors which have
helped to build up the industrial supremacy of England.
The infusion of new blood enriched and strengthened the
national life, while the technical skill and knowledge of the
industrial arts, possessed by the strangers within her gates,
enabled this country to wrest from her rivals the secrets of
important industries and become the workshop of the world.
The backward condition of sixteenth-century England in
many of the industrial arts is shown by the fact that when
Sir Thomas Gresham built the Royal Exchange in 1566,
he employed a Flemish architect and Flemish masons and
carpenters, and imported the wainscot, the glass, the stone
for paving, and nearly all the materials : in Holinshed's
phrase, " he bargained for the whole mould and substance
of his workmanship in Flanders "[4]. The services rendered

---

[1] Tucker, *Instructions* (ed. 1757), 21-22. Contrast *supra*, vol. ii. 446,
note 4.

[2] Dyer, *The Fleece* (1757), bk. iii. 88. Cartwright, the inventor of the
power loom and the combing machine, insisted that " whatever facilitates
labour multiplies the calls for it " : M. S., *A Memoir of Edmund Cartwright*,
202.

[3] J. B., *An Account of the French Usurpation upon the Trade of England*
(1679), 15.

[4] Holinshed, *Chronicles* (ed. 1807), i. 395 ; Burgon, *Life of Gresham*,
ii. 115-121. See also *infra*, p. 352.

by aliens affected every branch of the national economy. They introduced the 'new draperies' in the woollen industry [1]: they revived the decaying fortunes of the silk industry [2]: they started the making of fine linen [3]: they established the copper and brass industries [4]: they practically created the glass-making industry [5]: they promoted the growth of the steel and cutlery trades [6]: they developed the manufacture of china, paper, and cordage [7]: they provided the engineering skill to drain the Fens [8] and make harbours [9]: they improved the art of dyeing [10]: they were prominent as booksellers and stationers [11]: they furnished instruction in drawing and designing at the technical schools in Birmingham [12].

Although in course of time the alien immigrants were absorbed into the mass of the population, their coming aroused resentment among native artisans whose blind attachment to their own narrow interests, coupled with an intense dislike of innovations, proved an obstacle to indus- *Native opposition to aliens.*

---

[1] *Supra*, vol. i. 494 *seq.* In 1659 'spinners' were imported from Holland to make the finer kinds of cloth: *The Wiltshire Archæological and Natural History Magazine*, v. 48. About 1725 'Hamburg merchants' set up 'a new manufacture' for serges at Carlisle: *Hist. MSS. Comm. Portland*, vi. 131.

[2] *Supra*, vol. ii. 101.           [3] *Supra*, vol. ii. 110.
[4] *Supra*, vol. ii. 174.           [5] *Infra*, p. 367.

[6] Dutchmen and Frenchmen were engaged in the manufacture of steel: *Acts of the Privy Council*, 1558–1570, p. 333; *Hist. MSS. Comm. Lord De L'Isle and Dudley*, i. 316-317 (1565); *Tudor Economic Documents* (ed. Tawney and Power), i. 322 (c. 1603). For alien cutlers, see Lloyd, *The Cutlery Trades*, 101-104. Crowley employed metal-workers from Liège: *supra*, vol. ii. 179. German sword-makers from Solingen settled at Shotley Bridge near the end of the seventeenth century: *Victoria County History, Durham*, ii. 288-289.

[7] For paper, see *infra*, p. 352. For china, see Meteyard, *The Life of Josiah Wedgwood*, i. 108-109. Dutchmen and other aliens established here the manufacture of great cables and other kinds of cordage: Cunningham, *Alien Immigrants*, 217.

[8] *Supra*, vol. ii. 375. "Engineers are very scant in England": *Hist. MSS. Comm. Salisbury*, vi. 87 (1596).

[9] Flemish engineers were consulted about Dover Harbour: *Acts of the Privy Council*, 1581–1582, p. 139.

[10] Kepler, a Fleming, established a dye-house for scarlet at Bow in 1643. Another Fleming, Bauer, who came to England in 1667, "brought the art of dyeing woollen cloths to such perfection here that it has ever since retained its reputation": Burn, *The History of the French, Walloon, Dutch and other Foreign Protestant Refugees*, 258-259. But see *infra*, p. 385, note 2.

[11] Rogers, *Oxford City Documents*, 53.

[12] *House of Commons Journals*, xxviii. 496 (1759).

trial progress. Their attitude was shown in the reign of
Edward VI. when " five or six hundred men waited on the
mayor and aldermen of London complaining of the late
influx of strangers, and that by reason of the great dearth
they cannot live for these strangers, whom they were determined to kill up through the realm if they found no remedy " [1].
Under Elizabeth a protest was made in the name of the
citizens of London against the infringement of their custom
that " no man being a stranger to the liberties of the City
shall use handicrafts within the City " [2]. Two decades later
the remonstrance of ' sundry handicraftsmen and artisans '
that they were " being supplanted by the stranger, and their
living in a manner taken from them ", produced an inquiry
into the numbers and occupations of alien residents in
London [3]. The agitation against aliens was renewed in the
reign of James I. A petition in 1616 admitted that the
new-comers had devised ' many trades before to us unknown ',
but they did not fulfil the obligation to " entertain English
apprentices and servants to learn these trades, the neglect
whereof giveth them advantage to keep their misteries
to themselves " : moreover " their numbers causeth the enhancing of the prices of victuals and house rents ", and " no
tenement is left to an English artificer to inhabit in divers
parts of the City and suburbs " [4]. Near the end of the reign
a severe depression of trade [5] led to the appointment of
commissioners, whose function it was to make an annual
survey of aliens. Attention was drawn to the law which
forbade aliens to engage in handicrafts except as ' servants
to the English ', but they were to be permitted to ' enroll
themselves as servants ' to the King, paying " to our use as
a thankful acknowledgement of our royal favour such rates
and payments out of their earnings or gains to be distributed

---

[1] *State Papers Foreign*, 1547–1553, pp. 119-120 (1551). Flemish
weavers, who settled at Glastonbury in 1551, quitted the realm at Mary's
accession : *Somersetshire Archæological and Natural History Society's Proceedings* (1880), xxvi. part ii. 22.
[2] 1571 : *Tudor Economic Documents* (ed. Tawney and Power), i. 308-
309.
[3] 1592 : *Acts of the Privy Council*, 1591–1592, pp. 507-508.
[4] State Papers Domestic, James I., vol. lxxxviii. 112.
[5] *Infra*, p. 305.

and disposed of for the ease and comfort of our own people
. . . as shall be directed "[1].

After the Restoration the alien problem assumed a new *Arguments in favour of aliens.* aspect owing to the common belief that England was under-populated. The committee for trade, to which a petition against aliens had been referred (1660), reported that restraints on aliens would be hurtful as they had brought in many useful trades[2]. Alien immigration now figured prominently among the favourite proposals for the advancement of trade and industry; and to encourage it writers recommended an Act for the general naturalization of foreigners and for liberty of conscience[3]. They easily refuted the popular arguments against foreigners. " The general cry is that they eat the bread out of our mouths. They sell their goods when we can't, they work cheaper than we, live in holes, pay neither scot nor lot ; and if we should have many more of them, sure we should have nothing to do "[4]. To this it was replied : " Would not foreigners living here consume our corn, cattle, cloth, coals and all kind of things we use ? And would not that cause our lands to be better tilled and our trades increased ? Would they not bring several new trades with them or help to increase those we have ? Witness the Flemings in the time of Edward the Third, the colonies of Colchester, Canterbury and Norwich, the silk trade in Spitalfields, the tapestry-makers in Hatton Garden, Clerkenwell, and elsewhere, Mr. Todin, the rare pewterer in St. Martin's Lane, the husbandmen in the Fens, and divers others. And doth not every tradesman among them employ two or three English to attend them

[1] Rymer, *Foedera*, xvii. 438-439 (1622) ; *Remembrancia of the City of London*, 260.
[2] *State Papers Domestic*, 1660–1661, p. 363.
[3] " Imposing upon conscience . . . is a mischief unto Trade transcending all others ", since it affects " the soberest and most industrious " : *The Present Interest of England Stated. By a Lover of his Country* (1671), 13, 17-18, 25. In 1664 it was said : " Trade has decayed greatly since the Act of Restraint [the Conventicle Act] came out " : *State Papers Domestic*, 1663–1664, p. 603. See also Fortrey, *England's Interest and Improvement* (1663), 4, 13 ; *The Grand Concern of England explained in Several Proposals* (1673), 13-14 ; Child, *A New Discourse of Trade* (4th ed.), chapter vii. ; *Britannia Languens* (1680), 103 ; Schlatter, *Social Ideas of Religious Leaders*, 167 *seq.*
[4] Houghton, *England's Great Happiness : or a Dialogue between Content and Complaint* (1677), 8.

either in making tools, winding silk or such like, besides buying all their materials here?"[1]  Charles II. in 1672 issued a 'Declaration' inviting the subjects of the United Provinces to settle in England[2], and to facilitate their coming a Bill was introduced into Parliament for the naturalization of Protestant strangers[3]. In response to the invitation[4] a number of Dutch families came over : among them merchants, skippers with their vessels, artisans, a manufacturer of tiles and porcelain with sixteen workmen, and a master weaver with thirty workmen 'for making the finest cloth in Europe'[5].

*The Huguenots.*    Towards the end of the seventeenth century religious persecution in France caused an exodus of the most skilful and industrious section of the population ; and the exiles were welcomed by the English Government both as religious refugees and as economic assets. Their immigration constituted the third great landmark in the industrial history of England—the first being the influx of Flemings in the fourteenth century, and the second that of the Dutch and Walloons in the sixteenth century[6]. Declarations were issued by Charles II. in 1681, and by William and Mary in 1689, offering protection to 'distressed Protestants'[7]; and many thousands came over after the Revocation of the Edict of Nantes (1685). Some afterwards migrated to the colonies, yet in 1692 a parliamentary committee estimated the number of those settled in this country at 'upwards of thirty thousand'[8]. In London the principal French quarters were Spitalfields, Bethnal Green and Soho[9]; and they also settled, among other places, in Norwich where they intro-

[1] Houghton, *England's Great Happiness : or a Dialogue between Content and Complaint* (1677), 9-10. Similarly : Coke, *Treatise* (1671), i. 3-5.
[2] *State Papers Domestic*, 1672, p. 210.        [3] *Ibid.* 1672–1673, p. 530.
[4] Coke, *Treatise* (1675), iii. 53, and *Britannia Languens* (1680), 103, were mistaken in asserting that the invitation had no effect.
[5] *State Papers Domestic*, 1673–1675, p. 400 ; 1675–1676, p. 236 ; 1676–1677, pp. 351, 413. *Hist. MSS. Comm. Le Fleming*, 101.
[6] For the settlement of Flemings, Dutch and Walloons, see *supra*, vol. i. 452, 494. French Protestants also settled in England in the early seventeenth century : *State Papers Domestic*, 1619–1623, p. 265.
[7] *House of Commons Journals*, x. 666.
[8] *Ibid.* In 1718 one of the ministers of the Savoy Church estimated the number of French refugees at 'near 100,000 persons in the two kingdoms' : Smiles, *The Huguenots*, 318, note.
[9] Smiles, *The Huguenots*, 320.

duced the manufacture of crapes [1], and in Bristol where they made worsted cloths [2]. Some of the Huguenots were supported by the resources which they had brought with them, but the greatest part pursued the callings they had followed in France : " the making of silks, linens, hats, ' castile ' soap, white paper and other useful manufactures, by which they are become good subjects to their majesties and this nation reaps great benefit by them " [3]. They gave a permanent stimulus to industrial development ; and it was the son of a French refugee, Lewis Paul, who invented the first machine on which thread was spun by rollers—an anticipation of Arkwright's water-frame [4]. Nevertheless, in spite of the benefits which they conferred, dissensions were provoked by their presence. The ' London Prentices ' voiced ' their most sad complaint ' against the French weavers :

" You Weavers all I pray give ear.
A story true I will declare.
Our masters they do much repine,
Saying the French them undermine.
And get their trade away from them. . . .

" Our weaving trade is grown so dead,
We scarcely can get us bread. . . .
Because the French are grown so ill,
In selling their work at an under-price,
Which makes the tears run from our eyes.
And Weavers all may curse their fates
Because the French work under-rates " [5].

There was friction between the new-comers and the gilds whose privileges they infringed [6] ; and some towns endeavoured to exclude them on the pretext that their residence would be ' no advantage but a prejudice ' [7].

[1] *The British Merchant* (ed. 1721), ii. 275 ; James, *History of the Worsted Manufacture*, 166.
[2] Called ' cantaloons ' : *House of Commons Journals*, xi. 621 ; Cary, *A Reply to a Paper entituled, The Linen Drapers' Answer*.
[3] *House of Commons Journals*, x. 666.
[4] For Paul's claim to be considered the inventor, see Lipson, *The History of the Woollen and Worsted Industries*, 145 seq.
[5] *The Valiant Weaver* (1685).
[6] Clode, *Early History of the Guild of Merchant Taylors*, i. 79 (London); *Hist. MSS. Comm. Portland*, viii. 375-376 (Southampton).
[7] *Hist. MSS. Comm. Lincoln*, 109. Nearly 7000 Germans came over in 1709, but many removed to Pennsylvania : Macpherson, *Annals of Commerce*, iii. 6.

## (II)

### MONEY AND THE BALANCE OF TRADE

*Money and Wealth.*  It is a common charge against Mercantilism that it identified money with wealth [1] ; and the fact that confused thinking on the subject of money was not unknown, then as now, lends colour to the accusation. Money " is properly the wealth and strength of a State ", said one writer in 1622 [2] ; and some even advocated debasement of the coinage on the ground that it would enrich the whole nation, since there would be more money in the kingdom than before [3]. John Pollexfen, who held the responsible position of a Commissioner for Trade and Plantations, described gold and silver as ' the only or most useful treasure of a nation ' [4]. Joshua Gee, a merchant, observed : " So mistaken are many people that they cannot see the difference between having a vast treasure of silver and gold in the kingdom, and the mint employed in coining money, the only true token of treasure and riches, and having it carried away ; but they say money is a commodity like other things, and think themselves never the poorer for what the nation daily exports " [5]. Decker termed gold and silver ' the ultimate objects of trade ' : " and the more or less of these metals a nation retains, it is denominated rich or poor " [6]. It is a mistake, however, to attach undue importance to *obiter dicta* of this nature. They do not represent the best mercantilist opinion. Pollexfen was sharply criticized by Davenant [7] ; and Gee acknowledged that others held a different view. The Mercantile System must

[1] Under the Mercantile System " it was assumed . . . that wealth consisted solely of money " : Mill, *Principles of Political Economy* (ed. Ashley), 2. Cf. also the definition of the Mercantile System quoted *supra*, p. 2, note 1. See *supra*, vol. ii. Introduction, p. lxxvi, note 1.

[2] *The Belgicke Pismire* (1622), 65.

[3] Cradocke attempted to disprove the argument that prices would rise : *Wealth Discovered* (1661), 21-22. See also *The Use and Abuses of Money* (1671), 18-21 ; R. H., *The Prevention of Poverty* (1674), 15-16.

[4] Pollexfen, *England and East India inconsistent in their Manufactures* (1697), 6, 18. But later he modified the statement—' The only *or at least* most useful ' : *ibid.* 47.

[5] Gee, *The Trade and Navigation of Great Britain* (ed. 1730), 8.

[6] Decker, *Essay on the Causes of the Decline of the Foreign Trade* (ed. 1744), 1.        [7] Davenant, *Works* (ed. 1771), i. 353-354.

be interpreted, not by sentences divorced from their context, but by the general trend of mercantilist opinion as reflected in the whole range of economic literature and embodied in actual legislation. It must be remembered that seventeenth-century pamphleteers were not writing economic treatises [1], and their purpose was not a scientific analysis of the nature of wealth. They were controversialists engaged in partisan warfare ; and pamphlets struck off in the heat of a contest must not be too closely scrutinized, nor judged by occasional lapses and unguarded phrases. Take, for example, the classic of Mercantilism—Mun's *England's Treasure by Forraign Trade.* Its purpose was to expose the error of the bullionist school which opposed the export of bullion, and it showed how the export of money in trade was the means to increase treasure ; but, as will be seen, it recognized that other things constituted wealth besides gold and silver [2].

There is ample evidence that mercantilist writers as a whole did not share the crude fallacies commonly attributed to them. They were not ignorant of the functions of money, and they had grasped in its essentials the Quantity Theory [2a]. Thus the editor of *A Discourse of the Common Weal of this Realm of England* interpolated in the edition of 1581 the remark that " the prices of victuals and other wares in like sort is raised according to the increase of treasure " [3]. Similar statements are found in early seventeenth-century writers such as Malynes and Mun [4]. The latter categorically asserted : " All men do consent that plenty of money in a kingdom doth make the native commodities dearer, which as it is to the profit of some private men in their revenues, so is it directly against the benefit of the public " [5]. Petty

*[margin note: Mercantilist opinion about money.]*

---

[1] This appears to be the answer to Adam Smith's remark that " writers who begin by including lands, houses and consumable goods in wealth often forget them later " : *The Wealth of Nations* (ed. Cannan), i. 415-416 (marginal note).    [2] *Infra*, p. 65.

[2a] The Quantity Theory relates the value of money to its quantity. Mercantilist writers understood the principal function of money—to serve as an instrument of exchange : *supra*, vol. ii. Introduction, pp. lxxviii, lxxx.

[3] *A Discourse of the Common Weal of this Realm of England* (ed. Lamond), 187.    See also *infra*, Appendix, p. 495, No. 4.

[4] Malynes, *A Treatise of the Canker of England's Commonwealth* (1601), 10, 91 ; Mun, *England's Treasure by Forraign Trade* (1664), 43-44. Similarly : *Britannia Languens* (1680), 11.

[5] A rise in prices might give a stimulus to the home trade ; but it would work unfairly in regard to existing contracts, fixed incomes, and wages (allowing for the ' time lag '), and also affect adversely the export trade.

(*c.* 1665) affirmed that " money is but the fat of the body politic, whereof too much doth as often hinder its agility as too little makes it sick " [1]. Roger Coke (1675) defined money as " that by which all commodities are valued " and as " of no other use "; and he condemned the Act of Navigation, which permitted all nations to import money into England, yet imposed restrictions in the case of commodities, although ' much more valuable than money ' when they were employed in industry. Significant was his warning that " if we did too much abound in money, this would be a burthen to the nation and of ill consequence to the king and subject ", for commodities being valued ' according to the plenty of money ' those with fixed incomes would suffer from the rise in prices [2]. Houghton (1681) observed that " money was never made to be an idol " : its use was " no other than as a pawn, whereby I may procure any other commodity that I shall desire in lieu of some commodity I formerly parted with " [3]. Barbon (1690) described money as " an imaginary value made by a law for the conveniency of exchange : it is the natural stock that is the real value and rent of the land " [4]. Thomas (1690) declared that " we must consider money as the least part of the wealth of any nation, and think of it only as a scale to weigh one thing against another " [5]. Sir Dudley North (1691) pronounced money " a merchandise whereof there may be a glut as well as a scarcity ". It constituted " the weights and measures by which traffic is more conveniently carried on than could be done without them, and also a proper fund for a surplusage of stock to be deposited in ". In language reminiscent of Hume and Adam Smith he said : " Then let not the care of specific money torment us so much, for a people that are rich cannot want it " [6]. Davenant (1698) explained that money was the servant or measure of

---

[1] Petty, *Economic Writings*, i. 113 (also pp. 35, 192-193).
[2] Coke, *Treatise* (1675), iii. 44, 57-58.
[3] Houghton, *Husbandry and Trade Improv'd* (ed. 1728), iv. 26-27.
[4] Barbon, *A Discourse of Trade* (1690), 37.
[5] *Harleian Miscellany* (ed. Malham), ix. 406.
[6] North, *Discourses upon Trade* (1691), Preface (p. ix) ; 16-17. Cf. Adam Smith—" A country that has wherewithal to buy gold and silver will never be in want of those metals " : *The Wealth of Nations* (ed. Cannan), i. 401.

trade, the counters with which men reckon, but it was not indispensable since the real and effective riches of a country lay in its natural or artificial products ; and he pointed out that paper money performed ' all the offices of money ' [1]. In the next century Wood (1718) remarked that " men of the most extensive knowledge in all trading countries have defined and allowed gold and silver, or bullion, a commodity or merchandise " ; and he represented that a ' superfluous plenty ' of money would raise prices, and make us not " one jot richer than we are at present " [2]. These quotations, which can easily be supplemented [3], may perhaps serve to dispel the belief that the Mercantilists necessarily held the notion, in the words of Adam Smith, that " wealth consists in money, or in gold and silver " [4]. In this connexion it is noteworthy that as early as 1663 the export of bullion was expressly permitted by law,[5] while down to 1663 licences were readily obtained by merchants. The East India Company, for example, never complained that its operations were hampered by bullion restrictions : indeed its official apologist stated that the licences issued to it were in excess of its requirements [6]. Yet while the export of bullion was allowed, the export of wool was rigorously forbidden in spite of its high price abroad [7]. This indicates that the accumulation of treasure was subordinated to other economic considerations.

There are abundant indications that the bulk of mercantilist writers did not misconceive the true nature of wealth [7a]. Mun expressly stated that in a multitude of people " doth consist the greatest strength and riches both of king and kingdom " [8]. Petty declared (1662) that the wealth of England lay in land and people : ' fewness of people ' he

*Mercantilist opinion about wealth.*

---

[1] Davenant, *Works* (ed. 1771), i. 354-355, 444 ; ii. 106. See also *infra*, Appendix, p. 496, No. 1.

[2] Wood, *A Survey of Trade* (1718), 331-337.

[3] *E.g.* The British Merchant (ed. 1721), iii. 101 ; *Essays on Several Subjects* (1769), 118. See also *infra*, Appendix, p. 490, No. 1, and p. 496, No. 2.

[4] *The Wealth of Nations* (ed. Cannan), i. 415. And *supra*, p. 2, note 1.

[5] *Infra*, p. 73.

[6] Mun, *A Discourse of Trade from England unto the East Indies* (1621), 20. Similarly : *State Papers Domestic*, 1637–1638, p. 153.

[7] *Supra*, pp. 22 *seq.* ; and *infra*, Appendix, p. 496, No. 3.

[7a] Comprehensive views on wealth were expressed in Parliament in 1523 and 1621 : *supra*, vol. ii. Introduction, pp. lxxviii-lxxx.

[8] Mun, *England's Treasure by Forraign Trade* (1664), 31. Mun, like other writers, means ' industrious and laborious people ', *i.e.* producers of wealth : Thomas (*infra*, p. 66). Cf. *infra*, Appendix, p. 496, No. 4.

termed ' real poverty ', and he therefore included ' the value
of the people ' in his estimate of the national wealth [1].
" The stock and riches of the kingdom ", said an anonymous
writer in 1677, " cannot properly be confined to money, nor
ought gold and silver to be excluded from being merchandise
to be traded with as well as any other sort of goods " [2].
Even the author of *Britannia Languens* (1680), while he
stressed the importance of money, thought that Spain,
despite the wealth of the Indies, was ' for want of home
manufactures ' the poorest, weakest and least populous of
all nations [3]. Child (1690) maintained that it was ' multitudes
of people ' which ' principally enrich any country ' [4]. Barbon
(1690) asserted that the ' native staple ' of every country,
its natural and artificial products, constituted the ' riches '
of the country [5]. Similarly, Thomas (1690) held that " true,
solid and real wealth in respect to the nation is the land,
and what is upon or under its surface " ; but since lands and
houses without people are of no value at all, "only industrious
and laborious people are the riches of any nation " [6]. Sir
Dudley North (1691) observed that he who " raiseth most
fruits or maketh most of manufactory " will " enjoy most
conveniences, which is truly to be rich although there were
no such thing as gold, silver or the like " [7]. But it was
reserved for Davenant (1698) to attempt a comprehensive
definition of wealth. It consists of the fruits of the earth,
cattle, manufactured goods, buildings, shipping (' the working
tools of a trading people '), furniture, plate, jewels, pictures,
apparel, bullion and coined money. All these things, and
not gold and silver alone, may properly be termed the
' national stock ' or ' real treasure ' of a nation. In short,
" we understand that to be wealth which maintains the

---

[1] Petty, *Economic Writings*, i. 34, 108, 117.
[2] *The East India Trade a most profitable Trade to the Kingdom* (1677), 4.
[3] *Britannia Languens* (1680), 26, 238, 243. Cf. Coke, *Treatise* (1675),
iii. 3, 10, 21. See *supra*, pp. 8-9 ; vol. ii. Introduction, p. lxxx ; *infra*,
Appendix, p. 492, No. 1.
[4] Child, *A New Discourse of Trade* (4th ed.), p. xi. Similarly : Roger
North, *A Discourse of the Poor* (ed. 1753), 47.
[5] Barbon, *A Discourse of Trade* (1690), 5 ; Barbon, *A Discourse
concerning coining the New Money lighter* (1696), 4, 48-49.
[6] *Harleian Miscellany* (ed. Malham), ix. 406-407.
[7] North, *Discourses upon Trade* (1691), 2.

prince and the general body of his people in plenty, ease and safety " [1]. Writers in the eighteenth century gave expression to a similar view that wealth was ' every kind of useful possession ' [2].

It is undeniable that mercantilist writers attached great importance to gold and silver [2a], but the fact that they dwelt upon the dangers of an excess of money [3] in a country, indicates that the stress laid on money was not due to any confusion with wealth. In the first place, the precious metals were *nervi bellorum* [4], the sinews of war, which now was managed by the power of money. " War is quite changed from what it was in the time of our forefathers, when in a hasty expedition and a pitched field the matter was decided by courage. . . . Nowadays that prince who can best find money to feed, clothe and pay his army, not he that has the most valiant troops, is surest of success " [5]. " The mystery of war in having the last loaf ", it was remarked, " our ancestors understood. I wish we may have the last penny " [6]. There is no question that the Mercantilists attached importance to precious metals largely as an instrument of war : this is what they meant when they spoke of treasure as a ' pillar ' of ' national power ' [7]. It provided the ready means to buy arms and victuals and shipping ; to hire men in place of the old feudal levies ; and, in short, to make ' just and honourable wars, offensive or defensive ' (to quote a proclamation of 1661) [8]. When Gresham wrote to Burghley

*Reasons for the importance attached to the precious metals :*
*(i.) Sinews of war.*

---

[1] Davenant, *Works* (ed. 1771), i. 356-357, 377, 381-383 ; ii. 192-193.

[2] Wood, *A Survey of Trade* (1718), 332 ; Defoe, *A Plan of the English Commerce* (ed. 1728), 17-18 ; *The Case of the British and Irish Manufacture of Linen* (1738), 4 ; Tucker, *Instructions* (ed. 1757), 39 ; *An Estimate of the Manners and Principles of the Times* (1757), 151. For other testimony, see *House of Commons Journals*, i. 511, 636 ; xiv. 575.

[2a] Reasons for the prominence of treasure are analysed, *supra*, vol. ii. Introduction, pp. lxxxii-lxxxiv.

[3] *Supra*, pp. 63-4. 'A surfeiting diet': Davenant, *Works* (ed. 1771), i. 382.

[4] *Hist. MSS. Comm. Salisbury*, vii. p. 540 (1597) ; Malynes, *Saint George for England* (1601), Preface ; Mun, *England's Treasure by Forraign Trade* (1664), 173-174 ; Violet, *Humble Proposal against Transporting of Gold and Silver out of the Kingdom* (1661), 5 ; *The Use and Abuses of Money* (1671), 5.

[5] Davenant, *Works* (ed. 1771), i. 16, 348 ; v. 453. Similarly : Child, *A New Discourse of Trade* (4th ed.), 209. See *infra*, Appendix, p. 496, No. 5.

[6] *Hist. MSS. Comm. Portland*, iii. 535 (1693).

[7] *Britannia Languens* (1680), 238. See *infra*, Appendix, p. 497, No. 1.

[8] Bodleian Library : Fol. Θ. 660, No. 126.

that gunpowder and bow staves were 'better than any treasure'[1], he summed up the mercantilist position in a phrase. Best of all were the actual means of national defence : but the next best was the opportunity of purchasing them with a commodity universally acceptable. The connexion between money and munitions of war is shown in the simultaneous employment of Gresham as a financier to raise loans abroad, and as a merchant to buy gunpowder[2].

(ii.) *Basis of credit.* In the second place, the imperfect development of credit instruments in earlier times gave greater prominence to the utility of the precious metals[3]—especially owing to an exaggerated tendency to regard every economic disturbance as a monetary crisis, and every industrial fluctuation as due to the ' scarcity of money '. And later, when England had an extensive system of credit, as Davenant at the end of the seventeenth century claimed for her, the place of coin could not be entirely supplied by credit, since the latter derived its own existence from ' an expectation or assurance of money '[4]. In other words — the foundation of paper credit was a ' due proportion ' of coin[5]. Credit requires, wrote Davenant, " that there is . . . within the kingdom a sufficient quantity of the species to turn in trade, in the payment of rents and taxes, and in the manufactures, and whereby to keep the wheels of the machine in motion "[6]. Money, in fact, was the ' radical moisture ' of the commonwealth and the ' life of commerce and trade '[7]; for while

[1] *State Papers Foreign*, 1562, p. 260.

[2] *Ibid.* 1559–1560, p. 220. Gresham was apparently more successful as a financier than as a provider of munitions, for Lord Willoughby wrote to the Earl of Essex that what " of late years past Sir Thomas Gresham provided [was] fitter to kill the users than their enemies " : *Hist. MSS. Comm. Salisbury*, xiii. 606 (? 1596).

[3] Hume, writing near the middle of the eighteenth century, remarked that " the great plenty of bullion in France is, in a great measure, owing to the want of paper-credit " : *Essays : Of the Balance of Trade*.

[4] Pollexfen, *England and East India inconsistent in their Manufactures* (1697), 48.

[5] For Davenant's views, see *Works* (ed. 1771), i. 134, 165, 447; v. 453-454.

[6] *Ibid.* i. 448. Similarly : Locke, *Works* (ed. 1801), v. 148.

[7] Rymer, *Foedera*, xvii. 413 (1622) ; Misselden, *Free Trade* (1622), 28 ; Mun, *England's Treasure by Forraign Trade* (1664), 55 ; Fortrey, *England's Interest and Improvement* (1663), 42 ; Davenant, *Works* (ed. 1771), i. 379, 447 ; ii. 75. See *infra*, Appendix, p. 497, No. 2.

industrious inhabitants and the fruits of the earth constituted the ' true riches ' of a country, yet " to put a value
upon all this, and to put life and motion to the whole, there
must be a quick stock running among the people " [1]. Petty
explained that " the proportion of money requisite to our
trade is to be taken from the frequency of commutations " [2];
and an insufficiency of treasure to drive the nation's trade
diminished the trade and impoverished the nation. Even
Hume, who held that " it is of no manner of consequence
with regard to the domestic happiness of a State whether
money be in a greater or less quantity ", considered it
' good policy ' to keep it, if possible, still increasing on the
ground that this was favourable to industry [3]: similarly
Mun, a century earlier, had remarked on the economic
stimulus produced by a rise in prices [4].

The critics of mercantilist opinion in respect of money (iii.) *Other*
are apt to overlook certain vital considerations. One is *considerations.*
that modern economic practices postulate the free movement
of gold in two directions, inward as well as outward ; whereas
in the seventeenth century England could not freely import
bullion from every country, owing to the embargo laid by
some States on its export [5]. To this extent official regulations
to ensure an adequate supply of gold and silver were not
without justification ; and it must be noticed that they have
their counterpart in the present-day method of raising the
bank-rate in order to attract gold to this country [6]. Again,
changes in the level of prices consequent upon a decrease
in the quantity of money may have serious economic reactions, especially where contracts are framed on an assumption of stable prices. The want of money, it was apprehended,

---

[1] Davenant, *Works* (ed. 1771), i. 447.
[2] Petty, *Economic Writings*, i. 36.
[3] Hume, *Essays* (ed. Green and Grose), i. 315. For Hume's views on
money, see *supra*, vol. ii. Introduction, pp. lxxxiv-lxxxv ; *infra*, pp. 97-98,
497 (No. 3).
[4] Mun, *England's Treasure by Forraign Trade* (1664), 54-55.
[5] " It is death in Spain to export money " : Locke, *Works* (ed. 1801),
v. 72. And though Dutch policy might normally permit it, Dutch law—
according to the Venetian envoy in 1644—forbade the exportation of
money : *State Papers Venetian*, 1643-1647, pp. 130, 133. See *infra*,
p. 497 (No. 4).
[6] Adam Smith's criticism of Mercantilism is largely based upon the de-
batable assumption that no official ' attention ' is needed to " supply us with
all the gold and silver" wanted: *The Wealth of Nations* (ed. Cannan), i. 402.

would "beget a disvaluation of all our native commodities"[1];
although it is true that many complaints of the 'want of money'
mistook a falling off in demand for a real shortage of the
circulating medium [2]. It may be noticed, finally, that Petty
and Locke, in contrast with Sir Dudley North, considered
gold and silver different from other commodities because
they were not perishable, they commanded ' all the conveniences ' of life, and they were esteemed for wealth at all
times and places [3] ; and it still remains true that the precious
metals may have peculiar importance in a country whose
currency is based on a gold or silver standard.

*The Statute of Employment.* The export of money was repeatedly prohibited in the
Middle Ages [4] : hence the Elizabethan Government was pur-
suing a traditional policy when it recommended Parliament
in 1559 to revive the mediaeval Statute of Employment [5]
—' that excellent Statute ', Mun called it [6]—which enjoined
foreign merchants to employ the proceeds of merchandise
imported hither on native commodities. Nevertheless we must
not exaggerate the importance of the currency restrictions,
nor treat them as the essence of the Mercantile System. The
reasons for the restrictions were practical, not theoretical.
In the Middle Ages they were due to the scarcity of precious
metals to serve as instruments of exchange [7]. After the
influx of American silver another motive was assigned : they
were now intended to discourage ' the excessive import ' of
foreign commodities, and to foster native industries by com-
pelling merchants to export commodities of the realm in
place of money [8]. In any case the prohibition was largely a

---

[1] Sir Edward Coke in *House of Commons Journals*, i. 672, 716-717.
[2] *Infra*, pp. 310, 498 (No. 1). Cf. North, *Discourses upon Trade* (1691),
11-12.
[3] Petty, *Economic Writings*, i. 259-260, 269 ; Locke, *Works* (ed. 1801),
v. 12 ; North, *Discourses upon Trade* (1691), 13.
[4] *Supra*, vol. i. 531-533.
[5] *Hist. MSS. Comm. Salisbury*, i. 163. The complaints of alien merchants show that the Statute was in operation at the beginning of Elizabeth's reign : *State Papers Foreign*, 1560-1561, pp. 91-92. For a complaint
that the Statute was not observed (1571), see *Acts of the Privy Council*,
1571-1575, p. 25.
[6] Mun, *A Discourse of Trade from England unto the East Indies* (1621),
54. But see *infra*, p. 73. [7] *Supra*, vol. i. 482, 531-532, 619-620.
[8] This reason is assigned in *State Papers Domestic*, 1601-1603, p. 48 ;
*Tudor and Stuart Proclamations* (ed. Steele), i. No. 1157 (1615) ; *Newcastle*
[*contd.*]

dead letter. The Statute of Employment was difficult to execute even in the Middle Ages; and it had fallen into neglect by the end of Elizabeth's reign, since a proposal for its enforcement figured among the recommendations (1601) of a commission appointed to investigate the cause of " the large export of the treasure of this realm, and the not so ample import thereof as in times past "[1]. Apparently there was an attempt to revive the Statute of Employment in the next reign, for a protest made by the French ambassador in 1618 elicited the response from the Privy Council that " the employment of such moneys, as accrue by the sale of merchandises imported by strangers into this kingdom, upon the native commodities here, is founded upon an ancient Statute of this realm, whereunto not only the French but all other strangers are subject "[2]. Native merchants were also precluded by law from exporting money, though the restriction was evaded by the issue of licences[3]—the East India Company, in particular, was allowed to export as much as it required[4].

In the seventeenth century it came to be recognized that the attempt to retain gold and silver in a country by force of law was ' nugatory and vain '. Firstly : the law could not be enforced on aliens, among other reasons, on account of the inequalities of the customs duties. An alien merchant, who exported cloth from England, was required to pay more than double the duty imposed on natives[5], so that it became cheaper for him to buy cloth at an Englishman's hand abroad. And some commodities, such as corn, leather and tallow, either could not be taken out of the country by foreign merchants, or they were burdened with a heavy

*Restraints on the export of bullion inoperative.*

---

Merchant Adventurers, i. 44 (1622) ; Britannia Languens (1680), 38-39, 41, 43.

[1] State Papers Domestic, 1601–1603, pp. 47-48. Similar proposals were made under James I. : Acts of the Privy Council, 1615–1616, pp. 354, 366 ; Stowe MSS. 554, f. 45 ; Rymer, Foedera, xvii. 413-414 (1622).

[2] Acts of the Privy Council, 1618–1619, p. 10.

[3] State Papers Domestic, 1651–1652, p. 24. Proceedings were sometimes taken for unlawful transportation : ibid. 1619–1623, pp. 53, 169 ; 1638–1639, p. 199.

[4] Supra, vol. ii. 278.

[5] The Rates of Marchandizes as they are set downe in the Booke of Rates (Letters Patents, 8 James I.).

licence duty [1]. It is not surprising, then, to find that in 1611 aliens exported from London only one-quarter of the value of their imports [2]. Nevertheless the Government signally failed to see that its fiscal policy neutralized its bullionist policy. Secondly: the prohibition against the export of money made English merchants ' fearful ' of bringing their money into the kingdom where it would be detained, and induced them to deposit it instead at Amsterdam or Leghorn. Thirdly: the importance of leaving commerce ' to act in its own natural mode ' emphasized the unwisdom of restraints which reduced its volume, and so actually hindered the increase of treasure. Fourthly: in some countries, such as India, ' ready money ' was the most advantageous method of carrying on trade. Lastly: there was no danger that merchants would cease to export native wares if they were permitted freely to carry out money, for " the vending of English commodities doth not depend upon any other thing but the use and need which foreigners have of them " [3].

*Controversy between the bullionist and the mercantilist schools.* The establishment of the East India Company served to focus the controversy: the bullionist school, which opposed free trade in gold and silver [4], was confronted by the mercantilist school, which supported the removal of restraints. Mun's own writings serve to show how the mercantilist school gradually developed out of the bullionist school. In *A Discourse of Trade from England unto the East Indies*, published in 1621, while pleading for the right of the East India Company to export money, he praised ' that excellent Statute ' which required alien merchants to employ the

---

[1] " A Demonstration of the Merchants of Italy " (1576), in Schanz, *Englische Handelspolitik*, ii. No. 163 (p. 645).

[2] *Acts of the Privy Council*, 1615–1616, pp. 479-481. The additional duties paid by aliens were abolished in 1673 by an Act which provided that they should pay the same customs and subsidies as natives (except for coal) : *Statutes*, v. 791.

[3] On these points, see *State Papers Domestic*, 1654, p. 118 ; 1660–1661, p. 411 ; 1661–1662, p. 375. Fortrey, *England's Interest and Improvement* (1663), 33. Petty, *Economic Writings*, i. 57 ; ii. 442. Coke, *Treatise* (1675), iii. 58. North, *Discourses upon Trade* (1691), 13-14.

[4] *E.g.* T. Violet (an informer of dubious character who made charges against London merchants, which he was unable to substantiate : *State Papers Domestic*, 1637–1638, p. 153 ; 1659–1660, p. 448) ; *Britannia Languens* (1680), 39-40.

money they received in England upon native commodities [1].
Yet in a later and more famous work he described the Statute
of Employment as a ' remedy far worse than the disease '.
" The diversity of occasions and places which make an
ample trade ", he now wrote, " require that some men should
both export and import wares; some export only, others
import ; some deliver out [lend] their moneys by exchange,
others take it up ; some carry out money, others bring it in "[2].
At the Restoration, Parliament passed a resolution forbidding
the export of coin and bullion without licence [3] : but shortly
afterwards the Council of Trade reported in favour of making
the precious metals a free merchandise.   Although opposed
by the officers of the Mint, the proposal found an influential
advocate in Sir George Downing, who pointed out that
" money that in former time was only used as the measure
to value all commodities by is become now itself a commodity ".   In all ages experience had shown that the strictest
laws " cannot stop transporting gold and silver ", and three
great trades—the East India, Baltic and Levant—would be
lost if they were not transported [4].   These arguments, fortified by the examples of Holland, Hamburg, Venice and
Florence—which were said to allow free traffic in gold and
silver, yet ' abound with money '[5]—carried the day.   The
Act of 1663, by permitting the export of ' foreign coin or
bullion of gold or silver ', closed a chapter in a famous
controversy [6].   It did not, however, permit the export
of native coin ; and although the restriction was easily
evaded by melting [7], it caused large quantities of bullion

---

[1] Mun, *A Discourse of Trade from England unto the East Indies*
(1621), 54.

[2] Mun, *England's Treasure by Forraign Trade* (1664), 87-89.

[3] *House of Commons Journals*, viii. 39 (1660) ; Proclamation, 1661
(Bodleian Library : Fol. Θ.660, No. 126).

[4] *State Papers Domestic*, 1660–1661, p. 411; Violet, *Humble Proposal
against Transporting of Gold and Silver out of the Kingdom* (1661), 16-22.

[5] Roberts, *The Treasure of Traffike* (1641), 21, 24 ; Coke, *Treatise* (1671),
i. 71 ; Petty, *Economic Writings*, ii. 445 ; *Britannia Languens* (1680),
40.

[6] *Statutes*, v. 451.   In 1666 free coinage was established—a measure
criticized by Locke and Sir Dudley North : *ibid.* v. 598 ; Locke, *Works*
(ed. 1801), v. 90 ; North, *Discourses upon Trade* (1691), Preface, 11, 18.

[7] *Britannia Languens* (1680), 149 (in sect. ix.) ; Locke, *Works* (ed.
1801), v. 160, 199.

to ' lie dead ' instead of being brought to the Mint for coinage [1].

*Issues involved in the monetary problem.*    The monetary problem, as it was viewed in the sixteenth and seventeenth centuries, involved more complex issues than the movement of gold and silver in the ordinary way of commerce. The real source of anxiety lay in the conviction that money was enticed abroad by the unscrupulous conduct of other countries in ' crying up ' [2] the value of our money, and by the ' cunning handling ' of bankers in crying down the value of bills of exchange in order to bring about the export of money in place of bills [3].

*Ratios of foreign and English currencies.*    To take the first point. Genuine difficulties were created by the want of correspondence between the English and continental monetary systems. Thus a Dutch ' placard ', or proclamation, in 1586 fixed the exchange rates for foreign money—this was termed ' proclamation ' or ' permission ' money. The authorities, however, tolerated higher rates. The banks sometimes gave more for English money than the placard allowed—this was called ' bank ' money ; and debts were often discharged at a still higher rate known as 'current' money. The Dutch Government professed its inability to check practices by which English coins of gold and silver passed at too ' high a rate ' in Holland [4]. The complaint was also made that " our gold is transported into all the places of trade by the sea coast in France but specially into Normandy. The pieces of 22s. do pass in Normandy for 28s. though they want ten or twenty grains, for the French never weigh them, so the exporters gain by every piece six shillings " [5]. Various proposals to cope with the problem were canvassed : indeed Malynes declared that thirty-two methods

---

[1] *House of Commons Journals*, xxvi. 292. Cf. *State Papers Domestic*, 1668–1669, p. 501. An attempt in 1690 to revive the legal restrictions on the export of bullion was successfully opposed on the ground that the Act of 1663 was " one of the best Acts that ever was made for trade " : *House of Lords MSS.* 1690–1691, p. 181. See also *infra*, Appendix, p. 498, No. 2.
[2] *Sir Thomas Roe's Speech* (1641), in *Harleian Miscellany* (ed. Malham), iv. 457.    [3] For the exchanges, see *infra*, p. 80.
[4] *State Papers Domestic*, 1601–1603, pp. 47–48 ; Misselden, *Free Trade* (1622), 8-10 ; Misselden, *The Circle of Commerce* (1623), 101 ; Mun, *A Discourse of Trade from England unto the East Indies* (1621), 51.
[5] *Hist. MSS. Comm. Cowper*, ii. 76 (1635).

had been tried to prevent the export of money and to bring *Ratio* in bullion [1].   One was to vary the ratio between gold and *between gold and* silver.   The English currency system was one of bimetallism [2]; *silver.* but the ratio between the two metals, gold and silver, had been disturbed by the fall in the value of silver due to its influx from America.   In comparison with the ratios established abroad, gold in England was sometimes undervalued in relation to silver.   This caused an outflow of gold to other countries, where it exchanged for a greater quantity of silver than in this country [3].   Accordingly we get a series of monetary changes designed to raise the value of gold in proportion to silver.   In the twelfth century the proportion had been $1 : 9$; under Elizabeth it was $1 : 11 \cdot 79$ [4]; James I. changed it three times when it finally became $1 : 13 \cdot 34$ [5].   At one period in his reign the value of gold was apparently raised too high—with the result that silver was now undervalued and was not brought to the Mint : a proclamation of 1619 stated that ' turning silver into gold upon profit of exchange ' led to its transportation abroad [6].   After the Restoration the proportion was raised to $1 : 14 \cdot 48$ [7].

Another group of proposals was concerned with expedients *Purity* for altering the silver coinage in respect of its purity, weight *of the coinage.* or denomination.   No reputable writer ventured to recommend the first expedient—to debase the purity of the coinage by lowering the standard of fineness.   Henry VIII. and Edward VI. had adopted this device as a means of liquidating their debts [8].   Elizabeth signalized her accession by com-

---

[1] *State Papers Domestic*, 1641-1643, pp. 112-113.   Cf. *ibid.* 1651-1652, p. 26.

[2] The Act of 1816 made silver coins legal tender to the amount of 40s. only : Ruding, *Annals of the Coinage* (ed. 1840), ii. 116.

[3] *State Papers Domestic*, 1601-1603, pp. 47-48 ; *House of Commons Journals*, i. 528 (1621) ; Fortrey, *England's Interest and Improvement* (1663), 34.

[4] Except in 1601, when Elizabeth lowered it to 10.90.

[5] Ruding, *Annals of the Coinage* (ed. 1840), i. 11 ; Shaw, *The History of Currency* (2nd ed.), 69-70.      [6] Rymer, *Foedera*, xvii. 133.

[7] In 1816 it was $1 : 14\frac{288}{1000}$ : Ruding, *Annals of the Coinage* (ed. 1840), i. 11 ; Shaw, *op. cit.* 70.   The proportion could be raised by diminishing the weight of the gold coin.   Elizabeth coined the pound weight of ' crown gold ' (22 carats fine, 2 carats alloy) into £33 until 1601, when she coined it into £33 : 10s.; James I. into £41 ; Charles II. into £44 : 10s.: Ruding, *op. cit.* i. 338, 357, 379 ; ii. 13.

[8] *Supra*, vol. i. 167.

pleting the plan for restoring the standard, explaining to the
nation that the price of everything ' hath immeasurably and
daily risen ', and that the foreign exchanges had turned
against this country [1]. The withdrawal of base money from
circulation and the issue of a pure currency caused the
exchanges to rise in England's favour, the credit of which
Sir Thomas Gresham claimed for his own questionable de-

*Weight
of the
coinage.* vices [2]. The second expedient was to diminish the weight
of English money. Elizabeth in 1601 coined a pound weight
of the old standard silver into 62s. instead of 60s. Under
James I. it was proposed to coin it into 66s.; but the Privy
Council declared (1618) that it did not see any necessity to
alter the coinage, since there was no " such vast transportation of gold and silver into France and the Low Countries as
was supposed, neither there is any such notorious diminution
of treasure generally in the kingdom". Moreover it would
cause ' many inconveniences'. " The noise thereof through
the city of London and from thence to other parts of the
realm . . . hath already done hurt, and in some measure interrupted and distracted the course of general commerce ". The
project was again entertained by Charles I. in 1626—when he
issued a commission for the pound weight in silver to be
coined into 70s. 6d., though it is uncertain whether the commission was ever acted upon [3]—and by Parliament in 1690,
when a Bill was introduced for coining the pound weight in
silver into 65s., but dropped in committee [4].

[1] Ruding, *op. cit.* i. 335. The standard fineness of silver money was
11 oz. 2 dwts. fine and 18 dwts. alloy. Edward VI. and Mary had already
begun to restore the standard : *ibid.* i. 359. For Elizabeth's reform, see
Cunningham, *The Growth of English Industry and Commerce* (ed. 1907), ii.
127 *seq.* ; Feavearyear, *The Pound Sterling,* 71 *seq.* ; Read, " Profits on the
Recoinage of 1560–1 ", in *The Economic History Review,* vi. No. 2, 186 *seq.*
[2] " Did I not raise it [from 16s.] to 23s. ? " He proposed that the
Merchant Adventurers should be made to furnish the Crown with foreign
money at a fictitious (*i.e.* above the current) rate, which meant, of course,
inflicting the loss on English exporters : *State Papers Foreign,* 1558–
1559, pp. 153-154; *Hist. MSS. Comm. Salisbury,* i. 117; Burgon, *Life of
Gresham,* i. 96 *seq.,* 257, 335.
[3] For the project under James I., and the commissions issued by
Elizabeth and Charles I., see *Acts of the Privy Council,* 1618–1619, pp. 302-
303, 318-319 ; Ruding, *Annals of the Coinage* (ed. 1840), i. 12, 338, 357,
372-373, 382 ; Shaw, *Writers on English Monetary History,* 13 *seq.*
[4] *House of Lords MSS.* 1690–1691, 179 *seq.,* 205 *seq.* This proposal
is not noticed in Ruding, *Annals of the Coinage* (ed. 1840), ii. 30-32. In
1816 the pound weight was coined into 66s. : *ibid.* ii. 114, 119.

The main discussion turned on the third expedient—to *Denomina-* preserve the purity and weight of the metal but to raise the *tion of the* *coinage.* denomination of the coin, that is, to make it current at a higher value. It was represented that money was transported 'for the richness only'; and if it were 'dearly priced', no more would be taken out of the country [1]. Thus Sir Robert Heath declared that the root of the trouble was that " our moneys of gold and silver are of more value in their true intrinsical worth in all parts where we trade, than they are at home "; and he considered that the 'only effectual remedy' was " to countermine the policy of our neighbouring nations, who do enhance the values of their coins and so by consequence draw ours to them ". This was to be done, not by increasing the amount of alloy, nor by lessening the weight of the pure metal—" either of these ways would bring too much trouble upon us to vary as often as our neighbours please to vary "—but by " keeping the 12d. and 6d. of silver and the 20s. and 10s. pieces of gold, etc., in the same form and substance as now they are ", and altering 'the denomination of value' by proclamation according to 'the true intrinsical difference' between our money and foreign money [2]. The proposal to vary the denomination was vigorously assailed on the ground that it involved ' general detriment ' to the community [3]. It would produce a general rise in prices and inflict loss, in particular, on landlords in their rents and on creditors in their contracts [4]. In addition it would prove 'a business without end' [5], since other countries would raise their coins still further. In France the constant alteration of the coins by Louis XIV. " confounded all trade : nobody knew what his money was worth for a day together, nor what he was to buy or sell goods for " [6]. Spain had repeated recourse to the device. Portugal in a period of

---

[1] Schanz, *Englische Handelspolitik*, ii. 648 (? *temp.* Elizabeth).
[2] *State Papers Domestic*, 1640, pp. 498-500.
[3] Maddison, *England's Looking In and Out* (1640), 7.
[4] Misselden, *Free Trade* (1622), 106-107 ; *State Papers Domestic*, 1650, p. 130.
[5] Mun, *A Discourse of Trade from England unto the East Indies* (1621), 52.
[6] *Hist. MSS. Comm. Buckinghamshire*, 58. Cf. Macpherson, *Annals of Commerce*, ii. 716.

twenty-five years changed the value of her money three times : " and yet still we bring their money from them as heretofore, and sell our commodities to them for as much silver as ever ". The reason, as Child explained, was that foreign merchants altered the price of their goods in proportion as Portugal altered her coin : " the merchants still observing what the intrinsic value of the money is, not the name it is called by ". And so, he added, " it would be in England " [1].

*State of the coinage after the Revolution.* ' This old thread-bare and exposed project ', as Child termed it, was revived after the Revolution when the reform of the currency became an imperative necessity. During the Civil War Charles I. " went squirting up and down with his mints at Bristol, Shrewsbury, York, Oxford, Carlisle and many other places, and when these garrisons were surrendered the irons were carelessly neglected and came into the hands of knaves " [2], who coined counterfeit money. Moreover the technical deficiencies of the Mint were so great that some shillings weighed fourteen pence, and some not above eightpence [3]—with the result that the goldsmiths ' culled ' the heavy coins, which they melted down for plate or for export as bullion [4]. The state of the coinage was shown by a test made in 1695. There was brought into the Exchequer over a period of three months £57,200, which ought to have weighed 221,418 oz. 16 dwts. 8 grs. but actually weighed only 113,771 oz. 5 dwts.[5]. The depreciation of money due to bad or clipped coins was aggravated by the excessive issue of paper money during the French War [5a]. The effect was an ' exorbitant ' rise in the price of gold, guineas being current at 30s. apiece [5b] ; and the foreign exchanges were so depreciated that 4s. in the pound [6] was lost

---

[1] Child, *A New Discourse of Trade* (4th ed.), pp. xvi-xvii ; *House of Lords MSS.* 1690–1691, p. 206.

[2] *State Papers Domestic*, 1651–1652, p. 262.

[3] Fortrey, *England's Interest and Improvement* (1663), 35.

[4] An old complaint : *House of Commons Journals*, i. 527 (1621) ; Rymer, *Foedera*, xviii. 896 (1627) ; *State Papers Domestic*, 1651–1652, pp. 26, 243, 261, 263 ; Violet, *An Humble Declaration* (1643), 1 ; Violet, *A True Discovery* (1650) ; Violet, *The Advancement of Merchandize* (1651), 39.

[5] Lowndes, *An Essay for the Amendment of the Silver Coins* (1695), 106-107, 159.

[5a] This was pointed out in the Bullion Report of 1810 : Feavearyear, *The Pound Sterling*, 125, note.

[5b] *Infra*, Appendix, p. 498, No. 3.  [6] Lowndes, *op. cit.* 110-113.

upon the money remitted to Holland [1]. Domestic trade was severely handicapped and prices rose. Lowndes depicted the ' great contentions ' which " do daily arise amongst the King's subjects in fairs, markets, shops and other places throughout the kingdom about the passing or refusing of the same. . . . Persons, before they conclude in any bargains, are necessitated first to settle the price or value of the very money they are to receive for their goods ; and if it be in guineas at a high rate, or in clipped or bad moneys, they set the price of their goods accordingly " [2].

To meet this situation Lowndes, who spoke with the authority of a secretary to the treasury, recommended that the recoined money should become current at a higher rate—the crown to pass for 75d., the half-crown for 37½d., the shilling for 15d., and the half-shilling for 7½d. His contention was that an ounce of standard silver in bullion had risen in price from 5s. 2d. to 6s. 5d., while the crown, which contained almost an ounce of silver, still passed for 5s. : hence, the value of the silver in the crown being less than the price of silver in bullion, the coin was naturally melted down [3]. Locke denied that the price of silver had risen. " If the author means that an ounce of standard silver is risen to 6s. 5d. of our clipped money, I grant it him, and higher too. But then that has nothing to do with the raising our lawful coin which remains unclipped : unless he will say too that standard bullion is so risen as to be worth, and to actually sell for, 6s. 5d. the ounce of our weighty milled money. This I not only deny, but farther add that it is impossible to be so. For 6s. 5d. of milled money weighs an ounce and a quarter near. Can it therefore be possible that one ounce of any commodity should be worth an ounce and a quarter of the self-same commodity and of exactly the same goodness ? " Or " can it be supposed that a goldsmith will give one ounce and a quarter of coined silver for one ounce of bullion, when by putting it into his melting-

*Contro-versy between Lowndes and Locke.*

---

[1] On Aug. 16, 1695, the discount of an English bill drawn on Amsterdam was 36·9 per cent. : Rogers, *The First Nine Years of the Bank of England*, 38.

[2] Lowndes, *An Essay for the Amendment of the Silver Coins* (1695), 115.

[3] *Ibid.* 62, 68, 70, 77.

pot he can for less than a penny charge make it bullion ? "
" It is impossible that the value of coined silver should be
less than the value or price of uncoined "[1]. In short the
present price of bullion—the fact that bullion was not sold
by the ounce for less than 6s. 5d., " when that 6s. 5d. clipped
money paid for it does not weigh above an ounce "—proves
only that " the quantity of silver in money governs the value
of it and not the denomination : as appears when clipped
money is brought to buy bullion "[2]. Locke's argument,
reinforced by the contention that under Lowndes's scheme
prices would rise, and creditors and landlords suffer[3],
carried the day ; and in the recoinage of 1696 the denomination of the currency remained unchanged.

*The foreign exchanges.*     We have now to consider the monetary problem as it
was affected by the working of the foreign exchanges. In
the sixteenth century England's foreign trade was conducted
by means of bills of exchange, " whereby they that have
money in one country may deliver the same to receive
it again in another country at certain times and rates agreed
upon "[4]. They served a dual purpose : they saved the
risk and expense of transporting money abroad, and they
avoided breach of the laws against the export of money.
The convenience of the system was incontestable, since paper
subscribed by men of credit was considered equivalent to
money ; yet its practical working gave rise to an intense
controversy. " To many, if not to most merchants ", wrote
Scarlett in 1682, the subject of exchanges " remains a
mystery, and is indeed the greatest and weightiest mystery
that is to be found in the whole Map of Trade "[5]. The
opinion was widely held that a system, devised to prevent

---

[1] Locke, *Works* (ed. 1801), v. 153-154, 156.
[2] *Ibid.* 157. For replies to Locke, see Barbon, *A Discourse concerning
coining the New Money lighter* (1696) ; Temple, " Some Short Remarks
upon Mr. Locke's Book " (1696) in Somers, *Tracts* (ed. 1814), xi. 604.
[3] Locke, *Works* (ed. 1801), v. 86, 166. Similarly : *Hist. MSS. Comm.
Buccleuch*, ii. part ii. 721-722.
[4] Mun, *England's Treasure by Forraign Trade* (1664), 94. Cf. *infra*,
Appendix, p. 499, No. 1.
[5] Scarlett, *The Stile of Exchanges* (1682), Preface. On the foreign
exchanges, see Scarlett, *op. cit.* ; Marius, *Advice concerning Bills of Exchange* (ed. 1655) ; Hewitt, *A Treatise upon Money, Coins and Exchange*
(1740) ; and note 4 *supra*.

the export of money, was so manipulated by self-seeking individuals that it actually necessitated its export [1]. In the hands of bankers the exchanges, it was complained, were perverted from their ' true use '—the ' accommodating of merchants' affairs '—and became ' a trade ' [2]. The bankers operated on the money market in order to create an artificial scarcity or abundance of money; and when bills of exchange depreciated in value the effect was to encourage the export of specie, since " more will be given for our moneys carried in specie than can be had beyond the seas by bill of exchange ". In fact it was supposed that foreign exchangers designedly ' undervalued ' English bills, placing a lower value on them than on a corresponding amount of specie, in order to draw gold and silver out of the kingdom. " A low exchange is a cause of transportation of our moneys " [3]. Another evil was involved. It was held that " the exchange is the governor of prices of all wares interchangeably vented " between England and other countries [4], so that when the rate turned against this country, English goods became cheap abroad and foreign goods dear in England. The proposed remedy had the merit of simplicity, namely, that no one should make any exchange for money by bills of exchange ' under the true value of our money ' as fixed by public authority. Malynes [5], in particular, made the ' par of exchange ' the ' sole and sovereign remedy ' for all the maladies with which trade was afflicted. The criticisms, to which this proposal was exposed, served to elucidate the underlying factors, of whose operation the rate of exchange was in reality only the symptom.

A ' forced par ' was condemned as impracticable, just as *A forced par*. prices in a market cannot be ' prefixed '. The rate of exchange depended on time, whether the bill was for a shorter

---

[1] *State Papers Domestic*, 1650, p. 182.
[2] *Ibid.* 1601–1603, p. 48 ; Mun, *A Discourse of Trade from England unto the East Indies* (1621), 52.
[3] *State Papers Domestic*, 1598–1601, p. 88 ; 1601–1603, p. 48.
[4] *Tudor Economic Documents* (ed. Tawney and Power), ii. 182 (1551) ; iii. 347 (1564).
[5] In *The Maintenance of Free Trade* (1622) ; *A Treatise of the Canker of England's Commonwealth* (1601) ; and in *State Papers Domestic*, 1641–1643, p. 112.

or longer period ; on place, whether at an exchange centre bills were plentiful or scarce ; on persons, whether their credit was greater or less [1]. " These exchanges ", Mun explained, " are not contracted at the equal value of the moneys, according to their respective weights and fineness—first, because he that delivereth his money doth respect the venture of the debt and the time of forbearance ; but that which causeth an under- or over-valuing of moneys by exchange is the plenty or scarcity thereof in those places where the exchanges are made " [2]. If imports are in excess of exports, the demand for foreign bills will exceed the supply and their price will rise : and the converse. Thus the balance of trade, and not the manipulations of the bankers, was held to govern the rate of exchange. " In vain therefore hath Gerard Malynes laboured so long, and in so many printed books, to make the world believe that the undervaluing of our money in exchange doth exhaust our treasure, which is a mere fallacy of the cause, attributing that to a secondary means whose effects are wrought by another principal efficient "— it is " the over-balancing of our trade that carrieth away our treasure " [3]. Misselden further maintained that the price of goods was determined, not by the rate of the exchange, but by the intrinsic worth of the currency and by the demand and supply of commodities [4]. The general position taken up by Misselden and Mun was correct, though the arguments used in its support were sometimes defective [5]. In their anxiety to demonstrate the danger of a ' forced par ' of exchange, they even maintained that an adverse rate of exchange was actually beneficial to a country. They assumed that an alien merchant, bringing goods into this country, was placed at a disadvantage when he disposed of the money received here to English merchants or bankers, who paid him in foreign currency due to them abroad, inasmuch as he obtained less

---

[1] Misselden, *The Circle of Commerce* (1623), 98.

[2] Mun, *England's Treasure by Forraign Trade* (1664), 94-95.

[3] *Ibid.* 99, 103-104. A similar opinion had been expressed in 1564 (*Tudor Economic Documents*, ed. Tawney and Power, iii. 353), and in the report of a commission in 1601 (*State Papers Domestic*, 1601–1603, pp. 47-48).

[4] Misselden, *The Circle of Commerce* (1623), 20-21.

[5] *Ibid.* 107-108 ; Mun, *England's Treasure by Forraign Trade* (1664), 101.

for his English money owing to the unfavourable rate of exchange. Their argument overlooked the probability that alien merchants, if paid in a depreciated currency, would protect themselves by raising the prices of their wares. Nor did the doctrine, that the course of exchange 'always and in all countries '[1] was governed by the balance of trade, escape criticism. Barbon pointed out that " exchanges rise and fall every week, and at some particular times in the year run high against a nation and at other times run as high on the contrary ", according to the circumstances of the moment[2]; or, again, a war might turn the exchange against a country[3]. Moreover in the sixteenth and seventeenth centuries there was no 'settled' course of exchange to many countries, with which we nevertheless carried on a great trade[4].

The controversy over the exchanges assumed a practical bearing, when attempts were made to take the business of the exchanges out of the hands of ' the great moneyed men ' and place it under Government control, on the plea that " the greatest danger to a State is when money is made merchandise "[5]. In the Middle Ages the exchanger was a royal official[6], but repeated prohibitions failed to stamp out the practice of unauthorized exchanges, even when it was declared to be a capital offence. Henry VIII. in 1539 abolished all restraints upon private exchanges, and though reimposed in 1546[7] they remained ineffectual. On two other occasions it was sought to establish a Government monopoly of the exchanges. In 1576 Elizabeth appointed two haberdashers and a grocer to sanction all bills of exchange, subject to the stipulation that " the moneys of this realm may not be delivered under the just values of their standard "[8].

*Official exchangers.*

---

[1] *The British Merchant* (ed. 1721), iii. 106, 113.
[2] Barbon, *A Discourse concerning coining the New Money lighter* (1696), 39. Gresham had remarked that " the exchange riseth and falleth daily " : Burgon, *Life of Gresham*, i. 477.
[3] *E.g.* the War of the Spanish Succession : *The British Merchant* (ed. 1721), iii. 108 ; and *supra*, p. 79, note 1.
[4] Child, *A New Discourse of Trade* (4th ed.), 175.
[5] *Sir Thomas Roe's Speech* (1641) in *Harleian Miscellany* (ed. Malham), iv. 457.
[6] Ruding, *Annals of the Coinage* (ed. 1840), ii. 138 *seq.*
[7] *Ibid.* ii. 147-148.
[8] Proclamation, 1576 (Bodleian Library : Arch. G.C. 6, No. 174).

The merchants made a strong protest[1]. They objected to
the exchanger's fees and the scrutiny of their transactions [2] :
they affirmed that " the abundance of the deliverers or of
the takers make the exchange rise or fall " : and they uttered
the warning that any interference would either lead to the
use of specie in place of bills, or diminish the volume of trade.
Their remonstrance seem to have prevailed[3], and the office
lapsed [4] until Charles I. revived it in 1627 on the ground that
the exchange " ought to be our sole and appropriate right ",
although " ourself and divers our royal predecessors have for
some time now past tolerated an indifferent and promiscuous
kind of liberty to all " [5]. It is significant, however, to observe that bills of exchange were not brought under the
control of the exchanger, whose functions were confined to
coins and bullion [6] : it is evident, therefore, that the Government had become convinced of the futility of controlling
' merchant's exchange '. And even the goldsmiths were now
influential enough to prevent interference with the trade in
coins and bullion. Together with the merchants they laid a
complaint before the House of Commons, which condemned
the monopoly as ' an inconvenience and abuse in the execution ' [7]; and it was abandoned. Proposals for ' the well-
governing of the merchant's exchange ' cropped up occasionally [8], but assertions that English money was undervalued in
foreign bills of exchange were now dismissed as ' old incon-
siderate fancies, sufficiently refuted before ' [9].

The importance of the controversy over money lies in
the fact that it gave birth to the famous Theory of the

[1] Schanz, *Englische Handelspolitik*, ii. 642-647.

[2] " Our books shall be seen and our letters opened " : *ibid.* ii. 645.

[3] Tawney, Introduction to Wilson, *A Discourse upon Usury*, 153.

[4] In 1622 a declaration was issued that the King proposed to establish
a ' royal exchange ' : *State Papers Domestic*, 1619–1623, p. 417.

[5] Rymer, *Foedera*, xviii. 896. The office was given to the Earl of
Holland.

[6] The proclamation omits mention of bills of exchange.    Cf. also
Tawney, *op. cit.* 154.

[7] *State Papers Domestic*, Addenda, 1625–1649, p. 282 ; *House of
Commons Journals*, i. 917 ; *Remembrancia of the City of London*, 226.

[8] Maddison, *England's Looking In and Out* (1640), 26-28 ; *State Papers
Domestic*, 1651–1652, p. 243.

[9] *Britannia Languens* (1680), 236.

Balance of Trade [1], which in the seventeenth and eighteenth centuries became a corner-stone of the mercantilist theory of foreign commerce [1a]. The mercantilist school, as we have seen [2], adhered to the principle of free trade in the precious metals. It laid down two propositions—the most profitable use of money was to employ it in foreign trade [3]; and if exports exceeded imports the money in a country would not diminish but would increase [4]. Mun gave classic expression to these propositions in his simile of the husbandman. " If we only behold the actions of the husbandman in the seed-time when he casteth away much good corn into the ground, we will rather accompt him a madman than a husbandman : but when we consider his labours in the harvest, which is the end of his endeavours, we find the worth and plentiful increase of his actions " [5]. The title of Mun's book, *England's Treasure by Forraign Trade. Or, the Ballance of our Forraign Trade is the Rule of our Treasure*, was a reply to those " who bitterly exclaim when they see any moneys carried out of the realm " [6]. The export of money was actually the means to increase it by enlarging our trade on which we depended, in the absence of gold and silver mines, for any addition to our store of precious metals. Like any other commodity, money could be sent abroad, without apprehension of impoverishment, to serve as a productive stock : " for as money that circulates at home begets money to private men, so bullion circulating abroad begets bullion to a country " [7]. This was subject to the proviso that a favourable balance of trade, a surplus of exports over imports, brought money back into the country. In foreign trade, said Mun, " we must ever

[1] ' A melancholy subject ', Chalmers (*An Estimate of the Comparative Strength of Britain* (ed. 1782), 48) called it. " So much talked of, so little understood ", said Davenant, *Works* (ed. 1771), ii. 103.
[1a] Another corner-stone was its reaction upon agriculture, industry and navigation.
[2] *Supra*, p. 72.
[3] Coke, *Treatise* (1675), iii. 58 ; Petty, *Economic Writings*, ii. 441.
[4] Mun, *England's Treasure* (1664), 35-37 ; Misselden, *The Circle of Commerce* (1623), 34 ; *Britannia Languens* (1680), 11 ; *House of Commons Journals*, xii. 432 (1697) ; Puckle, *England's Path to Wealth and Honour* (1700), 29 ; *The British Merchant* (ed. 1721), i. 21.
[5] Mun, *England's Treasure by Forraign Trade* (1664), 50.
[6] *Ibid.* 34. Numerous Statutes deplored the carrying out of the realm of ' great masses of money ' : *e.g. Statutes*, iv. part i. 668 (1581).
[7] Davenant, *Works* (ed. 1771), ii. 117.

observe this rule : to sell more to strangers yearly than we
consume of theirs in value ", since " that part of our stock
which is not returned to us in wares must necessarily be
brought home in treasure "[1]. But " if the vanity and super-
fluity of our importation be greater than the exportation of
our home commodities will bear . . . money must necessarily
turn the scale ", and " our treasure must needs be wasted "
to make good the deficit, " notwithstanding all laws that
can be made "[2].

*The baro-*
*meter of*
*prosperity.*
The balance of trade became the barometer which registered the economic condition of the nation. It showed,
explained Misselden, " the difference of weight in the commerce of one kingdom with another, that is, whether the
native commodities exported and all the foreign commodities imported do balance or overbalance one another in the
scale of commerce. If the native commodities exported do
weigh down and exceed in value the foreign commodities
imported, it is a rule that never fails that then the kingdom
grows rich and prospers in estate and stock—because the
overplus thereof must needs come in, in treasure. But if the
foreign commodities imported do exceed in value the native
commodities exported, it is a manifest sign that then trade
decayeth and the stock of the kingdom wasteth apace—because the overplus must needs go out in treasure "[3]. The
balance of trade was, in short, the factor which governed
the importation or exportation of bullion. The conclusion
followed that a Government should regulate, not the flow of
precious metals, but the stream of commerce, directing it into
channels which would ensure a surplus of exports over imports. The conception of ' a well ordered trade ' dominated
the thought of the seventeenth century, as it had done the
later Middle Ages [4]; and writers still continued to speak
of the ' right ordering ' and the ' right management ' of our

---

[1] Mun, *England's Treasure by Forraign Trade* (1664), 11-12.  Similarly :
*The Petition and Remonstrance of the . . . Merchants of London trading to
the East Indies* (1628), 10 seq. ; Locke, *Works* (ed. 1801), v. 148, 160-
161.
[2] Stowe MSS. 554, f. 45 (1622) ; Fortrey, *England's Interest and Improvement* (1663), 27 ; *The British Merchant* (ed. 1721), iii. 123.
[3] Misselden, *The Circle of Commerce* (1623), 116-117.
[4] *Supra*, vol. i. 574 ; ii. 232.

trade [1]—but the end in view had now become primarily the realization of a favourable balance.

Misselden justly claimed that " this balance of the king- *History* dom's trade is no conceit or novelty, but hath been the wisdom *of the theory.* and policy even of elder times " [2]. Its history goes back to the fourteenth century, for in the reign of Richard II. an officer of the Mint, Richard Aylesbury, counselled that if trade were ' well and rightly governed ', so that the foreign merchandise which was brought into the realm did not exceed in value the native merchandise which passed out of it, the money already here would remain and plenty of money would come from abroad [3]. In the sixteenth century the theory had become firmly established. A discussion of ' Polices to reduce this Realme of Englande unto a Prosperus Wealthe and Estate ' (1549) set forth that " the only means to cause much bullion to be brought out of other realms " was to provide that we exported more than we imported [4]. The author of *A Discourse of the Common Weal of this Realm of England* (? 1549) wrote that " we must always take heed that we buy no more of strangers than we sell them, for so we should impoverish ourselves and enrich them " ; and he deplored the ' continual spoil ' of treasure which " goeth out of this realm " to pay for ' trifles ', that "we might either clean spare or else make them within our own realm " [5]. One of Cecil's correspondents (1551) claimed that " once brought to pass that the commodities of our realm and the travail of our people sold in foreign countries may exceed in value the foreign commodities brought in—so much shall our commonwealth be yearly gainers of them and they not of us, and we to live of them and they not of us, and our realm so much enriched of their money or otherwise and also keep our coin still " [6]. Burghley himself held the theory of the balance of trade, because he declared that " nothing robbeth the realm of England but when more merchandise

[1] Fortrey, *England's Interest and Improvement* (1663), 33 ; Wood, *A Survey of Trade* (1718), 337.
[2] Misselden, *The Circle of Commerce* (1623), 118-122.
[3] *Rotuli Parliamentorum*, iii. 127 *a* (1382). See *supra*, vol. i. 532, and Appendix.
[4] *Tudor Economic Documents* (ed. Tawney and Power), iii. 321.
[5] (Ed. Lamond), pp. 63-64.
[6] *Tudor Economic Documents* (ed. Tawney and Power), ii. 184-185.

is brought into the realm than is carried forth " [1]. Even the views expounded by Mun on the relation between the balance of trade and the foreign exchanges were anticipated long before, when it was officially pronounced (1564) that a favourable balance was ' the chiefest and the most profitable remedy ' to ' keep up the exchange ' [2]. In the seventeenth century the efforts of Malynes and Misselden to unravel the mysteries of the foreign exchanges [3], coupled with the attacks upon the East India Company, brought the theory into great prominence ; and with the almost complete extinction of the bullionist school as the result of the Act of 1663 [4], it became the accepted dogma of English economic opinion and the touchstone of national prosperity [5]. Its practical influence was not less profound. It provided the arguments on the basis of which the trade between England and France, when not actually prohibited, was placed under the severest restraints; and it was the partial revolt of economists against the theory which inaugurated the beginnings of the free trade movement. The practical fruits of the theory will be reviewed later : something must first be said as to its implications and assumptions.

*Distorted view of foreign trade.*       The theory tended, in its extreme form [5a], to foster a distorted view of foreign trade. It applied a single criterion for estimating the profit or loss in trade between nations. The balance alone measured the value of any trade : it was the ' one certain medium ' which indicated whether the kingdom gained or lost [6]. A country was enriched only by the treasure which the balance of trade brought into it—it was not enough to have a large volume of exports and imports ; the

[1] *Tudor Economic Documents* (ed. Tawney and Power), ii. 124.
[2] *Ibid.* iii. 353. Wheeler, *A Treatise of Commerce* (1601), 10, also held the doctrine of the balance of trade.
[3] *Supra*, pp. 81 *seq.*
[4] *Supra*, p. 73.
[5] Cf. *Tudor and Stuart Proclamations* (ed. Steele), i. No. 3079 (1656). One of the instructions given by Parliament to the Council of Trade in 1650 was " to consider of some way that a most exact accompt be kept of all commodities imported and exported . . . that a perfect balance of trade may be taken, whereby the commonwealth may not be impoverished " by an excess of imports over exports : *Acts and Ordinances of the Interregnum*, ii. 404.
[5a] For an enlightened view of foreign trade, see *supra*, vol. ii. Introduction, p. lxxxii.
[6] Child, *A New Discourse of Trade* (4th ed.), 164 ; *The British Merchant* (ed. 1721), i. 22.

'overplus' was the profit a nation made by commerce [1].
No gain accrued from domestic trade, "since by what is
consumed at home one loseth only what another gets, and the
nation in general is not at all the richer" : foreign traffic
alone increased the national wealth, and artisans should
therefore be employed on commodities intended for markets
abroad, not for home consumption [2]. This exaggerated view
merited the condemnation of Adam Smith, but two things
should be remembered. To-day foreign trade is vital to our
existence because it furnishes us with food and raw materials.
But until the 'Industrial Revolution' England raised her own
food supply and the raw material for her greatest industry ;
and although many necessaries came from abroad [3], imports
were largely in the nature of 'delicacies, superfluities or
trifles' [4], such as wines and silks. It was therefore natural
that foreign trade should be valued, less for the degree to
which it contributed to the amenities and comforts of life,
than for the addition which it made to the stock of precious
metals in an age when banking and credit facilities were
still incomplete. Again, not all Mercantilists ranked foreign
above domestic trade. "Our own consumption, the consumption of our own people, are the best and greatest market
for the product and manufactures of our own country".
This was Adam Smith's own doctrine [5], but it appears in the

---

[1] J. B., *An Account of the French Usurpation upon the Trade of England*
(1679), 4 ; Davenant, *Works* (ed. 1771), i. 16 ; ii. 199. In 1641 Sir T. Roe
said : "It is a true rule, if money increase, the kingdom doth gain by
trade ; if it be scarce, it loseth" (*Harleian Miscellany*, ed. Malham, iv. 456).
Tucker, *An Essay on Trade* (ed. 1753), p. iii. note, wrote : "The science
of gainful commerce consists ultimately in procuring a balance of gold
or silver to ourselves from other nations ". Smith, *Chronicon Rusticum-
Commerciale* (ed. 1747), ii. 533, summed up the doctrine thus : "In foreign
trade the balance is of much more consequence than the quantity ".
[2] Petty, *Economic Writings*, i. 295 ; Davenant, *Works* (ed. 1771), i. 102 ;
Brewster, *Essays on Trade and Navigation* (1695), 55, 96. It was even
held that trade within the Empire did not add to the national wealth :
*Hist. MSS. Comm. Various*, vi. 286 (*c.* 1763). See *infra*, Appendix, p. 499,
No. 2.
[3] *E.g.* materials for shipbuilding, Spanish wool, raw silk, drugs, dyeing
materials, etc.
[4] Bodleian Library : Fol. θ. 660, No. 126 (1661). The nature of our
imports had been criticized in the fifteenth century in *The Libelle of Englyshe
Polycye* (*supra*, vol. i. 585) ; and in the sixteenth century in *A Discourse
of the Common Weal of this Realm of England* (ed. Lamond), 63.
[5] *The Wealth of Nations* (ed. Cannan), i. 401 : "The inland or home
trade [is] the most important of all ". See *infra*, Appendix, p. 499, No. 3.

most unimpeachable exposition of mercantilist thought—
*The British Merchant* [1].

*Complaints of an adverse balance.*　More important in its practical bearings was the assumption on which the theory was based, namely, that it was possible to ascertain what was the balance of trade and to shape public policy accordingly. The complaint was common at all periods that imports exceeded exports, and that the country was being steadily impoverished by an adverse balance. " It is manifestly seen already by the customers' accounts in the Exchequer ", was Burghley's conviction, " that yearly the foreign commodities do surmount the commodities of the land " [2] ; and a currency commission reported in 1601 that there was an "overbalancing of foreign commodities imported above our home commodities vented out " [3]. During the great trade depression under James I. it was stated in Parliament that imports exceeded exports ' some hundred thousand pounds a year ' [4]. Misselden looked back to the fourteenth century as ' the golden age ' when the balance was in our favour, 'but the present time is like the iron age '. He gave the following figures for 1622 : ' the total exportations with charges amount to £2,320,436 ', and ' the total importations amount to £2,619,315 ' [5]. " This overbalancing ", said Malynes, " doth expel our moneys out of the realm " [6]. The disturbed condition of England after the Civil War reacted on the monetary situation. A correspondent in Holland wrote home : " Your expense for foreign goods is twice as much as the goods you export, and this in a few years will drain all your stock and not leave you a penny. We have more English gold in Amsterdam than you have " [7]. The Council of State

---

[1] *The British Merchant* (ed. 1721), i. 167. See *infra*, Appendix, p. 499, No. 4.

[2] *Tudor Economic Documents* (ed. Tawney and Power), ii. 124. Similarly : *ibid*. ii. 45, 184.

[3] *State Papers Domestic*, 1601–1603, p. 47.

[4] *House of Commons Journals*, i. 672, 752 (1624).

[5] Misselden, *The Circle of Commerce* (1623), 123, 128–130. The figures are not reliable, since the method of calculation was defective. Misselden's purpose in printing an Exchequer record of Edward III. was to show that the balance had now turned against us (and not to demonstrate the growth of commerce, as suggested by Miss Friis in her valuable monograph, *Alderman Cockayne's Project*, 11, note).

[6] Malynes, *The Maintenance of Free Trade* (1622), 22.

[7] *State Papers Domestic*, 1651–1652, p. 263.

appointed a committee ' to consider how the export of gold and silver may be hindered ' [1]; and a writer proposed that the Statute of Employment should be put in operation [2].

After the Restoration the complaints of the decay of trade grew in volume. Petty (1662) spoke of the trade in cloth as ' almost totally lost ' :   Coke (1671) enumerated other trades which were lost :  a writer in 1674 deplored the country's poverty due to " the necessity of parting every year with vast sums of money to make the balance of trade even, because we import much more than we export " : the address of a parliamentary candidate (1676) lamented " the general poverty . . . which, if not quickly remedied, will soon reduce us to the utmost misery " :  the author of *Britannia Languens* (1680) asserted that " our people generally more and more feel the want of money " [3].  Yet according to the Commissioners for Trade and Plantations, " trade in general did considerably increase from the end of the Dutch War in 1673 " to the Revolution [4]:  Child in *A Discourse about Trade*, published in 1690, affirmed that " in the gross we ship off now one-third part more of the manufactures, as also lead and tin, than we did twenty years past " [5] :  and Davenant expressed the opinion that between 1600 and 1688 " the stock of the kingdom was multiplied above fivefold, and particularly the species of money above fourfold " [6].  Petty himself in his later writings was at pains to show that " the interest and affairs of England [were] in no deplorable condition" :  " The buildings of London grow great and glorious . . .  actions [shares] in the East India Company

*Conflict of opinion as to the state of trade.*

---

[1] *State Papers Domestic*, 1649–1650, p. 430 ; *Acts of the Interregnum*, i. 1218.

[2] Chappel, *A Diamond or Rich Jewel presented to the Commonwealth of England* (1650), 4.

[3] Violet, *Humble Proposal against Transporting of Gold and Silver out of the Kingdom* (1661), 24 ; Petty, *Economic Writings*, i. 30 ; *Hist. MSS. Comm. Various*, i. 144 (1662); Fortrey, *England's Interest and Improvement* (1663), 12 ;  Coke, *Treatise* (1671), ii. Preface ;  R. H., *The Prevention of Poverty* (1674), 3-4 ; *State Papers Domestic*, 1675–1676, p. 499 (1676) ; *Britannia Languens* (1680), 1.   See also *infra*, Appendix, p. 500, No. 1.

[4] *House of Commons Journals*, xii. 432 (1697).

[5] Child, *A Discourse about Trade* (1690), Preface.   The book was licensed in 1689.   In his *Brief Observations concerning Trade and Interest of Money* (1668), 8, Child demonstrated the increase of ' the riches and splendour of this kingdom '.

[6] Davenant, *Works* (ed. 1771), i. 392-393.

are near double the principal money ; those who can give good security may have money under the statute-interest . . . the Exchange seems as full of merchants as formerly . . . the number of coaches and splendour of equipage exceeding former times ; the public theatres very magnificent . . . much land has been improved, and the price of food reasonable . . . men eat and drink and laugh as they use to do " [1]. Houghton, in an anonymous pamphlet, *England's Great Happiness* : or *a Dialogue between Content and Complaint* (1677), satirized the ' marks of poverty '—' multitudes of brave ships ', trade ' stretched as far as any trade is known ', ' abundance of more good debts abroad than credit from thence ', houses ' built like palaces ' in comparison with ' the last age ', and abounding with ' plenty of costly furniture ', rich jewels, ' shops and warehouses better furnished ' [2]. In the next century the belief in an adverse balance still gained currency. " The writings of Mr. Gee ", remarked Hume, " struck the nation with an universal panic, when they saw it plainly demonstrated by a detail of particulars that the balance was against them, for so considerable a sum as must leave them without a single shilling in five or six years. But luckily twenty years have since elapsed, with an expensive foreign war ; yet is it commonly supposed that money is still more plentiful among us than in any former period " [3]. A similar observation applies to the writers who represented the adverse balance in the years following the Restoration at two million pounds, which in a very few years would have completely drained the country [4]. This conflict of opinion as to the state of trade was inevitable, inasmuch as it was impossible to ascertain the true balance ; and the calculations, in which contemporaries indulged, resembled nothing so much as the making of bricks without straw.

In the first place, the official statistics of trade were extremely defective. No abstracts of accounts, showing the

---

[1] *Economic Writings*, i. 243-244 (*c.* 1676).
[2] Page 19. For Houghton's authorship, see *supra*, vol. ii. 396, note 6.
[3] Hume, *Essays* (ed. Green and Grose), i. 332.
[4] Cf. *Helps to a Right Decision upon the Merits of the late Treaty of Commerce with France* (1787), 14 *seq.* (This was written by W. Knox : see *infra*, p. 116, note 1.)

totals of exports and imports, were regularly kept at the *Official* custom-house until the appointment of an inspector-general *statistics of trade* of exports and imports near the end of the seventeenth *defective.* century [1]. Moreover the custom-house books did not record the real values of commodities but fictitious values. The Books of Rates, which were issued at different periods, assigned the prices at which duties on a percentage basis were to be levied : yet these prices did not correspond to market prices, which fluctuated constantly and over long periods of time underwent considerable change. The consequence was that some commodities were rated too high and others too low [2]. There was always a marked discrepancy between the fiscal values and current market prices—even in the reign of James I. imports were considered to be undervalued in the Book of Rates by one-third [3]. After the Revolution the newly appointed inspector-general of exports and imports (1696) drew up for statistical purposes an official valuation of goods [4] : but as the prices of commodities did not remain stationary, real values in the eighteenth century were often out of all proportion to the official valuation [5]. Thus for the purpose of investigating the balance of trade the custom-house statistics were unreliable. They afforded no accurate indication of true values, on the basis of which some comparison might have been instituted between exports and imports [6]. A single example will show the mistake of using the custom-house books to demonstrate that trade with any country was unprofitable when our imports exceeded in value our exports, and profitable when there was an excess of exports over imports. According to the customs

---

[1] In 1696 : Davenant, *Works* (ed. 1771), v. 349-350. Abstracts existed (for London) for 1662–1663 and 1668–1669 : *ibid.* v. 351. See *infra*, Appendix, p. 500, No. 2.

[2] *House of Lords MSS.* 1699–1702, p. 456. (Proposal of the Commissioners for Trade and Plantations for a new Book of Rates.)

[3] And exports by one-fifth : *Acts of the Privy Council*, 1615–1616, p. 479 ; Friis, *Alderman Cockayne's Project*, 207 (note 1), 213 (note 4).

[4] Davenant, *Works* (ed. 1771), v. 350. The Book of Rates had been revised in 1660 (*Statutes*, v. 184 *seq.*). Real values were first registered in the case of exports in 1798, and in the case of imports in 1854 : *Parliamentary Papers* (1898), lxxxv. 16, 51.

[5] *E.g.* haberdashery when exported was rated at about 9 per cent. of its real value. A list comparing official and real values in 1798 is given in Macpherson, *Annals of Commerce*, iv. 464.

[6] Child, *A New Discourse of Trade* (4th ed.), 166.

accounts the balance of trade between England and Ireland in the eighteenth century appeared favourable to the former [1]. Now Irish linen was rated in the English custom-house books at eightpence per yard, which was under one-half of its real value; and as it accounted for more than 50 per cent. of the exports from Ireland, the magnitude of the error in the valuation of this one commodity becomes apparent [2]. The custom-house books are defective, not only as regards values, but also in respect of quantities which were not accurately entered. When woollen manufactures were allowed to be exported duty-free after the Revolution [3], the merchants entered greater quantities of goods than they actually intended to ship abroad, either to gain reputation or to discourage others from sending to the same market [4]. Apart from inaccurate entries, the customs returns do not present a complete record of exports and imports. Certain commodities were expressly excluded, such as fish and bullion, the former paying no duty when exported nor the latter when imported [5]. Other commodities do not appear in the official record because they were smuggled in or out of the country. Smuggling was extensively carried on in the seventeenth and eighteenth centuries [6]; and the 'vast quantities' of goods clandestinely brought into the realm, or taken out of it, must seriously affect the accuracy of computations based on customs statistics. An estimate of exports should also include re-exports.

In addition to defects in the method of compilation, customs

---

[1] Whitworth, *State of the Trade of Great Britain* (1776), part ii. 19-20.

[2] See Lord Sheffield, *Observations on the Manufactures, Trade and Present State of Ireland* (ed. 1785), 278-279. Another example is Dutch linen (' fine Hollands '). This was rated (*temp.* Charles I.) at 5s. the ell; and when, at a later period, the Dutch manufactured a coarser linen not worth 2s. 6d. the ell, it was still rated on the old basis : *Hist. MSS. Comm. Buccleuch*, ii. part ii. 712 (1706).

[3] In 1700 : *supra*, p. 21, note 5.

[4] Davenant, *Works* (ed. 1771), v. 443-444 ; Cary, *An Essay towards Regulating the Trade* (ed. 1719), 84 ; Gee, *The Trade and Navigation of Great Britain* (ed. 1730), 117.

[5] Misselden, *The Circle of Commerce* (1623), 124 ; Cary, *An Essay towards Regulating the Trade* (ed. 1719), 84. See *supra*, vol. ii. 189, note 4.

[6] *Supra*, p. 23, and *infra*, p. 144. " Can we suppose that England this year (1760) bought goods from France only to the amount of £37 in return for goods to the amount of £209,946 ? " : Macpherson, *Annals of Commerce*, iii. 342, note.

statistics are necessarily inadequate since they do not take *Invisible exports.*
into account the invisible exports.  The latter consisted of
services performed by shippers and capitalists (which yielded
freights and interest on loans abroad), and the expenditure of
travellers [1a].  A writer pointed out in 1641 that an excess of
imports over exports need not involve the drain of gold and
silver because, as a result of the carrying trade, "good sums
of money are yearly raised by our nation abroad " [1].  It was
remarked that imports needed to be distinguished, accordingly as they were brought in English or in foreign shipping
—in the former case they should be valued only at their
' first cost and charges ' abroad ; in the latter case, ' with
the increase of the homeward freight' [2].  Another important
item in foreign trade was made up of the interest on oversea
investments.  In some branches of trade a series of ' favourable balances ' would have brought ruin on the trading community, for example, if our exports to the West Indies or
Hudson's Bay had continued permanently to exceed the
imports [3].  In these instances the excess of imports, or ' unfavourable balance ', constituted the profit earned by the
capital sunk in the sugar plantations, the fur trade and
other commercial enterprises : it was therefore a national
gain instead of a national loss.  Again, all outward cargoes
increased the volume of exports although they might be lost
at sea, captured by an enemy or confiscated by a foreign
Government ; or losses might be sustained through bad
markets, bankruptcies and other ' accidents ' [4].  In such
cases there would be a corresponding reduction in the value
of the homeward cargoes, imported in return for the outward
cargoes ; but the national loss would be masked by the illu-
sion of a ' favourable balance ', produced by a diminution in
the volume of imports.  Similarly, chance might enhance
the price of a cargo when sold abroad, and the commodities

[1a] See *infra*, Appendix, p. 501, No. 1.
[1] Robinson, *England's Safety in Trades Encrease* (1641), 50.  Similarly :
Misselden, *The Circle of Commerce* (1623), 124 ; Cary, *An Essay towards
Regulating the Trade* (ed. 1719), 85.
[2] Child, *A New Discourse of Trade* (4th ed.), 166.  Freights sometimes
amounted to nearly as much as the first cost of the goods : *House of
Commons Journals*, xiii. 723.
[3] Cf. Macpherson, *Annals of Commerce*, iii. 342-343.
[4] Child, *A New Discourse of Trade* (4th ed.), 166-167.

brought back in return might be of greater value than the commodities exported, yet the nation would be the gainer although the imports exceeded in value the exports [1].

*Triangular nature of trade.*  Enough has been said to show the difficulty of measuring the balance of trade, even when only the ' general balance ' of all exports against all imports was in question. It was still more difficult—in view of the triangular nature of trade under which commodities purchased in one country are often transported direct to a third country—to determine the ' particular balance ' of trade with separate countries. To give an example: we exported woollen manufactures to Portugal, and the sugar which we received in part payment was shipped to Italy [2], whence we brought back raw silk and other commodities [3]. On the surface it might appear as though the trade with Italy must involve the drain of bullion to pay for her raw silk, because the custom-house books would not disclose the payment actually made to Italy in goods ; and the balance of trade with Portugal might appear unduly favourable, owing to the diversion of Portuguese imports from these shores to Italy. Moreover custom-house entries would not reveal the profit which accrued from the Newfoundland trade [4], inasmuch as the fish was transported direct to Mediterranean countries. The proceeds were brought to England either in bills of exchange or in commodities [5]—in the latter case they would swell the imports, and might create the appearance of an unfavourable balance with Mediterranean countries. But England's trade with Holland affords the best example of the danger of facile generalizations, based on a hasty comparison of exports and imports. In the opening years of the eighteenth century the Dutch trade seemed singularly advantageous : the balance, formerly against us [6], turned in our favour, the

---

[1] *Ibid.*  [2] Some was brought to England.

[3] *Hist. MSS. Comm.* ix. part ii. 12 ; Cary, *An Essay towards Regulating the Trade* (ed. 1719), 85.

[4] The Commissioners for Trade and Plantations conjectured in 1707 that the fish from Newfoundland ' might amount ' to about £130,000 per annum : *House of Lords MSS.* 1706–1708, p. 255.

[5] Burke, *Observations on a Late State of the Nation* (ed. 1769), 49 ; Macpherson, *Annals of Commerce*, iii. 343.

[6] Davenant, *Works* (ed. 1771), v. 402, 404.

' overplus ' averaging nearly £1,400,000 per annum [1]. When, however, we examine the statistics of the trade with other countries we observe a marked falling off [2]. The explanation is that during the war with France the Dutch became, in a greater measure than before, the carriers of our goods since their ports were less exposed than our own to the danger of privateers [3] ; and actually this ' favourable balance ' was not beneficial to us, because it meant that the Dutch were intercepting the middlemen's profits in the branches of commerce interrupted by the war [4].

The more penetrating writers of the seventeenth century discerned the practical difficulties which must attend any investigation, based on custom-house returns, to ascertain the precise balance of trade. But Hume provided the classical exposition [4a] that, whatever the balance of trade, the apprehension of gold and silver permanently leaving a country was ' groundless '. His argument was based on the Quantity Theory of money : " Suppose four-fifths of all the money in Great Britain to be annihilated in one night . . . what would be the consequence ? Must not the price of all labour and commodities sink in proportion, and everything be sold as cheap as they were in [former] ages ? What nation could then dispute with us in any foreign market, or pretend to navigate or to sell manufactures at the same price, which to us would afford sufficient profit ? In how little time, therefore, must this bring back the money which we had lost, and raise us to the level of all the neighbouring nations ? Where, after we have arrived, we immediately lose the advantage of the cheapness of labour and commodities ; and the further flowing in of money is stopped by our fullness and repletion " [5]. Hume, however, neglects here to notice that a fall in prices, consequent upon the drain of money,

*Hume's ' refutation ' of the theory of the balance of trade.*

---

[1] The average of the years 1699–1705: Davenant, *Works* (ed. 1771), v. 417.
[2] The statistics are printed in Whitworth, *State of the Trade of Great Britain* (1776), part i.    [3] Davenant, *Works* (ed. 1771), v. 419, 435.
[4] Child, in the seventeenth century, remarked that Ireland, in spite of a favourable balance of trade, remained poor, because the excess of exports over imports represented the tribute paid to absentee landowners and others : *A New Discourse of Trade* (4th ed.), 167-168.
[4a] Hume was not the first to use the argument : *infra*, Appendix, p. 501, No. 2.    [5] Hume, *Essays* (ed. Green and Grose), i. 333.

might bring on an industrial crisis [1a]. In later times the mechanism of the foreign exchanges gave timely warning when the balance of trade turned against a country, and so discouraged over-trading. In earlier times confidence in the automatic operation of the foreign exchanges was lacking— not altogether without justification . so that even the demonstration that money cannot permanently abandon a country, would not have removed the apprehension that a temporary drain might dislocate the economic system, and create grave social problems with which Governments of the day were not fitted to cope. It was with the immediate effects of a fall in prices that writers of the seventeenth century were primarily concerned, when they depicted the consequences attendant upon the diminution of national treasure [1]: beyond this their analysis did not go. In other words—Hume demonstrated what would happen in ' the long run ', and the Mercantilists attached importance to ' the short run '. Both points of view are correct ; and in this respect it is unfair and misleading to speak—as it is the common practice —of the ' fallacy ' of Mercantilism [2a].

*Practical fruits of the theory.*     Behind the theoretical discussions on money there usually ranged a practical objective. The issue at stake between the ' Bullionists ' and the ' Mercantilists ' was whether the East India Company should be allowed to send gold and silver out of the country, while the most conspicuous application of the theory of the balance of trade was in relation to France. Not that France was the only country with which the balance of trade was unfavourable. Sweden, Norway, Denmark and the East Country ' always drained us of money ', the ' overbalance ' at the end of the seventeenth century approaching £300,000 [2]; and the balance with Russia

[1a] But see *supra*, vol. ii. Introduction, p. lxxxv, note 2.

[1] Locke was not the first to notice that a reduction of the currency would cause a fall in prices : *e.g. Britannia Languens* (1680), 126. And see *supra*, pp. 69-70. For the Quantity Theory of money : *supra*, p. 63.

[2a] See *infra*, Appendix, p. 501, No. 3.

[2] See the abstracts of exports and imports in *House of Commons Journals*, xiii. 723. Also *ibid.* xii. 432 ; *House of Lords MSS.* 1699-1702, pp. 455-456 (the amount stated for Denmark and Norway should be £50,000, not £150,000) ; Davenant, *Works* (ed. 1771), i. 397. In the reign of George III. the balance with Norway, Denmark and the East Country turned in England's favour : Whitworth, *State of the Trade of Great Britain* (1776), part ii. 6, 8.

was also against us [1]. But there were political factors to sharpen the edge of English animosity against France.

French trade had aroused misgivings as early as the *The French* reign of Elizabeth, owing partly to the alleged drain of money *trade.* and partly to the nature of the trade. The exports included cloth, tin, lead, herrings and coal : the imports consisted of luxuries such as wines and brandies, or of articles which entered into competition with native manufactures such as wrought silks, linen and paper [2]. Burghley condemned the French trade as ' hurtful to the realm '. " No country ", it was believed, " robbeth England so much as France ", and the annual export of ' fine gold ' was estimated at £100,000 [3]. In addition the wine trade encouraged ' the multiplying of taverns ' and diminished the consumption of ale and beer, " and consequently decayeth tillage for grain ". Finally, an argument which was to assume prominence after the Restoration, " it enricheth France whose power England ought not [to] increase " [4].

A commercial treaty concluded between England and *Growth of* France in 1606, and several times confirmed, provided that *tariffs.* the products and manufactures of one country could be freely carried into the other [5]. But English merchants met with opposition in France [6], and in 1648 trade was suspended. A French edict excluded wool and silk manufactures made

---

[1] Whitworth, *State of the Trade of Great Britain* (1776), part ii. 29-30. There was a favourable trade with the Mediterranean countries : *ibid.* part ii. 27-28, 31-34 ; *House of Commons Journals*, xii. 433.

[2] *Hist. MSS. Comm. Buccleuch*, i. 27-28 ; *The British Merchant* (ed. 1721), i. 18; Wood, *A Survey of Trade* (1718), 94. In the sixteenth century we also imported woad, salt and canvas : *Hist. MSS. Comm. Salisbury*, i. 165.

[3] *Hist. MSS. Comm. Salisbury*, i. 163, 165. Hitchcock in *A Pollitique Platt* (1580) maintained that French wares, ' besides the wines ', amounted to six times the value of English exports to France.

[4] *Tudor Economic Documents* (ed. Tawney and Power), ii. 124-125.

[5] Confirmed 1610, 1629, 1632 : *House of Commons Journal*, vi. 284-285. A treaty of 1572 conferred privileges on English merchants in France : *State Papers Rome*, 1572–1578, p. 15. In *Hist. MSS. Comm. Salisbury*, xiii. 574, there is a draft of a proposed treaty between France and England, of which the date is queried as May 1596. A treaty of 1600 is mentioned in *ibid. Cowper*, i. 128. An embargo was laid on French imports in 1626, when it was stated that " the French sell in England wines, of Gascony alone, to the value of 500,000 crowns annually " : *ibid. Skrine*, 85.

[6] *Acts of the Privy Council*, 1599–1600, p. 490 ; *State Papers Domestic*, 1633–1634, p. 282.

in England or Holland, and this country retaliated by an Act (1649) which laid an embargo on French wines and manufactures of wool and silk [1]. After three years the Council of State advised that commercial intercourse should be restored, and in 1657 Parliament repealed the Act [2]. Nevertheless the obstacles to trade did not disappear. The French Government, in order to develop native industries, increased the duties on English commodities, and restricted importation to a few ports which were inconveniently situated as distributing centres. The growth of tariffs is illustrated by the duty on cloth. When the treaty of 1632 was made, the amount of the French duty on an English broad cloth [3] was six livres : in 1644 it was raised to nine livres, in 1654 to thirty livres, in 1664 to forty livres, and in 1667 to eighty livres : while the duty on serge rose from one livre in 1632 to twelve livres in 1667 [4]. As a result the sale of cloth, which was said to account for one-third of our exports to France [5], was greatly diminished ; and the stage was thus set for a concrete application of the doctrine of the balance of trade.

*Three statements of the French trade.* The campaign for the prohibition of French imports was inaugurated by Samuel Fortrey in a book entitled *England's Interest and Improvement* (1663). He cited a memorial, alleged to have been laid before the French King, according to which our imports from France exceeded £2,600,000 a year, while our exports to France only amounted to £1,000,000, involving this country in an annual loss of £1,600,000, " whereby no doubt our treasure will be soon exhausted" [6]. The book created a deep impression [7], and it was henceforth assumed that the French trade was a losing

---

[1] *House of Commons Journals*, vi. 285 ; *Acts and Ordinances of the Interregnum*, ii. 239.

[2] *House of Commons Journals*, vii. 169 ; *Acts and Ordinances of the Interregnum*, ii. 1129.

[3] 31¼ yards : *The British Merchant* (ed. 1721), ii. 117. The livre was worth 1s. 6d. : *infra*, p. 107.

[4] *Britannia Languens* (1680), 194 ; *The British Merchant* (ed. 1721), ii. 117 ; *State Papers Domestic*, 1670, p. 600.

[5] *The British Merchant* (ed. 1721), ii. 153 ; Child, *A New Discourse of Trade* (4th ed.), p. xxii. The annual loss was represented as high as £400,000 : *State Papers Domestic*, 1677–1678, p. 70.

[6] Fortrey, *England's Interest and Improvement* (1663), 22-25. See *infra*, Appendix, p. 502, No. 1.      [7] Davenant, *Works* (ed. 1771), ii. 87.

trade.  In November 1674 ' A Scheme of the Trade as it is
at present carried on between England and France ' was
drawn up for the use of the ' Commissioners for the Treaty
of Commerce with France '.  The account covered the period
Michaelmas 1668 to Michaelmas 1669 ; and it represented
the exports to France at £171,021 : 6 : 8, and the imports
from France at £1,136,150 : 4 : 0, thus making the adverse
balance about a million pounds a year [1].  The origin of this
famous document, in which the adversaries of France found
one of their most formidable weapons, is uncertain.  The
author of *Britannia Languens* (1680) stated that it was " an
estimate of the French overbalance taken in England by
some English merchants from the entries of the port of
London " [2].  *The British Merchant* (1713) in one place
describes it as ' given in by the merchants ', and in another
place as ' a custom-house account delivered in almost forty
years ago by the chief officers of the customs ' [3].  The
Commissioners for Trade and Plantations stated in 1697 that
it was contained " in a report made by Sir George Downing,
then one of the Commissioners of the Customs, to the lords
of the Privy Council, then a Committee for Trade, dated the
9th of March 1675(–1676) " [4].  The Commissioners of the
Customs, again, declared in 1713 that it " could not be taken
from the custom-house books ", since it differed ' very much '
from their own accounts so far as they could be compared
with it [5].  In any case the 'Scheme' did not set the facts in
their true light.  French wines were valued at £12 : 10s. per
tun and French brandy at £20 per tun, which was apparently
greatly in excess of their prime cost abroad.  English exports, on the other hand, were valued at their prime cost,
on which basis French wines should have been valued at £7

---

[1] Printed in *State Papers Domestic*, 1673–1675, p. 435 ; *House of
Commons Journals*, xvii. 423-424 ; *The British Merchant* (ed. 1721), i. 181 ;
ii. 338 ; Somers, *Tracts* (ed. 1812), viii. 30-31 ; Cobbett, *Parliamentary
History*, iv. Appendix, No. xi. p. cxv.  See also *House of Commons
Journals*, xii. 432 ; xiii. 723.  *State Papers Domestic*, 1676–1677, pp. 18-19,
253 ; 1677–1678, p. 158.  Petty, *Economic Writings*, i. 297.  *The British
Merchant* (ed. 1721), i. 305.

[2] *Britannia Languens* (1680), 190-191.

[3] *The British Merchant* (ed. 1721), ii. 338, 407 ; iii. 303.

[4] *House of Commons Journals*, xii. 432.

[5] *Ibid*. xvii. 422-423.  Their own accounts are given, *ibid*. xvii. 394 *seq*.

or £8 per tun and French brandy at £9 per tun [1]. There was a tendency, in fact, to magnify imports by calculations based on their retail price in London, which included the prime cost, freight, customs, and the profit of merchants and retailers ; while exports were valued at their ' first cost ' only [2]. A third statement of the French trade is in a report drawn up in 1711 by the inspector-general of exports and imports. It is based on a manuscript in the custom-house and refers only to London, which was supposed to account for four-fifths of the trade of the kingdom [3]. It represents the imports from France (1668–1669) at £541,583 : 16s. and the exports to France at £108,699 : 4s.[4] : adding one-fourth for the trade of the outports, the adverse balance appeared to exceed half a million pounds, but the statement takes no notice of re-exports.

*Tariff war between England and France.* The economic rivalry of England and France fed the flames of a tariff war, which began under the Commonwealth but reached its climax after the Restoration. The French laid a tax of fifty sols [5] per ton upon English shipping ; made, as we have seen, successive additions to the duties on English commodities, amounting in 1667 to 50 per cent. or more of their value in the case of cloth [6] ; restrained their importation to particular ports ; and in 1686 placed a heavy imposition on our East India goods [7]. England retaliated by the Navigation Act of 1660, which was aimed at France as well as at Holland, and included among its provisions a duty of five shillings per ton on French shipping [8]. A few years later (1666), when France declared war against

---

[1] Child, *A New Discourse of Trade* (4th ed.), p. vi ; Davenant, *Works* (ed. 1771), v. 366-367. *The British Merchant* (ed. 1721), i. 341, claimed that the price of wine was £17 : 10s.

[2] For the undervaluation of exported calicoes, see *The British Merchant* (ed. 1721), i. 298, 310. [3] *Supra*, vol. ii. 249.

[4] Davenant, *Works* (ed. 1771), v. 351-353 (this also gives the returns for 1662–1663). See also *The British Merchant* (ed. 1721), ii. 70.

[5] In 1713 fifty sols were worth 2s. 6d., and at this period 3s. 9d. : *The British Merchant* (ed. 1721), i. 7-8, 18-19.

[6] *Britannia Languens* (1680), 194 ; Davenant, *Works* (ed. 1771), v. 369. For the duties, see *supra*, p. 100.

[7] Davenant, *Works* (ed. 1771), v. 368-369.

[8] *Statutes*, v. 249. Some indication of the amount of French tonnage is furnished by the ' demise ' of the duty in 1671 at a yearly rent of £1200 : *State Papers Domestic*, 1671, p. 163.

England[1], the King—in compliance with an address from the House of Commons—issued a proclamation excluding French products[2]; while in 1670 the Commons contemplated "laying such an imposition on French and other foreign goods and commodities as may discourage the bringing them in "[3]. Negotiations took place with France (1670) in which an effort was made to redress economic grievances. The Duke of Buckingham warned the French King that it was " impossible for him to have what he desires from England, till he has first satisfied the nation of his good intentions towards them by not pressing so hard upon us in point of trade ". But Colbert's influence proved too strong. " Mr. Colbert ", reported one of the English envoys, " is the occasion, I believe, of all the ill-usage our English merchants receive in France to weary them out of the trade and to encourage his own manufactures "[4]. He upheld the interests of the French clothiers, who had complained that the cheapness of English cloth flooded the French market : when the drapers remonstrated that they would lose their trade, they were told that *La commerce aujourdhuy en France est une matière d'estat*, and that to promote foreign fabrics was ' but to nourish their enemies '[5].

The shrinkage of English exports to France[6] led a com- *Prohibi-* mittee of the House of Commons in 1675 to recommend the *tion of French* prohibition of French commodities, if the French did not *imports*. reduce the impositions on English manufactures " at least to the same proportion and rate they were at the time of his majesty's happy restoration "[7]. The protests of manufacturers[8] and merchants grew into a demand (1676) for a new Parliament to deal with the economic situation. The

[1] January 1666 : *State Papers Domestic*, 1665–1666, pp. 237, 240.
[2] *House of Commons Journals*, viii. 632 ; *Tudor and Stuart Proclamations* (ed. Steele), i. No. 3481.
[3] *House of Commons Journals*, ix. 174. A ' tumultuous rising ' of the London apprentices was designed for 1st May 1670, as a protest against the French trade : *State Papers Domestic*, 1670, p. 176.
[4] *Hist. MSS. Comm. Buccleuch*, i. 482-487.
[5] *State Papers Domestic*, 1670, p. 601.
[6] Some figures are given in *ibid.* 1673–1675, p. 319.
[7] *House of Commons Journals*, ix. 365.
[8] The London silk weavers petitioned Parliament in 1671 to prohibit certain kinds of French silks : *Hist. MSS. Comm.* ix. part ii. 14. See *supra*, p. 18.

French, it was represented, had almost extinguished our trade with their own country by their tariffs on our manufactures, and they had spoiled our trade with Holland, Flanders and Germany by their wars ; they were ruining our home trade by large imports of silks, and draining the country of over a million pounds a year by the excess of imports over exports [1]. The economic argument was reinforced by political jealousies ; and in 1678 an Act of Parliament forbade the importation of French wines, brandy, vinegar, linen, cloth, silks, salt and paper, on the ground that they ' exhausted the treasure of the realm ' [2]. This famous Act, one of the landmarks in the history of Mercantilism, was looked upon in later years as the beginning of ' a remarkable era of English commerce' and ' a happy revival of English manufacture ' [3].

*Alternates with high duties.* Under James II. the prohibition of French imports was repealed (1685) [4], and though an additional duty was laid on French wines, it was only two-thirds of the imposition levied at the same time on other foreign wines [5]. At the Revolution the prohibition was renewed by the Act of 1689, which was continued in 1691 [6], and again in 1693 for three years " if the present war with France shall so long last " [7]. Peace was restored in 1697 [8], but French commodities were now burdened with very heavy duties. In the case of French wines the existing duties had been supplemented in 1693 by an imposition of £8 per tun [9]—this applied to wines taken as prize [10]—and in 1697 by a further imposition of

[1] " An Account of the proceedings at Guildhall " in *State Papers Domestic*, 1676–1677, p. 253.

[2] *Statutes*, v. 862. The prohibition was for three years and thereafter to the end of the first session of Parliament.

[3] Smith, *Chronicon Rusticum-Commerciale* (ed. 1747), i. 325.

[4] *Statutes*, vi. 10.                     [5] *Ibid.* vi. 2.

[6] *Ibid.* vi. 98 (1689), 247 (1691) ; *Tudor and Stuart Proclamations* (ed. Steele), i. No. 3988.

[7] *Statutes*, vi. 420 ; *House of Lords MSS.* 1692–1693, p. 384.

[8] Whitworth records no exports or imports for 1697, but gives returns for 1698–1702 : *State of the Trade of Great Britain* (1776), part ii. 13.

[9] *Statutes*, vi. 383.

[10] The impositions of 1693 did not affect the prohibition of French trade, but concerned French goods brought in by privateers : *The British Merchant* (ed. 1721), ii. 277. Cf. also Clark, *The Dutch Alliance and the War against French Trade*, 1688–1697, p. 70.

£25 [1]. Additional duties were also laid on brandy; and other French merchandise was nearly all charged with an imposition of 50 per cent. on its value—25 per cent. being levied in 1693 and another 25 per cent. in 1697 [2]. These duties amounted ' almost to a prohibition ', so that in 1697, when the Peace of Ryswick was negotiated, the English plenipotentiaries made no proposals for concluding a treaty of commerce with France, holding that " the balance of trade, as it now stands, is evidently on the English side " [3]. According to the custom-house returns for the year 1700 our imports from France were under £100,000, while our exports reached nearly £300,000 [4] : but that the former had actually fallen to this amount is improbable. When the Act of 1678 prohibited French wines, they were imported into England under the name of Spanish, Portuguese and Italian wines—this was done, it was said, by the direction of the Court and with the connivance of the customs officials, many of whom were ' indigent, mercenary and negligent ' [5]. After the prohibition was removed, false entries provided an escape from high duties : wines of Bordeaux were transported to San Sebastian, put in Spanish butts, and brought over to England as Spanish wines [6]. A large quantity of French goods, wines, brandy, silks and linen—" equal in value to a third part of all those that are entered at the custom-house ", is one estimate [7]—were also imported clandestinely [8] or brought by the Dutch [9].

The War of the Spanish Succession again put an end to

---

[1] *Statutes*, vii. 97.  On the wine duties, see also *Parliamentary Papers* (1898), lxxxv. 139.

[2] *Statutes*, vi. 383 (1693) ; vii. 97 (1697).

[3] *Hist. MSS. Comm. Bath*, iii. 127.

[4] Whitworth, *State of the Trade of Great Britain* (1776), part ii. 13.

[5] *Britannia Languens* (1680), 277-278.  *House of Commons Journals*, xii. 432 ; xiii. 206.  *The British Merchant* (ed. 1721), i. 338, 345-346.

[6] Justice, *A General Treatise of Monies and Exchanges* (1707), 5.

[7] *The British Merchant* (ed. 1721), i. 306.

[8] *House of Commons Journals*, xii. 210, 213.  Between 1675 and 1696 the total importation of brandy from abroad into London was roughly 42,000 tuns : between 1696 and 1712 it was roughly 5000 tuns (for London and the outports) : *ibid.* xvii. 362, 364.  This points to extensive smuggling. The prosperity of Lymington was attributed to the smuggling of French wines : *Hist. MSS. Comm. Portland*, ii. 287.

[9] Gee, *The Trade and Navigation of Great Britain* (1730), 13 ; *Hist. MSS. Comm. Portland*, v. 352.

the trade between France and England [1], though it was
found necessary to strengthen the prohibition by an Act of
Parliament in 1705 [2]. But when a Tory ministry came into
power, it repealed in 1711 the prohibition in respect of French
wines, subject to the proviso that they were paid for with
British goods [3]. Two years later it attempted to conclude
a commercial treaty [4] with France as part of the Peace of
Utrecht. The Ninth Article proposed—(1) to remove on
both sides all prohibitions not in force prior to 1664 ; (2) to
levy in England no higher duties on French than on other
foreign goods ; (3) to restore the French tariff of 1664 for
English exports to France, except that our woollen manufactures, sugar, salted fish and the produce of whales were
to be excluded from this tariff and made the subject of a
special agreement—pending this agreement they were to
come under the tariff of 1699 [5]. Another Article abolished
the duty on tonnage. A Bill was introduced into Parliament
to give effect to the treaty of commerce [6], and secured at
first a favourable reception [7]. Public opinion, however, was
aroused, and the Whig party seized the opportunity to make
political capital out of the Government's proposals. "Nothing
is more plain ", wrote Defoe to the Earl of Oxford, " than
that the disputes upon the subject of the commerce with
France are carried on, not merely as a dispute about trade,
which most of the people now so hot about it understand
little of, but as an arrow shot at the present administration ".
The other side claimed that this was not ' party against

[1] Whitworth records no imports from France for the years 1703-1710 :
*State of the Trade of Great Britain* (1776), part ii. 13.
[2] *Statutes*, viii. 360 ; *House of Lords MSS.* 1704-1706, p. 295. Ashley,
*Surveys Historic and Economic*, 299, dates the renewal of the prohibition
from the Act 3 & 4 Anne, but the Declaration of War forbade "all correspondence or communication with her majesty's enemies " : *House of
Commons Journals*, xiv. 431. See also Clark, " War Trade and Trade
War, 1701-1713 ", in *The Economic History Review*, i. No. 2, 268, 275-276.
[3] *Statutes*, ix. 388-389.
[4] Printed in *House of Commons Journals*, xvii. 331 *seq.*, and in *The
British Merchant* (ed. 1721), i. 43 *seq.*
[5] *House of Commons Journals*, xvii. 333, 340.
[6] Printed in *The British Merchant* (ed. 1721), i. 130 *seq.*
[7] *Hist. MSS. Comm. Polwarth*, i. 9-10. The produce of the duties
on French goods imported in 1713 was seven times that of 1712 : *House of
Commons Journals*, xvii. 554.

party, Tory against Whig'; and Defoe himself admitted that the opposition originated 'as a trading question'[1]. The case for the treaty was presented in *The Mercator* with which Defoe was closely identified[2]; the case against it in *The British Merchant*, in which "several ingenious merchants of long experience and well-skilled in trade joined together to contradict the impositions of this writer", who had "a knack of writing very plausibly"[3].

Against the treaty it was represented, first, that the removal of prohibitions and the reduction of duties were only partial. *Arguments against the treaty.* They applied to British goods but not to foreign goods re-exported from England; under this clause, therefore, the produce of the Levant or India could be excluded from France if carried in British shipping[4]. Secondly: cloth came under the tariff of 1699 and so paid a duty over one-third greater than that of 1664[5]. Apart from the handicap of a high duty, which served as 'an effectual prohibition', it was maintained that there would be no sale of English cloth in France because the low price of labour enabled French manufacturers to undersell foreign competitors[6]. Thirdly: the war had depreciated the French exchanges, the livre falling from eighteenpence to a shilling. This benefited French exporters but enhanced the price of English goods in France 50 per cent.[7], so that we should be inundated with French commodities while unable to market our own goods. For these reasons "the notion of establishing a trade with France, that shall be reciprocally

[1] *Hist. MSS. Comm. Portland*, v. 351-352: *The British Merchant* (ed. 1721), i. 202.

[2] "Mr. M——, who first set me upon that work and undertook the support of it, has declined any consideration for it ever since Lady Day last, so that I perform it wholly without any appointment for it, or benefit by it . . . though it is expensive to me "—Defoe to the Earl of Oxford (1714): *Hist. MSS. Comm. Portland*, v. 445.

[3] *The British Merchant* (ed. 1721), i. pp. x-xi.

[4] *Ibid.* i. 65, 234 *seq.*; ii. 149.

[5] Broad cloth paid 40 livres under the tariff of 1664, and 55 livres under the tariff of 1699: *ibid.* ii. 117-118, 300. The livre had depreciated in value, but the French Government was endeavouring to raise its value: *ibid.* ii. 118.

[6] *Ibid.* i. 6, 18, 307.

[7] The pound sterling was formerly equivalent to $13\frac{1}{2}$ livres, but now to 20; this made French goods cheap in England, and English goods dear in France: *ibid.* i. 19.

beneficial to each nation", was pronounced ' a thing impracticable '—" France will never permit us to import
thither any commodities, fish or manufactures that will in
any degree be detrimental to their product " [1]. While the
benefits conferred by the treaty thus appeared dubious, its
disadvantages were magnified. All the vested interests,
which had profited by the restrictions on French trade, raised
a storm of protest. French wines, it was alleged, would ruin
the trade with Spain, Portugal [2] and Italy, which sent wines
in exchange for cloth ; French silks would ruin the native
silk industry and the trade with the Levant, which sent
raw silk in exchange for cloth ; French linens would ruin
the trade with Germany, which sent linens in exchange for
cloth ; and finally, French brandy would prejudice the
plantations by lessening the demand for sugar and molasses
on the part of English distillers [3]. These trades were considered more valuable to England than the French trade,
for not only did they provide an outlet for our woollen
goods, but also the balance was thought to be in our
favour [4].

*Trade between England and France in the eighteenth century.* The arguments of the woollen and silk manufacturers
prevailed : the Bill of Commerce was defeated : and the
conclusion of a treaty with France was postponed for three-
quarters of a century. The commercial relations between
England and France during most years of the eighteenth
century are summed up in Adam Smith's calculation that
" 75 per cent. may be considered as the lowest duty to
which the greater part of the goods of the growth, produce
or manufacture of France were liable [5]. But upon the
greater part of goods those duties are equivalent to a prohibition. The French in their turn have, I believe, treated
our goods and manufactures just as hardly. . . . Those mutual

---

[1] *The British Merchant* (ed. 1721), ii. 442.
[2] For the argument based on the Methuen Treaty with Portugal, see
*infra*, p. 111.
[3] *House of Commons Journals*, xvii. 347-348, 379-380, 385-386, 391-393,
404, 408, 426-427.
[4] *The Trade with France, Italy, Spain and Portugal Considered* (1713), 5.
[5] The Acts of 1693 and 1697 alone accounted for a duty of 50 per cent.
on general French merchandise : *supra*, p. 105. For the duty on wine,
see *infra*, p. 114.

restraints have put an end to almost all fair commerce between the two nations " [1]. The official returns bear out this
statement. The highest figures are recorded in the middle
of the century, when in the years 1751–1754 the imports from
France entered in the custom-house books averaged about
£60,000, and the exports to France half a million. In later
years the imports remained on the whole stationary while
exports diminished by over one-half [2]. But, as Adam Smith
remarked, smugglers were now the principal importers of
British goods into France and of French goods into Great
Britain.[3]

The controversy over the French trade inaugurated the *The
'general'
and the
'parti-
cular'
balance
of trade.*
first phase of the Free Trade movement—the phase of
moderate tariffs and no prohibitions.[4] A group of economists, among whom were Child, North and Davenant, broke
away from the dogmas of their age, and associated themselves
with ideas which paved the way for the principles of the
Manchester School. They identified themselves with the
theory of the ' general balance ' of trade as opposed to the
' particular balance '. The distinction was already known
to Mun. " The balance of our trade is either general or
particular. The general is when all our yearly traffic is
jointly valued . . . the particular is when our trade to Italy,
France, Turkey, Spain and other countries are severally considered " [5]. According to the theory of the general balance,
an excess of imports over exports in the case of any particular
country was immaterial, provided the balance was favourable
with the world as a whole. The economists did not deny
that our trade with France was ' disadvantageous to this
nation ' ; but they considered it ' an endless and uncertain
speculation ' to isolate particular trades, and to measure their

---

[1] *The Wealth of Nations* (ed. Cannan), i. 438.
[2] Whitworth, *State of the Trade of Great Britain* (1776), part ii. 13-14.
It was stated in 1718 that since the rejection of the treaty of commerce
" the people of Great Britain have taken from France great quantities of
wines and brandies, etc., without having leave to import any of their
manufactures into that kingdom ": *Hist. MSS. Comm. Stuart*, vi. 443.
But the figures in Whitworth show an excess of exports to France over
imports.
[3] *The Wealth of Nations* (ed. Cannan), i. 438.
[4] On the term ' free trade ', see *supra*, p. 17, note 4.
[5] Mun, *England's Treasure by Forraign Trade* (1664), 96.

profit and loss to the nation singly without reference to the general trade of the country [1]. " Whatever overbalance France in particular might have upon us ", it was enough to know " beyond all dispute that England was every year a gainer in its universal trade " [2]. Thus while one school of thought condemned the trade with any country in which imports exceeded exports, a more progressive body of opinion considered the particular balance ' fallible and erroneous ', since an apparent ' losing trade ' might be ' a very necessary beneficial trade ' in its influence on other branches [3]. Our exports to the Baltic, for example, fell much below the value of our imports, but the latter consisted largely of naval stores without which our trade to other countries could not be carried on. However the Baltic trade, as the basis of all others, was admitted to be an exception even by those who upheld the theory of the particular balance [4]. It could not be pretended that French wines and silks came in the same category as naval stores : but there were other arguments *Arguments in favour of the French trade.* in their favour. In the first place, there was a re-export trade in French goods [5] ; and if we were to compete successfully with the Dutch, it was necessary that our ships should not be confined to British products but should carry a variety of cargoes, which was one of the secrets of Holland's predominance in the world's carrying trade [6]. In the second place, this country could not dispense with wines and brandy, linen and paper ; and the question was whether we should buy them in the best and cheapest market, France, or import them at a dearer rate through roundabout channels [7]. In the third place, there was involved in the French trade a vital principle, in the enunciation of which the modern theory of free trade began to assume shape and substance. " No imagination can be vainer than to think that trade is to be

---

[1] Davenant, *Works* (ed. 1771), i. 386 ; ii. 97.
[2] *Ibid.* v. 363.
[3] Child, *A New Discourse of Trade* (4th ed.), 164, 169-170.
[4] *The British Merchant* (ed. 1721), i. 28-29.
[5] Houghton, *England's Great Happiness : or a Dialogue between Content and Complaint* (1677), 6.
[6] *Infra*, p. 134.
[7] *Britannia Languens* (1680), 284 ; Davenant, *Works* (ed. 1771), v. 378-380.

ruled and circumscribed by art ; it must be suffered to take its own natural course, and not be interrupted by prohibitions or high duties equal to prohibitions, unless upon provocation from other countries ''. Those who seek to promote the consumption of their own native products '' by an universal discouragement of foreign goods will find themselves, in process of time, to have little or no trade, and that their own commodities shall remain a drug upon their hands ''. Moreover all branches of commerce are interdependent : one branch may seem prejudicial, yet '' to lop it off may kill another, which by secret fibres has relation to it '' [1]. To this was added the consideration that tariffs not only break links in the chain of commerce but they generally end in war [2].

The collapse of the ' free trade ' movement, engineered *The* by a Tory ministry in 1713, was largely due to the fear of *Methuen* losing a trade in which the balance was favourable to this *with* country, namely, the trade with Portugal. In the reign of *Portugal.* Charles II. we exported large quantities of cloth to Portugal [3] ; but owing to the heavy imposition laid upon refined sugar imported into England—coupled with an increase of the duty on Portuguese wine, which amounted to £20 : 10s. per tun and was almost prohibitive—the Portuguese Government endeavoured to set up a native cloth industry by forbidding the use of English cloth, with some exceptions, and by encouraging the immigration of English artisans [4]. To retain their threatened market the manufacturers and merchants in England pressed for a treaty of commerce, which should stimulate the consumption of Portuguese wines purchased

[1] Davenant, *Works* (ed. 1771), v. 387 ; i. 387.
[2] *Ibid.* v. 379.
[3] *House of Commons Journals*, xiv. 290. The exports of woollen manufactures, corn, fish, coal, lead, tin, etc., amounted yearly to £350,000 : *Hist. MSS. Comm.* ix. part ii. 12 (1671). James I. had appointed a consul in Portugal ' for the better government of that trade ' : *Acts of the Privy Council*, 1613–1614, p. 97.
[4] *State Papers Domestic*, 1671, pp. 118-120 ; 1678, pp. 235, 394 ; *Britannia Languens* (1680), 161 ; Davenant, *Works* (ed. 1771), ii. 37 ; v. 373. They began by prohibiting woollen cloth (except bays, etc.), hats and stockings. Later they admitted black cloth, which was not much in demand, and stockings and hats of finer quality : *House of Commons Journals*, xiv. 290. Yet they took about 180,000 stuffs a year, according to *An Essay on Wool and Woollen Manufacture for the Improvement of Trade* (1693), 10. See also *The British Merchant* (ed. 1721), iii. 18, 42, 82.

with English manufactures, in place of French wines purchased with English money[1]. Portugal demanded the reduction of the wine duty, but this would have involved a loss of revenue and raised difficulties in Spain, whose trade was considered equally beneficial to England[2]. Eventually the Methuen Treaty[3] was concluded in 1703, under which Portuguese wines paid only two-thirds of the duty charged on French wines[4]; and in return all our woollen manufactures were admitted into Portugal. This treaty was held in high favour. Our exports to Portugal, comprising ' vast quantities ' of cloth as well as corn, tin, lead, leather, and fish from Newfoundland, were more than doubled[5]: the returns were made in wine, sugar, oil and money. At Exeter, one of the chief manufacturing towns in the West of England, it was said that almost no other money was in circulation but Portuguese gold[6]. The Portuguese market was the more important because it embraced also Brazil, which was considered the basis of the trade[7].

The proposal made in 1713 to admit French wines on the same terms as other wines involved a breach of the Methuen Treaty, and it provoked a great outcry in the

[1] *Hist. MSS. Comm. Le Fleming*, 131 (1677) ; *House of Commons Journals*, x. 743 (1692).

[2] *House of Commons Journals*, xiv. 290-291.

[3] Printed in *ibid.* xiv. 290 ; xvii. 348-349 ; *The British Merchant* (ed. 1721), i. 209 *seq.*

[4] Actually they were already paying less than two-thirds : *The British Merchant* (ed. 1721), iii. 43, 49.

[5] According to *The British Merchant* (ed. 1721), iii. 24-25, our exports to Portugal increased from about £400,000 to £1,300,000. These figures are exaggerated. In 1700 exports amounted to £336,598 ; and in 1705 to £818,768 : *House of Lords MSS.* 1706-1708, pp. 253-255. (These totals do not include Newfoundland fish which was also sent to Portugal : *House of Commons Journals*, xv. 163.) Exports did not approach £1,300,000 until 1736 : Whitworth, *State of the Trade of Great Britain* (1776), part ii. 27. The statistics of the wine trade, 1675-1712, are given in *House of Commons Journals*, xvii. 363, 365 ; and from 1697 onwards in *Parliamentary Papers* (1898), lxxxv. 153 *seq.*

[6] *The British Merchant* (ed. 1721), ii. 18, 24 ; *The Consequences of Trade as to the Wealth and Strength of any Nation. By a Draper of London* (1740), 14.

[7] " A great part of the woollens sold in Portugal is for the Brazils, and the great consumption of woollens in the Brazils is by the negroes " : Decker, *An Essay on the Causes of the Decline of the Foreign Trade* (ed. 1744), 107. See also Defoe, *The Complete English Tradesman* (ed. 1727), ii. part ii. 66 ; Shillington and Chapman, *The Commercial Relations of England and Portugal*, 246 *seq.* And see *infra*, Appendix, p. 502, No. 2.

belief that Portugal would again prohibit our manufactures[1]. *French and Portuguese wines.* " Which is the wine ", it was asked, " that every Englishman will choose, Portugal or French wine, if the price of both should be the same ? " Portuguese wines were 'heavy and strong', and " we hankered after the old claret of Bordeaux ", although " the preserving our looms and the rents of Great Britain was of greater consequence to the nation than gratifying our palates with French wine " [2]. The statistics of the wine trade gave eloquent support to the argument. In 1683 the quantity of French wines entered at London amounted to 65 gallons, as compared with 16,772 tuns of Portuguese wine : in 1686, after the prohibition of French wines had been removed, the corresponding figures were 12,760 tuns (French) and 289 tuns (Portuguese) [3]. And the argument proved fatal in spite of the attempt to show that it was "specious with respect to our woollen manufactures, but not of any weight in the general argument of commerce " [4].

Down to the reign of George III. the volume of our exports to Portugal steadily grew, but then a remarkable shrinkage occurred due to increased duties, Portuguese sumptuary laws, the confinement of the trade with Brazil to Portuguese companies, and the competition of the Dutch and French [5]. *Commercial treaty with France (1786).* This weakened the force of the objection against a commercial treaty with France for the reduction of tariffs ; and when a Tory minister was once more in the saddle, public opinion was prepared for a change in the economic policy of

[1] *The Trade with France, Italy, Spain, and Portugal Considered* (1713), 13. Cf. *Seasonable Observations on the present Fatal Declension of the General Commerce of England* (1737), 9.
[2] French wines would be £2 a tun cheaper : *The British Merchant* (ed. 1721), i. pp. ix, 347-350 ; ii. 277. *An Essay on the Treaty of Commerce with France* (1713), 35.
[3] *House of Commons Journals*, xvii. 363. It should be noted that the quantities varied in different years.
[4] Defoe in *Hist. MSS. Comm. Portland*, v. 352 (1713).
[5] The exports fell to about one-half, while the imports remained stationary : Whitworth, *State of the Trade of Great Britain* (1776), part ii. 27-28. The port dues discouraged the English carrying trade to Lisbon : Macpherson, *Annals of Commerce*, iii. 425-426. French competition was complained of in 1735 : *Hist. MSS. Comm. Somerset*, 317. For Dutch competition : Decker, *An Essay on the Causes of the Decline of the Foreign Trade* (ed. 1744), 35. For the Portuguese companies : Shillington and Chapman, *The Commercial Relations of England and Portugal*, 282 seq.

the country. The treaty of commerce with France, which was signed September 1786, announced the intention of the contracting parties to put an end to " the prohibitions and prohibitory duties which have existed for almost a century between the two nations ". It provided that " the wines of France imported directly from France into Great Britain shall, in no case, pay any higher duties than those which the wines of Portugal *now* pay " [1]. This at once halved the duty on French wines, which had risen to about £96 per tun, though the preference given to Portugal in the Methuen Treaty was preserved in the Act of 1787. Under this Act the duty on French wines was still further reduced—it now varied from £25 : 4s. to £33 : 12s. accordingly as it was imported into London or the outports, and in British-built or foreign ships—but Portuguese wines only paid two-thirds of the French duty, that is, £16 : 16s. to £22 : 8s. [2]. Among other commodities the duties on all works of iron, steel, copper and brass were not to exceed 10 per cent. ; cottons and woollens, earthenware and pottery, were to pay 12 per cent. ; while manufactured articles mixed with silk remained prohibited on both sides [3].

*The beginnings of free trade not due to Adam Smith's influence.*       In concluding a treaty of commerce with France the younger Pitt may have been fortified in his opinions by *The Wealth of Nations* [4] ; but there appear to be no valid grounds for the common assumption that the beginnings of free trade were due to the influence of Adam Smith [5]. Pitt, who represented here the Tory tradition, was only resuming at the first opportunity the historic policy of the Tory party, and the decline of the Portuguese trade had now removed the practical obstacle which had been fatal to his predecessors. The debate in Parliament over the treaty proceeded on traditional party lines. Fox voiced the Whig sentiment that " France was the natural foe of Great

[1] Cobbett, *Parliamentary History*, xxvi. 233 *seq.*, 268 *seq.*
[2] *Parliamentary Papers* (1898), lxxxv. 139-140.
[3] Cobbett, *Parliamentary History*, xxvi. 237-238.
[4] Pitt first became acquainted with Smith in 1787 : Rae, *Life of Adam Smith*, 404 *seq.* In the debate on the French treaty *The Wealth of Nations* was not referred to by Pitt or Fox : *ibid.* 290-291.
[5] The proposal for a commercial treaty actually emanated from the French minister, Vergennes : Rose, *William Pitt and National Revival*, 347.

Britain " ; and he protested, as *The British Merchant* had done three-quarters of a century before, that we should lose the benefits derived from the Methuen Treaty which " had justly been considered as the commercial idol of England " [1]. Pitt, on the other hand, did not share the Whigs' apprehensions of French competition. " France had the advantage in the gift of soil and climate, and in the amount of her natural produce " ; but " our manufactures were so confessedly superior as to dread no competition " [2]. And even Burke, while opposing the treaty, admitted that " our capital gave us a superiority which enabled us to set all the efforts of France to rival our manufactures at defiance : the powers of capital were irresistible in trade " [3]. Pitt's view of the relative position of the two countries is borne out by the attitude of French and English manufacturers towards the treaty. Among French manufacturers ' this most pernicious treaty ' was execrated as " the most fatal stroke to their manufactures they ever experienced " [4]. The Chamber of Commerce of Normandy drew up a memorandum in which it dwelt upon " the perfection of the preparation and the merit of the spinning (united with cheapness) " of English cottons, the " advantages which the English possess over all the woollens of France ", and the " notable prejudice " to French potteries. " The opinion we develop upon this treaty is general and founded on a simple reflection—that France furnishes twenty-four millions of consumers against eight millions which England offers in turn " [5]. Among English manufacturers, in contrast with the national excitement in 1713, the passage of the treaty through Parliament in 1787 did not produce a single hostile petition, according to Eden who negotiated the treaty [6]. This he acclaimed as " a curious proof of the good sense and general information

---

[1] Cobbett, *Parliamentary History*, xxvi. 349, 398, 451.
[2] *Ibid.* 384, 389.
[3] *Ibid.* 487-488, 498.
[4] Young, *Travels in France* (ed. Maxwell), 94, 326.
[5] *Ibid.* 324. An earlier memorandum of the Chamber is described by Professor Sée in *The Economic History Review*, ii. No. 2, 308 *seq.*
[6] There was a petition from the ' General Chamber of Manufacturers ' for postponing consideration of the treaty with France, but it did not express hostility : Cobbett, *Parliamentary History*, xxvi. 377-378.

of the times in which we live " [1]. The real cause of the change, however, was not any theoretical demonstration of the benefits of free trade, but the confidence which English industrial interests now felt in their ability to meet foreign competition [1a]. When confidence in the natural protection afforded by superior efficiency was lacking, the manufacturers showed their former disinclination to dispense with legal protection [2]; and the teachings of Adam Smith then failed to evoke any response among them. In short, the beginnings of the free trade movement in England were dictated by practical considerations, in which abstract doctrines of economic freedom did not have the influence commonly assigned to them [2a].

### (III)

### THE NAVIGATION SYSTEM

*Early history of the Navigation Acts.*   The navigation system was a legacy of the Middle Ages. As early as the fourteenth century it was enacted that " none of the King's liege people do from henceforth ship any merchandise in going out or coming within the realm of England, in any port, but only in ships of the King's liegance " [3]; and the employment of foreign ships was forbidden under the Early Tudors [4]. The policy of protection provoked retaliation in other countries, the Emperor Charles V. placing a ban on English ships as a protest against the Statute of 1540 [5]. On this account one of Elizabeth's first measures was to repeal her predecessors' legislation, though with the proviso that goods imported in foreign vessels, ' masts, pitch, tar and corn only excepted ', should

---

[1] *Hist. MSS. Comm. Various*, vi. 198. Fox endeavoured to work up an agitation : *ibid. Rutland*, iii. 372-373. The anonymous pamphlet, entitled *Helps to a Right Decision upon the Merits of the late Treaty of Commerce with France* (1787), was written by W. Knox : *Hist. MSS. Comm. Various*, vi. 197-199.
[1a] Cf. *infra*, Appendix, p. 502, No. 3.
[2] Cf. the attitude of the ironmaster, Reynolds, towards Ireland in 1785 and towards France in 1786 : Rathbone, *Memoir of R. Reynolds*, 50, 287. Also see *infra*, p. 205, note 3.
[2a] See *infra*, Appendix, p. 503, No. 1.        [3] 1381 : *supra*, vol. i. 592.
[4] 1485, 1488, 1532 and 1540 : *supra*, vol. i. 592, 594.
[5] *State Papers Foreign*, 1563, p. 609.

pay aliens' customs [1]. The discrimination between native and alien shipping was intended, so it was explained, ' for avoiding of great deceit ' practised by natives in entering the goods of aliens in the custom-books in their own names ; but it served as a protective measure which induced even foreign merchants to employ English ships, in spite of higher freights [2], ' in order to be less troubled by the officers of custom '. As a consequence Philip II., citing the precedent set by his father in 1540, forbade " all of whatever nation they may be to lade any English ships in any port of the Low Countries " [3].

The freedom conferred by the Act of 1559 to use foreign *Under* ships was gradually curtailed, and the pendulum began to *Elizabeth,* swing back. It was alleged that the navy was decayed owing to the decline of ' the ancient navigation into the Levant ' [4], the concentration of the spice trade in the hands of the Portuguese, the restrictions laid by Spain on the use of foreign ships, and the augmentation of tolls in the Sound by the King of Denmark [5]. In 1563 it was made obligatory to employ native shipping in the coasting trade as well as for importing French wines and woad [6] ; and sometimes even the export of English commodities was confined to English vessels manned by English mariners, either as a result of instructions from the authorities or on the initiative of a trading company [7]. The privileges bestowed upon the Russia Company were also made to depend upon its employment of native shipping [8].

The Elizabethan Government, however, relied more *The Fish* upon indirect methods for promoting navigation. It fell *Days.* back upon the precedent set by an Act of Edward VI. enjoining " such abstinence [from meat] which hath been used in this realm " upon Fridays and Saturdays and in

---

[1] 1559 : *Statutes*, iv. part i. 375-376.
[2] Foreign freights were one-third or one-half lower : *State Papers Foreign*, 1564–1565, p. 529.
[3] 1563 : *ibid.* 1563, pp. 608-609.      [4] See *supra*, vol. ii. 335.
[5] *Tudor Economic Documents* (ed. Tawney and Power), ii. 104-105 (1563).
[6] *Statutes*, iv. part i. 423.
[7] (1) Corn : *ibid.* 425 ; *Hist. MSS. Comm. Pepys*, 190. (2) All commodities : *Acts of the Privy Council*, 1588, p. 3. (3) Trading company : *Newcastle Merchant Adventurers*, i. 43-44 (1593).
[8] *Supra*, vol. ii. 327.

Lent : " considering that due and godly abstinence is a means to virtue and to subdue men's bodies to their soul and spirit, and considering also specially that fishers, and men using the trade of living by fishing in the sea, may thereby the rather be set on work, and that by eating of fish much flesh shall be saved and increased " [1]. The intention to carry on Edward VI.'s policy was shown as early as 1559, when Parliament was exhorted to maintain " the old course of fishing by the straitest observation of Fish Days, for policy sake ; so the sea-coasts shall be strong with men and habitations, and the fleet flourish more than ever " [2]. Effect was given to this recommendation in an Act for the ' maintenance and increase of the navy ' (1564), which required ' every Wednesday in every week ', except Christmas week and Easter week, to be observed as a ' Fish Day '—" as the Saturdays in every week be or ought to be " ; and offenders were to be subject to the penalties laid down for " such as shall eat flesh upon Fridays, Saturdays or other Fish Days " [3]. The institution of Fish Days was intended " for the increase of fishermen and mariners, and repairing of port towns, and navigation " ; and it was expressly dissociated from any religious significance [4]. The local authorities were frequently pressed to enforce the observance of the law [5], but an open admission of failure was made in an Act of 1581, which alluded to the ' usual eating of flesh ' on Fish Days [6] ; and in 1585 Wednesday ceased to be one of the appointed Fish Days [7]. The

[1] *Statutes*, iv. part i. 65 (1549).

[2] *Hist. MSS. Comm. Salisbury*, i. 165.

[3] *Statutes*, iv. part i. 422 *seq.* One ' dish of flesh ' was permitted provided there were three ' dishes of sea-fish '.

[4] It was also intended to keep down the price of meat and preserve the young cattle : *Hist. MSS. Comm. Rye*, 102. In *A Brief Note of the benefits that grow to this realm by the Observation of Fish Days*, 1594 (in *An English Garner*, ed. Lang, 135), the maintenance of the Navy, the revival of decayed coast towns, and the check to the conversion of arable to pasture, were assigned as the reasons for the observance. The author was R. Hitchcock : *Hist. MSS. Comm. Salisbury*, v. 528. See also *State Papers Domestic, 1595–1597*, p. 540.

[5] *Acts of the Privy Council*, 1571–1575, p. 74; 1575–1577, p. 260; 1578–1580, pp. 14, 66.

[6] *Statutes*, iv. part i. 668.

[7] *Ibid.* iv. part i. 718-719. The penalties for eating flesh on the Fish Days were reduced in 1593 : *ibid.* iv. part ii. 855.

discredited policy of the Fish Days was revived in the seventeenth century. The first Parliament of James I. ordered their enforcement [1], and proclamations for their observance were issued as late as 1664 [2], but these repeated injunctions proved unavailing. None of the Fish Days, wrote Roger Coke in 1671, are observed [3].

An attempt was also made to stimulate native shipping *Other ex-* by forbidding subjects to import foreign-cured fish [4]. The *pedients.* sequel provides an interesting commentary upon the efforts to build up a mercantile marine by artificial expedients. " It was hoped and expected that the fishermen of this realm would in such sort have employed themselves to fishing, and to the building and preparing of such store of boats and shipping for that purpose, as that they should long ere this time have been able sufficiently to have victualled this realm with salted fish and herrings of their own taking, without any supply of aliens and strangers, to the great increase of mariners and maintenance of the navigation within this realm. Notwithstanding it is since found by experience that the navigation of this land is no whit bettered by means of that Act, nor any mariners increased nor like to be increased by it : but contrary wise, the natural subjects of this realm being not able to furnish the tenth part of the same with salted fish of their taking, the chief provision and victualling thereof with fish and herrings hath ever since the making of the same Statute been in the power and disposition of aliens and strangers, who thereby have much enriched themselves, greatly increased their navigation, and (taking advantage of the time) have extremely enhanced the prices of that victual to the great hurt and impoverishing of the native subjects of this realm, and yet do serve the markets here in very

---

[1] 1604 : *Statutes,* iv. part ii. 1058.

[2] 1619 : *Tudor and Stuart Proclamations* (ed. Steele), i. No. 1265. 1632: *State Papers Domestic,* 1631–1633, p. 260. 1640: *ibid.* 1639–1640, p. 370. 1663: *Mercurius Publicus,* No. iv. 49 (January 1662–1663). 1664 : *Tudor and Stuart Proclamations* (ed. Steele), i. No. 3390. See also *Hist. MSS. Comm. Various,* iv. 310 (1651).

[3] Coke, *Treatise* (1671), i. 18 ; Houghton, *Husbandry and Trade Improv'd* (ed. 1728), iv. 38 (1681).

[4] 1581 : *Statutes,* iv. part i. 668.

evil sort by little and little, housing and keeping their fish
as well on this side as beyond the seas till the prices be raised
to their liking.  And the merchants of this realm having
been wholly barred in their trades of providing of fish for
the service thereof, the navigation of this realm which was
intended to be augmented hath been rather impaired than
increased thereby, and the prices of fish greatly enhanced
to the great and general prejudice of the subjects "[1].
Accordingly the Act was repealed[2].  Nor was Elizabethan
legislation more successful in other directions since the
alien shipper was not driven from the coasting trade, as
directed by the Act of 1563[3].

*Under the
Early
Stuarts.*
Under the Early Stuarts the navigation policy was given
intermittent expression.  The obligation to employ native
shipping was enforced in the case of French wines[4], but
alien shippers continued to participate in the export
trade and they were especially prominent in the coal trade[5].
James I. issued proclamations in 1615 and 1622 enforcing
the Navigation Laws, which " of latter years have been
much neglected "[6]; and it was among the instructions
given to the Commission of 1622 to consider " how our laws
do now stand in force for the prohibiting of merchandise
to be imported in foreign bottoms, and to advise what is
fit to be done therein "[7].  Yet when a Navigation Bill was
introduced into the Parliament of 1621, it was rejected on
the ground that it ' restraineth multitude of merchants '.
In the discussion it was said that the Bill made a fair
show but was ' a Trojan horse ', which would ' overthrow
the navigation ' of the outports: in the West of England
" many ports have sixty sails of ships which cannot go into
the East Country for any masts, etc., so if the Dutch shall
not bring them, they cannot have them" and "their naviga-

---

[1] 1598 : *Statutes*, iv. part ii. 910.                    [2] *Ibid.*
[3] *Newcastle Merchant Adventurers*, i. 43 (1593).
[4] *Acts of the Privy Council*, 1613–1614, p. 158.
[5] Kayll, *The Trades Increase* (1615), 10-13.  See *supra*, vol. ii. 115.
[6] *Tudor and Stuart Proclamations* (ed. Steele), i. Nos. 1160 (1615), 1333
(1622) ; *Acts and Ordinances of the Eastland Company*, 152 (1622).  The
Eastland Company protested in 1615 : *Acts of the Privy Council*, 1615–
1616, p. 142.  But subsequently it supported the policy : *House of Commons
Journals*, i. 793 (1624); *State Papers Domestic*, 1619–1623, p. 211.
[7] Rymer, *Foedera*, xvii. 414.  See *infra*, p. 307.

tion shall be destroyed ". The Bill was also opposed by
the secretary of state " because of the reciprocal traffic
which is between them and us "[1]. However in 1630
Charles I. reissued his father's proclamation ' against the
shipping of merchandises in strangers' bottoms ', after he
had previously forbidden the alienation or part sale of
native vessels above fifty tons to foreigners[2]. But no
serious attempt seems to have been made to enforce the
navigation system ; and the neglect drew a remonstrance
from ' a great number of poor mariners ', who complained
that they were unemployed since French and Dutch shippers,
upon discharging their cargoes here, " relade back again at
under rates for far less than petitioners can live by, because
they go but with four men and a boy when the petitioners
cannot go under fourteen "[3]. A new note was struck
when the colonies were brought by the Early Stuarts
within the ambit of the naval protective system. In 1621
it was ordered that colonial tobacco must be landed first in
England before being taken to other countries ; in 1624
that it must not be carried in foreign ships ; in 1633 that
aliens must not engage in trade with Virginia[4] ; and in
1647 that all the ' goods of the growth ' of the plantations
must be exported in English bottoms[5]. These injunctions
laid the foundations of the old colonial system, based on
exclusion of the foreigner from the carrying trade.

The decade 1651 to 1660 witnessed two important *The Act*
measures, which not only developed in one comprehensive *of 1651.*
code the principles latent in earlier enactments, but provided the framework of English naval policy for nearly
two centuries. The Act of 1651[6] forbade any commodity

[1] *House of Commons Journals*, i. 642.
[2] Rymer, *Foedera*, xix. 130. Newcastle was permitted to employ
foreign vessels because of its losses during the war : *State Papers Domestic*,
Addenda, 1625–1649, p. 393 (c. 1630). Alienation forbidden (1626): *ibid.* 103.
[3] *State Papers Domestic*, 1634–1635, pp. 23-24, 498.
[4] *State Papers Colonial*, 1574–1660, pp. 26, 171 ; Beer, *The Origins of
the British Colonial System*, 192, 232-234.
[5] *Acts and Ordinances of the Interregnum*, i. 913.
[6] *Ibid.* ii. 559 seq. In 1650 ships of foreign countries were forbidden to
trade with the English plantations without licence, in order " to hinder the
carrying over of . . . enemies to this Commonwealth " : *ibid.* ii. 427.
Beer (*The Origins of the British Colonial System*, 374) regards the Act of
[contd.]

grown or manufactured in Asia, Africa or America to be
imported into England, Ireland or the plantations except
in ships which " belong only to the people of this commonwealth or the plantations . . . and whereof the master and
mariners are also for the most part of them of the people
of this commonwealth ", under penalty of forfeiting goods
and vessel. It also prohibited any commodity grown or
manufactured in Europe to be imported into England,
Ireland or the plantations except in ships which belonged
to ' the people of this commonwealth ', or in " such foreign
ships and vessels as do truly and properly belong to the
people of that country or place of which the said goods are
the growth, production or manufacture, or to such ports
where the said goods can only be or most usually are first
shipped for transportation ". It further enacted that no
goods of foreign growth or manufacture, ' brought into this
commonwealth in shipping belonging to the people thereof ',
should be shipped from any place other than where they
were grown or manufactured, or were usually ' first shipped
for transportation '. Three provisos were added. The
first safeguarded the right of the Levant and East India
Companies to import Mediterranean or Eastern commodities from their ' usual ports ', though not grown there.
The second made it lawful to " bring in from any of the
ports of Spain and Portugal all sorts of goods or commodities that have come from, or any way belonged unto,
the plantations or dominions of either of them ". The
third exempted from the operation of the Act silk or silk
wares brought by land from Italy, which it was permitted
to ship in English vessels from Ostend, Nieuport, Rotterdam, Middelburg, Amsterdam, ' or any ports thereabouts '.
In regard to the coasting trade the Act excluded any vessel
of which an alien was owner, part-owner or master. Subsequently the obligation to import commodities from the
place of their growth was dispensed with in the case of
naval stores such as hemp, pitch, tar, cordage, deal-boards

---

1650 as aimed at the Dutch carrying trade, but it was professedly intended
to prevent help being taken to the plantations, which were in ' rebellion '
against the Government of the Commonwealth.

and masts, which were allowed to be brought by all persons in any ship and from any port (1653) [1]; and licence was also given to export certain kinds of fish in foreign bottoms (1657) [2].

The Act as a whole was unpopular in influential quarters [3], and its enforcement does not appear to have been stringent. It caused a considerable rise in prices [4]; and the Government and merchants alike seemed content ' to let it sleep ', especially during the war with Spain when English trade was largely carried in Dutch ships to avoid Spanish privateers [5]. The ' commanders of ships in and about London ' complained to the Protector in 1658 that the Act " has been so eluded by strangers, and by devices to avoid the penalty, that many English ships are laid aside and some of the best broken up, our employment rejected, and trade chiefly carried on by aliens residing here and in foreign-built ships navigated by strangers, so that our seamen seek foreign employment. We appealed to Parliament in 1657, and they brought in a Bill to amend the Act but did not sit to complete it. Since the war with Spain we have traded thither, carrying out our manufactures and bringing in fruits, wines, etc., but the Dutch eat us out of our trade at home and abroad ; they refuse to sell us a hogshead of water to refresh us at sea and call us ' English dogs ', which doth much grieve our English spirits. They will not sail with us but shoot at us, and by indirect courses bring their goods into our ports, which wrongs not only us but you in your customs. We beg you to countenance the Act, and to make proclamation that all our vessels shall be manned with English subjects " [6]. To this the Customs Commissioners returned answer : " No law forbids manning English ships outward or inward bound with strangers,

*Not stringently enforced.*

---

[1] *State Papers Domestic*, 1652–1653, p. 442 ; Coke, *Treatise* (1671), ii. 118.

[2] *Acts and Ordinances of the Interregnum*, ii. 1099.

[3] *Acts and Ordinances of the Eastland Company*, 76 (1654). It was opposed ' by no mean ones '.

[4] *Newcastle Merchant Adventurers*, i. 179.

[5] Bland, *Trade Revived* (1659), 17 ; Brewster, *Essays on Trade and Navigation* (1695), 101.

[6] *State Papers Domestic*, 1658–1659, pp. 7-10.

but by the Navigation Act the trade with the plantations
is to be carried on in ships manned chiefly by English, and
with Europe by English ships or those of the country
whence the exports come ; so that Hollanders and other
foreigners, under colour of English bills of sale, have lately
carried on most of the trade of Europe with this nation,
and it is very difficult for seizer or informer to obtain
evidence to lead to conviction. No law forbids English
ships manned with foreigners to trade from one to another
of our ports unless a stranger be owner, part-owner or master,
so that English mariners are discouraged and seek employment elsewhere ". They concluded : " It would benefit
trade and navigation if it were enacted that English ships
be navigated only by Englishmen " [1].

*The Act of 1660.*   The Act of 1660 [2] sought to correct the defects or repair
the omissions which experience had brought to light in
the Act of 1651. It ordered that the master of an English
vessel and three-fourths at least of its crew must be English [3] ;
that all commodities exported from or imported into the
colonies [4] must be carried in ships owned by the people of
England, Ireland [5], Wales or the colonies ; that goods
imported in foreign ships, which were " of the built of that
country or place of which the goods are the growth, production or manufacture respectively ", should be deemed
aliens' goods and pay aliens' duties ; that no commodities
known as ' the enumerated commodities '—sugar, tobacco,
cotton wool, indigo, ginger, fustic or other dyeing wood
of the plantations—should be exported from any of the
colonies except to another English colony or to England,
Ireland [6] and Wales ; and that colonial merchants and
factors must possess British nationality.

Subsequent enactments can be grouped under three
heads, accordingly as they extended, modified, or suspended
the provisions of the Act of 1660. An important extension

[1] *Ibid.*                          [2] *Statutes,* v. 246-250.
[3] " Any of his majesty's subjects of England, Ireland and his plantations are to be accounted English and no others " : *ibid.* v. 395.
[4] For the restrictions imposed on the colonies by the Act of 1651, see
*supra,* p. 122.
[5] Ireland was subsequently excluded, *infra,* p. 128.
[6] See preceding note.

was made in 1662 when ships were required to be built in *Subsequent enactments.* the King's dominions as well as owned by his subjects, or else their cargoes paid aliens' duties[1]. Two years later it was laid down that 'no commodity of the growth, production or manufacture of Europe' should be imported direct into the plantations, but must be taken first to England or Wales, and shipped thence in English-built shipping whereof the master and three-fourths of the mariners at least were English[2]. In 1673 duties were imposed on enumerated commodities when shipped from one colony to another[3]. In other directions the stringency of the Act was relaxed. The obligation to import commodities direct from the place of their origin could not be maintained in view of the Dutch monopoly of the spice trade, and in 1662 permission was given to import spices from Holland[4]. A few years later the Treaty of Breda (1667) stipulated that all merchandise brought down the Rhine from Germany to the staple at Dordrecht should be deemed as if it were of the growth of Holland, and might therefore be transported to England in Dutch bottoms[5]. In the eighteenth century (1741) the Navigation Act was further modified to enable the Russia Company to import Persian commodities into this country through Russia[6]. On the other hand, the right to import Eastern commodities (raw silk and mohair yarn) from any Mediterranean port was confined in 1720 to Turkish ports in order to prevent trading by non-members of the Levant Company[7], so that the Act could be manipulated to protect vested commercial interests. The needs of the colonies also extorted concessions in respect of the enumerated commodities, which by the Act of 1660 had to be sent first to England. The list had been extended on subsequent occasions[8], and among the additions was rice

[1] *Statutes*, v. 394. The Act of 1696 excluded foreign-built ships from the colonial trade : *ibid.* vii. 103.
[2] *Ibid.* v. 449. This came into operation in 1664. [3] *Ibid.* v. 793.
[4] *Tudor and Stuart Proclamations* (ed. Steele), i. No. 3374.
[5] Macpherson, *Annals of Commerce*, ii. 531.
[6] *Statutes at Large*, vi. 163, 507. See *supra*, vol. ii. 350.
[7] *Statutes at Large*, v. 193-194 ; *House of Commons Journals*, xix. 269, 271, 275, 281, 316, 320-322.
[8] Rice and Molasses (1705) : *Statutes*, viii. 335-336. Beaver skins and other furs (1722) : *Statutes at Large*, v. 266. Copper ore (1722) : *ibid.* v.
[contd.]

which was formerly shipped direct to Spain and Portugal. The effect of making it an enumerated commodity was to spoil it before it reached the market abroad, and this, together with the double expense, reduced its consumption abroad, so that the market was captured by foreigners [1]. As a result of appeals to Parliament [2], Carolina was allowed in 1730, and Georgia in 1735 [3], to export rice direct to any part of Europe southward of Cape Finisterre, and subsequently [4] to any part of America southward of Carolina and Georgia. A similar liberty, inspired by fear of ' unlawful commerce between the plantations and foreign countries ', was given to the sugar colonies in 1739 to send their produce direct to any European port : " whereby the sugars will arrive at such ports sooner, with less charge, and in better condition for the consumption thereof ". The proviso was attached that the ship must first touch at some port in Great Britain, except when the ship went southward of Cape Finisterre [5]. Finally, in time of national emergency the Navigation Act was liable to be suspended, as during the Second Dutch War [6].

*Position of Scotland.*   The position of Scotland and Ireland under the Navigation Act raised problems which were only solved ultimately by their union with England. The extension of the Act to Scotland threatened to ruin her trade and shipping by placing her in the category of a foreign country. Her claim for exemption [7] was resisted on the grounds that the customs revenue would lose at least twenty thousand

---

275. Naval stores (pitch, tar, masts, etc.) (1729) : *ibid.* v. 524-525. Iron, lumber, coffee, cocoanuts, raw silk, hides and skins, etc. (1764) : *ibid.* vii. 462. In 1765 lumber was allowed to be sent direct to southern Europe : *ibid.* vii. 544-545.

[1] *House of Commons Journals*, xx. 62 : Gee, *The Trade and Navigation of Great Britain* (ed. 1730), 22.

[2] *House of Commons Journals*, xx. 62 (1722) ; xxi. 464 (1730).

[3] *Statutes at Large*, v. 553-554 (1730), 674-675 (1735).

[4] In 1764 South Carolina and Georgia ; in 1765 North Carolina : *ibid.* vii. 479, 543. In 1770 East and West Florida were allowed to export rice southward of Cape Finisterre : *ibid.* viii. 115.

[5] *Ibid.* vi. 115.

[6] 1665 : *Tudor and Stuart Proclamations* (ed. Steele), i. No. 3414. For the permission to use foreign vessels to import timber in 1668–1669, see *State Papers Domestic*, 1668–1669, pp. 290-291 ; Coke, *Treatise* (1671), i. 44 ; ii. 118.

[7] *State Papers Domestic*, 1661–1662, p. 74.

pounds a year if the Scots were allowed to bring in goods without paying alien, that is double, duties ; that if they had free trade with the colonies they might carry plantation produce abroad ; and that the objects of the Act, in general, would be frustrated since its very essence was to encourage English shipping [1]. A commission was set up (1668) ' for settling freedom of trade' between the two countries [2]. The Scottish commissioners claimed the right to participate in the English carrying trade, especially to the English colonies, and offered to give assurances that colonial products would be brought to England, except the small quantities consumed in Scotland [3]. Other demands included the removal of the high tariffs which impeded the traffic between the two kingdoms [4]. The English commissioners rejected the proposal for free trade to the plantations, " which are built up by the labour and expense of the English ", though the Scots could settle there as merchants or planters ; nor would they concede the right to import foreign commodities into England because this would diminish English navigation [5]. The negotiations lapsed [6], and Scotland maintained the heavy impositions which in retaliation she had laid on goods imported from England [7]. The latter greatly exceeded her exports to England, and English merchants trading to Scotland complained that they were ' now exposed to want and beggary ' [8]. The plantations were seriously incommoded since they were unable to obtain Scottish servants : in 1675 they complained that " intercourse with Scotland is almost wholly cut off by the Act of Navigation, for men will not bring servants when they may bring no other commodities " [9].

[1] *State Papers Domestic*, 1661–1662, pp. 135, 149.
[2] *Ibid.* 1667–1668, p. 156 ; *Statutes*, v. 630.
[3] *State Papers Domestic*, 1667–1668, pp. 179-180.
[4] There were heavy duties on Scottish cattle, linen, beer, etc., imported into England ; and salt paid sixteen times more than foreign salt : *ibid.* 1667–1668, p. 208.
[5] *Ibid.* 1667–1668, p. 285.
[6] Cf. *ibid.* 1673–1675, pp. 191, 215.
[7] *Ibid.* 1663–1664, p. 651 (1664).
[8] *Ibid.* 1663–1664, p. 651 ; Brown, *Miscellanea Aulica : Or a Collection of State Treatises* (1702), 200-202 ; Coke, *Treatise* (1671), i. 54 ; Keith, *Commercial Relations of England and Scotland*, 90-91.
[9] *State Papers American and West Indies*, 1675–1676, p. 304.

*Position of Ireland.* Ireland's position differed from that of Scotland. She was originally included in the Act of 1660 [1]; but in 1664 she was forbidden to export any of her products direct to the colonies except ' horses and victuals ', and another clause in the same Statute was interpreted to mean that the colonies could not send enumerated commodities direct to Ireland—an interpretation confirmed by the Act of 1671 [2]. After the Revolution (1696) it was further forbidden to import into Ireland any goods ' of the growth or product ' of the plantations, until they had first been landed in England or Wales [3]—this was construed to mean that non-enumerated commodities were now brought under the same ban as enumerated commodities. The effect of these enactments was to set up a barrier against the trade of Ireland with the British settlements [4]. One concession was made in 1705 when the export of Irish linens was permitted from any port of Ireland direct to any of the colonies [5]; and in 1731 Ireland was permitted to import direct from the colonies non-enumerated commodities [6]. In the last quarter of the eighteenth century Ireland regained a large measure of the commercial equality she had shared with England before the Restoration [7].

*Reasons for the permanent adoption of the navigation system.* In reviewing the Acts of 1651 and 1660 it must be noticed, first, that the principles embodied in them were not new. The legislation of nearly three centuries afforded numerous precedents for the protection of English shipping [8]: extensive privileges had been conferred on certain trading companies, the Levant and Eastland, shielding them from foreign competition [9]: there was a precedent for the exclusion of aliens from the colonial trade [10]: and even the

---

[1] *Supra*, p. 124.
[2] *Statutes*, v. 449-450, 748 ; *State Papers Domestic*, 1671–1672, p. 42.
[3] *Statutes*, vii. 106.
[4] *Hist. MSS. Comm. Fortescue*, i. 179. For a statement of Irish trade with the colonies, see *ibid. Lothian*, 301-310 ; also see *ibid. Egmont (Diary)*, i. *passim*.
[5] *Statutes*, viii. 351.  [6] *Statutes at Large*, v. 571.
[7] *Ibid.* viii. 595 (1778) ; ix. 73 (1780).  [8] *Supra*, pp. 116 *seq.*
[9] The Levant Company was given the sole right to import commodities from the Levant : *Tudor and Stuart Proclamations* (ed. Steele), i. No. 1160. The Eastland Company enjoyed a similar right for the commodities in which it dealt : *ibid.* i. No. 1333.
[10] *Supra*, p. 121.

policy of making England the staple for ' enumerated commodities ' was anticipated in the order of the Privy Council, in 1621, directing that tobacco and other commodities brought from Virginia should be first landed in England before being carried into any foreign parts [1]. The permanent adoption of the navigation system after the middle of the seventeenth century was due to the Civil War which, among other economic effects, enabled the Dutch to establish an undisputed ascendancy in the world's carrying trade. Owing to the distracted state of the country, combined with the insecurity of the seas which were infested with royalist privateers, English merchants could not keep their markets in Germany and the Baltic lands adequately supplied with woollen manufactures, whilst commercial intercourse with Russia suffered a complete eclipse [2]. In addition, England was unable to maintain her control of the colonial trade, which was largely captured by foreign shippers [3]. The Dutch benefited by the decline of English commerce, so that the Eastland merchants, who had originally opposed the attempt of James I. to enforce the Navigation Laws [4], were now foremost in pressing for their revival [5]. The Levant merchants, finding themselves exposed to Dutch competition, also claimed protection [6] ; and their demand that the produce of the eastern Mediterranean should be imported direct from the places of its growth, and not from the Netherlands, was given general application in the famous clause prohibiting the importation of all commodities except from the country of their origin [7]. Thus the Acts of 1651 and 1660 originated in the dislocation of English commerce caused by the Great Rebellion. They were the product of a situation essentially temporary in its nature, for there is no reason to suppose that English shippers would not have regained their former share of the

---

[1] State Papers Colonial, 1574–1660, p. 26.
[2] Coke, Treatise (1675), iv. Preface. Also supra, vol. ii. 331.
[3] Beer, The Origins of the British Colonial System, 352-358.
[4] Supra, p. 120, note 6.
[5] State Papers Domestic, 1651, pp. 273-274. See also the Company's letters in Acts and Ordinances of the Eastland Company, 76.
[6] State Papers Domestic, 1649–1650, pp. 11-12.
[7] Supra, p. 122.

carrying trade, and even extended it, as the need for meeting Dutch competition stimulated the versatility and enter-prise of English shipbuilders.  Just as the Dutch failed to establish an exclusive monopoly in the East Indies, in the Levant, or in Africa, so it is unlikely that they would have retained indefinitely the advantages which they had reaped from the Civil War.  The recovery would have taken time, since it was to be accomplished " by such means as God and Nature have ordained, viz. by increasing trade in England " [1]. But inability to take long views led the Governments of the Commonwealth and the Restoration to embark upon a policy which Elizabethan statesmen had condemned, and " Old Oliver entertained but coldly " [2].

*Effects of the Navigation Acts on:*

*(i.) the Baltic trade.*

A comprehensive indictment was framed against the navigation policy.  Roger Coke, its acutest critic, remarked that no one ' endued with less prescience than omniscience ' could foresee the mischiefs brought upon the nation by the Act of Navigation [3].  Among the ' mischiefs ' enumerated the most conspicuous was the handicap imposed on the Baltic trade, which had peculiar importance because it supplied England with the materials for shipbuilding—timber [4], hemp, flax, pitch and tar.  The trade was formerly driven, though not exclusively, by English merchants in exchange for manufactured goods [5].  They used foreign-built ships since native ships were not adapted for the Baltic, owing to our insular practice of making ' all ships serve for all trades ', whereas the Dutch built ships ' for every trade ' [6]. When the Act of Navigation sought to confine English

---

[1] Coke, *Treatise* (1675), iv. 75.

[2] *Ibid.* (1671), i. 43.  Cromwell caused the Act of 1651 to be modified : see *supra*, p. 123, and Coke, *A Detection of the Court and State of England* (ed. 1718), ii. 75.

[3] Coke, *Treatise* (1675), iii. 35.  Coke favoured the navigation system in certain branches of commerce : *ibid.* (1675), iv. 109.  His argument is repeated in *Britannia Languens* (1680).

[4] On the supplies of timber in England and the Baltic countries, see Albion, *Forests and Sea Power*, chapters iii.-iv.

[5] Coke, *Treatise* (1671), i. 43.  But Brewster denied that we lost the Baltic trade owing to the Act—" It was stealing from us " before, and was " quite lost by the year 1652 " : *Essays on Trade and Navigation* (1695), 99.  See *supra*, vol. ii. 320.

[6] " I could rarely discourse this point " : Coke, *Treatise* (1671), ii. 117-118 ; iv. 92-94.  Bland, *Trade Revived* (1659), 18.  *Supra*, vol. ii. 320.

merchants to English-built ships [1], the timber trade was partially captured by Scandinavian traders who sailed in Scandinavian bottoms [2]. The English could not oust their competitors on account of the difference in the cost of ship-building. According to Child a ' fly-boat ', which might cost elsewhere thirteen or fourteen hundred pounds, would cost here twenty-two to twenty-four hundred pounds [3]. Moreover the obligation, imposed by the Act, to buy foreign goods at their place of origin served to create a local monopoly ; and the Baltic countries seized the opportunity to raise their prices against English buyers. Timber, for example, was said to cost ' near double ', and we now paid for naval stores with ' the treasure of the nation ' [4]. At the same time increased duties were levied in the Sound by the King of Denmark, whose interest it was to make the Baltic trade ' insupportable ' to the English in order that his subjects might ' monopolize the trade ' [5]. Although the number of English vessels entering the Sound increased during the second half of the seventeenth century—a natural consequence of the expansion of trade after the Restoration —the percentage of Scandinavian ships trading to England was nearly trebled, while Dutch shipping maintained its ascendancy in the Baltic [6].

The advance in the price of naval stores increased the (ii.) *The cost of ship-building.* Coke relates that in 1650 he was *cost of ship-building* part-owner of a vessel of 100 tons, which was " fitted out to sea for £505 : four years after the same builder built another (both for the Newcastle trade) of 110 tons, and this ship fitted out to sea cost above £800. And the reason of this dearness the builder ascribed to the excessive prices of pitch, tar, cordage and sails " [7]. The title of the Act of Navigation thus appeared a misnomer: it sought ' the increase of navigation and mariners', but endeavoured to

---

[1] The Act of 1662 imposed aliens' duties on cargoes carried in vessels English-owned but foreign-built : *supra*, p. 125.

[2] *State Papers Domestic*, 1668–1669, p. 167 ; Coke, *Treatise* (1671), i. 44.

[3] Child, *A New Discourse of Trade* (4th ed.), 128. See Barbour, " Dutch and English Merchant Shipping in the Seventeenth Century " in *The Economic History Review*, vol. ii. No. 2, 275.

[4] Coke, *Treatise* (1671), i. 43-44 ; *Britannia Languens* (1680), 65.

[5] Coke, *Treatise* (1671), i. 44.   See *supra*, vol. ii. 320.

[6] *Infra*, pp. 135, 503 (No. 2).       [7] Coke, *Treatise* (1675), iii. 37.

confine both to English-built ships [1], the price of which was raised by restrictions on the import of timber and naval stores. The reason for dealing with foreign importers, or trading in foreign ships, was their comparative cheapness; yet instead of removing the obstructions responsible for high freights in England, the Act of Navigation only made English ships dearer than before owing to the enhanced cost of the materials for shipbuilding [2]. Again English shipwrights, it was said, knew only how to build men-of-war; and merchantmen were constructed so that they might serve as fighting ships, which made them unsuitable for the Baltic and fishing trades [3]. The Dutch, as we have seen, used different kinds of vessels for different trades [4]. Moreover the Act ran counter to earlier legislation [5] which had endeavoured to preserve English timber, reputed the best in the world, for particular purposes. The exclusion of timber brought from Holland or Hamburg [6], coupled with the dearness of Scandinavian timber, forced English shipbuilders to use up the native supply, which was rapidly becoming exhausted instead of being reserved for the royal navy and for ships of great burden engaged on distant voyages.

(iii.) *Industry and trade.*    The growth of a mercantile marine must depend on the volume of trade, but the navigation policy reacted adversely upon the industry and commerce of the country. It curtailed the market for our goods overseas because the high freights of English ships—" near double as dear built and sailed with near double the charge of the Dutch " [7]—in-

---

[1] *Supra*, p. 131, note 1.

[2] This is the argument in Coke, *Treatise* (1675), iv. 97 *seq.*; and in *Britannia Languens* (1680), 64 *seq.* Brewster, writing in 1695, denied that shipbuilding was made so much dearer : *Essays on Trade and Navigation*, 104.

[3] In the reign of James I. it was pointed out that an English ship was built 'for the defence of the realm', and the Dutch 'hoy' only 'for profit'. The latter (100 tons) could be worked by five men and a boy ; the former of the same burden needed twenty men : *Hist. MSS. Comm. Beaulieu*, 109.

[4] Petty, *Economic Writings*, i. 260-261 ; Fitzmaurice, *The Life of Sir William Petty*, 221. And *supra*, p. 130, note 6.

[5] *Statutes*, iv. part ii. 860 (1593) ; and *supra*, vol. ii. 157.

[6] On this point, see *infra*, p. 134, note 3.

[7] Coke, *Treatise* (1675), iii. 38 (also *ibid.* i. 36, 49-50) ; *Britannia Languens* (1680), 66-69.

creased the cost of raw materials imported from abroad, which in turn advanced the price of the finished products: it debarred other nations from trading with us except in their own ships and with commodities of their own growth or manufacture : and it hindered the concourse of traders and mariners to our shores, on which our commercial prosperity depended. Trade was further handicapped by the inability of shippers to make the most advantageous returns from the ports to which they carried English products, especially since conflicting interpretations of the term 'manufactured' rendered the goods of merchants liable to seizure by the customs officials [1]. Lastly, the system was alleged to concentrate the export trade in the hands of English merchants, who could export what commodities they pleased and at their own prices : and " as this law makes a few merchants masters of all the trade of England, so it makes mariners the merchant's masters " and " seamen's wages excessive ". To the rise in wages, combined with the dearness of ships, was sometimes attributed the loss of the trade to Russia and Greenland [2].

The irony of the situation was that the Dutch, against whom the Act of Navigation was specially aimed, benefited by the handicaps imposed on English shippers [3]. They continued to enjoy their former ascendancy in the Baltic, while they were not even excluded from trade with England— one branch of commerce being replaced by another and more lucrative branch. They had hitherto supplied England with hemp and flax brought from Riga, Reval and other places in the Baltic, with which the inhabitants on the east coast made ropes, nets and sails. These supplies now ceased. The Act prohibited the Dutch from bringing here raw materials from other countries : the people of the Baltic lands, whence came the best hemp and flax, did but

*(iv.) The Dutch carrying trade.*

---

[1] *E.g.* loaf sugar and combings of tow were seized in 1651 because they came from Holland : *Newcastle Merchant Adventurers*, i. 170.

[2] Coke, *Treatise* (1671), i. 48-50; iv. 112; *Britannia Languens* (1680), 65, 70 ; Brewster, *Essays on Trade and Navigation* (1695), 93, 97 ; *Newcastle Merchant Adventurers*, i. 179.

[3] The argument that the Navigation Acts ruined Dutch shipping was described by J. L. Ricardo as ' shipowners' logic ' : *The Anatomy of the Navigation Laws* (1847) 30.

little trade with us : and the English, for reasons mentioned above [1], were at a disadvantage in the Sound. Instead the Dutch now imported into England cordage, nets and sails, which the Act permitted them to do because they were manufactured in Holland ; so that 'many thousands' in England were deprived of their employment while the Dutch gained a more profitable trade [2]. In short the Act prevented England from obtaining, through Dutch agency, cheap supplies of raw materials which could have been worked up into manufactured goods ; but it did not prevent the Dutch importing raw materials into Holland, and re-exporting them to this country in a manufactured state. A parallel anomaly was the prohibition laid on English shippers against bringing timber from Hamburg since it was not grown there, although the timber would have been imported in English ships in exchange for our own commodities [3]. Instead it was brought from Scandinavia in Scandinavian ships by Scandinavian traders, who were paid in money—thus decreasing the employment of English shipping, and running counter to one of the cardinal doctrines of Mercantilism.

(v.) *The re-exportation trade.*     The Dutch enjoyed another advantage in trading with the Baltic [3a]. The basic principle of their commercial system was to encourage imports with a view to subsequent re-exportation. This enabled their ships to carry a varied cargo drawn from many countries—woollen manufactures, wines, spices, fish and salt. It gave them " a power of driving the trade of the world, where the commodities are not English or subject to the Crown of England " [4]. Davenant pointed out that there was no trade so advantageous as that of buying goods in one country to sell again in another. " There is gain by the freight ; it occasions consumption of our home product ; it breeds seamen,

---

[1] *Supra*, pp. 130-131.

[2] Coke, *Treatise* (1671), i. 48 ; ii. 117, 126-127 ; iii. 36-37 ; iv. 94-95. " Yarmouth before the Act of Navigation made yearly 2800 tons of cordage besides nets and sails ; now they make not ten, and neither nets or sails " : *ibid*. iv. 95.

[3] *State Papers Domestic*, 1668–1669, p. 291. Subsequently a ' special privilege ' was granted for importing Hamburg goods : *ibid*. 358.

[3a] For other advantages : *supra*, vol. ii. 320.

[4] Coke, *Treatise* (1671), i. 48 ; iii. 36, 54.

increases shipping, and improves navigation " [1]. The Act
of Navigation, however, put obstacles in the way of the
re-exportation of foreign commodities—other countries
could only send to England goods ' of their growth or manufacture ', and even then they had to pay aliens' duties,
while the high freights discouraged English merchants
from importing commodities not intended for home consumption. Hence English ships carried cargoes which
were less varied, and therefore less adapted to the Baltic
and Russian trades [1a]. Many places in the Sound, provided
by the Dutch with a variety of commodities, dared not buy
woollen manufactures from shippers who could not supply
them with other necessaries. Coke compares the numbers
of Dutch and English ships engaged in the Northern trade,
but his figures are not supported by the Sound Toll Accounts
which have thrown fresh light upon the subject. The
statistics of ships entering the Sound varied from year to
year. In 1671, when Coke issued Parts i. and ii. of his
*Treatise*, the Dutch ships numbered 872, and the English
106 ; but the year in which the rest of the *Treatise* appeared
(1675) coincided with an increase in the number of English
ships (364) and a decline in Dutch ships (434). In 1676 there
were 408 English and 467 Dutch ships ; but in 1683 the
figures were 325 (English) and 1102 (Dutch). The pre-
ponderance of Dutch shipping over the whole period is incontestable, so that the substance of Coke's contention
remains unaffected [2]. Our inferiority in the Northern trade
was not denied by the supporters of the Navigation Act,
though they attributed it partly to the high duties levied
in England on imports, which made them too dear for re-
exportation [3], and partly to the fact that the Dutch brought
back corn from the Baltic lands, whereas England normally
depended on her own produce [4]. To offset their advantages
in the Northern trade the Dutch were excluded from the
English colonies, but in the middle of the seventeenth century
the volume of the colonial trade was small, and they must
have found abundant compensation in the more complete
control which they acquired over the Baltic. It may be

---

[1] Davenant, *Works* (ed. 1771), i. 105-6.    [1a] Cf. *supra*, vol. ii. 320.
[2] Bang and Korst, *Tabeller over Skibsfart og Varetransport gennem
Øresund*, 1661–1783, i. 12, 16, 24. For Coke's figures, see *Treatise* (1675),
iii. 54; iv. 98. Cf. *Hist. MSS. Comm. Buckinghamshire*, 373-374; Davenant,
*Works* (ed. 1771), i. 397.    [3] For drawbacks: *infra*, p. 147.
[4] Brewster, *Essays on Trade and Navigation* (1695), 94, 97, 106.

observed, finally, that the Dutch were able to evade the Act
of Navigation by trading in the name of English merchants,
who acted in the capacity of factors for their Dutch employers [1], or (in the case of the Mediterranean trade) by
carrying goods to Leghorn and there putting them on board
an English ship [2].

*The political argument for the Navigation Act.* The argument in favour of the Navigation Act was
primarily political. The Speaker of the House of Commons
commended it to the King in 1660 with the assurance that
it would " enable your majesty to give the law to foreign
princes abroad. . . . And it is the only way to enlarge your
majesty's dominions all over the world ; for so long as your
majesty is master at sea, your merchants will be welcome
wherever they come " [3]. Adam Smith, after declaring that
" the Act of Navigation is not favourable to foreign commerce
or to the growth of that opulence which can arise from it ",
added : " As defence, however, is of much more importance
than opulence the Act of Navigation is, perhaps, the wisest
of all the commercial regulations of England " [4]. The
argument had been anticipated a century before by Child,
who described the Act as one of the ' most prudent ' ever
made. While acknowledging that in " the interest of the
greatest number " our products " should be taken from us
at the best rates, and foreign commodities sold us at the
cheapest ", by admitting foreign shippers, he contended
that " profit and power ought jointly to be considered " [5].
Navigation was regarded as ' the greatest strength ' of the
nation [6] : ' walls of wood ' as our best defence [7] : and the
maintenance of shipping as ' a principal means to advance
the honour, strength, safety and profit ' of the kingdom [8].
In a word, the carrying trade was the ' foundation of the

---

[1] Locke, *Works* (ed. 1801), v. 17.
[2] *Hist. MSS. Comm. Finch*, i. 93. Cf. *supra*, p. 125.
[3] *House of Commons Journals*, viii. 175.
[4] *The Wealth of Nations* (ed. Cannan), i. 429.
[5] Child, *A New Discourse of Trade* (4th ed.), 121-124.
[6] Malynes, *The Maintenance of Free Trade* (1622), 65.
[7] Davenant, *Works* (ed. 1771), i. 15. ' No wood no kingdom ' : Standish, *The Commons Complaint* (1611). Also *State Papers Domestic*, Addenda,
1625-1649, p. 543.
[8] Rymer, *Foedera*, xvii. 414 (1622).

navy ' [1], and its protection was therefore held to be justified on grounds of national security. The economic consequences of the Act were brushed aside somewhat summarily. The advantage of low freights could not be denied, but since the higher freights were earned by English shippers it was supposed that the nation benefited [2], and the national loss arising from the shrinkage of trade was minimized or ignored. The chief satisfaction was experienced in the reflection that " the Hamburger and Fleming, that run hackney all the world over, were a little stayed from coming hither, crowding so thick with all foreign commodities as they were wont to do " [3]. Child affirmed that, without the Act of Navigation, " you should see forty Dutch ships at our own plantation for one English ". On this account he acclaimed the Act as a *Carta Maritima* [4].

The argument that the Act of Navigation achieved its purpose in building up the maritime strength of the kingdom needs careful scrutiny. To begin with, its force is considerably weakened by Adam Smith's own admission that in the Dutch Wars—that is, before the Navigation Act " could have had time to produce any considerable effect "—England's navy was already superior to that of Holland, and " at least equal, perhaps superior, to the united navies of France and Holland "; and " its superiority, perhaps, would scarce appear greater in the present times " [5]. In other words, England's " great naval power could not, in either of those wars, be owing to the Act of Navigation " [6]; nor did ' the wisest of all the commercial regulations of England ' give her any greater margin of security than she had previously possessed. Apart from the question of security, the upholders of the navigation system appeared to be on surer ground when they made the confident claim that " we, by this Navigation Act, have gradually obtained a vast increase of shipping and mariners " [7]. Between

*Adam Smith's admission.*

---

[1] *Hist. MSS. Comm. Various*, vi. 191.
[2] Fortrey, *England's Interest and Improvement* (1663), 37. Similarly : Child, *A New Discourse of Trade* (4th ed.), 130.
[3] Fortrey, *England's Interest and Improvement* (1663), 36.
[4] Child, *A New Discourse of Trade* (4th ed.), pp. xxix-xxx.
[5] *The Wealth of Nations* (ed. Cannan), ii. 98.     [6] *Ibid.*
[7] Anderson, writing in 1764 : *The Origin of Commerce* (ed. 1764), ii. 110.

Reasons
for the
growth
of the
mercantile
marine.
the Restoration and the Revolution the tonnage of merchant ships was doubled [1]. The credit for this expansion is
given to the Act of 1660 ; and the criticism that the development took place in spite of the law, or at the expense of
other interests equally or possibly even more important, is
regarded [2] as ' largely academic ' and based on a series of
hypotheses that cannot be verified. But to attribute the
growth of shipping, in this period, to the Act of 1660 is to
overlook the fact that the quantity of foreign tonnage is
also represented to have doubled by the year 1688 [3], which
shows that native shipping did not increase at the expense of
foreign shipping. The growth of trade in the same ratio,
during the period in question [4], provides an adequate explanation of the expansion of tonnage both native and
foreign. England also profited by the difficulties of the
Dutch arising from their struggle with France, when part
of the carrying trade of Holland fell into English hands [5],
though the restrictions imposed by the Act of Navigation
made it impossible to take full advantage of the opportunity.
It must be remembered, further, that in certain branches of
commerce, such as the Levant and India among others,
no protection was needed for English shipping since the
strength and durability of native-built ships fitted them
for distant voyages [6]. There was, perhaps, a temporary
advantage in the exclusion of Dutch shippers from the
colonial trade [7], but against this must be set the handicaps in
the Baltic due to the greater cheapness and convenience,
and consequently lower freights, of foreign ships. In the
eighteenth century there was a marked decline in the
amount of foreign tonnage—in spite of the abolition of
differential duties on the export of English commodities
by aliens [8]—accompanied by a more than corresponding

---

[1] Infra, p. 139.
[2] E.g. Beer, The Old Colonial System, part i. vol. i. 13, note 1.
[3] Infra, p. 139. While the statistics for 1688 are untrustworthy, other
evidence supports the view that foreign tonnage increased : cf. infra, p. 139.
[4] Infra, p. 139.
[5] Scott, Joint-Stock Companies, i. 306.
[6] Coke, Treatise (1675), iv. 92-93. Brewster, Essays on Trade and Navigation (1695), 103-106 (' Three parts of the world ').
[7] Cf. infra, p. 173.                           [8] Supra, p. 72, note 2.

rise in native tonnage. Yet in view of the immense growth *Statistics of mercantile tonnage.* of British commerce the bulk of the carrying trade, especially to India, America and Africa, would probably have fallen to British shippers whether protected or not. The following statistics show the tonnage [1] of the ships cleared outwards, and the value of the cargoes exported, soon after the Restoration, at the Revolution, in the middle of the eighteenth century, and on the eve of the American War of Independence [2] :

|  | English Tonnage (Ships cleared outwards). | Foreign Tonnage (Ships cleared outwards). | Cargoes Exported. |
|---|---|---|---|
| 1663 | 95,266 * | 47,634 * | £2,022,812 † |
| 1688 | 190,533 | 95,267 | £4,086,087 |
| 1750 | 609,798 ‡ | 51,386 ‡ | £12,699,080 |
| 1774 | 798,864 | 65,192 | £15,916,343 |

\* The average of the years 1663 and 1669 (London only).
† The year 1663 (London only).
‡ The average of the years 1749–1751.

Even under the navigation system the same influences, which had formerly caused the rise and fall of native tonnage, continued to operate. Thus in 1696, during the war with France, the estimated tonnage of English and foreign ships ' arrived from and cleared to foreign parts ' was as follows for the port of London—90,496 (English) and 118,500 (foreign) [3]. Hence Davenant, who upheld the system, concluded that " strangers seem to have beaten us, in a manner, out of our own ports " [4]. The subsequent recovery of English

[1] The real tonnage is supposed to be about 50 per cent. above the registered : Macpherson, *Annals of Commerce*, iii. 340, note ; Chalmers, *An Estimate of the Comparative Strength of Britain* (ed. 1782), 45. Ships absent from port during the whole year are apparently excluded.
[2] The statistics of tonnage are taken from Chalmers, *op. cit.* Table facing p. 37. The returns of cargoes are taken from the Table given *supra*, vol. ii. 189 (except for 1688, for which see Chalmers, *op. cit.* Table facing p. 37 ; and cf. Davenant, *Works*, ed. 1771, ii. 270).
[3] Mich. 1695–Mich. 1696 : *House of Lords MSS.* 1695–1697, p. 421.
[4] Davenant, *Works* (ed. 1771), i. 396. For Davenant's figures, see *ibid.* 96. They also show an excess of foreign over native tonnage.

shipping supports the conclusion that the root causes of its prosperity, as of its occasional relapses, were independent of legislation and must be sought for in the general conditions affecting trade.

*Other expedients to stimulate shipping.*      In addition to the Navigation Acts two other expedients for the encouragement of native shipping attracted attention.  One was to free the carrying trade from the burden of customs duties : the other was to develop the fisheries. Both owed their inspiration to Holland, whose influence on England was most marked in the domain of commerce [1].

*Taxation.*      No change was more persistently advocated in the seventeenth and eighteenth centuries than the reform of the fiscal system, in order to stimulate the carrying trade. Taxes were of two kinds : direct and indirect.  The old methods of direct taxation—the mediaeval ' tenths and fifteenths' on movables, and the Tudor ' subsidies' on land and movables [2]—proved inadequate owing to their inelasticity.  They became ' fiscal expressions' for a fixed sum, and the quota assigned to the various localities remained unaffected by changes in the distribution of wealth.  One commissioner of taxes in the reign of Elizabeth averred that no one had been assessed " but is known to be worth at the least in goods ten times as much as he is set at, and six times more in lands than his assessment; and many be twenty times, some thirty and some much more worth than they be set at, which the commissioner cannot without oath help " [3].  Another stated that he could not induce the corporation of Chichester to have its property, " which is thought better than £100 by year, to be set at £3 in the subsidy, nor one childless alderman, who is better worth than £5000, to be assessed above £20 in goods " [4].  " The Englishman," declared Bacon, " is most master of his own valuation and the least bitten in purse of any nation in Europe " [5].  The

[1] For Holland's influence on England, see *supra*, p. 11.
[2] *Supra*, vol. i. 605-607.  A fifteenth and a tenth brought in about £39,000, and a subsidy £80,000.
[3] *Hist. MSS. Comm. Salisbury*, iii. 429 (1589); viii. 547 (1598).
[4] *Ibid.* v. 323 (1595).
[5] Dowell, *A History of Taxation* (ed. 1888), i. 158.

gross inequalities in the system of assessment inspired a proposal, in 1628, for an income tax of 2 per cent. upon incomes exceeding £125 per annum [1]. In 1640 Parliament instituted a system by which a fixed quota was levied on each county and borough ; and the practice was continued during the Interregnum (' monthly assessments ') [2], and after the Restoration—although Halifax asserted that its " inequality is so exorbitant between county and county " that it could not be rectified without a survey of the kingdom [3]. In some years Parliament substituted the method of a national pound rate equitably distributed over the whole country. Eventually in 1698 the principle of fixed quotas was finally adopted, but the proportion of the quota charged on each district within the county was henceforth determined by its share in the assessment of 1692 [4]. Originally an income tax on real and personal estate and on ' office or employment of profit ', it survived almost entirely as a tax on land [5].

The system of direct taxation, as it operated in practice, *Burden* was severely criticized by Sir William Petty, who complained *of the customs.* that taxes in England were levied ' chiefly upon land alone ', and not upon ' expense ' (consumption) as in Holland [6]. This view ignored the heavy burden of the customs. First, there was the ' old subsidy ', that is, tunnage and poundage : the former was a specific duty on imported wines, the latter an *ad valorem* duty of 5 per cent. on imports and exports as valued in the Book of Rates [7]. Current market prices, as we have already seen [8], often varied greatly from official values as entered in the Book of Rates, and the poundage duty of 5 per cent. on the official value of a commodity might work out at 20 or 25 per cent. of the price

---

[1] *State Papers Domestic*, 1628–1629, p. 435.

[2] *Statutes*, v. 145. For ' monthly assessments ', see Dowell, *A History of Taxation* (ed. 1888), iii. 72 seq.

[3] Halifax, *An Essay upon Taxes* (1693) in Somers, *Tracts* (ed. 1814), xi. 75.

[4] See *infra*, Appendix, p. 504, No. 1. " There goes £400 a year for the taxes ", wrote in 1712 the holder of a pension of £2000 : *Hist. MSS. Comm. Portland*, v. 153.

[5] There were other taxes analogous to a property tax—hearth-money or ' chimney-money ' (1662–1688) ; window tax (1696–1851) ; inhabited house duty (1778–1834 ; revived 1851) ; taxes on servants, carriages, animals, wearing hair-powder, etc. : Dowell, *op. cit.* vol. iii. bk. iii. On the hearth tax, see also Ogg, *England in the Reign of Charles II.*, ii. 429-430.

[6] Petty, *Economic Writings*, i. 301.

[7] *Statutes*, v. 184 seq. Cloth came under a special rate.

[8] *Supra*, p. 93.

paid by the merchant importer [1]. Secondly, other duties
were imposed in addition to the ' old subsidy ', so that the
total amount of the tax laid on an article might represent
a considerable percentage even of the retail price to the
consumer [2]. " In no part of the world ", exclaimed a
London merchant in the reign of Charles I., are traders
" so screwed and wrung as in England " [3]. Wine affords
the most striking example of these supplementary duties.
The ' old subsidy ' in 1660 was approximately £4 per tun : by
1784 successive imposts had raised the amount to approximately £46 for Portuguese and Spanish wines, and £96 for
French wines. Complications were introduced by the fact
that wine imported by an alien merchant or in an alien ship
paid a higher rate, and different rates were payable in the
outports from those levied at London [4]. The burden of indirect taxation was aggravated by the frauds of customs
officials [5], and by the practice of farming the customs, which
was not finally abandoned until 1671 [6] : " so as in conclusion
the poor people pay twice as much as the King receives " [7].
Some light on the amount of taxation, mainly indirect,
paid annually by artisans and labourers ' in the country ', is
afforded by the following calculations made in 1756 [8] :

---

[1] *E.g.* colonial tobacco was valued at 2od. per lb., on which the poundage was 1d., plus a further duty of 1d. After paying these duties it sold
here at one period for 4d. to 5d. per lb., so that the combined duties represented 40 to 50 per cent. of the selling price to the merchant : Beer, *The
Old Colonial System*, part i. vol. i. 130, 134, note 1 ; MacInnes, *The Early
English Tobacco Trade*, 186.

[2] The duty per lb. on colonial tobacco was raised to 5d. in 1685 and to
6d. in 1713. This was about 25 per cent. of the retail price in some cases:
Beer, *op. cit.* 160-161 ; Kennedy, *English Taxation*, 1640–1799, p. 32.

[3] *State Papers Domestic*, 1628–1629, p. 362.

[4] *Parliamentary Papers* (1898), lxxxv. 139.

[5] *Hist. MSS. Comm. Salisbury*, i. 148.

[6] A board of commissioners of the customs was appointed in 1671. The list
of commissioners from 1671–1895 is printed in *Parliamentary Papers* (1898),
lxxxv. Appendix iii. The new system had been adopted under the Commonwealth : *ibid.* 5 ; Hall, *A History of the Custom-Revenue in England*
(ed. 1892), i. 189-190 ; Atton and Holland, *The King's Customs*, i. 102-105.
In 1666 the customs were farmed for £390,000, while in 1671–1688 they
yielded net to the Crown an average of £555,752, but the increase is also
to be accounted for by the growth of trade : Davenant, *Works* (ed. 1771),
i. 370-371. See *infra*, Appendix, p. 505, No. 1.

[7] Petty, *Economic Writings*, i. 301 ; *Hist. MSS. Comm. Cowper*, i. 58.

[8] Massie, *Calculations of Taxes for a Family of each Rank, Degree or
Class for one year* (1756), Nos. 29-30. See *infra*, Appendix, p. 505, No. 2.

| | An Artisan. | | | A Labourer. | | | *Taxes paid by artisans and labourers.* |
|---|---|---|---|---|---|---|---|
| | £ | s. | d. | £ | s. | d. | |
| For Beer . . . | 0 | 6 | 6 | 0 | 4 | 7 | |
| Salt . . . . | 0 | 2 | 6 | 0 | 3 | 4 | |
| Sugar, etc. . . . | 0 | 3 | 0 | 0 | 2 | 0 | |
| Leather . . . | 0 | 1 | 11 | 0 | 2 | 2 | |
| Soap and candles . . | 0 | 3 | 10 | 0 | 1 | 3 | |
| Drugs, tobacco, etc. . | 0 | 5 | 0 | 0 | 2 | 6 | |
| Window tax . . | 0 | 2 | 4 | | (nil.) | | |
| | £1 | 5 | 1 | £0 | 15 | 10 | |

The wages of the artisan were reckoned at 7s. 6d. a week or
£19 : 10s. a year, and those of the labourer at 5s. a week or
£13 a year. Thus in both cases the taxes amounted to 1s. 3d.
in the £, or over 6 per cent. of their annual earnings.

Opinion was sharply divided as to the incidence and *Advocacy
of free
ports.*
effects of the indirect taxes. One view was that they were
'so many taxes upon trade and industry': another that
" all taxes whatsoever are in their last resort a charge upon
land ". Some contended, even as early as 1641, that
" the poor man's food . . . should be free of all charges":
others held that they stimulated the labourer to greater
exertions [1]. It was, however, in relation to the carrying
trade that the taxes levied on imports excited most discussion. For over a century the question was debated whether
imports should be admitted duty-free (or subject to a small
duty), and only pay a tax when taken out of bonded warehouses to be consumed at home. The greatness of Holland was
attributed to the wisdom she showed in ' sparing trade and
taxing home consumption '. The light duties levied upon
imports and exports, by drawing all nations to traffic with
her, made her the world's mart and her people the world's
carriers [2]. " Why may not this kingdom ", it was asked
(1647), " being so well situated, blest with so many fit and
convenient harbours, be made the magazine of Christendom

[1] Robinson, *England's Safety in Trades Encrease* (1641), 9; Petty,
*Economic Writings*, i. 91 *seq.* ; Davenant, *Works* (ed. 1771), i. 77 ; Decker,
*An Essay on the Causes of the Decline of the Foreign Trade* (ed. 1744), 6 *seq.* ;
Tucker, *An Essay on Trade* (ed. 1753), 38, 54, note. *Considerations on Taxes as
they are supposed to affect the Price of Labour* (1765), 6. And see *infra*, p. 277.
[2] Coke, *Treatise* (1671), ii. 122 ; iv. Preface, 115. Davenant, *Works*
(ed. 1771), i. 271.

and how ? " [1]  The answer was—make England a free port, allow foreigners and natives, upon payment of a small duty, to keep magazines of goods ready for transportation to other countries, and the trade of the world would centre here [2]. The contention that the lowering of customs would diminish the revenue [3], was met by Swift's maxim that in the arithmetic of the customs two and two make not four, but often make only one [4]. This meant that an increase of customs may diminish the actual yield in revenue, and conversely a decrease may enlarge it as a result of the growth of trade.

*Smuggling of tea.*  In place of customs duties it was proposed to substitute an excise, in the belief that it would make England ' an universal storehouse ' ; that it would increase the carrying trade, since the free importing and re-exporting of foreign goods ' creates a new trade and by consequence a new navigation ' ; that it would enable the merchant, who ' must always have by him a dead sum to answer the customs ', to manage a more extensive business than when his capital was thus locked up ; and finally, that it would check smuggling [5]. Tea afforded a conspicuous example of the loss of revenue due to smuggling [6]. The right of importing tea was vested in the East India Company, and the heavy duty with which it was burdened encouraged smuggling from France, Holland, Sweden and Denmark, where it was purchased with money and wool. It was computed that twenty thousand people were engaged in smuggling tea, the chief place of resort being Hawkhurst in Kent. They went armed, and the magistrates were intimidated from issuing warrants for their apprehension, and the officers of the customs from doing their duty. When the tea was landed, it was carried by ten or twelve persons in a body on horse-

---

[1] *Hist. MSS. Comm. Portland*, i. 406. Cf. *infra*, Appendix, p. 506, No. 1.
[2] *The Present Interest of England Stated. By a Lover of his Country* (1671), 11 ; *The Linen Drapers' Answer to . . . Mr. Cary his Essay on Trade.*  [3] Brewster, *Essays on Trade and Navigation* (1695), 31.
[4] Quoted in Hume, *Essays : Of the Balance of Trade.*
[5] Coke, *Treatise* (1671), i. 85-86 ; iv. 86. *Britannia Languens* (1680), 62, 118. Davenant, *Works* (ed. 1771), i. 30-31, 271-272. Decker, *An Essay on the Causes of the Decline of the Foreign Trade* (ed. 1744), 10-16, 56-60, 65-91. The proposal for free ports was criticized by Gee, *The Trade and Navigation of Great Britain* (ed. 1730), 111 *seq.*
[6] For wool smuggling : *supra*, pp. 23 *seq.* For tobacco smuggling : Hoon, *The Organization of the English Customs System*, 152 *seq.*, 170, 255, 261-262.

back into the inland counties where there was no danger of seizure. Here it was disposed of at certain markets to people who took a thousand pounds weight at a time. In addition there were men called ' duffers', who went on foot, " and have coats in which they can quilt a quarter of a hundredweight of tea, and bring it to London in that manner undiscovered, and these duffers supply the hawkers, who carry it about the town and sell it to the consumers " [1].

The excise was instituted during the Civil War (1643) *Excises.* when a duty was charged on tobacco, wines, spirits, beer, grocery, soap, paper and other commodities ; and it was maintained as " the most easy and indifferent levy that can be laid upon the people " [2]. Though its adoption is attributed to Dutch influence, the excise was not really new, because the exaction of tolls on things bought and sold at markets and fairs was an ancient practice [3]. None the less it was extremely unpopular with the nation, and in 1647 riots broke out in different parts of the kingdom [4]. After the Restoration the excise was retained on liquors [5] (except wine, which was charged with an additional customs duty), as compensation for the abolition of the revenue derived from feudal incidents. Other excises were added during the war with France after the Revolution [6]. Writers on the subject of taxation expressed conflicting sentiments as regards excises. Davenant held that " excises either directly or indirectly fall upon the whole body of the people " ; whereas Halifax considered that " a general excise upon home commodities is a real land tax ", inasmuch as it was imposed upon the produce of the land [7]. The former opposed ' high' excises in time of peace, on the

---

[1] *House of Commons Journals*, xxv. 101-109, 114. On the smuggling trade, see also *Hist. MSS. Comm. Dartmouth*, iii. 176-178, 214-215.

[2] *Acts and Ordinances of the Interregnum*, i. 202, 274, 466, 806 ; ii. 1186. An excise on cloth was advocated in 1637 : *State Papers Domestic*, Addenda, 1625-1649, p. 555.

[3] The parallel is pointed out in *Britannia Languens* (1680), 295.

[4] *Hist. MSS. Comm. Westmorland*, 492.

[5] Beer, ale, spirits, cider, tea, coffee, chocolate, etc.

[6] Dowell, *A History of Taxation* (ed. 1888), ii. 22-23, 53 *seq.* On the excise, see also Hughes, *Studies in Administration and Finance*, 116 *seq.* ; Kennedy, *English Taxation*, 1640-1799, pp. 51 *seq.*

[7] Davenant, *Works* (ed. 1771), ii. 199, 201 ; Halifax, *An Essay upon Taxes* (1693) in Somers, *Tracts* (ed. 1814), xi. 76-77.

ground that a rise in the cost of living would cause wages to advance. The latter condemned excises on native commodities as injurious to the export trade ; and he pointed out that the Dutch had few commodities of their own to export, " which renders this kind of tax most proper there though very destructive here ".

*Walpole's*
*excise*
*scheme*
In the eighteenth century an attempt was made to utilize the excise as the means of establishing the system of ' free ports '. Walpole in 1733 brought forward his famous excise scheme, which proposed to substitute excises for customs duties on wine and tobacco [1]. He contended that the scheme laid no new tax on the subject, but would facilitate the collection of existing taxes, " which laws were not effectual to collect " owing to the frauds of merchants, who imported ' at light weights ' and re-exported ' at heavy weights ', and to the collusion of customs officers whose meagre salaries increased the temptations of bribery. But a public outcry wrecked Walpole's proposals. " An exciseman ", wrote a correspondent, " has always been a most hateful officer to the inferior people, and should they be multiplied they will look upon them like the plagues of Egypt ". The opposition became so violent and so widespread, extending to the provinces, that Walpole withdrew his scheme amidst popular rejoicings. " They broke all the windows at the Post Office, rung their bells in all the churches, made bonfires, stopped every coach that came by, and made them cry : ' No excise ' " [2]. Although the policy of free ports was not adopted, its advantages were in some degree secured by means of drawbacks, under which the greater part of the duty paid on importation was repaid on re-exportation [3]. The system of drawbacks was

---

[1] He had previously (1723) reduced the duty on tea paid on importation, the full duty being paid only when taken out of the warehouse for home consumption : Dowell, *A History of Taxation* (ed. 1888), ii. 94 ; iv. 221. The younger Pitt carried out Walpole's policy : *ibid.* iv. 129, 257. Walpole also removed the duties on native commodities exported abroad, with certain exceptions : see *supra*, p. 21, note 5.

[2] For a contemporary account, see *Hist. MSS. Comm. Carlisle,* 95, 103-111. Also see *infra*, Appendix, p. 506, No. 2.

[3] James I.'s Book of Rates provided for the repayment of impositions (except on wines) : *The Rates of Marchandizes as they are set downe in the Booke of Rates,* 8-10 (Letters Patents, 8 James I.). After the Restoration

[contd.]

bitterly assailed by native manufacturers, who complained *Draw-*
that they were burdened with duties from which their *backs.*
foreign competitors were ' eased ' [1], but it enabled English
shippers to carry more varied cargoes than if the retention
of the duty on foreign goods, when re-exported, had compelled them to confine their cargoes to native commodities.
In the seventeenth century the fact that " we commonly
carry the product of England " only, had been considered
' one of our mistakes in trade ' [2] ;  and a system of drawbacks was necessary to make England " the emporium, or
warehouse, from whence other nations may be furnished
with foreign commodities of all sorts " [3].  There still remained, however, the officers' fees ' in and out ', and the
interest of the money ' lying dead for duties paid ' (until
' drawn back ') ;  and these were " so great a charge, the
natural interest of money being much higher with us than
in Holland, that the goods cannot come near so cheap from
us to any foreign market as from a free port where nothing
is paid in or out " [4].

The fisheries were universally recognized as one of the *The*
principal supports of a navigation system.  Among the *fisheries.*
causes of Holland's ' wealth and greatness ', contemporaries
singled out for special mention ' fishing on our coast ' and
' trafficking foreign commodities to and fro ' [5].  The Dutch
themselves styled the fishing trade ' the golden mines ' of
their country, which yielded them more treasure than did

---

only one-half was repaid :  *Britannia Languens* (1680), 151 (in sect. vi.),
174 ;  Child, *A New Discourse of Trade* (4th ed.), 184.   But later almost the
whole or greater part of the duty was repaid.   See Appendix, p. 506, No. 3.
    [1] *House of Commons Journals*, xxiv. 817-818 ;  *Britannia Languens*
(1680), 151 (in sect. vi.), 174 ;  *Hist. MSS. Comm. Portland*, v. 452.
    [2] Brewster, *Essays on Trade and Navigation* (1695), 97.
    [3] Robinson, *England's Safety in Trades Encrease* (1641), 20.   The policy
of drawbacks was advocated by Mun, *England's Treasure by Forraign
Trade* (ed. 1664), 30.   For a list of commodities entitled to drawbacks
in the middle of the eighteenth century, see Tucker, *Instructions* (ed.
1757), 33.
    [4] Decker, *An Essay on the Causes of the Decline of the Foreign Trade* (ed.
1744), 10.
    [5] Robinson, *England's Safety in Trades Encrease* (1641), 1 ;  Mun,
*England's Treasure by Forraign Trade* (ed. 1664),185, 188.

'the mines of Potosi or both Indies to Spain'[1]. The number of their fishing boats was estimated by Raleigh in 1618 at three thousand (involving, he computed, the employment of fifty thousand hands) ; and by later writers it was represented to exceed eight thousand, 'however it may seem incredible'[2]. Their activity gave rise to many protests. "From the Hollanders", wrote the secretary of state in 1634, "we suffer most by their intrusion on our fishings and pretence of *mare liberum*"[3]. The complaint was an old one, since in the time of Elizabeth it was asserted that English fishermen were fain to lay up their boats and seek other trades, while the Low Countries were enabled to maintain ships and mariners by fishing on the English coast[4]. The fishing in home waters was considered 'our natural wealth'[5], and the encroachment of strangers took bread out of the subject's mouth, and deprived the nation of "that infinite wealth which God hath made proper and peculiar unto us"[6]. At first the Dutch procured licences to fish but afterwards neglected to do so, although in 1609 commissioners were established at London and Edinburgh for the purpose of issuing licences to strangers[7]. Grotius defended the freedom of the seas ; and in reality he was only asserting a doctrine postulated by the English

[1] *State Papers Domestic*, Addenda, 1625–1649, p. 6 (1625) ; Evelyn, *Navigation and Commerce* (1674), 107, 110 ; Petty, *Economic Writings*, i. 257 ; Puckle, *England's Path to Wealth and Honour* (1700), 3-4.

[2] Raleigh, *Works* (ed. 1829), viii. 370 (the authorship of the *Observations* attributed to Raleigh is doubtful) ; *Hist. MSS. Comm. Cowper*, iii. 146-147 ; Coke, *Treatise*, iv. (1675), Preface, 87 ; De Witt, *The True Interest of Holland* (ed. 1746), 24.

Tobias Gentleman, *England's Way to Win Wealth* (1614), 14, wrote : "There have been seen and numbered . . . in sight at one time two thousand sails, besides them that were at sea without sight, which could not be numbered." The principal fleet was a thousand strong : *ibid.* 10-11. Later Evelyn declared that "more than 7000 [vessels] are yearly employed" in the fisheries : *Navigation and Commerce* (1674), 107.

[3] *State Papers Domestic*, 1634–1635, p. 69. Cf. *infra*, p. 507, No. 1.

[4] *State Papers Foreign*, 1564–1565, p. 528 ; *Hist. MSS. Comm. Rye*, 18 (1572).

[5] Mun, *England's Treasure by Forraign Trade* (ed. 1664), 22.

[6] Misselden, *Free Trade* (1622), 35 ; *Britannia Languens* (1680), 168.

[7] ΙΧΘΥΟΘΗΡΑ, or *The Royal Trade of Fishing* (1662), 30 ; Evelyn, *Navigation and Commerce* (1674), 113.

Government itself in 1602, when it instructed the ambassadors treating with Denmark to declare that " the Law of Nations alloweth of fishing in the sea everywhere " [1].

Repeated remonstrances were evoked by England's *Dutch fishing.* neglect to take advantage of ' a continual sea-harvest of gain and benefit ', which the bounty of Heaven had cast at our doors, "and we never yet stooped to take it up " [2]. The Dutch not only carried the herrings to all parts, but " to the ignominy and shame of our English nation " they " do vent our herrings amongst us here in England, and make us pay for the fish taken upon our own coast ready money "— half the fish sent to London being supplied by their vessels [3]. The reasons were widely canvassed why " the Dutch in numerous fleets for four months in the year follow the herring from Scotland to Yarmouth, whilst the wretched people upon our coast stand starving and looking on ", and why " even in the herring-fishing before Yarmouth we fish little above one fortnight, and in that fishing the Dutch employ above threefold the vessels we do and above two-fold the mariners " [4]. The question was a pressing one owing to the importance attached to the fisheries as a school for seamanship and the nursery of the navy [5], apart from the employment which they also gave to those engaged in building vessels, making nets, and curing fish. One explanation was that the Dutch busses, or fishing boats, were " great and strong and able to brook foul weather ", but " our cobbles, crayers and boats being small and thin-sided [were] easily swallowed by a rough sea " [6]. An English boat of equal dimensions with a Dutch boat cost 50 per cent. more to build, and was so heavy that it required one-third more sails and cordage, and more hands to manage it ; while the use of foreign timber and naval necessaries

---

[1] Rymer, *Foedera*, xvi. 433.
[2] Boroughs, *The Sovereignty of the British Seas* (ed. 1920), 94 (written in 1633) ; *Hist. MSS. Comm. Cowper*, iii. 146.
[3] According to *Hist. MSS. Comm. Rutland*, i. 470 (? 1623) ; Boroughs, *The Sovereignty of the British Seas* (ed. 1920), 102 ; Jenner, *London's Blame, if not its Shame* (1651), 9.
[4] Coke, *Treatise* (1675), iv. 87.
[5] *Statutes*, iv. part ii. 1058 (1604).
[6] Jenner, *London's Blame, if not its Shame* (1651), 11.

was discouraged by the Navigation Acts[1]. It was also represented that the Dutch had greater skill in cutting, packing and salting the fish ; and that the fish paid no freight when exported abroad, because it was carried in vessels which brought back corn and salt, and would otherwise have gone out empty[2].

*Efforts to encourage the fishing trade.*

Proposals for the encouragement of the fishing trade were pressed insistently upon the nation, accompanied by elaborate calculations of the anticipated profits. Robert Hitchcock in 1580 published his *Politic Plat*[3] under which a national loan was to be raised to build a herring fleet, and he quoted the remark of the Speaker of the House of Commons : " A Parliament hath been called for a less cause". Others recommended a joint-stock company[4] ; but though London capitalists paid lip-service to the project as " the most profitable work that could be devised ", they were reported to " despair of raising the money necessary ", being " engaged in other adventures "[5]. At length in 1632 the Society of the Fishery of Great Britain and Ireland was set up, the ' adventurers ' or shareholders including the lord treasurer[6]. Within two years the company had lost its capital and become deeply indebted. The failure of the enterprise was attributed to the mismanagement of the factory established at the Isle of Lewis, where the company bought land and erected houses for curing and packing their herrings, but ' the herrings failed to come '[7]. After

---

[1] Coke, *Treatise*, iv. (1675), 82, 99-100 ; Coke, *A Detection of the Court and State of England* (ed. 1718), ii. 59-60 ; ΙΧΘΥΟΘΗΡΑ, or *The Royal Trade of Fishing* (1662), 21. See also *supra*, pp. 131-132.

[2] According to Malynes, *Consuetudo vel Lex Mercatoria* (1622), 243-244. It was also alleged that English fishermen lacked enterprise and perseverance, preferring to live from hand to mouth : Keymor, *Observation made upon the Dutch Fishing about the year 1601* in *The Phenix* (ed. 1707), i. 229.

[3] Reprinted in *An English Garner* (ed. Lang.), 71, 93.

[4] E. S., *Britain's Buss* (1615), in *An English Garner* (ed. Lang), 306-307.

[5] *State Papers Domestic*, 1619-1623, pp. 517, 541. According to Malynes the trading companies opposed it, fearing that it would injure their trade abroad : *The Maintenance of Free Trade* (1622), 42.

[6] *State Papers Domestic*, 1631-1633, pp. 384, 510. A proposal for a ' corporation ' for the sale of fish was mooted in 1629, and a commission of inquiry was appointed in 1630 : *Hist. MSS. Comm. Ancaster*, 403-404 ; Rymer, *Foedera*, xix. 212.

[7] *State Papers Domestic*, 1639-1640, p. 440 ; Smith, *A True Narration of the Royall Fishings of Great Britain and Ireland* (1641). See also Elder, *The Royal Fishery Companies of the Seventeenth Century*, 54 *seq*.

the Restoration (1661) the King appointed a 'Council of the Royal Fishing of Great Britain and Ireland' to raise money by a lottery and by collections in churches; and three years later (1664) a company was erected with James Duke of York as governor [1]. Another company was set up in 1677, but during the war between France and Holland its vessels were seized by the French on the plea that they were Dutch-built and manned [2]. None of the companies owned the resources to withstand such reverses, and individual fishermen were discouraged by the attacks made upon them at sea [3]. In short the Dutch proved too strongly entrenched: they were able to crush potential rivals by selling the fish at a loss [4]: and before the seventeenth century was ended the conclusion had been reached, that the successful prosecution of the fishing trade could only be undertaken by the State [5]. In the eighteenth century another company, The Society of the Free British Fishery, was incorporated as late as 1750 [6]. The high hopes, with which its promoters embarked upon the undertaking, were satirized by Oliver Goldsmith in his essay, *On the Instability of Worldly Grandeur* (1759): " A few years ago the herring-fishery employed all Grub Street; it was the topic in every coffee-house and the burden of every ballad. We were to drag up oceans of gold from the bottom of the sea; we were to supply all Europe with herrings upon our own terms. At present we hear no more of this. We have fished up very little gold that I can learn; nor do we furnish the world with herrings as was expected. Let us wait but a few years longer, and we shall find all our expectations a herring-fishery "[7].

---

[1] ΙΧΘΥΟΘΗΡΑ, or *The Royal Trade of Fishing* (1662), 1 seq.; *State Papers Domestic*, 1663–1664, p. 549. The charter is printed in Carr, *Select Charters of Trading Companies*, 182.

[2] Carr, *Select Charters of Trading Companies*, 196; Collins, *Salt and Fishery* (1682), Epistle; Somers, *Tracts* (ed. 1814), xii. 37.

[3] *State Papers Domestic*, 1639–1640, pp. 440-441; see *The Petty Navy Royal* in *An English Garner* (ed. Lang), 49.

[4] *State Papers Domestic*, 1675–1676, p. 76.

[5] J. B., *An Account of the French Usurpation upon the Trade of England* (1679), 13. [6] *Statutes at Large*, vi. 474.

[7] Quoted in Samuel, *The Herring*, 132. See also DuBois, *The English Business Company after the Bubble Act*, 127 seq.

English enterprise might have contested more resolutely Dutch supremacy in the North Sea fisheries, had not English capital been largely diverted into other channels, in particular the woollen industry, coal-mining, and the Indian and Levant trades. None the less the fisheries were not entirely neglected. To begin with, England retained the red-herring trade partly because the fish had to be brought fresh on shore, which the Dutch were unable to do since their coast was too remote, and partly because the fish was smoked with wood which in this country was plentiful [1]. " No clothing comparable to the English bay, nor pheasant excelling a seasonable English red herring ", was the verdict of Spaniards in the seventeenth century [2]. In addition, the Newfoundland fisheries at the end of the seventeenth century employed about 140 ships and 5000 men [3]. Lastly, there was the Greenland whale - fishing which pursued a chequered career. Queen Elizabeth conceded the sole right of whale-fishing to the Russia Company in 1577 for the space of twenty years, and it was renewed by James I. in 1614 [4]. The Russia Company disposed of its privileges in 1620 to a group of its own members, who composed the Greenland Company [5]. The latter's monopoly was contested by the Dutch who sent armed vessels, and by Hull which claimed to have been the first in the field. Under the Commonwealth the Company was confirmed in its monopoly of the fishing from Bell Sound to Horn Sound, in spite of the arguments of its adversaries that it contained only

[1] Child, *A New Discourse of Trade* (4th ed.), pp. xxvi-xxvii. For the Yarmouth trade, see Tobias Gentleman, *England's Way to Win Wealth* (1614), 26 *seq.*

[2] Roberts, *The Merchants Mappe of Commerce* (1638), 258. The herring was styled the ' king of fish ' : Robinson, *England's Safety in Trades Encrease* (1641), 16.

[3] *House of Commons Journals*, xi. 681 (1697) ; *Statutes*, vii. 515. The French and Dutch repaired to Cornish ports to buy Newfoundland fish : *State Papers Domestic*, 1633–1634, pp. 318–319 ; 1625–1649, p. 543. *Hist. MSS. Comm. Salisbury*, vii. 385. On French competition at Newfoundland, see Coke, *A Detection of the Court and State of England* (ed. 1718), ii. 58-59.

[4] *Tudor and Stuart Proclamations* (ed. Steele), i. No. 1149 ; *State Papers Domestic*, Addenda, 1625–1649, p. 92 ; Carr, *Select Charters of Trading Companies*, 28.

[5] *State Papers East Indies*, 1617–1621, p. 346; Scott, *Joint - Stock Companies*, ii. 58, 69.

fifty-five members, that it provided scarcely more than *Whale-* half of the shipping, that it advanced prices, and that it *fishing.* failed to furnish sufficient supplies of oil and fins, thus forcing the country to import from Holland[1]. The Company, however, was unable to prevail against the Dutch. When the whales resorted to the bays near the shore the English, occupying the best bays, held the advantage; but when the whales kept further from the land, amidst the ice, the enterprise became more perilous and the Company grew discouraged[2]. During the Great Rebellion the men engaged in the whale-fishery were employed in the war, and in the second half of the seventeenth century the Greenland trade was counted by Child among the lost trades. In 1673 it was therefore thrown open, and at the same time the Navigation Acts were relaxed " in regard there are at present great want of harpiniers and seamen skilled and exercised in the trade of whale-fishing "—only one-half of the men, instead of three-fourths, now being required to be English[3]. Although some expeditions were sent out to Greenland, the concessions which had been made by Parliament failed to revive the trade, and after the Revolution another joint-stock company was incorporated (1693) to carry on the whale-fisheries[4]. This fared no better, and in 1702 the trade was again thrown open[5]. The South Sea Company attempted to revive the trade but its ventures proved unfortunate[6].

[1] *Acts of the Privy Council, 1618–1619,* pp. 2, 49, *Tudor and Stuart Proclamations* (ed. Steele), i. No. 3089 (1658) ; *State Papers Domestic,* 1653–1654, pp. 362, 377–379, 419–421.
[2] Macpherson, *Annals of Commerce,* ii. 287. For a description of whale-fishery, see *House of Commons Journals,* xxv. 829.
[3] *Statutes,* v. 792 ; Child, *A New Discourse of Trade* (4th ed.), Preface ; *House of Commons Journals,* xxv. 829.
[4] *Statutes,* vi. 405 *seq.* (' The Company of Merchants of London trading to Greenland ').
[5] *Ibid.* vii. 151 ; viii. 50. *House of Commons Journals,* x. 773.
[6] *House of Commons Journals,* xxv. 829 ; Macpherson, *Annals of Commerce,* iii. 130, 178-179.

(IV)

### THE OLD COLONIAL SYSTEM

*Conception of a self-supporting empire.*   In harmony with the fundamental principles of Mercan-tilism, there gradually developed the conception of a self-supporting empire. The resources of England were in-adequate to supply her with the raw materials required in certain industries, such as shipbuilding, and her depend-ence upon alien sources infringed the cardinal maxim of the Mercantile System. The foundation of colonies pro-vided the means by which foreign commodities could become ' native ' to this country [1] : it opened up the vision of an empire knit together by economic ties, in which each part sustained and nourished the whole, and the mother country and the colonies were made complementary to one another. From this standpoint colonial legislation must be treated, not as a mosaic of disjointed fragments, but as the expression of co-ordinated lines of policy. There is a tendency to look upon colonial policy as purely opportunist ; and it may be admitted that particular measures were often dictated by political or fiscal exigencies. This, however, is what we should expect. In the working out of a comprehensive system which extended over many decades, the circum-stances of the moment would naturally throw into sharper relief the expediency of stressing one or other of its varied aspects ; but this does not disprove the hypothesis that the main features of colonial legislation can be related to a policy explicitly enunciated and consciously pursued. The following quotations will show that the broad concep-tion of imperial economic relationships was firmly enter-tained, though its application in detail was determined by general considerations of national policy. At the Re-storation the legislature announced the intention of the mother country to make the colonies " yet more beneficial and advantageous unto it, in the further employment and increase of English shipping and seamen, [and] vent of

---

[1] Thomas, *An Historical Account of the Rise and Growth of the West-India Colonies* (1690), in *Harleian Miscellany* (ed. Malham), ix. 426.

English woollen and other manufactures " [1]. Fortrey, whose book issued in 1663 attracted wide attention, defined the purpose of plantations to " increase the wealth and trade of this nation, either in furnishing us with what we are otherwise forced to purchase from strangers, or else by increasing such commodities as are vendible abroad " [2]. After the Revolution the newly-appointed Commissioners for Trade and Plantations were instructed to inquire how colonies might be rendered most beneficial, and they reported that " it was the intent in settling our plantations in America, that the people there should be only employed in such things as are not the product of England to which they belong, except for so much as should be wanting for their own sustenance and supply of provisions to their neighbours " [3]. And Cary summed up the whole situation in the words : " I take this kingdom and all its plantations to be one great body " [4].

There was a consensus of opinion that the colonies *Benefit* existed to serve as ' an inexhaustible mine of treasure ' to *of the colonies* their mother country in consuming its manufactures, and *to the* producing commodities which would prevent the drain of *mother country.* money abroad to purchase foreign wares, or by their sale outside the realm bring back money from foreign parts [5]. Nor did these expectations prove illusory. It was estimated that before England had any sugar plantations of her own she paid Portugal a great sum per annum for sugar [6], whereas now she not only supplied her own wants but exported large quantities abroad. Similarly, Virginian tobacco furnished both the home and foreign markets. In addition the price of sugar was said in 1690 to have fallen by two-thirds, and that of tobacco by six-sevenths [7]. In other directions the

[1] *Statutes*, v. 449 (1663).
[2] Fortrey, *England's Interest and Improvement* (1663), 39.
[3] *House of Commons Journals*, xii. 427 (1699) ; xiii. 298.
[4] Cary, *An Essay towards Regulating the Trade* (ed. 1719), 48.
[5] Davenant, *Works* (ed. 1771), i. 106 ; Thomas in *Harleian Miscellany*, (ed. Malham), ix. 426 (1690).
[6] £400,000 is the estimate mentioned in *The Groans of the Plantations* (1689), 33, and in *The Case of His Majesty's Sugar Plantations* (Somers, *Tracts*, ed. 1812, vol. viii. 480), but the estimates of pamphleteers are not reliable.
[7] Thomas, *op. cit.* 412, 425 (1690). Tobacco fell from 4s. or more to 7d. per pound.

colonies proved a source of profit to the mother country. Occupying the ' northern, cold and barren parts ' of America, they " brought them " within a century " to be the richest, the most improved and the most flourishing ", in marked contrast with the Spanish possessions, at whose door ' the sin of diligence ' could not be laid [1]. Already at the Restoration the Commissioners of the Customs reported that " the plantations are his majesty's Indies, without charge to him raised and supported by the English subjects, who employ above two hundred sail of good ships every year, breed abundance of mariners, and begin to grow into commodities of great value and esteem ", one of which (tobacco) " pays more custom to his majesty than the East Indies four times over " [2]. At the end of the seventeenth century the colonies were considered ' a main branch ' of England's wealth [3] : their growing population provided an expanding market for our manufactures : the duties on their exported produce were, at any rate at first, a source of revenue [4] : and the carrying trade was computed to maintain one-half or two-thirds of English shipping ' in a safe and healthy navigation ' [5]. The available statistics confirm the evidence of contemporaries. The population of the colonies was estimated at 300,000 in 1698, and at two and a half millions on the eve of the American War of Independence [6]. At the former period colonial exports to England, as entered in the custom-house books, were officially valued at £871,832, and colonial imports from England at £786,854 [7] : the corresponding figures for 1774

---

[1] Defoe, *A Plan of the English Commerce* (ed. 1728), 303-306.

[2] 1661 : *Acts of the Privy Council*, Colonial Series, 1613–1680, pp.319-320.

[3] Davenant, *Works* (ed. 1771), i. 397. Similarly : Wood, *A Survey of Trade* (1718), 135.

[4] *Supra*, p. 142, note 1. Thomas in 1690 stated that the price of tobacco was 7d. per lb. to the merchant, out of which " the King has 5d." : *Harleian Miscellany* (ed. Malham), ix. 425. See *infra*, p. 507, No. 2.

[5] Child, *A New Discourse of Trade* (4th ed.), 203 ; Thomas, *op. cit.* 431 ; *The Case of His Majesty's Sugar Plantations* in Somers, *Tracts* (ed. 1812), viii. 481 ; *The Groans of the Plantations* (1689), 26. See also *House of Commons Journals*, xii. 433 ; *Considerations on the Propriety of imposing Taxes in the British Colonies* (1766), 80.

[6] Davenant, *Works* (ed. 1771), ii. 22; *Hist. MSS. Comm. Various*, vi. 290.

[7] Mich. 1697–Mich. 1698: *House of Lords MSS.* 1699–1702, pp. 432-434 (including Newfoundland). Real values were higher.

were £5,020,963 and £4,444,443 [1]. Expressed in the form of percentages—the colonies accounted for 15 per cent. of the oversea trade of the mother country in 1698, and for 33 per cent. in 1774 [2].

The public estimation of the value of a colony was *Types of* measured by the degree of pliability with which it fitted *colonies.* itself into the scheme, whereby the American settlements were required to supplement the resources of the mother country. A distinction was accordingly drawn between two groups of colonies [3]. The first, comprising Virginia, Maryland, Barbados and Jamaica, among the rest, produced commodities such as tobacco, sugar, cotton, cocoa, ginger and dyeing woods ; and they took from us clothing, household furniture and provisions. The second, more particularly New England—stigmatized by Child as ' the most prejudicial plantation to this kingdom ' [4]—raised corn and cattle, together with a few masts, furs and train-oil, of which the annual value was small. " By tillage, pasture, fishing, manufactures and trade ", said a writer in 1690 [5], " they to all intents and purposes imitate Old England. . . . If any, such only should be neglected and discouraged who pursue a method that rivals our native kingdom, and threatens, in time, a total independency thereupon ". Moreover it entered into competition with the mother country in the carrying trade, and in supplying provisions to the West India Islands [6]. Yet even this group absorbed large quantities of English manufactured goods, so that it satisfied at least one canon of the old colonial system in

[1] Christmas 1773–Christmas 1774 : Macpherson, *Annals of Commerce*, iii. 564. These totals do not include colonial trade with Scotland and other countries.

[2] For the total trade in 1698 : *House of Lords MSS.* 1699–1702, p. 435. For 1774 : Macpherson, *Annals of Commerce*, iii. 564. On the statistics of American colonial commerce, see Johnson, *History of Domestic and Foreign Commerce of the United States* (ed. 1922), 112 *seq.*

[3] *House of Commons Journals*, xii. 433 ; Child, *A New Discourse of Trade* (4th ed.), 230-231 ; Davenant, *Works* (ed. 1771), ii. 21, 25 ; Wood, *A Survey of Trade* (1718), 142-143 ; Gee, *The Trade and Navigation of Great Britain* (ed. 1730), 20 *seq.*

[4] Child, *A New Discourse of Trade* (4th ed.), 229 (but cf. p. 233).

[5] Thomas in *Harleian Miscellany* (ed. Malham), ix. 432.

[6] On the trade between New England and the island plantations, see Harlow, *A History of Barbados*, 268 *seq.*

providing a market for the products of the parent state ;
while the mutual dependence of the two groups, the one
furnishing the other with provisions and so enabling it to
raise commodities for a European market, gave almost equal
importance to both [1].  New England also carried on a trade
in timber with Spain and Portugal, thus invading the monopoly of the Baltic lands, and she could therefore claim a
place among the colonies ' profitable ' to the mother country [2].
After the middle of the eighteenth century a change becomes
apparent in the relative position of the different colonies.
Our exports to the continental colonies grew rapidly, while
those to the West Indies appeared in comparison almost
stationary [3];  and among the continental colonies it is
noteworthy that in some years the exports to New England
even exceeded those to the tobacco plantations of Virginia
and Maryland [4].  The change had a momentous consequence
since the discussion over the retention of Canada instead of
the French West Indies, after the Seven Years' War, turned
on the question whether colonies were more important as
sources of supply or as markets for English manufactures [5].

*The
'colonial
pact'.*        The economic system, on which the British Empire was
based for two centuries, must be interpreted in the light
of the services which England rendered to her oversea dependencies.  The mother country furnished the colonies
with their first settlers :  she found the capital for their
development :  she ensured them a protected market for
their produce :  she safeguarded their trade-routes :  and she
defended them from hostile attacks.  In return for these services she laid down regulations, designed to repay her for the
benefits she conferred.  These regulations were often selfish
and even ungenerous :  they were nearly always unwise and

[1] This was recognized by Davenant : *Works* (ed. 1771), ii. 24.  Also
by Wood, *A Survey of Trade* (1718), 145.
[2] Gee, *The Trade and Navigation of Great Britain* (ed. 1730), 104-105.
[3] *The Interest of Great Britain Considered with regard to her Colonies*
(1760), in Macpherson, *Annals of Commerce*, iii. 317.
[4] 1754 and subsequent years : Whitworth, *State of the Trade of Great
Britain* (1776), part 1. 58 *seq.*
[5] For this discussion, see Beer, *British Colonial Policy, 1754–1765*,
chapter viii.

inexpedient : but it may be fairly debated whether the colonies, in spite of the subordination of their economic interests to the welfare of the motherland, did not receive from the ' colonial pact ' more than they were asked to concede.

The principal argument in defence of the old colonial *Emigrants* system was that the population of the colonies was largely *included :* drawn from the mother country. The stream of emigrants, (i.) *Religi-* *ous re-* which flowed from England in the seventeenth century, *fugees.* comprised three main categories. Some went, as William Penn wrote, " to enjoy their consciences more quietly, others out of necessity, and lastly, some involuntarily as being delinquents " [1]. The first category, composed of religious dissidents, was actuated by the desire ' to be free of the Church's power and out of her reach ' [2]. The movement had already set in by the end of the sixteenth century, when the Privy Council gave permission for ' sectaries ' to settle in Canada [3] ; and early in the next century a great number of Puritans including the Pilgrim Fathers, ' disliking many things in practice here in respect of Church ceremony ', settled in New England [4]. The efforts of Archbishop Laud to enforce conformity with the ritual of the Established Church upon the children of Protestant refugees, who came here in the reign of Elizabeth, caused an exodus from Norwich to New England, and the number of emigrants is said to have exceeded two thousand [5]. It was reported in 1634 that six hundred persons intended to sail from Ipswich [6], and instructions were issued by the commissioners for the plantations to check ' such promiscuous and disorderly departing ', and allow no one to leave the kingdom without permission, and only after attestation that he conformed to the discipline of the Church of England [7]. At a later period " many of the military saints

[1] *Hist. MSS. Comm. Portland*, iv. 79 (1704).
[2] *Ibid.* 80.
[3] *Acts of the Privy Council*, 1597, p. 6.
[4] *State Papers Colonial*, 1574–1660, p. 157.
[5] In 1636 : Moens, *The Walloons and their Church at Norwich*, 93-94.
[6] *State Papers Domestic*, 1633-1634, p. 450.
[7] 1634 : *Hist. MSS. Comm. Rye*, 195-196. In 1637 a proclamation was issued : *Tudor and Stuart Proclamations* (ed. Steele), i. No. 1745.

at his majesty's restoration (flying thither richly laden
with the plunder of Old England) carried over great riches ;
so as now New England is become a bank of money and a
magazine of men and arms, and can effectually arm and
maintain sixty thousand stout men well disciplined " [1].
Besides New England, the religious factor was conspicuous
in the foundation of Maryland and Pennsylvania.

(ii.) *Paupers and debtors.* The second category of emigrants had its origin in destitution or the hope of economic advancement.  The settle-
ment of paupers in the colonies appeared the most promising
solution of a social problem, with which the existing machinery of poor relief was inadequate to cope.  In 1618, for
example, it was reported that London intended to ship to
Virginia a hundred young boys and girls, who lay starving in
the streets, at an estimated charge of five hundred pounds [2].
At different times the City entered into contracts with the
Virginia Company for the transportation of poor children,
the cost being shared between them [3].  The proposal was
even mooted that every parish should raise a fund to assist
the emigration of vagrant children, who were suffered " to
run idly up and down, in breaking of hedges, gathering of
wool, pelting of sheep, and in harvest-time gleaning and
filching of corn, and such other lewd or worse course, seeking
also their meat from house to house ".  Its author calculated " the charge for furnishing forth each child, the
voyage and maintenance for each child until its labour
becomes profitable . . . at not less than ten pounds " [4].
Another suggestion was to send to the colonies people in
general who were ' burthensome '—" but send them in
time ;  don't let them run the gauntlet through all the
gaols in the kingdom " [5].  Apart from paupers, debtors

---

[1] ·*Hist. MSS. Comm. Pepys*, 270 (undated).  The number is exaggerated.
According to one statement the ' standing militia ' consisted of 10,000 foot
and 1000 horse ;  " they can on occasion raise 20,000 more."  Other
estimates give smaller figures : *State Papers America and West Indies*,
1675–1676, pp. 220, 408, 465.
[2] *State Papers Colonial*, 1574–1660, p. 19 ; *Acts of the Privy Council*,
1619–1621, p. 118.
[3] Beer, *The Origins of the British Colonial System*, 47-48.  See also
Brown, *The Genesis of the United States*, i. 252 *seq.*
[4] *Hist. MSS. Comm. Beaufort*, 134-135 (*temp.* James I.).
[5] *Miscellaneous Reflections upon the Peace and its Consequences* (1749),
59-60 ; Gee, *The Trade and Navigation of Great Britain* (ed. 1730), 58 *seq.*

found in emigration the means of escaping their liabilities :
" If money is named, immediately they threaten us with
going off straight to New England, and in reality away they
go " [1].

The third category of emigrants consisted of Irish and (iii.) *Pris-*
Scottish prisoners of war transported under the Common- *oners of war
and de-*
wealth [2], Quakers [3], and delinquents.   Offenders were trans- *linquents.*
ported overseas as early as 1617 [4].   The Law of Settlement
(1662) empowered justices of the peace, with the leave of
the Privy Council, to sentence ' disorderly persons and
sturdy beggars ' to transportation for a period not exceeding
seven years [5] ;  in 1671 it was provided that offenders in
certain cases could elect to be transported to one of the
plantations for seven years [6] ;  under the Habeas Corpus Act
persons convicted of felony might pray to be transported [6a] ;
and in 1718 it became legal to sentence offenders to
transportation [6b].   " They strive at the sessions-house ", said
Yarranton, " for persons to carry to Barbados or Virginia " [7].

Two other elements in the colonial population were (iv.) *Fish-*
fishermen and aliens.   The masters of ships engaged in *ermen and
aliens.*
the Newfoundland fishery were represented as " very
negligent in bringing their men home, whereby they save
the charge of their passage ;  and those men, so left, are
enticed " by expectation of great wages " and carried to
New England " [8].   Again, in the reign of James I. certain
aliens, including Walloons and Frenchmen, agreed to settle

[1] *Hist. MSS. Comm. Various*, viii. 400 (1729).   For earlier complaints :
*State Papers Domestic*, 1633–1634, p. 450.
[2] *State Papers Domestic*, 1649–1650, p. 95 ;  1650, p. 346.
[3] *Hertford County Records*, i. 166 ;  Child, *A New Discourse of Trade*
(4th ed.), 199.                    [4] See *infra*, Appendix, p. 507, No. 3.
[5] *Statutes*, v. 402.   For examples, see *Hist. MSS. Various*,
i. 145, 147 ;  *Middlesex County Records*, iii. 334.   For the Law of Settlement : *infra*, p. 457.          [6] *Statutes*, v. 709.          [6a] *Statutes*, v. 937.
[6b] *Statutes at Large*, v. 113.   On the later history of transportation to
the colonies, see *The Law Quarterly Review*, vi. 401 *seq*.
[7] Yarranton, *England's Improvement* (1677), 173.   William Penn
declared that Virginia ' especially ' had been " frequented by the necessitous and much stocked with criminals " :  *Hist. MSS. Comm. Portland*,
iv. 79.   Actually there were many settlers of social standing, ' sprung
directly from the squirearchy of the mother country ' :  Bruce, *Social Life
of Virginia in the Seventeenth Century*, 23 *seq*.   Cf. Bruce, *Economic History
of Virginia in the Seventeenth Century*, i. 597-607, where the transportation
of condemned persons to Virginia is considered exceptional in the early
seventeenth century, but more frequent in ' the first years following
the Restoration '.   See also Channing, *A History of the United States*,
i. 239.
[8] *House of Commons Journals*, xiii. 725.

in Virginia [1]; and later the Huguenots, driven from their country by persecution, were encouraged by the English Government to transport themselves " at great hazard and expense ", as their petition of 1696 relates, " into England and America, where they have improved the English colonies by trade and great labour, and especially Carolina and New York which are chiefly inhabited by French Protestants " [2]. One writer (1662) recommended that foreigners should be encouraged to settle in the plantations, since " we only (or generally) send thither the very rubbish and off-scouring of his majesty's dominions; persons for the most part bred up to nothing but idleness and all manner of vice " [3]. In ordinary circumstances emigration was not attractive to Englishmen, owing to the length and discomforts of the voyage [4], the strange and hostile environment in America, and the servitude imposed on those who lacked independent means as the price of their transportation [5]. After the Civil War many of ' the worsted party ' betook themselves to the plantations, while the change of government at the Restoration occasioned another exodus [6], but in the eighteenth century it was said that " there are few in England, who have tolerable bread, who would hire themselves to go to America " [7].

Unscrupulous methods were sometimes practised in order to obtain recruits for the colonies. Information was sent to the Privy Council in 1618 by a magistrate in Somersetshire that a " messenger of the chamber had pretended a commission to press maidens to be sent to the Bermudas and Virginia ". His proceedings bred " such terror to the

[1] *State Papers Colonial*, 1574–1660, p. 498 ; *Documents relative to the Colonial History of the State of New York*, iii. 9 (also *ibid.* v. 52-54).

[2] *House of Commons Journals*, xi. 491.

[3] *Short Notes and Observations drawn from the present decaying condition of this Kingdom in point of Trade* (1662), 9. Bacon had complained of this in his *Essay : Of Plantations*.

[4] A ' speedy journey ' to New England in 1638 occupied ' seven weeks and odd days ' : *Hist. MSS. Comm. Kenyon*, 56. See also *infra*, p. 197, note 1.

[5] Bruce, *Economic History of Virginia in the Seventeenth Century*, i. 631 ; Weeden, *Economic and Social History of New England*, i. 84.

[6] Child, *A New Discourse of Trade* (4th ed.), 198-199.

[7] *Hist. MSS. Comm. Shrewsbury*, 92 (*c.* 1750).

poor maidens that forty have fled from one parish to obscure
places, and their parents do not know what has become of
them " [1]. An ordinance issued during the Civil War made
it lawful, in view of the ' great want of servants ' in the
plantations, for any one to transport thither persons willing
to serve there, provided that their names were registered
in the custom-house, that no force was used, and that
apprentices were not enticed to desert their masters, nor
children under age admitted without their parents' consent [2]. As a result evil notoriety was earned by a class of
men, known as ' spirits ', who used to decoy persons away
from their friends by ' romantic promises ', carry them to
the plantations, and there sell them against their will ' for
their passages ' for three to seven years, during which period
they were ' to all intents and purposes slaves ' [3]. After
the Restoration the mayor of Bristol petitioned the King
for power to examine all shipowners and servants or passen-
gers on ships going to the plantations, to ascertain if they
went of their own free will, and to keep a register of them
" to avoid the abuse of husbands or wives running away
from each other, children being spirited away, apprentices,
rogues, etc. escaping in that way " [4]. The merchants, on
their part, complained that " evil-minded people take the
opportunity of the general belief of the wicked custom of
spiriting away servants for the plantations to embark
voluntarily, receiving money, clothes, etc.", and then at
" some port profess to be carried off without their consent " [5].
In other cases ' societies of ill men ' professed to procure
servants for the plantations, who were sworn before a justice
of the peace that they were not married nor in service, and
that they had bound themselves as servants at ' the Plantation Office ' : " yet afterwards the merchants and masters

---

[1] *State Papers Colonial*, 1574–1660, p. 19.
[2] 1647 : *Acts and Ordinances of the Interregnum*, i. 912.
[3] *State Papers Domestic*, 1638–1639, p. 271 ; Chappel, *A Diamond or Rich Jewel, Presented to the Commonwealth* (1650), 16 ; *Hist. MSS. Comm. Stopford-Sackville*, ii. 19 (1775). For examples of spiriting, see *State Papers Domestic*, 1664–1665, p. 140 ; *Middlesex County Records*, iii. 239, 326, 331 ; iv. 276.
[4] *State Papers Domestic*, 1661–1662, p. 441. See *infra*, Appendix, p. 508, No. 1.
[5] *State Papers Domestic*, 1663–1664, p. 639. See *infra*, Appendix, p. 508, No. 2.

of vessels have been often prosecuted " as kidnappers,
" though it is absolutely necessary that the plantations
should be supplied with servants and workmen—there are
so many tricks and troublesome suits that merchants cannot
safely agree for them " [1]. The passage of a servant cost
five pounds or more, while clothes and other necessaries
involved about the same amount : " their time may not
be above five years, and is commonly but four " [2].

*The popu-*
*lation prob-*
*lem in*
*England.*
The public attitude towards emigration had a decisive
influence in shaping the policy of the mother country towards
the colonies. Down to the Restoration it was generally believed that England was over-populated. Confronted with
the social problems created by enclosures and other economic
changes of the sixteenth century, Elizabethan writers enumerated among the ' benefits ' of plantations the emigration of
those " which do now live idly at home, and are burthenous,
chargeable and unprofitable to this realm " [3]. Under James
I. it was again repeated that " there is an overplus of
people " [4] ; and Fuller in 1642, alluding to the depopulation
produced by enclosures, exclaimed : " Long since had this
land been sick of a pleurisy of people, if not let blood in their
Western plantations " [5]. After the Restoration, under the
influence of expanding trade, there was a complete change of
sentiment. The conviction became widespread that England
was under-populated [6]. " There is nothing so much wanting
in England as people ", said the author of *The Grand Concern
of England Explained* (1673). " The two last great plagues,
the civil wars at home, and the several wars with Holland,

---

[1] *House of Commons Journals*, xiii. 653, 814 (1702).
[2] *The Groans of the Plantations* (1689), 17. When the emigrants had
to be equipped with tools, etc., the cost was increased. The total expenditure on each settler would then be about £20 : see Beer, *The Origins of
the British Colonial System*, 49-51. Also see Bruce, *Economic History of
Virginia in the Seventeenth Century*, i. 629 *seq.*
[3] Hakluyt, *The Principal Navigations* (ed. 1904), viii. 112.
[4] *Hist. MSS. Comm. Beaulieu*, 109 ; *ibid. Exeter*, 167.
[5] Fuller, *The Holy State* (ed. 1642), 101. The remark is repeated in
*Considerations concerning Common Fields and Inclosures. By Pseudomisus*
(1654), 40. " England is a kingdom very populous ", wrote Cooke, *Unum
Necessarium* (1648), 7. Bland spoke of England's ' supernumerary people ' :
*Trade Revived* (1659), 11.
[6] Petty, *Economic Writings*, i. 68, 242, 287, 301 ; ii. 605. And following notes.

Spain and France, have destroyed several hundred thousands of men . . . besides vast numbers have transported themselves, or been transported, into Ireland and other our foreign plantations "[1]. Many writers, including Evelyn and Roger Coke, spoke of " the ruinous numbers of our men daily flocking to the American plantations", which "rob us of our people to the weakening the nation"[2]; and the statute-book itself bore testimony to the belief that " this kingdom hath and doth daily suffer a great prejudice by the transporting great numbers of the people thereof to the plantations "[3]. Davenant estimated the number of people in the dominions at three hundred thousand[4], a figure which appeared to afford some ground for apprehension.

It is impossible to determine with any precision the population of England in the seventeenth and eighteenth centuries. Contemporary estimates are conflicting. "I give no heed to those guesses ", remarked Defoe, " there being no rule or foundation to make such an estimate upon "[5]. In the latter part of the seventeenth century Gregory King calculated the population at 5½ millions ; Petty variously computed it at 6 and 7⅔ millions ; Davenant at 7 and 8 millions ; Barbon at 7 millions[6]. In any case the statements of post-Restora-

*Size of the population of England.*

---

[1] *The Grand Concern of England explained in Several Proposals* (1673), 13.

[2] Evelyn, *Navigation and Commerce* (1674), 112 ; Coke, *Treatise* (1671), i. 16, 27-28, 90 ; iii. 75 ; *Britannia Languens* (1680), 173 ; J. B., *An Account of the French Usurpation upon the Trade of England* (1679), 16 ; *The Prevention of Poverty : or, New Proposals* (1677), 4. A different view was expressed by Child, *A New Discourse of Trade* (4th ed.), 195-196 ; and by Houghton, *Husbandry and Trade Improv'd* (ed. 1728), iv. 36 *seq.*

[3] *Statutes*, v. 748 (1671).

[4] Davenant, *Works* (ed. 1771), ii. 22. *Britannia Languens* (1680), 121, 176, actually spoke of " those millions of people which we have lost or been prevented of by the plantations ".

[5] Defoe, *A Plan of the English Commerce* (ed. 1728), 172.

[6] Petty, *Economic Writings*, i. 105, 267, 291 ; ii. 460, 544 ; King, *Natural and Political Observations and Conclusions upon the State and Condition of England, 1696* (ed. Chalmers), 36, 47 ; Davenant, *Works*, (ed. 1771), i. 19, 69 ; ii. 184 ; Barbon, *A Discourse of Trade* (1690), 47 ; Macpherson, *Annals of Commerce*, iii. 701 *seq.* ; Macaulay, *The History of England*, chapter iii. For the eighteenth century, see Chalmers, *An Estimate of the Comparative Strength of Britain* (ed. 1782), 144 *seq.* ; Eden, *The State of the Poor* (1797), i. 333-335 ; iii. Appendix No. xiv. ; Rickman, *Comparative Account of the Population of Great Britain* (Census Returns, 1831), 8-12. See also Gras, *The Evolution of the English Corn Market*, 75 ; Brownlee, " The History of the Birth and Death Rates in England [contd.]

tion writers, that the colonies were depopulating England, were incorrect if they implied an actual decline in population. It may be safely affirmed that the reverse was true, and that population was growing—in the seventeenth century[1] at a slow rate ; and in the later eighteenth century more rapidly [2] owing to a fall in the death-rate brought about by the reduction in infantile mortality[3], the spread of medical knowledge[4], the improvement in the standard of living[5] and other factors. However, the growth of population in the hundred years following the Restoration failed to keep pace with the expansion of trade and industry ; and the shortage of hands largely explains the introduction of machinery into the textile manufactures [6]. As early as 1663 Fortrey expressed the opinion that England could support double the population ' were they rightly employed ' [7] ; while Davenant, more cautiously, considered that the kingdom could bear ' a full third part more of inhabitants ' [8]. The view that England was ' prejudiced by the paucity of people '[9] had an important bearing on imperial policy, because the old colonial system was based on the assumption that the mother country was entitled to reap substantial benefit from her colonies, to compensate for the sacrifice entailed in the loss of population[10]. Moreover the prospect of economic gain to the parent state was precisely the argument employed in defence of emigration.  " 'Tis strange we should be thought to diminish the people of England ", said one writer, " when we do so much

---

and Wales taken as a Whole, from 1570 to the present time ", in *Public Health* (vol. xxix.), June and July 1916 ; Gonner, " The Population of England in the Eighteenth Century ", in *Journal of the Royal Statistical Society*, new series, lxxvi. part iii. 261 *seq.* For the population of London, see *supra*, vol. ii. 249, note 5.   Also see *infra*, Appendix, p. 508, No. 3.

[1] Davenant, *Works* (ed. 1771), ii. 2.

[2] See Griffith, *Population Problems of the Age of Malthus*, and Buer, *Health, Wealth, and Population in the Early Days of the Industrial Revolution.*

[3] *Infra*, p. 435.

[4] Simon, *English Sanitary Institutions*, chapter vii.

[5] *E.g.* the consumption of fresh meat : *supra*, vol. ii. 374.

[6] Lipson, *The History of the Woollen and Worsted Industries*, 135-6, 164.

[7] Fortrey, *England's Interest and Improvement* (1663), 39.

[8] Davenant, *Works* (ed. 1771), i. 74; Wood, *A Survey of Trade* (1718), 313.

[9] *Britannia Languens* (1680), 159 (in sect. vii.).

[10] Child, *A New Discourse of Trade* (4th ed.), 209-210 ; Gee, *The Trade and Navigation of Great Britain* (ed. 1730), 77.

increase the employments [there] " [1]. It was maintained that every emigrant to the sugar plantations occasioned the consumption of more English commodities than did several persons at home [2].

The colonies were founded without any ' public charge ' to the State [3], but individuals in the mother country furnished the capital for the development of their resources. Money was needed to finance voyages of exploration [4], as well as for the settlement and maintenance of emigrants until they grew self-supporting. The plantations became a field for capitalist enterprise, and moneyed men sank, and often lost [5], their capital in them as a form of investment. They were actuated by the hope of discovering precious metals, of raising commodities for the English market, and of developing the fishing trade for which there existed both an English and a continental market. Not that colonies were founded only for purposes of profit-making. There was a mixture of motives. The writer of a letter to the secretary of state in 1633 remarked that the settlers in different colonies " went not forth upon the same reasons nor for the same end ". He distinguished two kinds of colonies—the one (Virginia) planted ' only for profit ' ; the other (New England) where the emigrants " went upon two other designs, some to satisfy their own curiosity in point of conscience, others (which was more general) to transport the Gospel " [6]. Yet even the promoters of Virginia based their appeal for support on the ground of ' the enlargement of Christian religion ' [7]; while

*Investment of capital in the colonies.*

---

[1] *The Groans of the Plantations* (1689), 29. Similarly : Houghton, *Husbandry and Trade Improv'd* (ed. 1728), iv. 38 ; Wood, *A Survey of Trade* (1718), 155-156 ; Defoe, *A Plan of the English Commerce* (ed. 1728), 363-365.

[2] Four, said Child, *A New Discourse of Trade* (4th ed.), 205. Seven, thought Davenant, *Works* (ed. 1771), ii. 20. Ten, according to Thomas, in *Harleian Miscellany* (ed. Malham), ix. 413 (1690). Cf. also Bennett, *Two Letters and Several Calculations on the Sugar Colonies and Trade* (1738), 55. Young considered this a ' ridiculous notion ' : *The Farmer's Letters* (ed. 1768), 308.

[3] *Acts and Ordinances of the Interregnum*, i. 571. But Jamaica, New York and Canada were acquired by the State. See *infra*, Appendix, p. 509, No. 1.

[4] Raleigh's expeditions, on which £40,000 is said to have been spent, were joint-stock undertakings : Scott, *Joint-Stock Companies*, ii. 244.

[5] *E.g. Hist. MSS. Comm. Cowper*, ii. 38.

[6] *Ibid. Cowper*, ii. 38.  [7] *Ibid. Buccleuch*, i. 99 (1611).

New England sought to attract 'gentlemen of ability', who might ' advance their own estates ' as well as propagate the Gospel [1]. Ultimately colonial expansion must be viewed as an expression of that spirit of adventure which in the Middle Ages had sought an outlet on the battlefields of France. The outburst of national energy, which marked the spacious days of Elizabeth, was not a new phenomenon: its significance lies rather in the fact that the vitality, which had hitherto dissipated itself in worn-out channels, was now expended in other and more fruitful directions. The discovery of the New World revealed to the nation its true element, the sea, and the expansion of the English race lay in the logic of History. But whatever the motive for colonization, it was the financial resources of the mother kingdom, which provided the means for undertaking it and for maintaining the trade of the plantations [2].

*Cost of establishing a colony.* Some light is thrown upon the cost of establishing a colony in a seventeenth-century estimate of the expenses incurred in ' the First Plantation of New England '.

" For the passage of persons thither . . . . £95,000
For the transportation of neat, horses, sheep, swine, goats, besides the price they cost . . . . 12,000
For provision of food before they could bring the woods to tillage . . . . . . . 45,000
For nails, glass and other iron works before they had iron mills . . . . . . . . 18,000
Their great artillery, arms and ammunition . . 22,000

£192,000

" Besides what the adventurers laid out in England. Most of those who did cast into this Bank were those who were in this transmigration ; and their charges amounted to much more than double the above-mentioned sums. About twenty years ago 'twas calculated to above £400,000 " [3].

The outlay in respect of ' first cost ' on a sugar plantation of a hundred acres was estimated at £5625 [4]—a figure which,

---

[1] *E.g. Hist. MSS. Comm. Cowper*, i. 449 (1632).
[2] *Ibid. Cowper*, ii. 38.
[3] *Ibid. Pepys*, 270 (undated).
[4] Thomas in *Harleian Miscellany* (ed. Malham), ix. 420 (1690).

like the rest, must be related to the current monetary values. The large sums involved meant that the beginnings of colonial enterprise had to be conducted on a joint-stock basis, and the form of organization which had become familiar in foreign trade was now applied in a new direction. The most important company engaged in the work of colonization was the Virginia Company. Incorporated in 1609, its membership numbered 56 City companies and 659 individuals [1]. Within a dozen years it had expended over £100,000 ' without return either of profit or of any part of the principal itself ' [2]; and in 1625 it was dissolved [3].

The mother country rendered another service to the colonies [4] : she set up a protected market. The most conspicuous example of the protection given to colonial products was tobacco, its production being forbidden in this country primarily in the colonial interest. No doubt there was a mixture of motives. The Government was not indifferent to the revenue arising from the customs paid on imported tobacco ; and the original prohibition of home-grown tobacco in 1619 may be traced to the bribe offered by the Virginia Company in the shape of a higher duty [5]. Yet we must avoid the common mistake of finding in the financial exigencies of the Crown a complete explanation of the policy of the Early Stuarts. Their persistent discouragement of tobacco-growing in the plantations [6] shows that they were actuated by a genuine desire to promote the interests of the colonies, as they understood them. After all, any loss of revenue on imported tobacco could have been made good by an excise on English tobacco such

*A protected market for the colonies*

---

[1] Scott, *Joint-Stock Companies*, ii. 249, 251. A lottery was one of the means of raising capital : *Hist. MSS. Comm. Buccleuch*, i. 122.

[2] Beer, *The Origins of the British Colonial System*, 222.

[3] Scott, *Joint-Stock Companies*, ii. 288. Two colonies had been authorized, the second to be established by the western ports. The early attempts proved unsuccessful, but in 1620 the Council for New England was formed, and continued until 1635 : *ibid.* ii. 298-305.

[4] Colonial merchants also received long credits : see Rees, " Mercantilism and the Colonies " in *The Cambridge History of the British Empire*, i. 594 ; Andrews, *The Colonial Background of the American Revolution*, 104 *seq.*; Clark, *British Opinion and the American Revolution*, 27-30 ; Nettels, " British Policy and Colonial Money Supply ", in *The Economic History Review*, iii. No. 2, 233.

[5] Scott, *Joint-Stock Companies*, ii. 273. [6] *Infra*, p. 181.

as was actually levied in 1653 [1]; and the maintenance of an unpopular policy in the face of widespread opposition, protracted to the end of the seventeenth century, was clearly due to the conviction that the welfare of the plantations was bound up with the maintenance of their English market. Other reasons assigned for the prohibition were evidently intended to reconcile the nation to the sacrifice it was called upon to make : it was alleged that English tobacco was ' not so good and wholesome ' as foreign-grown, that it destroyed the fertility of corn-land, and that it occupied soil required for other crops [2]. Despite these arguments public sympathy was on the side of the English grower. In the Parliament of 1621 Sir Edward Coke declared that the restraint imposed on the ' setting of tobacco ' was opposed to the liberty of the subject, while another member affirmed that ' very good and wholesome tobacco ' was grown here [3].

*Tobacco-growing in England.* It took, indeed, nearly a century to stamp out the planting of tobacco in England. A stream of statutes and proclamations seemed ineffectual to achieve the purpose [4]; and the services of the militia and even of the regular troops had to be requisitioned year by year to trample down the growing crops [5]. The prohibition first applied to the vicinity of London, and it was made general in 1619 [6]; yet under the Commonwealth we even hear of the export of English tobacco [7], and complaint was made to Cromwell " of the great damage that hath accrued to the English plantations

---

[1] *House of Commons Journals*, vii. 348.

[2] *Statutes*, v. 297 ; *Tudor and Stuart Proclamations* (ed. Steele), i. Nos. 1268 and 1677.

[3] *House of Commons Journals*, i. 579, 605. See *infra*, Appendix, p. 509, No. 2.

[4] *E.g. Statutes*, v. 297 (1660), 452 (1663), 747 (1671). *Tudor and Stuart Proclamations* (ed. Steele), i. Nos. 1268 (1619), 1677 (1634). *Acts and Ordinances of the Interregnum*, ii. 580 (1652). *State Papers Domestic*, 1629–1631, p. 475 ; 1635–1636, pp. 568-569 ; 1658–1659, p. 55 ; 1677–1678, p. 363. *Hist. MSS. Comm. Beaufort*, 510 (1655) ; *ibid. Various*, i. 153 (1676).

[5] *Hist. MSS. Comm. Portland*, ii. 144 (1662) ; *Acts of the Privy Council, Colonial Series*, 1613–1680, p. xxiii ; *Victoria County History, Worcestershire*, iv. 456.

[6] *Tudor and Stuart Proclamations* (ed. Steele), i. No. 1268. The Virginia Company secured the concession by payment of a higher duty : *supra*, p. 169.

[7] *House of Commons Journals*, vii. 348 (1653).

abroad by the great quantities of English tobacco "[1]. After the Restoration it was asserted that the cultivation of tobacco in England ' doth continue and increase '[2] ; and there were reported to be hundreds of offenders whose proceedings were connived at by the local authorities, who as landowners participated in the profits [3]. Gloucestershire and Worcestershire were the principal centres of tobacco-growing, but eighteen counties received orders, at one time or another, for the destruction of English-grown tobacco ; and the orders were issued at least as late as 1694 [4]. This persistence on the part of native growers was a measure both of the profitable nature of the commodity, and of the sacrifice entailed in giving the colonies a monopoly of the English market at the expense of the English farmer : and the one and the other must be borne in mind when the disabilities of the colonies are considered. The monopoly was further strengthened by restrictions on foreign tobacco. An attempt to exclude Spanish tobacco entirely (1624) was modified (1627) in favour of a limited importation, but it was burdened with a heavy duty [5]. Another instance in which the interests of the English producer were sacrificed to the colonies was the exclusion of English fishermen from the New England fisheries. New England claimed a monopoly of the fishing on her coasts, and she received the support of the home Government despite the opposition raised in Parliament [6]

In addition the colonies were given preferential treatment under the English fiscal system—they enjoyed partial or complete immunity from customs duties. Virginia secured the concession (1609) that all commodities shipped thither should go duty-free [7]. New England obtained

*Fiscal immunities*

---

[1] *Hist. MSS. Comm. Beaufort*, 511 (1655).
[2] *Statutes*, v. 747 (1671).
[3] Latimer, *Merchant Venturers of Bristol*, 172 (1666).
[4] *Acts of the Privy Council*, Colonial Series, 1613–1680, p. xxiii ; 1680–1720, p. xix. For 1696, see *infra*, Appendix, p. 509, No. 3.
[5] *Tudor and Stuart Proclamations* (ed. Steele), i. Nos. 1385, 1505 ; *State Papers Colonial*, 1574–1660, pp. 83, 125. In 1631 Spanish tobacco paid 2s. per lb., Virginian 9d. ; in 1632 Virginian tobacco paid only 4d. : *State Papers Domestic*, 1629–1631, p. 476 ; 1631–1633, p. 291.
[6] Beer, *The Origins of the British Colonial System*, 274–278.
[7] *State Papers Colonial*, 1574–1660, p. 8.

(1644) exemption from taxes on her trade with this country, inwards as well as outwards [1]. Colonial products, where they were not admitted into England without payment of customs, were often more lightly burdened than foreign products, for example, Virginian tobacco paid a smaller duty than Spanish [2]. On some colonial articles brought into this country, not only was the duty remitted but a bounty was also paid [3]. Moreover the duties levied on European goods imported into England were, with certain exceptions, almost entirely repaid when the goods were re-exported to the colonies [4]. Hence the colonial consumer enjoyed an advantage over the English consumer, who at the same time paid a higher price for colonial products— tobacco, sugar and rice among others — since the latter were guarded from foreign competition by preferential tariffs. And finally the colonies, in the words of the statute-book, were " maintained and protected at a great expense of the treasure of this kingdom " [5]. Cary expressed a view widely held in the eighteenth century, when he defended the right of the mother country to draw profit from the colonies because she sent fleets and regiments to their aid, " towards which they contribute but little " [6].

*The Acts of Trade.*　　The Acts of Trade, which governed the economic relations between England and her colonies, were designed to serve a threefold purpose—(1) to keep the colonial trade in the hands of the mother country in order to benefit English shipping ; (2) to make the colonial industries supplement the economic resources of the parent State ; and (3) to develop

---

[1] *Acts and Ordinances of the Interregnum*, i. 571. Other plantations like Virginia, Bermudas, Barbados, etc., paid no duty on goods imported from England : *ibid.* i. 912.

[2] *Supra*, p. 171, note 5.　　　[3] *Infra*, p. 185.　　　[4] *Infra*, p. 193.

[5] *Statutes*, viii. 354 (1704). It was estimated that the " expenses we have been put to in consequence of our possessing colonies on the continent of North America " amounted to 40 millions from the accession of the Hanoverians to 1788, " in addition to the charges of at least two wars which cost us above 240 millions more, and which were entered into principally on their account " : Sinclair, *The History of the Public Revenue* (ed. 1803), ii. 100-101.

[6] Cary, *An Essay towards Regulating the Trade* (ed. 1719), 51. Similarly: *Acts of the Privy Council*, Colonial Series, vi. 43.

a colonial market for English manufactures. All three objects had a common basis founded on the conviction that trade, as William Penn wrote, was " the benefit England chiefly has by these colonies " [1].

In order to establish a monopoly of American commerce, *(i.) Monopoly of the colonial trade.* the Acts of Navigation sought to confine the oversea trade of the colonies to the mother country. The restriction was thought justified on the grounds that it was " the usage of other nations to keep their plantations' trade to themselves" [2], and that it was the only means of enabling England to derive economic advantage from her dependencies [3]. This contention was reinforced by the political argument, advanced in the infancy of the colonies and repeated subsequently, that " these colonies, if they fall into the practice of trading independently of England, may erect themselves into independent commonwealths " [4]. The irony of events turned a policy, intended to strengthen the Empire, into one of the factors responsible for its dissolution. Yet even Roger Coke held that " the Act of Navigation with reason prohibits the trade of our plantations to foreigners"; and Child, who professed free trade opinions, considered colonies harmful unless they were kept in a state of subjection and their trade confined to the mother country by ' severe laws ' [5].

The clauses in the Navigation Acts affecting the colonies *How far a grievance.* were noticed above [6]. How far they constituted a genuine grievance cannot be easily determined. The exclusion of the Dutch, who were strongly entrenched in the colonial trade [7], was resented by the planters. " When ", said a writer in 1657 [8], " the Dutch traded thither the planters

---

[1] *Hist. MSS. Comm. Portland*, iv. 30 (*c.* 1701).

[2] *Statutes*, v. 449 ; Child, *A New Discourse of Trade* (4th ed.), 210. Cf. *The Regulations lately made concerning the Colonies* (1765), 89 : " No nation would tolerate colonies upon any other conditions ".

[3] *House of Commons Journals*, xii. 433 ; Child, *A New Discourse of Trade* (4th ed.), 125.

[4] Davenant, *Works* (ed. 1771), i. 397.

[5] Coke, *Treatise* (1675), iv. 113 ; Child, *A New Discourse of Trade* (4th ed.), 125, 192, 210.

[6] *Supra*, pp. 122, 124.

[7] " Before the Act of Navigation there went ten Dutch ships to Barbados for one English " : Child, *A New Discourse of Trade* (4th ed.), 211. Cf. also Brewster, *Essays on Trade and Navigation* (1695), 99-100.

[8] Gatford, *Publick Good without Private Interest* (1657), 14.

bought shoes at twelve pounds of tobacco ; since they were prohibited the English made them to pay fifty pounds of tobacco for the like ; and so in proportion for other commodities.  And then, if any of the plantations sent tobacco hither, they had the freight thereof for £4 per ton, but upon the prohibition of the Dutch they sometimes paid £14 per ton and most constantly £8 or £9 per ton ", that is, freights were doubled and sometimes even trebled.  " And whereas the Dutch would then give the planters threepence per pound for their tobacco . . . since that the tobacco, for the most part of it, will not yield above an half-penny per pound there ; and when it comes to England it will scarce pay the freight and custom, by reason of the want of that vent which it formerly had before the Dutch planted tobacco in their own territories, which they did not till that prohibition."  The American colonies, it was urged, were in need of customers : why, then, should the Dutch be prevented from dealing with them ?

*Enumerated commodities.* The policy of making England the staple for certain colonial products, known as ' enumerated commodities ' [1], was designed to give her the first claim upon them, as well as to control their export to European countries.  It was also partly intended to raise a revenue, though the latter would not necessarily have suffered if the plantations had been permitted to send their produce direct to foreign markets, especially as a large part of the duty on colonial goods brought to England came to be repaid when they were re-exported [2] ; while the nation would have profited from the enlargement of trade, which was now contracted by the "greater charge by longer voyages, double risks, and the expense of time and labour in loading and unloading " [3].  The restriction was a serious handicap, in particular, to the colonies which traded with southern Europe.  The sugar plantations complained that the obligation to convey their sugar to England, which consumed only half of it [4], before taking the other half elsewhere,

---

[1] *Supra*, p. 124.
[2] On tobacco three-quarters, on sugar one-half : Beer, *The Old Colonial System*, part i. vol. i. 37.
[3] Thomas in *Harleian Miscellany* (ed. Malham), ix. 442 (1690).
[4] *State Papers America and West Indies*, 1675–1676, p. 304.

ruined their trade to the Straits since it increased the price [1]. A celebrated pamphlet, *The Groans of the Plantations* (1689), observed : " As for confining the plantation trade to English ships and Englishmen, though it be to our particular loss (for the Dutch were very beneficial to us), yet we took it in good part in regard our great and dear Mother of England hath by it such vast advantages. But that English ships and Englishmen should not be permitted to trade to their best convenience and profit is a thing we cannot understand " [2]. When the governor of Barbados pressed the home authorities to allow liberty of trade to any market, he drew upon himself a severe censure for his ' dangerous principles ' [3]. Yet relief was not obtained until 1739, when their inability to ' carry on the sugar trade on an equal footing with foreign sugar colonies ' at length received recognition, and they were allowed to deal direct with the South of Europe [4]. A few years before a similar concession had been made in regard to rice [5]. The position in respect of tobacco was different, inasmuch as England appeared a natural staple for a commodity which was consumed in northern Europe. But the grievance was ventilated that the re-exported tobacco, which was said to amount to two-thirds of the total quantity [6], was burdened with additional freight, insurance, commission and other shipping charges, whilst its value was depreciated owing to the glut of the

[1] *The Groans of the Plantations* (1689), 5 ; *The Case of His Majesty's Sugar Plantations* in *Somers, Tracts* (ed. 1812), viii. 480.

[2] *The Groans of the Plantations* (1689), 5. Cf. Petty, *Economic Writings*, i. 299.

[3] 1676 : *State Papers America and West Indies*, 1675–1676, pp. 368, 424, 474–475, 485, 510.

[4] *Statutes at Large*, vi. 115, 119. The Bristol merchants opposed the application of the West Indian planters : Latimer, *Merchant Venturers of Bristol*, 187.

[5] See *supra*, p. 126.

[6] Thomas in *Harleian Miscellany* (ed. Malham), ix. 425 (1690) ; Wood, *A Survey of Trade* (1718), 144. The annual export of tobacco from Virginia and Maryland averaged (*c.* 1700) 60,000 to 70,000 hogsheads (an hogshead usually contained 5 cwt.) : *House of Commons Journals*, xiii. 724. France and Spain annually took nearly 20,000 hogsheads : *ibid.* xvi. 93. In 1766 the figure given is 90,000 hogsheads, averaging each 952 lb.: *Considerations on the Propriety of imposing Taxes in the British Colonies* (1766), 72, 79. According to Adam Smith, " we imported about 96,000 hogsheads and the home consumption was not supposed to exceed 14,000 " : *The Wealth of Nations* (ed. Cannan), ii. 2.

commodity in the English market[1]. The tenacity, with which the system of ‘ enumerated commodities ’ was upheld, is shown in the view that its general abandonment " might be dangerous, if not fatal, to Great Britain " [2]. The critics of the system, on the other hand, adopted the standpoint that England should distinguish between revenue and commerce : " If we get a great revenue by means of America, what signifies who gets advantage by their trade ? For example, if we draw several millions of revenue by their tobacco, why should we grudge that France should get a few hundred thousand pounds by their trade ? " [3]

*Illicit trading.* The fruit of the navigation system was the illicit trade which sprang up with the connivance of the American authorities. Smuggling was considered a venial sin, and it doubtless explains the acquiescence of the colonists in restrictions, which they speedily found intolerable when any stringent attempt was made to enforce them. Newfoundland, where the nations of Europe forgathered, served as a convenient meeting-place. Thither the New England men, acting as the carriers for the plantations, brought tobacco, sugar and other ‘ enumerated commodities ’, and sold them to the fishing ships, which conveyed them direct to foreign markets without first landing them in England or paying duty. In the same way colonial markets were supplied with European commodities, which had been taken to Newfoundland and sold to the plantation ships there. These breaches of the law were committed openly, and the ‘ fishing admirals ’ at Newfoundland, according to the Commissioners for Trade and Plantations, were ‘ generally the greatest offenders themselves ’ [4]. The New England shippers also traded direct with European countries, exchanging colonial products for manufactured goods. In particular, they carried on ‘ a very large and extensive trade ’ with the French and Dutch in Europe. ‘ A settled

---

[1] *Considerations on the Propriety of imposing Taxes in the British Colonies* (1766), 72-73 ; *Hist. MSS. Comm. Egmont (Diary)*, i. 151.

[2] *Hist. MSS. Comm. Various*, vi. 96 (1768).

[3] *Ibid. Stopford-Sackville*, ii. 103 (1778).

[4] *House of Commons Journals*, xiii. 725 ; *House of Lords MSS.* 1706-1708, p. 289.

course of traffic' was said to exist between the northern colonies and the ports of Marseilles and Toulon. Timber and other materials for shipbuilding, together with rice, skins and furs, were conveyed direct to the arsenals of France ; and the returns were made in goods of the growth and manufacture of France or other foreign countries, which were taken to America ' without ever touching in Great Britain '. A similar trade was conducted with Holland[1]. These evasions of the Navigation Acts meant that the English trader, who paid a duty on colonial goods, was exposed to the competition of the illicit trader, who escaped the payment of duty and so could furnish foreign markets at lower prices [2].

The most signal failure of the Navigation Acts to confine *The Molasses Act.* the trade of the plantations exclusively to the mother country was seen in the intercourse between the English colonies and their foreign neighbours. The Molasses Act, which sought to prohibit this intercourse, excited more discontent than perhaps any other part of the old colonial system : yet the fact must be remembered that it was passed in response to the entreaties of an important group of colonies. The Molasses Act is instructive, also, because it revealed the inherent contradictions of English colonial policy, which pursued divergent and incompatible aims. The northern colonies were accustomed to supply the French and Dutch West Indies with provisions, fish and lumber ; and the trade was especially lucrative since the chief returns were molasses which were used to make rum [3]. Now it was in the interests of the mother country to permit an intercourse, which was extremely profitable to the northern colonies and enabled them to purchase English goods. On the other hand, the sugar colonies protested strongly against the encouragement given to their foreign rivals to raise commodities which competed with their own. Thus two fundamental issues were involved—one was the develop-

[1] *House of Commons Journals*, xxvi. 107.
[2] On these points see *ibid*. xiii. 504, 725 ; Child, *A New Discourse of Trade* (4th ed.), 231-232 ; *The Present State of the British Empire* (1768), 288-289.
[3] Foreign manufactured articles were also among the returns : *House of Commons Journals*, xxiv. 818.

ment of an oversea market for English goods, which necessarily depended upon the ability of the colonies to buy; the other was the maintenance of England as the channel of trade between her colonies and foreign countries or plantations. The attention of Parliament was drawn to the question in 1731. The sugar-planters represented that " of late years [divers subjects] carried on a trade to the foreign sugar colonies in America, from whence they are supplied with sugar, rum, molasses and their other productions, instead of those from our own colonies . . . and as this new method of trade increases and enriches the colonies of other nations, so it is injurious to the trade of this kingdom and greatly impoverishes the British sugar colonies "[1]. The root of the trouble was that the French sugar plantations were in a position to undersell their English rivals, since they were not allowed to send rum to Europe where it would have competed with French brandy. Moreover the northern colonies, trading direct with their neighbours, escaped any duties charged on foreign commodities when brought first to England as the Navigation Acts directed. The northern colonies retorted that a great part of the profits of their intercourse with foreign plantations centred in England, in payment of the manufactures received from this country; that its cessation would be the destruction of their shipping, several thousand tons being engaged in the trade ; that the French would be forced to supply their own colonies with lumber, fish and other necessaries, so that French navigation would reap the benefit ; finally, that it would place a dangerous monopoly in the hands of British sugar-planters, and—assuming their ability to supply, not only the British market of which they already had the monopoly, but the American market as well—they would exact prohibitive prices. A Bill was introduced into Parliament in 1731 to forbid the importation of foreign sugar, rum or molasses into Great Britain and Ireland or any of the dominions, but it failed to pass the House of Lords [2]. Two years later

[1] *House of Commons Journals*, xxi. 641-642.
[2] Wood, *A Survey of Trade* (1718), 137-138 ; *The Present State of the British Empire* (1768), 289-290 ; Macpherson, *Annals of Commerce*, iii. 171-177.

the Molasses Act, without prohibiting the trade, laid heavy duties upon it [1].

The sequel is related in a series of petitions presented to Parliament two decades later. The sugar-planters took their stand by the general principles enshrined in the navigation system. " In the making of [the Navigation] Laws, always looked upon as the bulwark of the British commerce, the legislature of Great Britain had, as the petitioners conceive, two great and important objects in view—one the increase of naval power by making British shipping and British subjects the sole carriers of the whole British commerce ; the other the appropriating and securing to Great Britain all the emoluments arising from the trade of her own colonies " [2]. The desire to guard ' these two great sources of her wealth and power ' from any invasion had inspired the Act of 1733, but notwithstanding its provisions the British in North America, " as though they thought themselves independent of Great Britain ", imported vast quantities of sugar, rum and molasses from the French and other foreign sugar colonies without paying the duties imposed by the Act. Counter-petitions on behalf of the northern colonies protested that prices had doubled since the Act was passed [3]. The Molasses Act remained in operation, though disregard of the revenue laws was so general in America that the commodity was imported in large quantities without paying any duty [4]. In 1764 the importation of foreign rum was prohibited, but the duty on molasses was halved in order to discourage smuggling [5].

One effect of the Navigation Acts must not be overlooked. They admitted colonial ships to the same privileges as English ships, in spite of the fact that the colonies themselves passed laws discriminating against English shipping [6]. This encouraged the colonies to build

*Conflict of interests in the colonies.*

*Colonial shipping.*

---

[1] *Statutes at Large*, v. 616. The duty on foreign molasses imported into the colonies was 6d. per gallon.

[2] *House of Commons Journals*, xxvi. 107.

[3] *Ibid.* xxvi. 168-169, 183-184.

[4] *The Regulations lately made concerning the Colonies* (1765), 79.

[5] *Statutes at Large*, vii. 458, 460. In 1766 it was reduced to 1d. per gallon : *ibid.* vii. 620.

[6] Beer, *The Old Colonial System*, part i. vol. i. 64, 206 ; vol. ii. 246.

ships of their own [1], and enabled New England in particular
to develop a flourishing shipbuilding industry, which was
attracting attention in the reign of Charles II. " Our
planters of New England ", said a writer in 1680, " having
gotten a considerable navigation of their own, do trade
from port to port in America, and have in a manner beaten
us out of that kind of employment in those parts " [2]. No
American plantation was so ' apt ' for building ships as New
England, or so qualified for ' breeding ' seamen, due partly
to the ' natural industry ' of the people and still more
to the fisheries. Child thought that there was " nothing
more prejudicial, and in prospect more dangerous, to any
mother kingdom than the increase of shipping in her
colonies " [3]. His opinion was shared, for obvious reasons,
by the Thames shipbuilders who complained to Parliament in 1724 that they were seriously injured by colonial
competition [4]. Though they attributed the decay of their
industry to American competition, another explanation
may be given. During the war with France many new
ships were built to repair the losses at sea, and the shipbuilding industry was inflated beyond its normal dimensions.
After the war the number of ships was in excess of peace-
time requirements, and a severe depression set in [5]. It is
unlikely, in any case, that the development of American
shipping injured the English shipbuilding industry. The
latter had a monopoly of men-of-war for the royal navy,
colliers for the coal trade, and ships for distant voyages—
India, the Levant and the South Seas, as well as a share of
the vessels which visited Barbados, Jamaica and Virginia.
Colonial-built ships were used in New England, Newfoundland and the American coasting trade [6]. They were also
employed in the timber trade to Portugal and Spain,
but these, on the home journey, were refitted in this

---

[1] For a graphic description, see Morison, *The Maritime History of
Massachusetts*. Also see Bishop, *A History of American Manufactures*,
i. 36 *seq.*

[2] *Britannia Languens* (1680), 175.

[3] Child, *A New Discourse of Trade* (4th ed.), 232-233.

[4] Ashley, *Surveys Historic and Economic*, 313 ; Giesecke, *American
Commercial Legislation before 1789*, 70.

[5] Gee, *The Trade and Navigation of Great Britain* (ed. 1730), 105-106.

[6] The American coasting trade was confined to English, Irish and
colonial ships : *Statutes*, vii. 103 (1696).

country, and repairing old ships was considered as profitable as building new ones owing to the high price of timber [1].

The second feature of the colonial system was to encourage the colonies, in accordance with 'the true design and intention of those settlements', to "apply their industry to the cultivation . . . of such products as may be proper for the soil of the colonies, and do not interfere with the trade or produce of Great Britain " [2]. The view that the plantations should concentrate on particular products was strongly entertained from the infancy of the colonies. Here the history of tobacco is instructive. In the early part of the seventeenth century the use of tobacco had become general in this country [3], despite a strong current of opposition voiced by James I. himself. "Tobacco and ale ", said a member of Parliament in 1621, are "now made inseparable in the base vulgar sort : these accompanied with idleness, drunkenness, sickness, decay of their estates " [4]. The authorities of Virginia defended its cultivation on the plea that the people were forced to follow that 'contemptible weed' to enable them to support themselves [5]. But the Early Stuarts were persuaded that the colonies could not prosper if they relied on tobacco alone, and neglected other things 'of greater consequence' [6]; and though "contented [as one of their proclamations intimated] to tolerate the use of tobacco of the growth of those plantations for a time, until by more solid commodities they be able to subsist otherwise " [7], they repeatedly enjoined the plantations to turn their attention to 'staple' commodities. "The King", wrote Charles I. to the authorities of Virginia, " is much troubled . . . that this plantation is wholly built

*(ii.) Colonial industries to be supplementary.*

---

[1] Gee, *The Trade and Navigation of Great Britain* (ed. 1730), 105-106. Half of the New England shipping was said to be engaged in the European trade : Macpherson, *Annals of Commerce*, iii. 165. Some colonial vessels were sold here : Beer, *The Old Colonial System*, part i. vol. ii. 266, 312.

[2] *House of Lords Journals*, xxiv. 412 ; *House of Commons Journals*, xiii. 448.

[3] *Tudor and Stuart Proclamations* (ed. Steele), i. No. 1268 ; *Hist. MSS. Comm. Various*, i. 87.

[4] *House of Commons Journals*, i. 605.

[5] *State Papers Colonial*, 1574–1660, p. 39 (1623).

[6] *Ibid.* 63 (1624).          [7] Rymer, *Foedera*, xvii. 668 (1625).

*Opposition to tobacco.* upon smoke " [1] ; and the Somers Islands were admonished that, considering the care taken to encourage the inhabitants to plant 'real' commodities, the King marvelled that they applied themselves wholly to tobacco [2]. Public opinion, as expressed in parliamentary debates, showed that the Stuarts voiced a widespread sentiment. A proposal was debated in the Parliament of 1621 to 'banish' tobacco and 'help Virginia by some other means', and it found support among those who 'loveth England better than Virginia'; but it was urged that Virginia should be allowed ' a certain time for it ', or ' else we overthrow the plantation ' [3]. Attempts were made to confine the importation of tobacco to London, and to fix the quantity at what " the King shall declare to be competent, his majesty not thinking it fit to admit of an immeasurable expense of so vain and needless a commodity, which ought to be used as a drug only, and not so vainly and wantonly as an evil habit of late times has brought it to " [4]. The restriction may have been partially intended to raise money by the grant of licences to import tobacco elsewhere. In any case it led to extensive smuggling in the English Channel, and was therefore modified in 1639 by the addition of some other ports including Bristol [5]. After the Restoration the attempt to divert the colonies from growing tobacco was abandoned ; and so marked was the change of opinion, and so large the revenue drawn from this product, that the Commissioners for Trade and Plantations in 1707 even proposed to ' hinder ' the colonies " from applying their labour to any other product or manufacture than that of tobacco " [6].

The staple commodities to which the colonies were admonished to devote their energies included, first and foremost, naval stores—masts, hemp, flax, tar, pitch, turpentine

---

[1] *State Papers Colonial*, 1574–1660, p. 86 (1627). Similarly : *ibid.* 125, 239, 250.
[2] *Ibid.* 125 (1631).          [3] *House of Commons Journals*, i. 581.
[4] *State Papers Domestic*, 1629–1631, p. 475 ; *State Papers Colonial*, 1574–1660, p. 125 ; MacInnes, *The Early English Tobacco Trade*, 54.
[5] Latimer, *Merchant Venturers of Bristol*, 130.
[6] *Acts of the Privy Council*, Colonial Series, 1680–1720, p. 515. In 1768 the revenue from tobacco was said to be near £300,000 a year : *The Present State of the British Empire*, (1768), 308.

—' the foundation and support ' of the navy and merchant Naval service [1]. The importance attached to naval stores is ex- stores. plained in the preamble of an Act of Parliament passed to encourage their production. "The royal navy and the navigation of England, wherein under God the wealth, safety and strength of this kingdom is so much concerned, depends on the due supply of stores necessary for the same, which, being now brought in mostly from foreign parts in foreign shipping at exorbitant and arbitrary rates . . . may be provided in a more certain and beneficial manner from her majesty's own dominions " [2]. At first Virginia was contemplated as a source of supply, and the Early Stuarts exhorted her to turn her attention to naval stores [3]. Sir Dudley Digges, in defending the East India Company from the charge of exhausting native timber, alluded to the possibility of the Company obtaining shipbuilding materials from Virginia [4]; and in 1609 a ship arrived from thence laden with wood, pitch and tar [5]. New England, however, was soon recognized as offering more inviting prospects, and the earliest settlers cherished the hope that they would "raise good profit, not only by our fishing trade, but by hemp, flax, pitch, tar, potashes, soap-ashes, masts, pipestaves, clapboards and iron " [6]. Yet although masts were occasionally brought from New England [7], it was not until after the Revolution that the question of importing naval stores from America was given serious attention. William Penn, the founder of Pennsylvania, wrote : "If the Crown would encourage every climate in those things it is proper for, we could produce silk, oranges and lemons, fruit and wine, as well as others of us hemp, flax, tar, masts, and abundance of crooks, knees and stately plank for shipping. The mines of England have destroyed much of the timber of England,

---

[1] House of Commons Journals, xi. 595.
[2] 1704 : Statutes, viii. 354.
[3] State Papers Colonial, 1574–1660, pp. 86, 269.
[4] Digges, The Defence of Trade (1615), 30.
[5] State Papers Colonial, 1574–1660, p. 7.
[6] Hist. MSS. Comm. Exeter, 167 (1623). Ibid. Cowper, i. 449 (1632); ii. 38-39. State Papers Colonial, 1574–1660, p. 156.
[7] State Papers Domestic, 1671–1672, p. 223 ; 1672–1673, p. 551. A Short Account of the Present State of New England (1690), 4.

and here is enough of both. If great undertakers there
would fall upon it here, we might supply England"[1]. Others
represented New England to be superior to the Baltic
countries for timber[2] and other shipbuilding materials,
and urged that the exploitation of her resources would
make her " of the most useless and unprofitable plantation
of this nation the best and most advantageous "[3].

*Company-*
*promoting.*        The 'great undertakers', whose interest Penn was
anxious to enlist, had taken the matter up as early as 1688.
Headed by Sir Matthew Dudley, they endeavoured to float
a company with a capital of £100,000 to bring naval stores
from the American colonies. The capital was subscribed,
but they failed to obtain a charter of incorporation owing
to the opposition of a rival group of financiers (including
Sir Joseph Herne)[4], two of whom offered to supply American
stores without a charter. This put a stop to Dudley's
undertaking, though in eighteen months only ' one small
ship half laden with naval stores ' was brought to London.
Dudley and his partners renewed their proposal in 1702.
The Commissioners for Trade and Plantations agreed that
the undertaking could be best carried on by a joint stock,
but ' clogged ' their consent " with divers unusual clauses
absolutely obstructive to all manner of trade. And though
they withdrew all these except one, requiring that no person
should dispose of his interest therein within five years "
—doubtless as a guarantee of good faith—Dudley, " knowing that no one would so tie himself ", desisted[5]. This is
Dudley's own account ; but the Government evidently
feared that the promoters, under colour of supplying the
country with naval stores, were seeking a privileged position
in the plantation trade which could be turned to their
private advantage, or that their real object was to float
a company for purposes of ' stock-jobbing '. For these

[1] *Hist. MSS. Comm. Portland*, iv. 31 (*c.* 1701).
[2] On the timber supplies in the colonies, see Albion, *Forests and Sea
Power*, chapter vi.
[3] Brewster, *Essays on Trade and Navigation* (1695), 87-88.
[4] For Herne, see *infra*, p. 215.
[5] *Hist. MSS. Comm. Portland*, viii. 164-165 ; *House of Lords MSS.*
1704-1706, p. 93 ; *Acts of the Privy Council*, Colonial Series, 1680-1720,
pp. 196 *seq.*

reasons it gave a lukewarm reception to another proposal, emanating from a different source, to establish a company for trading with the colonies [1].

Although the activities of the company promoter were officially discouraged, the Government was not indifferent to the importance of empire development. The Commissioners for Trade and Plantations, in accordance with their instructions (1696) to ascertain how naval stores could best be procured from the colonies [2], reported that they had applied themselves to the problem : the Navy Board conducted an investigation into the resources of the empire [3] : and samples of naval stores were brought from America [4]. The policy eventually adopted took the shape of bounties, which became the normal method of encouraging colonial production. The system of bounties was devised to serve a threefold purpose. The development of the outlying parts of the empire would free the mother kingdom from a dangerous dependence upon foreign countries [5] : the energies of the colonists, absorbed in producing raw materials, would be safely diverted from manufactures : and the Baltic lands would lose a monopoly which enabled them to exploit the market—it was stated in 1720, for example, that the Danes had raised the price of deal boards 100 per cent. within four years [6]. Thus the institution of bounties, which Adam Smith in general condemned, was intended to make the supply of naval stores cheaper, less precarious, and a means of employing the colonies. The system was inaugurated by the Act of 1704 owing to Sweden's refusal to allow the export of naval stores save in her own ships [7].

*Bounties on colonial products.*

[1] *Acts of the Privy Council*, Colonial Series, 1680–1720, pp. 465 *seq.* See also Lord, *Industrial Experiments in the British Colonies of North America*, 30 *seq.*
[2] *House of Commons Journals*, xiii. 298.          [3] *Ibid.* xiii. 301.
[4] *Ibid.* xi. 595 ; *State Papers Domestic*, 1696, pp. 309-310. A contract was made with a London merchant to supply ' masts, yards and bowsprits ' for the navy : *ibid.* p. 98.
[5] " Hemp being absolutely necessary for shipping, England is at Russia's mercy " : *Hist. MSS. Comm. Various*, vi. 292.
[6] *House of Commons Journals*, xix. 316.
[7] *Hist. MSS. Comm. Various*, vi. 292. A very considerable fall in price was said to have resulted from the bounty (*ibid.* 292-293), owing to the increased importation of naval stores from the colonies : *House of Lords MSS.* 1706-1708, p. 309.

As a result bounties were granted on tar, pitch, turpentine, masts, yards and bowsprits imported from the American colonies. Then the materials for manufacturing cordage and sail cloth, namely, hemp and undressed flax, were included ; but the culture of hemp did not succeed, and the bounty fell into oblivion though it was revived in 1764. Timber was added to the list in 1766 [1]. Apprehension in the eighteenth century of a world shortage in the supply of raw materials caused the system of bounties to be extended to other colonial products : indigo (1749) and raw silk (1770) [2]. The latter was one of the commodities which the Early Stuarts had pressed upon the attention of the Virginia Company as ' a rich and solid commodity preferable to tobacco ', and the colony had been enjoined to cultivate mulberry trees, breed silkworms, and set up silk works [3]. Encouragement of colonial produce also took the form of a removal, or reduction, of customs duty. Thus raw silk, prior to receiving a bounty, was admitted duty-free (1750), as well as potashes and pearl ashes used in the making of soap (1751), while colonial coffee enjoyed a preferential tariff (1735) [4].

(iii.) *Monopoly of the colonial market.* The third feature of the colonial system was the development of a market in America for English manufactures. The European market seemed precarious in view of the efforts of foreign countries to establish their own manufactures ; and, as in our own day, one argument for a colonial empire was expressly based on the contention that " most of the neighbouring nations in Europe, by prohibiting or discouraging our manufactures, make it necessary that all proper encouragement should be given towards the increasing our colonies " [5]. As the early hopes of discovering precious metals in North America faded away, they gave

---

[1] *Statutes*, viii. 354-356 (1704) ; *Statutes at Large*, vii. 477 (1764), 540 (1766) ; *The Regulations lately made concerning the Colonies*, (1765), 54.
[2] *Statutes at Large*, vi. 411 (1749) ; viii. 85-86 (1770). For silk, see *supra*, vol. ii. 100. The scramble for cotton led to a sharp rise in prices (c. 1750) : *Reports from Committees of the House of Commons*, ii. 292.
[3] *State Papers Colonial*, 1574–1660, pp. 31, 57, 269. It was also urged to plant vines : *ibid.* 57, 86.
[4] *Statutes at Large*, v. 596 (1735) ; vi. 469 (1750), 577 (1751).
[5] *House of Commons Journals*, xxv. 850. See also *infra*, pp. 295-296.

place to the more solid anticipations that the New World would 'create a new commerce'[1]. The prospect of a market for English commodities was one of the main attractions of the colonies, and they soon ranked among England's best customers. They took from the mother country woollen goods, which accounted for one-half the value of the total exports of English manufactures to the colonies [2], ' an infinite quantity of iron wares ready wrought ', shoes, hats, horses, flour, beer, cheese and butter [3]. On the other hand, voices were raised in America against depending exclusively on the production of food-stuffs and raw materials. " The balance of our trade with England is now greatly against us, and will continue to be so till we find out other returns. . . . It is trade and manufactures make a country rich and populous " [4].

The problem of preventing the colonies from developing *Repression* their own manufactures was a constant preoccupation with *of the woollen* the authorities in England ; and it supplied one of the *manufac-* motives for encouraging the production of raw materials. *ture.* The reciprocal relations, which in the view of contemporaries should subsist between the mother country and the colonies, were set forth in a letter written by George Grenville to William Knox in the eighteenth century but reflecting a standpoint familiar in the seventeenth century : " I perfectly agree with you ' that we ought to take our materials for manufactures from our colonies, although we should pay higher prices for them or be obliged to reduce the price of them to our manufacturers by bounties '. . . . The giving to them every possible encouragement to produce raw materials for our use would, in my opinion, be the most proper as well as the most effectual means of diverting them from manufacturing themselves to a great extent " [5]. The

---

[1] Defoe's phrase : *A Plan of the English Commerce* (ed. 1728), p. ix. Cf. Cary, *An Essay towards Regulating the Trade* (ed. 1719), 50.

[2] Beer, *The Commercial policy of England towards the American Colonies*, 81 (*c.* 1717).

[3] A list is given in *The Groans of the Plantations* (1689), 28-29. About one-quarter of the exports from the mother country to the colonies consisted of foreign goods : Beer, *British Colonial Policy*, 1754-1765, p. 282.

[4] *House of Commons Journals*, xxiii. 116. For Thomas Jefferson's views : *infra*, Appendix, p. 509, No. 4.

[5] *Hist. MSS. Comm. Various*, vi. 95-96 (1768).

commodities which the colonies were to be discouraged from manufacturing included textiles, woollen and linen, iron, hats and leather [1]. Not content, however, to rely upon her superior economic efficiency, the mother country embarked upon the policy of repressive legislation. The most conspicuous example was the treatment of the woollen industry. As early as 1638 the beginnings of a cloth manufacture in America are noted, many of the settlers ' having been clothiers in England ' [2]. After the Revolution the Commissioners for Trade and Plantations reported that New England and other northern colonies had applied themselves ' too much ' to the improvement of woollen manufactures amongst themselves [3]. At their instigation Parliament inserted a clause in the Act of 1699, which provided that no wool, woollen yarn or woollen manufactures, ' being of the product or manufacture of any of the English plantations in America ', should be exported from the colonies or even transported from one colony to another : " and we have since understood ", they stated (1700), " that the said restraint has had a very good effect " [4]. But in a subsequent report (1707) it was admitted that the northern colonies " do not only clothe themselves with woollen goods, but furnish the same commodity to the more southern plantations, notwithstanding the prohibition in the Act of (1699) " [5].

*Repression of the iron industry.* The iron manufacture ranked next in the category of prohibited industries. At first the production of iron in America was encouraged. " No better iron in the world ", Sir Edwin Sandys, a leading member of the Virginia Company, told the House of Commons in 1621. The Company erected in Virginia three or four iron works, which cost four thousand pounds and were said to be ' in great forwardness ' [6]. About the same time the ' Company of the New-

---

[1] Gee, *The Trade and Navigation of Great Britain* (ed. 1730), 80-81.
[2] Beer, *The Origins of the British Colonial System*, 285, note 3.
[3] *House of Commons Journals*, xii. 427.
[4] *Statutes*, vii. 528 ; *House of Commons Journals*, xiii. 299.
[5] *House of Lords MSS.* 1706-1708, p. 250.
[6] *House of Commons Journals*, i. 622 (1621) : *State Papers Colonial*, 1574-1660, pp. 39, 57.

foundland Plantation ' was permitted " to transport thither the materials to make bar iron, as iron ore, stone and cinders, as also the instruments for that work, that thereby they might be encouraged to go on in their purpose of erecting iron works in that plantation " [1]. Even more significant was the proposal made by the governor of Virginia to the Privy Council, in 1633, that skilled artisans should be transported ' to set the iron works on foot ' [2]—a request which would have been inconceivable a century later when the emigration of ' manufacturers ' was viewed with extreme jealousy [3]. The rupture with Sweden shortly after the accession of George I. brought the question of American iron into sudden prominence, and opened up a controversy which lasted until the War of Independence settled it, and other controversies, in summary fashion. The annual consumption of iron in Great Britain now amounted to forty thousand tons, according to a contemporary statement [4], and more than half came from abroad, especially Sweden [5]. The shortage of fuel rendered it difficult to increase the home supply ; while the interruption of trade in the Baltic, coupled with the action of the Swedes in laying an additional duty of nearly 25 per cent. [6] on exported iron, revealed the inexpediency of depending on foreign countries—apart from the drain of money abroad to pay for it [7]. The American colonies abounded with wood and iron ore, while the climate was healthy and provisions cheap, so that with due encouragement a sufficient quantity of pig iron could be made to supply the forges of the mother country at reduced cost. The proposal was restricted to pig iron, but the ironmasters were at once up in arms. They protested that any encouragement of the iron manufacture in the colonies would inevitably tend to the ruin of the iron trade of this kingdom. " No forbidding clause or restraint, if iron be made in the plantations ",

[1] *Acts of the Privy Council*, Colonial Series, 1613–1680, p. 34.
[2] *State Papers Colonial*, 1574–1660, p. 160.  [3] *Supra*. p. 47.
[4] *House of Commons Journals*, xix. 103.  [5] *Supra*. vol. ii. p. 161.
[6] Macpherson, *Annals of Commerce*, iii. 73.
[7] Between two and three hundred thousand pounds per annum is one estimate : Gee, *The Trade and Navigation of Great Britain* (ed. 1730), 68.

they contended, " can prevent their manufacturing of it in those countries where there is coal in such plenty and conveniences for it " ; and we should therefore lose both the making of pig and bar iron, and the manufacture of iron wares [1]. To meet their objection a Bill was introduced into Parliament, which forbade the making of bar iron and the manufacture of iron wares. This would have destroyed all the iron works in the colonies, and rendered it an offence for a smith to fashion even ' a bolt, spike or nail ' : but the Bill failed to pass [2].

*Rival interests of ironmongers and ironmasters.*
The controversy grew acute in 1737. The ironmongers complained that bounties were paid on the importation of tar, pitch, turpentine, hemp, masts, yards, and bowsprits, but none upon iron imported into this kingdom from our American colonies, " where it is capable of being produced in every respect equal in goodness to the best iron from Sweden ". Their anxiety to stimulate the importation of American iron was due to the fear of losing the American market for iron wares. New England had erected furnaces, forges and slitting mills, and not only made bar iron but manufactured it into ' axes, nails and sundry other species ', with which they supplied themselves and their neighbours. This injured the iron manufacturers in the Midlands, whose trade had " always increased and flourished till lately in proportion to the American plantations, but now greatly declines for want of its usual demands " [3]. To discourage the colonies from working up their iron it was proposed to create a market in England for their raw material, though the contention that the export of bar iron from America would prevent it being manufactured there assumed that American bar iron could be sent to England, worked up here, and then returned to the colonies to be sold there cheaper than the American ironmonger could manufacture it. This assumption failed to take account of two things.

---

[1] *House of Commons Journals*, xix. 118. Also *ibid*. xviii. 691, 733, 745-749.
[2] 1719 : Macpherson, *Annals of Commerce*, iii. 72-73.
[3] *House of Commons Journals*, xxii. 772-773, 776, 828 ; xxiii. 15. It was also reported that English iron workers in the metal trades had emigrated to the colonies : *ibid*. xxii. 776.

One was the cost of carriage. In addition to the transport of bar iron from the forges to the coast, its freight from New England to London was said to be 40s. per ton with port charges ; its carriage from London to the Midlands, where the iron was manufactured, was about 30s. ; the carriage of the manufactured iron to London was 70s. to 80s. by land and 40s. by water. The freight to America is not stated nor the cost of its distribution there, though it was affirmed that iron wares were liable to rust by water carriage. Moreover the iron passed through many hands : the American factor, the English importer, the bar ironmonger in the provinces, the manufacturer, the London dealer, the English exporter, the American dealer. The cost of carriage and re-carriage, and the profits of the different venders who handled the commodity, were considered insuperable obstacles to the export of bar iron from America to be manufactured in this country [1].

A dozen years later the conflict of rival interests ended *The Act* in a victory of the iron manufacturers over the ironmasters. *of 1750.* The Act of 1750 encouraged the production of pig iron and bar iron in the colonies by allowing it to be imported into England duty-free [2], in order to furnish the needs of the iron manufacturers. And it endeavoured to safeguard the interests of the latter by forbidding the erection of any new colonial " mill or other engine for slitting or rolling of iron, or any plating forge to work with a tilt hammer, or any furnace for making steel " [3]. The Act had an instructive sequel, which not only exhibited in all its crudity the selfish spirit animating this restrictive legislation, but also illus trated anew the unfavourable reactions produced on the mother country itself. In 1764 the Commissioners for Trade and Plantations expressed the opinion that the export of coal from England very much enhanced its price to the consumer at home, and to relieve the burden upon

[1] *House of Commons Journals*, xxiii. 109, 113.
[2] *Statutes at Large*, vi. 490-491. The exemption from duty on bar iron applied only to London, but in 1757 it was extended to all ports : *ibid.* vii. 144 ; *Hist. MSS. Comm. Le Fleming*, 357. For parliamentary petitions in support of and against the Act, see *House of Commons Journals*, xxv. 1018-1022, 1038-1039.
[3] This was disregarded in America : *infra*, Appendix, p. 510, No. 1.

English manufactures it recommended that the colonies should be supplied with coal from Cape Breton. But the apprehension gained ground that the development of coal-mining in America would provide her with the means of establishing an iron manufacture, and two years later it was decided not to authorize nor encourage the opening of the mines at Cape Breton [1].

*Export of hats prohibited.*   The ban was also visited upon the export of hats. This action was taken in 1732 as a result of the London Felt-makers' petition, in which they represented that " the inhabitants of the plantations in America, being supplied with beaver skins at less expense than the petitioners, have been induced to set up a manufacture of hats, and are thereby enabled not only to supply the foreign markets but even to send over hats to Great Britain " [2]. The comparative cheapness of their raw material, which was burdened with neither customs nor freight, enabled the American hat-makers to " afford hats five shillings cheaper there than here in England ". Some indication of the size of the American unit of production is given in the evidence of a witness before a committee appointed to investigate the question. He stated that he had worked at Boston with a master hatmaker, who commonly finished forty beaver hats in a week. Four or five apprentices, the number kept by most of the hatmakers, were employed in the trade besides journeymen, and they were bound only for two to four years. The wage paid for making a hat was 1s. 3d. : the corresponding wage in England was 4s. 6d. or 5s. [3]. The Act of 1732 forbade the export of hats from the British plantations " to any other of the British plantations or to any other place whatsoever ", and restricted colonial hat-makers to two apprentices [4] : but in spite of the prohibition, we are told a generation later, hats manufactured in New England found a good though clandestine market in the rest of the colonies [5].

---

[1] *Acts of the Privy Council,* Colonial Series, vi. 363; *ibid.* 1766–1783, pp. 18-20.
[2] *House of Commons Journals,* xxi. 802.          [3] *Ibid.* xxi. 824.
[4] *Statutes at Large,* v. 594-595.
[5] *The Present State of the British Empire* (1768), 288.

Other examples show that official opinion in England *Other in-dustries dis-couraged.* had become definitely committed to the view that " every attempt in the colonies to check or interfere with the manu- factures of this country ought, in policy and reason, to be discouraged and suppressed " [1]. Colonial legislation, which seemed likely to promote native industries, was frowned upon : thus an Act of the Virginia legislature was dis- allowed because it relieved the exporters of dressed hides from ' certain duties paid upon their importation ', and an Act of the South Carolina legislature because it proposed a bounty on linen made in the colony [2]. The English manu- facturer enjoyed another advantage in the colonial market— he was partially protected from foreign competition. The Act of Navigation provided that European products must be shipped to the colonies from England only [3]. Nearly all the duties levied on them in England were paid back on their re-exportation to the colonies, except in the case of some foreign products such as manufactured iron and steel, cordage, sail cloth and paper, which meant that in these commodities the English producer enjoyed a preference [4]. On the other hand, the mother country paid bounties on certain goods, for example, linen made in Great Britain and Ireland ; and this diminished the price to the colonial purchaser.

It was a mistaken policy on the part of the mother *Mistaken policy of England.* country to exhibit this jealous spirit towards American industries, despite the defence [5] that she depended upon her manufactures to provide the resources which enabled her to give protection to her oversea dominions. English manufacturers had no valid ground for fearing colonial competition : the superior quality and cheapness of their goods were their best protection. The cost of making woollen cloth was stated by the Commissioners for Trade and Plantations in 1732 to be 50 per cent. greater in

---

[1] *Acts of the Privy Council*, Colonial Series, 1766–1783, p. 37.
[2] *Ibid.* 37, 319-320.  See *infra*, Appendix, p. 510, No. 2.
[3] *Supra*, p. 125.
[4] Beer, *British Colonial Policy*, 1754–1765, pp. 194-195, 201.  The drawback was 97½ per cent. (in 1764 reduced to 95 per cent.) of the amount paid : *ibid.* 281-282.
[5] *E.g.* Gee, *The Trade and Navigation of Great Britain* (ed. 1730), 79.

America than in England, and that of linen cloth 20 per cent., owing to the high price of labour [1]. Nor were the authorities at home incapable of recognizing the true principles of imperial economic relationships, as is shown by the report of the Commissioners for Trade and Plantations on a proposal, made in 1706, to compel American planters to clothe their servants and slaves in English woollen manufactures : " Wares and merchandises of any sort to be sent from England for the supply of your majesty's plantations ought rather to be recommended to your subjects there by their proper goodness, usefulness and cheapness, than be imposed upon them at a rated price by the power and compulsion of laws, which would be the greatest discouragement to trade " [2]. Coercion, in any case, was bound to fail because the Acts of Trade could not be properly executed in America : they were unpopular there since they were deemed unjust, and American juries refused to convict [3]. The alternative to coercion was to encourage as much as possible the production of raw materials, which would divert the energies of the colonists into other channels, and enable them to afford English manufactured articles [4]. Once the colonies were genuinely ripe for industrial development the impotence of artificial restraints would have been speedily revealed. In the circumstances legislative interference was important, not so much in the infliction of actual economic injury—though this was not always insignificant [5] —as in demonstrating the political subjection of the colonies to external control.

The extent to which economic factors were responsible for the American Revolution cannot easily be measured. At first sight it is natural to attribute the disruption of

[1] Macpherson, *Annals of Commerce*, iii. 187. See *infra*, Appendix, p. 510, No. 3.
[2] *Acts of the Privy Council*, Colonial Series, vi. 46.
[3] *Hist. MSS. Comm. Stopford-Sackville*, ii. 103. Yet the Acts of Trade were not ' innocuous nor negligible ' : see *Acts of the Privy Council*, Colonial Series, 1720–1745, p. ix.
[4] *Hist. MSS. Comm. Various*, vi. 293.
[5] " We extremely suffered by the Act of 1696 ", wrote William Penn : *ibid. Portland*, iii. 602. (For the Act of 1696, see *Statutes*, vii. 103 *seq*.) See also *supra*, note 3. For currency grievances, see *infra*, Appendix, p. 511, No. 1.

England's first empire to a policy avowedly designed to *How far economic factors were responsible for the American Revolution.* make the oversea settlements 'duly subservient and useful'[1]. Yet contemporary English opinion held that the colonies "felt the benefit more than the burden" of the Acts of Trade[2], and the view appears on the whole well-founded. Irksome as their disabilities may seem on paper, the working of the system was not unduly onerous in practice. It was modified by concessions such as those which enabled the colonies to carry on trade direct with southern Europe in certain 'enumerated commodities', or it was evaded with the open connivance of the American authorities. This lax administration of the system helped to bring the authority and prestige of the mother country into disrepute ; and habitual disregard for the laws of the parent state fostered a spirit of independence, which made any attempt at enforcement of the laws appear a gross act of tyranny. The efforts to suppress smuggling and administer the Acts of Trade with greater rigour, by substituting vice-admiralty courts for juries[3] and employing the navy[4], were the more deeply resented because the colonies had grown accustomed to the latitude which alone made the Acts tolerable. Against their disabilities, real or nominal, must be set the reciprocal advantages which the colonies enjoyed in the shape of the protection, the credit and the market of the mother country. The old colonial system, as the ruthless destruction of tobacco-growing in England demonstrated, was far from one-sided. Nor were even their disabilities unattended by compensating features. Behind the shelter of the Navigation Laws which protected her from alien competition, New England built up an important shipbuilding industry[5]. These considerations may fairly lead us to conclude that, though individuals

---

[1] *House of Commons Journals*, xiii. 448 (Report of the Commissioners for Trade and Plantations, 1701).

[2] *Hist. MSS. Comm. Fortescue*, i. 504 (1789).

[3] *House of Commons Journals*, xiii. 300 ; *Hist. MSS. Comm. Portland*, iii. 602. On the vice-admiralty courts : *infra*, Appendix, p. 511, No. 2.

[4] *Statutes at Large*, vii. 444 ; *Acts of the Privy Council*, Colonial Series, 1745–1766, pp. 560, 690. See also Beer, *British Colonial Policy*, 1754–1765, chapter xi., and Andrews, *The Colonial Period of American History*, iv. chapters vi.-vii.      [5] *Supra*, p. 180.

chafed against the restraints laid upon them, the colonies
would not have cut themselves adrift from the mother
country on the ground of economic grievances alone : and
this conclusion is fortified by the absence, in the Declaration
of Independence, of all reference to the Acts of Trade beyond
an allusion of doubtful significance [1].

*Other causes of the American Revolution.* The seeds of revolution were sown at the birth of the
colonies. The Puritan exiles manifested from the first a
marked spirit of independence ; and as early as 1633 the
objection was being voiced against New England that in
time " they will revolt from their allegiance " [2]. Although
then described as ' a causeless fear ', the apprehension
remained. " It very much concerns the nation of Great
Britain ", wrote an American correspondent eighty years
later, " to take some speedy care of us . . . lest in time the
seed of rebellion should spring up ", and the people " put
in practice what they now can only talk of " [3]. The economic growth of the colonies, combined with the removal
of the French danger, provided the conditions which made
possible a declaration of independence ; and the greatest
exercise of tact and patience alone could have averted it.
Accordingly, in weighing up the causes of the American
Revolution other elements besides the economic must be
considered—the independent character of the early settlers,
which created a tradition of self-assertion and self-reliance [4] ;
the enjoyment of autonomy, which strengthened and developed this tradition, and so ripened the seeds of revolt [5] ;
the absence of close and continuous relations with the
mother country [6], whose authority could not be properly

[1] The allusion to laws " for cutting off our trade with all parts of the
world " may only refer to the Boston Port Bill : Beer, *British Colonial
Policy*, 1754–1765, p. 306, note 2.    See also Andrews, *The Colonial Background of the American Revolution*, 128 (and the admirable discussion in
*ibid.* Essay iv.).    And *infra*, Appendix, p. 511, No. 3.

[2] *Hist. MSS. Comm. Cowper*, ii. 38-39.

[3] *Ibid. Portland*, v. 200 (1712).    Defoe dismissed the ' notion ' of
revolt as 'absurd and without foundation ' : *A Plan of the English Commerce* (ed. 1728), 143, 354-357.    Similarly : Gee, *The Trade and Navigation of Great Britain* (ed. 1730), 71-72.

[4] " New England has shown an uncommon stiffness" : Gee, *op. cit.* 72.

[5] Cf. *Hist. MSS. Comm. Fortescue*, i. 504.

[6] Cf. *ibid. Buckinghamshire*, 297.

enforced in distant lands [1], and in whose concerns the colonies felt no vital interest ; the destruction of the French power in America, which removed the most serious obstacle to secession. But whatever the causes of the loss of the American colonies, the old colonial system—based on the principle that "colonies are a strength to their mother kingdom . . . while they are kept dependent on it" [2]—had outlived its day. The new standpoint was indicated by Burke when he wrote : " A great empire cannot at this time be supported upon a narrow and restrictive scheme either of commerce or government " [3].

## (v)

### IRELAND

The old colonial system had its counterpart in England's treatment of Ireland where Mercantilism, conceived in the narrowest spirit, produced its bitterest fruits. The economic relations between the two countries were dominated and poisoned by jealousy of Irish competition, and the fact that Ireland had been planted with English settlers [4] did not prevent the enactment of measures detrimental to her well-being. Even enlightened and experienced writers like Child, one of the greatest figures in the business world of the seventeenth century, considered that England was affected adversely by the progress of Ireland, which supplied foreign markets with wool, meat and corn " at cheaper rates than we can afford to the beating us out of those trades " [5]. Davenant predicted, as the effect of Irish competition, that " rents must everywhere fall . . . the poor

*Relations between England and Ireland.*

[1] The journey from Portsmouth to Charleston (South Carolina) occupied seven weeks in 1756: *ibid. Various*, vi. 245-246. See also *supra*, p. 162, note 4.

[2] Davenant, *Works* (ed. 1771), ii. 10, 24.

[3] Burke's letter (1778) is printed in Latimer, *Merchant Venturers of Bristol*, 196. For the views of the Elder Pitt and Franklin, see *supra*, vol. ii. Introduction, p. xcix.

[4] For the plantation of Ulster by London companies in the reign of James I., see Scott, *Joint-Stock Companies*, ii. 338 *seq.* ; Johnson, *The History of the Worshipful Company of the Drapers of London*, iii. 16-50, 123-139, 266-271, 374-424; O'Brien, *The Economic History of Ireland in the Seventeenth Century*, 22 *seq.* Also *Hist. MSS. Comm. Cowper*, i. 95 ; *ibid. Beaulieu*, 107.

[5] Child, *A New Discourse of Trade* (4th ed.), 49.

must want employment . . . half our foreign trade must forthwith cease " [1]. Both writers overlooked the fact that Ireland, if she entered into competition with England, at the same time provided a valuable market for English commodities [2]. But behind the façade of economic nationalism, stripped bare of trappings and pretences, lay the sombre influences of racial domination and religious bigotry, which kept apart in relentless antagonism the two nations whom Nature and History had linked together in indissoluble union. These complex forces created the atmosphere in which the clamour of sectional interests yielded an abundant crop of repressive legislation. Irish cattle, Irish wool and Irish cloth were the three commodities which opened up a fertile field of embittered controversy [3].

*Irish cattle.*

The importation of Irish cattle into England had attracted hostile notice in the early decades of the seventeenth century, when complaint was made that it ' decayed' the breed of English cattle, depressed the value of land, and drained the kingdom of ' great store ' of money. A Bill against importation was introduced into the House of Commons in 1621, but was rejected on the ground that it would raise the cost of living and curtail the Irish demand for English manufactures [4]. After the Restoration the political situation reinforced the economic argument, and in 1664 a penalty of £2 was levied per head of ' great cattle ' imported during the latter half of the year. Three years later another Act forbade the importation of cattle from Ireland or ' any other place beyond the seas ' [5]. In spite of the warning that it ' will beggar this kingdom ' [6] (Ireland), the prohibition remained in force for nearly a century [7],

---

[1] Davenant, *Works* (ed. 1771), ii. 253.

[2] For the amount of the trade between England and Ireland near the end of the seventeenth century, see *House of Lords MSS.* 1697–1699, pp. 133-134.

[3] For the restrictions imposed on Irish trade by the Navigation Acts, see *supra*, p. 128.

[4] *House of Commons Journals*, i. 527, 615, 625 ; *State Papers Domestic*, 1619–1623, pp. 393, 498.

[5] *Statutes*, v. 451 (1664), 597 (1667), 641.

[6] *Hist. MSS. Comm. Egmont*, ii. 9. For the Irish objections to the Act, see *State Papers Ireland*, 1666–1669, pp. 185-188, 289-293, 533-542.

[7] It was removed ' for a limited time ' in 1759 and in subsequent years, and permanently in 1776 : *Statutes at Large*, vii. 260 ; viii. 460.

but its effects proved injurious to England as well as to Ireland[1].

Firstly : it was prejudicial to landowners because *Effects of the prohibition of Irish cattle.* "the breeding lands of England are not able to raise a sufficient stock for the feeding [lands], six months feeding being as much as four years breeding " ; and owing to the scarcity the breeders charged more for lean cattle than they yielded when fatted, "which makes feeding lands worth little or nothing ". Secondly : it was detrimental to navigation and the customs revenue—the former since three or four hundred ships had formerly been employed in the carrying trade ; the latter because it diminished the volume of trade between the two countries. Thirdly : the victualling of ships, native and foreign, was transferred from England to Ireland where beef was sold at 12s. the barrel of 2½ cwt., while in England 23s. the cwt. was paid[2] ; and it caused vexation that " the Dutch and French now victual much cheaper in Ireland than the English can in England ". Fourthly : " as if the mischief of these Acts would never have an end ", the prohibition turned the trade of Ireland into a wrong channel. It " made Ireland lessen their great cattle and increase their sheep, so that they have prodigious quantities of wool, which with their hides and tallow is mischievous to England in three ways "—by exporting it abroad to be worked up in foreign countries ; by sending it to England where it competed with our own ; and " by setting up woollen manufactories in Ireland where, having wool, hides and tallow cheaper than we, and all sorts of provisions at a much less rate, they must have workmen for half the price ". The final argument has a special interest in its assumption that labour is the cause of value : " The riches of a nation arising from the labourer, artificer and manufacturer, from their labour money is first raised

---

[1] For the case against the Act, see *State Papers Domestic*, 1673–1675, pp. 166 *seq.* ; *ibid.* 1667–1668, p. 46 ; *House of Commons Journals*, xxiv. 447, 465 ; Coke, *Treatise* (1671), i. 53-68 ; iii. 39-40 ; Petty, *Economic Writings*, i. 185, 299 ; *Britannia Languens* (1680), 53, 162-167 ; Collins, *A Plea for the bringing in of Irish Cattle* (1680), 4, 6, 9 ; *The Grand Concern of England explained in Several Proposals* (1673), 16 *seq.* ; Davenant, *Works* (ed. 1771), ii. 257.

[2] In 1674 : *State Papers Domestic*, 1673–1675, p. 167.

to pay the tenant and through him the landlord. Now to check the labourer is to stifle the riches of the nation in embryo ; and how much the prohibition has . . . done this is to be considered " [1]. It had diminished the demand for English manufactures, hops and beer taken in exchange for Irish cattle [2] ; and, in addition to the loss of an important market, the industrial population in England " cannot feed so well since provisions are dearer ", nor produce so cheaply—a matter already recognized in the seventeenth century as " very important to a country that subsists so much by manufactures ". These arguments foreshadowed the demand that the agricultural interest must not be allowed to override the national interest [3]. Almost the solitary voice on the other side was Houghton, who maintained that the consumption of home products would raise rents [4]. The fall in rents had been the main argument in favour of protection, although Cobden's view, that the agriculturist did not benefit by protection, was anticipated by those who pointed out that the value of land depended on the state of trade—" which is ever so much better . . . by how much the freer it is "—a prosperous people being able to afford the farmer better prices for his produce [5].

*Irish wool.* A different policy was pursued in respect of Irish wool. Its export to England was actively encouraged [6] in order to prevent the growth of an Irish woollen industry, but elsewhere it was prohibited [7]. The embargo on Irish cattle, however, stimulated the production of wool, which was shipped to foreign parts under the pretence that it was

[1] *State Papers Domestic,* 1673–1675, p. 168.
[2] The value of Irish cattle imported into England was estimated at £80,000 to £90,000 per annum ; and the value of English exports to Ireland, prior to the prohibition, at £204,000: *ibid.* 1673–1675, pp. 168-169. For another estimate, see *ibid.* 1667–1668, p. 46 ; and for Petty's calculations, *ibid.* 1673–1675, p. 169.
[3] Davenant concluded that the prohibition " is wholly beneficial to the northern and western counties and has improved their land, and is hurtful to the rest of England " : *Works* (ed. 1771), i. 46 ; ii. 257.
[4] Houghton, *Husbandry and Trade Improv'd* (ed. 1728), iv. 82 *seq.*
[5] Coke, *Treatise* (1671), i. 58, 64 ; iii. 40-41. Also *supra,* p. 33.
[6] Letter of Charles II. in *State Papers Domestic,* 1672, p. 337. See *infra,* Appendix, p. 511, No. 4.
[7] *Acts of the Privy Council,* 1615–1616, p. 639 ; *Tudor and Stuart Proclamations* (ed. Steele), i. No. 1600 (1630) ; *Acts and Ordinances of the Interregnum,* i. 1061 (1648).

destined for England[1]. To check this practice, certain ports were appointed in England and Ireland to serve as the sole channels of the wool trade between the two countries[2]: a proposal was even made to form a company to buy up all the surplus wool of Ireland " that comes to the ports " there[3]: yet no device was successful in stamping out smuggling[4]. Ireland was allowed to export yarn to England as well as wool, though in the case of yarn the sentiments of manufacturers were divided. A parliamentary committee in 1708 described the importation of Irish worsted yarn as 'a growing evil' because it was sold for 14d. a pound, while English worsted yarn of similar quality cost 20d.[5] It met, therefore, with violent opposition from woolcombers and was said to be disliked by weavers who worked by the piece, being alleged to be weaker and to involve more time in repairing broken threads[6]. Nevertheless, in spite of the protests of the graziers and the disturbances created by the workmen, Irish yarn continued to be imported and in 1740 was freed from the payment of customs duty[7].

Restrained from transporting cattle to England, or wool *Irish cloth.* anywhere but to England, the Irish people turned their energies to butter-making and cloth-making. To protect the home market of the English farmer, and the foreign market of the English manufacturer, the Act of 1681 prohibited the export of Irish butter and cheese to England, and the Act of 1699 prohibited the export of Irish woollen

---

[1] *Hist. MSS. Comm. Ormonde*, ii. 268, 385 ; iv. 116-117. *State Papers Domestic*, 1677–1678, p. 71 ; 1694–1695, p. 457.
[2] *Statutes*, vii. 526 (1699). The restriction to specified ports was removed in 1753 : *Statutes at Large*, vii. 12.
[3] 1674 : *State Papers Domestic*, 1673–1675, pp. 170-171 ; *An Account of the late Design of buying up the Wool of Ireland in Company* (1674).
[4] *Remarks on the . . . Necessity of preventing the Irish Wool being run* (1730) ; *Hist. MSS. Comm. Buckinghamshire*, 303 (1770).
[5] *House of Commons Journals*, xv. 476-477, 533, 544, 553 ; xvi. 137, 553, 569, 575. Irish combed wool was 1d. per lb. cheaper.
[6] *The Interest of England Consider'd with respect to the Woollen Manufactures* (1731), 19.
[7] *House of Commons Journals*, xvi. 569 ; xxi. 693 ; xxiii. 358 ; *Statutes at Large*, vi. 87 ; *The Grasier's Complaint. By a Lincolnshire Grasier* (1726). For the disturbances caused by the importation of Irish yarn, see Dunsford, *Historical Memoirs of Tiverton* (1790), 208, 230 *seq.*

manufactures except to England [1]. The policy of discouraging the Irish woollen industry was not new. In the reign of Charles I. there had existed in Ireland ' some small beginnings towards a clothing trade ', which Strafford checked for fear " they would beat us out of the trade itself by underselling us, which they were well able to do " [2]; and after the Restoration, according to Petty, the ' clothing trade ' was even less than before the Civil War [3]. But when the Irish farmers, cut off from the English market, concentrated attention on grazing, wool and meat became plentiful and cheap, the price of wool being four shillings a stone less than in England [4]; and this abundance of raw material, coupled with cheapness of living, attracted English artisans from the West of England and induced Irish refugees, who had settled here during the wars of the Revolution and acquired experience in making cloth, to return home [5]. " These erected then a manufactory (great in respect to Ireland) at Dublin [6], which hath been carried on ever since and increases daily. There came also over, much about the same time, sixty families from Holland setting up another at Limerick, which by occasion of the succeeding wars decayed. But, after these, more of the English clothiers came and fixed about Cork and Kinsale, where they continue and are grown not inconsiderable. Some French have since resorted to Waterford to make druggets there and other commodities of their fashion. And about a year or two ago some merchants of London raised another manufacture at Clonmel, managing it by their agents [7]. . . .

---

[1] *Statutes*, v. 941 ; vii. 524 (These Acts came into operation in 1681 and 1699 respectively). Coke, *Treatise* (1671), i. 62.

[2] Knowler, *The Earl of Strafforde's Letters and Despatches* (1739), ii. 19.

[3] Petty, *Economic Writings*, i. 209.

[4] *State Papers Domestic*, 1672, p. 337.

[5] *House of Commons Journals*, x. 611. The Duke of Ormond employed Graunt in 1667 to procure 500 Walloon families about Canterbury and transport them into Ireland : Carte, *The Life of James, Duke of Ormond* (ed. 1851), iv. 284.

[6] Sheffield, *Observations on the Objections made to the Export of Wool from Great Britain to Ireland* (1800), 23, speaks of a settlement of English clothiers at Dublin ' about 1664 '.

[7] A company is said to have been formed in London with a joint stock of £100,000 ; Yarranton, *England's Improvement* (1677), 101-102.

There is more cry than wool in all this matter : for I dare
and do assure you that, modestly speaking, the whole
quantity of what we work up in Ireland amounts not to the
half of what any one clothing county in England does " [1].

Alarmed at this new development the English woollen *Fear of*
manufacturers, who claimed ' by prescription and posses- *Irish com-*
*petition.*
sion ' the sole right of making cloth, raised a great outcry ;
and the instruments of the emigrant weavers were destroyed
by mobs [2]. Irish competition was dreaded because labour
was cheap. In England a wool-comber earned nine to ten
shillings a week, the wool was prepared with oil costing $7\frac{1}{2}$d.
to 8d. a pound or more, and " the woman that spins it
would think sixpence a day small wages ". In Ireland " the
spinner would be content to earn threepence a day, and herself goes through the whole process from the sheep's back
until the worsted is ready for the loom, preparing it with the
worst butter at twopence or threepence a pound mixed with
a mucilaginous juice got from fern roots ". The weaving
was also done very cheaply as " the women of every peasant
manufacture clothing and blankets for the family " [3].
But if Ireland appeared to possess some advantages in the
' first cost ' of woollen manufactures, she was handicapped
in other respects—" the convenience of markets, the distance of ports, the opportunity of shipping, the dyeing and
particular preparations of some sorts of cloths, with many
other things relating to trade in those manufactures " [4].

After the Revolution the manufacturers of the West *The Act*
Country protested to Parliament that Ireland was under- *of 1699.*
mining English trade, and that ' vast numbers of our workmen ' were emigrating to Ireland where they were " able
to undersell the petitioners at least 20 per cent." [5]. The

[1] *A Letter from a Gentleman in Ireland to his Brother in England* in
Smith, *Chronicon Rusticum-Commerciale* (ed. 1747), i. 303-304. Similarly :
*House of Lords MSS.* 1697–1699, pp. 108 *seq.*
[2] *State Papers Domestic*, 1675–1676, pp. 277, 329.
[3] *Hist. MSS. Comm. Stopford-Sackville*, i. 257-258. This was written
in 1779, but it represents the situation a century earlier : *e.g. House of
Commons Journals*, xviii. 686 ; *House of Lords MSS.* 1697–1699, pp.
108 *seq.*
[4] Report of the Commissioners for Trade and Plantations in *House of
Lords MSS.* 1697–1699, p. 388.
[5] *House of Commons Journals*, x. 611 (1692) ; xii. 37, 64 (1698).

Commissioners for Trade and Plantations expressed the opinion that the Irish woollen industry was " wholly incompatible with the fundamental trade of England, on which the prosperity of this nation so much depends " [1]. Both Houses of Parliament petitioned the King that " the wealth and power of this kingdom do, in a great measure, depend on the preserving the woollen manufacture as much as is possible entire to this realm ", and " it becomes us, like our ancestors, to be jealous of the establishment and the increase thereof elsewhere " [2]. In vain it was urged that the proposed restrictions would " greatly prejudice the trade of England and ruin the Protestant interest of Ireland " : in vain it was pointed out that " dearness of wages does not destroy manufactures, but always is an evidence that they thrive " [3] : and in vain the warning was uttered [4] that it was impossible to prevent Ireland exporting her wool, if she were discouraged from manufacturing it. In 1699 the export of Irish woollen manufactures was prohibited except to England [5] ; and " the Irish woollen fabrics ", in the words of Arthur Young, " were destroyed by one of the most infamous Statutes that ever disgraced a legislature " [6]. A generation after its enactment it was said to have " laid the foundations of all the misfortunes of both kingdoms ". It drove Irish workmen abroad [7] where they set up their trade, and—so ran the current opinion—" taught our neighbours to steal from us a manufacture we entirely engrossed before ". A writer pointed out that the English persecution in trade had the same effect as the French

[1] *House of Commons Journals*, xii. 427.
[2] 1698 : *ibid.* xii. 338 ; xix. 237.
[3] *Ibid.* xii. 407 ; *Some Thoughts on the Bill*, etc. (1698) ; *The Substance of the Arguments for and against the Bill* (1698).
[4] As early as 1662 : *Short Notes and Observations drawn from the present decaying condition of this Kingdom in point of Trade*, 8.
[5] *Statutes*, vii. 524.  *Supra*, p. 202, note 1.
[6] Young, *The Question of Wool Truly Stated* (1788), 21.  Ireland continued to make coarse stuffs for home consumption : Murray, *A History of the Commercial and Financial Relations between England and Ireland*, 108-109.
[7] *House of Commons Journals*, xvi. 569 (1711) ; *Some Thoughts on the Woollen Manufactures of England* (1731), 6.  The depopulation of the South and West of Ireland was attributed to the prohibition : *The Commercial Restraints of Ireland Considered in a Series of Letters* (1780), 134.

persecution in religion, in causing an exodus of Ireland's
most industrious sons. He showed the fallacy of the argument on which the suppression of the Irish woollen industry
had been based. Assuming that Ireland did work cheaper
than Yorkshire or Lancashire, would it hurt the British
Empire " more than it hurts her that Yorkshire or Lancashire should work cheaper than Devonshire or Cornwall ?
Can any man of open understanding consider Ireland but
in the light of four or five great counties, added to England
advantageously for water carriage, cut by a large navigable
river ? " [1]

The Act of 1699 remained in operation until 1780 [2]. *Irish linen*
Its survival on the statute-book for over three-quarters of
a century testified to the tenacity of the vested interests
affected [3]; but a menacing political situation at last drove
home the lesson that it was time for England " to awaken
from the dream that by impoverishing Ireland she enriches
herself " [4]. Meanwhile, to compensate Ireland for the
injury to her woollen manufacture, she was promised
' countenance, favour and protection ' for her linen manufacture, in order to make it " the general trade of that
country as effectually as the woollen manufacture is, and
must be, of England " [5]—although Davenant pointed out
that many countries, which bought our woollen goods, would
be unable to do so " unless we deal for their linens " [6].
The policy was initiated by Strafford, who expressed to
Charles I. his ambition " to leave your subjects there in
much happier condition than I found them, without the
least prejudice to your subjects here ". He wished to lay

---

[1] *A Representation of the State of Trade of Ireland* (1750) in Bischoff,
*History of the Woollen and Worsted Manufactures*, i. 141. Similarly :
*Essays on Several Subjects* (1769), 140-141.
[2] *Statutes at Large*, ix. 71-72.
[3] *Hist. MSS. Comm. Stopford-Sackville*, i. 257-258 ; *ibid. Lothian*, 331 ;
*ibid. Rutland*, iii. 373. See also *An Account of the Proceedings of the Merchants,
Manufacturers and others concerned in the Wool and Woollen Trade of Great
Britain* (1800), and Rathbone, *Memoir of Richard Reynolds*, 50. For the
opposition of the ' General Chamber of Manufacturers of Great Britain '
to Pitt's Irish policy (1785), see Bowden, *Industrial Society in England
towards the End of the Eighteenth Century*, 169 seq.
[4] *Hist. MSS. Comm. Stopford-Sackville*, ii. 103.
[5] *House of Commons Journals*, xii. 428 ; xiii. 299 ; xix. 237-238.
[6] Davenant, *Works* (ed. 1771), ii. 256.

" aside the manufacture of wools into cloth or stuff there ",
and " set up the manufactury of hemp and flax ".   " The
women ", he remarked, " are all naturally bred to spinning,
the Irish earth is apt for bearing of flax, and this manufacture would be in the conclusion rather a benefit than
other to this kingdom.   I have therefore sent for the flax-
seed into Holland. . . . I have sent for workmen out of the
Low Countries and forth of France, and set up already
six or seven looms " [1].  After the Revolution the undertaking to encourage Irish linens assumed the form of a
compact [2], to which effect was given in 1696 when Ireland
was permitted to export to England hemp, flax, linen yarn
and linen cloth duty-free [3].  The progress of the Irish linen
industry was further stimulated by the settlement of
Scottish dissenters and French Huguenots [4].

---

[1] Knowler, *The Earl of Strafforde's Letters and Despatches* (1739), i. 93 ;
ii. 19-20.  The Duke of Ormond also encouraged the linen manufacture
in Ireland and procured workmen from Brabant and France :  Carte, *The
Life of James, Duke of Ormond* (ed. 1851), iv. 284-285.

[2] *Hist. MSS. Comm. Lothian*, 331.

[3] *Statutes*, vii. 156.

[4] *A Letter from a Merchant.* . . . *The Case of the British and Irish
Manufacture of Linen* (1738), 13-14.  See also Gill, *The Rise of the Irish
Linen Industry*, 15 *seq.*

# CHAPTER V

## THE CONTROL OF INDUSTRY

THE industrial policy of the State in the sixteenth, seven- *Province* *and* teenth and eighteenth centuries, in contrast with its com- *methods of* mercial policy as embodied in the Mercantile System, is *State* *action.* not known by any distinctive name: but it was, none the less, based on certain well-defined principles [1]. The State inherited from the mediaeval gilds the tradition of authoritarian control in the sphere of industry, and the assumption of new responsibilities by Queen Elizabeth and her successors was made inevitable by the profound changes which were taking place in the economic structure of society. The growth of capitalism and the movement of industry away from the old urban centres were inter-related phenomena, and together they imperilled the whole system of industrial regulation as it had been built up in the Middle Ages. The creation of a national code was intended not to supersede, but to strengthen and supplement, the local codes of the mediaeval gilds; and the Statute of Apprentices (1563) and other legislative enactments were in their essentials nothing more than the application, on a wider scale, of principles which had been put into operation by municipal bodies. The province of State action—which has steadily grown, in spite of occasional and temporary reactions, from the sixteenth century down to the present day—embraced problems relating to wages, apprenticeship, unemployment, trade unionism, the technical processes of industry, and the encouragement of new industrial arts. The methods of control included both direct supervision through the agency of public officials, and the delegation of authority to cor-

[1] See *supra*, vol. ii. Introduction, pp. cii-cv.

porate bodies or individuals. In the following sections these problems and methods will be examined in detail : but first something must be said about the origin of capital and the system of finance, which helped to create the necessary conditions for industrial growth.

## (1)

### CAPITAL AND FINANCE

*Origin of capital.*

The origin of capital has been a subject of much speculation. On the Continent its genesis has been sought for in the rents of landlords, which created a surplus for investment in trade and industry. In England, too, landlords were to be found willing to sink capital in productive enterprises, though the latter were usually connected with the soil, for example, the Willoughbys of Nottinghamshire engaged in coal-mining[1]. Speaking generally, the capital which found its way into manufactures was drawn, in this country, not from rents but from trade. In the early Middle Ages England possessed in her natural products, especially wool— ' the goddess of merchants ', as Gower called it[2]—some indispensable commodities; and it was in the export abroad of wool, together with corn, tin and lead, that she laid the foundations of her wealth. The gains which accrued from trade were invested in manufactures, so that in England commerce, the child of agriculture, became the parent of industry. The remarkable expansion of the woollen manufactures in the fifteenth century converted England into a country whose staple export was cloth in place of wool, the manufactured article instead of its raw material ; and this revolution was already bringing great wealth to the kingdom before the close of the Middle Ages[3]. Henceforth commerce and industry reacted upon each other ; and capital began to play an increasingly important part in the development of both. The progress of capitalism[4] before the

---

[1] *Infra*, p. 214. Some monasteries carried on coal-mining : Savine, *English Monasteries on the Eve of the Dissolution*, 123-124 ; Nef, *The Rise of the British Coal Industry*, i. 134-136.
[2] *Supra*, p. 22. [3] *Supra*, vol. i. 459-461.
[4] See *supra*, vol. ii. Introduction, pp. xiii-xiv, xxxviii-xxxix.

Reformation forbids us to regard the capitalist spirit as a product of the Puritan movement. Nevertheless Puritanism contributed to the development of capitalism, since the aversion of the Puritan from pleasure not only promoted thrift but increased his absorption in business affairs. As a seventeenth-century writer remarked : " Amongst the Reformed the greater their zeal, the greater is their inclinations to trade and industry as holding idleness unlawful " [1]. Petty observed that the dissenters were " for the most part thinking, sober and patient men, and such as believe that labour and industry is their duty towards God " [2].

In the sixteenth and seventeenth centuries wealth in *Growth of* England grew rapidly ; and this provided the requisite *wealth in* *England.* basis for the accumulation of capital [2a]. Sir John Hawkins, the treasurer of the navy, thought in 1584 that native wealth had increased threefold since the accession of Elizabeth [3]. " The realm ", it was said, " aboundeth in riches, as may be seen by the general excess of the people in purchasing, in buildings, in meat, drink and feastings, and most notably in apparel " [4]. Davenant made precise calculations as to the advance made in the next century. He estimated that the 'stock' or wealth of England was about 17 million pounds in 1600, 28 millions in 1630, 56 millions in 1660, and 88 millions in 1688, while the annual income of the country at the end of the century was represented at 43 millions [5]. These figures are hypothetical, but there is no question as to the expansion of wealth in the seventeenth century. Child, writing after the Revolution, noted as evidence of national prosperity that the quantity of merchant shipping was doubled, and the volume of exports enlarged by one-third, within twenty years [6]. The increase of wealth was

[1] *The Present Interest of England Stated. By a Lover of his Country* (1671), 24. For Weber's thesis, see Tawney, *Religion and the Rise of Capitalism*, 319 ; Sée, *Modern Capitalism*, 39-40. Cf. *infra*, Appendix, p. 512, No. 1.

[2] Petty, *Economic Writings*, i. 262.

[2a] For changes in prices and their influence on capital : *supra*, vol. ii. Introduction, pp. xvi-xix.

[3] Wright, *Queen Elizabeth and Her Times* (1838), ii. 232.

[4] 1579 : Murdin, *A Collection of State Papers relating to Affairs in the Reign of Queen Elizabeth* (1759), 327.

[5] Davenant, *Works* (ed. 1771), i. 250, 375. Gregory King's figures were 25 millions (1600), 37 (1630), 64 (1664), 86 (1688) : *ibid.* ii. 276.

[6] Child, *A New Discourse of Trade* (4th ed.), pp. xxxvi-xxxvii. Cf. Petty, *Economic Writings*, i. 271. Also *supra*, pp. 91, 138.

largely drawn from three branches of trade : European, Colonial, and East Indian.  Davenant, assuming that the annual addition to the national wealth at the time of the Revolution was two millions, distributed the amount in the proportions of £900,000 (Colonial), £600,000 (East Indian), and £500,000 (European) [1].

*Privateering expeditions.*

Wealth came to England by other channels than trade. In the middle of Elizabeth's reign a writer spoke of " the great store and plenty of treasure, which is walking in these parts of the world, far more in these our days than ever our forefathers have seen in times past.  Who doth not understand of the infinite sums of gold and silver which are gathered from the Indies and other countries, and so yearly transported unto these coasts ? " [2]  These ' infinite sums ' came into English hands largely through the sacking of Spanish galleons.  " Twelve millions brought in ", said a member of Parliament in 1621, " in the Queen's time by gentlemen of worth—the spring that furnished the kingdom " [3].  Francis Drake brought back from his journey round the world gold and silver bullion out of which was provided, in part, the original capital of the Levant Company [4].  The bait of Spanish treasure proved irresistible— ' the Indies fleet ' laden with gold, silver and jewels was reputed in 1570 to be worth six million pounds, and " this whole fleet ", it was promised, " with God's grace shall be intercepted and taken within these three months " [5].  In the financing of privateering expeditions the Queen, her ministers, her court and others participated on a joint-stock basis, which served to familiarize the nation with the methods of a joint stock [6].  A correspondent wrote to

[1] Davenant, *Works* (ed. 1771), i. 93-94.  Gregory King calculated the annual increase at £2,400,000 : *ibid.* ii. 184 (Scheme B).  In 1677 it was estimated that the East India trade added £500,000 to the national wealth : *The East India Trade a most profitable Trade to the Kingdom* (1677), 7-8.

[2] *A Discourse of the Common Weal of this Realm of England* (ed. Lamond), 187.  (This passage appears in the edition of 1581.)

[3] *House of Commons Journals*, i. 528.

[4] *State Papers Domestic*, 1547–1580, p. 691 ; Scott, *Joint-Stock Companies*, i. 80-86.

[5] *Hist. MSS. Comm. Pepys*, 173.

[6] In an expedition of 1592 the Queen had a tenth share : *ibid. Bath*, ii. 38-40.

Burghley in 1586 : " Men in authority, to recover their unthriftiness, sell their lands, buy ships, and command the captain and company not to return without assurance of a very great sum " [1]. A successful venture might multiply the original capital ten or a hundred fold [2]. Cecil, who was secretly interested in several expeditions, drew over £7000 from a prize captured in 1601 in return for an ' adventure' (investment) of over £700 [3].

Whether England on the whole benefited by these privateering expeditions is open to question. The opinion was current under James I. that the country "never throve so well as when at war with Spain " [4]. " Nothing is thought to have enriched the English more ", wrote the Venetian ambassador in 1618, than " the wars with the Spaniards in the time of Queen Elizabeth " [5]. Two Elizabethan views may be contrasted. The one (1598) categorically affirmed that "the war with Spain hath been profitable. . . . How many millions we have taken from the Spaniard is a thing notorious. Which that they have been all gains for England I think it not difficult to prove " [6]. The other (1600) recognized that the precious metals could be obtained from Spain either by traffic or by force : " By traffic . . . we may not as long as we continue in war with them. . . . By force is full of cost, hazard and peril " [7]. Against the profits derived from privateering expeditions must be set the cumulative effects of the disturbance of trade on the Continent provoked by Spanish hostility ; and the commercial crisis of 1586 [8] was only part of the price which England paid. " The trade with Spain ", wrote the Spanish ambassador to King Philip in 1580, " is of the greatest importance to the English . . . it being the principal source of their

*Their effects on trade.*

---

[1] *State Papers Domestic*, Addenda, 1580-1625, p. 181.

[2] The treasure brought back by Drake in 1580 is supposed to have exceeded £600,000 (of which Elizabeth received nearly half), the capital outlay being under £5000 : Scott, *Joint-Stock Companies*, i. 81-82.

[3] *Hist. MSS. Comm. Salisbury*, xi. 539. For other ventures of Cecil's, see *ibid.* xii. 234, 453, 599 (" I pray you conceal . . . my name ").

[4] *State Papers Domestic*, 1623–1625, p. 185.

[5] *State Papers Venetian*, 1617–1619, p. 416.

[6] *Hist. MSS. Comm. Salisbury*, viii. 212.

[7] *Ibid.* x. 395.      [8] *Infra*, p. 303.

wealth and strength, which consists mainly in the great number of their ships. . . . They have no other trade so profitable, both on account of the vast sums of specie they bring, which they can get from no other place, and the richness of the merchandise which they carry. This makes them almost the masters of commerce in other parts as well, as they have the monopoly of the shipping " [1]. The interruption of this trade had disastrous effects upon the country ; and it was said in 1602 that " the Queen's inducement to peace is not so much to free herself from the expenses of the war, which are partially covered by the prizes she makes, but in order to secure a free commerce, and to allow her subjects to increase their capital " [2]. Roger Coke, writing after the Restoration, expressed the opinion that the nation in the reign of James I. " became incredibly enriched, more than it was in Queen Elizabeth's reign ", and he attributed the growth of wealth to the peace with Spain and the opening up of trade with Virginia, Barbados and the East Indies [3].

*Foreign invest- ments.* One source of capital in England was foreign investments [4], particularly on the part of the Dutch, who were able to obtain a higher rate of interest in this country than in Holland [5]. In the early seventeenth century Dutch capitalists provided the money for schemes of land drainage in England [6] : they participated (1614) in the First Joint Stock of the East India Company [7] : they assisted the Company of Merchant Adventurers with a loan to enable it to buy back its charter from the King in 1617 [8] :

---

[1] *State Papers Spanish*, 1580–1586, p. 8.

[2] *State Papers Venetian*, 1592–1603, p. 509 (Letter of the Venetian ambassador in France).

[3] Coke, *Treatise* (1675), iv. Preface.

[4] Contrast Marshall, *Industry and Trade* (ed. 1920), 735 : " The only markets for loans at that time were local or at best national ". See also *infra*, Appendix, p. 512, No. 2.

[5] Barbon, *A Discourse of Trade* (1690), 33, 84-85, speaks of a difference of 3 per cent. German capital was invested in the copper-mining industry : *supra*, vol. ii. 174.

[6] *Supra*, vol. ii. 375.

[7] Scott, *Joint-Stock Companies*, ii. 103. In 1773 proprietors of £1000 stock or more numbered 487 (English) and 325 (foreign) : Macpherson, *Annals of Commerce*, iii. 541, note.

[8] Friis, *Alderman Cockayne's Project*, 415 ; and *infra*, p. 381. It may be safely assumed that the foreign loan was made by the Dutch.

they financed merchants [1] and fishermen [2]: and in the Parliament of 1624 a Bill for reducing the rate of interest to 8 per cent. was opposed expressly on the ground that " this will draw much money out of the kingdom, the Dutch having much here " [3]. The disturbed condition of England on the eve of the Civil War caused foreign capitalists, " who were wont to furnish great sums of money at interest ", to call in their loans which English merchants had employed in trade [4]. After the Restoration it was stated that a great part of the money used in trade and for the rebuilding of London was Dutch money [5]. As regards the amount of foreign money invested in England, a parliamentary committee was informed in 1669 that " Alderman Bucknell had above £100,000 in his hands, Mr. Meynell above £30,000, Mr. Vandeput at one time £60,000, Mr. Dericost always near £200,000 of Dutch money, lent to merchants at 7, 6 and 5 per cent. when money was at 8 per cent." [6]. This infiltration of foreign capital aroused jealousy, and it was now used as an argument in favour of a legal reduction in the rate of interest that ' neighbour-countries ' would " make no profit out of us by that means " [7]. England, however, still continued to attract foreign capital. "People abroad ", it was remarked in 1721, " will be glad to keep their money here and transmit more to us, because the interest is higher and the principal more secure than in any other part of the world " [8]. " It is well known ", said a writer in 1728, " that foreigners have a large share in our public funds, amounting (by the best information I can get) to about seven or eight millions " [9]. But by this time England was herself exporting capital abroad—apart from what she sent to her own colonies, which she had

---

[1] *Sir Thomas Roe's Speech* (1641), in *Harleian Miscellany* (ed. Malham), iv. 457.
[2] *Hist. MSS. Comm. Ancaster*, 404 (1629).
[3] *House of Commons Journals*, i. 679. See *infra*, pp. 225, 512 (No. 3).
[4] *State Papers Domestic*, 1640–1641, p. 524 ; 1650, p. 179.
[5] *Hist. MSS. Comm.*, viii. part i. 134. [6] *Ibid.*
[7] Fortrey, *England's Interest and Improvement* (1663), 42.
[8] *Hist. MSS. Comm. Various*, viii. 298. About 1782 the interest on the national debt paid to foreigners was calculated at £1,200,000, and that paid to natives at £6,600,000 : *Annals of Agriculture*, i. 37.
[9] *The Wealth and Commerce of Great Britain considered* (1728), 4. See *infra*, p. 512 (No. 4).

supplied with capital from their foundation [1]. " Our merchants ", wrote Gee in the early years of the eighteenth century, " not only had money enough to carry on their trade, but supplied foreign princes, lent money upon bottomry and upon commodities in all countries, the remittances from whence swelled the balance of trade so much in our favour " [2]. And before the end of the century it was proudly claimed that " London is now what Amsterdam has been " [3].

*Capital invested in industry.*    Money made in one branch of trade served to finance other branches : thus the profits of the Levant trade helped to furnish the original capital of the East India Company [4]. Industry drew capital from two sources : the gains of the producer who handled the raw materials, and the gains of the merchant. Even in the fifteenth century the successful wool-producer invested his profits in industry—for example, the Tames of Fairford, sheep-masters, built up a prosperous cloth manufacture [5]. Sir Thomas Gresham, merchant and financier, engaged in the iron industry and erected a paper-mill, as also did Spilman, the German jeweller of Queen Elizabeth [6] : Bacon tells of ' a nobleman in England ' who was ' a great sheep-master, a great timber-man, a great collier, a great corn-master, a great lead-man, and so of iron ' [7] : the Willoughbys of Nottinghamshire, who were landowners, engaged in coal-mining and the making of iron and glass [8] : Dud Dudley, the ironmaster, had as his partners in 1651 a merchant and a linen-draper [9]. We find also examples of the integration of industry [10]—as far back as the fourteenth century a London lime-burner appears to have

---

[1] *Supra*, p. 167.

[2] Gee, *The Trade and Navigation of Great Britain* (ed. 1730), 6. In the later eighteenth century English capital was invested in the French funds and even in the Crimea : *Annals of Agriculture*, xv. 547-548 ; xvi. 110. See *infra*, Appendix, p. 513, No. 1.

[3] *Hist. MSS. Comm. Charlemont*, ii. 169 (1791).

[4] *Supra*, vol. ii. 273.        [5] *Supra*, vol. i. 182, 479.

[6] *State Papers Domestic*, 1598–1601, p. 505 ; Burgon, *Life of Gresham*, ii. 425-426, 444. For Spilman, see *infra*, p. 352, note 2.

[7] Bacon, *Works* (ed. Spedding), vi. 461.

[8] See *Hist. MSS. Comm. Middleton, passim.*

[9] Dudley, *Mettallum Martis* (1665), 20-21. For Dudley, see *supra*, vol. ii. 160.

[10] See Index, *s.v.* Industry (integration).

leased a Northumberland colliery, sea-coal being used in *Indications* lime-burning [1]; and a glass-maker, Joshua Henzey, in the *of the capitalist* seventeenth century entered into partnership with Robert *spirit.* Foley, the great ironmaster, probably to obtain fuel for his glass-furnaces [2]. There are, indeed, abundant indications that the capitalist spirit, as evinced in the conception and execution of large and speculative enterprises, is older than the ' Industrial Revolution '. In the sixteenth century there already existed ' captains of industry ', such as John Winch-combe, William Stumpe, Peter Blundell and Humphrey Chetham, among many others [3]; far-sighted merchants such as Sir Edward Osborne, who played a leading rôle in establish-ing trade with the Levant [4]; financiers such as Sir Thomas Gresham, who negotiated Government loans and manipulated the foreign exchanges. In the seventeenth century there emerged into prominence many notable figures in the capitalist sphere, including Sir Edwin Sandys [5], Sir Josiah Child and Sir Ambrose Crowley [6]. One example of capitalist enterprise in the reign of William III. discloses a type which is often considered as the creation of modern finance. This was Alderman Sir Joseph Herne—a financier through whom the English Government made payment abroad of subsidies to the Allies in the war against France ; an army contractor who supplied provisions to the forces in Ireland and Flanders ; a company promoter who established a company of copper-miners, a company of glass-makers, a company of the ' Royal Fishery of Ireland ', and a company of merchants trading to North-West America ; and finally, a merchant and shipowner engaged in trade with Italy [7].

One of the principal incentives to the accumulation and *The joint-* employment of capital was the system of joint stocks, which *stock system.* had been foreshadowed in the mediaeval *societas* or partner-ship, and in the ' common bargains ' of the gild merchant [8].

---

[1] Galloway, *Annals of Coal Mining*, i. 39, 50.
[2] *Victoria County History, Worcestershire*, ii. 280.
[3] *Supra*, vol. ii. 6. Chetham belongs mainly to the seventeenth century.
[4] *Supra*, vol. ii. 336. [5] *Supra*, p. 188. [6] *Supra*, vol. ii. 178.
[7] *State Papers Domestic*, 1690–1691, pp. 316, 456, 459, 469, 482, 527, 540 ; 1691–1692, pp. 3-4, 353 ; 1693, p. 94. See *infra*, Appendix, p. 513, No. 2.
[8] *Supra*, vol. i. 271 ; Scott, *Joint-Stock Companies*, i. 1, 15.

We see the logical development of the latter in the plans for municipal trading at King's Lynn [1], and in the scheme put forward by the inhabitants of Portsmouth for " making a joint stock towards the attainment of trade, traffic and commerce unto that town, to be employed in the way of merchandising " [2]. The joint-stock company provided a broader basis of membership than urban gilds, and a more formal organization than the *societas*. There was a rapid growth of the system in the second half of the sixteenth century, when several industrial and trading companies were erected [3] and even privateering expeditions were organized on a joint-stock basis [4]. Within the framework of the regulated company itself, as we have seen, corporate trading on the part of its members was not excluded [5] ; and it is significant that interlopers sometimes conducted their illicit trade on a joint-stock footing [6].

*Merit of joint stocks.*

The merit of the joint-stock system was that it enabled the capital invested in industry and trade to be drawn from a wide area. As the preamble to a Statute in 1662 recited : " Divers noblemen, gentlemen and persons of quality, no ways bred up to trade or merchandise, do oftentimes put in great stocks of money into . . . public societies, and receive the proceed of those stocks sometimes in ready moneys, sometimes in commodities, which they usually sell for money or exchange again, by which means the trade of those companies is much encouraged " [7]. At first the number of shares in a company was strictly limited ; and new capital was obtained, not by increasing the number of shares, but by calling up fresh sums on the original shares. The shares, however, could be broken up into fractions ; and since they were transferable, even in the sixteenth century, the burden could be distributed over a wider circle [8]. The transferability of shares was undoubtedly one of the main causes of

---

[1] 1656 : *State Papers Domestic*, 1656–1657, p. 22.
[2] 1632 : *Hist. MSS. Comm. Cowper*, i. 474.
[3] *Supra*, vol. ii. 174, 195.     [4] *Supra*, p. 210.
[5] *Supra*, vol. ii. 227. See also *infra*, Appendix, p. 513, No. 3.
[6] In 1614 English merchants traded in cloth to Antwerp on a joint stock: *Acts of the Privy Council*, 1613–1614, p. 643. Also see *supra*, vol. ii. 297.
[7] *Statutes*, v. 419.
[8] Scott, *Joint-Stock Companies*, i. 37, 44, 442–443.

the popularity of the joint-stock system. It has been estimated that at the accession of Elizabeth the capital invested in joint-stock undertakings was about £10,000 ; that in 1695 it exceeded 4 millions ; that in 1717 it was over 20 millions ; and that in 1720 it was about 50 millions [1]. The nominal capital was greater than the sum actually devoted to trade, owing to the practice of making loans to the State, though the resources of the companies were supplemented by the loans which they themselves raised [2]. It is not surprising that this remarkable increase in the capitalization of joint-stock companies, especially after the Revolution, aroused misgivings in view of the opportunities which it seemed to afford for " that new mistery . . . we call stock-jobbing " [3]. The Commissioners for Trade and Plantations framed a strong indictment in their report to Parliament in 1696 : " The pernicious art of stock-jobbing hath of late so wholly perverted the end and design of companies and corporations—erected for the introducing or carrying on of manufactures—to the private profit of the first projectors, that the privileges granted to them have commonly been made no other use of by the first procurers and subscribers, but to sell again with advantage to ignorant men drawn in by the reputation, falsely raised and artfully spread, concerning the thriving state of their stock. Thus the first undertakers getting quit of the company, by selling their shares for much more than they are really worth to men allured by the noise of great profit, the management of that trade and stock comes to fall into unskilful hands ; whereby the manufactures, intended to be promoted by such grants and put into the management of companies for their better improvement, come from very promising beginnings to dwindle away to nothing, and be in a worse condition than if they were perfectly left free and unassisted with such laws or patents " [4]. As a result

*Stock-jobbing.*

---

[1] Scott, *Joint-Stock Companies*, i. 336, 394, 439 (cf. also 418-419).

[2] *Supra*, vol. ii. 247, 293, and *infra*, p. 238.

[3] Defoe, *The Villainy of Stock-Jobbers Detected* (1701), 4. For other attacks on stock-jobbery, see *Angliæ Tutamen* (1695), which enumerates different projects for companies ; and Davenant, *Works* (ed. 1771), i. 432.

[4] *House of Commons Journals*, xi. 595.

of the South Sea Bubble, an Act was passed which required every company to possess a charter [1]. This imposed a grave handicap on joint-stock enterprise on account of the expense involved. In default of a charter, an industrial or commercial undertaking was carried on by articles of partnership alone—a procedure attended by serious drawbacks. First, the capital was held liable for the private debts of the individual partners, " and subject to be torn in pieces upon the bankruptcy of any of them " [2]. Secondly, it was believed, whether rightly or wrongly, that a charter gave the shareholders the privilege of limited liability, for an application made in 1764 was based expressly on the plea that " many gentlemen, who are now willing to subscribe largely for extending and improving the manufactory [of cambrics], will not advance their money if they are to be answerable for more than they subscribe, which they must be in case of common partnership " [3].

*Extensive use of credit.*    The volume of capital invested in trade, whether domestic or foreign, depends in a vital degree upon the extent and facility of credit transactions. Credit is the life-blood of industry and commerce — it was described in 1640 as ' the life of a merchant ' [4]—and it enables trade to be conducted on an infinitely larger scale than if every transaction were carried out on a cash basis. The credit system already existed in the Middle Ages [5], and its importance grew enormously in the sixteenth and seventeenth centuries. Time bargains became the rule, and book-credit was universally given, frequently for long periods—in the woollen industry the wool dealer and the cardmaker gave credit to the clothier, the clothier to the draper (six to fifteen

---

[1] *Supra*, vol. ii. 369. See *infra*, Appendix, p. 513, No. 4.
[2] *State Papers Domestic*, 1691–1692, pp. 287, 344, 523.
[3] *House of Commons Journals*, xxix. 785. In 1662 limited liability was established for certain trading companies: *Statutes*, v. 419. For the history of the limited liability concept, see DuBois, *The English Business Company after the Bubble Act*, 94 *seq.*, 152-153.
[4] *State Papers Domestic*, 1640, p. 241.
[5] *Supra*, vol. i. 616, note 1.

months) [1], and the draper to the merchant [2]. The amount was often considerable—one London cloth merchant in the reign of Elizabeth absconded to Ireland owing the clothiers £1500 [3]; another in the next reign, who was trusted with £20,000 worth of cloth, went bankrupt [3a]; and a wholesale linen-draper in the reign of Anne became insolvent for £70,000 [4]. The expansion of the credit system was promoted by the great increase in the number of merchants in the sixteenth century, who traded either on borrowed capital or on credit : but it was easily abused. Complaint was often made that merchants over-traded, ' over-running themselves upon credit ', necessitating the frequent intervention of the Privy Council on their behalf when pressed by their creditors [5]. The merchants of Ipswich were held up as an example of the evil effects of excessive credit. They bought their cloth ' upon time ', " and by reason they go so much upon credit they are enforced . . . to sell, giving fifteen or eighteen months' day of payment for their cloths ; and having sold them they then presently sell their bills so taken for cloth, allowing after the rate of 14 or 15 and sometimes 20 per cent." [6]. It was on the ground of this ' unprofitable course of merchandise ' that Burghley and Gresham had proposed to confine the Company of Merchant Adventurers to " those that be richer, and that will deal and trade like merchants with their stocks [*i.e.* capital], and not with the exchange [*i.e.* on credit] as all the young merchants do " [7]; and the trading companies endeavoured to set limits to the credit

---

[1] *Supra*, vol. ii. 22 (note 2), 28. For the cardmakers, see *The Clothiers' Reason against . . . prohibiting . . . foreign Wool Cards*. In the eighteenth century the ironmasters of Furness gave over 14 months' credit : Fell, *The Early Iron Industry of Furness*, 330-331. See *infra*, Appendix, p. 514, No. 1.

[2] Thus in July 1580 a London draper sold kersies worth £600, which were to be paid for in April : *Acts of the Privy Council*, 1581–1582, p. 103.

[3] *Ibid.* 1591–1592, p. 559. [3a] *Ibid.* 1619–1621, p. 79 (1619).

[4] *Hist. MSS. Comm. Portland*, iv. 167 (1705). In 1637 a merchant owed £1700 to Coggeshall clothiers : *State Papers Domestic*, 1636–1637, p. 368. See *infra*, Appendix, p. 514, No. 2.

[5] *Acts of the Privy Council*, 1575–1577, pp. 224-225 ; 1578–1580, p. 171 ; 1597–1598, p. 550. It also intervened on behalf of insolvent clothiers : *State Papers Domestic*, 1619–1623, pp. 395, 471 ; 1629–1631, p. 419.

[6] Raleigh, *Works* (ed. 1829), viii. 367.

[7] Burgon, *Life of Gresham*, i. 463 (1553) ; *Tudor Economic Documents* (ed. Tawney and Power), ii. 47 (? 1564).

system by fixing the period for which credit might be given [1].
Yet all efforts to restrict the use of credit proved ineffectual.
At the close of the seventeenth century the Commissioners
for Trade and Plantations stated that " a great part of trade
is carried on by credit " [2]. Barbon affirmed that in all
trading centres more wares were sold upon credit than for
' present money '. " Most of the retail traders ", he remarked, " buy upon . . . credit, and are usually trusted
for more than double they are worth " [3]. Defoe even declared that two-thirds of the trade of England was conducted on a credit basis, and that English tradesmen understood how to manage credit better than any other tradesmen
in the world [4]. English merchants not only took credit
at home but gave it abroad, and this produced a twofold
result—it promoted the development of oversea trade, and
strengthened England's hold upon foreign markets, which
in some cases were heavily indebted to her [5].

*Bills of debt.* The instrument of credit transactions in domestic trade
was the bill of debt or inland bill of exchange [6]. Down to
the end of the seventeenth century bills of debt were ' the
loosest things in trade ' [7], since they could not be ' protested ' for non-payment. Moreover, during a great part
of the century, they were not readily transferable. Malynes,
writing in 1622, stated that the ' laudable custom ' of transferring bills of debt from one person to another " is not

---

[1] *Supra*, vol. ii. 225 (the Merchant Adventurers) ; *Acts and Ordinances of the Eastland Company*, 55.

[2] *House of Commons Journals*, xii. 435.

[3] Barbon, *A Discourse of Trade* (1690), 27-28. Similarly : Davenant, *Works* (ed. 1771), i. 442.

[4] Defoe, *The Complete English Tradesman* (ed. 1732), i. 339, 343.

[5] *Ibid.* 338-339. For colonial indebtedness, see *supra*, p. 169, note 4. For Portuguese indebtedness, see Westerfield, *Middlemen in English Business*, 386. For Spain, see *infra*, Appendix, p. 514, No. 3.

[6] For foreign bills of exchange, see *supra*, pp. 80 *seq.* Another type of bill, called ' Dry Exchange ', was ' Usurer's Exchange ', *i.e.* a loan of money " upon interest with condition to receive the same sum of moneys, with a certain profit, at a certain time, and in the same place ". The ad-vantages to the usurer were (1) that the bill mentioned only the sum to be paid, not the sum received, so that it could not be known what interest he exacted ; (2) if the bill were not met punctually, he could take immediate action ' by attachment and arrest ' : Scarlett, *The Stile of Exchanges* (1682), 4, 266-268.

[7] Defoe's phrase : *The Complete English Tradesman* (ed. 1732), i. 351.

practised in England ", though ' altogether used ' by the Merchant Adventurers abroad [1] : Misselden in the same year recommended that the buying, selling and transferring of bills of debt should be made legal [2] : Roberts (1641) deplored " the great stock of the kingdom which continually lieth in all negotiators' hands in dead bills and bonds " without circulating in trade [3] : Child (1668) attributed the prosperity of the Netherlands, among other factors, to a law permitting the transference of bills from one to another, whereas in England men were " accustomed to buy and sell goods by verbal contracts only " [4]. In 1669 a measure was introduced into Parliament to make inland bills of exchange transferable like foreign bills of exchange, but it dropped with the close of the session [5]. Five years later another Act was drafted, which stated that many ' inconveniences ' occurred to merchants " for want of power to assign their bills . . . in satisfaction of their debts "; but it was not proceeded with [6]. However the custom of merchants prevailed, and before the close of the seventeenth century inland bills of exchange appear to have become in practice readily transferable [7]. They were invested with legal sanction by the Act of 1698, which provided that they should be protested for non-payment, after which the holder could recover payment, together with interest and charges, from whomever the bill had been received [8]. A subsequent Act (1705) made promissory notes also assignable by endorsement, and allowed action to be taken on them as in the case of inland bills of exchange [9]. This not only effected economies in the transmission of money, but enabled capital to circulate more rapidly, since the holder of the bill could

[1] Malynes, *Consuetudo vel Lex Mercatoria* (1622), 96-99.
[2] Misselden, *Free Trade* (1622), 117-118.
[3] Roberts, *The Treasure of Traffike* (1641), 54.
[4] Child, *Brief Observations concerning Trade and Interest of Money* (1668), 6 ; Child, *A New Discourse of Trade* (4th ed.), 7, 136. Similarly : *Hist. MSS. Comm. Portland*, i. 406 (1647) ; Potter, *The Trades-Man's Jewel* (1650).
[5] *Hist. MSS. Comm.* viii. part i. 137.
[6] *Ibid.* ix. part ii. 40.
[7] On the development of the negotiable character of bills, see Holdsworth, *A History of English Law*, viii. 140 *seq.*
[8] *Statutes*, vii. 371.     [9] *Ibid.* viii. 353.

now anticipate the day of payment by discounting the bill or assigning it in payment of his own debts [1]. The development of banking in the seventeenth century, as we shall see [2], created another form of credit instrument, bank-notes and goldsmith's notes, which became current in lieu of specie, and by facilitating large payments ' eased ' the course of trade. These various kinds of paper credit made the national wealth more liquid, and in quickening trade and industry they served in the nature of new resources.

*Trading on borrowed capital.*  Where a merchant or manufacturer or shopkeeper did not trade on his own capital or on book-credit, or when either of these was inadequate, there remained open to him a third recourse—to trade on borrowed capital [3]. " How many merchants and shopkeepers ", exclaimed Mun, " have begun with little or nothing of their own, and yet are grown very rich by trading with other men's money" [4]. Bacon declared that " it is certain that the greatest part of trade is driven by young merchants upon borrowing at interest " [5]; and the extent of capital loaned for productive purposes might be very large, for example, a gunfounder under the Commonwealth employed a capital of £30,000 on which he paid interest [6]. But before the use of borrowed capital could become general two things were needed—the abandonment of the mediaeval attitude towards usury ; and the establishment of a banking system.

*The problem of usury.*  The problem of usury assumed a new aspect in the sixteenth century. Hitherto the ethical issues involved in the taking of interest had been the most widely canvassed ; yet though they still continued to engage attention, their importance steadily diminished. Writers still spoke of the

---

[1] Child had predicted that it would " effectually increase the useful stock [capital] of the nation at least one-third part ": *A New Discourse of Trade* (4th ed.), 139.

[2] *Infra*, pp. 231, 242.

[3] The writer of a letter in 1555 remarks—" Here is in London many merchants bankrupt ; as I learn, my aunt will not trust no more any merchants ": *Hist. MSS. Comm.* iii. 37.

[4] Mun, *England's Treasure by Forraign Trade* (1664), 144.

[5] Bacon, *Essays : Of Usury.*

[6] *State Papers Domestic*, 1651, p. 62.

' damnable sin of usury ', but their protestations went un-
heeded : the main current of thought swept by them concerned with issues that were fundamentally economic.   The
questions, which exercised the minds of men in the sixteenth
and seventeenth centuries, concerned primarily not the law-
fulness but the rate of interest.   Ought the rate of interest
to be fixed by law ?   And what machinery was required to
bring together lender and borrower, and to mobilize the
resources of the community so as to create ' a fund of credit ' ?
The answer to these questions was worked out by gradual
stages, in the course of which was evolved the modern banking
system.

The prohibition of usury rested on the assumption that *Reasons*
money was barren :   its abandonment was dictated by the *for per-*
*mitting*
recognition that " it is only idle moneys, locked up in a chest *interest.*
and unemployed, that is unfruitful and barren " [1].   " 'Tis a
vain thing ", observed Selden, " to say money begets not
money, for that no doubt it does " [2].   The demand for money
came principally from two classes—traders and landowners.
The trader, who had no capital of his own and might not
borrow it, " must either sit still, or buy at time " (*i.e.* on
credit), " which is interest under another name " [3].   Where
money was expended on capital goods or in trade, it was the
means to create further wealth, and the lender in charging
interest only asserted a right to share in the wealth produced
with his assistance.   Thus Malynes wrote :   " If I deal with
a merchant that maketh gain of my money with his trade
and commerce, and is well able to pay me again, being chiefly
enriched by my means, why should not I in reason have part
of his benefit and advantage when by my goods he is grown
rich ? " [4]   In the case of the landowner whose choice lay
between a mortgage and the forced sale of his estates, the
payment of interest might appear not only the lesser of two
evils, but even an equitable return to the lender for the service
he had rendered.   This idea that interest was lawful, where

---

[1] Scarlett, *The Stile of Exchanges* (1682), Preface.   Cf. Barbon, *A Discourse of Trade* (1690), 31-32.
[2] *Table Talk of John Selden* (ed. Pollock), 135.
[3] North, *Discourses upon Trade* (1691), 8-9.
[4] Malynes, *Consuetudo vel Lex Mercatoria* (1622), 330.

the borrower turned the money to good account, produced a
phase of money-lending of which we get a glimpse in Derbyshire in the reign of James I.   Here a debtor paid interest
on a loan, if he acknowledged that he had enjoyed a benefit
from it ;  otherwise the creditor took his money back at the
end of a certain period without interest, and lent it to another.
Lenders chose their debtors with discretion, so that they
actually made 10 per cent. on their money while helping
others ' in their distressed estates '.   The writer of the letter,
in which this account is given, adds :  " I have cause to thank
them . . . that lent me money after that rate in my need,
for otherwise I had had no foot of land at this hour " [1].
None the less interest continued to be regarded as ' the fruit
of another man's labour ' ;  and usurers were stigmatized as
" the true drones of a commonwealth, living upon the honey
without any labour " [2].   It was reserved for Locke to suggest
that " to receive profit from the loan of money is as equitable
and lawful as receiving rent for land, and more tolerable to
the borrower ", whose labour was less arduous than that of
a tenant, while his returns were likely to be much greater [3].

*Legal rates*
*of interest.*    In practice no distinction was possible between productive and unproductive loans ; and the toleration of the one,
in the interests of traders and manufacturers, necessarily
extended to the other.   An Act fixing the maximum rate
of interest at 10 per cent. had been passed in 1545, but
repealed in 1552 [4] :  it was revived by Parliament (1571) in
a Statute which still denounced usury as ' forbidden by the
law of God ' [5], and gave the lender no legal right to enforce
a contract for interest.   In the debate on the Usury Bill
the change of opinion was expressed by a member who said
that " the mischief is of the excess, not otherwise " ; and to
forbid interest was to hamper trade, by keeping apart those
with money and those with the skill to use it [6].   The actual

---

[1] *Hist. MSS. Comm. Cowper*, i. 54 (1605).
[2] Davenant, *Works* (ed. 1771), i. 57.
[3] Locke, *Works* (ed. 1801), v. 36-37.
[4] *Supra*, vol. i. 619.
[5] *Statutes*, iv. part i. 542.
[6] D'Ewes, *The Journals of all the Parliaments during the Reign of
Queen Elizabeth* (1682), 172.

rate was sometimes much above 10 per cent. : in 1588 even 20 per cent. was paid [1]. Under James I. a proposal to limit the rate of interest to 8 per cent. was defeated in 1621 partly on religious, partly on economic grounds—the former because it tolerated usury ; the latter because it would distress merchants and " undo most of the gentry of England, will bring down the price of land, no man will lend money, and so many mortgages may be lost " [2]. Three years later the proposal was revived : on this occasion it was urged that it would lead to the withdrawal of foreign capital from England, and to the investment of English capital abroad [3]. The argument in favour of the reduction was one frequently employed after the Restoration, namely, that the low rate of interest in Holland was " the reason why we are beaten out of trade by the Low-Country men " [4]. This argument carried the day and interest was fixed at 8 per cent. (1625), " provided that no words in this law contained shall be construed or expounded to allow the practice of usury in point of religion or conscience " [5]. Under the Commonwealth the rate was reduced to 6 per cent. [6] : this was confirmed at the Restoration [7] : but an attempt to lower it to 4 per cent. in 1669 proved a failure [8]. In 1714 the rate was brought down to 5 per cent.[9]. This was done partly to relieve the landowners burdened by the war with a heavy load of indebtedness ; partly to bring the English rate nearer to the Dutch ; and partly in the belief that a high rate of interest on loans discouraged the investment of money in trade.

These enactments provoked a sharp conflict of opinion as to whether there was a natural rate of interest against which legislation was ineffective. The demand for State

---

[1] Hist. MSS. Comm. Middleton, 567.
[2] House of Commons Journals, i. 611.          [3] Ibid. i. 679, 775.
[4] Ibid. i. 775. The rate of interest in Holland in 1622 was 6 and 7 per cent. according to Misselden, Free Trade (1622), 117.
[5] The Act came into operation in 1625 : Statutes, iv. part ii. 1223-1224.
[6] 1651 : Acts and Ordinances of the Interregnum, ii. 548.
[7] 1660 : Statutes, v. 236.
[8] Hist. MSS. Comm. viii. part i. 134 ; ibid. Kenyon, 83.
[9] Statutes, ix. 928. From the record of a trial in 1691 it would seem that 5 per cent. was considered the proper rate for mortgages : House of Lords MSS. 1692–1693, pp. 288-289.

regulation was inspired by the low rate in Holland, where in the later seventeenth century it was 3 or 4 per cent.[1]. " This ", declared Child, " is the *causa causans* of all the other causes of the riches of that people " ; and he predicted that if the rate were as low in England, we should become "as rich and considerable in trade as they now are "[2]. The cheapness of money gave the Dutch many advantages over their competitors. It enabled them to build and equip their ships at a smaller cost ; to undersell other traders ; and to hold large stocks—it was said that a dearth of corn in England or elsewhere enriched Holland, the great ' magazine and storehouse ' of Europe, ' seven years after '. The English merchant was therefore seriously handicapped by the fact that the price of money was much higher in this country than in Holland[3]. Other writers condemned " the vanity and fruitlessness of making civil positive laws against the laws of nature ", and considered it best for the State to leave borrowers and lenders to make their own bargains. They pointed out, first of all, that interest always carries with it insurance for risk. Where the security was hazardous, " a kind of insurance must be interwoven with the simple natural interest, which may advance the usury very conscionably unto any height below the principal itself "[4] ; while those who gave good security—for example, the East India Company—borrowed under the legal rates. And next, they held that the natural fall of interest is the effect of trade. " It is not low interest makes trade ", said Sir Dudley North, " but trade increasing, the stock of the nation makes interest low "[5]. Misselden had given utterance to a similar view nearly three-quarters of a century earlier : " As it is the scarcity of money that maketh the high rates

[1] So it was commonly stated (*e.g.* Locke, *Works*, ed. 1801, v. 67) ; but Sir Dudley North was ' certainly informed ' that " the current interest between merchant and merchant, when they disburse money for each other's account, is 6 per cent.", and that money lent at 3 and 4 per cent. was " upon mortgages " : *Discourses upon Trade* (1691), 5.

[2] Child, *A New Discourse of Trade* (4th ed.), 8-9.

[3] Coke, *Treatise* (1671), ii. 123-124 ; *Britannia Languens* (1680), 53 ; Barbon, *A Discourse of Trade* (1690), 79 *seq.*

[4] Petty, *Economic Writings*, i. 48, 304.

[5] North, *Discourses upon Trade* (1691), 4. Similarly: Hume, *Essays: Of Interest.* " Stock " means capital.

of interest, so the plenty of money will make the rates low better than any statute for that purpose "[1]. Their third line of argument was that usurers would foreclose their mortgages, that mercantile credit would be ruined and foreign money withdrawn, and that money would not be forthcoming on public emergencies [2]. The compulsory abatement of interest would profit only ' the vast-moneyed traders ', who would squeeze out small men and engross trade in their own hands ; it would encourage extravagance on the part of landowners who spent more than their income ; it would lead to evasion and perjury ; it would inflict loss on all who deposited their money with bankers —the incomes of widows and orphans, especially, would suffer—since they would only receive the legal rate ; and, to crown all, borrowers would still be compelled to pay the natural price for money in accordance with the law of demand and supply.

Once usury was brought within the pale of the law, if *Early* not of social morality, the ground was prepared for the rise *history of banking.* of banking in its modern form. The early history of banking in England is obscure. The usurer was a well-known figure in mediaeval society, but we cannot say whether he was accustomed as a normal and regular practice to receive deposits or to make advances with money entrusted to him by others : it was presumably his own capital that, as a rule, he loaned [3]. The crucial question is when the system of deposit banking first became general. It may be safely assumed that there was a transitional stage, in which the services of a financial intermediary were requisitioned to make a temporary arrangement for the disposal of money in an advantageous way. Thus in 1590 the ' portion of a young maid ' was loaned through the agency of a scrivener [4]. The scrivener's occupation as a clerical expert, engaged in drawing up bills and bonds, gave him opportunities for

---

[1] Misselden, *Free Trade* (1622), 117.

[2] *Hist. MSS. Comm.* viii. part i. 134.

[3] It is, of course, more than likely that landowners, merchants and others did entrust their surplus wealth to the mediaeval money-lender, and received remuneration from him. See also *supra*, vol. i. 617, note 3.

[4] *Acts of the Privy Council*, 1590, p. 359 ; 1590–1591, p. 95.

arranging credit transactions ; and a commission on usury
in the reign of Charles I. was specially instructed to punish
scriveners, who charged more than was allowed " for procuring
moneys to be lent " [1]. In some cases money may also have
been deposited with the scrivener [2] ; but in general he
appears to have acted as a broker between lender and
borrower. Money-lending was not confined to scriveners,
for banking had not yet become a specialized profession [3].
In Elizabeth's reign Sir Thomas Gresham, among his varied
activities, was a banker with whom money was deposited
on interest [4] : Pallavicino, a ' gentleman of Genoa ' settled
in England, was a prominent financier [5] : the estates of the
Earl of Essex, whose debts exceeded ten thousand pounds
in 1597, were mortgaged to a mercer and three wine merchants [6] : and even the Dean of Windsor was accused of
' letting his money to use ', a charge which he repudiated [7].
Under the Early Stuarts brokers and ' friperers ', as well as
scriveners, are mentioned as " taking greater sums of money
for the loan and forbearance of money upon bonds and
other securities, than permitted by law " [8]. After the
Restoration, and even in the eighteenth century, the scrivener
still conducted financial operations [9]. Defoe described the
tactics of the scrivener, who offers a tradesman " to lodge
some money in his hands. So he calls it, pretending 'tis
from a client who has some money to dispose of " [10].   How-

[1] State Papers Domestic, 1637–1638, pp. 602-603. The scrivener acted
as a broker in other matters: e.g. the sale of skins to leather-sellers: ibid.
1638–1639, p. 245.
[2] On this point, see Tawney, Introduction to Wilson, A Discourse
upon Usury, 99-101 ; Richards, The Early History of Banking in England,
15-18. For the varied activities of a Restoration scrivener, see Hist.
MSS. Comm. Hodgkin, 21.
[3] Tawney, op. cit. 86 seq. Chetham, the great clothier, made advances
of money : Raines and Sutton, Life of Humphrey Chetham, i. 120.
[4] He allowed Burghley's son-in-law (Lord Oxford) 10 per cent. and
then 12 per cent. for his money : Burgon, Life of Gresham, ii. 412-413.
[5] Acts of the Privy Council, 1580–1581, p. 356.
[6] Hist. MSS. Comm. Salisbury, vii. 283.
[7] State Papers Domestic, 1601–1603, pp. 272-273. For the transactions
of an Elizabethan usurer (George Stoddard), see Hall, Society in the
Elizabethan Age, 48 seq.
[8] State Papers Domestic, 1637–1638, p. 603.
[9] Coke, Treatise (1671), i. 80 ; Britannia Languens (1680), 234; Davenant, Works (ed. 1771), i. 79 ; Defoe, The Complete English Tradesman
(ed. 1732), i. 373.        [10] Defoe, op. cit. i. 373.

ever, by the middle of the seventeenth century the scrivener was eclipsed in importance by the goldsmiths.

The goldsmiths did not create the banking system, as *The gold-* it is sometimes asserted, but they played an important *smiths.* part in its development. Various factors contributed to the evolution of the goldsmith into a banker. One of their functions was to deal in foreign money of which they kept supplies; another was to ' cull ' and weigh English coins which passed through their hands, melting down the weighty coins for plate or for export as bullion [1]. They thus became accustomed to financial business, and on occasion they doubtless made advances, while their strong-rooms provided obvious facilities for the safe custody of their customers' money. The distrust aroused among native and foreign merchants by Charles I.'s seizure of the bullion in the Mint, until then accounted ' the safest place and surest staple in these parts of the world ' [2], coupled with the insecurity of property during the Civil War, extended the practice of entrusting money to the goldsmiths' charge. Their ordinary business was at a standstill, " the trade of plate being then but little worth, most of the nobility and gentry and others melting down their old plate rather than buying new " [3]. Accordingly they embraced the opportunity to become " the merchants' cash-keepers, to receive and pay for nothing, few observing or conjecturing their profit they had for their pains " [4]. Some of them, " who had the highest credit, undertook to receive gentlemen's rents as they were returned to town, and indeed any man's money, and to allow them some interest for it though it lay for a month only or less, the owners calling for it by a hundred or fifty pounds at a time as their occasions and expenses wanted it. This new [5] practice giving hopes to everybody to make profit of their money until the hour they spent it, and the conveniency as they thought to com-

[1] *Supra*, p. 78.
[2] *State Papers Domestic*, 1640–1641, p. 524. See *infra*, p. 315.
[3] *The Mystery of the New Fashioned Goldsmiths or Bankers* (1676), 3.
[4] *Ibid.* 3.
[5] The practice of making deposits was not new : see *supra*, p. 228, note 4.

mand their money when they pleased, which they could
not do when lent at interest upon personal or real security—
these hopes, I say, drew a great cash into these new goldsmiths' hands " [1].

*Deposit
banking.*

Under the Commonwealth the goldsmiths, ' especially
those in Lombard Street ', were spoken of as " the greatest
merchants and London cashiers, who will receive any man's
money for nothing and pay it for them the same or the next
day " [2]. In order to encourage deposits the goldsmiths
began to pay interest, and under Charles II. they gave 6 per
cent.[3]. This ' trade of bankering ', as it was called, grew so
popular that, according to Child, " most men as soon as they
can make up a sum of £50 or £100 send it in to the goldsmith " [4]. Those with money at their disposal found the
system more attractive than loans on mortgage, where the
absence of a land register made the security uncertain, and
" it was so troublesome and chargeable getting their moneys
again when they had occasion to use it " [5]. Roger North
relates that his brother, Sir Dudley North, upon his return
from Turkey near the end of Charles II.'s reign, " found
divers usages in London very different from what had been
practised in his time there . . . as, first, touching their
running cash which, by almost all sorts of merchants, was
slid into goldsmith's hands ; and they themselves paid and
received only by bills, as if all their dealings were *in banco.*
He counted this a foolish, lazy method, and obnoxious to
great accidents ; and he never could bring himself wholly
to comply with it. For, having taken an apprentice, one
Fairclough, the son of a Presbyterian old usurer, he paid and
received all by his cash-keeper in his own counting house, as
merchants used to do. But, at length, he was prevailed on
to use Benjamin Hinton, a Lombard-street man ; and, for
acting therein against his conscience, was punished with the
loss of about fifty pounds. But others lost great sums by
this man ; and his breaking made a great shake upon the

---

1 *The Mystery of the New Fashioned Goldsmiths or Bankers* (1676), 5.
2 *State Papers Domestic*, 1651–1652, p. 263.
3 Child, *A New Discourse of Trade* (4th ed.), 33. Also *infra*, p. 235.
4 Child, *op. cit.* p. xxxix.
5 Yarranton, *England's Improvement* (1677), 17.

Exchange. I remember he hath come home . . . in great amazement at his own greatness ; for the banking goldsmiths came to him upon the Exchange with low obeisances, ' hoping for the honour '—' should be proud to serve him ', and the like ; and all for nothing but to have the keeping of his cash. This pressing made him the more averse to that practice ; and, when his acquaintance asked him where he kept his cash, he said : ' At home ; where should he keep it ? ' They wondered at him, as one that did not know his own interest. But, in the latter end of his time, when he had left the City and dealt more in trusts and mortgages than in merchandise, he saw a better bottom and used the shop of Sir Francis Child, at Temple-bar, for the paying and receiving all his great sums " [1]. The basis of deposit banking was public confidence in the personal credit and integrity of the banker, and when public confidence was shaken there at once appeared the phenomenon of a ' run on the banks '. The presence of the Dutch in the Medway in 1667 caused a panic. " There was such astonishment that everyone went to his goldsmith to recall his moneys, but they were all sent back empty-handed " [2]. According to Pepys, however, the goldsmiths did not refuse to pay out money [3], while the King gave an assurance of their solvency and declared that the Exchequer would meet its obligations to them [4].

*'A run on the banks'.*

The goldsmith issued to the depositor a ' note '. These ' goldsmith's notes ' were of two kinds [5]. One, ' the running cash note ', was a receipt on which were entered the amounts deposited and the amounts withdrawn : this was the precursor of the modern ' pass-book '. The next step was to dispense with the personal application of the depositor, and allow him to address an order to the goldsmith to pay the

*Goldsmith's notes.*

*(in margin)* like Tom Brown.

---

[1] North, *The Lives of the Norths* (ed. Jessopp), ii. 174-175.
[2] *State Papers Domestic*, 1667, p. 246.
[3] Pepys, *Diary* (ed. Wheatley), vi. 362.
[4] *Tudor and Stuart Proclamations* (ed. Steele), i. No. 3493. Printed in Turnor, *The Case of the Bankers and their Creditors* (ed. 1675), 135.
[5] On the ' goldsmith's notes ', see Bisschop, *The Rise of the London Money Market*, 53-61 ; Martin, " *The Grasshopper* " *in Lombard Street*, 127-128. Dr. Bisschop (*op. cit.* 67) considers that the discounting of bills " did not come into prominence until much later ", but it was already common in 1676 : *The Mystery of the New Fashioned Goldsmiths or Bankers* (1676), 4.

bearer a stated amount : an early example of this, the precursor of the modern cheque, is dated 1675 [1]. The other
kind of note was a ' promissory note ' in which the goldsmith undertook to pay a certain sum.  These ' promissory
notes ' were transferable, and they served the purpose of a
modern bank-note, from which they differed in the respect
that they were issued for irregular instead of fixed amounts.
Although the money deposited with goldsmiths was due
either ' at sight ' or within a short period, they did not keep
it in their coffers, but issued most of it to make advances to
merchants and the Crown, depending upon their customers
to bring in money as fast as it was taken out [2].  " Having
thus got money into their hands, they presumed upon some
to come as fast as others were paid away ;  and upon that
confidence of a running cash (as they call it), they begun to
accommodate men with moneys for weeks and months upon
extraordinary gratuities, and supply all necessitous merchants, that over-traded their stock, with present money
for their bills of exchange, discounting sometimes double,
perhaps treble interest for the time as they found the merchant more or less pinched " [3].  More important than the
merchants—or even the needy landowners living in excess
of their income, who still remained the chief borrowers of
money according to Sir Dudley North [4]—the financial needs
of the Crown proved the decisive factor in the evolution of
the banking system.

*Govern-
ment bor-
rowings.*  Mediaeval kings had borrowed in times of stress from
foreign bankers as well as from their own subjects, so that
the practice of raising Government loans was no novelty in
the sixteenth century.  But the debasement of the currency
in the first half of the century, and the influx of American
silver in the second half, altered the traditional level of
prices, and the sovereign was no longer able, even in ordinary
times, to ' live of his own '.  Elizabeth had recourse to
borrowing on a large scale, and the expedients adopted by

---

[1] Printed in Richards, *The Early History of Banking in England*, 50-51.
[2] According to Sir Dudley North, a banker who owed £10,000 seldom
kept £1000 in specie : *Discourses upon Trade* (1691), 21.
[3] *The Mystery of the New Fashioned Goldsmiths or Bankers* (1676), 4.
[4] North, *Discourses upon Trade* (1691), 6-7.

her successors for supplying the deficiencies of their income involved them in a constitutional struggle with Parliament, which attributed their difficulties to extravagance. After the Restoration Charles II., debarred from raising money by illegal taxation, systematically anticipated supplies. The long wars with France, which began under William III., forced Parliament at last to face the real situation, and the solution was found in the creation of a funded debt on the basis of which was erected the Bank of England.

In the sixteenth century the English Government nego- *Antwerp,* tiated loans in Antwerp, then the world's money market. *the world's* The financial agent of the Crown under Elizabeth was Sir *market.* Thomas Gresham, through whom business was conducted with foreign bankers, and the city of London furnished the security[1]. While Elizabeth's credit was better than that of her predecessors—she paid 12 per cent. whereas they had paid 14 per cent.[2]—the ' money-men ' of Antwerp were not always ready to lend money owing to the insecurity of her position. In 1562 Gresham wrote : " Here is such great doubts cast upon our estate as the credit of the Queen's majesty and all the whole nation is at a stay, and glad is that man that may be quit of an Englishman's bill " [3]. The course of events described above [4], which led in 1564 to the departure of the Merchant Adventurers from Antwerp, increased the disinclination of foreign bankers to make loans to the English Government : the rate of interest rose to 16 per cent.[5] : and in 1566 Gresham announced his intention of returning home. " I do see and feel already that here is no more money to be had at no price ; by reason I have gone through all the money-men by one practice or other, and specially

---

[1] *E.g. State Papers Foreign,* 1558–1559, p. 13. The foreign bankers included the Fuggers, Jasper Schetz 'and his brethren', and Lazarus Tucker : Burgon, *Life of Gresham,* i. Appendix, Nos. x.-xi. ; Ehrenberg, *Capital and Finance in the Age of the Renaissance,* 116, 190.

[2] Burgon, *Life of Gresham,* ii. 32-33. Gresham stated in 1566 that the loans he had negotiated since Elizabeth's accession amounted to £1,100,000 : *ibid.* ii. 418.

[3] *Ibid.* ii. 13. Contrast Ehrenberg, *Capital and Finance in the Age of the Renaissance,* 346 : " On the Continent its credit remained unshaken during the most severe crises ".

[4] *Supra,* vol. ii. 199.

[5] Scott, *Joint-Stock Companies,* i. 53.

with all them which I was wont to deal withal—as the Fuggers, Schetz, Paul van Dall, Rellinger, Lixall, the heirs of Lazarus Tucker, and divers other " [1]. The inability to raise money abroad had two significant effects. It forced the nation to rely in a larger measure upon its own resources— by 1570 Gresham had succeeded in raising a loan of over £21,000 in the City at 12 per cent., though the Queen was required to give " her accustomed bonds for the discharging of the Statute of Usuries, which [wrote Gresham] I would wish might be presently set at liberty, if it were possible, for the better accomplishing of her highness' enterprise " [2]. This loan was furnished by individuals and apparently was voluntary, in contrast with the loan of £30,000 exacted from the Merchant Adventurers at the beginning of the reign [3]. As a corollary, a change of policy in respect of usury was forced upon Elizabethan statesmen : and, in order to enable London to take the place of Antwerp as the bankers of the English Government, the Act of 1571 was passed which to all intents and purposes sanctioned the payment of interest [4]. Failure to repay punctually the loans made by her subjects impaired the Queen's credit, but she was apparently able near the end of her reign to raise a loan in the City at 10 per cent. [5]

At first the Government relied largely upon the mercantile classes for raising loans. It was observed by the Venetian ambassador in 1610 that English merchants had " acquired great power, on account of the need which the King and his ministers always have of them in realizing the revenue and the subsidies " [6]. The emergence of the gold-

---

[1] Burgon, *Life of Gresham*, ii. 158.

[2] *Acts of the Privy Council*, 1571–1575, pp. 53 *seq.* ; Burgon, *Life of Gresham*, ii. 342-343. Loans were also raised in Germany (Burgon, *op. cit.* ii. 418) and at Lyons (Scott, *Joint-Stock Companies*, i. 91). In 1572 the Queen still owed over £20,000 at Antwerp : *Hist. MSS. Comm. Salisbury*, ii. 19.

[3] *Newcastle Merchant Adventurers*, i. 89. See *supra*, vol. ii. 242.

[4] " That being done . . . I would not doubt but that there would be more money found in London than in Antwerp " (Clough) : Burgon, *Life of Gresham*, ii. 180-181. For the Act of 1571 : *supra*, p. 224.

[5] 1598 : *Acts of the Privy Council*, 1598–1599, p. 337 ; *Hist. MSS. Comm. Salisbury*, viii. 511 ; Burgon, *Life of Gresham*, ii. 420.

[6] *State Papers Venetian*, 1607–1610, pp. 475, 481.

smiths as Government bankers took place under the Common- *Goldsmiths*
wealth, and they supplied Cromwell's ' wants of money *become*
upon great advantages ' [1].  After the Restoration the King *ment*
relied habitually upon them for advances in anticipation *bankers.*
of the revenue, although this did not exclude loans from the
trading companies as before [2].  According to Clarendon [3],
" the bankers did not consist of above the number of five
or six men [4], some whereof were aldermen and had been
lord mayors of London. . . . They were a tribe that had
risen and grown up in Cromwell's time, and never were
heard of before the late troubles, till when the whole trade
of money had passed through the hands of the scriveners :
they were for the most part goldsmiths, men known to be
so rich and of so good reputation that all the money of the
kingdom would be trusted or deposited in their hands ".
The relations between the Government and the bankers are
thus described.  As soon as an Act of Parliament was passed
the bankers were called into the presence of the King, " and
told ' that the King had occasion to use such a sum of ready
money within such a day '. . . . Whereupon one said :
' He would within such a time pay one hundred thousand
pounds ' ;  another more, and another less, as they found
themselves provided ;  for there was no joint stock amongst
them, but every one supplied according to his ability.
They were desirous to have 8 in the hundred ", but professed to " leave the interest to the King's own bounty,
declaring ' that themselves paid 6 in the hundred for all
the money with which they were entrusted ', which was
known to be true " [5].  The legal rate was 6 per cent., yet
the King paid 10 or 12 per cent., the rate of interest growing
as his credit deteriorated owing to the extent of his borrowings [6]—in 1676 it was said that the bankers received ' above

[1] *The Mystery of the New Fashioned Goldsmiths or Bankers* (1676), 5.
[2] *State Papers Domestic*, 1665–1666, p. 357.
[3] *The Life of Edward, Earl of Clarendon* (ed. 1827), iii. 7.
[4] *I.e.* the principal goldsmiths who had dealings with the King.  The
number of goldsmiths engaged in deposit-banking was much larger.
(There were 44 in 1677 : Westerfield, *Middlemen in English Business*,
378.)
[5] *The Life of Edward, Earl of Clarendon* (ed. 1827), iii. 8-9.
[6] Child, *A New Discourse of Trade* (4th ed.), 19.

20, and sometimes 30 in the hundred '[1]. The loan, together with the interest to be paid on it, was charged on various branches of the revenue, the bankers being given an assignment of " the payment of the first money that should be payable upon that Act of Parliament . . . or tallies upon the farmers of the customs or excise, or such other branches of the revenue as were least charged ; having the King's own word and the faith of the Treasurer that they should be exactly complied with "[2].

*The Exchequer 'shut up'.* Confidence in ' the King's own word' was rudely shaken, when the Exchequer was ' shut up ' (18 December 1671) and an order suspended payments due to the bankers for a period of twelve months[3] : this was done in expectation of a rupture with the Dutch. The goldsmiths thereupon suspended payment to their own clients, who included merchants from the West of England[4] ; and bills of exchange were returned to Italy dishonoured[5]. " The common faith of a nation violated", wrote Turnor. He met the plea that the bankers had exacted greater interest than the law allowed—and had therefore forfeited their loans—with the argument that an Act of 1671[6] had sanctioned higher rates, by levying a tax of 15s. per cent. on loans for which the King was required to pay more than 6 per cent. ' as interest, consideration, gratuity or otherwise ' ; and in any case the loss fell upon the bankers' clients[7]. Evelyn attributed the responsibility for this breach of faith to Clifford, who " hinted to me as a confidant that his majesty would shut up the Exchequer . . . but, says he, it will soon be open again and everybody satisfied. For this bold man, who had been the sole adviser of the King to

---

[1] *The Mystery of the New Fashioned Goldsmiths or Bankers* (1676), 5.
[2] *The Life of Edward, Earl of Clarendon* (ed. 1827), iii. 9.
[3] *State Papers Domestic,* 1671–1672, pp. 68, 87.
[4] *Ibid.* 1671–1672, p. 73. " When the Exchequer was first shut, few people failed, but imputed that for a cause " : Houghton, *A Collection of Letters for the Improvement of Husbandry and Trade,* ix. 94 (1682).
[5] Andréadès, *History of the Bank of England,* 40. For details of the debt due to the goldsmith bankers, see Richards, *The Early History of Banking in England,* 67 seq.      [6] *Statutes,* v. 693.
[7] Turnor, *The Case of the Bankers and their Creditors* (ed. 1675), i, 114-117. For a defence of the stoppage, see *State Papers Domestic,* 1673–1675, pp. 502-503.

invade that sacred stock (though some pretend it was Lord Ashley's counsel, then chancellor of the exchequer), was so over-confident of the success of this unworthy design against the Smyrna merchants as to put his majesty on an action, which not only lost the hearts of his subjects— and ruined many widows and orphans whose stocks were lent him—but the reputation of his Exchequer for ever, it being before in such credit that he might have commanded half the wealth of the nation. The credit of this bank being thus broken did exceedingly discontent the people, and never did his majesty's affairs prosper to any purpose after it " [1]. The suspension of payments was prolonged by a subsequent declaration beyond the original date [2], and in 1675 the creditors of the goldsmiths laid their distressed condition before Parliament. Some, they stated, were widows and orphans, others had saved to maintain themselves in their old age, others had put their estates into the goldsmiths' hands until their children came of age to apprentice them or bestow them in marriage [3]. The King undertook to assign ' the hereditary excise ' for ' the payment and satisfaction ' of the bankers' debt [4], and the interest was punctually paid until about a year before his death. The payment then ceased, but eventually (1705) it was made part—in origin the oldest part—of the national debt [5].

The ' stop of the Exchequer ' affected the King's credit [6], and it had its nemesis in the rate of interest which Charles II. was now required to pay [7]. Evidently a system, under

[1] Evelyn, *Diary* (ed. Dobson), ii. 340. Arlington declared that he " knew not who directed it ; all concurred in it ": *State Papers Domestic*, 1673–1675, p. 106 But it is also said that the majority of the Council opposed it : *Calendar of Treasury Books*, iii. part i. p. lix.

[2] *State Papers Domestic*, 1672–1673, p. 266. " All my money in the Exchequer has been detained from me these sixteen months, and not a penny of interest paid since I lent it ", wrote Dr. E. Chamberlayne : *ibid.* 1672, p. 657.

[3] *Ibid.* 1675–1676, p. 369 ; *Hist. MSS. Comm. Finch*, ii. 8.

[4] *State Papers Domestic*, 1676–1677, p. 537 ; 1677–1678, p. 152.

[5] See *Calendar of Treasury Books*, iv. pp. xiv-xv ; Sinclair, *The history of the Public Revenue* (ed. 1801), i. 398-401. The undertaking given by Charles II. to pay interest to the bankers in 1677 is printed in Hilton Price, *A Handbook of London Bankers* (ed. 1891), Appendix, pp. 426-431.

[6] Cf. the quotation from Halifax, *infra*, p. 240.

[7] *Calendar of Treasury Books*, v. part i. p. ix. Also *supra*, p. 235. Creditors of the Crown were given ' tallies ' charged on separate branches of

[*contd.*]

which the Government raised mortgages on the revenue from private bankers at ruinous rates, could not continue indefinitely, apart from the objections felt by the House of Commons on constitutional grounds. Nor was the alternative system more satisfactory of bringing pressure to bear upon trading companies, such as the Merchant Adventurers and the East India Company, to make advances [1] as the condition of their privileges, because it starved them of the capital necessary to carry on their real function, which was trading not lending. The outbreak of war with France after the Revolution brought these difficulties to a head, and in spite of the opposition of the private bankers a public bank was erected to serve as the agency for Government borrowings. Although the Bank of England was not founded until 1694, proposals for the erection of a bank had been made as early as the sixteenth century. One proposal apparently contemplated a State bank with a capital of £100,000, though Elizabeth had not the money to start it [2]; while Fitzherbert devised a plan for a ' common bank ', for which the capital was to be raised by a species of death duties [3]. In the next century (1611) James I. granted a patent for the setting up of a public office to be called ' The Public Register for General Commerce ', which was intended to bring together borrowers and lenders. The scheme did not involve a deposit bank, since the lenders were not to leave their money in the custody of the office, but it sought the elimination of the scrivener and the broker. " Whereas many conscionable men would willingly expose their moneys for eight or nine in the hundred, but cannot make it known and therefore do put their stocks into the hands of brokers or scriveners to employ for them ; so it is that those brokers do for the most part take ten in the hundred for those moneys, which the owners do afford

---

the revenue; and as these tallies were heavily discounted, creditors charged a correspondingly high rate of interest. However, in 1678 London undertook to lend the King £100,000 at 7 per cent. and a similar sum at 8 per cent. : *Hist. MSS. Comm.* vii. 470.     [1] *Supra*, vol. ii. 242, 310.
    [2] *State Papers Domestic*, 1598–1601, p. 88.
    [3] *Hist. MSS. Comm. Salisbury*, i. 133-134 (? 1553). A proposal was made about the year 1627 for a national bank, the capital to be raised by taxes : *State Papers Domestic*, 1627–1628, pp. 493-494.

at a cheaper hand, thereby wronging both the lender and borrower ". Accordingly it was proposed that those who had money to lend should have it registered at an office, and " such as repair unto this register to borrow may also receive notice . . . if the security be good " [1].

Modern banking was not destined, however, to develop *Later* on the lines either of a compulsory levy or of an institution *proposals.* which simply registered loan transactions. The true lines of its development were foreshadowed in 1641 when Robinson recommended the erection of a deposit bank, where money could be deposited on interest at 5 per cent. and loaned out to borrowers [2]. After the outbreak of the Civil War proposals of this kind multiplied fast, the example of Holland with a famous bank at Amsterdam being cited in support [3]. Two schemes put forward in 1661 have a particular interest. One advocated a bank with " a coinage of its own called bank money " [4]; the other a land bank, " wherein the security of lands may pass and be held of equal value or credit with any other species whatsoever " [5]. Most of the proposals aimed at the expansion of credit in the interests of merchants, but some had in view the financing of the Government. A project for a ' Bank of England ', in the reign of Charles II., bears a striking resemblance in certain details to the one adopted in the reign of William and Mary. In order to relieve the national revenue of its debts, a loan of two million pounds was to be raised at 6 per cent. ; special privileges were to be accorded to the lenders as an inducement to lay down their money ; but the revenues assigned for the payment of interest were also to provide for extinguishing the principal [6]. Conspicuous among the

[1] The patent was granted to Sir A. Gorges and Sir W. Cope : Gorges, *The Publicke Register for Generall Commerce* (1611).

[2] Robinson, *England's Safety in Trades Encrease* (1641), 34.

[3] Benbrigge, *Usura Accommodata* (1646) ; *Hist. MSS. Comm. Portland,* i. 406 (1647) ; Chappel, *A Diamond or Rich Jewel, Presented to the Commonwealth* (1650), 8 ; Lambe, *Seasonable Observations humbly offered to his Highness the Lord Protector* (1657), 10 *seq.*

[4] D'Ouvilly, " A Bank of Exchange " in *State Papers Domestic,* 1661–1662, p. 78.

[5] Cradocke, *Wealth Discovered* (1661), 8. Petty also advocated ' inbanking 20 millions worth of land ' : *Economic Writings,* i. 312.

[6] *Hist. MSS. Comm. Hodgkin,* 326 (*temp.* Charles II.). For another proposal, see *State Papers Domestic,* 1673–1675, p. 186.

advocates of public banks, erected on the basis of money or securities such as plate ' and other durable commodities ', was Sir William Petty. In answer to the question : " what remedy is there if we have too little money ? " he replied : " we must erect a bank, which well computed doth almost double the effect of our coined money " [1]. One experiment at a public bank, which ' made a mighty stir ', was actually tried : it was in some respects a curious anticipation of Robert Owen's scheme of ' labour exchanges ' and ' labour notes '. It took the form of a ' bank of credit ', which circulated bills of credit on merchandise deposited therein, the depositor being allowed credit to the extent of two-thirds or three-fourths of the market value of his deposit, for which he paid 6 per cent. interest. It was thus intended that manufacturers and tradesmen might deposit their goods, and by ' raising a credit on their own dead stock ' increase their trade until they had ' a good market '. The bank was short-lived : Houghton spoke of it at the beginning of 1683 as ' now establishing ', but it is said to have collapsed the same year [2].

*Founding of the Bank of England.* The Bank of England was founded as a consequence of the Revolution of 1688, which by making England a participant in the continental struggle against France created the national debt. The Government did not know where to turn for money to carry on the war [3], and eagerly embraced the proposal made by William Paterson for a loan of £1,200,000 to the State at 8 per cent. in return for the incorporation of the subscribers as a bank [4]. Halifax threw cold water upon the idea of a national funded debt—" the breach of the Exchequer credit by King Charles and ever since, and the frequent breaking of the bankers, will make men very shy of parting with their money upon new projects at a distance " [5] ; and the private bankers endeavoured to

[1] Petty, *Economic Writings*, i. 26, 311-312 ; ii. 446.

[2] Houghton, *Husbandry and Trade Improv'd* (ed. 1728), iv. 145; Macpherson, *Annals of Commerce*, ii. 612 ; Westerfield, *Middlemen in English Business*, 380-381 ; Scott, *Joint-Stock Companies*, iii. 202.

[3] *State Papers Domestic*, 1694-1695, p. 197 (Godolphin to the King).

[4] Andréadès, *History of the Bank of England*, 65.

[5] Halifax, *An Essay upon Taxes* (1693) in Somers, *Tracts* (ed. 1814). xi. 76.

defeat the project by offering ' any rates ' to get money into their hands and prevent the subscriptions [1]. In spite of their efforts the whole £1,200,000 was subscribed in ten days [2]; and the founding of the Bank of England was authorized by the Act of 1694 which permitted the subscribers, as a corporation, to issue notes, buy and sell bullion, deal in bills of exchange, and make advances on merchandise—in short, to use their stock ' for issue, for loans and for discount ', but not to engage in commerce [3].

The history of the Bank of England is an epitome of the financial history of England since the Revolution ; and it enjoys the distinction shared by few other institutions that not only from the first did it occupy a dominating position, but its importance to the community has steadily grown until to-day it is both the Government's banker and the bankers' banker. Its services may be enumerated under five heads. First of all, the Bank of England encouraged the accumulation of capital and the circulation of hoarded wealth, by giving depositors a sense of security hitherto lacking [4]. According to contemporaries two to three million pounds were lost in the previous thirty years owing to the bankruptcy of goldsmiths and scriveners [5], so that safe depositing had become a national necessity. Secondly : the Bank of England was instrumental in reducing the rate of interest on loans whether to the State or to merchants. The goldsmiths paid depositors 6 per cent. and charged borrowers 12 per cent. or more [6] ; the Bank of England paid 4 per cent.[7] and charged the Government at first 8, then 6, ultimately 3 per

*Services rendered by the Bank of England*

---

[1] *State Papers Domestic*, 1694-1695, p. 197.

[2] Godfrey, *A Short Account of the Bank of England* in Somers, *Tracts* (ed. 1814), xi. 4. The subscribers numbered about 1300 : *ibid.* 3. The directors called up 60 per cent. of the subscriptions and paid the rest in bank bills : Rogers, *The First Nine Years of the Bank of England*, 19, 25-26.

[3] *Statutes*, vi. 489-490.

[4] Wood, writing in 1718, says that people did not " as formerly " keep " sums in chests by them " : *A Survey of Trade*, 341.

[5] Godfrey, *A Short Account of the Bank of England* in Somers, *Tracts* (ed. 1814), xi. 7. " Not less than two millions within five and twenty years " : Barbon, *A Discourse of Trade* (1690), 29. Several failures were reported in 1676 : *Hist. MSS. Comm.* vii. 468. Also see Houghton, *Husbandry and Trade Improv'd* (ed. 1728), iv. 153.

[6] *Supra*, p. 235.

[7] Rogers, *The First Nine Years of the Bank of England*, 18.

cent.[1]. Godfrey, the first deputy-governor of the Bank, pointed out that "those who are concerned in the Bank cannot fail to lessen the interest of money for it's their own interest to do it, else they cannot employ it ; and their fund being settled at 8 per cent. per annum, the lower they bring all other interest they make the stock of the Bank the more valuable ; and it must be allowed that it is the only fund that ever was settled in England which has lessened the interest of money". This lowering of interest raised the value of land, increased trade, and afforded a guarantee against the exploitation of ' public, or private men's, necessities '[2]. Thirdly : the Bank of England provided the requisite conditions for the issue of paper money. This was considered the main purpose of banking, "which is to furnish the kingdom with an imaginary coin to serve the uses of that which is really so "[3]. The banks at Amsterdam and Venice "make payments easy by preventing the continual trouble of telling over money, and cause a great despatch in business "; while in London the absence of a bank had forced merchants to use goldsmith's notes, which circulated from hand to hand, and were so convenient that their credit was kept up in spite of great losses[4]. The Bank of England was able to enlarge the currency and expand the basis of credit ; and so extensive had the use of paper money (bank-notes and goldsmith's notes) become by 1697, according to a pamphlet published then, that " all foreign and inland bills of exchange and all

---

[1] In 1709 the Bank lent £400,000 free of interest (*Statutes*, ix. 115), which meant that the Government paid 6 per cent. on the total amount borrowed. In 1742 another loan (£1,600,000) free of interest reduced the rate on the original loan to 3 per cent. (*Statutes at Large*, vi. 173). The credit of the Government in regard to the floating debt was improved by the introduction (1696) of Exchequer Bills charged on the total revenues, whereas the ' tallies ' (*supra*, p. 237, note 7) were charged on separate branches which might prove insufficient : *State Papers Domestic*, 1696, pp. 220, 222 ; Ehrenberg, *Capital and Finance in the Age of the Renaissance*, 353-356. See *infra*, Appendix, p. 514, No. 4.

[2] Godfrey, *A Short Account of the Bank of England* in Somers, *Tracts* (ed. 1814), xi. 4-6. Davenant, on the other hand, asserted that the ' funds ' diverted money too much from the channels of trade, and raised it " above the price which either our foreign or domestic trade can afford to pay for it " : *Works* (ed. 1771), i. 23-24.

[3] Rogers, *The First Nine Years of the Bank of England*, 76, quoting a pamphlet dated 1697.

[4] Barbon, *A Discourse of Trade* (1690), 28-29.

great payments were made in these notes "[1]. Gradually the issue of bank-notes became more important than the receipt of deposits : near the end of the eighteenth century the deposits at the Bank of England did not exceed £1,500,000, while its note issue amounted to £9,500,000 [2]. These bank-notes were issued for fixed amounts, namely, £20 ; in 1759 notes for £15 and £10 were introduced ; and in 1794 notes for £5 [3]. At first there was an over-issue of paper in bills and notes, which resulted in depreciation, and the early difficulties of the Bank were due to inadequate covering in the shape of specie [4] ; in 1696 clothiers complained that they were forced to take bank-notes, which would not pass again without heavy discount [5] ; ultimately the issue of notes was regulated by the Act of 1844. Fourthly : the Bank of England not only caused money to circulate which might otherwise have been hoarded—' paper credit ' induced people, who formerly kept their money in chests, to part with it more readily [6]—but it could be trusted not to impair the standard of the currency. It was said that if the money lodged with the goldsmiths had been deposited in the Bank, it would not have been so ' scandalously clipped ', and the nation would have been spared the recoinage [7]. Fifthly : the foundation of the Bank of England had a steadying influence on the foreign exchanges, and foreign bills were discounted at more reasonable rates [8]. It may be noted, finally, that the Bank of England had profound constitutional and political significance—the former in bringing Government borrowings under Parliament's control ; the latter in identifying the interests of the moneyed classes with the Revolution settlement [9].

[1] Rogers, *The First Nine Years of the Bank of England*, 75 ; Wood, *A Survey of Trade* (1718), 340.

[2] 1797 : Bisschop, *The Rise of the London Money Market*, 119.

[3] In 1797 notes were issued for £2 and £1 : Gilbart, *The History, Principles and Practice of Banking* (ed. 1882), i. 43, 45, 48.

[4] Rogers, *The First Nine Years of the Bank of England*, pp. xvi, xviii, 71, 73, 83, 87-88, 135.   [5] *House of Commons Journals*, xi. 582, 635.

[6] *Supra*, p. 241, note 4.

[7] Godfrey, *A Short Account of the Bank of England* in Somers, *Tracts* (ed. 1814), xi. 5. For the recoinage, see *supra*, p. 80.

[8] Rogers, *The First Nine Years of the Bank of England*, pp. xviii, 84.

[9] Godfrey, *A Short Account of the Bank of England* in Somers, *Tracts* (ed. 1814), xi. 4, 8. This was shown in 1715 : *Hist. MSS. Comm. Stuart*, i. 520 ; ii. 69.

Country
banks.

The founding of the Bank of England did not put an end to private banking which still continued—in Ireland two bankers became insolvent in 1734 for nearly two hundred thousand pounds [1]—but it checked any further development of joint-stock banking. Two Acts, passed in 1697 and 1709, conferred on the Bank the practical monopoly of joint-stock banking. The first enacted that, during the continuance of the Bank of England, no other bank was to be erected or permitted by Act of Parliament [2]. The second deprived any corporate body, which numbered more than six persons, of the right to issue paper money payable at demand or within six months [3]. As a company which was not incorporated by Act of Parliament was denied certain legal privileges [4], and as the issue of paper money was then considered the primary end of banking, the Bank remained the only joint-stock bank down to the nineteenth century. This monopoly of the Bank of England retarded the development of a banking system in the provinces, owing to the failure of the Bank to establish country branches ; and the provinces also suffered from the fact, noted by Child, that " the trade of bankers being only in London does very much drain the ready money from all other parts "[5]. However, wealthy provincial merchants were accustomed to open accounts with London bankers for the convenience of making payments in London, and they thus came to undertake banking business since they were in a position to render services to their customers and friends, while their vaults afforded safe custody for money confided to their care [6]. This explains the different origin of London and country banks. In London it was the goldsmith who developed into a banker, and even in the late eighteenth century eminent bankers kept a goldsmith's shop [7]. In the provinces mer-

---

[1] *Hist. MSS. Comm. Portland*, vi. 57.

[2] *Statutes*, vii. 226. The scheme for a national land bank in 1696 was a failure, the subscriptions " not amounting to above £36,000, and none of that like to be paid " : *State Papers Domestic*, 1696, p. 321.

[3] *Statutes*, ix. 130.     [4] See *supra*, p. 218.

[5] Child, *A New Discourse of Trade* (4th ed.), 52. For the difficulties experienced by the ironmasters of Furness in obtaining specie, see Fell, *The Early Iron Industry of Furness*, 332-342.

[6] Bisschop, *The Rise of the London Money Market*, 145-148. See *infra*, Appendix, p. 515, No. 1.     [7] Pennant, *Of London* (1790), 361.

chants, manufacturers and shopkeepers turned bankers. The Nottingham bank, one of the oldest in the country, was started in the latter part of the seventeenth century by Smith a mercer : the Old Gloucester Bank was founded by Wood a chandler : the Edinburgh banks were established by Coutts a corn-dealer, Mansfield a linen-draper, Cuming a cloth merchant, and Alexander a tobacco merchant : the Norwich bank owed its origin to the Gurneys worsted manu-facturers : in Liverpool banks were erected by merchants and linen-drapers, and in Darlington by worsted manu-facturers : in Birmingham ironmasters are associated with the beginnings of banking : in Bristol a bookseller carried on a banking business [1]. In this connexion it may be observed that two of the joint-stock banks now in existence bear the name, one of an ironmaster (Lloyd), the other of a linen-draper (Barclay) [2]. The real development of banking in the provinces belongs to the second half of the eighteenth century. About the year 1750, according to Burke, there were barely a dozen bankers out of London [3] : in 1800 the country banks numbered 386 [4], while 71 had stopped pay-ment in 1793 [5]. Thus in Bristol the first bank formed under a proper deed of partnership was established with six partners in 1750, and within a quarter of a century Bristol contained five banking houses [6]. The country banks issued

---

[1] Nottingham : Easton, *The History of a Banking House (Smith, Payne & Smiths)*, 36. Gloucester : Fox Bourne, *English Merchants*, 333. Edin-burgh : *ibid.* 333 seq. ; Graham, *The One Pound Note*, 71-72. Norwich : Bidwell, *Annals of an East Anglian Bank*, 13-14. Liverpool : Hughes, *Liverpool Banks and Bankers*, 51, 56, 91 seq. Darlington : Phillips, *A History of Banks, Bankers and Banking in Northumberland, Durham and North Yorkshire*, 134, 346. Birmingham : Lloyd, *The Lloyds of Birming-ham* (3rd ed.), 20 seq. Bristol : Cave, *A History of Banking in Bristol*, 3, 9.

[2] Lloyd, *The Lloyds of Birmingham* (3rd ed.), 20 seq. ; Matthews and Tuke, *History of Barclays Bank Limited*, 35.

[3] Burke, *Two Letters . . . on the Proposals for Peace with the Regicide Directory of France* (1796), 80. " They are now ", he wrote in 1796, " in almost every market town " : *ibid.* 80.

[4] Thornton, *An Enquiry into the Nature and Effects of the Paper Credit of Great Britain* (1802), 154. According to Macleod, *A Dictionary of Poli-tical Economy*, i. 119, there were ' about 400 ' in 1793. The growth of country banks is indicated by Arthur Young's remark in 1793 that " the number of banks, even in villages, became an object of general ridicule before the war was thought of " : *Annals of Agriculture*, xxi. 93.

[5] Sinclair, *The History of the Public Revenue* (ed. 1803), ii. Appendix, 63.

[6] Cave, *A History of Banking in Bristol*, 9, 12.

notes[1]; and it was the over-issue of paper, without an adequate cash reserve, which brought on severe financial crises. The private banks in London, on the other hand, generally discontinued the issue of notes, and cheques took their place [2].

*Loans to small producers.* The creation of banks helped to provide capital for men who conducted business on a large scale, but it left untouched the problem of the small producer and the small trader. As a rule the latter had very little capital of their own or none at all; and they had to fall back on two alternatives. They could buy goods ' at time ', that is, on credit, from richer men willing to trust them; but the prices they were charged involved the payment of a high rate of interest amounting to 10 and 12 per cent.[3]. Or, instead of buying goods ' at time ', they could buy money ' at time ', that is, raise loans on interest. Here the problem was to find a lender; and in this connexion we get bequests of money to be employed in loans to poor men, advances made by corporate bodies, and pawnbroking establishments. In the Middle Ages money was sometimes bequeathed to give ' young beginning men ' a start in life [4]; and legacies for this purpose, administered by municipal authorities or trading companies, became common in the sixteenth and seventeenth centuries. One of the most famous was the bequest made near the end of the sixteenth century by Sir Thomas White, lord mayor of London and founder of St. John's College, Oxford. It provided that annually a sum of one hundred pounds was to be lent free of interest for the space of ten years to four young men, preferably those engaged in cloth-making; the bequest circulated among twenty-four towns, each of which received it in turn once in twenty-four years [5]. In addition to charitable funds

---

[1] A Nottingham bank-note is dated 1728 : Easton, *The History of a Banking House* (*Smith, Payne & Smiths*), 101, 103.
[2] Bisschop, *The Rise of the London Money Market*, 157, 161.
[3] North, *Discourses upon Trade* (1691), 7.
[4] *Supra*, vol. i. 460.
[5] Clode, *Early History of the Guild of Merchant Taylors*, ii. 178 ; *Hist. MSS. Comm. Exeter*, 232-233. For other examples, see *Reading Records* (ed. Guilding), iii. 17, 149 ; *Northampton Records* (ed. Cox), ii. 307 ; *York Merchant Adventurers* (ed. Sellers), 288 ; *Norwich Records* (ed. Tingey),ii

[contd.]

provided by philanthropists, the gilds in the Middle Ages
and beyond sometimes placed their resources at the disposal
of their members. The gild merchant of Lynn evidently
served as the bank of the community, for a long list of
members were in its debt to the extent of over £1200 :
the Merchant Adventurers of Newcastle loaned the Company's money at 4 per cent. : and the journeymen shoemakers of Oxford were entitled to borrow from the common
' box ' [1]. Sometimes, also, the municipality itself made
advances. Oxford, Coventry, Nottingham and Liverpool
lent money to individuals [2], and the corporation of Kendal
deposited funds with the ironmasters of Furness [3]. In
rural districts, as late as the seventeenth century, the
village community fulfilled the function of a credit bank
in loaning to its members cattle and sheep and money,
for which interest was charged [4].

And finally, there were pawnbroking establishments. *Pawn-*
In the fifteenth century there existed on the Continent *broking.*
*montes pietatis*, or charitable loan funds, from which loans
were made to the poor on the security of pledges [5]. In
England the *mons pietatis* was, if not unknown, at least
rare. Perhaps the nearest approach to it was ' The Charitable Corporation for Relief of Industrious Poor ', founded
in 1699 by philanthropic persons with the object of assisting
the ' industrious poor ' with small sums upon pledges at
' legal interest ' (6 per cent.) [6]. However the purpose of
the *mons pietatis* was met, when the authorities of a parish
or municipality assumed responsibility for the provision

---

pp. cix, cxiv ; Seyer, *Memoirs of Bristol*, ii. 140 ; Noake, *Worcester in Olden
Times*, 25 ; *Hist. MSS. Comm. Various*, i. 47 ; *Victoria County History,
Surrey*, ii. 346.

[1] *Hist. MSS. Comm. King's Lynn*, 228-230 (1409) ; *Newcastle Merchant
Adventurers*, i. 232 (1687) ; *Records of Oxford* (ed. Turner), 8 (1512).

[2] Oxford : *Records* (ed. Turner), 418, 425. Liverpool : *Municipal
Records* (ed. Picton), 1700–1835, p. 147. For Coventry and Nottingham,
see *supra*, vol. ii. 121.

[3] Fell, *The Early Iron Industry of Furness*, 334 (eighteenth century).

[4] Addy, *Church and Manor*, 314 *seq.*

[5] Ashley, *An Introduction to English Economic History and Theory* (ed.
1909), ii. 447-449.

[6] The charter of incorporation (1708) is printed in Carr, *Select Charters
of Trading Companies*, 256 *seq.* See also Scott, *Joint-Stock Companies*, i.
364 ; iii. 380.

of loans on the security of articles held in pledge. In such cases they either acted themselves in the capacity of pawn-brokers [1] or appointed official pawnbrokers. Thus at Berwick an order was issued in 1598 prohibiting all pawn-broking, save by two 'credible and honest' brokers who were to keep a register of transactions [2]. These cases were doubtless exceptional. In general, pawnbroking was carried on by private individuals, and the importance which it attained in the life of the working community is reflected in the evidence of a witness before a parliamentary committee in 1746. He described the business as an 'in-dispensable necessity' to several classes of persons—" the very poor sort of people, such as persons who cry fish, fruit or other wares about the streets ", and obtained from pawn-brokers the money to buy the commodities in which they dealt; 'the middling sort of tradesmen', who borrowed from pawnbrokers to pay their journeymen's wages, support their credit and maintain their families, which they could not otherwise do " by reason of the great credit they are obliged to give their customers "; artificers and handi-craftsmen, who were thus enabled to buy materials to carry on their business; journeymen with nothing but their wages to depend on, who must perish when sick or out of employment " if there were no such profession " [3]. " I cannot comprehend ", wrote Campbell, how " the poor labouring tradesman in this metropolis . . . can live with-out the pawnbroker " [4].

## (II)

### WAGES

The fundamental trait of capitalism is the wage-system under which a worker sells, not the fruits of his labour, but the labour itself—a distinction of vital economic significance [5]. The wage-system did not arise in industry on account of the

---

[1] For examples, see Addy, *Church and Manor*, 316-317.
[2] *Hist. MSS. Comm. Various*, i. 3-4, 25.
[3] *House of Commons Journals*, xxv. 46.
[4] Campbell, *The London Tradesman* (1747), 296. For bankruptcy, see *infra*, Appendix, p. 515, No. 2.
[5] Cf. *supra*, vol. ii. Introduction, pp. xxvi-xxix.

introduction of machinery. In three out of the four main branches of the textile manufactures—wool-combing, spinning and weaving—machinery was not used until near the end of the eighteenth century [1]; and in the fourth, cloth-finishing, it was still exceptional [2]. The origin of the wage-system lay in the divorce of the workers from the ownership of the material on which they worked—a process which had begun in the woollen industry at least as early as the fourteenth century [3]. When the material became the property of a capitalist employer, he thereby secured the right to dispose of the finished product; and the manual craftsman was transformed from an independent producer into a labourer working for hire. This change of status was attended with momentous consequences: it created the basis for the perennial struggle between capital and labour. The antagonism of these two great forces was not the outcome of the ' Industrial Revolution ', as it is often supposed. The history of past centuries reveals examples [4] of strained relations between employers and employed, which equal, if they do not surpass, in bitterness those afforded by the nineteenth century. In one form or another ' labour unrest ' has manifested itself in industry for five hundred years. The workman's labour is a perishable commodity; he cannot withhold it for any length of time or he will starve. Hence there easily arises the possibility of exploitation, and from the fifteenth century down to our own day the energies of the working classes have been absorbed in the effort to establish and maintain a ' standard of life '. The conflict of capital and labour was fought out over three main grievances—low wages, payment in kind, and unemployment. The hours of labour, though excessively long, were seldom advanced as a source of grievance against the employers, since the work was mainly done in the homes of the artisans [5].

*Origin of the wage system.*

[1] Inventions like Paul's spinning and carding machines did not come into general use: Lipson, *The History of the Woollen and Worsted Industries*, 148-149, 155.
[2] For the gig mill, see *supra*, p. 51.
[3] *Supra*, vol. i. 468 *seq.*
[4] *Supra*, vol. i. 407, and *infra*, pp. 393 *seq.*
[5] For a complaint against long hours of labour, see *supra*, vol. ii. 58, note 3.

*Complaints of low wages.*     The most important grievance was low wages. In the fifteenth century a popular pamphlet on *England's Commercial Policy*, one of the earliest expressions of industrial discontent known to us, summed up in a telling phrase the economic position of the textile workers under the new conditions of production :

" The poor have the labour, the rich the winning " [1].

In the sixteenth century (1539) the Suffolk and Essex weavers attributed their destitute state to a conspiracy of ' the rich men ', the clothiers, " to hold and pay one price for weaving of cloths " [2]. In the seventeenth century (1621) a member of Parliament complained in the House of Commons that clothiers " give not the poor competent wages—threepence a day and no more to divers " [3]. A famous ballad, which is said to have been chaunted about the streets in the time of Charles II. [4], recited in rude rhymes the grievances of the workers in cloth against their employers. It is entitled *The Clothier's Delight ; Or, the Rich Men's joy and the Poor Men's sorrow. Wherein is exprest the craftiness and subtility of many Clothiers in England by beating down their Workmen's wages.* The opening verses run :

" Of all sorts of callings that in England be,
     There is none that liveth so gallant as we ;
     Our trading maintains us as brave as a knight,
     We live at our pleasure, and take our delight ;
     We heapeth up riches and treasure great store,
     Which we get by griping and grinding the poor.
     And this is a way for to fill up our purse,
     Although we do get it with many a curse.

" Throughout the whole kingdom, in country and town,
     There is no danger of our trade going down,
     So long as the Comber can work with his comb,
     And also the Weaver weave with his lomb ;

---

[1] *Supra*, vol. i. 481.       [2] *Supra*, vol. i. 474.
[3] *House of Commons Journals*, i. 609.
[4] Macaulay, *The History of England* (ed. 1906), i. 322.

The Tucker and Spinner that spins all the year,
We will make them to earn their wages full dear.
   And this is a way for to fill up our purse,
   Although we do get it with many a curse.

" In former ages we us'd to give,
So that our work-folks like farmers did live ;
But the times are altered, we will make them know
All we can for to bring them all under our bow ;
We will make to work hard for sixpence a day,
Though a shilling they deserve if they had their just pay.
   And this is a way for to fill up our purse,
   Although we do get it with many a curse " [1].

What was the attitude of the State towards the wage *State re-*
problem created by the growth of capitalism ?  In the *gulation*
*of wages*
fourteenth and fifteenth centuries the right to regulate wages *in the*
was a recognized feature of gild activity [2].  In the nineteenth *Middle*
*Ages.*
century the exercise of this right became the bone of contention between capital and labour.  In the intervening
period, the sixteenth, seventeenth and eighteenth centuries,
the State assumed the function of maintaining the ' standard
of life ' of the working community.  It would not admit the
claim of the wage-earners to determine the conditions of
their labour [3], but as a compensation it shouldered, at any
rate in principle, the responsibility of securing to every man
a just remuneration for his work.  The system of State
regulation of wages was actually in operation before the
sixteenth century, though in earlier times it was apparently
limited to unskilled labour outside the craft gilds.  Its history
goes back to the middle of the fourteenth century, when the
Government was called upon to face the difficult situation
arising from the mortality among workers in agriculture.  In
1349 the Ordinance of Labourers enjoined labourers to
accept the wages current before the Black Death.  In 1351,
and again in 1388, the Statute of Labourers specified the
maximum rates of payment [4].  But in 1390, recognizing the

[1] Quoted in Burnley, *The History of Wool and Wool-combing*, 161 *seq.*
[2] *Supra*, vol. i. 335.  For municipal wage regulation, see *ibid.* 384.
[3] *Infra*, pp. 395, 405, 408.
[4] *Statutes*, i. 307 (1349), 311 (1351) ; ii. 57 (1388).

need for local variations in accordance with the cost of living, Parliament imposed the duty of assessing wages upon the justices of the peace [1]. The new Act was presumably intended to abolish the statutory maximum laid down in previous legislation, for the justices were authorized to make their assessments ' by their discretion according to the dearth of victuals ' [2]; and an example has survived (Norfolk, 1431) in which they definitely fixed higher rates than those of 1388 [3]. Under Henry VI. the principle of a statutory maximum was revived in the Act of 1445, which ordered that the " wages of servants, labourers and artificers shall not exceed the assessing that followeth " [4]. It has been conjectured that the justices continued to assess wages subject to the statutory maximum [5]. As regards rural districts there appears to be no evidence to show whether this was so or not, though the town authorities sometimes enforced the statutory maximum, and at other times issued schedules of wages which exceeded it [6].

*The Statute of Apprentices.*    The Early Tudors continued the system of a statutory maximum [7], but at the accession of Elizabeth a change of method became manifest. The rise in prices in the sixteenth century had rendered obsolete the statutory limits on wages contained in the earlier enactments ; and any attempt to put them into operation would have accelerated the rural exodus. It was the policy of the Elizabethan Government to encourage agriculture and to prevent the drift from the country into the towns. It is therefore significant that its first legislative programme included the confirmation of the Act of 1390, " ordering the justices at every session to appoint by proclamation the wages of workers " [8]. The Bill introduced for

---

[1] *Statutes*, ii. 63. Confirmed in 1427 and 1429 : *ibid.* ii. 234, 244.
[2] *Ibid.* ii. 63.
[3] McArthur, " A Fifteenth-Century Assessment of Wages " in *The English Historical Review*, xiii. 301.
[4] *Statutes*, ii. 338.
[5] McArthur, " The Boke longyng to a Justice of the Peace " in *The English Historical Review*, ix. 313-314.
[6] Putnam, " Northamptonshire Wage Assessments of 1560 and 1667 " in *The Economic History Review*, vol. i. No. 1, 129.
[7] *Statutes*, ii. 585 (1495) ; iii. 124 (1515).
[8] *Hist. MSS. Comm. Salisbury*, i. 162 (1559).

the purpose into the Parliament of 1559 proved abortive [1] ; but the justices in Northamptonshire (1560) and in Buckinghamshire (1561), at the Queen's ' special commandment ', framed a schedule of wages higher than the statutory rates prescribed by an Act of Parliament which was as yet unrepealed [2]. These two assessments afford unmistakable evidence that, even before the Statute of Apprentices authorized the change, there was a return in some of the counties [3] to the principle first laid down by the Act of 1390, under which the justices of the peace were given a free hand to fix the maximum rates. Legal sanction for the innovation was soon forthcoming. The famous enactment, known as the Statute of Apprentices (1563), stated that the wages ' limited and rated ' in the Acts still in force were now ' in divers places ' too small, and could not " conveniently without the great grief and burden of the poor labourer and hired man be put in good and due execution ". Accordingly it discarded the principle of a statutory maximum, and gave unrestricted power to the magistrates in the localities in order, as the preamble recites, to " yield unto the hired person both in the time of scarcity and in the time of plenty a convenient proportion of wages " [4]. It authorized the justices of the peace of every county and city at the annual Easter sessions, " calling unto them such discreet and grave persons of the said county or of the said city or town corporate as they shall think meet, and conferring together respecting the plenty or scarcity of the time and other circumstances necessary to be considered ", to appoint the wages of labourers and artificers " by the year or by the day, week, month, or otherwise, with meat and drink or without meat and drink ". The penalty for giving wages above the

---

[1] *The Economic History Review*, vol. i. No. 1, 126.

[2] Miss Putnam has printed the Northamptonshire assessment in *ibid*. 124 *seq*. The Buckinghamshire assessment is printed in *Tudor Economic Document* (ed. Tawney and Power), i. 334 *seq*.

[3] The towns had already, in some cases, discarded the statutory maximum : *supra*, p. 252. In 1562 a carpenter in Middlesex was indicted for his refusal to accept work at the " wage of twelvepence a day, against the form of divers Statutes and Ordinances in this case provided " : *Middlesex County Records*, i. 43.

[4] *Statutes*, iv. part i. 414 *seq*.

maximum fixed by the justices was ten days' imprisonment and a fine of five pounds, and the penalty for accepting such wages was twenty-one days' imprisonment.

*Institution of a minimum wage.*

The Statute of Apprentices was ambiguously worded, and left room for doubt whether it embraced within its scope ' all manner artificers, workmen and workwomen ', or only " such as did work about husbandry ". To remove this doubt several Bills were drafted in 1593, fixing minimum rates for those engaged in the woollen industry. One [1] stated that spinners and weavers were impoverished ' for lack of sufficient wage ', and laid down a new scale of remuneration. This Bill differed from the Statute of Apprentices in the important respect that it substituted a minimum for a maximum wage. It required a minimum wage to be enforced in the districts where it was necessary, but when higher wages were already being paid they were to be maintained. The Bill never became law ; presumably the attempt to fix rates for the whole country was considered impracticable. Instead an Act was framed (1598), which gave the justices authority " to rate wages of any labourers, weavers, spinsters, and workmen or workwomen whatsoever, either working by day, week, month, year, or taking any work at any person or persons' hand whatsoever " as piecework [2]. The Act was confirmed in the next reign (1604) with two significant additions. The first instituted a minimum wage : " If any clothier or other shall refuse to obey the . . . assessment of wages, and shall not pay so much or so great wages to their weavers, spinsters, workmen or workwomen as shall be so set down, rated and appointed . . . that then every clothier and other person and persons so offending shall forfeit and lose for every such offence to the party grieved ten shillings." The second provided that " no clothier being a justice of peace . . . shall be any rater of any wages for any weaver, tucker, spinster or other artisan that dependeth upon the making of cloth " [3]. These two clauses are an indication that the Government was actuated in its legislation by a genuine desire to safeguard

---

[1] *State Papers Domestic*, Addenda, 1580–1625, p. 349 ; *Tudor Economic Documents* (ed. Tawney and Power), i. 371 *seq.*

[2] *Statutes*, iv. part. ii. 913.      [3] *Ibid.* 1022-1024.

the economic interests of the industrial population ; and this
inference is strengthened by the fact that the weavers and
spinners themselves pressed for the compulsory assessment
of wages.  In 1623, for example, the textile workers of
Wiltshire petitioned the justices in these terms : " May it
please you to be informed of the distressed estate of most of
the weavers, spinners and others that work on the making
of woollen cloths, that are not able by their diligent labours
to get their livings, by reason that the clothiers at their will
have made their works extreme hard and abated wages what
they please.  And some of them make such their workfolks
to do their household businesses, to trudge in their errands,
spool their chains, twist their list, do every command, without giving them bread, drink or money for many days'
labours ".  They asked the justices " to appoint certain grave
and discreet persons to view the straitness of works, to assess
rates for wages according to the desert of their works, now
especially in this great dearth of corn, that the poor artificers
of these works of woollen cloth may not perish for want of
food whiles they are painful in their callings ".  The justices
ordered the publication of the table of wages " in order that
workmasters and workmen alike may take notice thereof,
and that the workmen who desire that the same rates may
stand may be the better satisfied " [1].  The justices themselves
lacked the technical knowledge necessary for drawing up
tables of rates, but the Act provided that they should obtain
expert assistance.  In Wiltshire, in 1602, proposals were
drafted by a committee of clothiers and weavers, and submitted to the justices for ratification ; and in 1635 the grand
jury, to ' discharge our consciences ', made recommendations
for an increase in the wages paid to workers in husbandry [2].

The problem how far the authoritarian regulation of *How far*
wages was in actual operation has been much discussed.  We *wage regu-*
*lation was*
shall see that there is an unbroken continuity in the history *enforced.*
of wage assessments in this country, in one branch or another
of industry, down to the third decade of the nineteenth
century [3] : but the difficulty is to determine the extent to

---

[1] *Hist. MSS. Comm. Various*, i. 94.          [2] *Ibid.* 162, 169.
[3] *Infra*, p. 270, note 5.

which the Statute of Apprentices was generally administered, as distinct from local and intermittent action on the part of the magistrates. Evidence of the latter is available throughout the seventeenth and eighteenth centuries : as to the former it may be said that the first century of the Act was the period in which it was most commonly enforced. The working of the system depended primarily upon the hold which the monarchy, acting through the agency of the Privy Council, maintained over the local authorities. Under Elizabeth and the Early Stuarts the Council actively intervened on behalf of distressed artisans, and there was frequent recourse to the machinery of wage regulation. The fall of the absolute monarchy created a new and obscure situation.

*Under Elizabeth.*
Wage assessments exist for every decade of Elizabeth's reign [1]. Although the action of the Buckinghamshire magistrates in 1561, in appointing ' governors of labourers ' to

[1] 1560 (Northamptonshire) : *The Economic History Review*, vol. i. No. 1, 131.
1561 (Buckinghamshire) : *Tudor Economic Documents* (ed. Tawney and Power), i. 334.
1563 (Kent) : *Archæologia Cantiana*, xxii. 316 (printed also in *The English Historical Review*, xli. 270). See *infra*, p. 515, (No. 3).
1563 (Rutland) : Rogers, *A History of Agriculture and Prices*, iv. 120.
1563 (Lincoln) : *Hist. MSS. Comm. Lincoln*, 55.
1563 (Southampton) : *Tudor and Stuart Proclamations* (ed. Steele), i. No. 576.
1564 (Exeter) : *Hist. MSS. Comm. Exeter*, 50.
1570 (Hull) : *Tudor and Stuart Proclamations* (ed. Steele), i. No. 654.
1576 (Canterbury) : *ibid*. i. No. 703.
1586 (London) : *Tudor Economic Documents* (ed. Tawney and Power), i. 363.
1592 (Hertfordshire) : *Hertford County Records*, i. 8.
1593 (East Riding of Yorkshire) : Eden, *The State of the Poor* (1797), iii. p. xc.
1593 (Chester) : Morris, *Chester*, 367-368 ; Eden, *op. cit.* iii. p. xciii.
1594 (Devonshire) : Hamilton, *Quarter Sessions from Queen Elizabeth to Queen Anne*, 12.
1594 (Essex) : Webb, *The Parish and the County*, 455, note 2.
1594 (Canterbury) : *Tudor and Stuart Proclamations* (ed. Steele), i. No. 868.
1595 (Cardiganshire) : *ibid*. i. No. 875.
1595 (Lancashire) : *ibid*. i. No. 876.
1595 (Higham Ferrers) : *ibid*. i. No. 877.
1595 (New Sarum) : *ibid*. i. No. 878.
1596 (Chester) : Morris, *Chester*, 367-368 ; Eden, *op. cit.* iii. p. xciv.
1602 (Wiltshire) : *Hist. MSS. Comm. Various*, i. 162.
For other assessments : *infra*, Appendix, p. 516, No. 1. For the operation of the system in London, see McArthur, " The Regulation of Wages in the Sixteenth Century " in *The English Historical Review*, xv. 445 *seq.*

make a monthly report on the observance of their rates [1], was doubtless exceptional, there are clear indications that the system was enforced [2]. At the end of the century the scope of the Statute was widened expressly on the ground that it had been found ' beneficial for the commonwealth ' [3]. The solicitude displayed by the Tudor Privy Council, in watching over the interests of the wage-earners, is reflected in a letter which it addressed to the justices of the peace in 1595 : " We are given to understand that sundry workfolks with their families . . . are like to be very much distressed by reason the clothiers in this time of dearth do not anything increase their wages. We pray you very heartily to deal earnestly with the clothiers in this behalf, procuring them to yield to such reasonable increase of wages to the said workmen and artificers, as they may have no just cause to think themselves uncharitably dealt with, and thereupon such inconveniences to follow as by like occasion is accustomed " [4].

The system of wage regulation continued in operation *Under the* under the Early Stuarts, the assessments being particularly *Early Stuarts* numerous during the period of Charles I.'s personal government [5]. More than once the Privy Council intervened on

---

[1] *Tudor Economic Documents* (ed. Tawney and Power), i. 334.
[2] *Middlesex County Records*, i. 50 (1564), 63 (1568) ; *Hist. MSS. Comm. Various*, vii. 139 (1571) ; *Acts of the Privy Council*, 1588, p. 168. At Warwick in 1586 the charge was given to the jury to determine if any person had " taken wages contrary to the meaning of the Statute " : *The Book of John Fisher* (ed. Kemp), 156.
[3] *Supra*, p. 254.
[4] *Acts of the Privy Council*, 1595–1596, p. 44.
[5] 1603 and 1605 (Wiltshire) : *Hist. MSS. Comm. Various*, i. 162-168.
1610 (Norfolk) : *The English Historical Review*, xiii. 522.
1610 (Rutland) : Eden, *The State of the Poor* (1797), iii. p. xcv.
1619 and 1621 (Lincolnshire) : *Hist. MSS. Comm. Rutland*, i. 455, 460.
1630 (Norwich) : *State Papers Domestic*, 1629–1631, p. 396.
1630 (Suffolk) : *The English Historical Review*, xii. 307.
1631 (Hertford) : *Hist. MSS. Comm. Hertford*, 160.
1631 (St. Albans) : Clutterbuck, *History of the County of Hertford*, i. p. xxii.
1632 (Herefordshire) : *Hist. MSS. Comm. Portland*, iii. 31.
1632 (Gloucester) : Rogers, *A History of Agriculture and Prices*, vi. 694.
1633 (Dorsetshire) : *Sussex Archæological Collections*, i. 75, note ; Roberts, *Social History of the Southern Counties*, 207.
1634 (Derbyshire) : Cox, *Three Centuries of Derbyshire Annals*, ii. 239.
1635 (Wiltshire) : *Hist. MSS. Comm. Various*, i. 169.
For other assessments : *infra*, Appendix, p. 516, No. 2. There are several references to the enforcement of the system under James I. in the North Riding : *Quarter Sessions Records* (The North
[contd.]

occasions which seemed " to concern the common good of the poorer sort ".  In 1614 it drew the attention of the justices of Wiltshire to the weavers' complaint of "the small wages given them by the clothier, being no more than what was accustomed to be paid forty years past, notwithstanding that the prices of all kind of victual are almost doubled from what they were.  It is thought fitting that, having called the clothiers before you, you examine the truth of this complaint, and finding it to be as is informed, to use your best endeavours for the proportioning of their wages unto the state of these present times, as in all other trades it is observed " [1].  The incident demonstrates that the formal reissue of the wage-schedule year by year, usually without alteration [2], was defeating the purpose of the Elizabethan Statute, which required the justices to take into account ' the plenty or scarcity of the time '.

*Intervention of the Government.*    One instance of Government intervention presents several features of interest.  In 1631 the textile workers in the eastern counties laid their grievances immediately before the Council, complaining that " the poor spinsters, weavers and combers of wool in Sudbury and the places near adjoining thereunto in the counties of Suffolk and Essex, are of late by the clothiers there (who are now grown rich by the labours of the said poor people) so much abridged of their former and usual wages, that they (who in times past maintained their families in good sort) are now in such distress by the abatement of their wages in these times of scarcity and dearth, that they are constrained to sell their beds, wheels and working tools for want of bread ".  The Council appointed commissioners to investigate and redress the grievances of the petitioners ; and it added the instruction that " in case any particular person shall be found (either out of the hardness of his heart towards the poor, or out of private ends or humours) refractory to such courses as the commissioners

---

Riding Record Society), i. 114, 141, 202, 220; ii. 53.  In 1631 the Derbyshire justices reported : " We do not find upon our enquiry that the Statute for labourers and ordering of wages is deluded " : Bland, Brown and Tawney, *English Economic History : Select Documents*, 388.

[1] *Acts of the Privy Council*, 1613–1614, pp. 458, 653.

[2] *Infra*, p. 276.

shall think reasonable and just, that then they bind over every such person to answer the same before the Board ". The commissioners afterwards reported to the Council that they had summoned before them the ' saymakers ', and demanded the reason why they had reduced the wages of their workfolk. " Their answer was that all of that trade in other parts of the kingdom did the like ; but if it might be reformed in all other parts, they were content to give such wages as we should set down ". This response served incidentally to reveal how excessive competition exerted an adverse influence upon the rates of wages. The commissioners accordingly drew up a scale, which they recommended the Government to make general throughout the kingdom [1].

These examples of State interference with wages indicate *Its economic reactions.* that the Government was ready to support the interests of workmen against their employers, so that the Elizabethan Statute cannot be regarded as purely one-sided in its operation. At the same time, however, the justices were instructed that ' perverse and ill-disposed workmen ' were to be forced to accept ' reasonable and ordinary wages ' [2]. In some cases the intervention of the central authority was attended by economic reactions which it was unable to control. This was shown at Colchester when the Privy Council appointed a commission " to take such course for raising the wages of the poor as was taken at Sudbury ". It was " found by experience that the raising of the wages cannot advance the relief of the poor, but will prove inconvenient, for that they will not be set on so much work as if the wages were at the usual rate " [3]. The same lesson was apparently demonstrated on another occasion. In 1629 the Earl of Warwick informed the Council that weavers in East Anglia had complained to him that their masters had enlarged the size of the cloth without augmenting wages. He recommended, as a means of " settling peace among the people ", that bays should be made of one length and that the workmen should be paid

---

[1] *State Papers Domestic*, 1631–1633, p. 22 ; Bland, Brown and Tawney, *English Economic History : Select Documents*, 357-360.

[2] *Hist. MSS. Comm. Cowper*, i. 471 (1632).

[3] *State Papers Domestic*, Addenda, 1625–1649, pp. 430-431 (? 1631).

reasonable wages [1]. After an interval the Council decided on a general increase in the wages of textile workers to correspond with changes in the measurement of the work. Accordingly a proclamation in 1636 ordered an advance of twopence in the shilling to be paid to spinners and " all labourers and other artificers employed about the trade of clothing and yarn-making ". Within a year, significantly enough, the proclamation was repealed [2]. None the less the Government continued to insist that the workers should receive ' competent wages ' for their work [3].

*Wage regulation during the Interregnum.* During the Interregnum the Statute of Apprentices remained in force as is shown by several assessments [4]. The Civil War, among its other economic effects, caused a rise in prices which necessitated an advance in wages. The Derbyshire scales in 1648 show a general increase of about 50 per cent. over those issued in 1634 [5] ; and the justices of Essex (1651) expressly alluded to " the prices at this time of all kind of victuals and apparel, both linen and woollen, and all other necessary charges wherewith artificers, labourers and servants have been more grievously charged with than in times past " [6]. The intention of the Long Parliament to carry on the traditions of the absolute monarchy was announced in an important resolution of the House of Commons in 1649, enjoining " the lord mayor (for the time being) of the city of London, and all justices of peace within

---

[1] *State Papers Domestic*, 1629–1631, p. 20.
[2] Rymer, *Foedera*, xix. 730 *seq.* ; xx. 41, 94.
[3] Instructions to the Commission of Enquiry into the woollen industry : *State Papers Domestic*, 1638–1639, p. 23.
[4] 1647 (West Riding of Yorkshire) : *The Economic Journal*, xxiv. 221. 1648 (Nottinghamshire) : *Journal of George Fox* (ed. 1852), i. 65-66. 1648 (Derbyshire) : Cox, *Three Centuries of Derbyshire Annals*, ii. 240. 1651 (Essex) : *The Particular Rates of Wages* (British Museum : 816 m. 15. 44).
1654 (Devonshire) : Hamilton, *Quarter Sessions from Queen Elizabeth to Queen Anne*, 163.
1655 (Wiltshire) : *Hist. MSS. Comm. Various*, i. 169 ; *Records of the County of Wiltshire* (ed. Cunnington), 290.
1655 (London) : *The English Historical Review*, xv. 455.
1658 (North Riding of Yorkshire) : *Quarter Sessions Records* (The North Riding Record Society), vi. 3.
For other assessments : *infra*, Appendix, p. 516, No. 3. There is a reference to offences against the Statute in 1655 in *Hertford County Records*, i. 112.
[5] *Victoria County History, Derbyshire*, ii. 183.
[6] *The Particular Rates of Wages* (British Museum : 816 m. 15. 44).

the said city and liberties thereof . . . forthwith to put in execution the several Statutes of 5 Eliz. cap. 4 and 1 Jacobi cap. 6, made and enacted for the rating and settling of the wages of the several artificers within the limits aforesaid, for their better relief and subsistence in these dear times. . . . And that care be taken annually to do the same, if need require, according to the tenor of the said laws. And all justices of peace in the several counties of this commonwealth and dominion of Wales are, in like manner, required to do the same " [1]. In other, and more personal, ways pressure was being put on the magistrates to adjust the rates of wages to the new conditions, as a vivid passage in George Fox's *Journal* serves to illustrate : " At a certain time (1648) when I was at Mansfield, there was a sitting of the justices about hiring of servants ; and it was upon me from the Lord to go and speak to the justices that they should not oppress the servants in their wages. So I walked towards the inn where they sat ; but finding a company of fiddlers there I did not go in, but thought to come in the morning when I might have a more serious opportunity to discourse with them, not thinking that a seasonable time. But when I came again in the morning they were gone, and I was struck even blind that I could not see. I inquired of the innkeeper where the justices were to sit that day; and he told me, at a town eight miles off. My sight began to come to me again ; and I went and ran thitherward as fast as I could. When I was come to the house where they were and many servants with them, I exhorted the justices not to oppress the servants in their wages, but to do that which was right and just to them ; and I exhorted the servants to do their duties, and serve honestly, etc. They all received my exhortation kindly ; for I was moved of the Lord therein " [2].

The reign of Charles II. has been regarded [3] as ' the posterior limit, for England generally ', of the practice of wage regulation, but there is evidence to show that the system was widespread after the Restoration. Assessments

*Under Charles II.*

---

[1] *House of Commons Journals*, vi. 180.
[2] *Journal of George Fox* (ed. 1852), i. 65-66.
[3] Cunningham, *The Growth of English Industry and Commerce* (ed. 1907), ii. 44.

have been preserved for Essex (1661), Worcestershire (1663), Northamptonshire (1667), Middlesex (166–), the West Riding (1672), Hertfordshire (1678), Lincolnshire (1680), Suffolk (1682), Warwickshire (1684), Somersetshire (1685), Wiltshire (1685), Buckinghamshire (1687), etc.[1] The survival of wage assessments is purely a matter of accident : others will doubtless come to light : and in any case it must not be inferred that the system was not put in execution in any county unrepresented in the list of known assessments [1a]. That the public faith in the system had not lapsed is shown by the presentment made by the grand jury of Worcestershire in 1661 : " We desire that servants' wages may be rated according to the Statute, for we find the unreasonableness of servants' wages a great grievance, so that the servants are grown so proud and idle that the master cannot be known from the servant, except it be because the servant wears better clothes than his master "[2]. Allusions to wage regulation occur in post-Restoration writings, but they are indecisive. Petty in one place observed that " it is unjust to let any starve when we think it just to limit the wages of the poor, so as they can lay up nothing against the time of their impotency and want of work ". This suggests that the Statute was in force, yet elsewhere he remarked : " Now the price of labour must be certain, as we see it made by the Statutes

[1] 1661 (Essex) : Eden, *The State of the Poor* (1797), iii. p. cii.
1663 (Worcestershire) : *Hist. MSS. Comm. Various*, i. 323.
1667 (Northamptonshire): *The Economic History Review*, vol. i. No. 1, 133.
166– (Middlesex) : Cunningham, *The Growth of English Industry and Commerce* (ed. 1912), iii. 887.
1672 (West Riding of Yorkshire) : Heaton, *The Yorkshire Woollen and Worsted Industries*, 313.
1678 (Hertfordshire) : *Hertford County Records*, i. 292.
1680 (Lincolnshire) : *Victoria County History, Lincolnshire*, ii. 336.
1682 (Suffolk) : Eden, *The State of the Poor* (1797), iii. p. ciii.
1684 (Warwickshire) : Rogers, *A History of Agriculture and Prices*, vi. 699.
1685 (Somersetshire) : *Hist. MSS. Comm.* vii. 698.
1685 (Wiltshire) : *ibid. Various*, i. 174-175 ; *Records of the County of Wiltshire* (ed. Cunnington), 294.
1687 (Buckinghamshire) : *Victoria County History, Buckinghamshire*, ii. 70.
For other assessments : *infra*, Appendix, p. 516, No. 4. There are references to assessments in the North Riding in 1680, 1681, 1691, and 1692 : *Quarter Sessions Records* (The North Riding Record Society), vii. 34, 45, 50, 128, etc.  [1a] See *infra*, Appendix, p. 518, No. 1.
[2] *Hist. MSS. Comm. Various*, i. 322. In 1674 the enforcement of the Statute was recommended : *State Papers Domestic*, 1673–1675, p. 495. See *infra*, Appendix, p. 518, No. 2.

which limit the day wages of several workmen, the non-observance of which laws, and the not adapting them to the change of times, is by the way very dangerous and confusive to all endeavours of bettering the trade of the nation " [1]. Roger North, again, implies that the system was not obsolete but ineffective [2]; and this is probably a correct view of the situation. It is at least certain that the official scales lagged behind the wages actually paid, and that the economic rates normally exceeded the legal rates, though at all periods of wage regulation the disparity existed [3].

The eighteenth century is represented by a number of assessments [4], but there appears little doubt that the system was not in general operation. As will be seen [5], it died out in the woollen industry both in the West of England, where capitalism was most deeply entrenched, and in the West Riding of Yorkshire ; and special legislation was needed to establish it in the tailoring industry in 1721 and in the silk industry in 1773 [6]. The judges in their legal decisions were seeking to limit the scope of the Statute of Apprentices to workers in agriculture, and ignoring subsequent enactments by which it was expressly applied to industry [7]. In 1704 they pronounced that " the Statute extends only to servants in husbandry, not to gentlemen's servants, nor to

*In the eighteenth century.*

---

[1] Petty, *Economic Writings*, i. 20, 52.
[2] *Infra*, p. 275.           [3] *Infra*, p. 275.
[4] 1703–1708 (West Riding of Yorkshire) : Rogers, *A History of Agriculture and Prices*, vii. part ii. 610–614.
  1710 (Warwickshire) : *Victoria County History, Warwickshire*, ii. 180.
  1713 (Devonshire) : Hamilton, *Quarter Sessions from Queen Elizabeth to Queen Anne*, 273.
  1722 (West Riding of Yorkshire) : Rogers, *op. cit.* vii. part ii. 614.
  1724 (Kent) : *The English Historical Review*, xliii. 405.
  1724 (Nottinghamshire) : *Victoria County History, Nottinghamshire*, ii. 295 ; *Nottinghamshire County Records* (ed. Copnall), 65.
  1725 (Lancashire) : *Annals of Agriculture*, xxv. 305.
  1728 (Gloucestershire) : *infra*, p. 266.
  1732 (Kent) : Rogers, *op. cit.* vii. part ii. 623.
  1732 (Gloucestershire) : *ibid.* 623.
  1732 (Shropshire) : *The Economic Journal*, iv. 516.
  1750 (Westmorland) : *Hist. MSS. Comm. Le Fleming*, 357.
  1754 (Lincolnshire) : *Victoria County History, Lincolnshire*, ii. 346.
  1756 (Gloucestershire) : *infra*, p. 269.
  1765 (Warwickshire) : *Victoria County History, Warwickshire*, ii. 181.
  1765 (Buckinghamshire) : *ibid. Buckinghamshire*, ii. 84.
For other assessments : *infra*, Appendix, p. 518, No. 3.
[5] *Infra*, p. 266, note 1.           [6] *Infra*, pp. 270, 405–406.
[7] *Supra*, p. 254 ; *infra*, pp. 281, 519 (No. 1).

journeymen with their masters " [1]. The decay of the system
as a normal function of the economic organism may be inferred
from the recommendation, made in 1724 by a parliamentary
committee, that " some more effectual method be provided
for obliging the justices of the peace to assess the wages of
servants and labourers mentioned in the Statute of the Fifth
of Queen Elizabeth ; and also for the better preventing of
any agreement, promise, gift or payment of wages contrary
to such assessment " [2] ; as well as from the categorical
statement (1751) of Fielding, who was a London magistrate,
that the law had " grown into utter neglect and disuse " [3].
Yet the wording of an Act passed in 1747 suggests that the
Statute of Apprentices was not considered obsolete, for it
provides that all disputes over wages should be heard by the
justices of the peace, " although no rate or assessment of
wages has been made that year by the justices " [4]. The
authority to fix wages remained vested in the justices, and
appeal could be made to them by masters or men [5]. On the
whole, the situation is no doubt accurately represented in a
remark made by a writer in 1787 : " In some places, as I
am informed, [the Statute of Apprentices] now is carried into
execution, but . . . has been in others totally neglected " [6].

*Movement towards laissez faire.*    The history of wage regulation, more especially in industry, affords clear indications that the fall of the abso-
lute monarchy was the turning-point in the evolution of
capitalism. The Early Tudors had sought to set limits to
the growth of industrial capitalism [7] ; and their immediate
successors, while abandoning the attempt to check the de-

---

[1] *The English Reports*, xci. 384 (3 Anne).

[2] *House of Commons Journals*, xx. 257.

[3] Fielding, *An Enquiry into the Causes of the late Increase of Robbers*
(2nd ed. 1751), 85.

[4] *Statutes at Large*, vi. 353.

[5] Thus in 1705 the Newcastle Hostmen, owing to the ' excessive wages '
demanded by ship-carpenters, resolved to ' move ' the justices of the
peace ' for redress herein ' : *Newcastle Hostmen*, 167-168. For appeals of
the men, see *infra*, p. 266. For appeals of the masters, see *infra*, Appendix,
p. 519, No. 2.

[6] Kirby, *A Letter to a Member of Parliament* (1787), 6. The Statute was
described as ' a sleeping law ' and ' very long disused ' in *Annals of Agriculture*, xiii. 243, note (1790) ; xxiv. 561 (1795).

[7] *Supra*, vol. i. 317-318, 479-480, 505-507.

velopment of a capitalist class, endeavoured to regulate its activities. After the Revolution of 1688, however, capitalism was allowed a freer hand in industry. The control of the State over economic life did not relax, but it was manifested in a different direction. The energies of Parliament were absorbed in the effort to provide those conditions which seemed necessary to maintain the stability and prosperity of the staple industries ; to secure for them ample supplies of raw material and the undisputed possession of markets at home and abroad ; in short, to control the commercial basis of industry. It was less concerned to regulate the conditions of labour and to promote in an active manner the social welfare of the working classes. This had been in a peculiar degree the province of the Privy Council, which in Tudor and Stuart days repeatedly intervened on behalf of oppressed artisans ; but after the Great Rebellion the authority of the Council was fatally impaired. The effect was felt as early as 1665, when attention was drawn to the " great negligence and remissness in too many justices of the peace in the exercise of the trust committed to them " [1]. Once the Council ceased to exercise its former control, the economic system of which it had been the pivot began to disintegrate. The industrial legislation of the sixteenth century was allowed to fall into disuse, and the spasmodic efforts to revive it only threw into sharper relief the contrast between the old order and the new. The Revolution completed the process of disintegration, and Parliament came directly under the influence of a capitalist regime which now demanded its liberation from the shackles of State control. Under the influence of changed political conditions the State moved steadily in the direction of *laissez faire*, and the capitalist classes did not hesitate to challenge its right to dictate to them the terms on which they should employ their labour. The whole industrial outlook of the eighteenth century was permeated by a growing economic individualism which resisted, or ignored, occasional attempts to fetter the unrestricted freedom of action which it henceforth claimed. And the success of Adam Smith's *Wealth of Nations* was largely due to the fact that he gave

[1] *Hist. MSS. Comm. Rye,* 465.

articulate expression to ideas, towards which the leaders of industry had long been feeling their way.

*Changed attitude of the State.* Two examples of wage regulation after the Revolution will illustrate the new attitude of the State towards industrial problems. In 1728, when the system had passed out of living memory in the textile industry of the West Country [1], the justices of Gloucestershire revived it at the quarter sessions and fixed the wages of weavers. Their assessment was ignored by the clothiers, who no longer feared as in earlier times a summons before the Privy Council, and formed a union to resist the authority of the magistrates [2]. Nearly thirty years later in 1756, a landmark in economic history, the whole question of State regulation of wages was re-opened, and the case was fought out between the advocates and opponents of legal minimum rates. The starting-point of the controversy was an application made to Parliament on behalf of the weavers of Gloucestershire, in which it was complained that their employers paid them truck wages [3]. A committee of the House of Commons, after hearing the evidence of the weavers, reported favourably on the petition, and Parliament proceeded to pass an Act against the payment of wages in kind. The weavers in their evidence had seized the occasion to voice the complaint that the clothiers had neglected to obey the order issued by the justices of Gloucestershire in 1728 ; and Parliament thought to strengthen the hands of the justices, whose authority had been thus defied, by re-enacting for the woollen industry the assessment clauses of the Elizabethan Statute [4]. The clothiers, who had been taken by surprise, fought strenuously against the Act. They drew up a document which their workmen were asked to sign, in which the latter acknowledged themselves well satisfied with their wages, and agreed to remain at work upon the terms at

---

[1] A clothier at Stroudwater informed a parliamentary committee in 1757 that he " never heard of any rate for wages being made by the justices of the peace before " 1728 : *House of Commons Journals*, xxvii. 730. In the West Riding the textile clauses were omitted from 1672 onwards : Heaton, *The Yorkshire Woollen and Worsted Industries*, 313-315. Cf. also Tawney, " The Assessment of Wages in England by the Justices of the Peace" in *Vierteljahrsschrift für Sozial- und Wirtschaftsgeschichte*, xi. 332, 555.

[2] *House of Commons Journals*, xxvii. 503, 730.

[3] *Ibid.* 468.                   [4] *Statutes at Large*, vii. 118.

which they were then employed [1]. Shortly afterwards the justices held their quarter sessions, and both sides presented petitions to the court. The weavers complained that the clothiers had ignored the rates fixed by the justices at the beginning of the reign (1728), " well-knowing that . . . the weavers could not bear the expense of applying to this court on every breach thereof". Their sufferings had since increased owing to the great reduction in their wages, "insomuch that the weavers cannot get above fourpence for sixteen hours' labour upon many sorts of work " [2]. The clothiers responded with a counter-petition in which they protested against the compulsory assessment of wages ; and the grounds, on which their opposition was based, throw light on the practical difficulties of wage control. Their argument was partly technical, partly economic, partly political.

The technical objection raised by the clothiers was that the system of compulsory assessment was not workable, because it was impossible to settle beforehand equitable rates [3]. The piece-lists drawn up by authority fixed the price of weaving according to the number of threads contained in the warp or chain [4] ; but the true value of weaving could not be ascertained on the basis of the number of threads alone. Many factors needed to be considered : the number and size of the threads, the weight of the chain, the fineness of the weft, the breadth of the cloth, and the mode of manufacture —the qualities and kinds of cloth being " too various to be reduced to any regular or fixed standard " [5]. The legal rates also made no allowance for degrees of technical skill : the indifferent weaver was remunerated at the same rate as the superior weaver, although the value of cloth depended largely upon the standard of workmanship [6]. Some of the technical

*Arguments against wage control :*
*(i.) technical objections.*

---

[1] *A State of the Case . . . relating to the . . . Rising of the Weavers in the County of Gloucester* (1757), 6-7.

[2] *Ibid.* 8-10.

[3] *House of Commons Journals*, xxvii. 683.

[4] An example will be found in *Hist. MSS. Comm. Various*, i. 162.

[5] *House of Commons Journals*, xxvii. 730 ; *A State of the Case . . . relating to the . . . Rising of the Weavers in the County of Gloucester* (1757), 14, 21-23.

[6] *House of Commons Journals*, xxvii. 731.

points raised by the clothiers were perhaps valid, but others were not. The justices doubtless lacked the technical qualifications for drafting elaborate and complicated piece-lists, and the principles upon which they proceeded, however suited to the circumstances of more primitive epochs, erred on the side of exaggerated simplicity ; but the combined wisdom of clothiers and weavers ought not to have been unequal to the task of framing fair and equitable rates [1].

(ii.) *Economic objections.*    In their economic plea for Freedom of Contract the clothiers seem to have caught the spirit, as they certainly anticipate the language, of a later age. " We think it . . . repugnant ", they declared, " to the liberties of a free people and the interest of trade that any law should supersede a private contract honourably made between a master and his workman " [2]. They postulated the doctrine of Industrial Freedom : " Trade is a tender plant that can only be nursed up by liberty ". " Why must the first manufacture in the kingdom, for such the woollen is justly esteemed, be put under unnecessary restrictions ? " [3] The system of assessment was condemned as both superfluous and pernicious. It was superfluous because labour was sufficiently protected by the law of competition—" when trade is in a flourishing state, labour will always find its value ". It was pernicious because " every law which tends towards raising the price of labour, as it must in the end necessarily advance our manufactures, will be greatly prejudicial to the trade of this nation " [4]. The weavers were told that their demand for higher wages would recoil upon their heads, since it would drive the manufacturers to raise the prices of their commodities, which " have not for some time past, nor can now be, sold abroad

---

[1] Cf. the Wiltshire committee : *supra*, p. 255.

[2] *A State of the Case . . . relating to the . . . Rising of the Weavers in the County of Gloucester* (1757), 16. A weaver told the committee of 1757 that " if it was left open for clothiers and weavers to make their own bargains, it would be more advantageous for the trade in general " : *House of Commons Journals*, xxvii. 731. But another in 1803 said : " Our necessity was our masters' opportunity, so that they reduced the price when we could not tell which way to shift elsewhere " : *Parliamentary Papers* (1802–3), vii. 62, 68.

[3] *A State of the Case . . . relating to the . . . Rising of the Weavers in the County of Gloucester* (1757), 15.

[4] *Ibid.* 13, 33.

at such low prices as those of other countries " [1]. The argument, that our foreign markets could only be maintained by cheap labour, passed for current coin during the ' Industrial Revolution ', when it was insufficiently recognized that the prosperity of industry depends, not upon very low wages nor long hours, but upon productive efficiency.

The third, an anti-democratic, line of argument adopted by the clothiers was calculated to make its appeal in the quarters to which it was addressed. The Act was declared subversive of authority. " The weavers by this Act will be rendered more our masters than we are now theirs. A levelling and turbulent spirit . . . ought never to be countenanced amongst the common people " [2]. The short space of time, which had elapsed since the Act was placed on the statute-book, had been long enough to show that these fears were not ill-founded. " Instead of preventing unlawful combinations it has encouraged caballing, fomented discontent, and produced confusion and riot " [3]. *(iii.) Political objections.*

The clothiers seem to have marshalled their case so effectively that the justices were won over to their standpoint and refused to issue any order. Their decision greatly disappointed the weavers, who having secured an Act of Parliament in their favour had confidently expected the magistrates to put it in execution. A strike ensued which lasted six weeks, and the whole county was in a state of uproar [4]. In order to pacify the strikers, the justices sanctioned a scale of wages [5], and the men returned to work. The triumph of the weavers was short-lived, for few employers observed the assessment but continued to pay their men upon the old footing [6]. The clothiers of Gloucestershire soon began to agitate for a repeal of the Act. Supported by the clothiers of Somersetshire and Wiltshire, they carried their case to Parliament (1757) where they represented the *Significance of the repeal of the Act of 1756.*

---

[1] *House of Commons Journals*, xxvii. 683.

[2] *A State of the Case . . . relating to the . . . Rising of the Weavers in the County of Gloucester* (1757), 14.

[3] *Ibid.* 34.

[4] *Ibid.* 24 ; *House of Commons Journals*, xxvii. 730.

[5] The rates are given in *House of Commons Journals*, xxvii. 732.

[6] *A State of the Case . . . relating to the . . . Rising of the Weavers in the County of Gloucester* (1757), 30.

"ill consequences which have arisen" from the Act, "by virtue whereof the justices of the peace . . . have power to make rates for the payment of wages "[1]. They repeated the arguments which had served them so effectively in their legal duel with the weavers, and their solicitations prevailed. Parliament, turning a deaf ear to the prayer of the weavers not to subject them ' to the arbitrary will and power of the clothiers '[2], annulled the measure which it had passed in the previous year[3]. Its action was almost in the nature of an economic revolution. For nearly two centuries[4] the right of the State to fix wages had been recognized as a cardinal principle of industrial regulation ; and though in practice the right had fallen into disuse, its survival on the statute-book had vested in the authorities a reserve of power, to which they could always turn in the last resort for the protection of the working classes. The repeal of the Act of 1756 signified that the system of wage assessment was now definitely discarded in the premier industry of the country. The principles of *laissez-faire* received legislative sanction in the woollen manufacture half a century before they were adopted as the authoritative basis of State action. Nevertheless, Parliament was not guided by any conscious theory of non-intervention in industrial matters. Sixteen years later (1773) it passed, on behalf of the journeymen silk weavers of London and Middlesex, an Act which embodied the very principle of State control of wages now abandoned in the case of the woollen industry[5]. It also established (1770) ' one fixed and settled price ' for the hire of ' coal-heavers ' employed in unloading ships laden with coal, and empowered the authorities of London to alter the rates[6]. Its policy was thus largely

[1] *House of Commons Journals*, xxvii. 683, 703.
[2] *Ibid.* 741, 753.
[3] *Statutes at Large*, vii. 143 (1757).          [4] See *supra*, p. 253.
[5] *Statutes at Large*, viii. 259. In London they were to be fixed by the lord mayor, recorder and aldermen ; and in Middlesex by the justices of the peace. Master weavers were forbidden to give ' more or less ' wages. The Spitalfields Act was not repealed until 1824 : *Statutes of the United Kingdom*, ix. 742. The effect of the Act was to stimulate the migration of the industry to other parts : *Annals of Agriculture*, ii. 106 ; x. 453. On the Spitalfields silk industry, see George, *London Life in the Eighteenth Century*, 176 *seq.* ; Clapham, " The Spitalfields Acts " in *The Economic Journal*, xxvi. 459 *seq.*
[6] *Statutes at Large*, viii. 135-136. For the Act of 1768 fixing tailors' wages : *infra*, p. 406.

opportunist but the trend of its thought is unmistakable ; for good or evil it was moving steadily in the direction of Freedom of Contract.

The Statute of Apprentices has been criticized on various grounds. The historian of English labour saw in it " the most powerful instrument ever devised for degrading and impoverishing the English labourer ", in " allowing those who are interested in keeping him poor to fix the wages on which he shall subsist " [1]. Eighteenth-century economists based their condemnation on the principles of *laissez-faire*. " The Statutes for regulating wages and the price of labour ", wrote Dean Tucker in the middle of the century, " are another absurdity and a very great hurt to trade. Absurd and preposterous it must surely appear for a third person to attempt to fix the price between buyer and seller without their own consents. For if either the journeyman will not sell his labour at the fixed or statutable price or the master will not give it, of what use are a thousand regulating laws ? Nay, how indeed can any stated regulations be so contrived as to make due and reasonable allowance for plenty or scarcity of work, cheapness or dearness of provisions, difference of living in town or country, firing, house-rent, etc. ; also for the goodness or badness of the workmanship, the different degrees of skill or despatch of the workman, the unequal goodness of materials to work upon, state of the manufacture, and the demand or stagnation at home or abroad ? . . . And yet, were even this possible, a great difficulty still recurs, viz. who shall, or how can you, force the journeyman to work or the master to give him work, unless they themselves shall mutually agree about it ?—And if they agree, why should you, or I, or anyone else interfere ? " [2] Employers, as we have already noticed [3], stressed the technical difficulties of assessment. The workers, when they thought themselves strong enough to regulate their own wages by combined action, claimed that " the true value of every man's work and labour must be proportioned to his capacity and

*Criticisms of the Statute of Apprentices.*

---

[1] Rogers, *A History of Agriculture and Prices*, v. 628 ; Rogers, *Six Centuries of Work and Wages* (ed. 1912), 398-399. See *infra*, Appendix, p. 520, No. 1.

[2] Tucker, *Instructions* (ed. 1757), 34-35.  [3] *Supra*, p. 267.

industry, which makes it impracticable, or at least very inequitable, by any positive law to put an equal value on every man's labour ". " If the justices shall settle the men's wages, how is it possible that each man shall be rewarded according to his merit ? . . . Every man will be paid alike and there will be no encouragement for merit." They also expressed the fear that " indifferent workmen will never be employed by reason that the masters are obliged to give them certain wages, which may possibly be more than such a man can deserve "[1].

*Theories of wages.* Discussion of the authoritarian regulation of wages turned mainly on two questions. The first concerned the principle by which the assessment of wages should be governed. The Statute of Apprentices was based on the understanding that ' in the time of scarcity and in the time of plenty ' the labourer's standard of life should remain uniform. To the end of the seventeenth century the theory was generally maintained that the cost of living should determine the remuneration of labour [1a]. One writer asserted that " where the one riseth, the other doth so likewise ; as at London and in other places, where provisions are dearest, labour is dearest"[2]. Another asked : " If the manufacturer buys his victuals at excessive rates, at what rates must he sell his manufacture or how shall he live ? "[3]. A later generation flung scorn upon the orthodox theory of wages. " The squires of Norfolk ", said Burke, " had dined when they gave it as their opinion that [wages] might or ought to rise and fall with the market of provisions "[4]. The theory was now held that wages depended upon supply and demand. We find, as early as 1738, an expression of the view that " the price of labour, like other commodities, must always depend upon the proportion there is between the quantity ready to be sold and the quantity ready to be purchased "[5].

[1] Galton, *Select Documents : The Tailoring Trade*, 9-10 (1721), 30 (1745). This view was shared by some employers : *ibid.* 75-77.
[1a] For the adoption of a sliding scale, see *infra*, Appendix, p. 520, No. 2.
[2] Collins, *A Plea for the bringing in of Irish Cattle* (1680), 10. Similarly : Puckle, *England's Path to Wealth and Honour* (1700), 26 ; Cary, *An Essay towards Regulating the Trade* (ed. 1719), 96.
[3] *Britannia Languens* (1680), 156 (in sect. vii.).
[4] 1795 : Burke, *Thoughts and Details on Scarcity* (ed. 1800), 5-6, 13.
[5] *A Letter from a Merchant. . . . The Case of the British and Irish Manufacture of Linen* (1738), 20.

The second question prominent in the discussion of wages *Doctrine* was whether the national interest was best served by a low *of the economy* or a high price of labour. One section of opinion affirmed *of high wages.* that " 'tis a certain maxim that cheapness of labour [1a], and consequently the cheapness of goods, is the only means to increase their consumption either at home or abroad ", and so enlarge the demand for labour [1]. Another section anticipated the modern doctrine of the economy of high wages. " If you would reduce the price of our manufacture ", wrote Defoe, " by reducing the wages of the poor, who are the workers or manufacturers, it is not possible but that you will reduce the value and goodness of the manufacture. If you expect the poor should work cheaper and not perform their work slighter and more overly, as we call it, and superficially, you expect what is not in the nature of the thing. . . . This, therefore, is beginning at the wrong end of trade ; but the true way is keep up the goodness of your manufacture so as to make it excel in quality, and its exceeding in price will be no deficiency in trade. Things are not dear or cheap according as they sell for more or less, but according as the price they sell for bears a proportion to the goodness or meanness of the goods sold " [2]. Child's point of view was similar. He characterized a proposal to ' retrench the hire ' of labour, which was based on the plea that " dearness of wages spoils the English trade ", as " an honest, charitable project and well-becoming a usurer ". He considered high wages " an infallible evidence of the riches of that country ", and remarked that the Dutch " give generally more wages to all their manufacturers by at least twopence in the shilling than the English ". Low wages drove people abroad : " and so the Dutch have drained us of our seamen and woollen manufacturers, and we the French of their artificers and silk manufacturers " [3]. The sentiments voiced by Child and

[1a] But not necessarily a low standard of living : see *infra*, Appendix, p. 520, No. 3.

[1] *The British Merchant*, No. 5 (1719). Similarly : Fielding, *An Enquiry into the Causes of the late Increase of Robbers* (2nd ed. 1751), 88, 93. See also *supra*, vol. ii. 55.

[2] Defoe, *A Plan of the English Commerce* (ed. 1728), 60. See also Cary, *An Essay towards Regulating the Trade* (ed. 1719), 97-99.

[3] Child, *A New Discourse of Trade* (4th ed.), pp. x-xi. Similarly : Collins, *A Plea for the bringing in of Irish Cattle* (1680), 10-11. Fielding
[*contd.*]

Defoe were hardly typical of their age, but the prosperity of
those parts of England where wages were highest afforded
convincing testimony of their soundness.  It was, for example, the high rates paid at Birmingham which led Arthur
Young to discover that the cost of labour is not to be
measured ' by the pay *per diem* ', and to draw the inference
that though the master " must be a great friend to low wages
in theory, he will not be so in practice, for such lowness is
merely nominal ; it is the cheapness of barbarity, backward-
ness and ignorance ; it is a cheapness that keeps the men
poor and wretched, without making the masters rich " [1].
And Burke concluded that " the price of labour rises with
the growth of manufacture, and is highest when the manufacture is best " [2].

*State con-
trol of
wages a
safeguard
against op-
pression.*
Although contemporary opinion was sharply divided on
the subject of wages, some general conclusions may be
suggested.  Firstly : in practice the tendency of State control
of wages was to protect ' the humble and truly laborious '
from undue oppression [3].  The best proof that the laws relating to wages were not regarded by the workers in a hostile
light is the fact that they themselves pressed on several
occasions for their enforcement [4].  When the ' Industrial
Revolution ' menaced the handicraftsmen with a rapid deterioration in their standard of life, their first instinct was to
turn to the traditional machinery by which that standard,
as they believed, had been safeguarded in the past.  We may
reasonably infer that the system of wage regulation was not
associated in the minds of the working classes with any bitter
memories or inherited aversion.

Secondly : the Statute of Apprentices did not prevent a
rise in wages.  The schedules of wages issued by the justices
may have had the temporary effect of depressing the earnings
of the better-paid workmen to the general level, since the

criticized Child in *An Enquiry into the Causes of the late Increase of Robbers,*
(2nd ed. 1751), 85 *seq.*  See also *supra*, pp. 7, 204 (note 3).
[1] *Annals of Agriculture*, iii. 268-269 ; xvi. 534-535.
[2] *Ibid.* iii. 268, note.
[3] Fielding, *op. cit.* 90.
[4] *Supra*, pp. 258, 266.  The opposition of the journeymen tailors
appears exceptional : *supra*, pp. 271-272.

schedules did not distinguish between different grades of *Rise in wages not prevented.* merit : but the effect could only have been temporary. Employers speedily found that it was necessary to exceed the statutory level in order to attract the more competent workmen. Thus in Buckinghamshire the wages paid to artisans in the latter part of the sixteenth century were sometimes double the amount specified in the assessment [1]. We must therefore avoid the assumption that the legal rates, authorized by quarter sessions, were identical with the economic rates which actually prevailed [1a]. There is, indeed, evidence that the justices of the peace sometimes ignored their own assessments. In one case, which subsequently came before the judges, an employer was ordered by the magistrates to pay the wages due to a servant ' for work and labour in husbandry ', although " it does not appear to be Statute wages, and such only are within their jurisdiction " [2]. On another occasion the justices required a master to pay his servant the wages owing to her, which exceeded the maximum they had themselves prescribed [3]. Nor, again, must the distinction be pressed between the Act of 1563 which embodied the principle of a maximum wage, and the Act of 1604 which instituted a minimum wage for the textile industries : in practice the authorities do not seem to have distinguished closely between them [4]. Where the justices sanctioned scales which ran counter to the popular sentiment, they remained inoperative. " The poor ", said Roger North towards the end of the seventeenth century, " laugh at them and cry : ' Statute work against Statute wages '. For laws will not make nor influence prices in open market ". The justices, he added, had tried to enforce their assessments, " but in vain, as all know by experience " [5]. This expression of opinion from a singularly competent observer is valuable

[1] *Victoria County History, Buckinghamshire*, ii. 68. For other examples of the disparity between ' Statute ' and economic wages, see *supra*, vol. ii. 388 ; Rogers, *A History of Agriculture and Prices*, v. 827-8 ; *infra*, pp. 407 (note 1), 521 (No. 1).

[1a] See *infra*, p. 521 (No. 2).

[2] *The English Reports*, xci. 383 (1 Anne).

[3] *Victoria County History, Buckinghamshire*, ii. 71.

[4] Cf. the wording of the Wiltshire assessment of 1655 in *Hist. MSS. Comm. Various*, i. 173. And for Yorkshire, see Heaton, *The Yorkshire Woollen and Worsted Industries*, 110-112.

[5] North, *A Discourse of the Poor* (ed. 1753), 64. See *infra*, p. 521 (No. 3).

testimony that the Act did not keep down the wages of English labour.  Child, also, observed that our ancestors " did exercise such policy of endeavouring to retrench the price of labour by a law, although they could never effect it " [1].

*Wages not dependent upon prices.*    Thirdly : the effort to establish a relation between the price of provisions and the price of labour, so that wages should vary according to the state of the harvest, rising in time of scarcity and falling in time of plenty, proved unsuccessful.  The justices, in fact, did not attempt the task, and as a rule contented themselves with the annual reissue of the old scales mostly without alteration in spite of variations in prices.  Thus in Wiltshire the rates appear to have remained unchanged from the accession of James I. to the Commonwealth, except that in 1635 changes were made in the wages of agricultural labourers ; in 1655 a new schedule was framed ; and in 1685 agricultural rates were revised [2]. Roger Coke remarked (1671) that when provisions were cheap, labourers refused to work for less wages than when they were dear [3] ; and one of the objects of combinations in the eighteenth century was ' to support the old price ', that is, resist any attempt to reduce the price of labour whatever the price of provisions [4].  Petty declared that, so far from wages falling when food was plentiful, the reverse was true. " It is observed by clothiers and others who employ great numbers of poor people, that when corn is extremely plentiful, that the labour of the poor is proportionably dear.  And scarce to be had at all, so licentious are they who labour only to eat or rather to drink " [5].  The view was therefore

[1] Child, *A New Discourse of Trade* (4th ed.), p. xii.

[2] *Hist. MSS. Comm. Various*, i. 161.  The editor of the Calendar (*ibid.* 67) infers that there was " little change in the social condition of the people and in prices during that period ", but the legal rates were not necessarily identical with the economic rates.

Other examples of the reissue of assessments without change are Kent (*The English Historical Review*, xli. 273), Middlesex (*ibid.* xliii. 402) ; West Riding of Yorkshire (*The Economic Journal*, xxiv. 232), St. Albans (Gibbs, *The Corporation Records of St. Albans*, 17, 25), Exeter (*Hist. MSS. Comm. Exeter*, 50).  And for further examples, see *infra*, Appendix, p. 521, No. 4.

[3] Coke, *Treatise* (1671), i. 75.

[4] *Considerations on Taxes as they are supposed to affect the Price of Labour* (1765), 67.        [5] Petty, *Economic Writings*, i. 274.

common from the time of the Restoration that an abundant
harvest was the cause of poverty in a nation [1]—a paradox
of which the explanation was that, since " the nominal price
of a day's labour in money hardly ever varies with the price
of provisions ", the low cost of provisions resulted in " labouring less and not cheaper ". " The poor ", it was asserted,
" do not labour upon an average above four days in a week
unless provisions happen to be very dear " [2]. The argument
assumed that the poor worked only to satisfy the bare
necessaries of life ; and it implied a static condition of society
in which the masses had not yet acquired a taste for luxuries,
and therefore lacked the stimulus to exert themselves for the
satisfaction of new wants. The important conclusion follows
that it would be erroneous to apply to eighteenth-century
England the theory of the ' Iron Law ' of wages, which was
based on the widely different conditions supposed to exist in
eighteenth-century France. In this country wages were not
ground down to a minimum level of subsistence, but the
working classes laboured only sufficiently to maintain a
traditional standard of life [2a].

Connected with low wages was another evil which per- *Truck*
sisted for many centuries, namely, the payment of truck *wages.*
wages. Artisans were often obliged by their employers to
take part of their wages in provisions or goods rated at extravagant prices [3], sometimes greatly in excess of their real
worth [4]. Some clothiers forced their weavers to become their
tenants and pay rents for their houses, whether they occupied
them or not : others made them buy their bread and other

---

[1] *State Papers Domestic*, 1663–1664, p. 412 ; 1666–1667, p. 105 (" Want
promotes trade more than plenty, as it forces to labour "). Similarly :
Houghton, *Husbandry and Trade Improv'd* (ed. 1728), iv. 382 *seq.* ; Gee,
*The Trade and Navigation of Great Britain* (ed. 1730), 38. For a different
view : Collins, *A Plea for the bringing in of Irish Cattle* (1680), 10-11.

[2] *Considerations on Taxes as they are supposed to affect the Price of Labour*
(1765), 6-15. Young strongly held this view : *The Farmer's Letters* (ed.
1768), 36-37 ; *Tour through the North* (ed. 1771), iii. 193 ; iv. 311. See
also *Annals of Agriculture*, iii. 419 ; xiii. 366 ; xv. 236. But contrast
*infra*, p. 522 (No. 1).          [2a] See *infra*, p. 522 (No. 2).

[3] *House of Commons Journals*, xiv. 67 ; xx. 627 ; xxiii. 89. Hale,
*A Discourse touching Provision for the Poor* (1683), 18. Coal-miners complained of being paid in corn and other commodities at rates far above the
market price : *Newcastle Hostmen*, 127. See also *supra*, vol. ii. 51, 172-3.

[4] *Supra*, vol. i. 481.

necessities at particular shops [1]. Another device was to defer
the payment of wages until they amounted to a considerable
sum, and then compel the workpeople to take promissory
notes payable at a future date ; this not only drove the workmen into debt, but they also had to forfeit part of their
earnings in order to get the notes discounted [2]. The workers
kept up a ceaseless stream of protests against these evil
practices, and for centuries the legislature passed laws against
them. As early as 1464 Parliament, following the precedent
set by the municipal authorities half a century before,
ordered employers to pay their workfolk ' lawful money for
all their lawful wages ' [3]. This injunction was revived at
intervals in the succeeding centuries [4] ; but it did not suppress
a system which inflicted great hardships upon workmen, and
was the burden of repeated complaints to Parliament [5]. One
reason for the failure of the laws against truck was the want
of a summary method of punishing those who disobeyed the
law: when the magistrates imposed penalties on employers, the
latter removed the trials to Westminster, and the expense of
carrying on prosecutions in such circumstances was beyond
the resources of the poor [6]. An incident, which occurred in
1637, showed the inadequacy of the ordinary legal remedies.
A baymaker of Colchester, who paid his workpeople in
commodities, was ordered by the mayor and justices to pay a
sum of money on account of their excess value. Upon his
refusal he was again summoned before the court, when his
attorney announced his intention to spend a hundred pounds
on lawsuits rather than make restitution. On this occasion
the Privy Council intervened, and committed the offender to
prison until he had paid his workmen double the amount due
to them, in addition to the costs of the prosecution [7].

[1] House of Commons Journals, xviii. 280; The Gentleman's Magazine, ix. 9.
[2] House of Commons Journals, xxvii. 503.          [3] Supra, vol. i. 481.
[4] Statutes, iii. 28 (1512) ; iv. part i. 490 (1566) ; viii. 220 (1702) ; ix.
687 (1712).  Statutes at Large, v. 32 (1715) ; v. 435 (1726) ; vi. 138 (1740),
etc.
[5] House of Commons Journals, xiv. 67, 139 ; xix. 181-182 ; xx. 627 ;
xxiii. 89 ; xxiv. 88-89, 117 ; xxvii. 468. The practice continued into the
nineteenth century : e.g. Parliamentary Papers (1805), iii. 125. A worker's
complaint (1792) against truck wages is printed in Ashton, An Eighteenth-
Century Industrialist, 12.
[6] House of Commons Journals, xxvii. 468, 503.
[7] State Papers Domestic, 1637, pp. 44, 88-89, 115.

## (III)

### TECHNICAL TRAINING

In the Middle Ages the responsibility for the technical *Appren*
*ticeship*
training of workmen rested with the craft gilds : in the *made com*
sixteenth century it was assumed by the State.  The Statute *pulsory by*
*the State*
of Apprentices [1]—turning local law, the custom of the (1563).
locality, into national law, the custom of the country—made
the institution of apprenticeship compulsory on all engaged
in industry.   It provided that " it shall not be lawful to any
person or persons, other than such as now do lawfully use
or exercise any art, mistery or manual occupation, to set up,
occupy, use or exercise any craft, mistery or occupation now
used or occupied within the realm of England or Wales,
except he shall have been brought up therein seven years [2]
*at the least* as apprentice . . . nor to set any person on work
in such mistery, art or occupation, being not a workman at
this day, except he shall have been apprentice ".   The State
thus recognized the claim of the qualified workman to be
protected from unskilled competitors, but a check was imposed upon capitalism since it limited the supply of labour.
The Act laid two other restrictions upon capitalism.   It did
not venture to define the number of apprentices which a
master might take into his employment [3], discarding
in this respect a vital principle of the gild system, yet it
compelled every master in the woollen, tailoring and
shoemaking industries, who had three apprentices, to keep
one journeyman ;  " and for every other apprentice above
the number of the three apprentices one other journey-

---

[1] *Statutes*, iv. part i. 419 *seq.*  See *infra*, p. 522 (No. 3).

[2] For the actual length of apprenticeship, see *supra*, vol. ii. 37-38, 218 ;
*infra*, p. 523 (No. 1).   In 1578 an apprentice was bound to a mariner for
three years to learn the art of navigation : *Hist. MSS. Comm. Various*,
iv. 264.

[3] The marginal note that " persons in market towns may take *two*
apprentices " (*Statutes*, iv. part i. 419) is erroneous.   The Statute reads :
" to have in like manner *to* [*i.e.* as] apprentice or apprentices the child or
children . . ."   Subsequent legislation fixed the number of apprentices
in the case of the hatmakers (1566 : *ibid.* iv. part i. 495) ; the Norwich
weavers (1662 : *ibid.* v. 373) ; and the London silk weavers (1773 : *Statutes
at Large*, viii. 260).  Also *infra*, p. 523 (No. 2).

man " [1]. The proportion of journeymen to apprentices was fixed, partly to protect the former from the competition of cheap labour, and partly to ensure that artisans did not spoil the material entrusted to them through the incompetence of half-trained assistants. It was also made illegal for a merchant trading oversea, mercer, draper, goldsmith, ironmonger, embroiderer or clothier, ' dwelling in any city or town corporate ', to take an apprentice (other than his own son) whose father or mother did not possess freehold of the annual value of forty shillings ; or, dwelling in a market town, freehold worth sixty shillings. A country weaver, living outside a city, corporate town or market town, could only take as apprentices the sons of sixty-shilling freeholders [2]. This attempt, based on mediaeval precedent, to organize the industrial life of the country on a class basis by excluding the children of ' husbandmen and labourers ', is explained by the current opinion that " through the idleness of those professions so many embrace them that they are only a cloak for vagabonds and thieves, and there is such a decay of husbandry that masters cannot get skilful servants to till the ground without unreasonable wages " [3] ; while the concession made to ' cities and towns corporate ' was intended to discourage the migration of industry to new centres.

*Modified by legislation.* The operation of the Statute of Apprentices was modified in two ways—by legislation and judicial decisions. The Civil War created the problem of the discharged soldiers, which necessitated a relaxation of labour restrictions. Some were apprentices who had not served out their time, others had never been bound apprentices. An Ordinance of the Commonwealth (1654) admitted ex-service men to any handicraft or trade ' in any city or town corporate or in any

---

[1] The Act of 1662 required Norwich weavers who kept two apprentices to employ two journeymen : *Statutes*, v. 373. Similarly, the Act of 1671 for the Kidderminster stuff weavers : *ibid.* 712. See *infra*, Appendix, p. 523, No. 3.

[2] Or his own son. This restriction did not apply to weavers in Cumberland, Westmorland, Lancashire and Wales, " weaving friezes, cottons or housewives' cloth only ".

[3] *Hist. MSS. Comm. Salisbury*, i. 163. For mediaeval legislation, see *supra*, vol. i. 321.

other place whatsoever ' [1] ; and the precedent then set was imitated on subsequent occasions [2]. While the Statute was thus limited in one direction, its scope was extended in another—for example, in 1653 it was applied to the printers of books [3].

The trend of judicial decisions evinced clearly the desire *Modified* to diminish as much as possible the force of the Statute of *by judicial* *decisions.* Apprentices, which (it was said in 1669) " has been by most of the judges looked upon as inconvenient to trade and to the increase of inventions " [4]. As Blackstone, writing in 1765, observed : " The resolutions of the courts have in general rather confined than extended the restriction. No trades are held to be within the Statute but such as were in being at the making of it ; for trading in a country village apprenticeships are not requisite ; and following the trade seven years is sufficient without any binding " [5]. These ' resolutions of the courts ' were frequent in the seventeenth century [6], and they were in harmony with the attitude of the common law towards restraints on trade [7]. The law courts gave the utmost latitude to the interpretation of the Statute, in order to weaken the restrictions which it imposed on economic enterprise. Tolley's Case (1615) affords an example of the legal reasoning which was employed. " It was agreed and resolved that an upholster is not a trade within that Statute. For first, it is not a trade that is mentioned in any of the branches of the Statute, howsoever in all parts of the Statute there is mention made of sixty-one several trades and misteries ; and if the artisans, which at that time were assistants under the committees for the expressing of all manner of trades, [had] thought that the trade of an upholster had been such a trade that required art and skill for the exercising of it, they would not have

---

[1] *Acts and Ordinances of the Interregnum*, ii. 1006-1007. The local authorities had already taken the initiative : *Hist. MSS. Comm. Rye*, 217 (1651).

[2] *Statutes*, v. 241 (1660) ; vii. 528 (1698) ; ix. 791 (1712).

[3] *Acts and Ordinances of the Interregnum*, ii. 697-698.

[4] Privy Council Register, 29th Oct. 1669 (printed in Unwin, *Industrial Organization*, Appendix A, vii.).

[5] Blackstone, *Commentaries on the Laws of England* (ed. 1765), i. 415-416. See *infra*, Appendix, p. 523, No. 4.

[6] *The English Reports*, lxxxiii. 1279 ; xci. 518-519, 680.

[7] For the common law, see *supra*, p. 263 ; and *infra*, pp. 348-351, 360, 365. Also *supra*, vol. ii. Introduction, pp. cxxi, cxxxiii-cxxxv, 432 (note 3).

failed to make mention of it. . . . Thirdly, the trade of an upholster doth not require any art or skill for the exercising of it, inasmuch as he hath all things made to his hand, and it is only to dispose them in order after such time as they are brought to him ; . . . and so he is like to Æsop's bird, which borroweth of every bird a feather, his art resting merely in the overseeing and disposition of such things which other men work, and in the putting of feathers into a tick, and sewing them up when he hath done, the which one that hath been an apprentice unto it but seven days is able to perform. And the intent of this Statute was not to extend unto any other trades, but such as required art and skill for the managing of them ; and therefore it was adjudged in the Exchequer upon an information against one, in the 42 year of the reign of the late Queen Elizabeth, that a coster-monger was not a trade intended by the Statute of 5 Elizabeth because his art was in the selling of apples, the which re-quired no skill or experience for the exercise of it. So an husbandman, tankard-bearer, brickmaker, porter, miller and such like trades are not within the Statute of 5 Elizabeth cap. 4, so as none may exercise them but such a one that hath been an apprentice by the space of seven years ; for they are arts which require rather ability of body than skill. But a brewer and baker are within the Statute because it concerneth the health of men's bodies to have good bread baked and beer brewed, and so it is fit that they should have skill for the exercise of them " [1]. In 1655 the frame-work knitters were held to be outside the Statute, since " the trade was not a corporation " in the fifth year of Elizabeth [2] ; and a decade later the tobacco-pipe makers, who had not been incorporated until 1620, sought to be brought under the Act, expressly in order that " none may follow the trade who have not been apprentices seven years " [3]. The legal attitude towards another part of the Statute, requiring apprentices in certain occupations to be sons of freeholders [4], is indicated by the opinion of the recorder of Newcastle (1741) : " 'Tis probable

[1] *The English Reports*, lxxx. 653-654.
[2] *State Papers Domestic*, 1655-1656, p. 77.
[3] 1664 : *ibid.* 1664-1665, p. 116.      [4] *Supra*, p. 280.

when 5 Elizabeth was made, it might be then intended that
if the father had forty shillings per annum he might give his
son a competent fortune to set up in trade, and the master
would be better secured.    But, say the books, such an estate
now is scarce sufficient to make the son a cobbler.    So that
this day it seems a matter quite indifferent whether such
certificate be or no " [1].

The Statute of Apprentices remained on the statute-book *Enforce-
for two and a half centuries.    Its observance was primarily a ment of
matter of local custom, and the growth of an infinite variety ship.*
of practices can best be shown by a survey of evidence drawn
from different parts of the country [2].    As early as 1575
breaches of the Act had created dissensions between the
bakers and brewers of Rye.    The former complained that
in spite of ' good and wholesome laws ' requiring ' each sort
of people ' to " use the trade and living wherein they have
been lawfully trained up ", brewers turned bakers without
having served an apprenticeship " contrary to all law, equity
and good conscience ".    The authorities, finding that " by
no reasonable persuasion . . . those brewers would leave
baking ", and that the principal offender who baked and
brewed " is (God be thanked) grown to good wealth, and the
whole company of the bakers thereby utterly impoverished ",
issued a decree based on the principle that " the state of a
commonwealth is preferred before the private gain of a few " [3].
A few years later (1585) the weavers of Hereford represented
that they were " like to fall into utter ruin ", and they attributed their distressed condition partly to the admission of
persons not duly apprenticed [4].    In London the Act was
said in 1593 to be " now so far out of order at this present
that there must be a remedy or else it will breed, as all men
do know, a further inconvenience " ; and an office was set
up in London licensed by the lord mayor for the registra-
tion of apprentices [5].    Nevertheless in Hertfordshire, in 1598,

[1] *Newcastle Merchant Adventurers*, i. 258.
[2] On the survival of apprenticeship in the woollen industry, see *supra*,
vol. ii. 39 *seq.*, 72 *seq.*
[3] *Hist. MSS. Comm. Rye*, 45-48.
[4] *Ibid. Hereford*, 335.                   [5] *Ibid. Salisbury*, iv. 385.

several victuallers were presented for following the occupation of a baker, "not having been apprenticed thereto for a term of seven years "; in Wiltshire, in 1603, the ' orders agreed upon for the occupation of weavers ' laid down detailed regulations on apprenticeship ; in Lincolnshire, in 1618, a list was drawn up of apprentices who had been bound to farmers [1].

*The corporation of ' honest London tradesmen '.* Breaches of the Act suggested to a needy monarch the means of filling an exhausted treasury; and in 1619 James I. appointed a commission to grant pardons " to such as use trades whereto they have not been apprenticed, and for dispensing with them to continue the same for their lives, notwithstanding the Statute " [2]. In the next reign the financial embarrassments of the Crown dictated a more ambitious project for profiting by evasions of the law. This took the form of a corporation of ' tradesmen and artificers ', confined to those who had served an apprenticeship or compounded for their failure to do so. The scheme was unfolded in a proclamation : " Whereas a great number of people, as well aliens as others our subjects born, who never served as apprentices in any trade, craft or occupation, have intruded into places " within London and without, " and there without restraint or order . . . practise and exercise several trades, misteries and handicrafts, by means whereof the said places are much pestered with inmates and become noisome and contagious, wares are falsified and sophisticated, and the tradesmen and artificers . . . who have served as apprentices according to our laws are very much impoverished ", the latter are therefore constituted a corporation, and no one else may set up any occupation, " or use any trading by retail there, or be admitted into the corporation, unless he shall first serve as an apprentice there by the space of seven years ". But as for those, proceeds the proclamation, who " have not served apprenticeships, in regard the punishment whereunto they are liable if we should put our laws in execu-

---

[1] *Hertford County Records,* i. 26-27 ; *Hist. MSS. Comm. Various,* i. 74 (Wiltshire) ; *ibid. Rutland,* i. 455.

[2] Four commissioners were appointed for seven years : *Tudor and Stuart Proclamations* (ed. Steele), i. No. 1242 ; *Hist. MSS. Comm. Rutland,* i. 455. For their activities, see *infra,* Appendix, p. 523, No. 5.

tion would much impoverish them . . . we therefore . . . have
further ordained that they also may be admitted into the
said freedom in such manner as by our said letters patents
is ordained, and after such admittance shall and may freely
use their trades " [1]. The corporation of ' honest London
tradesmen ' was constituted by letters patent in 1636 : its
membership extended to all tradesmen ' buying and selling
by retail ', who inhabited within three miles of the city of
London [2]. It was provided that the King should be paid
four shillings for everyone who had served a seven years'
apprenticeship, twenty shillings for those who had not been
apprenticed, and five pounds for an alien : but henceforth
none were to be admitted without apprenticeship. The sum
of £3340 was collected for the King, of which he actually
received £2300. " The business was good ", commented
one of its promoters, " but became perverted by admitting
those who had no right ; but the unpardonable fault was
[this was said in 1654] that it raised money for the King
without consent of Parliament " [3].

In the provinces informers were equally on the alert *Informers*
to discover breaches of the Statute [4]. In 1640 the clothiers *against breaches of*
in the West Riding of Yorkshire, among whom the legal *the law.*
binding of apprentices was still practised [5], were thrown
into a state of consternation by the threat of prosecution for
taking apprentices whose fathers did not own forty-shilling
freeholds, and for not maintaining the proportion of journeymen to apprentices : " which will tend to their utter undoing
if some remedy be not speedily had, there being not one
clothier in the county but is guilty of the penalties of the said
Statutes ". The restrictions, they protested, were " never
observed in the county of York and cannot be for many
reasons " [6]. It would be wrong to infer from the statement
of the Yorkshire clothiers that the legal proportion of journeymen to apprentices was universally ignored. About the

[1] Rymer, *Foedera*, xx. 113-114.
[2] *State Papers Domestic*, 1638–1639, p. 20.
[3] *Ibid.* 1654, pp. 265-266.
[4] *Hertford County Records*, i. 59, etc.
[5] *State Papers Domestic*, 1637, pp. 274-275.
[6] *Ibid.* 1640, p. 501.

same time the Privy Council inquired into the grievances of the journeymen in the silk industry. Its report described as unfounded the allegation that the masters kept many apprentices and few journeymen, " for upon examination we find none of them to have exceeded their orders whereby they are limited, and that in the· total they have more journeymen than apprentices " [1].

*Effects of the Civil War.*    The Civil War relaxed the bonds of society and weakened the respect for traditional economic practices. In Wiltshire the ' ancient weavers ' of Westbury complained in 1647 that " now in these disordered times many apprentices, having forsaken parents and masters under colour of following the wars, the wars being ended, refuse to serve out their time, but before they are eighteen or twenty years old betake themselves to marriage and the gaining a loom's work for themselves ; whereby the ancienter weavers are many times by—put beside of their work, and sometimes the master under-crept by him who should be his servant " [2]. In other parts of the country the like complaint was raised against persons exercising ' misteries and trades ' to which they had not been apprenticed [3]. After the Restoration several Acts were passed for the regulation of trade in which apprenticeship still remained obligatory : in 1662 laws were framed for the Norwich worsted industry and the West Riding broad cloth industry, requiring a seven years' apprenticeship [4]. County sessions rolls continue to record the presentment of offenders for following occupations in which they had not served a seven years' apprenticeship—the Hertfordshire list includes a maltster for using the trade of a grocer, a yeoman for exercising the craft of a ' common brewer ', a cordwainer, a weaver and a dyer [5]. Nevertheless one writer, who spoke

---

[1] *State Papers Domestic*, 1639, pp. 458-459 ; 1639–1640, p. 38.
[2] *Hist. MSS. Comm. Various*, i. 114.
[3] *Ibid. Rye*, 230 ; *Hertford County Records*, i. 102, 110, 112 ; and *infra*, p. 287.      [4] *Statutes*, v. 372, 427.
[5] *Hertford County Records*, i. 155, 171, 202, 255. In 1657 the inhabitants of Westbury petitioned against the indictment of three women for ' burling ' cloth without serving an apprenticeship : *Hist. MSS. Comm. Various*, i. 135. At Nottingham there were frequent presentments in the seventeenth century : *Records of Nottingham*, iv. 325 ; v. 103, 136, 329, 331, 387 397, 402. Similarly Surrey : *Surrey Quarter Sessions Records*, 1659–1661, (Surrey Record Society), 134 *seq.*

with some authority, declared (1671) that " there is few of the relations to clothing which doth observe such an exact rule of apprenticeship . . . notwithstanding it is enjoined in a very strict and penal manner"[1]. Even the organized misteries found it difficult to protect their vested interests. The Company of Woolmen—that is, Wool-packers—of London voiced their grievance in 1664 that " during the late troubles many persons never apprentices, inexperienced and not sworn into the Company ", had taken up the trade of packing wool[2]. The combers of Coggeshall in Essex complained that boys learnt their art without being bound apprentices. Although the justices granted an injunction in 1664 it had no effect, and in 1686 the combers started a fund to prosecute ' intruders ' into their trade :

> " From such as would our rights invade
> Or would intrude into our trade
> Or break the law Queen Betty made
> Libera nos Domine "[3].

After the Revolution industrial capitalism claimed the right, not only to make its own contract with labour in respect of wages and length of service[4], independent of any external interference, but also to draw freely upon an unlimited supply of labour. The first step in this direction was the repeal in 1694 of the clause in the Statute of Apprentices, confining apprenticeship among country weavers to the sons of sixty-shilling freeholders[5]. Four years later the proposal was mooted for the introduction of a Bill, "for the freedom of trade without seven years' service, and to prevent vexatious indictments on penal Statutes"[6]; and the attitude of the State on this question was soon disclosed. At the beginning of the eighteenth century Parliament openly abandoned the legal

*Apprenticeship after the Revolution.*

---

[1] [Carter], *England's Interest by Trade Asserted* (1671), 33.
[2] *State Papers Domestic*, 1663–1664, p. 469. On the enforcement of apprenticeship by the gilds after the Restoration, see Dunlop, *English Apprenticeship*, 110 seq.
[3] *Hist. MSS. Comm. Various*, viii. 577-581.
[4] *Supra*, p. 265, and *infra*, p. 318.
[5] *Statutes*, vi. 463. See *supra*, p. 280.
[6] *Hist. MSS. Comm. Cowper*, ii. 382. At the Weavers' Hall 1795 apprentices were bound in 1680–1684, and 808 in 1696–1700 : *A Brief History of Trade in England* (1702), 130-131.

enforcement of apprenticeship, in the response which it gave
to the numerous petitions of wool-combers and weavers in
different parts of the kingdom, who complained that " great
numbers of persons of all other trades have intruded into
the petitioners' trade, so that they cannot get a livelihood ",
and that many of these intruders take fourteen or more
apprentices to work for them for a year or two, after which
they become journeymen " to the ruin of such as have legally
served apprenticeships to the said trade " [1]. The legislature
declined to take any action, and pronounced the maxim
which was to mould its economic policy throughout the
century : " *Trade ought to be free and not restrained* " [2]. The
House of Commons even rejected the recommendation made
by its own committee appointed to investigate the grievances
of the weavers of Taunton, who asserted that weavers took
five, six or seven apprentices together, while " many intrude
into that trade who never served their apprenticeships
thereto ". The committee's report stated that there were
about fifteen hundred woollen weavers in Taunton and about
two thousand within a radius of five miles, " and not half
of them have served apprenticeships to the weaving trade " :
it therefore proposed that woollen and worsted weaving
should be confined to those only who were qualified by
apprenticeship. This proposal was still the law of the land,
yet it failed to be accepted ; and leave was given to bring
in a Bill to repeal all laws restraining persons, who had not
been apprenticed, from working in the woollen industries [3].

*Trend of parlia-mentary opinion.*      The trend of parliamentary opinion towards industrial
freedom was displayed on other occasions [4]. In 1707 the
governors of the Dutch Bay-Hall in Colchester—mindful
of the high premium, forty or fifty pounds, often paid with
an apprentice—restricted the making of bays to " such as
have served seven years to the trade of bay-making ". The

---

[1] *House of Commons Journals*, xiii. 338, 365, 376, 383, 404, 416, 657.
The petitions came from London, Peterborough, Leicester, Cirencester,
Somerset and Devon.
[2] 1702 : *ibid.* xiii. 783.          [3] 1702 : *ibid.* xiv. 31, 67-68, 70.
[4] A stream of petitions vainly urged the enforcement of apprenticeship :
*ibid.* xviii. 171 (1715) ; xix. 181 (1719) ; xxi. 153 (1728) ; xxiii. 639, 648,
664-665, 686 (1741) ; xxiv. 88, 117, 124, 132 (1742), etc.

House of Commons resolved (1715) that the trade should be free to all who had served their apprenticeship to any branch of the woollen manufacture in Colchester [1]. It was significant, too, that a clause in an Act of 1725, making a seven years' apprenticeship compulsory on all makers of broad cloth in the West Riding of Yorkshire, was repealed in 1733 [2]. A reversal of policy in the opposite direction, due to the special circumstances of the occupation, is seen in the case of the watermen and lightermen engaged on the River Thames. In 1705 Parliament removed the restrictions which prevented watermen taking apprentices under eighteen years old [3], or more than one apprentice at a time. In 1737 fresh restrictions on the age and number of apprentices were imposed, owing to complaints that they were taken for the sake of a small premium—" three parts of the apprentices are taken for no more than two or three pounds "—at twelve and thirteen years old, " not having strength nor being of size sufficient for the labour required in such occupation " : it was also enacted that the apprentices of watermen must serve seven years and lodge with their masters—thus reviving a custom once general but now fast disappearing [4]. The payment of a premium with apprentices had by this time grown into a normal practice in all occupations. Although attended with obvious drawbacks, as the example of the watermen shows, it served to make masters more willing to take beginners into their service, and to accept the responsibility for their instruction and oversight. The amount paid to a master was sometimes considerable. A baymaker received forty or fifty pounds with an apprentice, a clothier ' the best part of two hundred pounds ' or even twice that figure, a merchant several hundred pounds, while an apothecary in 1661 stipulated for forty pounds and clothes for the apprentice [5]. It was perhaps indicative of Parliament's attitude towards apprenticeship that in 1710 the premium

---

[1] *House of Commons Journal*, xviii. 280-281.
[2] *Statutes at Large*, v. 385, 641.
[3] The son of a waterman could be apprenticed at the age of sixteen.
[4] *Statutes*, viii. 511 (1705) ; *Statutes at Large*, vi. 54 (1737) ; *House of Commons Journals*, xxii. 791-792, 830.
[5] Baymakers : *supra*, p. 288. Clothiers : *The Interest of England . . .*
[contd.]

was burdened with a tax of sixpence in the pound on every
sum of fifty pounds or under, and a shilling in the pound on
sums over fifty pounds. This duty, which was to be paid by
the master, did not apply to premiums received in respect
of parish apprentices ' placed out at the common or public
charge of any parish ' [1].

*Report of a parliamentary committee (1751).* In the middle of the eighteenth century the House of
Commons appointed a committee " to inquire into the laws
relating to trade and manufactures ". Its report, which
registered an important stage in the development of economic
thought, showed how complete was the change of sentiment
towards the Elizabethan Statute. " There are other laws
of great importance which deserve consideration—particularly such as require the serving an apprenticeship for seven
years before any person can set up a particular trade and
occupation; which were at first well intended for securing
the goodness and consequently the value and estimation of
our several manufactures in foreign parts, and to prevent
the disparagement of them by unskilful workmen. But
since the improvement of trade in general, it is found that
all manufactures find their own value according to their
goodness ; and that scarce any prosecutions have been
carried on upon these Statutes, but against such as have
excelled in their own trades by force of their own genius,
and not against such as have been ignorant in their professions—which is the reverse of the intent of such laws and
a great obstruction to industry and improvements. These
obstructions arise partly from the laws above-mentioned,
and partly from particular franchises and by-laws of corporations. But your committee are of opinion, if the legal
restraints were once removed, the particular by-laws would
soon be reversed : as they cannot but observe that the most
useful and beneficial manufactures are principally carried on,
and trade most flourishing, in such towns and places as are
under no such local disabilities " [2]. More than half a century

---

considered in a Dialogue between Sir T. Flourishing and T. Castdown (1701),
23 ; Parliamentary Papers (1802–3), vii. 145. Merchants : supra, vol. ii.
192. Apothecaries : Hist. MSS. Comm. Kenyon, 69. Other examples are
given below : infra, Appendix, p. 524, No. 1.
   [1] Statutes, ix. 193-194. See infra, Appendix, p. 524, No. 2.
   [2] House of Commons Journals, xxvi. 292 (1751).

elapsed before general effect was given to the recommendation [1]; but in the traditional spirit of English institutional
development, piecemeal legislation continued to sap the
foundations of the old order.   In 1713 the brandy-distillers
had been exempted from the operation of the Act [2] : in 1777
the dyers in Middlesex, Essex, Surrey and Kent were permitted to employ journeymen who had not been apprenticed,
and the hatters were no longer required to serve an apprenticeship [3].

While parliamentary opinion thus moved steadily in the *Indict-*
direction of *laissez-faire*, the local authorities remained *ments against*
wedded to ' ancient customs, franchises and liberties '.   In *offenders.*
significant contrast with the maxim, pronounced by the
legislature in 1702, that " trade ought to be free and not
restrained " [4], stands the sweeping ordinance established
by the ' mayor and commonalty ' of Salisbury in 1706.   This
enjoined that " no person whatsoever, not being free of the
said city, or having served as an apprentice within the said
city by the space of seven years, shall . . . by any colour, way
or means whatsoever, directly or indirectly, by himself or
any other, use or exercise any art, trade or mistery " within
the city [5].   Throughout the eighteenth century ' vexatious
indictments ' continued to be brought against those who
took up a trade to which they had not served an apprenticeship.   In Hertfordshire the list comprises a glover, a clock-
maker, a butcher, a fellmonger and a tallow chandler ; in
Hampshire a Romsey clothier was indicted (1704) ' for the
unlawful use of the art or mistery of clothier ', but secured
a verdict in his favour since he had exercised his trade for
thirty years ; in Bedfordshire, where a baker, a barber, a
shoemaker and a tailor figured among the offenders, cases
occur to the end of the century ; and there are other indications that the machinery of the law was intermittently put

---

[1] The apprenticeship clauses of the Statute of Apprentices were
repealed in 1814 for all industries : *supra*, vol. ii. 76, note 3.

[2] *Statutes*, ix. 900.

[3] *Statutes at Large*, viii. 512 (dyers), 550 (hatters).   Cf. *Reports from
Committees of the House of Commons*, ii. 376.

[4] *Supra*, p. 288.

[5] *Hist. MSS. Comm. Various*, iv. 252-253.   For similar regulations at
Tiverton (1692), see *State Papers Domestic*, 1691–1692, p. 115.

into operation [1]. Nevertheless in some places a different
spirit prevailed. " Almost in every town in England where
trade flourishes greatly ", it was remarked in 1779, " they
never ask whether a man has served his apprenticeship " ;
and to this, together with the absence of settlement restrictions, was attributed the rise of Leeds, Manchester, Halifax
and Birmingham [2] —though even Leeds enforced the system
of apprenticeship in the woollen industry down to the middle
of the eighteenth century [3].

*The justifi-*
*cation for*
*compulsory*
*apprentice-*
*ship.*
In the course of a memorable debate in Parliament on
the repeal of the Statute of Apprentices (1814), the exponents
of the new economic doctrines seized the occasion to fling
scorn upon the old-fashioned principles which had held sway
in the sixteenth century. " The reign of Queen Elizabeth ",
it was proclaimed, " though glorious, was not one in which
sound principles of commerce were known " [4]. The criticism
is vitiated by the implied assumption that Elizabethan
statesmen were presented with a blank sheet, on which they
could inscribe any kind of legislative programme in disregard
of the psychology and traditions of the society for which
they legislated : in short it lacks the sense of historical
realities. The conception of industrial freedom which commended itself to the nineteenth century was not necessarily
suited to a different order of society. In the sixteenth
century the institution of apprenticeship still remained the
basis of industrial organization, and a violent breach with
its traditions was unthinkable on the part of the Tudor
monarchy, which in every aspect of its economic policy
pursued the consistent aim of protecting the social fabric
from the dissolving forces of the new commercialism [5].
Industry was still conceived, as it had been in the Middle
Ages, in the light of a public service. It was an ' art ', or—

[1] *Hertford County Records*, i. 402 ; ii. 25, 89, 149, 178. *Bedfordshire
County Records*, i. 32. *Victoria County History, Hampshire*, v. 487. *Ibid.
Bedfordshire*, ii. 105. *Ibid. Lincolnshire*, ii. 348.
[2] *Victoria County History, Yorkshire*, iii. 453. For the settlement laws,
see *infra*, pp. 457 *seq.*
[3] Heaton, *The Yorkshire Woollen and Worsted Industries*, 309-310.
[4] Hansard, *The Parliamentary Debates*, xxvii. 564.
[5] See *infra*, p. 300, note 4.

as we should now describe it—a 'profession'; and, as in
most modern professions, compulsory training was imposed
to protect alike the interests of the public and the interests
of the skilled worker.  This twofold purpose of apprenticeship finds expression in an Elizabethan document: "The
prentice that is bound for less than seven years doth not
commonly prove to be an expert artificer, so that thereby
ignorance and imperfection in divers arts and occupations
do enter; yet many are bound for five, four, three, yea two
years or less, and then take upon them to bring up others
under them, whom they make as evil and as unskilful workmen as themselves, which doth not only impair good and
perfect workmanship or knowledge in occupations, but also is
a means whereby the number of artificers do so multiply that
one of them do as it were eat out and consume another "[1].

Under the Early Stuarts the virtues of apprenticeship
were still being inculcated [2]: but after the Restoration a
growing volume of public opinion, responding to the needs
of an expanding trade, advocated the removal of restraints
on industry, many of which were now clearly antiquated.
Child announced the gospel of industrial freedom: "To
improve and advance trade" we must "begin the right way,
casting off some of our old mistaken principles in trade, which
we inherit from our ancestors who were . . . unskilful in the
misteries of and methods to improve trade".  Among the
'common errors' of his day, he included the notions that
"none shall use any manual occupation except he has been
apprentice to the same", and that "to suffer artificers to
have as many apprentices as they will is to destroy trade "[3].
Other writers attacked restrictions on the binding of the
children of 'poor people', that is, those not owning a forty
or sixty-shilling freehold: "which clause apparently shuts
out at least five parts of the people in six from the woollen
manufacture, and by consequence tends to the depopulation
of our inland towns".  A seven years' apprenticeship was

*Change
of public
opinion.*

---

[1] *Tudor Economic Documents* (ed. Tawney and Power), i. 355 (? 1573).
[2] Misselden, *Free Trade* (1622), 61.
[3] Child, *A Discourse about Trade* (1690), 47; Child, *A New Discourse
of Trade* (4th ed.), pp. xli-xliv, 78-79.  The fourth edition reads 'any
natural occupation'.  The first edition reads 'any manual occupation'.

now considered too long a term of ' drudgery and slavery ', which drove many youths into ' other more easy and ready employments ' [1]. The disinclination of Parliament to enforce the system of apprenticeship thus represented a genuine change of sentiment, which continued to find expression in the next century—as, for example, when Dean Tucker included among the ' bad laws ' relating to trade "that absurd Statute of the Fifth of Queen Elizabeth, which restrains persons from exercising those very trades they may have the happiest genius for " [2].

## (IV)

### UNEMPLOYMENT

*The problem of unemployment.*

We have seen that the growth of capitalism created the problem of unemployment as early as the sixteenth century [3]. Here we are concerned, not with the normal ebb and flow of trade, and its regular reaction upon the volume of employment, but with the abnormal interruptions which we call commercial crises. The earlier phases of our industrial development exhibit phenomena identical with those which we are apt to regard as peculiar to the nineteenth century. England's commerce, in becoming world-wide [4], found itself exposed to the vicissitudes of a world economy, and the course of her economic life was profoundly disturbed by occurrences remote from her territory. Hence the apprehension with which the progress of industry was viewed by the early economists, who preferred to see the prosperity of this country broad-based on land rather than on the shifting foundations of trade. "We have too great a clothing commonwealth ", said a member of Parliament in 1614 [5], and Mun voiced the general uneasiness when he wrote : " Clothing . . . is the greatest wealth and best employment of the poor of this kingdom, yet nevertheless we may peradventure employ ourselves with better safety, plenty and

---

[1] Coke, *Treatise* (1675), iii. 22 ; *Britannia Languens* (1680), 159-160 (in sect. vii.) ; *The Trade of England Revived* (1681), 7.
[2] Tucker, *Instructions* (ed. 1757), 34.    [3] *Supra*, vol. ii. 64.
[4] For the extent of English foreign trade, see *supra*, vol. ii. 184 *seq.*
[5] *House of Commons Journals*, i. 491.

profit in using more tillage and fishing, than to trust so wholly
to the making of cloth ; for in times of war, or by other
occasions, if some foreign princes should prohibit the use
thereof in their dominions, it might suddenly cause much
poverty and dangerous uproars, especially by our poor people,
when they should be deprived of their ordinary maintenance " [1]. A similar view was expressed by Westcote, a contemporary of Mun : " Every rumour of war or contagious
sickness (hindering the sale of these commodities) makes a
multitude of the poorer sort chargeable to their neighbours,
who are bound to maintain them " [2].

Tariffs and wars were now revealed as economic factors *Foreign*
of cardinal importance. The protection which Holland *Tariffs.*
gave to her woollen industry in the early part of the seventeenth century [3] helped to bring about one of the severest
industrial crises in English history [4], and it figured prominently among the causes leading up to the Dutch Wars. The
Restoration Parliament asserted that the ' immoderate and
excessive imposts ' levied upon English cloth by the Dutch
constituted, " in effect, little less than a plain inhibition of
the trade of those manufactures into Holland "; and it
urged the King to procure their removal ' by treaty or otherwise ' [5]. France adopted a protectionist policy expressly
designed to exclude English cloth from her markets, and it
greatly embittered the relations between the two countries [6].
Sweden laid a duty of over 50 per cent. upon English woollen
manufactures in order to encourage her own industries [7].

[1] Mun, *England's Treasure by Forraign Trade* (1664), 181-182.
[2] Westcote, *A View of Devonshire in 1630* (ed. 1845), 62.
[3] Even in the sixteenth century various towns in the Low Countries
passed ordinances excluding English cloth, " which is like to prove great
injury to England. This has stimulated greatly the manufacturers of cloths
in these parts, and Spanish and other wools are also in demand " : *Letters and
Papers, Foreign and Domestic, of Henry VIII.*, vol. iv. part ii. 1557 (1527).
[4] *Infra*, p. 305. The Dutch laid an imposition of 32s. (' consumption
money ') on fine English cloth, ' and so proportionably ', while in the
Spanish Netherlands, 24s. (' licence money ') was exacted : *House of
Commons Journals*, i. 689, 773, 780 (1624). The clothiers represented the
Dutch imposition at 45s. : Stowe MSS. 354, f. 65 (1622). For the impositions in 1650, see *State Papers Domestic*, 1650, p. 21.
[5] 1660 : *House of Commons Journals*, viii. 149 ; *State Papers Domestic*,
1660-1661, p. 255.
[6] For the French tariffs on English cloth, see *supra*, p. 100.
[7] 1680 : *House of Commons Journals*, xii. 432.

The erection of tariff walls in the Old World served, indeed, as one of the main arguments for the development of a colonial empire in the New World [1].

Wars affected English industry in two ways [1a]. They inflated certain branches, such as iron and ship-building, so that the conclusion of peace brought on a depression of trade—this happened after the War of the Spanish Succession [2] and the Swedish War [3]. Moreover the disturbance of trade, and the strain upon the financial solvency of continental houses, had a marked effect even when England was not an actual participant in the war. On the eve of the Thirty Years' War two houses at Elbing and Hamburg, holding eighty thousand pounds' worth of English goods, suspended payment, thereby inflicting severe losses on the Eastland merchants [4]. The outbreak of the war found England unprepared to meet an interruption of her trade in Central Europe, since her position in the Dutch market was being severely shaken, and the combined influence of these factors had disastrous results upon the manufacturing districts in England [5]. "The course of trade", wrote Misselden, "is stopped and hindered that merchants cannot pass without peril from place to place, and the moneys become so variable that when a merchant hath sold his cloth and hopeth to have gained something thereby, by that time that the term for payment is expired he receiveth less in value than the cloths cost, by the raising and rising of the moneys" [6]. The Second Dutch War had its repercussions upon trade, and a Norwich correspondent informed the Government that "the people are mad for peace, and unless it come soon, those manufacturing parts cannot subsist" [7]. The situation was aggravated by the Fire of London because the capital was the great cloth depository of the kingdom. "Many poor Coventry clothiers are undone by it", a letter related, "their whole estate lying there in cloth" [8]. Another remarked : "Many of our

---

[1] *Supra*, p. 186.    [1a] See *infra*, p. 524 (No. 3).    [2] *Supra*, p. 180.
[3] Ashton, *Iron and Steel in the Industrial Revolution*, 130.
[4] *Acts and Ordinances of the Eastland Company*, p. li (1617).
[5] *Infra*, p. 305.    [6] Misselden, *Free Trade* (1622), 52.
[7] *State Papers Domestic*, 1666–1667, p. 550.
[8] *Ibid.* 110. Later it was reported that "the dead-hearted clothiers are pricking up their ears, expecting a trade" : *ibid.* 235.

clothiers have lost many thousand pounds' worth of cloth
[and] given off all trading, so that we begin already to feel
the loss by the multitude of poor " [1]. Under William III.
the misfortunes of the war with France in its early stages
deepened, even if they did not originate, the depression of
trade ; and the woollen industry was said to be ' much
decayed ' and ' quite down '. The foundation of the Bank
of England, together with an improvement in the political
situation, apparently restored confidence, for a revival of the
cloth trade was noted soon afterwards [2].

In the next century barely one or two decades enjoyed *Eighteenth-*
uninterrupted peace. The War of the Spanish Succession *century wars.*
created, while it lasted, a fictitious prosperity owing to the
demand for manufactures and foodstuffs to meet the needs
of our armies abroad and the requirements of countries
whose tillage and industries were interrupted by the war [3].
The real situation, however, was disclosed when the period
of inflation was ended, and the workhouse made its appearance as the permanent legacy of the war [4]. The accession of
George I. brought to the throne an enemy of Sweden, and
the fruits of his hostility were manifested in the West
Country. " In Exeter and other parts of Devonshire ", it
was reported, " great numbers of clothiers had got together
in a very audacious manner and refused to pay any more
taxes unless there were a new Parliament, and the prohibition
taken off as to the commerce with Sweden, by which they say
all their manufactories are ruined. Some troops were sent
by the Government against them " [5]. A quarter of a century
later, when England was at war with Spain, the clothing
towns pressed their representatives in Parliament to give
' most serious attention ' to the woollen manufacture, " the
decay of which is so sensibly felt in these parts by the
starving condition to which many thousands of his majesty's
subjects are reduced " [6]. At the close of the Seven Years'

[1] *Hist. MSS. Comm. Portland*, iii. 298.                    [2] *Ibid.* 548, 564.
[3] Wood, *A Survey of Trade* (1718), 200-201.
[4] *Infra*, p. 477. The ruin of the famous Colchester bay trade, and the
dissolution of the Dutch corporation there, was attributed to the war :
Cromwell, *History of Colchester* (1825), 289.
[5] *Hist. MSS. Comm. Stuart*, v. 262 (1717) ; vi. 107.
[6] *Ibid. Somerset*, 124 (1742).

War eighteen great houses in Amsterdam failed for many millions, and several houses failed at Hamburg and Stockholm, " which it is afraid will affect many more in London, Paris, etc." [1]—a striking indication of the interdependence of the financial centres of Europe. The Seven Years' War also ruined the carrying trade and caused ' a prodigious diminution ' in our shipping, for the enemy's privateers exposed our merchant ships to such risks that the ships of neutral countries could be hired at a much cheaper rate [2]. Moreover the currency had been inflated during the war, and this caused a rise in prices, followed by labour unrest and an advance in wages. " Was there not a coinage of fifty millions of paper money during the late war, and a vast increase of real money by rich captures and an extended commerce to the amount of many millions more ? Have not the prices of butter, cheese, eggs, meat, and even corn, gradually advanced upon us according to the great increase of our paper and money currency ? For the more we abound in money, of the less value it is (for it will have its market price as well as any other commodity) ; and as it decreases in its value by its plenty, you must give more of it in weight or tale to purchase what you want ; and this has, and (as the evil goes on) will raise the prices of estates, of rents and of everything else " [3]. The baneful effects of war were again to be demonstrated before many years had elapsed. The War of American Independence diminished the volume of English commerce [4], while the prospect that European countries would be drawn into it at once created apprehensions of " the utmost ill consequences to the export trade of the woollen manufactures of the West Riding of Yorkshire "[5]. A letter written by John Wesley in 1775 described the situation produced by the American War. " In every part of England where I have been (and I have been East, West, North and South within these two years) trade in general

---

[1] *Hist. MSS. Comm. Shrewsbury,* 94 (1763).          [2] *Ibid. Various,* vi. 287.
[3] *Aris's Birmingham Gazette,* 1766 (quoted in Ashton, *Iron and Steel in the Industrial Revolution,* 134).
[4] Cf. the statistics in Macpherson, *Annals of Commerce,* iii. 564, 585, 599, 614, 632, 651, 673.
[5] *Hist. MSS. Comm. Lonsdale,* 139.

is exceedingly decayed, and thousands of people are quite unemployed. Some I know to have perished for want of bread ; others I have seen creeping up and down like walking shadows. I except three or four manufacturing towns, which have suffered less than others. . . . Even where I was last, in the West Riding of Yorkshire, a tenant of Lord Dartmouth was telling me : ' Sir, our tradesmen are breaking all round me, so that I know not what the end will be '. Even in Leeds I had appointed to dine at a merchant's ; but before I came, the bailiffs were in possession of the house. Upon my saying : ' I thought Mr —— had been in good circumstances '—I was answered : ' He *was* so ; but the American War has ruined him ' '' [1].

Apart from the influence of wars and tariffs, the pheno- *The trade cycle.* menon of the trade cycle was already known. Defoe's graphic description has a familiar ring [2] : '' Upon some sudden accident in trade here comes a great unusual demand for goods, the merchants from abroad have sudden and unusual commissions, the call for goods this way or that way increases, this makes the factors send large orders into the country, and the price of goods always rises according to the demand. The country manufacturer looks out sharp, hires more looms, gets more spinners, gives more wages, and animated by the advanced price is not content to answer his new orders only, but he continues the excursion he had made into the country for spinners, etc., runs on to an extremity in quantity as far, or perhaps farther, than his stock will allow ; and in a word, gluts the market with the goods. The accident of trade which from abroad filled the merchant's commissions and the factor's orders being over, those demands are also over, and the trade returns to its usual channel ; but the manufacturer in the country who had run out to an unusual excess in his business, without regard to the circumstances of it, having not stopped his hand as his orders stopped, falls into the mire, his goods lie on hand, the poor which he called from the plough and the dairy to spin and weave are cast off again, and not finding

---

[1] *Hist. MSS. Comm. Dartmouth*, iii. 220.
[2] Defoe, *A Plan of the English Commerce* (ed. 1728), 257-258.

their way presently back to their old drudgery lie and starve for want of work, and then they cry out trade is decayed, the manufactures are lost, foreigners encroach upon us, the poor are starved, and the like ".

*Attitude of the State towards unemployment.* We may distinguish three periods in the attitude of the State towards the problem of unemployment. The first, embracing the Tudors and Early Stuarts, was one of active intervention ; the second, extending from the Civil War to the close of the nineteenth century, was marked by *laissez-faire* ; the third, the twentieth century, has witnessed the revival of the principle of intervention though in an altered form. The reason for State action in the first period, besides the fact that it carried on mediaeval gild traditions [1], is indicated in Burghley's remark that " by lack of vent tumults will follow in clothing counties " [2]. It was the fear of " what commonly followeth of idleness " [3] that prompted the Government of the day to pursue a policy which aimed above all things at stability, and discouraged economic change of any kind because it created social unrest [4]. The dangers of unemployment had been revealed in 1525 when Wolsey endeavoured to raise war taxes [5] :

" Upon these taxations,
The clothiers all, not able to maintain
The many to them longing, have put off
The spinsters, carders, fullers, weavers, who,
Unfit for other life, compell'd by hunger
And lack of other means, in desperate manner
Daring the event to the teeth, are all in uproar
And danger serves among them " [6].

At the same time there was present a genuine desire to safeguard ' the poor man's labour, his inheritance ' [7].

[1] *Supra*, vol. i. 347-348.
[2] *Hist. MSS. Comm. Salisbury*, ii. 251 (1579).
[3] *Ibid. Pepys*, 58 (1565).
[4] As was shown in its attitude towards sheep-farming, the migration of industry, the growth of capitalism, etc.
[5] Holinshed, *Chronicles* (ed. 1808), iii. 709.
[6] Shakespeare, *King Henry VIII*.
[7] Sir E. Sandys's phrase : *House of Commons Journals*, i. 527 (1621). On the motives influencing the Government, see also *infra*, p. 448. The
[*contd.*]

The methods of intervention were threefold. The first *Long en-*
took the form of an attempt to secure continuity of employ- *gagements.*
ment by insisting on long engagements. In the Middle Ages
it was usual to engage workmen for protracted periods, sometimes even for three or four years [1]. The principle received
legal recognition in the Statute of Apprentices (1563), which
provided that no person should be " taken into service . . . to
work for any less time or term than for one whole year " in
occupations which included agricultural labourers, textile
workers, shoemakers, cutlers, bakers, brewers, millers and
many others. A servant could not be dismissed nor leave
his employment before the end of his term, " unless it be
for some reasonable and sufficient cause to be allowed "
before a magistrate. The penalty imposed for a breach of
the law was forty shillings if a master broke the contract,
and imprisonment if a servant were the offender [2]. A decade
later it was said that " men of these occupations are, notwithstanding this Act, hired by the day, the week, the month
or other time less than a year . . . in most places the Statute
remaineth utterly unobserved as if there were no such law
at all " [3]. This statement was too sweeping if it included
agricultural labourers : the hiring of farm workers at the
annual fair or ' statute ' lasted into the nineteenth century [4].
An account of these ' statute hirings ' was given by a Yorkshire farmer, Henry Best, in 1641 : " About a fortnight or
ten days afore Martinmas, the chief constable of every
division sendeth abroad his precepts to all petty constables,
willing them to give notice to all masters and servants
within their several constableries how that he intendeth to
sit at such a place on such a day ", for the attendance of
" masters that want servants, and servants that want

---

recognition of labour as a source of national wealth (Furniss, *The Position
of the Laborer in a System of Nationalism*, 22) was doubtless an influential
factor.
    [1] *Supra*, vol. i. 336.
    [2] *Statutes*, iv. part i. 415-416. Annual engagements were required in
1561 by the justices of Buckinghamshire, *i.e.* prior to the Statute of
Apprentices : *Tudor Economic Documents* (ed. Tawney and Power), i.
336.
    [3] *Tudor Economic Documents* (ed. Tawney and Power), i. 360-362.
    [4] In some places the ' statute ' fair is held at the present day.

masters ".  Best relates that on one occasion he " heard a servant asked what he could do, who made this answer—

> ' I can sowe,
> I can mowe,
> And I can stacke,
> And I can doe,
> My master too,
> When my master turnes his backe ' " [1].

We get a glimpse of the working of the system under the Commonwealth in a draft order to the high constables of Hertfordshire.  It instructed them to appoint a ' statute ' for hiring servants, and to keep a register of all the servants hired there ; to give to all such servants a certificate showing with whom they are hired, for what wages, and where they dwell ; and to return a list of the names of the servants and of their masters, and their abodes, to the justices [2].  Sometimes it was expressly laid down that, except on ' extraordinary occasions ', servants were only to be hired at the ' set statute ' [3] :  thus the magistrates in Nottinghamshire ordered in 1724 that all hiring of servants should take place at the ' statutes ' [4].  Yet the practice was not universal : in Devonshire there was ' no fixed time or place of hiring ' farm servants when Marshall made his investigations in the middle of George III.'s reign [5].  In industrial occupations annual engagements were more difficult to enforce.  The best example of their survival is to be found among coalminers, who contracted in the Yearly Bond to give a year's service [6].  In the Yorkshire woollen industry it was not unknown, even at the end of the eighteenth century, to hire journeymen for twelve months [7] ; but where the work was done in the homes on a piece-wage basis, as among the West Country weavers, fixed terms of engagement were impossible.  There remained two alternatives—either the authorities must provide work for the unemployed ; or they must exert

---

[1] *Rural Economy in Yorkshire in 1641, being the Farming and Account Books of Henry Best* (ed. Robinson), 134-136.
[2] *Hertford County Records*, i. 116 (1656).      [3] *Ibid.*
[4] *Victoria County History, Nottinghamshire*, ii. 295.
[5] Marshall, *The Rural Economy of the West of England* (1796), i. 109.
[6] *Supra*, vol. ii. 124.  For unemployment in the coal-mining industry, see *infra*, Appendix, p. 525, No. 1.      [7] *Supra*, vol. ii. 36, 76-77.

pressure upon merchants to buy, and manufacturers to produce, even when trade was bad. The former alternative was part of the poor law system, and will be described in another chapter [1]. The latter can best be illustrated by reference to some notable examples taken from the years 1528, 1586, and 1622.

In 1528 the trade in the Netherlands was interrupted *The crisis* by the declaration of war. The clothiers were urged to keep *of 1528.* their workfolk in employment, but they declared that they could not hold out more than two or three weeks unless the merchants continued to buy as usual [2]. Wolsey summoned the merchants of London before him and thus addressed them : " Sirs, the King is informed that you use not yourselves like merchants, but like graziers and artificers ; for where the clothiers do daily bring cloths to your market for your ease, to their great cost, and there be ready to sell them, you of your wilfulness will not buy them as you have been accustomed to do. What manner of men be you ? I tell you that the King straitly commandeth you to buy their cloths as beforetime you have been accustomed to do, upon pain of his high displeasure " [3].

In the last quarter of the sixteenth century arose a more *The crisis* serious situation, which was made the occasion for a tentative *of 1586.* experiment in an ' open trade ' [4]. The political enmity between Elizabeth and Philip II. was detrimental to the commercial interests of England, since the Spanish monarch controlled or influenced the chief European markets for the sale of English cloth [5] ; and the seizure of Spanish treasure can scarcely have been adequate compensation for the losses sustained in trade [6]. At the end of 1586 the economic crisis came to a head. Burghley in a letter to the lord chancellor expressed apprehension that " this great matter of the lack of vent not only of cloths, which presently is the greatest, but of all other English commodities which are restrained

---

[1] *Infra*, p. 429.
[2] *Letters and Papers, Foreign and Domestic, of Henry VIII.*, vol. iv. part ii. 1868, 1881.
[3] Hall, *Chronicle* (ed. 1809), 745-746.
[4] A trade open to all merchants, instead of being confined to privileged companies.
[5] *State Papers Spanish*, 1580-1586, p. 651.    [6] *Supra*, p. 211.

from Spain, Portugal, Barbary, France, Flanders, Hamburg
and the States, cannot but in process of time work a great
change and dangerous issue to the people of the realm, who
heretofore in time of outward peace lived thereby, and without it must either perish for want or fall into violenc: " [1].
The West Country clothiers were driven to dismiss their
workpeople, though some kept the men at work to their own
loss [2]. The Privy Council, after holding an investigation,
charged the clothiers to resume their trade ; and it laid down
the principle—upon which it repeatedly insisted—that those
who in prosperous periods gained by their trade were not
at liberty to leave it off in periods of stress [3]. At the same
time, however, it enjoined the Merchant Adventurers to buy
" at such reasonable prices as they were accustomed ". The
Company gave an assurance that " there should be no cause
for the clothiers to leave their work unoccupied ", and undertook to raise a loan at " their common charge, with which
money they would buy up all such cloths weekly as the
particular merchants for lack of ready money should not
be able to buy " [4]. The promise was apparently unfulfilled
and the trade was therefore thrown open. The Queen concurred in Burghley's proposal to restore to the merchants of
the Steelyard their ' ancient liberty ' of buying cloth, and
native merchants who did not belong to the Company were
allowed to export cloth to Germany and the Low Countries [5].
Burghley claimed that his device for ' setting merchants
and clothiers at liberty ' was a success [6]. The Company, on
the other hand, asserted that " the malady was never a whit
the better " [7] ; and it met the attack on its monopoly by
suspending its trade altogether [8].

The industrial depression continued until the end of

---

[1] 1587 : Nicolas, *Memoirs of the Life and Times of Sir Christopher
Hatton* (1847), 470. Cf. also *Hist. MSS. Comm. Ancaster*, 91.

[2] *State Papers Domestic*, 1581–1590, p. 402. See also Rymer, *Foedera*,
xx. 627, for the exclusion of English cloth.

[3] *The Book of Orders* (1586), 14. See *infra*, p. 442, note 1.

[4] *Acts of the Privy Council*, 1586–1587, pp. 272-274.

[5] *State Papers Domestic*, 1581–1590, pp. 410-413 ; *Acts of the Privy
Council*, 1589–1590, pp. 217-218. Also see *supra*, vol. ii. 262.

[6] *State Papers Domestic*, 1581–1590, p. 413.

[7] Wheeler, *A Treatise of Commerce* (1601), 46, 56.

[8] *House of Commons Journals*, i. 220.

Elizabeth's reign. A letter from the Earl of Bath to the *Its long* Privy Council described the state of Devon in 1596 : " I *duration.* live here in a country full of poor people that depend most upon clothing ; but by reason of the present want of traffic, spinsters, weavers and all others belonging to the trades are grown to great poverty and like daily to decay. I hear much complaining of it, and it is feared that in short time it will turn into some inconvenience amongst us " [1]. The long duration of the depression has been attributed to the spirit of monopoly ; but this explanation overlooks the fact that, when the cloud lifted in the next reign, the Merchant Adventurers still retained their privileges. The cause was political rather than economic. The war with Spain closed important markets against us, exposed merchant vessels to the risk of capture at sea [2], increased the burden of taxation, and drained away the national resources in men, money and ships into unprofitable channels. In addition the last decade of the century included several years of dearth [3]. Accordingly it is not surprising that industry was unable to recover from its stagnation.

One of the most memorable depressions in the annals of *The crisis* the English textile industries began in 1620 [4], and lasted *of 1620–* four to five years [5]. The export trade declined by one- *1624.* third ; the price of wool fell ; clothiers, even those reputed the wealthiest, were brought to the verge of bankruptcy ; and unemployment was widespread [6]. In one Wiltshire town forty-four looms stood idle for half a year— " by which means eight hundred persons, twenty at the least for each loom in weaving, spinning and spooling, are now miserably distressed for want of employment " [7]. The distress was general throughout the kingdom : " The whole common-

---

[1] *Hist. MSS. Comm. Salisbury*, vi. 35.

[2] Scott, *Joint-Stock Companies*, i. 98.  [3] *Supra*, vol. ii. 400.

[4] *State Papers Domestic*, 1619–1623, p. 144 ; *Acts of the Privy Council*, 1619–1621, pp. 197, 206.

[5] It was debated in the Parliament of 1624 : *House of Commons Journals*, i. 752.

[6] *Ibid.* i. 752 ; *State Papers Domestic*, 1619–1623, pp. 149, 480. Mun stated that " we lost at the least half our clothing for foreign parts " : *England's Treasure by Forraign Trade* (1664), 18.

[7] *Hist. MSS. Comm. Various*, i. 94. Estimates of the number of persons to whom each loom gave employment are conflicting : see *supra*, vol. ii. 17 (and note 3), and *infra*, p. 306.

wealth suffereth ", said a royal edict [1]. Many thousands of spinners, weavers, fullers and cloth-workers [2] were affected, and disturbances seemed likely. " We much fear ", wrote the justices of Gloucestershire to the Privy Council, " that the peace hereof will be very shortly endangered notwithstanding all the vigilance we use or can use to the contrary ", since workmen " do wander, beg and steal, and are in case to starve as their faces (to our great griefs) do manifest " [3]. The unemployed went in groups to the houses of the rich, demanding food and money, and seized provisions in the market-place [4].

*General distress.* The Privy Council actively bestirred itself. It issued a circular letter to the justices of the clothing counties, enjoining them to call the clothiers together, and require the latter to keep their workfolk in employment under penalty of a summons before the Council. The clothiers were not to be allowed to dismiss their men ' at their pleasure ', for those who made profit when trade was good must be content to suffer loss when trade was bad [5]. The justices of Suffolk reported that they had summoned the clothiers who lived themselves in great want and misery, being ' much decayed in their estates ' on account of their losses due to merchants going bankrupt, the sale of their cloth at ' under-prices ', and the large quantity of cloth still lying upon their hands. In twenty out of two hundred townships in the county there was cloth unsold worth £39,282 ; in twelve alone the clothiers had lost £30,415 by bankruptcies ; and similar losses were experienced elsewhere [6]. The clothiers of Gloucestershire, pressed to employ their workpeople a month longer, consented to do so for a fortnight. They stated that there were 1500 looms in the county, each employing sixteen hands who received little more than a shilling a week apiece,

---

[1] Rymer, *Foedera*, xvii. 411.
[2] The parliamentary committee for trade reported in 1624 that 12,000 cloth-workers were out of work : *House of Commons Journals*, i. 711.
[3] *The Wiltshire Archæological and Natural History Magazine*, xxii. 80.
[4] *State Papers Domestic*, 1619–1623, p. 346.
[5] *Ibid.* 343 (1622) ; *Hist. MSS. Comm. Rye*, 439.
[6] *State Papers Domestic*, 1619–1623, p. 362 (1622) ; *Hist. MSS. Comm. Rye*, 439-440.

"which is much too little " [1]. In some cases the justices bore testimony that the employers recognized their responsibilities. " The clothiers here do yet continue to keep their poor in work as in former times they have done, although it hath been to their great losses ; and so they are contented to do as long as they may occupy their trade without undoing of themselves " [2]. Money was borrowed to pay wages [3] ; and it was recorded that " one Will Bennett, a very ancient and good clothier, doth offer to live by brown bread and water rather than his great number of poor people should want work, if he had means to keep them in work " [4]. Other measures were taken to deal with the situation. Merchants were ordered to buy up as much cloth as possible, and wool dealers to sell wool at moderate prices ; clothiers were protected from the importunity of their creditors ; the justices were instructed to raise a fund, where necessary, to put the unemployed on work although the impoverishment of the country made this difficult [5]. Finally in 1622 a commission, composed of twelve persons, was set up to ascertain the causes of and remedies for the decay of trade ; and two representatives of the clothiers of each ' clothing ' county were summoned to London to give evidence before it [6].

This commission, the first of its kind to make a detailed *Report of a* investigation of the causes of unemployment, held numerous *royal com-* *mission on* conferences with clothiers, drapers, merchants, customs *unemploy-* officials and landowners. After " many days spent in this *ment.* weighty service ", it drew up a comprehensive report [7] reflecting the diversity of opinions expressed by the different interests consulted. The reasons assigned for the stagnation of trade were as follows : (1) " The making of cloth and other draperies in foreign parts in more abundance than in former

---

[1] *State Papers Domestic*, 1619–1623, p. 358 (1622).
[2] Leonard, *The Early History of English Poor Relief*, 115.
[3] *Victoria County History, Oxfordshire*, ii. 196.
[4] *Ibid. Gloucestershire*, ii. 159.
[5] *State Papers Domestic*, 1619–1623, pp. 343, 358, 471.
[6] *Ibid.* 382, 410, 452 ; Rymer, *Foedera*, xvii. 411. A rate was levied on the clothiers to discharge the expenses of their representatives : *Quarter Sessions Records for the County of Somerset*, i. 316, 321.
[7] British Museum : Stowe MSS. 554, f. 45.

times, being thereunto chiefly enabled by the wools and other materials transported from the kingdoms of England, Scotland and Ireland, we conceive to be the chiefest cause that less quantity of ours are vented there ". (2) " The false and deceitful making, dyeing and dressing of our cloth and stuffs, which disgraceth it in foreign parts". (This was attributed by the drapers to the corruption or remissness of the aulnagers, the sale of cloth privately instead of in public markets, and the intrusion of ' inexperienced persons ' into the industry [1].) (3) " The heavy burthen upon our cloth whereby it is made so dear to the buyer, that those that were wont to furnish themselves therewith in foreign parts either buy cloth in other countries, or clothe themselves in a cheaper manner than our cloth can be afforded " [2]. (4) " The clothiers apprehend that staplers, jobbers and brokers of wool are also a cause . . . by deceitful mingling [of wool], and often selling it from hand to hand before it comes to the clothiers " [3]. (5) " The present state of the times by reason of the wars in Germany is conceived by many to be some present impediment to the vent of our cloth, partly by the interruption of passages, partly for want of money occasioned by foraging of the countries ". (6) " The policies of the Merchant Adventurers which bring upon themselves suspicion of combination in trading, and the smallness of their number which do now usually buy and vent cloth, and the like policies of other merchants ". (The clothiers attached particular responsibility for the ' deadness of trade ' to the close corporations of merchants, " which limit the times, persons, numbers and prices to be observed in buying cloths " [4].) (7) " The scarcity of coin at home and the baseness of foreign coins compared unto ours ". (8) " The

[1] *State Papers Domestic*, 1619–1623, pp. 400–401. For the aulnagers, see *infra*, p. 328.

[2] The burden was threefold—customs duties, charges levied by the trading companies, and foreign tariffs. Owing to these various dues an English cloth was said to cost in Holland £4 : 13 (and in the Spanish Low Countries £5 : 1) more than a Dutch cloth : Stowe MSS. 354, f. 65. Cf. also *House of Commons Journals*, i. 752, 780–781 ; and *supra*, p. 295, note 4.

[3] Mun alludes to the high price of wool, which made cloth ' exceeding dear ' : *England's Treasure by Forraign Trade* (1664), 18.

[4] *Hist. MSS. Comm. Rye*, 440 ; Stowe MSS. 354, f. 65 ; *State Papers Domestic*, 1619–1623, pp. 358, 362.

want of means of return for our merchants especially out
of the Eastland countries, which discourage them to carry
out cloth thither because they can neither sell for ready
money nor barter for vendible commodities " [1]. (9) " The
too little use of wearing cloth at home, and the too much
of silks and foreign stuffs which over-balance our trade ".
The report omits mention of the most important cause of
the crisis—the disastrous interference of James I. with the
cloth industry, of which an account will be given below [2].

The remedies proposed by the commission covered a *Remedies*
range not less comprehensive than its survey of the causes. *proposed*
*by the com-*
They included—(1) an embargo on the export of wool ; *mission.*
(2) the revision of the laws relating to the manufacture of
cloth, in order " that those that are fit for the present times
may be quickened " ; (3) the establishment of a corporation
in every county, composed of " the most able and sufficient
men of the same, whereby they may be authorized to look
fully to the true making, dyeing and dressing of cloth and
stuff in every shire " ; (4) the prevention of the use of ' false
dyeing stuff ', and that " dyeing stuffs be not made dear
by patentees . . . else the dyed cloth will continue dear" ;
(5) the restraint of ' wool jobbers ' ; (6) the compulsory
wearing of native cloth ; (7) the abolition of the import
duties on English cloth levied abroad, and of the ' private
impositions ' exacted by the Merchant Adventurers at home,
"to the endearing of the cloth exported"; (8) the encouragement of the fisheries and the employment of English shipping;
(9) the reform of the trading companies ; (10) the confinement of money within the country and the regulation of
the currency ; (11) and lastly, " the most important remedy
(as we conceive) is to provide against the overbalance of
trade ".

These various proposals have been considered in their *Their sig-*
appropriate place: their interest for us here lies in the con- *nificance.*
temporary analysis presented of a phenomenon, destined to
become a recurring feature of England's industrial develop-

---

[1] Cf. *supra*, p. 135.
[2] *Infra*, pp. 378-83, 525 (No. 2). Contrast Shaw, *The History of Currency*
(2nd ed.), 144 : " The crisis was purely a monetary or currency crisis ".

ment[1]. The catastrophe of a trade depression on a national scale was sufficiently new to excite the gravest apprehensions, which are reflected in the wide scope of the suggested remedies. Two points, however, may be noticed in this place. Money stringency, which was treated not as a symptom, but as a cause, was the most widely accepted explanation of the economic crisis : thus early was manifested the belief in the influence of currency phenomena on the cycle of trade. Again, the interruption of trade was attributed in part to the war in Germany ; and to whatever extent the outbreak of the Thirty Years' War was responsible for a commercial crisis in this country, it was an indication that the economic life of England was now vitally affected by disturbances in the European system. It is revealing, in this connexion, to find the opinion expressed by the commission that " the wasting of the several parts of those countries by the wars, the consumption of their stock, disturbance of their trade, are profitable means to open the way for our better vent when it shall please God to send peace " [2]. Only after repeated experiences has the lesson been learnt that a Continent impoverished by war is not the best customer for a nation that lives by its trade. Out of the commission's report emerged a noteworthy result in the creation of a standing Committee on Trade (1622), appointed to investigate the methods of carrying out the commission's proposals, and generally to find means " to advance and quicken trade, raise again the native commodities of our kingdom, encourage traders, clothiers and the wool growers and manufacturers, or to remove the impediments or discouragements thereof " [3].

The above incidents exhibit in a conspicuous light the

[1] For other views on the decay of trade, see Misselden, *Free Trade* (1622), 28, 41, 50-52 ; Malynes, *The Maintenance of Free Trade* (1622), 104 ; *Hist. MSS. Comm. Cowper*, i. 126.
[2] Stowe MSS. 554, f. 45.
[3] Rymer, *Foedera*, xvii. 410 *seq.* The appointment of committees or councils of trade to advise the Government in economic matters was an indication of the growing importance of industry and commerce. On their history, see Andrews, *British Committees, Commissions, and Councils of Trade and Plantations, 1622–1675* ; Bieber, *The Lords of Trade and Plantations, 1675–1696* ; Basye, *The Lords Commissioners of Trade and Plantations, 1748–1782* ; Andrews, *The Colonial Period of American History*, iv chapter ix. Also see *supra*, p. 14, note 3.

methods of authoritarian intervention in times of industrial *Other trade* depression, nor do they stand alone. Thus in 1564 the *depressions.* clothiers of Reading and Newbury were warned by the Privy Council not to abandon their trade, throwing their men out of work [1] ; and in 1607 the weavers in Wiltshire solicited the aid of the local magistrates " touching certain grievances conceived to be offered by the clothiers in putting some of them from work, whereby they are left without means to relieve them and their families " [2]. The period 1629–1631 was one of falling trade, aggravated by famine. The justices of Essex wrote to the Council that the distress among the manufacturing population in certain areas was likely to affect above thirty thousand persons ; while in the neighbouring county of Suffolk the clothiers informed the judges that they were unable to continue their trade, as their cloth was not being bought by the Levant and Russia Companies. Pursuing its usual tactics, the Council again instructed the justices of the peace to charge the clothiers " that have in former times gained by that trade, not now in this time of dearth to leave off trade whereby the poor may be set on work " [3]. Another industrial depression occurred a few years later. " Great parts of the estates of sundry persons of this country ", it was reported from the West of England, " do now lie dead in London in woollen manufactures " [4]. In Essex the baymakers, at the request of the justices, raised loans to keep their trade going, but it was said that "many of them who were work-masters are become workmen " [5]. A commission, which was appointed to inquire into the state of the cloth trade (1638) [6], represented the causes of decay to be the transportation of wool, the use of machinery [7], frauds in manufacture, and the high import duties on English cloth levied in foreign countries. The fiscal exactions of the

[1] *State Papers Domestic*, 1547–1580, p. 243.
[2] *The Wiltshire Archæological and Natural History Magazine*, xxii. 223.
[3] *State Papers Domestic*, 1628–1629, p. 521 ; 1629–1631, pp. 8, 403, 481 ; 1631–1633, p. 14. *Orders for the preventing and remedying of the Dearth of Grain* (1630), 15.
[4] *State Papers Domestic*, 1639, p. 85 ; *Hist. MSS. Comm. Exeter*, 80.
[5] *State Papers Domestic*, 1637, p. 64.
[6] *Hist. MSS. Comm. Portland*, viii. 2-3. (The report is dated 1640.)
[7] *Supra*, p. 51.

Crown are not mentioned, but it was perhaps significant of the waning power of the monarchy that the authorities in one industrial centre, Exeter, did not hesitate to speak out freely : " The great sums of money that of late years have been raised and paid out of this country have much emptied the stores of the meaner sort of people ", whose impoverishment had the effect of reducing the demand for foreign commodities " imported from beyond the seas in return for English merchandise sent thither "[1]. In addition the political turmoil was beginning to make itself felt. " Trading both at home and abroad declineth very fast ", it was reported in 1639 ; and two years later a petition to the House of Commons, complaining of the decay of trade, received several thousand signatures [2]. But the situation had now passed beyond the control of monarchy and parliament alike.

*Economic significance of the Civil War.* We have noticed the more important disturbances which affected the course of English economic development, arising from foreign wars, tariffs and errors of statesmanship [3]. The greatest disturbance of all was due to the Civil War, which left permanent traces upon the economic system. The dislocation of trade, though serious enough while it lasted, was transient [4]. When Cromwell turned out the Long Parliament, " the kingdom was arrived at the highest pitch of trade, wealth and honour that it in any age ever yet knew. The trade appeared by the great sums offered then for the customs and excise, nine hundred thousand pounds a year being refused. The riches of the nation showed itself in the high value that land and all our native commodities bore, which are the certain marks of opulency " [5] ; and the

---

[1] *State Papers Domestic*, 1639, pp. 85-86. Cf. *supra*, p. 17, note 2.

[2] *Hist. MSS. Comm. Cowper*, ii. 226, 278, 280.

[3] The reference is to James I.'s interference with the cloth industry : *supra*, p. 309, and *infra*, p. 378.

[4] But the ' destruction of the clothing trade ' at Reading was attributed to the Civil War : Coates, *The History and Antiquities of Reading* (1802), 457 ; *Britannia Languens* (1680), 163. Pontefract attributed to the Civil War the loss of a ' very great ' cloth trade : *House of Commons Journals*, xii. 96.

[5] *The World's Mistake in Oliver Cromwell* (1668) in *Harleian Miscellany* (ed. Malham), vii. 349.

A Venetian ambassador—" the first ambassador of your Serenity who has been to London since the abolition of the royal authority "—spoke in

[contd.]

legal rate of interest was reduced to 6 per cent. [1]. Nevertheless the dissolution of the bonds which held industrial society
together had a profound influence. A violent shock was
given to institutions which had controlled and regulated the
economic system, and while the process of change had already
begun, it was enormously accelerated by the relaxation of
the traditional checks and restraints. For a decade the
central administration was unable to exercise any effective
control over economic affairs : for a decade the economic
functions of the local administration were largely in abeyance [2]. When a settled government was at length established, it was unable to revive in their fullness the authoritarian traditions which had enabled Elizabeth and the Early
Stuarts to destroy or penalize enclosures ; to bring pressure
to bear on employers ; to require local authorities to provide
work for the poor; to insist on technical training for artisans;
to regulate wages ; to place individuals or corporations in
control over a branch of industry ; and in other ways to
exert influence on the economic life of the community. After
the Restoration the movement towards *laissez-faire* in industry acquired increasing momentum [3] until the ' Industrial Revolution ' necessitated a return, in an altered form,
to the principle of State intervention.

The causes of the Civil War were primarily religious and
constitutional, but the economic factor was not absent.
The political self-assertion of the middle classes, born of

---

1656 of " the copious and flourishing trade of London. . . . Ships frequent
it in such numbers that on my arrival more than 2000 were counted up
and down the famous River Thames ". He added : " It is true that since
the change of government the splendour and greatness of London have
suffered a considerable change. The throng of the most illustrious nobility
which made it brilliant, being now persecuted and depressed, is scattered
about the country. The exquisite Court, once the most sumptuous and
joyous in the world, frequented by noble ladies and abounding in the most
refined entertainment, is now changed for the perpetual marching and
countermarching of troops, the ceaseless noise of drums and trumpets, and
numerous companies of officers and soldiers at their various posts " :
*State Papers Venetian*, 1655–1656, pp. 299, 308.

A letter written in 1654 remarked : " Who had seen it [London] in
the King's time, and looked upon it now, would discern a great change in
it " : Thurloe, *State Papers* (1742), ii. 670.

[1] *Supra*, p. 225.                    [2] Cf. *Hist. MSS. Comm. Various*, i. 110.
[3] On the growth of industrial freedom in England, see *supra*, vol. ii.
Introduction, pp. cxv-cxxviii, cxxxi, cxxxv-cxxxvi.

a sense of economic power, was nourished and inflamed by economic grievances. In 1640 a petition was laid before the municipal authorities at Newcastle in the name of the merchants of the town, including the warden of the Merchant Adventurers, urging that the two burgesses chosen by the corporation for the ensuing Parliament should receive instructions for their guidance [1]; and at the same time an address was presented to the burgesses themselves. The list of instructions contained, first, a demand for the maintenance of ' the orthodox faith of our Church ', but this was not part of the original draft and was apparently inserted *pro forma*. The instructions were mainly concerned with the economic grievances which had alienated the trading classes from the monarchy. "What burdens the entrenching upon the freedom of the subjects by monopolies of soap, salt, coal, tobacco, starch and many other such like are palpable, together with the new great impost on wine, lead and all other commodities ", as well as " the grievances of butlerage, increase of custom-house fees, pretermitted dues and all other impositions set down in the book of rates above the subsidy of tunnage and poundage. We also groan all heavily under the taxes and assessments for ship-money and other intolerable burdens. . . . All these are so felt by the merchants and others that our estates are squeezed from us, and we now become only to have the name to be rich but are in truth miserably poor. And lastly, this particular body suffers in regard, within the walls and without, strangers are suffered to injure both merchants and tradesmen in their privileges " [2].

In addition to the patents of monopoly [3] and the imposition of taxes, which excited widespread resentment, two more recent measures (1640) adopted by Charles I. to obtain money must be noticed. Failing to raise a loan in the City at 8 per cent. [4], he pressed the East India Company to sell

---

[1] The practice of giving instructions to M.P.'s was common in the seventeenth century : see Lipson, "The Elections to the Exclusion Parliaments" in *The English Historical Review*, xxviii. 68-69. Also *supra,* vol. ii. 403.

[2] *State Papers Domestic*, 1639–1640, pp. 600-604.

[3] For the patents of monopoly, see *infra*, pp. 352 *seq.*

[4] *State Papers Domestic*, 1640, p. 31.

him its stock of pepper at 2s. 1d. per lb. to be paid for over *Aliena-* a period of two years, and then threw the pepper on the *tion of the moneyed* market at 1s. 8d. per lb. ' ready money '[1], while he was *classes.* unable to meet the instalments owing to the Company as they fell due[2]. More important was the seizure of the bullion brought by merchants and goldsmiths to the Mint to be coined. It amounted to over £100,000 ; and although the King undertook to pay 8 per cent. interest, his action " put the merchants into great disorder " since their credit would be ruined if they failed to meet their obligations here and abroad. Eventually a compromise was reached whereby the King retained £40,000 as a loan, but henceforth native and foreign merchants forbore to deposit bullion in the Mint, which until then was " accounted the safest place and surest staple in these parts of the world "[3]. The antagonism of the moneyed classes was fatal to Charles I.'s prospects of victory. " What means ", the writer of a letter asked in 1642, " has he to keep the machine going, while the Parliament holds all the money of the kingdom ? "[4] There are other indications that the alignment of parties reflected conflicting economic interests [4a]—as, for example, when a landlord threw in his allegiance with the King, and his tenants enlisted in the parliamentary forces[5].

The Civil War inflicted considerable injury upon the community. There was much wanton destruction of property : iron works were demolished, sheep slaughtered, towns burnt, the country plundered and ' harrowed '[6]. Transport was rendered insecure whether by land or sea :

[1] He bought the pepper for £63,283 : 11 : 1 and sold it for £50,626 . 17 : 1. This involved an apparent loss of £12,656: 14s., but as the Company was not to be paid immediately the King saved the interest (8 per cent.), so the net loss was calculated at £6581 : 0 : 10 : *State Papers Domestic*, 1640–41, p. 522.

[2] *The Court Minutes of the East India Company*, 1640–1643, pp. xii-xiii.

[3] The amount seized is variously given as (1) about £100,000, (2) £110,000, and (3) £130,000 : *State Papers Domestic*, 1640, pp. 451, 544 ; 1640–1641, p. 524. The compulsory loan is given as £40,000 in Ruding, *Annals of the Coinage* (ed. 1840), i. 392.

[4] *Hist. MSS. Comm. Franciscan*, 162, 232.

[4a] See *supra*, vol. ii. Introduction, p. cxxiii.

[5] *Hist. MSS. Comm. Beaufort*, 551.

[6] *Ibid. Various*, i. 115 ; *ibid. Portland*, i. 465, 713 ; Nicholls, *Iron Making in the Forest of Dean*, 41. For the condition of England during the Civil War, see James, *Social Problems and Policy during the Puritan Revolution*, 35 *seq.* ; Hine, *The History of Hitchin*, i. 192 *seq.* ; Coate, *Cornwall in the Great Civil War and Interregnum*, 223.

clothiers were discouraged from sending their cloth to market since it was liable, even under convoy, to be seized by the enemy [1]. Dread of the King's men-of-war deterred fishermen from voyaging to the North Sea ' to take fish ', or to Yarmouth ' to take herrings ' [2]. Merchants were ruined by the confiscation of their ships and goods in foreign parts [3]. "We have lost 1800 ships and their ladings ", they complained under the Protectorate, " chiefly caused by the subjects of this commonwealth who have gone to the enemy, taken up commissions, and assisted them like parricides " [4]. The money-market was disorganized, not only by the demands made upon it by the belligerents, but also by the withdrawal of foreign investments. Investors abroad, who were " wont to furnish great sums of money at interest ", called in their loans, and their example was followed by English investors who for security transferred a large part of their resources to the Continent [5]. This caused the foreign exchanges to move against England at a time when munitions had to be bought abroad. It also meant that merchants were unable to obtain credit ; and, to add to their difficulties, the payment of money due to them in Scotland and Ireland was suspended, while in England country tradesmen could not discharge the debts they owed them [6]. The manufacturers, in their turn, suffered from the decay of trade. They could not procure payment from their debtors, who sheltered themselves behind the plea that this was ' no time to pay money ' [7]. In 1643 the Gloucestershire clothiers declared that they were ' in a most distressed condition '. Some were completely ruined ; others had the residue of their estates in the hands of London merchants, " without which we cannot keep our workfolks in work " ; and all had lost their credit, because they were severed from their principal market

---

[1] Corbet, *An Historical Relation of the Military Government of Gloucester* (1645) in *Bibliotheca Gloucestrensis* (ed. Washbourn), i. 137-138. *Hist. MSS. Comm.* vi. 186.

[2] *Hist. MSS. Comm. Rye*, 215. The fishing trade at Newfoundland was also hindered : *ibid.* vi. 107.

[3] *State Papers Domestic*, 1650, p. 178.

[4] *Ibid.* 1657–1658, p. 245.

[5] *Ibid.* 1640–1641, p. 524 ; 1650, p. 179.

[6] *Ibid.* 1640–1641, p. 524.    [7] *Hist. MSS. Comm.* iv. 62.

and could not dispose of their cloth [1]. Even before the actual clash of arms, the sense of insecurity and uncertainty—the ' fears and distractions ' of the time—had resulted in a ' general decay of trade '. A portent of the future was the petition presented ' in the name of thousands of poor people in and about the city of London ', which pleaded that " they wanted bread ; they must not starve ". A conference of the two Houses was held, and Hollis warned it that " this was but the beginning of evils—like a small cloud which, if it be not prevented, will soon cover the sky " [2]. Another petition from clothiers in Suffolk and Essex stated that the ' fears ' which oppressed London, " in whom the breath of our trade and livelihood consisteth, have so blasted their hopes that the merchants forbear exportation, our cloths for the most part for the space of these eighteen months remain upon our hands, our stocks lying dead therein, and we can maintain our trading no longer. The cries for food of many thousands of poor, who depend on this trade, do continually press us " [3]. As a result the emigration of capital, already mentioned, had its sequel in the emigration of natives and aliens destitute of work or ' fearing the issue of the sad distractions ' [4]. More important still, the difficulties experienced by some of the trading companies, in supplying their oversea markets, afforded the Dutch an opportunity for entrenching themselves more firmly in the carrying trade of the world [5] ; and the fresh

[1] *A Petition presented unto His Majestie. . . . By High Sheriffe of the County of Gloucester* (1643), 1-2. In 1645 merchants spoke of the ' deadness of trade ': *House of Commons Journals*, iv. 171. In 1659 *The Declaration of Thomas Lord Fairfax and the rest of . . . York* deplored the ' ruin of the clothing trade of this county '. During the siege of Colchester the bay-makers were allowed to hold a market outside the town : *Hist. MSS. Comm. Buckinghamshire*, 285 (1648).

[2] 1642 : *House of Lords Journals*, iv. 559, 581.

[3] *The Humble Petition of the Clothiers . . . of Suffolk and . . . Essex* (1642).

[4] *House of Commons Journals*, iii. 238 (1643) ; *State Papers Domestic*, 1650, pp. 178-179.

[5] *State Papers Domestic*, 1650, p. 178. See also *supra*, pp. 129, 173 ; *infra*, p. 526 (No. 1).

" Artisans and substantial persons are daily seeking refuge in these parts [*sc.* Holland] from England, bringing population, skill and wealth to the country. . . . The war of England increases their population, their business and their possessions " : *State Papers Venetian*, 1643-1647, pp. 36, 43 (' Advices from the Hague ', 1643). The Venetian Secretary in England wrote—" Those people are not losing their opportunities of gain. They
[*contd.*]

jealousies which this provoked, culminating in the Navigation Acts of 1651 and 1660, and in the wars with Holland, must be counted among the consequences of the Great Rebellion. When the Civil War was ended, the labour market was flooded with disbanded soldiers, who found themselves without employment. As apprentices took up arms, so their masters received other apprentices in their stead : " and now many of the first being returned again hath increased the number exceedingly " [1].

*Economic legacies of the Civil War.*    The permanent economic legacies of the Civil War, as distinct from its immediate effects, included the reform of taxation—the abolition of feudal incidents, the adoption of the excise, and the new form of land tax [2] ; the stimulus given to agricultural improvements [3] ; the relaxation of industrial restraints [4] ; and the increased parochialism in the methods of poor relief [5]. These are considered elsewhere : but one change must be noticed here. The Civil War brought to an end the system under which employers were required by the State to keep their men at work in times of industrial depression. The attempt to secure continuity of employment was abandoned. The right of the employer to expand or contract his business freely according to the market for his goods, to take on men when trade was brisk and to dismiss them when trade was dull, was no longer questioned by the State. Instead the machinery of the poor law was used to relieve the distress created by unemployment. The fact that the workers could no longer appeal with any assurance of success to the magistrates, to protect them against dismissal, threw them upon their own resources. They began to form benefit clubs, and in doing so forged one of the links in the chain of trade unionism [6].

---

have two principal strokes in mind, one to gain the control of the fisheries and of the sea, to the very great prejudice of this Kingdom at a time when the King is unable to prevent it, and Parliament will not disoblige them for its own ends " : *State Papers Venetian*, 1643–1647, p. 38 (1643).

[1] *Abbreviate of the Weavers' Business* (1648), 7.
[2] *Supra*, pp. 141, 145.          [3] *Supra*, vol. ii. 373.
[4] *Supra*, p. 286 ; and *infra*, p. 324.
[5] *Infra*, p. 454.          [6] *Infra*, pp. 386 *seq.*

(v)

## The Standardization of Industry

The economic activities of the State were not confined to *State control of industrial processes.* regulating the conditions of labour : they also embraced the sphere of production by prescribing the processes of manufacture. The minutest rules were framed respecting the nature of the materials, the use of mechanical appliances, and the form of the finished product. Yet the very multitude of laws with which the statute-book was burdened served, in the absence of an efficient administrative machinery, to defeat its own purpose. " There are now many laws in force concerning the making of cloth ", the Government confessed in 1622, " which for their number and contradiction do perplex and entangle the makers of cloth, and make it hard to be discerned what the law is in many particulars " [1]. An abstract published in 1792 of ' laws relating to the growers of wool and to the manufacturers of, and dealers in, all sorts of woollen commodities ', enumerated the titles of three hundred and eleven laws then on the statute-book [2]. " It were better ", said Misselden, " to have fewer laws with better execution " [3].

A later age, as we shall see [4], condemned State control *A system of regulation justified.* of industry on the ground that it hampered individual enterprise. Much of the criticism was just, since the community had by then grown ripe for a larger measure of industrial freedom and for greater elasticity in the working of the economic machine. We must not, however, infer that in earlier centuries the individual could have been safely left, in the conduct of his business affairs, to the promptings of enlightened self-interest and the conviction that honesty was the best policy. Even when we have liberally discounted the preambles to Acts of Parliament, and the obsession of merchants that every trade depression was due to the iniquities of manufacturers, there remain sufficient

---

[1] Rymer, *Foedera*, xvii. 412 ; Stowe MSS. 554, f. 45.
[2] Bischoff, *History of the Woollen and Worsted Manufactures*, i. 6.
[3] Misselden, *The Circle of Commerce* (1623), 136.
[4] *Infra*, p. 325.

indications that the state of the industry justified a system
of regulation, though not necessarily the particular forms
which it assumed. One indication was the practice abroad
of ' taring ', that is, making abatements in the price for
defects in the cloth bought from English merchants [1]. Another was the protests made by foreign Governments—the
Estates of Holland in 1589 complained of ' great defects and
frauds ' ; the French King in 1601 confiscated faulty English
cloth ; the Senate of Hamburg in 1649 addressed a remonstrance to the Council of State [2]. These protests give
substance to the contention that the ' ancient estimation '
abroad of English cloth, and therefore its sale, suffered in
consequence of ' ill and deceitful making ' [3]. Misselden,
an official of the Merchant Adventurers, wrote in 1632 to the
secretary of state : " Our English cloth grows more and more
in disgrace, and causeth the Dutch to go on with more
courage in their making of cloth " [4]. A decade later a committee of the House of Commons reported that " the greatest
reason for the not venting of [Suffolk] cloths was that, in
fourteen or fifteen thousand cloths that they made yearly,
nine or ten thousand of them were falsely made " [5]. A
memorandum dated 1651, entitled ' Reasons for reforming
the inland trade under certain supervision ', exhibits the
standpoint of the age. It represented that " the generality
of English exports are bad " owing to the malpractices of the
makers, upon whose shoulders it placed the responsibility
for " the deadness of trade and want of employment "—a
matter of vital concern to a nation of which two-thirds
depended upon manufactures of one kind or another [6]. " In
one port of Spain alone, within these few years, we used to
vent twelve thousand pieces of says, serges and such like
woollen stuff, but now scarcely two thousand, and so on in

---

[1] State Papers Domestic, 1629–1631, p. 446. Also supra, vol. ii. 236.
[2] Acts of the Privy Council, 1589–1590, p. 288 ; 1600–1601, p. 388.
State Papers Domestic, 1649–1650, p. 270.
[3] Rymer, Foedera, xvii. 412.
[4] Hist. MSS. Comm. Cowper, i. 465. Similarly : Sir Thomas Roe's
Speech (1641) in Harleian Miscellany (ed. Malham), iv. 459.
[5] House of Commons Journals, ii. 528.
[6] The estimate doubtless includes the producers of wool and other raw
materials, and those who handled the commodities at every stage.

other parts, the Dutch having taken up a truer way of making them ". The writer concluded that the interests of our trade abroad demanded the regulation of our industries at home, because foreign nations " cannot be obliged to traffic with our people if we will cozen them ; nor can we expect a currency of price in other countries for our manufactures if they be not of any certain goodness " [1]. While there thus appeared a solid basis for the complaints made against the manufacturers, the policy of industrial supervision also harmonized with the tradition that economic affairs should be ' orderly governed '.

The branch of industry chiefly affected by national *A standard* regulation was the woollen manufacture, though every *of quality.* branch was in some degree brought under control [2]. An intricate network of rules was devised, which was intended to standardize the making of cloth, that is, to establish a uniform standard of quality and dimensions. In regard to quality it was forbidden to mingle different kinds of wool, or ' yarns of divers spinnings ', in the same cloth ; or to employ other fraudulent methods of manufacture .[3] The preamble to the Act of 1552 described how clothiers " study rather to make many than to make good cloths " ; and " instead of substantial making of cloth do practise sleight and slender making—some by mingling of yarns of divers spinnings in one cloth ; some by mingling fell wool and lamb's wool, or either of them, with fleece wool ; some by putting too little stuff ; some by taking them out of the mill before they be full thicked ; some by overstretching them upon the tenter and then stopping with flocks such breaks as shall be made by means thereof ; finally, by using so many subtle sleights and untruths as when the cloths so made be put in the water to try them, they rise out of the same neither in length nor

---

[1] *State Papers Domestic*, 1651–1652, p. 88. The writer was possibly the author of a scheme ' to settle a government in our manufactures ', which was considered by a commission of thirty London merchants shortly before the Civil War : *Hist. MSS. Comm. Portland*, i. 405-406.

[2] *E.g.* Leather: *Statutes*, iv. part i., 368-369 (1559), 429 (1563) ; iv. part ii. 1039 (1604) ; vii. 239-240 (1697). Silver and gold thread : *ibid.* vii. 420 (1698). Honey and wax : *ibid.* iv. part i. 670 (1581). There were also ' surveyors ' of coal, iron and lead.

[3] *Ibid.* iv. part i. 136 (1552) ; iv. part ii. 975 (1601).

breadth as they ought to do " [1]. In spite of a series of repressive enactments, Parliament did not succeed in destroying the evils which it lamented. They still flourished in the seventeenth century when John May, an aulnager's deputy, enumerated in detail the deceits practised in the woollen industry in his day—the mixing of various sorts of wool, which in his opinion made the cloth uneven ; and the frauds of weavers, fullers, dyers and cloth-finishers, such as using a coarser yarn for the middle than the ends of the cloth, " which is so far as commonly the merchant or buyer looks into them " [2].

*Statutory dimensions.*     The system of statutory dimensions was dictated partly by the desire to safeguard the interests of the purchaser, but it was also intended to prevent defrauding of the customs by exporting cloth of excessive length [3]. Inaugurated as early as the twelfth century, it was in existence as late as the eighteenth century [4]. In practice, however, the ' assize of cloth ' was largely a dead letter. Even in the sixteenth century the Government had found it difficult to enforce the law. In 1537 the lord chancellor was warned by the clothiers that if they were compelled to make cloth according to the assize, they must forbear cloth-making because it was impossible to keep the breadth of the cloth limited as the Act required, nor could the weavers afford to provide the necessary ' lomes and slees '. In reply he " bade them take heed and beware, for . . . if by obstinacy or wilfulness they left their cloth-making, any murmur or sedition among the people for lack of work would be laid to their charge. To this they said obediently they would do what they could ". Nevertheless it was considered expedient to suspend the operation of the Act [5]. The lord mayor of

---

[1] *Statutes*, iv. part i. 136.

[2] May, *A Declaration of the Estate of Clothing* (1613), 24 *seq.* For similar accounts, see Leake (1577) in *Tudor Economic Documents* (ed. Tawney and Power), iii. 210 *seq.* ; and W. S., Gent., *The Golden Fleece* (1656).

[3] *Statutes*, iv. part i. 601 (1572).

[4] *Ibid.* iv. part i. 724 (1585) ; iv. part ii. 1137 (1607) ; ix. 82 (1709). For mediaeval legislation, see *supra*, vol. i. 446, 462. The sizes varied according to the nature of the cloth (whether ' broad ', or ' narrow ', or ' kersies ', etc.), and the period.

[5] *Letters and Papers, Foreign and Domestic, of Henry VIII.*, xii. part ii. 265, 304.

London in 1631 made a test examination of thirty-nine cloths which were on sale at Blackwell Hall, and found that only eight conformed to the legal dimensions [1]. Nor is this surprising, since the manufacturers were clearly bound to observe the tastes and fashions of their oversea markets. They also had to observe the laws of the country with which they traded, and these might conflict with English laws; for instance, an edict of the Polish Parliament enjoined cloth to be made of sizes which did not correspond with the official standard in England [2].

Insuperable difficulties also attended the effort to pro- *Over-stretching of cloth.* hibit the 'over-stretching' of cloth. In order to stamp out the practice of straining or stretching cloth unduly, Parliament resolved on the drastic remedy of prohibiting the use of tenter-frames on which cloth, after being fulled, was stretched in the open air to dry [3]. The Act of 1598 forbade the use of any tenter 'of what sort or kind soever' north of the Trent; and three years later, owing to the confiscation of defective cloth by the French King, the prohibition was made general for the whole country as regards unwrought cloth [4]. The clothiers were at once up in arms. They declared that it was impossible to bring the cloth to perfection without using tenters to 'even' it in length and breadth [5], nor were they willing to forgo the opportunities of profit which the practice afforded. Moreover the obligation to weave cloth in definite sizes, which the clothiers maintained was not feasible on account of differences in the wool and in fulling, induced them to stretch the cloth, when under the standard, in order to avoid the penalty [6]. In spite of repeated admonitions addressed by the Privy Council to the justices of the peace, the Act was not put in execution; cloth was brought to market 'rather worse than better' [7];

---

[1] *State Papers Domestic*, 1629–1631, p. 502.
[2] *Ibid.* 1637, p. 396.
[3] Lipson, *The History of the Woollen and Worsted Industries*, 141.
[4] *Statutes*, iv. part ii. 920 (1598), 975-976 (1601) ; *State Papers Domestic*, Addenda, 1580–1625, p. 465-466. The Act of 1552 had forbidden the use of any 'engine' for stretching cloth : see *supra*, vol. i. 484.
[5] *Hist. MSS. Comm. Salisbury*, xi. 583.
[6] *House of Commons Journals*, xxx. 262-263.
[7] *State Papers Domestic*, 1601–1603, p. 46.

and in 1624 the use of tenters was again permitted by law [1].
On another occasion the manufacturers showed their determination to observe no restrictions which did not accord
with their interests. In 1633 the clothiers of Gloucestershire
dismissed their workfolk in protest against a proclamation,
ordering that " no cloth shall be hung for drying in any rack
or tenter that has any lower bar ". This was intended to
prevent stretching, but the clothiers claimed that " the
want of a lower bar enforces their cloths to become faulty
in length and breadth by reason of the wind and sun's working upon them in the drying " [2]. Though the Government
sought by means of proclamations to give ' new life to the
Statutes ' [3], their influence was at best transient. The
resistance of manufacturers to paternal legislation reminds
us once again that economic practice cannot be interpreted
from the pages of the statute-book [4] : and it warns us not
to date the beginnings of *laissez-faire* in industry from the
belated repeal of laws, which in actual fact had always been
honoured more in the breach than in the observance [5].

*The doctrine of industrial freedom.*  After the Restoration the doctrine of industrial freedom
gained an increasing hold over the minds of the governing
classes. For one thing, the waning power of the Privy
Council weakened irreparably the existing mechanism of
control. For another, the Civil War proved, as we have
already seen [6], a powerful dissolvent of traditional economic
ideas : the reaction against authority in the constitutional
sphere extended inevitably to the economic sphere, and
encouraged a critical attitude towards State interference.
And further, the principle itself of national regulation of
industry was discredited by the Tudor and Stuart practice
of employing private individuals as the agents of the State.

---

[1] *Statutes*, iv. part ii. 1226.
[2] *State Papers Domestic*, 1633–1634, p. 166.
[3] *Ibid.* 1629–1631, p. 446. (This refers to the proclamation of 1618 :
*Tudor and Stuart Proclamations* (ed. Steele), i. No. 1223.)
[4] See *supra*, p. 319 ; and vol. i. 232, 235, 292, 378.
[5] The repeal of industrial legislation in 1809 (the woollen industry) and
1813–1814 (other industries) was due to the activities of ' informers and
attorneys ', who ' rummaged out obsolete but existing laws ' : *Hist. MSS.
Comm. Fortescue*, vii. 133 ; Lipson, *The History of the Woollen and Worsted
Industries*, 212.
[6] *Supra*, p. 313.

The history of the aulnage, as will be shown [1], demonstrated how rapidly the inspection of commodities was liable in private hands to degenerate into a tax on commodities [2]. Although voices were still heard demanding the execution of ' the good old laws ' [3], economists were beginning to proclaim the doctrine that " industry has its first foundation in liberty " [4]. The policy of standardizing industry was severely condemned by Child, who expressed the views of the manufacturers when he pleaded for freedom in industry. " All our laws ", he wrote, " that oblige our people to the making of strong, substantial (and, as we call it, loyal) cloth of a certain length, breadth and weight, if they were duly put in execution would, in my opinion, do more hurt than good because the humours and fashions of the world change, and at some times, in some places (as now in most), slight, cheap, light cloth will sell more plentifully and better than that which is heavier, stronger and truer wrought ; and if we intend to have the trade of the world we must imitate the Dutch, who make the worst as well as the best of all manufactures, that we may be in a capacity of serving all markets and all humours.   I conclude all our laws limiting the number of looms, number or kind of servants, and times of working, to be certainly prejudicial to the clothing trade of the kingdom in general ".   He recommended that clothiers should be left at liberty " to make what cloth and stuffs they please, how they will, where and when they will, of any lengths or sizes " [5].

The Revolution was followed in this, as in other directions, by a complete relaxation of industrial restraints.   " As the

---

[1] *Infra,* p. 328.

[2] Child, *A New Discourse of Trade* (4th ed.), 3.

[3] *Short Notes and Observations drawn from the present decaying condition of this Kingdom in point of Trade* (1662), 2 ;  Coke, *Treatise* (1671), i. 88. A writer in 1677 complained that formerly " our clothes were made strong to endure many years and . . . left as legacies to . . . friends and children, who did not despise to wear the clothes of their ancestors " : *Reasons for a Limited Exportation of Wool,* 13.   But the decay of the woollen industry at Worcester was attributed to " the obstinacy of the workmen, who persisted in making a thick heavy cloth instead of a light and spongy " : Green, *The History and Antiquities of Worcester* (1796), i. 290-291.

[4] Davenant, *Works* (ed. 1771), ii. 35.

[5] Child, *A New Discourse of Trade* (4th ed.), 159-161.   Similarly : *House of Lords MSS.* 1702-1704, p. 99.

*Relaxation of industrial restraints.* worthy makers of those good laws are now asleep ", it was complained in 1691, " so are their laws too ", and every man may make his cloth at his own choice [1]. " Nowadays ", remarked Davenant, " laws are not much observed which do not in a manner execute themselves " [2]. The position, as it existed in the middle of the eighteenth century, was aptly summed up in a parliamentary report on ' the laws relating to trade and manufactures ' : " A great part . . . ought to be entirely repealed—many as being grown out of use, and scarce ever put in execution but on malicious and frivolous prosecutions ; others entirely local ; others, though perhaps well calculated for the times in which they were made, yet now become prejudicial to Trade in its present state ; others quite useless " [3]. In 1738 Parliament discarded the system of statutory dimensions for the West Riding of Yorkshire in the case of narrow cloth, and in 1765 in respect of broad cloth [4]. At the opening of the nineteenth century a clothier told a parliamentary committee in effect that at this time manufacturers made goods to suit every customer and every climate [5]. The attempt to standardize industry was thus necessarily abandoned. It was manifestly impossible to manufacture cloths according to statutory dimensions, in view of the variety of materials exported abroad to meet the tastes of foreign buyers ; nor was it considered imperative to prevent the straining and stretching of cloth, because the manufacturer was the one most interested in maintaining the credit of his cloth, and therefore the most concerned not to stretch nor strain it injuriously ; while lastly, the employment of various ingredients forbidden by law [6] was now required owing to improvements

[1] *Reasons of the Decay of the Clothing Trade* (1691), 2.
[2] Davenant, *Works* (ed. 1771), ii. 205. ' Nowadays ' is 1699.
[3] *House of Commons Journals,* xxvi. 292 (1751). Similarly : Tucker, *Instructions* (ed. 1757), 33 *seq.*
[4] *Statutes at Large,* vi. 81 (1738) ; vii. 564 (1765) ; *House of Commons Journals,* xxx. 262 *seq.* The searchers were to stamp the cloth with its actual measurements. The Leeds authorities protested that the Act of 1765 would be ' ruinous to the credit of the manufacture ' : *ibid.* xxx. 385.
[5] *Parliamentary Papers* (1802–3), v. 259.
[6] Cf. the Act of 1581 against " certain deceitful stuff used in the dyeing of cloth " : *Statutes,* iv. part i. 671.

in the art of dyeing [1]. The argument in short was that, however useful State control of industry might have been in earlier times to give credit to the industry by preventing abuses, competition could henceforth be trusted to secure this end. " The interest of the seller ", ran the maxim of trade, " is sufficient security to the buyer for fair dealing ". The doctrine of Adam Smith was anticipated by Dean Tucker when he wrote : " The self-love and self-interest of each individual will prompt him to seek such ways of gain, trades and occupations of life as, by serving himself, will promote the public welfare at the same time " [2].

We have now to consider the methods adopted by the State to carry out its industrial policy. They were four in number—the direct intervention of the Government ; the creation of an administrative staff ; the employment of the craft gilds as agents of national supervision [3]; and the delegation of authority to private individuals [4]. The direct intervention of the Government assumed various forms. The Privy Council under Elizabeth and the Early Stuarts frequently brought pressure to bear upon the local authorities, and administered sharp reproofs for their neglect to enforce the law [5]; or sometimes it summoned manufacturers to Westminster to answer in its presence the charges of ' false making of cloth ' [6]. Royal commissions were also set up to hold inquiries into the state of the textile industries. One commission was established by James I. in 1622 [7], and others during the personal government of Charles I.[8]. This kind of control was necessarily intermittent, and it was intended at best to supplement the activities of an administrative staff.

*Methods of industrial control.*

---

[1] These points were all mentioned by a witness giving evidence before a parliamentary committee in 1803 : *Parliamentary Papers* (1802-3), vii. 381-382.

[2] Tucker, *Instructions* (ed. 1757), 31-32.     [3] *Infra*, pp. 330 *seq.*
[4] *Infra*, pp. 352 *seq.*     [5] *Supra*, p. 323.
[6] *Acts of the Privy Council*, 1578–1580, pp. 126, 160, 168. In 1635 merchants asked the Privy Council to instruct J.P.'s to summon the makers before them " and to deal effectually with them for their true making " : *State Papers Domestic*, 1635, p. 307.     [7] See *supra*, p. 307.
[8] 1630, 1633, 1638 : *State Papers Domestic*, 1633-1634, p. 21 ; 1638–1639, p. 23. For a commission's report (1640), see *Hist. MSS. Comm. Portland*, viii. 2.

It is an indication of the importance of the woollen industry that it gave rise to the appointment of State officials, as early as the thirteenth century, to execute the regulations prescribed by the law. These officials were known as aulnagers, and their functions were to test the dimensions and quality of each piece of cloth, sealing what was sound, and confiscating what was defective [1]. In the seventeenth century the office was farmed by the Duke of Lennox, who under James I. became aulnager for woollen cloth, worsteds and the new draperies [2]. His deputies did not trouble themselves about the size and quality of the cloth but were content as a rule to enforce payment of the duty. The manufacturers purchased the seals, which they affixed to their cloths without submitting them for inspection. The seals were publicly sold by the bushel, it was stated in Parliament in 1624, so that ' the instrument of right ' was now ' the instrument of deceit '. The original design of the institution was entirely lost sight of, the makers having " an uncontrolled liberty to make bad cloth of what materials they will " [3]. Hence there arose the demand for its abolition on the ground that it was now useless, and survived only as an instrument of extortion and oppression [4]. In 1699 Parliament enacted that the aulnage should cease after the expiry of the grant renewed to the Duke of Lennox in 1664 for sixty

[1] *Supra*, vol. i. 461-462.

[2] *Acts of the Privy Council*, 1613–1614, pp. 129, 380. He became aulnager for the new draperies in 1605 : *Tudor and Stuart Proclamations* (ed. Steele), i. No. 1017. The new draperies came under the aulnage in 1594 : *State Papers Domestic*, 1591–1594, p. 523. The legality of Lennox's patent for the new draperies was questioned : *A Record of some Worthie Proceedings in 1611* (published 1641), 35 ; *House of Commons Journals*, x. 128, 174 (1689).

[3] *Tudor Economic Documents* (ed. Tawney and Power), i. 190 (1576) ; *State Papers Domestic*, 1619–1623, p. 247 ; *House of Commons Journals*, i. 709 (1624) ; Child, *A New Discourse of Trade* (4th ed.), 3 ; Haynes, *A View of the Present State of the Clothing Trade in England* (1706), 83.

[4] *State Papers Domestic*, 1651–1652, p. 480 ; *House of Commons Journals*, xi. 16, 21 (1693). There were complaints that they entered drapers' shops to search the cloth, and exacted excessive fees : *Acts of the Privy Council*, 1613–1614, p. 165 ; *House of Commons Journals*, i. 709 (1624) ; *ibid.* x. 169-176 (1689) ; *House of Lords MSS.* 1692–1693, pp. 34 *seq.* ; *Hist. MSS. Comm. Various*, i. 84, 88 ; *Victoria County History, Lancaster*, ii. 377 ; Heaton, *The Yorkshire Woollen and Worsted Industries*, 177 *seq.* and 198 *seq.*

years ; accordingly in 1724 it lapsed [1]. The supersession of the aulnager was facilitated by the fact that his functions had already been taken over by another set of officials [2]. The Act of 1552 ordered the municipal authorities to appoint searchers, who were to inspect and seal the cloth ; and near *The searchers.* the end of Elizabeth's reign similar officials were instituted in rural districts by the justices of the peace [3]. The searchers were instructed to enter all houses and workshops where cloth was made, but they in their turn became negligent in the discharge of their duties. " They have set the seals of their office ", complained Misselden, " to cloths they never searched nor saw " ; and he stated that the seals were bought and sold ' as in a market ', and affixed to the cloth by the manufacturer [4]. In the early eighteenth century the obligation was also placed on the fuller to measure and stamp the cloth brought to his mill [5]. Public searchers existed in other branches of industry besides cloth-making. The Act of 1563 laid upon the local authorities the duty of appointing searchers to examine all leather offered for sale, to seal it when it was ' sufficiently and well tanned ', and to ' make true search and view ' of all boots, shoes, saddles and other wares made of tanned leather [6].

Neither the direct intervention of the Government, nor the system of inspection by public officials, proved an effective method of enforcing industrial regulations. The

[1] *Statutes,* vii. 610-611.

[2] Cf. *State Papers Domestic,* Addenda, 1625-1649, p. 519.

[3] *Statutes,* iv. part i. 139 (1552) ; iv. part ii. 921 (1598), 976 (1601). The aulnagers retained their powers of search.

[4] Misselden, *Free Trade* (1622), 44-46. Searchers ceased to be appointed outside the corporate towns : W. S., Gent., *The Golden Fleece* (1656), 48, 92 ; Smith, *An Essay for Recovery of Trade* (1661), 8. See also *infra*, Appendix, p. 526, No. 2.

[5] *Statutes,* ix. 82 (1709), 686 (1712). An elaborate machinery was set up in the West Riding of Yorkshire in 1765. Searchers were to measure and seal the cloth at the fulling mills ; inspectors were to examine the cloth (after it had left the fulling mill) in the workshops of cloth-dressers, in tenter grounds and in warehouses ; and lastly, there were to be supervisors of the searchers and inspectors : *Statutes at Large,* vii. 564 *seq.*, 581 *seq.* A register was kept of the cloth milled in Yorkshire, which was considered ' the barometer of the woollen trade of Yorkshire ' : see the statistics printed in Bischoff, *History of the Woollen and Worsted Manufactures,* ii. Appendix, Table IV. For inspectors under the Worsted Acts : *supra*, vol. ii. 49.

[6] *Statutes,* iv. part i. 432-433. A parliamentary committee recommended in 1728 that the London magistrates should appoint searchers of tiles and bricks : *House of Commons Journals,* xxi. 78.

*Traditional* State therefore utilized also the traditional method, which
*methods of* was to leave control in the hands of merchants and manu-
*control.* facturers themselves, not in their capacity as individuals,
but as organized in a corporation. One function of the
trading companies, as we have seen [1], was to supervise the
quality of the wares exported abroad; and Blackwell
Hall, where the cloth brought to London was exposed for
sale, provided them with opportunities for inspection [2].
More important still were the gilds which continued to
survive, though with varying degrees of authority and
prestige, throughout the sixteenth, seventeenth, and into the
eighteenth century.

## (VI)

### THE CRAFT GILDS

*Survival*      In the middle of the sixteenth century the Venetian
*of the*
*craft gilds.* envoy in London wrote home : " The whole population is
divided into ' companies ', termed in Venice ' schools ', or
fraternities, of artificers . . . nor can any one enter these
companies until he has served those of the trade during six
or seven years " [3]. There are abundant indications of the
survival of the craft gilds after the sixteenth century.
The ordinances of the Tailors' Company at Lincoln, dated
1679, might have been framed three centuries earlier. They
provide that all members of the company must be freemen
of the city ; no tailor was to set up or do any work ' before
agreement ' with the master of the company and the mayor ;
' foreign ' tailors must pay forty shillings to the company ;
two searchers were to be appointed to inspect defects in
garments on complaint by a customer ; a scale of prices
was laid down ; tailors were forbidden to work in private
houses, " without it be for one day to do his customer a
pleasure " ; ' evil words and misbehaviour ' in the presence
of the master of the company were to be punished by fine
or imprisonment [4]. Numerous gilds at Hull in the seven-

---

[1] *Supra*, vol. ii. 235.                    [2] *Supra*, vol. ii. 25.
[3] *State Papers Venetian*, 1534–1554, p. 344 (1551).
[4] *Hist. MSS. Comm. Lincoln*, 108. For the ordinances of the textile
workers of Coggeshall, see *ibid. Various*, viii. 573 *seq.*

teenth century enacted by-laws in the traditional form [1]. In London, in the eighteenth century, the Hatters exercised jurisdiction within a radius of ten miles ; none but a ' free ' hatter could work at the trade ; and the number of apprentices which a master might take together was limited to two [2]. At the end of the eighteenth century, in Exeter, " almost every other man you met wore an apron of emerald green serge, girded and tied with a scarlet woollen band—they all belonged to the Gild of Incorporated Weavers, Fullers and Shearmen, who were alone permitted to exercise their craft " [3]. Sometimes the authority of the gilds was confirmed by Act of Parliament. Thus in 1563 the Curriers' Company was empowered to examine and seal all leather curried in London : the Companies of Haberdashers, Cappers and Hatters were required in 1566 to make joint inspection of caps and hats within the London area : the Dyers' Company in 1726 (and even as late as 1783) was authorized to appoint searchers in London [4]. At other times a royal proclamation was issued in support of a gild, for instance, Elizabeth in 1596 forbade anyone to ' wind or fold ' wool without obtaining licence from the Woolmen or Wool-packers' Company [5].

The vitality of the gild principle is shown by the numerous *Stuart incorporations.* grants of incorporation made in the seventeenth century to newly-formed or old established crafts. Under James I. the grants embraced Feltmakers (1604), Musicians (1604), Turners (1604), Fruiterers (1605), Gardeners (1605), Pinmakers (1605), Shipwrights (1605), Woodmongers (1605), Butchers (1606), Curriers (1606), Plumbers (1611), Founders (1614), Apothecaries (1617), Scriveners (1617), Bowyers (1621), Starchmakers (1622). Charles I. added Upholsters (1626), Tilers and Bricklayers (1627), Playing-card Makers

---

[1] Lambert, *Two Thousand Years of Gild Life*, 209, 240, 281, 311, 322, 326, 341, 357. For Witney : *infra*, Appendix, p. 526, No. 3.
[2] 1752 : *Reports from Committees of the House of Commons*, ii. 376.
[3] *All the Year Round* (ed. Dickens), xiv. No. 340, p. 319.
[4] *Statutes*, iv. part i. 431-432, 494 ; *Statutes at Large*, v. 452, ix. 290. See also *infra*, Appendix, p. 526, No. 4. In 1641 the Shrewsbury " corvisours " complained that leather was not publicly searched as ' in other cities ' : *Hist. MSS. Comm. Shrewsbury*, 64.
[5] *Tudor and Stuart Proclamations* (ed. Steele), i. No. 883. The prohibition was renewed after the Restoration : *State Papers Domestic*, 1663-1664, p. 469.

(1628), Silk Throwers (1629), Spectacle-makers (1629), Clock-makers (1631), Silkmen (1631), Combmakers (1636), Worsted Combers of Exeter and Devon (1637), Beaver-makers (1638), Distillers (1638), Glaziers (1638), Glovers (1638), Gunmakers (1638), Hatband-makers (1638), Horners (1638), Soapmakers (1638), and Coachmen (1639) [1]. On the eve of the Long Parliament the Government hastily revoked grants to Brick and Tile-makers, Butchers, Combmakers, Gutstring-makers, Hatband-makers, Horners, Spectacle-makers and Tobacco-pipe Makers [2].

*Motives for creating companies: (i.) financial gain.* Three main categories of companies may be distinguished according to the motive which inspired their creation. In the first category the Government was evidently seeking opportunities of profit. The ostensible reason for incorporating the Starchmakers was to remedy abuses such as using wheat, but the Crown exacted an annual rent in return for the monopoly conferred upon them [3]. Incorporation became in fact, as we shall see [4], the recognized method of evading the Statute of Monopolies passed in 1624.

In the second category the Government showed a genuine desire to promote the interests of the artisan element

---

[1] Apothecaries : Hazlitt, *The Livery Companies*, 348. Beaver-makers : Rymer, *Foedera*, xx. 230. Bowyers : Hazlitt, *op. cit.* 375. Butchers : *ibid.* 401. Clockmakers : *ibid.* 419. Coachmen : *State Papers Domestic*, 1639, p. 161. Combmakers : Hazlitt, *op. cit.* 111. Curriers : *ibid.* 459. Distillers : *Remembrancia of the City of London*, 111. Feltmakers : Hazlitt, *op. cit.* 484. Founders : Williams, *The Founders' Company*, 25. Fruiterers : Hazlitt, *op. cit.* 508. Gardeners : *State Papers Domestic*, 1634–1635, pp. 339–340. Glaziers : Hazlitt, *op. cit.* 518. Glovers : *infra*, p. 333. Gunmakers : Hazlitt, *op. cit.* 528. Hatband-makers : *ibid.* 116. Horners : *ibid.* 531. Musicians : *ibid.* 568. Pinmakers : *State Papers Domestic*, 1603–1610, p. 211. Playing-card makers : Hazlitt, *op. cit.* 593. Plumbers : *ibid.* 596. Scriveners : *ibid.* 615. Shipwrights : *ibid.* 620. Silkmen : *Tudor and Stuart Proclamations* (ed. Steele), i. No. 1645. Silk Throwers : *supra*, vol. ii. 102. Soapmakers : Hazlitt, *op. cit.* 140. Spectacle-makers : *ibid.* 623. Starchmakers : *State Papers Domestic*, 1619–1623, p. 394. Tilers and Bricklayers : *Acts of the Privy Council*, 1627, p. 46. Turners : Hazlitt, *op. cit.* 649. Upholsters : *ibid.* 655. Woodmongers : *supra*, vol. ii. 140, note 7. Worsted Combers (Devon) : *State Papers Domestic*, 1636–1637, p. 461 ; 1637, p. 381.

In some cases gilds were founded on application to the municipal authorities : *Records of Oxford*, 331 (1569) ; *Hist. MSS. Comm. Southampton*, 95 (1617).

[2] Rymer, *Foedera*, xx. 341, 345 (1639).

[3] *State Papers Domestic*, 1619–1623, p. 394 ; Macpherson, *Annals of Commerce*, ii. 369.

[4] *Infra*, pp. 361-362.

in the gilds, which was seeking a separate organization in (ii.) *Revolt of the handicraft element.* order to escape capitalist control. A cleavage had developed between the handicraft and trading sections in the gild [1]; and the superior resources of the latter, which controlled the supply of raw material and the sale of the finished product, reduced the small masters to a condition of economic dependency. Thus the leather-workers, who obtained incorporation as the Glovers' Company in 1638, complained that the leather-sellers, " if once they put their griping hands betwixt the grower or the merchant " and the users of leather, " never part with the commodities they buy till they sell them at their own pitched rates, without either regard or care whether the workman be able to make his money thereof or no " [2]. In encouraging the independent organization of working masters, the policy of the Early Stuarts harmonized with the general trend of their social activities on behalf of the poorer classes [3]. Parliament itself intervened to protect the artisan skinners from the merchants, who engrossed the supply of skins, " and so draw the whole trade into their own hands and work the same in their own houses " [4]. The revolt of the handicraft element was widespread in the first half of the seventeenth century, and its manifestations were especially marked under the Commonwealth, when the political upheaval created a social ferment. The London Weavers afford a conspicuous example of the division of interests in the gild. At the conclusion of the Civil War ' the commonalty of the corporation of Weavers of London ' hastened to frame an indictment against the governing body, which they charged with various offences, such as admitting members who had not served an apprenticeship, exacting high fees for admission, depriving the commonalty of the right to elect their rulers, and squandering the resources of the company [5]. A few years later (1652)

---

[1] *Supra*, vol. i. 423.
[2] Unwin, *Industrial Organization*, 129-130 ; Unwin, *The Gilds and Companies of London*, 254.
[3] *Supra*, pp. 258, 306, and *infra*, pp. 449 *seq.*
[4] *Statutes*, iv. part ii. 1085 (1606) ; *Remembrancia of the City of London*, 93 (1606).
[5] *The Case of the Commonalty of the Corporation of Weavers of London truly Stated*, 3-7. The rulers of the company replied in the *Abbreviate of the*
[*contd.*]

the ' commonalty ' of the Founders' Company complained that they were " extremely trodden and kept under foot by the power and will of the master and wardens and assistants ", who were " not able to judge of anything relating to the trade . . . they being men of other callings [1], of which three-thirds parts of the assistants do consist ". Their attack was met with the counter-charge that " their levelling minds and proud imperious wills " were seeking " an equal power with the court of assistants in government and authority " ; and " where was it ever known . . . that the people which should be ruled should seem to instruct their rulers ? " [2] On the surface the revolt appeared to be a democratic movement for the control of the government of the companies, but the grievances of the ' commonalty ' really sprang from the ' engrossing ' of trade by the wealthy members of the gild.

(iii.) *Corporate regulation of industry.* In the third category the Government was only responding to petitions, which had behind them the support of a deeply-rooted tradition in favour of regulating industry on a corporate basis. We may take as an example the charter granted to the Worsted Combers of Exeter and Devon. The company was to consist of all persons who had used the trade of worsted combing for the past three years, and it was to be governed by a master, wardens, and a council drawn in equal numbers from the city and the county [3]. In cases of this kind Parliament was not opposed to the system of incorporation, provided it was not tainted with financial gain to the promoters. In 1624 the Cutlers of Hallamshire were constituted a company by an Act which empowered them to make by-laws and to appoint searchers. The preamble to the Statute indicates how strongly entrenched was the mediaeval idea of the corporate regulation of industry. It

---

*Weavers' Business* (1648). There were earlier complaints (1636 and 1641) : *Hist. MSS. Comm.* iv. 55.

[1] See *infra*, p. 340.

[2] Williams, *The Founders' Company*, 32-37, 108-111. There were fresh differences in 1697 : *ibid.* 130-133. There were controversies in 1649, among the Merchant Taylors : Clode, *Early History of the Guild of Merchant Taylors*, i. 73.

[3] *State Papers Domestic*, 1637, p. 381.

deplored the fact that ' divers persons ' engaged in making
cutlery, " not being subject to any rule, government or
search of any others of skill in those manufactures, have
refused to submit themselves to any order, ordinance or
search ", but " have taken liberty to themselves to . . . take
as many apprentices and for what term of years " they think
fit, whereby " the whole trade and the exact skill formerly
exercised therein is like in a short time to be overthrown " [1].
The erection of industrial companies thus accorded with
the prevailing economic sentiment [2], which held that the
gild system had " worked great good . . . in respect that the
government of every artificer and tradesman being committed to men of gravity, best experienced in the same
faculty and mistery, the particular grievances and deceits
in every trade might be examined, reformed and ordered " [3].
Even under the Commonwealth this sentiment remained
powerful. The Council for Trade, investigating complaints
of ' abuses and deceits ' in different branches of industry,
reported (1651) that some occurred for want of incorporation ; others for want of sufficient power in their corporations to search for and punish offenders, or assess their
members or commodities to defray the charge of search ;
others through taking in men of different trades under one
company [4]. Subsequently the ' Trade Committee ' recommended the incorporation of the Needlemakers of London
to prevent ' the great fraud used in making needles ' [5]. The
Needlemakers were incorporated in 1656, and after the
Restoration fresh companies were created—the Tobacco-
pipe Makers (1663), the Glass-Sellers (1664), the Patten-
makers (1670), the Tinplate-workers (1670), the Wheel-
wrights, (1670), the Gold and Silver Wire-drawers (1693),
and the Fanmakers (1709) [6]. In addition several corpora-

---

[1] Statutes, iv. part ii. 1242–1243.
[2] Except where it was related to some insidious financial project : see
infra, pp. 361-362.
[3] Ordinances of the Faversham Mercers' Company : Gross, The Gild
Merchant, ii. 89 (1616).
[4] State Papers Domestic, 1651, p. 444.
[5] Ibid. 1656–1657, p. 64 (1656).
[6] Hazlitt, The Livery Companies, 148, 479, 515, 526, 572, 583, 647, 667.
In 1692 steps were taken to incorporate the grocers, mercers, and woollen
[contd.]

tions were established by the legislature[1]—an indication that the principle of gild control over industry continued to enjoy parliamentary sanction in the second, as it had done in the first half of the seventeenth century.

*Proposals for the re-organization of industry on a gild basis.*    The most striking proposal made in the seventeenth century for the reconstruction of industry on the basis of corporations, armed with powers of control and search, was put forward in 1622. A royal commission, appointed to inquire into the causes of the trade depression, recommended that " a corporation in every county be made of the most able and sufficient men of the same, whereby they may be authorized to look fully to the true making, dyeing and dressing of cloth and stuffs in every shire, and not trust to mean men by whose conjectures many faults are committed to the great disgrace of our drapery "[2]. This recommendation, had it been adopted, would have brought rural industry under gild control, and reversed the whole trend of industrial development since the end of the fifteenth century[3]. Three years later a warrant was actually issued to ' draw up corporations ' for thirty-two counties where the new draperies were manufactured[4]. The proposal was revived in a modified form by another commission in 1640 : it advised the erection of corporations in sixty towns, which should appoint paid officers to supervise the clothing industry of the district, and assume responsibility for the " losses, damages and penalties of all faulty cloths or stuffs that are suffered to pass their seal "[5]. These bodies were to be constituted upon the model of the Dutch Bay-Hall at Colchester, which was more successful than most gilds in preserving its authority. The name of this famous society of baymakers betrays its origin. It dated from the sixteenth century when Col-

---

and linen drapers of Tiverton in one gild : *State Papers Domestic*, 1691–1692, p. 114. Their ordinances are printed in Boyce, *Historical Memoirs of Tiverton*, Bk. v. Appendix, No. vii. 44-48. Other examples : *infra*, p. 527 (No. 1).

[1] *Supra*, p. 334 ; and *infra*, pp. 337-339, 527 (No. 2).
[2] Stowe MSS. 554, f. 45.          [3] *Supra*, vol. i. 505-507.
[4] *State Papers Domestic*, Addenda, 1625–1649, p. 4.
[5] *Hist. MSS. Comm. Portland*, viii. 3.    For a proposal to control wool-combing, see *ibid. Portland*, iii. 74 (1641).    See also *infra*, p. 527 (No. 3).

chester received a large influx of immigrants, who introduced into the town the new draperies. The strangers followed the practice already adopted at Sandwich and other places for the ' true and upright making and ensealing ' of bays and says. At Sandwich the first step taken by the foreign weavers, who settled there early in Elizabeth's reign [1], was to appoint from their midst twelve men ' of the discreetest and best skill ' to attend a hall—assigned to them by the authorities of the town—at certain hours of the day to view the bays and other stuffs brought there for inspection, and to affix various seals, indicating the place of manufacture and the quality and size of the cloth [2]. The privileges of the Dutch Bay-Hall, which included the right of search and power to make by-laws, were confirmed by Act of Parliament in 1660 [3]. Colchester became renowned for the manufacture of bays [4]; and its prosperity was attributed to the success of the Hall in maintaining, by the strictest scrutiny, the deserved reputation of its wares [5].

The policy advocated under the Early Stuarts for the *Clothing corporations.* general reconstitution of industry on a gild basis did not materialize, though some attempts were made to establish clothing corporations in particular centres. The clothiers, cloth-workers, weavers and tailors of Bury St. Edmunds received a charter, but they petitioned for its withdrawal and for the suppression of the corporation, on the ground that it was utilized as a means for extorting money [6]. An Act of Parliament in 1650 erected a corporation within Norwich and the county of Norfolk, composed of two presidents, twelve wardens and forty assistants, all of whom were

---

[1] *Supra*, vol. i. 498.

[2] *Hist. MSS. Comm. Salisbury*, iv. 573-574. It was said that " the same order and course here used was taken from hence by tradition to Norwich, Colchester, Maidstone, Canterbury and other places ".

[3] *Statutes*, v. 253-254. On the organization of the Dutch Bay-Hall, see *Victoria County History, Essex*, ii. 388 seq.

[4] Defoe, *A Tour of Great Britain* (ed. 1724), i. Letter i. 20, 44.

[5] *Reasons of the Decay of the Clothing Trade* (1691), 3 ; Haynes, *A View of the Present State of the Clothing Trade in England* (1706), 82. See *infra*, Appendix, p. 527, No. 4.

[6] 1609 : *Hist. MSS. Comm. Bury St. Edmunds*, 141. Applications for incorporation were received from the ' Broad Weavers and Clothiers ' of Coventry and the Walloon Weavers of Canterbury : *State Papers Domestic*, 1663-1664, p. 611 (Coventry) ; 1675-1676, p. 426.

to be master weavers. This body was given comprehensive powers to govern the worsted industry, to make by-laws, and to enter any house, shop or warehouse belonging to weavers, merchants and retailers, in order to " search and view the yarn and stuffs whether they be ordered and made according to the laws, orders and ordinances of the trade " [1]. After the Restoration, despite local hostility [2], the organization was revived in its essentials by the Act of 1662 [3]. Again, in 1671, Parliament enacted that for the purpose of regulating the making of Kidderminster stuffs, "there shall be chosen one president, four wardens and eight assistants " to frame ordinances for the ' good government ' of the manufacture, subject to the approval of the judges of assize. Cloth, as at Norwich, was to be brought to a hall to be examined and sealed, and authority was given to enter houses and workshops of workmen and dealers [4]. More significant than the examples just cited was the experiment tried in Yorkshire of broadening the basis of the gild, so as to make it a partnership between the purely industrial element and the State.

*Control shared between Industry and the State.*

The general level of the woollen industry in Yorkshire as regards quality and skill was low, and the manufacturers gained an evil notoriety for the use of prohibited materials [5]. To provide a remedy for abuses a Bill was introduced into Parliament in 1656, constituting the makers of ' broad mixed woollen cloth ' within the West Riding of Yorkshire ' a body politic and corporate ', but it was rejected [6]. After the

---

[1] Except russels and fustians : *Acts and Ordinances of the Interregnum*, ii. 451-455 (Yarmouth and Lynn were exempted). For the earlier organization of the Norwich weavers, see *supra*, vol. i. 433.

[2] *The Argument against the Bill for Regulating the Stuffs in Norfolk and Norwich.*

[3] *Statutes*, v. 370 *seq.* Wardens who had the oversight of the manufacture were still being appointed in 1768 : *The Present State of the British Empire* (1768), 68.

[4] *Statutes*, v. 710 *seq.*

[5] *Letters and Papers, Foreign and Domestic, of Henry VIII.*, vol. vi. 500 ; vii. 616. Also *supra*, vol. ii. 12-13 ; and *infra*, p. 527 (No. 5).

[6] *House of Commons Journals*, vii. 467, 588. The York gild of coverlet-makers had been given power of search throughout the county by the Act of 1543 : *supra*, vol. i. 505. The Leeds corporation sought increased powers over the cloth manufacture in 1639 : *State Papers Domestic*, 1639-1640, p. 251.

Restoration a corporation of ' Broad Woollen Clothiers '
was set up, consisting of all the justices of the West Riding
together with two masters, ten wardens, twelve assistants
and the commonalty. It was vested with the power of
making by-laws for " the better spinning, working, making,
fulling and milling of woollen cloth ", which might tend to
" the good credit and advancement of the trade ". It was
also to appoint searchers of cloth, who could enter any house,
workshop or warehouse of clothiers, drapers and cloth-
workers in order to inspect the cloth " that it be of a due
weight, length and breadth according to the Statute ".
One important limitation of its authority must be observed.
The corporation was expressly debarred from imposing
" any other or lesser rates or wages upon any inferior workmen, servants or labourers to be employed by them or any
of them in the manufacture, than such as shall be from time
to time allowed and approved of by the justices of the peace
in their quarter sessions, according to the laws and statutes
touching labourers " [1]. Thus both the constitution and
the powers of the Yorkshire corporation exhibited a significant departure from those of the mediaeval craft gilds. It
was not exclusively an industrial body since it embraced
the public authorities, and it was definitely forbidden to
interfere with wages. In short it foreshadowed a new form
of industrial association, in which control is shared between
Industry and the State.

In the eyes of contemporaries the survival of the gild *The right
of search.*
system had its justification in the maintenance of a standard
of quality and workmanship . " The fundamental ground
of incorporating handicraft trades and manual occupations
into distinct companies ", declared a London company in
the seventeenth century, " was to the end that all persons
using such trades should be brought into one uniform government, and corrected and regulated by expert and skilful
governors " [2]. When the gilds of Salisbury were re-organized

[1] 1662 : *Statutes*, v. 425 *seq.* The corporation expired in 1685 : Heaton,
*The Yorkshire Woollen and Worsted Industries*, 234.
[2] Jupp and Pocock, *The Carpenters' Company*, 313. See also *supra*,
p. 335.

in 1612, it was carefully stipulated that each gild must nominate searchers who were to be sworn in open court [1] In the course of time it proved increasingly difficult to carry out this primary function, especially in the metropolis. Owing to redemption and the right of patrimony [2], it frequently happened that " he who is titular of this or that fraternity never was bred up in it . . . the law of the City imposing an absolute necessity that all, who are free of the City, should carry the name of some one or other of their brotherhoods " [3]. Moreover the Statute of Apprentices, which enacted that none should use any art in which he had not been apprenticed, did not, according to the common interpretation, ' touch the City's liberties ' whereby a free-man of London was enabled to follow all ' lawful trades ' [4]. As a consequence the London companies contained members drawn from a variety of trades : one of the masters of the Founders' Company was an ale-house keeper, so that it is not surprising that the ' master and wardens ' were charged with neglect of their duty to make diligent inspection of ' all brass weights, and brass and copper works ' [5]. And even when the gild authorities were ' diligent ' in regard to the members of their own company, they could not easily control the members of another company : during the latter half of the sixteenth century the Merchant Taylors, engaged in cloth-finishing, successfully resisted the claim of the Cloth-workers' Company to examine their work [6]. In the reign of Elizabeth (1571) fourteen of the smaller companies represented to the civic authorities that in ancient times the wardens of every handicraft had the " search and punishment of all persons occupying the art " ; and they urged that all who exercised a handicraft, but were " free of another

---

[1] Haskins, *The Ancient Trade Guilds and Companies of Salisbury*, 237.
[2] Redemption means admission by purchase, and patrimony means admission by right of birth.
[3] *The Cities Advocate* (1629), 57. See *supra*, vol. i. 431.
[4] *Remembrancia of the City of London*, 91. Also *supra*, vol. i. 358, note 7 ; and *infra*, Appendix, p. 528, No. 1.
[5] Williams, *The Founders' Company*, 130. Other members included a brewer (113), a carman (118), a stationer (152), a fishmonger (155), and a clockmaker (156). Similarly : Jupp and Pocock, *The Carpenters' Company*, 496, 555.
[6] Clode, *Early History of the Guild of Merchant Taylors*, i. 199-203.

company, should thenceforth observe and keep the ordinances of the company of handicraftsmen as touching their
wares and works made, and to pay their fines and duties to
the said company of handicraftsmen ", while their apprentices
should be admitted at the expiration of their term to the
company whose mistery they used [1].

Under the Early Stuarts the aid of the Government was *Incompat-*
invoked to uphold the claim of the ' handicraft ' companies *ible with
the rights*
to make their membership compulsory on all who practised *of London*
their trades [1a]. In 1605 when the Cooks' Company received *freemen.*
a charter from the King, the court of aldermen ordered
every cook to be translated into the Cooks' Company [2].
Subsequently the court resolved to rescind the decree ' for
some known inconveniences ', but the Cooks obtained a
fresh charter from the Crown confirming it. Thereupon
the court appealed to the Privy Council which suppressed
the new charter [3]. In 1622 the Privy Council issued an
order requiring all freemen of London, who used the art of
weaving without being free of the Weavers' Company, to
be translated into that Company [3a]. Like the Cooks' patent,
this infringed the cherished privilege of the freemen of
London to carry on any occupation [4]; and the civic authorities protested that the order "would cause much trouble
and suits at law, and be a bad example for other companies " [5]. The Privy Council again intervened on behalf
of the Brewers' Company in 1630, but the court of aldermen reported that the members of other companies were
" utterly unwilling to submit to such a translation ", though
ready to submit to search. It further represented that
" a general translation from one company to another . . .

[1] Clode, *Early History of the Guild of Merchant Taylors*, i. 204-206.
[1a] For Cloth-workers, see *infra*, Appendix, p. 528, No. 2.
[2] *Second Report of the Commissioners appointed to inquire into the
Municipal Corporations* (1837)—*London Companies*, 180 ; Unwin, *The
Gilds and Companies of London*, 264.
[3] 1614 : *Remembrancia of the City of London*, 96-98 ; *Acts of the Privy
Council, 1613–1614*, pp. 591, 601. The Cooks, however, appealed to the
order of 1605 in a remonstrance to the Goldsmiths' Company in 1653 :
Kramer, *The English Craft Gilds*, 168, note 41.
[3a] *Acts of the Privy Council, 1621–1623*, p. 263.
[4] *The English Reports*, lxxx. 651. Also *supra*, p. 340.
[5] *Remembrancia of the City of London*, 103. The order only ratified two
orders previously made by the court of aldermen itself in 1617 and 1619,
but held in abeyance.

would be a great breach of the whole frame of the City's government " [1].

*Conces-*   Under the Commonwealth the ' handicraft ' companies
*sions to the* renewed their former petitions to the rulers of the City that
*handicraft*
*companies.* all persons using their trades, who were free of other companies, should " bind their apprentices to the respective companies whose trades they use " ; but owing to the influence of the great companies the petitions were rejected [2]. However, the principle for which they contended was conceded in the case of the Glovers' Company, in whose favour an act of common council in 1650 required all glovers, free of other companies, to bind their apprentices to a member of the Glovers' Company, though they were allowed to retain the services of the apprentices [3]. A similar regulation appears in the charter of the Frame-work Knitters' Company (1663) [4] ; and it was repeated by the civic authorities on behalf of the Carpenters' Company in 1693 [5]. A greater concession was won by the Founders in 1753, when an act of common council provided that henceforth no person should practise the trade of a founder unless first admitted to the Founders' Company [6]. This did not affect the rights of founders who were already members of other companies, and the Founders' Company proceeded to invite them to become ' love brothers ' [7]. But it evidently failed to bring all founders under its control, for in 1831 a committee appointed to inquire whether founders could be forced to belong to the Founders' Company, " they being freemen or not of another company ", reported that " it does not appear by the charter that the court can compel founders to take up their freedom in this company " [8]. Another London

---

[1] *Remembrancia of the City of London,* 108. Similarly for the Poulters' Company : *ibid.* 108-109.

[2] 1653 : Jupp and Pocock, *The Carpenters' Company,* 310, 635. 1658 : Williams, *The Founders' Company,* 115-116. For the earlier petitions, see *supra,* p. 340.

[3] *Second Report of the Commissioners appointed to inquire into the Municipal Corporations* (1837)—*London Companies,* 284.

[4] Felkin, *A History of the Machine-Wrought Hosiery,* 70.

[5] Jupp and Pocock, *The Carpenters' Company,* 268, 312-315.

[6] Williams, *The Founders' Company,* 150-151, 176. The Clockmakers' Company had a similar order : *ibid.* 156.

[7] *I.e.* members of the Founders' Company ' without any fee or expense ' : *ibid.* 152 (1755), 155.        [8] *Ibid.* 174-175.

company, the Carpenters, had abandoned in despair the attempt to enforce membership nearly a century before [1].

In spite of the difficulties of exercising an effective control over industry, the right of the London companies to make search did not lapse [1a]. *Survival of the right of search.* The ordinances of the Clothworkers' Company (1639) provided that the officers, ' once every quarter in the year at the least ', should enter into houses and shops ' to oversee ' that cloth-finishers " do their work well, lawfully, surely and workman-like for the common wealth and profit of the king's majesty's subjects " [2]. The Founders continued to hold ' view and search ' in the seventeenth century, and the election of searchers is recorded as late as 1746 [3]. The Carpenters appointed ' viewers ' of buildings during the eighteenth century, until their duties were taken over by district surveyors under the Building Act of 1774 [4]. The Tinplate-workers carried out a search as late as 1773 [5]. In the provinces, as we should expect, the records show that gild functions were in some instances performed and in others neglected. At Salisbury in 1624 the ' viewers ', chosen to ' view and try the workmanship ' of an applicant for membership of the Tailors' Gild, failed to give their opinion until his admission, when they " delivered in their bill that they do not find him a workman ; which is like to redound to the reproach of the wardens and also to the scandal of the whole company " [6]. The duty of search was easily abused, when the searchers made their visits in private and engaged in ' covert dealing ' [7]. Cases of obstruction were frequent [8], and with the passage of time there was increasing doubt as to the legal validity of the rights claimed by the gilds [9]. In so far as the piecemeal nature of the evidence warrants any generalizations, it appears correct to

---

[1] Jupp and Pocock, *The Carpenters' Company*, 565-566 (1739).

[1a] See also *supra*, p. 331 ; and *infra*, p. 528 (No. 3).

[2] *The Ordinances of the Clothworkers' Company*, 116-117. Similarly : *The Charters of the Clothworkers' Company*.

[3] Williams, *The Founders' Company*, 92, 110, 113, 118, 150.

[4] Jupp and Pocock, *The Carpenters' Company*, 193. Also pp. 155-157, 516, 527.

[5] Unwin, *The Gilds and Companies of London*, 348.

[6] Haskins, *The Ancient Trade Guilds and Companies of Salisbury*, 180.

[7] *Hist. MSS. Comm. Shrewsbury*, 64.

[8] Kramer, *The English Craft Gilds*, 163 *seq.*

[9] *Infra*, pp. 348 *seq.*

say that the system of inspection was in frequent operation in the seventeenth century, but ceased to be a regular and normal practice as the eighteenth century ran its course, though it did not die out completely

*Disabilities of non-free-men.* It is the fate of all institutions which have outlived their period of usefulness, that their defects grow more marked as their decay progresses. The later history of the gilds illustrates this universal tendency. In proportion as their power for good waned, the tenacious hold which they maintained on their privileges exerted a more baneful influence. In virtue of these privileges the right to set up in trade, or work at a skilled occupation, in any borough was confined by charter or prescription to those who were both members of a gild and freemen of the borough. The disabilities imposed on ' foreigners ' [1] were not without justification in earlier times [2], but they served to hinder the mobility of labour and capital, by placing impediments in the way of those who sought to follow their occupation in another locality. The dynamic forces which animate a progressive community were held in check by the obsolete restraints of a static society. The general nature of these restraints can best be shown by a few examples. At Grimsby in 1583 it was ordered that no labourer, who came to live in the town, should be allowed to work until he was admitted by the authorities ' to work as a labourer ' ; and no artificer or tradesman, taking up his residence at Grimsby, could ' work of his occupation or set up and keep a shop ' without the permission of ' Mr. mayor and his brethren ' [3]. At Southampton in 1607 an Act of Parliament confirmed the charter of Henry VI. forbidding non-freemen to buy or sell commodities, except provisions for their own use [4]. At Salisbury in 1615, and again in 1658, every citizen was required to

---

[1] " Such they call all those who are not sons, or apprentices of seven years' standing, to a freeman in the same town " : *Britannia Languens* (1680), 97. The freedom of a borough was obtained by birth, purchase (*supra*, p. 340, note 2), service (apprenticeship), gift, and marriage : *First Report of the Commissioners appointed to inquire into the Municipal Corporations* (1835), 18-19. See also *supra*, vol. i. 265, note 2.

[2] See *supra*, vol. i. 438.     [3] *Hist. MSS. Comm. Grimsby*, 278, 281.

[4] *Statutes*, iv. part ii. 1148.

belong to one or other of the companies : in 1628 no one was to be admitted to any company "until he shall be sworn a free citizen " : in 1706 a stringent order debarred non-free-men from keeping a shop, or exposing for sale any wares by retail, or using 'any art, trade or mistery whatsoever '. The jealousy displayed by the Salisbury authorities towards 'strangers ' was extreme—it was prohibited to put them in possession of any house or shop for business purposes, or to send work out of the city ; and a shoemaker might not even sell boots and shoes made outside the city. Yet when the workmen in Salisbury took advantage of the situation to demand higher wages, the regulation against the employ-ment of country labour was relaxed ; and citizens were allowed to engage carpenters, masons, tilers and labourers living in the country, until the town workmen were willing to serve at " such reasonable rates and wages as the work-men which inhabit the country will serve for "[1]. Similarly at Hull, if the weavers would not work ' at reasonable rates and in reasonable time ', it was permitted to send work out of the town[2]. Apart from concessions of this kind, the corporate towns continued to adhere to their policy of exclusiveness. Thus at Lincoln in 1686 an order was taken against opening any shop or using any occupation ' by foreigners not free of the city '[3]. At Bury St. Edmunds in 1689 a petition was signed by many of the free burgesses, complaining of the badness of trade and the poverty of the town, and desiring that the admission of 'foreigners' to trade in the place might be stopped[4]. At Lancaster in 1690 the representatives of a score of trades, alleging that " they had received great prejudice by foreigners intruding among them ", sought incorporation to strengthen their privileges [5].
We must not suppose that the disabilities placed on non-

---

[1] *Hist. MSS. Comm. Various*, iv. 237-239, 242, 252-253. The Coventry Weavers' Company opposed the dyeing and dressing of Gloucestershire cloths at Coventry : *Victoria County History, Warwickshire*, ii. 255.

[2] Lambert, *Two Thousand Years of Gild Life*, 210 (1673).

[3] *Hist. MSS. Comm. Lincoln*, 111.

[4] *Ibid. Beaufort*, 132. The cloth of Blackburn clothiers was seized at Preston : Abram, *A History of Blackburn*, 202 (*temp.* Charles II.).

[5] *State Papers Domestic*, 1690–1691, p. 61. See the account given in *Autobiography of William Stout of Lancaster* (ed. 1851), 30-31.

*Reasons for the disabilities of non-freemen.*

freemen were invariably due to economic jealousy [1a]. In some cases the object was to prevent residents escaping their share of municipal taxes and municipal offices [1]. The charter granted to Salisbury in 1612 ordered that no one should ' exercise any art, occupation or mistery ' in the city who was not ' a free citizen ', and it explained the prohibition on the ground that " merchants, artificers and others, inhabitants of other cities, for their private gain sell their merchandise in the city, and stay as long as it is pleasing to them without any payment or taxation towards the maintenance of the city "[2]. At Winchester ' by ancient custom ' the mayor and aldermen annually assessed artificers and others engaged in trade in the city, ' and not free thereof ' : at Wallingford in 1681 fines varying from 40s. to £15 were imposed upon persons ' for trading, not being a freeman '[3] : at Norwich ' all makers of stuffs, makers of wool into yarn, master weavers and master wool-combers ' were required by an Act of Parliament (1722) to become freemen of the city, in order that municipal offices might not " fall to persons who are not the chief manufacturers or the most substantial inhabitants "[4]. Hence, while the town government usually supported the authority of the gilds, it punished severely those which admitted non-freemen to their ranks : in 1698 the London court of aldermen prohibited for twelve months " any person to be admitted into the freedom of this city in the Company of Founders "[5]. The fine for entrance into the burgess-ship of the borough was often small [6], and where this was the case it doubtless helped to make the obligation to take up the freedom more tolerable. None the less the objection to the system remained that the municipality was at liberty to exclude on any pretext whomever it pleased. An entry in the minutes of the town council of Nottingham (1629) needs no comment : " This company are not willing

---

[1a] For Quakers, see *infra*, Appendix, p. 528, No. 4.

[1] *State Papers Domestic*, 1672–1673, p. 344.

[2] Haskins, *The Ancient Trade Guilds and Companies of Salisbury*, 78.

[3] Gross, *The Gild Merchant*, ii. 247 (Wallingford), 264 (Winchester: 1650). Walford, *Gilds* (ed. 1888), 123 (Winchester: 1671).

[4] *Statutes at Large*, v. 311.

[5] Williams, *The Founders' Company*, 131-133.

[6] *E.g. Hist. MSS. Comm. Grimsby*, 278 ; *ibid. Various*, vii. 102 (Dunwich).

that Cornelius Launder shall be made burgess in regard there be already two pewterers in the town, who have children and apprentices that are ready to set up trade themselves ; and therefore no necessity as yet to give him admittance as a burgess " [1].

The restraints on internal trade and industry were *Condemned by Restoration writers.* vigorously assailed by a group of Restoration writers [2], who had emancipated themselves from many of the dogmas enshrined in the economic system of their day. Child denounced as a 'common error' the notion that "no man ought to live and trade in a corporation, that is not a freeman of the place " [3]. Roger Coke condemned corporations as obstacles to the progress of trade ; and he deplored that towns which might have been 'seminaries for employment of people' were grown 'poor and unfrequented' [4]. The author of *Britannia Languens* lamented that "most of our ancient corporations and gilds [are] become oppressive oligarchies ". They exacted arbitrary fines of admission, so that " beginners in manufacture and other trades, being foreigners and having but small stocks, can never obtain freedom, and without it are burthened and plagued with by-laws, penalties, distresses and seizures. Nay, if a man be exquisite in his trade, he shall hardly get a freedom for money in a corporation where there are more free of the same trade, for then he is looked on as a dangerous person and likely to eat the bread out of their mouths, as they phrase it " [5]. The progress of Birmingham was attributed to the fact that it admitted all comers [6].

The influence of these opinions began to make itself felt. *Attitude of Parliament.* The Fire of London had already compelled the legislature to make a breach in the traditional system by sanctioning the employment of ' foreigners ' in rebuilding the City. The

---

[1] *Records of Nottingham,* v. 137.
[2] Even in the sixteenth century the restrictions on industry had met with criticism : *A Discourse of the Common Weal of this Realm of England* (ed. Lamond), 128-129 ; *Tudor Economic Documents* (ed. Tawney and Power), iii. 276.
[3] Child, *A New Discourse of Trade* (4th ed.), pp. xlii, 182.
[4] Coke, *Treatise* (1671), i. 70 ; iii. 24, 29, 67.
[5] *Britannia Languens* (1680), 97-98.
[6] Tucker, *An Essay on Trade* (ed. 1753), 87-88. Also *infra,* p. 466.

Act of 1667 allowed workmen, who were not freemen of
London, to have ' the same liberty of working ' as freemen
until the buildings were finished, and after seven years the
privilege was to be enjoyed for life [1].
The Carpenters'
Company in vain depicted the ' sad consequences ' of enter-
taining ' foreigners ', and demanded that no person who had
not served seven years to the art of carpentry should be
employed, and that ' foreign ' carpenters who had served
seven years might only work as labourers and not as ' master
workmen or undertakers ' [2].
The attitude of the legislature
was again shown in 1705, when a parliamentary committee
adjudicated upon the privileges of two East Anglian towns.
Yarmouth and King's Lynn both claimed the custom of
' foreign bought and foreign sold ', by which the freemen
alone had the right to deal in all commodities brought
into the town—for example, non-freemen were obliged to sell
their coal to freemen only. The committee resolved that this
custom was ' a monopoly and a very great grievance and
oppression ' to the inhabitants of neighbouring counties [3].

*Attitude of the law courts.* The attitude of the law courts was on the whole unfavourable to privileges and monopolies of any kind as being ' in
restraint of trade ' [4]. This was demonstrated in 1695. The
burgesses of Droitwich claimed, on the strength of their
charters, the sole right to sink salt-pits ; and they exploited
their position by restricting the supply of salt to keep up the
price. A landowner infringed the monopoly by sinking pits
on his own land. The corporation brought an action but
lost it : other landowners began to sink pits : and the price
of salt fell from two shillings a bushel to fivepence [5]. The
gilds were subject to official scrutiny in virtue of the Act
of 1504 [6], which required them as late as the end of the

---

[1] *Statutes*, v. 606.

[2] Jupp and Pocock, *The Carpenters' Company*, 278-279, 312, 508.

[3] *House of Commons Journals*, xiv. 510-513. For the practice of ' Hain-
ing ', see *ibid*. 513.  Parliament in 1581 and 1598 condemned the ordinances of the London Fishmongers restraining persons from buying and
selling fish, but sanctioned them, except as regards ' salted fish or herrings ',
in 1601 : *Statutes*, iv. part i. 669 ; iv. part ii. 911, 974.

[4] See *supra*, p. 281 and note 7.

[5] *Victoria County History, Worcestershire*, ii. 260-261.

[6] *Supra*, vol. i. 420. The Commission of 1622 was authorized to
examine gild ordinances : Rymer, *Foedera*, xvii. 413.

eighteenth century to submit their ordinances to the high authorities for approval [1]. Yet sometimes [2] a court of justice pronounced ordinances to be ' against law ' [3], even though they had been sanctioned by the lord chancellor, lord treasurer, or the chief justices. It laid down the principle that, despite the Act of 1504, craft ordinances needed to be " affirmed as good or disaffirmed as unlawful " by a court of law [3a]. Sheppard, writing in 1659, explained that by-laws were ' good and binding ' only if ' in pursuit ' of custom or prescription : thus when the London authorities made a by-law that no one should take the son of an alien as his apprentice, it was adjudged (1595) ' a void order ', since the " covenants and bonds of binding that apprentice were good " [4]. At Newcastle, where the Merchant Adventurers claimed the custom of ' foreign bought and foreign sold ' [5], a committee in 1726 reported that open shop was kept by 114 persons, most of whom were not freemen : and " knowing by experience that indictments are tedious and expensive "—one lawsuit was protracted for seven years—it was content to recommend only that a weekly assessment should be laid upon the offenders. It is significant to observe both the extent to which shop-keepers ignored the custom in a place where the spirit of monopoly was deeply entrenched, and the confession of impotence in dealing with them by recourse to litigation. The Merchant Adventurers of Newcastle also contended that even the freemen of the town must buy corn through their agency, but when a case came before the court of ex-chequer (1730) a verdict was returned against the Company. Nevertheless the latter continued to defend its privilege of exclusive trading, but it did so indirectly—throughout the first three-quarters of the eighteenth century it prosecuted

[1] 1675 : *State Papers Domestic*, 1675–1676, p. 426. 1692 : Boyce, *Historical Memoirs of Tiverton*, Bk. v. Appendix, No. vii. 44. 1782 : Williams, *The Founders' Company*, 161.

[2] 1620 : *Acts of the Privy Council*, 1619–1621, p. 208 ; *State Papers Domestic*, 1619–1623, p. 235 (Ipswich Cloth-workers and Tailors) ; Sheppard, *Of Corporations, Fraternities and Guilds* (1659), 98–104 (Weavers of Newbury : *temp.* James I.). [3] Sheppard, *l.c.*

[3a] Wagner, " The Common Law and Free Enterprise ", in *The Economic History Review*, vii. No. 2, 219, note 2. (Also *ibid.* 217-219 for the Merchant Taylors of London, *temp.* Elizabeth.)

[4] Sheppard, *op. cit.* 81-87, 104. [5] *Supra*, p. 348.

traders who did not belong to the Company for infringing
the Statute of Apprentices [1]. Near the end of the century,
however, traders at Newcastle were claiming immunity
expressly on the plea that they had been left undisturbed
in their business for many years [2].

*Other judicial decisions.*    Other judicial decisions reflect the varying currents of
legal opinion. At Winchester in 1705, when the mayor
brought an action against a non-freeman, one of the judges
declared that " a custom to exclude people from exercising
a trade was a strange custom " [3] : on the other hand, the
right of exclusive trading was upheld at Colchester in 1732,
at Devizes in 1748, and at Bath in 1766 [4]. When Northampton consulted its deputy recorder in 1739 as to its power
of debarring non-freemen, he replied : " I know my Lord
Chief Justice Holt (that oracle of the law) hath often set
himself against such exclusion of foreigners, saying it was
against the liberty of the subject, and that it was a grievance
that there were any corporations in England that should
pretend to exclude any persons who have been bred up to
a trade " [5]. The uncertainty that existed as to the legal
position is shown by the frequency with which counsel's
opinion was taken regarding the validity of by-laws " to
hinder foreigners from trading in the town ". Thus Nottingham in 1698 ordered that " special care shall be taken to
prosecute and suppress all foreigners from and for using any
trade within the town ". Although this injunction was
' allowed and approved of ' by the judge at the assizes, the
town council resolved four years later " to take advice forthwith about the by-law " [6]. The gilds evidently shared in
the general uncertainty, for at Andover the Haberdashers'
Company agreed " to take the opinion of some counsel on
the validity of their ancient orders . . . and how far they
have a power to compel the admission of persons refusing to

---

[1] See *infra*, p. 351, note 5.

[2] *Newcastle Merchant Adventurers*, i. pp. xlv, 241, 249, 253, 255, 261,
note.

[3] Gross, *The Gild Merchant*, ii. 269. See *infra*, Appendix, p. 529, No. 1.

[4] *Newcastle Merchant Adventurers*, i. p. xliv, note.

[5] *Northampton Records*, ii. 317.

[6] *Records of Nottingham*, v. 397, 399 ; vi. 9. Legal advice had been
taken in 1647 : *ibid.* v. 252.

become free of the Company "[1]. Yet almost to the last moment some of the gilds continued to fight for the retention of their privileges. As late as 1827 the Merchants' Company in York prosecuted a druggist for selling articles of foreign produce : the judge, however, decided that the plaintiffs had failed to prove a custom 'from time immemorial'[2]. A few years later came the end. The Municipal Corporations *The Municipal Corpora-* Act of 1835 laid down that " every person in any borough *tions Act* may keep any shop for the sale of all lawful wares and mer- *(1835).* chandises by wholesale or retail, and use every lawful trade, occupation, mistery and handicraft for hire, gain, sale or otherwise, within any borough "[3]. The Act removed the restraints on trade, real or nominal, which still persisted in many places [4]; but the freedom which it conferred as a legal right had already been, in practice, largely attained. Economic forces had already drained away the vitality of the gilds until there remained nothing but an empty shell [4a]. One illustration will suffice : in 1752 a master feltmaker informed a parliamentary committee that he employed six ' foreigners ' to one freeman, and in 1755 the Feltmakers' Company formally abolished the restriction on the employment of ' foreign ' workmen [5]. " The insensible progress of society", wrote Eden in 1797, "has reduced chartered rights . . . to a state of inactivity ; and both private and national interests have superseded the necessity of having recourse to antiquated customs. . . . Corporations now seldom enter into litigation, except upon occasions when their *elective* franchises are concerned "[6].

[1] Gross, *The Gild Merchant*, ii. 350-351 (1807).
[2] *York Merchant Adventurers*, 316-321. The Mercers' Company at Shrewsbury brought an action in 1823 : Hibbert, *The Influence and Development of English Gilds*, 134.
[3] *Statutes of the United Kingdom*, xiii. 1016. In 1761 Parliament had thrown open the trade of a fishmonger to "any person although not brought up in the trade of a fishmonger " : *Statutes at Large*, vii. 373.
[4] *First Report of . . . the Municipal Corporations* (1835), 20.
[4a] For the causes of the decline of the craft gilds, see *supra*, vol. ii. Introduction, pp. cxxxi-cxxxiii.
[5] Unwin, *Industrial Organization*, 224. The neglect of the Statute of Apprentices also made for freedom, for when it was in operation it could be used to indict non-freemen : Child, *A New Discourse of Trade* (4th ed.), 151.
[6] Eden, *The State of the Poor* (1797), i. 436-437. He denied Adam Smith's statement that ' many large incorporated towns ' shut out all workmen who had ' no exclusive privilege '.

## (VII)

### THE PATENTS OF MONOPOLY

*Categories of patents: (i.) inventions.*    One method of State control of industry, which assumed great prominence in the second half of the sixteenth and the first half of the seventeenth century, was the delegation of authority to an individual or to a group of individuals acting in a corporate capacity. This method of control gave rise to what is commonly known as the patents of monopoly which, as the fruits of the royal prerogative, raised issues no less important in their constitutional than in their economic bearings. Although the patents granted by Elizabeth and the Early Stuarts gained evil notoriety, they must not be merged in a general condemnation. Four categories may be distinguished. Bacon described the first, to which no exception could be taken, where " any man out of his own wit, industry or endeavour finds out anything beneficial for the commonwealth "[1]. The definition must be understood to mean not only original discoveries but the introduction of technical processes from abroad. To the category of inventions as thus defined belong the earliest patents of Elizabeth. In the sixteenth century England was behind the Continent in her knowledge of some industrial arts, for example, cloth-finishing, glass-making, paper-making, and mining[2]. Her

---

[1] D'Ewes, *The Journals of all the Parliaments during the reign of Queen Elizabeth* (1682), 644. Similarly : Noy, *Reports and Cases* (1669), 182.

[2] For mining, see *supra*, vol. ii. 174. For cloth-finishing and glass-making, see *infra*, pp. 367, 375.

Various attempts were made in the sixteenth century to establish the manufacture of paper in England. Elizabeth granted her German jeweller, John Spilman, the sole right of building paper-mills and collecting rags, but he complained that his monopoly was infringed by others (*State Papers Domestic*, 1598–1601, p. 505 ; 1601–1603, pp. 43-44, 108. His mill was erected at Dartford about 1588 : Rye, *England as seen by Foreigners*, p. lxxii). There were paper-makers in Middlesex in the reign of Charles I. who employed thirty-six servants (1636 : *State Papers Domestic*, Addenda, 1625–1649, p. 537. The servants' wages amounted to £10 a week). Paper for books was made at Wolvercote (Oxford) as early as 1666 (*Victoria County History, Oxfordshire*, ii. 226). A great stimulus was given to the industry by the French immigrants, among them Henry de Portal, who set up a paper manufactory in Hampshire (*ibid. Hampshire*, v. 489. See also *ibid. Buckinghamshire*, ii. 111 *seq.* ; *House of Lords MSS.* 1690–1691, pp. 74, 435). At the end of the seventeenth century Davenant observed
[*contd.*]

dependence upon foreign countries infringed the principles of Mercantilism. It involved, according to the popular notion, the drain of bullion to pay for the imported commodities ; and the preambles of Elizabethan Statutes allude repeatedly to the necessity of husbanding the monetary resources of the kingdom [1]. Moreover in the case of commodities like gunpowder the protection of infant industries could be defended on the ground of national security. In the grant of patents of this kind Elizabeth was following in the footsteps of her predecessors. The most conspicuous precedent was the patent given to John Kempe, a Flemish capitalist who settled in England in the reign of Edward III., in order to revive the decaying woollen industry [2] ; and other patents were conferred on aliens in the fourteenth and fifteenth centuries, which were really passports or guarantees of protection. Elizabeth developed the system on the basis of exclusive privileges ; and the numerous grants issued in the first decade of her reign indicate a deliberate policy on the part of her advisers to make England economically self-sufficing, so far as her natural resources permitted. They include patents to mining prospectors [3] and to makers of glass [4], alum [5] and saltpetre [6], among the rest [7]. It was expressly stipulated that a proportion of native workmen should be employed ; and the provision that prices should not be extortionate, coupled with other safeguards, shows

that " as to ordinary paper . . . we are very much improved in that manufacture, though we are not come up to the French perfection " (Works, ed. 1771, vol. v. 372). The formation of joint-stock companies, which had been advocated a century earlier, afforded further indications of progress (The Commissioners for Trade and Plantations stated in 1697 that one corporation made about 100,000 reams p.a. of white paper : House of Commons Journals, xii. 435. Scott, Joint-Stock Companies, iii. 69, quotes an estimate of 60,000 reams (c. 1710). For an early proposal to form a joint-stock company, see Tudor Economic Documents, ed. Tawney and Power, ii. 251). The workmen engaged in paper-making were paid eight or nine shillings a week (1702 : House of Commons Journals, xiii. 747). In spite of the advance made, the French were still said in the middle of the eighteenth century to excel us in writing-paper, and the Genoese in printing-paper (Campbell, The London Tradesman (1747), 126). For a description of paper-making, see Celia Fiennes, Through England on a Side Saddle, 101.

[1] E.g. infra, p. 365.          [2] Supra, vol. i. 452.
[3] Supra, vol. ii. 174.          [4] Infra, p. 367.
[5] Infra, p. 372.          [6] Infra, p. 358.
[7] Steel : infra, Appendix, p. 529, No. 2. A list is given in Hulme, " The History of the Patent System " in The Law Quarterly Review, xii. 145 seq.

that Burghley was genuinely anxious to prevent the evils of monopoly [1].

The second category of patents took the form of licences relaxing the rigidity of the law, for instance, those permitting the export of unfinished cloth [2]. This category on the whole was beneficial; yet grave abuses crept in when authority was given to an individual to compound with offenders for their breach of certain Acts of Parliament [2a], such as those which forbade the use of gig mills in cloth-finishing [3], or enjoined the compulsory growing of hemp [4]. These Acts were found unworkable, and in default of their repeal it was advisable to grant a dispensation, but in private hands the opportunities for extortion were unlimited.

The third category of patents comprised the bestowal on an individual of powers of supervision over an industry or trade. Thus Sir Walter Raleigh enjoyed the right to issue licences for keeping taverns and retailing wines [5]. The function of regulating the sale of wine was a necessary one, and it was exempted from the censure visited upon monopolies by the Act of 1624 [6]; nevertheless the delegation of governmental functions to private persons seeking their own profit tended to create a kind of feudalism in industry. The abuse of this method of control was best exemplified in the grant of the aulnage made by James I. to the Duke of Lennox. The purpose of the aulnage, as we have seen [7], was to ensure that the manufacturers of cloth conformed to a given standard of quality and dimensions; but the Duke's agents sold the seals to the clothiers without any examination of the cloth. No parallel can therefore be drawn between such patents and the inspection of workshops by mediaeval gilds or the inspection of factories by government officials. As administered in practice the patent was utilized, not to promote the good of the industry, but to fill the coffers of the patentee.

The fourth category of patents provoked the main op-

---

[1] Carr, *Select Charters of Trading Companies*, p. lix.
[2] *Infra*, p. 376.          [2a] See *infra*, Appendix, p. 529, No. 3.
[3] *Supra*, p. 51.          [4] *Supra*, vol. ii. 109.
[5] For an example of a licence to a tavern-keeper, see *Hist. MSS. Comm. Bath*, ii. 22.
[6] *Statutes*, iv. part ii. 1214.     [7] *Supra*, p. 328.

position. It was created where a settled trade was handed (iv.) *Control of a settled trade.*
over to one or more persons for the sake of personal gain.
Malynes gives as ' the truest definition ' of a monopoly the
following : " A kind of commerce in buying, selling, changing
or bartering, usurped by a few and sometimes but by one
person . . . whereby . . . the liberty of trade is restrained
from others [and] the monopolist is enabled to set a price of
commodities at his pleasure "[1]. Or, as defined in the
Parliament of 1604, it was " a private or disordered engrossing for the enhancing of prices, for a private purpose, to a
public prejudice "[2]. The essential feature of this group of
patents was the setting up of a monopoly in an industry
which was already established. In some cases the fourth
category developed out of the first—a patent for a new
process might extend, as it did in glass-making and soap-
making[3], into the control of the whole industry. In other
cases, for example, Darcy's patent for playing-cards[4], there
was no claim that the patentees had invented anything ;
and their interest in the trade of which they secured control
was founded entirely on the hope of personal profit—" All
their pretences public good," said a member of Parliament
in 1614, " their end private gain "[5]. The action of the
Crown in granting such patents was dictated by a variety of
motives. Professions of reforming abuses in an industry,
although generally nothing more than the insincere lip-
service of the promoters, sufficiently harmonized with the
traditions of the mediaeval craft gilds to give their projects
a semblance of justification. Thus Richard Drake, for his
services in ' Sir Francis Drake's voyage ', received a patent
for " the brewing of such stuff as serveth for making of
vinegar and *aqua-vitæ*, being now compounded, be it spoken
with reverence, of the most noisome " ingredients[6]. Again
the patent for starch-making, issued first to an individual
and then to a company, affected to be a remedy against the

---

[1] Malynes, *Consuetudo vel Lex Mercatoria* (1622), 214.
[2] *House of Commons Journals*, i. 985.
[3] *Infra*, pp. 363, 369.
[4] *Infra*, p. 360.
[5] *House of Commons Journals*, i. 472.
[6] *Hist. MSS. Comm. Salisbury*, iv. 457 (? 1593).

' waste and consumption ' of wheat [1]. Moreover the Crown wished to reward servants [2] and gratify favourites ; while any revenue, which came to the exchequer from the patents, might be plausibly represented as compensation for the loss of customs duties on articles of which the importation was now prohibited, or as an excise imposed to make good the deficiencies of parliamentary taxation. In any case Elizabeth and James I.[3] reaped only a scanty harvest from the patents. Charles I., however, raised larger sums because he used them deliberately as a machinery for the collection of an excise on commodities [4].

*The 'projector'.*

Taking the patents as a whole, the driving force behind them lay in another direction. The system of monopolies yielded the same opportunities for patent-hunting, which at a later period were provided by company-promoting ; and the ' projector ' was as notorious at the beginning of the seventeenth century as the ' stock-jobber ' at the end [5]. The description of a ' projector ' in 1641 runs thus : " He employs all his time, labour, study and experience only to search out the abuses of every place, profession and mistery whatsoever. Next his greatest study is to propose the fair outside of a reformation ; and this he begins with a petition to his majesty, with such mighty pretences of enriching the kingdom that he dares most impudently to affirm that it shall bring to his majesty, his heirs and successors for ever many thousands yearly—yea, and employment for all the poor people of the realm (which how well all these late projects have effected, I leave to judicious censure). . . . The issues proceeding of these his pains and labour . . . are commonly called or known by the name of projects " [6]. Two

---

[1] *Supra*, p. 332. One patent (1622) is printed in Carr, *Select Charters of Trading Companies*, 117. The patentees themselves are said to have used wheat : Price, *The English Patents of Monopoly*, 16, note.

[2] Elizabeth's coachman was licensed to export old ' bowtes ', shoes and slippers. He sold the licence for 200 marks : *Hist. MSS. Comm. Salisbury*, vii. 166.

[3] The Crown revenue from patents under James I. is estimated at about £900 (Scott, *Joint-Stock Companies*, i. 149), though it is supposed that hardly £50 was annually derived from true monopoly rents : Price, *The English Patents of Monopoly*, 16, 31, 32 (note). For James I.'s losses on alum, see *infra*, p. 372. [4] *E.g.* wine : *infra*, p. 371.

[5] For stock-jobbing, see *supra*, p. 217.

[6] Brugis, *The Discovery of a Projector* (1641), 1-2.

prominent 'projectors' in the reign of James I. were Sir Arthur Ingram, identified with the alum project [1], and Sir Lionel Cranfield, afterwards lord treasurer. A letter written by Cranfield to Ingram, after discussing a number of projects, concludes : " One rule I desire may be observed between you and me, which is that neither of us seek to advance our estates by the other's loss, but that we may join together faithfully to raise our fortunes by such casualties as this stirring age shall afford " [2]. The ' stirring age ' of Elizabeth and the Early Stuarts provided innumerable openings for 'undertakers', though many of the patentees reaped only a harvest of disappointments. Indeed it was one of the chief evils of the patent system—apart from the dislocation of the industry affected, the check to private enterprise, and the exploitation of the consumer—that it diverted capital into unproductive channels in an age when the wise direction of the national resources was imperatively demanded. Chief Justice Coke in his *Charge* delivered at the Norwich Assizes [3] declared that the monopolist " for the most part useth at a dear rate to pay for his foolishness. For some of that profession have been so wise to sell twenty, thirty or perhaps forty pound land a year, and bestow most part of the money in purchasing of a monopoly : thereby to annoy and hinder the whole public weal for his own private benefit. In which course he so well thriveth as that by toiling some short time, either in starch, vinegar or *aqua-vitæ*, he doth in the end thereby purchase to himself an absolute beggary ; and for my own part, their purposes and practices considered, I can wish unto them no better happiness ".

The unpopularity of the patents was a measure of the *Unpopularity of patents.* abuses for which they were held responsible. The price of all articles which came within their ambit showed a considerable increase [4]. This rise in price has been represented as the inevitable sacrifice entailed in the protection of infant industries, but the justification would at best only cover

---

[1] *Infra*, p. 372.     [2] *Hist. MSS. Comm. Various*, viii. 5 (1607).
[3] *The Lord Coke His Speech and Charge* (1607).
[4] D'Ewes, *The Journals of all the Parliaments during the reign of Queen Elizabeth* (1682), 647-648. For an example (brushes), see *Hist. MSS. Comm. Salisbury*, iv. 457.

patents comprised in the first category. Probably not even these, since the fundamental defect of the patent system lay in the malpractices of its administrators, and even a good patent could be turned to evil account by the agents of the patentee. The most notorious case was saltpetre. Elizabeth and her successors showed anxiety to provide for the making of gunpowder within the realm, and numerous patents were granted for obtaining saltpetre [1]. The danger of depending for supplies upon other countries was a real one. Gresham had experienced difficulty in shipping munitions from the Low Countries in the early years of Elizabeth's reign [2]; and besides the unwillingness of foreign Governments to suffer gunpowder to pass out of their dominions, there was always the possibility of its interception at sea. The argument based on national security was reinforced by the claim that English gunpowder could be sold at two-thirds of the price paid for the foreign commodity, namely, at eightpence a pound [3]. To obtain saltpetre the patentees and their agents were authorized to enter private houses and other buildings, in order to search for it [4]. The ' insolence ' of the ' saltpetre-men ' became a crying evil. The patent, Cecil confessed in the Parliament of 1601, " digs in every man's house " [5]. A report made to the Admiralty in 1630 stated that there was no part of their commission, which the saltpetremen and their servants had not extremely abused. " As in digging in all places without distinction, as in parlours, bedchambers, threshing and malting floors, yea, God's own house they have not forborne ; so they respect not times—digging in the breeding time in dove-houses and working sometimes a month together, whereby the flights of doves are destroyed ;

---

[1] See Carr, *Select Charters of Trading Companies*, pp. lviii, lxxx-lxxxi.

[2] Burgon, *Life of Gresham*, i. 294, 319, 323 ; ii. 22. Difficulty was also experienced in supplying the deficiency created by the Cadiz expedition : *State Papers Domestic*, 1598–1601, pp. 470-471.

[3] *State Papers Domestic*, 1598–1601, pp. 470-471. A saving of £5000 a year on 100 lasts : *Hist. MSS. Comm. Salisbury*, xii. 63-64. But the Act of 1640 allowed anyone to make or import gunpowder on the ground that the price had been " excessively raised " through its having been " engrossed " : *Statutes*, v. 131.

[4] *Hist. MSS. Comm. Leeds*, 97 ; Rymer, *Foedera*, xviii. 23.

[5] D'Ewes, *The Journals of all the Parliaments during the reign of Queen Elizabeth* (1682), 653.

and without respect to harvest time [digging] in barns and in malting houses, when green malt is upon the floor ; and in bedchambers placing their tubs by the bedside of the old and sick, even of women in childbed and persons on their death-beds. They have undermined walls and seldom fill up the places they have digged " [1]. Cecil acknowledged in the House of Commons that there was no patent " whereof the execution hath not been injurious ", and that exactions unauthorized by the grant had been levied on ' poor ignorant people ' by means of ' letters of assistance ' from the Privy Council [2].

Opportunities for extortion and oppression were multi-plied by the lavishness with which Elizabeth granted monopolies : her profusion appeared inexcusable even in the eyes of her own ministers. " I caused a collection to be made ", wrote the lord treasurer to Cecil on the eve of the meeting of Parliament in 1601 " and do find the number to be very great, and most of them so unfit and so odious, neither profitable to her majesty nor good for the common-wealth "[3]. He proposed to anticipate the protest of Par-liament by calling in many of the patents[4]. When the Commons met the storm burst. A long list of patents was recited : it included salt, starch, vinegar, glass, steel, tin, cards and saltpetre among others. " The principallest commodities ", said one member, " are engrossed into the hand of those blood-suckers of the commonwealth " ; and another speaker cried out that " if order be not taken for these, bread will be there before the next Parliament "[5]. The Queen recognized the strength of the opposition, and issued a proclamation (1601) frankly confessing that " some

*Lavish grants of patents.*

---

[1] *State Papers Domestic*, 1629–1631, p. 245. See also *Hist. MSS. Comm. Leyborne–Popham*, p. xiii ; *ibid. Cowper*, ii. 74 ; *Victoria County History, Surrey*, ii. 307.

[2] D'Ewes, *The Journals of all the Parliaments during the reign of Queen Elizabeth* (1682), 652.

[3] *Hist. MSS. Comm. Salisbury*, xi. 324-325.

[4] Bacon stated in Parliament (1601) that since the last Parliament (1597) " at least fifteen or sixteen, to my knowledge, have been repealed : some by her majesty's own express commandment, upon complaint made unto her by petition ; and some by *Quo Warranto* in the Exchequer " : D'Ewes, *The Journals of all the Parliaments during the reign of Queen Elizabeth* (1682), 645.

[5] *Ibid.* 646, 648, 650.

of the grants were not only made upon false and untrue suggestions contained in her letters patents, but have been also notoriously abused to the great loss and grievance of her loving subjects ". Many of the patents were declared void ; and, more important still, liberty was given to those wronged by any which remained " to take their ordinary remedy by her highness's laws of this realm " [1]. This undertaking, to allow the law courts to determine whether any monopoly was injurious to industry and trade, served to extend the influence of the common law upon economic life. Hitherto the Crown had resisted any attempt to submit its prerogative to the arbitrament of the law courts : thus shortly before the proclamation appeared, the Privy Council had ordered stay to be made of a suit which was brought to test the validity of the patent held by Edward Darcy for the manufacture and sale of playing-cards, in order that the Queen's prerogative " may not be called in question " [2]. The proclamation removed the ban, and Darcy himself sought the protection of the courts against a haberdasher, who was infringing his patent, in a celebrated Case of Monopolies [3]. The right of the common law to determine the validity of patents of monopoly, which Elizabeth conceded in 1601, was given statutory force in the Statute of Monopolies (1624) [4] ; yet two years later the Stuart Government refused to allow Mansell's glass patent to be tried before the judges [5]. Its refusal was a recognition of the fact that the common law was tending to look with disfavour upon restraints on trade [6], and was therefore incompatible with the exercise of the royal prerogative in economic affairs.

James I. signalized his accession by suspending monopolies [7], but the barn was swept clear only to make room for

[1] Proclamation, 1601 (Bodleian Library : Arch. G.C. 6, No. 415).
[2] *Acts of the Privy Council*, 1601–1604, p. 237.
[3] 44 Elizabeth : Noy, *Reports and Cases* (1669), 173 *seq.*
[4] *Statutes*, iv. part ii. 1212.
[5] Price, *The English Patents of Monopoly*, 77. For the glass patents, see *infra*, p. 367.
[6] See *supra*, p. 281 (and note 7). But even in the seventeenth century the judges still approved of regulations to promote the ' well ordering of trade ' : *infra*, p. 365.
[7] Except those held by companies : *Tudor and Stuart Proclamations* (ed. Steele), i. No. 944.

more obnoxious entrants. "As a garden, clean weeded, *The* weeds next year "[1], so Parliament was confronted every *Statute of Mono-* session with a fresh crop of patents. Chamberlain wrote in *polies* 1620 : "For proclamations and patents they are become so (1624). ordinary that there is no end, every day bringing forth some new project or other. . . . Whereas at the King's coming in there were complaints of some eight or nine monopolies then in being, they are now said to be multiplied to so many scores "[2]. The Statute of Monopolies (1624) pronounced illegal all monopolies "for the sole buying, selling, making, working or using of anything ", though an exception was made in favour of inventors and companies [3]. Abundant precedents existed for issuing patents to companies not only in foreign trade but also in domestic industries [4]. Public opinion, still powerfully influenced by the corporate character of mediaeval society, sharply distinguished between the exclusive privileges bestowed on individuals and those conferred on companies. If the Queen, said Bacon, grants a monopoly to a number of burgesses or to a corporation, that must stand : "that forsooth is no monopoly "[5]. In Darcy's Case of Monopolies the counsel for the defence acknowledged that "when there be many sellers, although they be all free of one company, as goldsmiths, clothiers, merchants, drapers, tailors, shoemakers, tanners and such like, who have settled governments and wardens and governors to keep them in order, they were never accounted a monopoly "[6]. Hence the exclusion of companies from the Statute of 1624 was sanctioned by public sentiment : nevertheless its effect was to provide patent-hunters with a loophole for escape, and

---

[1] *House of Commons Journals*, i. 491.

[2] State Papers Domestic, James I., vol. cxvi. 13.

[3] *Statutes*, iv. part ii. 1212-1213. Other exceptions included grants relating to printing, saltpetre, ordnance, alum, glass and iron, and to the Newcastle Hostmen. The statement in Levy, *Monopoly and Competition*, 20, note 2, that "the Act [of 1624] forbade all monopolies whether for individuals or bodies corporate or politic whatsoever" overlooks the proviso in favour of companies in clause 9.

[4] *E.g.* the Mines Royal and the Mineral and Battery Companies : *supra*, vol. ii. 174.

[5] D'Ewes, *The Journals of all the Parliaments during the reign of Queen Elizabeth* (1682), 645.

[6] Noy, *Reports and Cases* (1669), 182. For Darcy's case, see *supra*, p. 360 ; also cf. Wagner, "Coke and the Rise of Economic Liberalism ", in *The Economic History Review*, vi. No. 1, 35-42.

henceforth they sheltered themselves under cover of a charter of incorporation. Thus James I. granted William Shipman the sole right of planting madder, which was used in dyeing ; his successor incorporated Shipman ' and his assigns ' as the Society of Planters of Madder of the City of Westminster [1]. The reign of Charles I. witnessed a great extension of the system of incorporation, as well as a deliberate attempt to utilize it for the purpose of raising indirect taxation. No more unfortunate machinery could have been devised, since it involved the maximum amount of interference with established trades, while the greater part of the money extorted from the consumer was intercepted by the monopolists [2]. In this way it combined with other economic grievances [3] to alienate the trading classes from the Crown, and to inflame popular opinion against the King and his advisers. In 1640 the ' mountains of monopolies ' began to ' go down apace ' [4], but the enemies of the monarchy had been provided with a handle. In his indictment of Stuart rule Pym laid marked stress upon the ' infinite mischiefs ' produced by ' the great inundation of monopolies '—" the impairing the goodness and enhancing the price of most of the commodities and manufactures of the realm, yea, of those who are of most necessary and common use, as salt, soap, beer, coals and infinite others ; that, under colour of licences, trades and manufactures are restrained to a few hands; [that monopolies] have been very chargeable to the kingdom and brought very little treasure into his majesty's coffers " [5].

The working of the patent system can best be illustrated by a study of a group of patents which attracted most attention, namely, soap, salt, glass, wine, alum, and cloth-finishing.

*The soap patent.* The manipulation of the soap industry affords a striking example of the mixture of motives which inspired the economic activities of the Early Stuarts : the desire to

---

[1] Carr, *Select Charters of Trading Companies*, p. lxxix.
[2] *Infra*, pp. 364, 371.          [3] *Supra*, pp. 314 *seq.*
[4] *State Papers Domestic*, 1640–1641, p. 260 ; *Hist. MSS. Comm.* Kenyon, 60.
[5] Pym, *The Kingdome's Manifestation* (1643), 12, 20.

create new sources of revenue, which would make the Crown independent of parliamentary control, was associated with a policy of industrial protection designed to make the kingdom economically independent. The attempt to combine in a single scheme aims widely dissimilar was invariably disastrous. A genuine, if mistaken, national object lent colour to specious projects for raising revenue ; while the latter not only blinded the Government to the dangers which lay ahead, but caused it to persist in its policy long after the dangers had become a reality. In 1631 a group of ' gentlemen soap-boilers ' [1], never ' bred up to the trade ', was incorporated under the name of the Society of Soapmakers of Westminster, which used native materials to work a new process for soap [2]. It was ordered that no foreign soap should be imported, and that native soap should be made with vegetable instead of fish oil ; the Society was armed with powers to search and stamp the soap of the independent producers ; and no soap was to be made elsewhere than in the city of London, Westminster and Bristol [2a]. Subsequently the production of soap was confined to the Society and those licensed by it, so that a project for working a new process developed into control of the whole trade [3]. The Society undertook to pay the King £4 (afterwards £6) per ton[4]; and as he lost the duties which he formerly received on the prohibited materials, he was entitled to reasonable compensation. The price of the soap was not to exceed 3d. per lb.[5], which gave security to the consumers against exploitation ; and the payment to the Crown was to come out of the profits of the new process.

On paper the scheme thus protected a native industry— at the expense, however, of the Greenland Company [6]— against foreign competition and against dependency on

---

[1] Wilkins, The Sope-Patentees of Londons Petition Opened and Explained (1646) ; Wilkins, A Looking-Glasse for Sope-Patentees (1646).

[2] Its charter is printed in Carr, Select Charters of Trading Companies, 136.

[2a] For Bristol : infra, Appendix, p. 529, No. 4.

[3] Rymer, Foedera, xix. 381 seq., 504 seq., 566 seq., 592 seq.

[4] A Short and True Relation concerning the Soap-business (1641), 4, 23-24.

[5] Ibid. 5, 11.

[6] It was injured by the restraint on the use of whale oil : State Papers Domestic, 1634–1635, pp. 392-393.

*Degener-*
*ates into an*
*excise*
*scheme.*

foreign materials, while it safeguarded the consumers from
a rise in price and the Crown from a loss of revenue. It
attempted, in short, to accomplish too many things, and the
sequel betrayed the wide gap that often exists between the
optimistic prospectus of a company promoter and his actual
performances. The invention proved a failure in spite of
over eighty testimonials (including four countesses and five
viscountesses) that the new soap was better [1]. In 1634 the
old soap, made with fish oil, was selling privately at 6d., 8d.,
10d. and 12d. the pound owing to ' the extreme badness ' of
the new soap [2]. A number of independent soap-boilers were
summoned before the Star Chamber for resisting the patent,
using fish oil, opposing the searchers, and selling soap not
stamped with the Society's seal [3]. They were condemned to
imprisonment and a heavy fine, but before long the Society
itself was empowered to make soap with fish oil [4]. Eventually (1637) the independent soapmakers of London offered
to pay the King £8 per ton, and in return for a sum of
£43,000 the Westminster Society surrendered its patent [5].
In its place was erected a new company, the Society of
Soapmakers of London, consisting of those engaged in the
trade [6]. As a consequence the price of soap was increased
over 50 per cent. to meet the charge of the royalty paid to
the King and the compensation due to the old company.
Coarse soap, formerly sold at 2¼d. per lb. wholesale and at
2½d. retail, was raised to 3¼d. wholesale and 4d. retail ; and
' sweet or best ' soap advanced from 2½d. to 3¾d. wholesale,
and from 3d. to 5d. or 6d. retail [7]. The attempt to improve
the soap industry by a new process thus degenerated into
an excise scheme of the most reprehensible kind, in which
the sum extracted from the consumers was out of all proportion to the amount which reached the exchequer. At the
meeting of the Long Parliament the price of soap fell ' 2d.

---

[1] Rymer, *Foedera*, xix. 509.
[2] *A Short and True Relation concerning the Soap-business* (1641), 17-18.
[3] *Ibid.* 7 *seq.*          [4] *Ibid.* 18, 20.
[5] *Ibid.* 25-26 ; Rymer, *Foedera*, xx. 181 *seq.*
[6] Its charter (dated 1637) is printed in Carr, *Select Charters of Trading
Companies*, 160.
[7] *State Papers Domestic*, 1639-1640, p. 602.

in 5d.' [1], yet the new corporation escaped condemnation doubtless owing to the fact that its membership comprised, not ' gentlemen soap-boilers ', but the actual producers. And it was accorded the protection of the law courts. A legal decision pronounced in 1656 [2] shows that even under the Commonwealth the judges were not unfavourable towards the principle of industrial regulation : " I know very well that common and vulgar judgments run high against all such patents, and condemn them before they understand them, as being contrary to the liberty of the subject and the freedom of trade. But they that consider them better are not so hasty and rash in their censures : for certainly upon a serious consideration all such patents and by-laws as tend most to the well-regulating and ordering of trades and the better management of them, so that the benefit of them may be derived to the greater part of the people though with a prejudice to some particular persons, have always been allowed by the law. But patents which tend to the engrossing of trade, merchandise and manufacture, though of never so small value, into one or a few hands only, have always been held unreasonable and unwarrantable ". Accordingly the patent of the London Soapmakers was conceived " not to be within the Act against Monopolies ".

Salt, like soap, was an article of primary necessity [3]. A considerable supply was drawn from abroad, involving the drain of " great sums of money to the impoverishment of this realm by wasting and conveying of the treasure and coin of this realm into foreign parts " [4]. To encourage the English manufacture of salt, a patent was granted in 1566 to a native of Antwerp [5], domiciled in England, to make salt by a new process. An Act of Parliament assigned the patent to a group which included Cecil (Burghley), the Earl of Pembroke and the Earl of Leicester, but did not prohibit the importation of foreign salt nor the making of native salt by the old

*The salt patent.*

---

[1] *Hist. MSS. Comm. Kenyon*, 59.

[2] Hardres, *Reports of Cases adjudged in the Court of Exchequer* (1693), 55.

[3] For the process of salt-making, see *Hist. MSS. Comm. Portland*, vi. 105-106, 109, Collins, *Salt and Fishery* (1682); and Postlethwayt, *Dictionary of Trade and Commerce, s.v.* Salt. Salt was made by boiling down the liquid from the brine springs, by evaporating sea water, and (later) by dissolving rock salt. The patents refer to sea salt.

[4] *Statutes*, iv. part i. 523.      [5] Francis Bartye.

process [1]. Another patent issued in 1586 to Thomas Wilkes, one of the clerks of the Privy Council, had all the worst features of a monopoly, for it gave him the sole right to make and sell white salt in King's Lynn, Boston and Hull for the needs of these ports and of ' the counties thereunto adjacent ' [2]; and the effect was shown three years later when King's Lynn complained that the price of salt had been doubled [3]. In the Parliament of 1601 the salt patent was singled out for special attack, one member affirming that the price of salt had risen in his county from sixteen pence to fourteen and fifteen shillings a bushel [4].

*Its injurious effects.*     James I. apparently contented himself with patents for " the making of bay and white salt by a new kind of invention " [5]. In the next reign (1635) the salt trade of the coast from Southampton to Berwick was placed in the hands of a company, ' the Society of Saltmakers at the North and South Shields ', which undertook to pay the King a duty of ten shillings per wey in return for the exclusion of foreign salt [6]. The scheme demonstrated the mercantilist methods of achieving economic self-sufficiency. It was to be accomplished, not as to-day by means of tariffs or subsidies, but by the prohibition of imports coupled with the concession of exclusive privileges to an individual or company. Thus it vested complete control of the market in the hands of a single producer, since protection from foreign competition was combined with the suppression of independent enterprise at home. The sequel is instructive. The price of salt, which was three pounds west of Southampton, reached as much as six pounds on the east coast [7], and the rise was

---

[1] *Statutes*, iv. part i. 523-524 (1566). For the early history of the salt industry, see Hughes, *Studies in Administration and Finance*, 19 *seq.*, and *The English Historical Review*, xl. 334 *seq.*
[2] *Tudor Economic Documents* (ed. Tawney and Power), ii. 254.
[3] *Hist. MSS. Comm. Salisbury*, iii. 395.
[4] D'Ewes, *The Journals of all the Parliaments during the reign of Queen Elizabeth* (1682), 647.
[5] 1614 : *Acts of the Privy Council, 1613–1614*, p. 567.
[6] Its charters are printed in Carr, *Select Charters of Trading Companies*, 142, 167. In 1636 another company was formed, the Saltmakers of Great Yarmouth : *ibid.* 148. See also Hughes, *op. cit.* 88 *seq.*
[7] Price, *The English Patents of Monopoly*, 114-116 ; Scott, *Joint-Stock Companies*, ii. 468-470.

detrimental to the interests of the fishing industry, one of the pillars of the Mercantilist State. Moreover the project was injurious to shipping, equally a pillar of Mercantilism. The masters of Trinity House protested against the prohibition of foreign salt, on the ground that the greatest part of the shipping was employed in trade to southern Europe, and " for freight home they expose themselves to fortune, encouraged by their certain loading of salt when all better employment fails. If the importation of salt fails, a third part of the merchant ships in this land will want employment . . . for if the certainty of relading salt be taken away the voyage will not be undertaken " [1]. The argument illustrated afresh the inherent contradictions of a policy, which adopted facile solutions without regard to their reactions upon other branches of the national economy. The salt patent was eventually revoked by the Long Parliament [2].

The glass industry provides a signal instance of the abuse *The glass* of the patent system. A legitimate desire to encourage a *patent.* new process assumed the form of an attempt to control the trade as a whole, and disproportionate risks were taken for the sake of an uncertain advantage. Down to the reign of Elizabeth the glass made in England was of a coarse quality and the finer varieties were imported. In 1567 a patent was granted for twenty-one years to Anthony Beckn and Jean Carre of Antwerp to make ' great glass '. They procured workmen from Lorraine and erected three glass-houses, two in Sussex and one in London, but owing to dissensions among the partners the project was a failure and the workmen returned to France [3]. Seven years later a patent was given to an Italian, Verselini, to manufacture drinking glasses, yet again nothing material was accomplished [4]. The real impetus to the glass industry came from French refugees, probably Huguenots, who carried on the trade without any patent. They belonged to the glass-making families of Lorraine (Henzey and Tyzack) and Normandy (Bungar),

---

[1] *State Papers Domestic*, 1635–1636, p. 44.
[2] *House of Commons Journals*, ii. 58-59.
[3] *State Papers Domestic*, Addenda, 1566–1579, p. 34 ; *Tudor Economic Documents* (ed. Tawney and Power), i. 302-307. On the history of glass-making in England, see Hartshorne, *Old English Glasses*.
[4] Price, *The English Patents of Monopoly*, 69.

and became the chief producers of glass in this country [1]. One problem which confronted the glass-makers was the scarcity of fuel; and the glass industry, like the iron industry [2], migrated to new centres, from Surrey and Sussex to the Forest of Dean and then to Staffordshire and Worcestershire, as the supplies of timber became exhausted. The question of an alternative fuel was growing urgent [3], when it was discovered that the difficulties, which retarded the use of coal in the iron industry, could be more readily surmounted in the case of glass. The adoption of coal led to an important development which is commonly associated exclusively with the 'Industrial Revolution'—the migration of industry to coal-producing areas. Towards the end of James I.'s reign works for the manufacture of glass were established at Newcastle [4], a confirmation of Gray's claim (1649) that the coal trade of Newcastle " hath made this part to flourish in all trades " [5]. The patents already in existence, which had served no useful purpose, were now supplemented by fresh grants conferring the exclusive right to employ coal in the production of glass.

*Higher prices and worse quality.*     The unpopularity of the glass patents provoked an outcry in the Parliament of 1614 : " Now to glass, after to iron, after to all other trades. This is like taking away the millstone from the poor ". A parliamentary committee reported the statement of the merchants that " if all these patents might be called in, which now are for making glasses, that should be sold here (by importation for 3¼d.) which now costeth 16d." [6]. The claims of the different patentees produced friction [7] but they were bought out, and in 1615 a new patent was issued with which Sir Robert Mansell, who ultimately obtained complete control, now became identified. The position of the new patentees was strengthened by a proclamation which forbade both the use of wood in the

---

[1] Price, *op. cit.* 67 *seq.* See also *Victoria County History, Surrey*, ii. 295 *seq.* A glass-house was established near Hastings by Frenchmen : *Acts of the Privy Council*, 1581–1582, p. 281.
[2] *Supra*, vol. ii. 158 *seq.*
[3] Standish, *New Directions for the Planting of Timber* (1613), 4.
[4] *State Papers Domestic*, 1623–1625, p. 215.
[5] Gray, *Chorographia* (1649), 26.
[6] *House of Commons Journals*, i. 469, 472.
[7] *Acts of the Privy Council*, 1613–1614, pp. 29, 162, 497, etc.

melting of glass, and the importation of foreign glass [1]. These restrictions placed the glass industry in the hands of Mansell and his partners, who alone had the right to employ coal in making glass. Although Mansell was allowed to retain his monopoly until 1642—it was exempted from the Act of 1624 [2]—his association with the industry was unfortunate. He introduced no new process since the glassmakers had already begun to use coal : he claimed to have sunk thirty thousand pounds in the industry [3], though the chief producers, the Bungars, Henzeys and Tyzacks, were presumably in a condition to finance the industry themselves : he suffered severely from the Scottish occupation of Newcastle [4], yet apart from this his losses seem to have been primarily due to incompetency, not to the deliberate expenditure of the far-seeing entrepreneur. The glaziers complained of " the dearness, badness and scarcity of glass, and the want of full size "—even the members of the Privy Council confessed " their own experience that glass was not so fair, so clear nor so strong as the same was wont to be " [5] —and the yearly rent of £1500, which was to be paid to the Crown, fell into arrears [6]. Once the industry was released by the Long Parliament from the strangle-hold of monopoly [7], the art of glass-making showed progress ; and after the Restoration, Evelyn described the glass blown in this country as " of finer metal than that of Murano at Venice " [8]. The manufacture of sheets of plate glass is said to have been established by a Frenchman, Abraham Thevenart, after the Revocation of the Edict of Nantes [9]. Towards the end of the seventeenth century the glass-makers organized them-

---

[1] *Tudor and Stuart Proclamations* (ed. Steele), i. No. 1164. The patent of 1624 allowed any person to import foreign glass, but that of 1634 restricted importation to Mansell : Price, *The English Patents of Monopoly*, Appendix, 225, 235.

[2] *Statutes*, iv. part ii. 1214.

[3] *State Papers Domestic*, 1640–1641, p. 65.

[4] *Ibid.* 1640–1641, p. 65. Mansell had three furnaces near Newcastle in 1640, and he seems to have employed there sixty alien workmen : *ibid.* 1640–1641, p. 65.

[5] *Ibid.* 1637–1638, pp. 153-154.

[6] *Ibid.* 1640–1641, p. 65 ; *Hist. MSS. Comm. Leeds*, 91-92.

[7] *House of Commons Journals*, ii. 530, 596.

[8] Smiles, *The Huguenots*, 331.

[9] *Ibid.* ; Cunningham, *Alien Immigrants*, 243.

selves in companies [1] ; and those who opposed the ' free trade ' treaty with France in 1713 claimed that we had " absolutely and entirely made [the manufacture of glass] our own " [2].

*The wine patent.*  The wine trade in 1637 gave birth to a project which ranked among the most unpopular measures sanctioned by Charles I. in his efforts to replenish an exhausted treasury. The authorship of the scheme was commonly attributed to Alderman Abel, master of the Vintners' Company, and Richard Kilvert, ' a most politic projector ', who are represented in a contemporary tract as debating the pretext " upon which we may ground the begging of this patent "— " Marry, thus : we must first pretend both in the merchant and vintner some gross abuses and these no mean ones neither, for the reforming and rectifying of which we are petitioners for this patent. And that the merchant shall pay to the King forty shillings upon every tun ere he shall vent it to the vintner ; in lieu of which, that the vintner may be no loser, he shall raise the price also of his wines. . . . It is no matter how the subject suffer, so we get and gain by it. Now to cover this our craft . . . because all things of the like nature carry a pretence for the King's profit, so we will allow him a competent proportion of forty thousand pounds per annum ; when the power of the patent, being punctually executed, will yield double at least, if not treble that sum, and return it into the coffers of the undertakers " [3]. The dialogue was a satire on the methods of patent-promoting ; but another pamphlet, in defence of Alderman Abel, stated that the plan " proceeded originally from the generality of the vintners " [4]. According to a third, the vintners' own account, the project was not contrived by them : the initiative was taken by the Government, which in 1632 proposed an imposition of four pounds per tun. When the vintners refused their assent, a decree

[1] Scott, *Joint-Stock Companies*, iii. 110.
[2] *The British Merchant* (ed. 1721), ii. 276.
[3] *A Dialogue or accidental discourse betwixt Mr. Alderman Abell & Richard Kilvert* (1641), 6. See also *The Last Discourse betwixt Master Abel & Master Kilvert* (1641).
[4] *A True Discovery of the Projectors of the Wine Project* (1641).

was procured in the Star Chamber " prohibiting vintners to dress meat and restraining them from divers benefits of their trade ; and this was prepared as a lash to over-awe them ". The infringement of the decree gave the court a handle against the vintners, and under the threat of a prosecution they yielded [1].

Whatever the origin of the scheme, its main features were not disputed. In 1637 the Company of Vintners agreed to pay a duty of forty shillings on every tun of wine sold in the kingdom, in return for a monopoly of the retail trade in wine—merchants being forced to sell only to retail vintners, and coopers being restrained from buying or selling wines. The vintners were also allowed to ' dress and sell ' victuals, beer and tobacco, and to raise the price of wine by one penny a quart on French wines, and by twopence a quart on Spanish wines [2]. The impost of forty shillings a tun was farmed to a number of vintners for £30,000 a year, although —according to Pym—the quantity of wine sold was 45,000 tuns, on which the duty would amount to £90,000, thus giving the farmers a profit of £60,000 [3]. Actually the whole profit which the project brought the King in the space of three years was only £19,606 [4]. For the sake of this meagre return, the consumers were left to be exploited by a corporation armed with a monopoly of the trade and the right to raise prices. An increase of one penny per quart would have produced £4 : 4s. a tun, so that the vintners, who were only required to pay the farmers of the duty £2, gained £2 : 4s. on every additional penny ; and actually they charged more than one penny above the old price. Pym stated that the latter was advanced by twopence : on this basis the consumers paid altogether £378,000, of which the King was nominally entitled to £30,000 though he received much less [5]. Thus the wine project, like the soap patent,

*Manipulation of the wine trade.*

[1] *The Vintners' Answer* (1642), 2-4.
[2] *A True Discovery of the Projectors of the Wine Project* (1641) ; *House of Commons Journals*, ii. 218.
[3] Pym, *The Kingdome's Manifestation* (1643), 20.
[4] *House of Commons Journals*, ii. 218 (1641).
[5] This calculation is based on a sale of 45,000 tuns, and reckoning 252 gallons to the tun : *A True Discovery of the Projectors of the Wine Project*

[*contd.*]

illustrates how industry was manipulated to bring in revenue to the Crown at a cost to the consumers which was utterly disproportionate.

*The alum patent.* The monopolies were generally vested in private hands. The most conspicuous example of an industry which became a Crown monopoly was the alum industry : it shed an unfavourable light on the competence of James I. and his ministers for the management of a State enterprise. Alum, ' a very necessary commodity' used to dye cloth, was imported from abroad. In 1564 Elizabeth, " desirous that the hidden riches of the earth should by search and work of men skilful be found and brought to the use and commodity of her realm ", granted a patent to Cornelius de Vos " to dig, search and work the ores of alum and copperas ". Two years later an Act of Parliament assigned the patent to Lord Mountjoy on the ground that Cornelius de Vos was " of no sufficient wealth and ability to bring the ores to such effect and perfection as was requisite " [1]. Mountjoy's efforts were apparently fruitless, but early in the next reign alum deposits were discovered in Yorkshire. At first (1607) a group of patentees, financed by London capitalists, secured the right to work them : then in 1609 the King took the mines into his own hands and farmed them out. The importation of foreign alum was prohibited [2], and although it was promised that the native product should be sold at reasonable rates, prices rose considerably while the quality deteriorated. The contractors became insolvent, and in 1613 the King appointed his own managers for the mines. In two years the Crown lost heavily—it is estimated that about £100,000 was invested by the King [3], and either appropriated by the agents or expended unprofitably. The mines were once more put out to farm (1615), and a letter written by one of the farmers to another in 1619 shows the disastrous state

---

(1641), 23, 25 ; Pym, *The Kingdome's Manifestation* (1643), 20. (Pym's own estimate of £360,000 assumes £8 per tun, instead of £8 : 8s.)

[1] *Statutes*, iv. part i. 522-523. Operations were carried on in the Isle of Wight : Price, *The English Patents of Monopoly*, 82. There were alum works in Dorsetshire : *Acts of the Privy Council*, 1581–1582, pp. 339, 341. See *infra*, Appendix, p. 530, No. 1.

[2] In 1609 : *Tudor and Stuart Proclamations* (ed. Steele), i. No. 1082. For the alum project : Turton, *The Alum Farm* ; Price, *op. cit.* 82 *seq.*

[3] Price, *op. cit.* 101. But see *infra*, Appendix, p. 530, No. 2.

of the enterprise : " I am undone by this business, and so will you be if you cannot work yourself out of it. . . . I go in fear of the workmen, who clamour for pay and will only be satisfied with all that is due to them ; it being a lamentable thing to see a multitude of poor snakes tattered and naked and ready to starve for want of food and clothes, not finding any credit for bread and drink because they are unpaid for three months and some four, and doing daily sore labour for nothing but tickets, which they set before their wives and children to feed them when they ask bread, saying they get naught else, and some of them this day in my sight arrested and carried to prison for their diet " [1].

Among other commodities which were constituted royal *Other patents.* monopolies were gold and silver thread, playing cards, pins and tobacco. A patent for the sole right to make gold and silver thread was granted in 1611 on the pretext that imported bullion alone would be used in the manufacture. The industry was taken over by the Crown in 1618, but the commissioners appointed by the King acted with flagrant dishonesty—' sophisticating ' the thread by mixing gold and silver with lead ; melting bullion of the realm instead of importing bullion ; and crushing opposition relentlessly by imprisoning independent wire-workers and seizing their tools [2]. Two of the commissioners, Mompesson and Michell, were afterwards condemned in the Parliament of 1621. The manufacture of playing cards was not undertaken directly by the Crown's agents. It was left in the hands of the London Company of Playing-card Makers, with which the King entered into an agreement " for a constant weekly buying and taking off from them of their manufactures of cards and dice " [3]. The alleged reason for the contract was " the better employment and relief of the cardmakers and dicemakers " : its real purpose was to secure the trading profits of the industry for the Exchequer. In the case of the pin-making industry [4] Charles I. undertook in 1640 to supply

[1] *Hist. MSS. Comm. Various*, viii. 15-16. For the later history : *infra*, Appendix, p. 530, No. 3.
[2] *House of Commons Journals*, i. 538-542 ; *Hist. MSS. Comm.* iii. 16 ; *ibid. Buccleuch*, i. 208. [3] Rymer, *Foedera*, xx. 145.
[4] Under James I. a patent was promoted to restrain the importation of foreign pins, supply the Pinmakers' Company with capital, and take off

[contd.]

capital to the amount of ten thousand pounds for the purchase of pins, and in return the Pinmakers' Company engaged to use only wire provided by the King. This double
arrangement was designed to yield a profit on the sale both
of the raw material and the finished product. The King,
however, at once farmed his share in the enterprise to a
capitalist [1]. The tobacco monopoly had a chequered history
—at one time held by private individuals, at another time
by the Crown ; its fiscal purpose strongly marked, yet not
obscuring other motives of a more unalloyed character. The
sole right to import tobacco was first conceded in 1615 to
two individuals, then in 1620 to a group of capitalists, and
the following year to the collector of the tobacco impost.
The Virginia and the Bermuda Companies remonstrated
against the tobacco monopoly, and in 1622 it was conferred
upon them, though owing to dissensions among their members the contract was soon rescinded. It was next proposed
(1624) to make tobacco a Crown monopoly ; and this took
effect in the reign of Charles I., who appointed commissioners
in 1627 with the exclusive right to buy tobacco from the
importers and to sell it in England on the King's behalf [2].
The royal monopoly was intended to benefit the Exchequer ;
none the less other motives influenced the King in bringing
the trade under Government control, as is shown by his
pressing the colonies to devote themselves to more substantial commodities [3]. The colonies disliked equally the
monopoly and the recommendation to curtail production :
they ignored the latter, but they could not evade the former
despite their protests against it.

*Patent for cloth-finishing.* The most famous patent is associated with Alderman
Cockayne's ' unhappy project ' for dyeing and dressing
cloth [4]. It was more important than any other because it

its hands the whole output : *Remembrancia of the City of London,* 519,
521-526.
  [1] Unwin, *Industrial Organization,* Appendix A, iii.
  [2] On the Stuart regulation of the tobacco industry, see Beer, *The
Origins of the British Colonial System,* 117 seq.          [3] *Supra,* p. 181.
  [4] For the process of dressing cloth, see Lipson, *The History of the
Woollen and Worsted Industries,* 141-142. Cloth-dressers were also termed
cloth-finishers, cloth-workers, shearmen, and croppers : *supra,* vol. ii. 53.

affected the premier industry of the country, and its consequences were more enduring and widespread. The true significance of this experiment, however, will be missed if it is treated simply as a monumental example of Stuart folly. James I. may have been largely influenced in his support of Cockayne by the hope of financial gain to the Crown—it is impossible, as it is unprofitable, to weigh precisely the complex motives that actuated the Early Stuarts in their economic policy. Nevertheless the fact remains that the aim of fostering a native cloth-finishing industry was something more than a mere fiscal expedient [1] : it was a mercantilist conception debated from the fifteenth to the eighteenth century. James's intervention proved disastrous, yet it had the approval of his wisest councillor, Bacon ; and there appears no reason to doubt the sincerity of his desire that " the reducing of the trade of white cloths, which is but an imperfect thing towards the wealth and good of this our kingdom, unto the trade of cloths dyed and dressed might be the work of our time " [2]. The root of the trouble was that ' the most part ' [3] of the cloth exported from England was sent abroad in a raw state, undyed and unfinished. This brought the merchants into collision with the cloth-workers. The same principle was involved as in the export of wool : just as wool was the raw material of the makers of cloth, so white undressed cloth was the raw material of the dyers and cloth-finishers. In each case the conflict was between the producers of raw or half-manufactured material and the merchants handling it on the one hand, and the users of the material on the other ; and in each case the State supported the claims of the latter. An instructive difference must, however, be noticed. The makers of cloth succeeded in establishing a monopoly, since they provided the graziers with a home market for English wool ; the cloth-finishers did not succeed in establishing a monopoly, since they were unable

---

[1] For a different view, see Unwin, *Industrial Organization*, 185 (" The cloth-working project was only part of a wider policy of indirect taxation "). Cf. also *infra*, p. 378, note 5.

[2] Carr, *Select Charters of Trading Companies*, 78.

[3] *Acts of the Privy Council*, 1558–1570, p. 304. See *supra*, vol. ii. 228, note 5 ; and *infra*, p. 377.

to provide the principal exporters of cloth with a foreign
market for English-dressed cloth.

The series of enactments against the export of cloth in
an unfinished state commence in the fifteenth century [1], and
culminate in the Act of 1536, which ordered that no white
cloth above the value of four pounds and no dyed cloth
above the value of three pounds should be exported ' un-
barbed, unshorn and unrowed ' [2]. The efforts of the clothiers
and cloth merchants to obtain a repeal of this Statute failed
—according to Chapuys, the imperial ambassador in England—because the King derived a great profit from licences
permitting transportation [3]. But the depreciation of the
currency caused the price of cloth to rise, so that in the reign
of Elizabeth cloth made of the coarsest wool, formerly sold
for four pounds the piece, advanced to seven or eight
pounds ; [4] and, as the law stood, it could no longer be sent
abroad unless dyed and dressed. The Queen therefore issued
licences to enable white cloth to be taken out of the country
notwithstanding the Statute. The grant to the Merchant
Adventurers in 1564 empowered them to ship 30,000 cloths
a year ' not wrought or dressed ', of which 25,000 were to be
above £3 and under £6 in value per cloth, and 5000 were to
be above the value of £4 per cloth [5]. Two years later, in
order to pacify the cloth-finishers, Parliament enacted that
one cloth ' wrought and dressed ' was to be exported for
every nine cloths exported by licence unwrought ; and that
Kentish and Suffolk cloths were not to be sold abroad
unfinished under any licence [6]. Other licences were given to
individuals, including Walsingham and Raleigh. The Company of Merchant Adventurers is said to have instigated
some of the patentees to sue for licences, which it afterwards
bought from them [7]. The Company in this way exceeded its

---

[1] For the Acts of 1467, 1487, 1512 and 1523, see *supra*, vol. i. 455
(and note 4), 485 (note 4).　　　　[2] *Statutes*, iii. 545.
[3] *Letters and Papers, Foreign and Domestic, Henry VIII.*, vol. xvii. 183
(1542).
[4] *State Papers Domestic*, 1591–1594, p. 321 ; Misselden, *The Circle of
Commerce* (1623), 56.
[5] *Statutes*, viii. 752 ; *House of Commons Journals*, xv. 458.
[6] *Statutes*, iv. part i. 489.
[7] *State Papers Domestic*, 1598–1601, pp. 383-384 ; *ibid.* Addenda,
1580–1625, pp. 385, 402-403.

original grant, and at the end of the sixteenth century was reputed to transport annually 56,000 cloths, of which only 300 were dressed instead of the proportion of one in ten [1].

The cloth-finishers importuned the Government inces- *Inferiority of English dyeing and finishing.* santly against the merchant exporters, who provided them with no employment and disregarded the obligation laid upon them by the Act of 1566 [2]. It was affirmed that the export of finished cloth would " set many thousands of poor people more on work for dressing and dyeing, and likewise employ more ships and mariners for bringing in dyeing stuffs " [3]. A statement attributed to Sir Walter Raleigh computed that England shipped yearly about 80,000 un-dressed and undyed cloths together with 50,000 white bays and kersies, which found employment for " near fifty thousand people in foreign parts " [4]. The Merchant Adventurers defended the export of white rough cloth on the ground of the inferiority of English workmanship in the dyeing and finishing industries [5]. " The dressing and dyeing of our cloths beyond seas far surpasses that done here, and makes the people continue wearing our cloth ; but take that away, and they are like to fall from cloth and wear stuffs of other countries " [6]. The cloth merchants informed the Privy Council in 1541 that the cloth-finishers dressed cloth so ill, that the people of the Low Countries would no longer buy English cloth: " at least there was not a piece of dressed cloth from here, that did not sell there for two ducats less

---

[1] *State Papers Domestic*, 1598–1601, p. 204. Another estimate was 500 cloths dressed for the Company : *ibid.* Addenda, 1580–1625, p. 401.

[2] *Ibid.* 1598–1601, pp. 204, 207 ; *Acts of the Privy Council*, 1558–1570, pp. 277-278 ; *House of Commons Journals*, i. 711, 771.

[3] Raleigh, *Works* (ed. 1829), viii. 369.

[4] *Ibid.* 366, 368-369. A member of the House of Commons declared in 1614 that " they gain above £700,000 per annum by dyeing and dressing of our cloths " : *House of Commons Journals*, i. 491. Roger Coke said £480,000 : *Treatise* (1671), i. 16. These can only be guesses since the cost of finishing cloth varied. A parliamentary committee was informed in 1707 that by exporting Wiltshire cloths undressed and undyed we lost 15 per cent., Gloucestershire cloths dressed and undyed 10 per cent., fine Worcestershire cloths (undressed and undyed), 100 per cent.: *House of Commons Journals*, xv. 459.

[5] A Portuguese inventor who was attempting certain experiments in dyeing was licensed to move freely in the kingdom : *Acts of the Privy Council*, 1575–1577, p. 381 (1577).

[6] *State Papers Domestic*, 1598–1601, p. 208.

than if it were not dressed, and besides the loss of these two ducats they lost other two in getting them ready "[1]. Half a century later the governor of the Merchant Adventurers stated that the obligation to dress every tenth cloth involved a charge of eight shillings a piece : " and yet every piece of such dressed cloth is ten or twelve shillings less in value when sold beyond seas, than if undressed "[2]. In the case of dyeing the water was often unsuitable ; and the refugees from the Low Countries in the reign of Elizabeth sought permission to export cloth undyed " till we find suitable water for dyeing : none yet found keeps the colours bright and fresh, and we think it were better to send them abroad to dye than have them spoiled here "[3]. The interests of the cloth-makers were pronounced to be more important than those of the cloth-finishers, " who do not number a tenth part of the cloth-makers ". Moreover the cloth-finishers had the dressing of the cloth worn in England, and of that usually transported to Russia, the Baltic lands, France, Spain, Italy and Turkey—the principal markets for unwrought cloth being those supplied by the Merchant Adventurers, namely, the Netherlands and Germany [4].

*Cockayne's project.* The dispute came to a head in the reign of James I. Alderman Cockayne brought forward a project by which all cloth was to be dyed and dressed at home before being allowed to leave the kingdom [5]. It was estimated that the country would save £700,000 a year [6] ; and to make the scheme more attractive, it was baited with the promise of additional revenue to the Crown [7]. The Merchant

[1] *Letters and Papers, Foreign and Domestic, Henry VIII.*, vol. xvi. 410.
[2] *State Papers Domestic*, 1591–1594, p. 321 (1593).
[3] *Ibid.* Addenda, 1566–1579, p. 32 (1567).
[4] *Ibid.* 1595–1597, p. 330 ; *ibid.* Addenda, 1580–1625, p. 401. Cloth made in Kent and Suffolk had also to be dressed in England, whatever the market for which it was destined : *supra*, p. 376.
[5] Miss A. Friis (*Alderman Cockayne's Project*, Preface, 231, 238-239, 284) makes the interesting suggestion that the project was inspired by the hostility of the Eastland Company, which exported to the Baltic cloth dressed in England (*supra*, vol. ii. 319), while the Dutch sent thither English cloth which they bought from the Merchant Adventurers and themselves dressed. The part assigned to the artisan cloth-workers (Unwin, *Industrial Organization*, 124) seems exaggerated.
[6] *House of Commons Journals*, i. 491. See *supra*, p. 377, note 4.
[7] 5s. on every cloth dressed, and the duties on dye-stuffs : Friis, *Alderman Cockayne's Project*, 239, 338.

Adventurers were summoned before the Privy Council to decide whether they would agree to abandon their trade in undyed and undressed cloth, " or leave the market free unto such as will undertake the said course ". They pronounced the scheme ' infeasible ', but their objections, based on mis-givings which proved well-founded, were over-ruled ; and they were called upon to resign their charter into the King's hands, in spite of their warning that "the loss will redound to our utter undoing and to the decay of the best-settled trade in Europe "[1]. In the House of Commons the scheme met with hostile criticism. " If to be done with a pen or an argument at Council Table ", said a member sarcastically, " Mr. Alderman Cockayne will do it ". Nor was the pro-posal to bring in five thousand foreign workmen to perform the work viewed with favour — " we have too great a clothing commonwealth already "[2]. However the King was now definitely committed. A proclamation issued in July 1614 ordered that no broad cloth, undyed or undressed, was to be exported after November 2nd ; and when the Merchant Adventurers refused to surrender their charter, their privi-leges were suspended by another proclamation in December[3]. A New Company was incorporated, consisting of Cockayne and his supporters, under the name of ' The King's Mer-chants Adventurers of the New Trade of London '[4]. It was joined by some members of the Old Company, whose capital was embarked in the trade, though their past experience led them to entertain little hope of success in the sale of dressed cloth[5]. The New Company undertook to send abroad six thousand dressed and dyed cloths in the first year, twelve thousand in the second, and eighteen thousand in the third[6].

The effects of this ill-starred venture were soon disclosed. *Its failure.* The clothiers complained that the cloth lay on their hands unsold ; the cloth-workers protested that they were in a worse

[1] *Acts of the Privy Council,* 1613–1614, pp. 303–304, 538, 586 ; *House of Commons Journals,* i. 491.
[2] *House of Commons Journals,* i. 491 (1614).
[3] *Tudor and Stuart Proclamations* (ed. Steele), i. Nos. 1148, 1154.
[4] Its charter is printed in Carr, *Select Charters of Trading Com-panies,* 78.
[5] *State Papers Domestic,* 1611–1618, p. 291.
[6] *Acts of the Privy Council,* 1615–1616, pp. 190, 218.

plight than before [1]. The promoters of the scheme put the
blame on the Old Company which, they alleged, had shipped
in the previous year more than the normal quantity of goods
expressly in order ' to clog the trade' and close the foreign
market against the New Company [2]. Permission to export
undressed and undyed cloth failed to relieve the situation [3],
and the New Company pressed for fresh concessions which
led the Privy Council to the conclusion that " the Company
themselves, by demanding things unreasonable and inconvenient, do hold the work not feasible " [4]. The King
began to recognize that he had been ' much abused ', but to
uphold the New Company he promised to put forty thousand
pounds into the enterprise himself : *sed ubi est ?* comments
the writer of a letter [5]. In July 1616 the New Company
claimed that it had exceeded the proportion of dyed cloths
fixed for the first year [6] ; yet in September the cloth market
was at a ' stand ', and the Privy Council was already lament-
ing " the alteration of that trade from a flourishing estate to
that which now it is come unto " [7]. Under constraint the
New Company, although ' sore burdened ', agreed to buy up
the cloth, but declared ' plainly' to the King and the Council
that " we are not able nor dare undertake to proceed in this
forced course any longer than till Christmas. . . . This un-
exampled compulsion of buying at the unreasonable pleasure
of the clothier " would make English cloth become dear and
give place to the Dutch in foreign markets [8]. The following
year the bubble was pricked and the scheme collapsed,
despite Bacon's counsel to " blow a horn to let the Flemings
know your majesty will not give over the chase " [9]. His
opinion was that the cause of failure lay, not in the project
itself, but in the instruments employed—the personnel of the
New Company ; and he recommended that the Old Com-

[1] *State Papers Domestic*, 1611–1618, p. 287.
[2] *Acts of the Privy Council*, 1615–1616, p. 30.
[3] Carr, *Select Charters of Trading Companies*, 95.
[4] *Acts of the Privy Council*, 1615–1616, pp. 412, 416-417.
[5] *State Papers Domestic*, 1611–1618, p. 395 (1616).
[6] *Acts of the Privy Council*, 1615–1616, pp. 658-659.
[7] *Ibid.* 1616–1617, pp. 4, 7.
[8] *Ibid.* 1616–1617, pp. 17-18 ; *Hist. MSS. Comm. Buccleuch*, i. 176.
[9] *The Letters and the Life of Francis Bacon* (ed. Spedding), vi. 74.

pany should be drawn into it, since " I do not yet believe the work impossible or inconvenient " [1]. The King confessed that " time discovereth many inabilities which cannot at first be seen ", and added : " We intend not to insist and stay longer upon specious and fair shows which produce not the fruit our actions do ever aim at .*. . perceiving that the former grounds proposed to us by the undertakers of that work consisted more in hopes than in effects " [2]. The New Company was dissolved in 1617, and the Old Company was restored to its privileges for which it paid a fine of fifty thousand pounds [3]. To raise the money it laid heavy charges on cloth, which added to the difficulties experienced by the merchant exporters in recapturing the trade they had lost [4]. Thus ended an ill-fated experiment on which the verdict was written by Misselden : " In charity we may think it was good in the purpose, though it proved ill in the practice " [5].

The disturbance of the cloth trade produced effects which *Effects of Cockayne's project.* exercised a baneful influence long after the primary cause had disappeared. The attempt to force dressed cloth upon foreign markets evoked immediate opposition abroad. The English ambassador in the United Provinces was informed in January 1614 that " the announcements which have been brought from England of the prohibition of the [export] of undyed cloths have greatly disturbed the Orders [of Holland]. There were some who advocated the abolition of English cloths from these provinces " [6]. The prediction of ' harsh consequences ' was fulfilled in an edict of the States General prohibiting the importation of dressed and dyed cloth into the United Provinces [7], and when the news arrived in England

---

[1] *Hist. MSS. Comm. Eglinton,* 96-97.

[2] State Papers Domestic, James I., Proclamations Collection No. 50A (August 12, 1617).

[3] *State Papers Domestic,* 1611–1618, pp. 481, 499, 500, 514 ; *Tudor and Stuart Proclamations* (ed. Steele), i. No. 1200. It was said that the Company paid altogether £70,000 : *House of Commons Journals,* i. 531. In the earlier negotiations £100,000 had been spoken of, but the state of trade caused the merchants to " waive that offer " : *Hist. MSS. Comm. Bath,* ii. 63. See also *supra,* vol. ii. 247, note 7 ; and *infra,* Appendix, p. 530, No. 4.

[4] For the amount of the Company's charges, see *supra,* vol. ii. 225, note 5.

[5] Misselden, *Free Trade* (1622), 41.

[6] *Hist. MSS. Comm. Buccleuch,* i. 148, 151. The prohibition did not actually come into operation until November 1614 : *supra,* p. 379.

[7] *Acts of the Privy Council,* 1615–1616, p. 220.

word was passed to a prominent landowner to dispose of his wool without delay[1]. Seizing the opportunity presented to them by the misguided policy of the English Government, the Dutch set to work to develop their own cloth manufacture[2]. As early as March 1614 it was reported that they had resolved upon " the erecting of a drapery in several towns here, if they may not have whites out of England, and they have destined very large sums of money to that end "[3]. They erected looms and fulling mills ' at great charges ', and considerable success attended their efforts[4]. It is, however, significant that the cloth trade to Holland in 1620 was not much below its volume in 1614 on the eve of Cockayne's experiment, whereas the cloth trade to Germany had fallen by more than one-half[5]. We may therefore conclude that the result of Cockayne's project was to extend the market for Dutch cloth in Germany : the Merchant Adventurers themselves stated in 1622 that Dutch cloth, though coarse, was greatly used in Germany[6]. Yet other factors besides Dutch competition must be taken into account. The falling off in the German demand for English cloth may be partly attributed to the outbreak of the Thirty Years' War, which made traffic unsafe for English merchants, while it affected trading conditions generally[7]. Moreover, a stimulus had been given in Germany, as in Holland, to the native manufacture of cloth[8]. Finally, it must be remembered that the decline in the export of broad cloth may also

---

[1] *Hist. MSS. Comm. Buccleuch*, i. 249.

[2] A cloth industry was already in existence : *supra*, p. 295, note 3. According to the notes taken at a Privy Council meeting in 1614, " the Low Countries make 20,000 cloths a year, and Germany as many " : Friis, *Alderman Cockayne's Project*, Appendix D, 460.

[3] *Hist. MSS. Comm. Buccleuch*, i. 156.

[4] The Dutch were said in 1640 to make 30,000 cloths a year : *State Papers Domestic*, 1639–1640, p. 417.

[5]

| | Hamburg. | Middelburg. |
|---|---|---|
| 1614 | 46,000 cloths | 34,500 cloths |
| 1620 | 21,000  ,, | 32,000  ,, |

These figures are approximate : Friis, *Alderman Cockayne's Project*, 383 (also pp. 98, 129).

[6] *State Papers Domestic*, 1619–1623, p. 387.

[7] *Ibid.* Also *supra*, p. 296 ; and *infra*, Appendix, p. 530, No. 5.

[8] Battie, *The Merchants' Remonstrance* (1644), 4.

be connected with the growth of the ' new draperies ' [1], which to some extent were taking its place. Whatever the contributory causes may have been, the shrinkage in the broad cloth trade was responsible for one of the gravest commercial crises in English industrial history, which began in 1620 and lasted several years [2]. Two decades later the export trade had not yet recovered [3]. After the Restoration Roger Coke affirmed that in addition to great quantities of coarse cloth, the Dutch now " made most of the fine cloth used in these parts of Europe ", while even in England " we are come to wear much of their fine cloths, especially blacks ". This improvement in the Dutch manufacture he attributed to the workmen whom they procured from England, Flanders and other places [4]. Thus James I.'s ill-advised interference with the cloth trade gave a permanent stimulus to the woollen industry abroad—" the first and greatest occasion [so the clothiers described it in 1622] both to increase the drapery beyond the seas and to decay it in our kingdom " [5]. Moreover the cloth-finishers were worse off than before, since the States General did not revoke its proscription of English dressed cloth [6]. The Merchant Adventurers removed the ' stint ' on the export of dyed and dressed cloth in 1618 [7] ; but complaint was made in Parliament that not more than four of them were actually engaged in this trade, and it was therefore thrown open in 1624—at the instigation, it was said, of ' divers of the New Company ' [8].

The subsequent history of the oversea trade in white

[1] For the ' new draperies ', see *supra*, vol. i. 494.

[2] *Supra*, p. 305.

[3] " The cause whereof was that unhappy project of dyeing and dressing of cloth by Sir William Cockayne and others " : Battie, *The Merchants' Remonstrance* (1644), 4. Similarly : Coke, *Treatise* (1675), iii. 11 ; *Britannia Languens* (1680), 158-159 (in sect. xi.).

[4] Coke, *Treatise*, ii. (1671), 111-112 ; *Britannia Languens* (1680), 161.

[5] Stowe MSS. 354, f. 65.

[6] According to *Veneris* (1662), 11, it was in force in 1662. But it may be inferred from *State Papers Domestic*, 1635, p. 524, that the prohibition was not maintained throughout the period. See also *supra*, vol. ii. 212. And subsequently medleys (cloths dyed in the wool) were admitted into Holland : *House of Commons Journals*, xv. 460.

[7] *Supra*, vol. ii. 238.

[8] *House of Commons Journals*, i. 698, 702 ; *State Papers Domestic*, 1634-1635, p. 313. The Company recovered its privileges in 1634 : *supra*, vol. ii. 263.

*Later history of the export of unfinished cloth.* cloth can be briefly sketched. We have seen that Elizabeth granted licences to export undressed cloth not only to the Merchant Adventurers but to individuals. Among the latter was the Earl of Cumberland, who received a patent in 1601 to export undressed cloth for ten years on payment of an annual rent of a thousand pounds [1]; subsequently the period was extended by James I. The Company entered into an arrangement with the Earl by which the licence was taken off his hands, though after its restoration in 1617 it found that its own licence to ship 30,000 cloths was sufficient to cover all the white cloth which the foreign markets could absorb. The Earl complained to the Privy Council, which ordered (1617) that the two licences should be joined together, and that the Earl should receive 16d. on every white cloth transported under the number of sixty thousand, and 2s. 8d. on each additional white cloth if that number were exceeded [2]. This ' composition money ' was one of the ' burdens upon cloth ', which advanced its price and diminished its sale abroad [3]; it was vented as a grievance in the Parliament of 1624, which proposed that the Company's own licence should be raised from 30,000 to 50,000 [4]. Upon the expiry of the term for which the Earl's patent was granted, it was transferred to the Duke of Lennox. The Company in 1632 leased it for seven years at a rent of £2600, and within four and a half years sustained a loss of £2500 [5].

Under the Commonwealth the Merchant Adventurers appealed to the Council of State for protection against the London cloth-workers, who had instituted a prosecution against them for neglect of the Act of 1566 which required one cloth in ten to be dressed [6]. In the reign of Charles II.

[1] *State Papers Domestic*, 1601–1603, p. 80. The patent did not apply to cloths of Kent or Suffolk. The Earl received 2s. 2d. on each undressed cloth exported under his licence : *Acts of the Privy Council*, 1601–1604, p. 488. The amount was fixed at 2s. 8d. in the charter to the New Company in 1615 : Carr, *Select Charters of Trading Companies*, 96.

[2] *Acts of the Privy Council*, 1616–1617, p. 363 ; *State Papers Domestic*, 1639, p. 540.

[3] Stowe MSS. 554, f. 45 ; *ibid.* 354, f. 65.

[4] *House of Commons Journals*, i. 706, 780.

[5] *Ibid.* i. 773 ; *State Papers Domestic*, 1636–1637, p. 106 ; 1639, p. 540 ; 1639–1640, p. 234. Subsequently they paid a tax on each cloth : *House of Commons Journals*, xv. 458.

[6] *State Papers Domestic*, 1652–1653, p. 309.

the cloth-workers renewed their agitation. The Government *End of the* was besieged in 1674 with petitions from every side. The *controversy.* cloth-workers and dyers repeated the familiar arguments that the export of white cloth enriched other nations by enabling them to manufacture commodities of our growth, ' while we remain idle ' : the cloth-makers pointed to the failure of the experiment under James I., and contended that the making of cloth was more important than the finishing of it : the factors at Blackwell Hall certified that the Merchant Adventurers now sent abroad far more cloth dyed and dressed than in the rough—a statement confirmed by a parliamentary committee in 1707[1]. The change was attributed to a Dutchman, Brewer, who came over to England in 1667 with his servants and introduced improvements into the dyeing and finishing of cloth[2]. The agitation failed[3]; and two years later (1676) Charles II. empowered the Countess of Portland for thirty-one years to license the export of undyed and undressed cloth, without limitation as to number or price[4]. In 1707 this patent expired, and the officers of the customs put a stop to the shipment of all white cloths including those covered by the original licence of the Merchant Adventurers. The legality of their proceedings was questioned by a committee of the House of Commons, which drew up a long report on the subject. To remove doubts as to the exact legal position, an Act was passed in the same year making it lawful for any person to export white woollen cloth, but a duty of five shillings per cloth was imposed as a measure of protection to the native dyers and finishers[5]. This brought to an end a controversy which had lasted for two centuries and a half.

The dispute over the export of undressed cloth has a parallel in that over the export of undressed skins. The

[1] *State Papers Domestic*, 1673–1675, pp. 301-302, 315-316, 454 ; *House of Commons Journals*, xv. 460.
[2] Macpherson, *Annals of Commerce*, ii. 529. But see *supra*, p. 57, note 10.
[3] The dyers petitioned against the export of undyed serges in 1693 : *State Papers Domestic*, 1693, p. 6.
[4] *House of Commons Journals*, xv. 458.
[5] *Ibid.* xv. 405, 439, 456 *seq.* ; *Statutes*, viii. 751-752. Gloucestershire white dressed cloths had been burdened with a duty of 5s. under the Countess of Portland's patent, and Wiltshire white undressed cloth with 1s. 4d. : *House of Commons Journals*, xv. 458-459.

*Export of undressed skins.* 'handicraftsmen of the Mistery of Skinners of London' demanded that certain kinds of skins [1] should not be transported before they were tawed and dressed. The merchants objected that " these sorts of skins will not sell tawed beyond the seas ". It was stated that the tawyers counted but twenty-eight persons ; and that the patentees, who were only ten in number, designed to obtain the sole transportation of skins, which would enable them to buy at their own price. As among the cloth-finishers the dispute produced, or was the expression of, a cleavage in the ranks of the Skinners' Company, the artisan element pressing for prohibition, and the trading element being opposed to restrictions [2]. The incident not only throws light upon the forces which were dissolving the traditional forms of industrial organization, but it reflects the divergent issues represented by the manufacturing and mercantile interests, the former being identified with protection, the latter with free trade [3].

## (VIII)

## TRADE UNIONISM

*Factors in the rise of trade unionism.* We have seen above that the later seventeenth century witnessed a definite trend towards a policy of *laissez-faire* in industry. Under the influence of a growing economic individualism, fostered by the development of capitalism, the State began to assume a different attitude towards labour problems, particularly those relating to wages, unemployment and technical training—with the consequence that the industrial legislation of the sixteenth century was allowed gradually to fall into disuse [4]. This change of public policy was one of the factors in the rise of trade unionism [5]. It forced the workers to shoulder re-

---

[1] Grey cony-skins and morkins.

[2] *Hist. MSS. Comm. Buccleuch*, i. 179 (? 1616). See also *ibid. Salisbury*, iv. 91-92.

[3] The London Pewterers petitioned in 1593 against the export of unwrought tin—" The twentieth part of the tin carried forth is not wrought into pewter, but goeth forth unwrought " : *ibid. Salisbury*, iv. 463 ; v. 137-138.

[4] *Supra*, pp. 265, 287, 313, 318.

[5] Another factor was the increasing difficulty of attaining mastership: cf. *supra*, vol. ii. 55.

sponsibilities which had hitherto been the province of the
State alone, and to rely upon their own efforts for the
maintenance of the ' standard of life '. It transformed
the relations of capital and labour [1a], which were no longer
shackled by an external authority but were left free to
determine, according to their strength, the rates of wages
and the general conditions of employment. It is significant,
at any rate, that the Revolution of 1688, which brought to
a final close the era of benevolent autocracy, should have
been followed within a few years by an outburst of trade
union activity. We shall hardly be wrong if we recognize
in these manifestations whose history we have now to relate,
not indeed a new spirit [1], but a sign of the growing self-
assertion of the working classes provoked into expression by
the instinct of self-preservation.

We may glance, first, at the antecedents of trade union- *Ante-*
ism. As far back as the fourteenth century associations of *cedents of*
wage-earners, known as journeymen or yeomen gilds, are *unionism.*
found in London [2], and in the next two centuries they
became frequent in provincial towns. In general they failed
to maintain their independence ; and their subordination to
the authorities may be illustrated from the ordinances of a
seventeenth-century gild at Gloucester. " It has seemed fit
to us the mayor and aldermen . . . with the consent of the
present warden and stewards of the company of weavers and
of others the masters of the said company . . . to allow
that the journeymen of the said trade in the said city may
in quiet and orderly sort at any time hereafter congregate
and meet together . . . and choose two honest and discreet
journeymen . . . to be their stewards for the year ensuing,
which stewards shall have power and authority to assemble
and call together all the journeymen . . . using the trade
of weaving . . . to confer among themselves of all such good
means and orders as best may be for the good of their
society. . . . The said company of journeymen shall not
hereafter do or cause to be done any act prejudicial or
hurtful towards the wardens and his company or brethren of

---

[1a] On the conflict of capital and labour, cf. *supra*, vol. ii. Introduction,
pp. xxx-xxxii.

[1] See *supra*, vol. i. 392 *seq*.

[2] *Supra*, vol. i. 402 *seq*.

the said art and trade of weavers, either by raising, altering or changing their wages, or otherwise, by colour of anything herein contained " [1]. The journeymen gilds, where they survived, developed into organizations of small masters, and the latter have been regarded as furnishing the link between gilds and trade unions [2]. But although the traditions of the hatters' union—to take an oft-quoted example—connected them with the Feltmakers' Company [3], there is no historical continuity as a general rule between the older industrial associations and the trade unions of a later date. The hatters do not appear to have been a typical example ; and the origins of trade unionism must be sought for in other directions.

*Early references to labour unrest.* The activities of the journeymen gilds had called forth the Act of 1548, which anticipated the Combination Laws of the eighteenth century by imposing severe penalties upon those who associated together to " do their works but at a certain price and rate " [4]. The Act did not prevent combinations as is shown in the charge made to a grand jury in 1638, instructing it to inquire "whether any artificers, workmen or labourers have promised or agreed together to make or do their works, but at certain rates. The end of these unlawful agreements ", proceeded the judge, " is but to deceive the people by setting excessive prices upon their works or commodities " [5]. We get occasional glimpses of these ' unlawful agreements '. A letter from the Privy Council to the commissioners for the Mines Royal in 1614 stated that " divers inhabitants about the mines, that were gravers and carriers of peat and turf to the number of two hundred persons, who heretofore made great suit to be set on work, and did strive amongst themselves which of them should serve in the most loads of peat and other provisions, have of late (notwithstanding they had received their allotments for this year what everyone would bring in, and received part of their imprest money or wages for the same beforehand) combined together not to work, dig or carry

---

[1] *Hist. MSS. Comm. Beaufort*, 416-418 (1602).
[2] Unwin, *Industrial Organization*, 200 seq.
[3] *Ibid.* 215.                    [4] *Supra*, vol. i. 405.
[5] *Hist. MSS. Comm. Verulam*, 193.

any peat or other like provisions, unless they might have the prices raised a fourth part more than formerly was given and they had agreed to accept " [1]. An embryonic union among shoemakers was disclosed in 1619 when one, Robert Ratcliffe, was presented at the Nottingham sessions " for giving oath, and enticing divers and sundry shoemakers' servants to agree and swear to several articles that in their combination they did agree unto, the said Ratcliffe administering oath himself not to work their three-sole shoes under three shillings and their two-sole shoes under two shillings and sixpence. . . . *Item* we present Henry Newcome for consenting and enticing many other to the like " [2]. The institution of an oath was a traditional feature of shoemakers' combinations. Nearly a century before a number of journeymen shoemakers at Wisbech, withdrawing from the town, bound themselves by oath not to work under certain rates, and threatened that none should " come into the town to serve . . . but we will have an arm or a leg of him, except they will take an oath as we have done " [3].

After the Restoration, perhaps owing to the decay of central control, references to labour unrest grow more frequent. The ' clerk of the ropeyard ' at the Portsmouth dockyard complained to the navy commissioners in 1663 that he had been " much obstructed in the discharge of his duty by the mutiny of the workmen. By hasty spinning they finish what they call a day's work by dinner-time and refuse to work till four o'clock. Yesterday twenty-five of them left the work to go to the alehouse, where they still remain ". He requested authority to dismiss a couple of the ringleaders in case of opposition. The ropemakers in their defence stated that the clerk had " such malice implacable towards them that they cannot endure it, calling

*After the Restoration.*

---

[1] *Acts of the Privy Council*, 1613–1614, p. 535.
[2] *Records of Nottingham*, iv. 362.
[3] 1538 : *Letters and Papers, Foreign and Domestic, Henry VIII.*, vol. xiii. part i. 537 ; part ii. 21, 31, 33. In 1545 the wife of a merchant of the Staple wrote from Glapthorne to her husband : " Your eight wool-winders be at [the] point to go their ways, saying that they will not work no more for 2s. a sack, for they do not get 4d. a day ". They asked 4s. a sack, as they had in London, and to find themselves in meat and drink : *ibid.* xx. part ii. 176.

them dogs, rebellious rogues, and using much other reviling language, causing their creditors in the town not to trust them, and bringing in two of his own servants, who spoil the hemp in spinning ". As a result of the ' mutiny ' among the spinners in the dockyard, two of the ringleaders were discharged [1]. In London the tendency among journeymen to combine together is revealed in the earliest records of the Feltmakers' Company, which contain an ordinance (1667) enjoining the master and wardens to " present to the court of lord mayor and aldermen a table of rates " that " the journeymen may not by combination or otherwise excessively at their pleasure raise their wages ". The ordinance was ineffective, for in 1698 the journeymen feltmakers confessed that they had held meetings " wherein we have conspired and combined together to enhance the prices for making of hats, for which several of us now stand indicted " [2]. An attempt on the part of the London sawyers to obtain incorporation in 1670 as an independent organization was successfully resisted by the carpenters, joiners and ship-wrights, who represented that the sawyers worked for hire on the employer's material, and their incorporation would be " drawn into an evil precedent " for other labourers to masons, bricklayers and plasterers; and " if the said labourers be incorporated the smallest combination or confederacy amongst them can give a check to any of his majesty's or his subjects' works " [3]. At Colchester, in 1676, the weavers made a demonstration directed apparently against an un-popular employer. " They were assembled ", wrote a corre-spondent to the secretary of state, " by the blowing of a horn about two in the morning, and so went round the town till they were three or four hundred ". They eventually dispersed, but " the trained bands were raised which were kept up about three weeks ". Six of the ringleaders were convicted—" I do not believe all of them are worth ten pounds " [4]. The following year an incident is recorded at Trowbridge, where a party of men marched through the

---

[1] *State Papers Domestic*, 1663–1664, pp. 242, 244, 276.
[2] Unwin, *Industrial Organization*, Appendix A, pp. 246, 250.
[3] Jupp and Pocock, *The Carpenters' Company*, 307-309.
[4] *State Papers Domestic*, 1675–1676, pp. 513-514.

streets headed by a fiddler, calling on all who were of their side to follow them, their object being to raise wages from 6s. per week to 6s. 6d. for working twelve hours a day [1]. That associations were not confined to workmen is indicated by an injunction, issued in 1696, to prosecute employers who entered into combinations directed against their workmen, " as it is said to be done at Colchester " [2].

In tracing the first beginnings of trade unionism, mention *Friendly* must also be made of friendly societies. This important *societies.* institution provided the means whereby workmen and their families, who fcll into a distressed condition, might obtain relief without recourse to the parish. It was significant in two ways—it marked the growth of a spirit of independence and self-reliance among workmen, who endeavoured by concerted action to meet the misfortunes of life ; and it created the nucleus for trade unionism since benefit clubs easily developed into industrial associations. In the Middle Ages the craft gilds served as friendly societies [3], and they bequeathed to the modern world the principle of a mutual insurance fund supported by voluntary subscriptions. In the reign of Elizabeth maimed and superannuated mariners were given pensions from a ' chest ' at Chatham maintained by the contributions of sailors [4] ; and in 1618 the Merchant Adventurers of Bristol levied a penny in the pound upon the wages of their seamen ' towards the relief of poor seafaring men ' in the Company's almshouse [5]. In the eighteenth century there were numerous friendly societies in existence. " There are in the metropolis and in many other parts of the kingdom ", it was stated in 1767, " societies or clubs of young labouring men who appropriate a trifling part of their weekly earnings towards raising a fund for the support of their members " in case of sickness, accidents or age [6]. Near the end of the eighteenth century London contained six

[1] *Hist. MSS. Comm. Various,* i. 155.
[2] *State Papers Domestic,* 1696, p. 205.
[3] *Supra,* vol. i. 342.
[4] Macpherson, *Annals of Commerce,* ii. 188. See also *State Papers Domestic,* 1638–1639, p. 6.
[5] Latimer, *Merchant Venturers of Bristol,* 79.
[6] *An Inquiry into the Management of the Poor* (1767), 74.

hundred friendly societies, Sheffield fifty-two, Lancaster eighteen, Carlisle six [1]. Writing in 1797, Eden observed that " since the commencement of the present [eighteenth] century friendly societies have been gradually extended to most parts of Great Britain ", and he added : " In the North of England instances may be found of clubs of this kind which have existed above an hundred years " [2]. His statement is borne out by the example of the keelmen of Newcastle mentioned above [3]. The legislature recognized the importance of friendly societies, in 1793, by an Act which conferred upon them a legal status and protected their funds, provided their rules were submitted for confirmation to the justices of the peace in quarter sessions [4].

*Weavers' unions.*    The combinations formed among textile workers in the eighteenth century were the forerunners of the great trade unions of the nineteenth century. The ostensible purpose of these unions was to serve as benefit clubs for the relief of the sick. In Gloucestershire the members of a club paid twopence a week and received six shillings a week in times of sickness ; and in Wiltshire they were paid seven shillings [5]. But benefit clubs, as we have said, readily assumed the character of trade societies, for when men who are engaged in the same occupation meet together at regular intervals, they inevitably begin to discuss trade grievances ; and the consciousness of unity, inspired by their co-operation for purposes of mutual insurance, soon makes its influence felt in other directions. Our knowledge of the early trade union movement is derived mainly from the accounts given by the employers in their petitions to Parliament, which were naturally biassed. One of the earliest petitions dates from the year 1707. It represented that within the past four or five years " the weavers (who are very numerous) have in most towns, where the woollen manufactures are made,

---

[1] Eden, *The State of the Poor* (1797), i. 461 ; ii. 58, 310. For other instances, see *ibid.* i. 616 *seq.* Eden estimated that the London societies averaged 80 members each. For Sheffield, see Lloyd, *The Cutlery Trades*, 239.
[2] Eden, *op. cit.* i. 600.
[3] *Supra*, vol. ii. 127. For another example : *infra*, p. 531 (No. 1).
[4] *Statutes at Large*, xii. 388 *seq.* The rules of a friendly society in Norfolk (1784) are printed in *Annals of Agriculture*, xix. 262 *seq.* See *infra*, p. 531 (No. 2).    [5] *Parliamentary Papers* (1802–3), vii. 24-25.

formed themselves into clubs, particularly at Taunton, and have a common seal, tipstaffs and colours, which they display at pleasure, and meet as often as they think fit at their club-house being an inn at Taunton ; and four or five persons appointed as their supervisors (if any of their club are about to be prosecuted) give them a certificate under their hands and common seal, and money out of their common stock, to travel from their families, whereby their families have become chargeable to their several parishes ; and by their arbitrary proceedings they hinder many honest labourers, who refuse to join in their club, from using their lawful employments whereby they might get a comfortable maintenance for their families". The Taunton club, proceeds the petition, "have committed many outrages and riots, and put many of her majesty's subjects in great danger of their lives, forced many from their habitations, broken the common gaol and also private houses, and rescued several persons who were committed for the said crimes " [1]. At Bristol the journeymen " in imitation of others in divers places of the kingdom " had formed a ' confederacy ', which put forward the demands that no master weaver should take an apprentice without its leave ; that the apprentice must be enrolled in its books ; and that a master should not employ a journeyman before he became a member of the confederacy, or brought a certificate that he was ' confederated ' at some other place [2]. The Government ordered an inquiry to be held and the offenders to be prosecuted [3]. On several occasions in the next two decades the employers in the West of England renewed their attack upon the unions. They affirmed that trade was ' very much incommoded ' by " riotous and tumultuous clubs and societies of workmen, who hinder labourers in the woollen manufactures from working therein except they have such exorbitant prices as the clubs prescribe ", and who " threatened the masters to pull down their houses and burn their work unless they would agree with their terms " [4].

[1] *House of Commons Journals*, xv. 312. Similarly, Tiverton : *ibid.* 312.
[2] *Ibid.* 312.          [3] *Hist. MSS. Comm. Portland*, iv. 393-394.
[4] *House of Commons Journals*, xviii. 715 (1718) ; xx. 268 (1724).

*A parlia-
mentary
inquiry
into trade
unionism.*
The employers' efforts were at length crowned with success. The ' mayor, capital burgesses and assistants ' of Tiverton, ' being the principal merchants and traders in the woollen manufactures there ', presented a petition in 1726 asserting that the wool-combers and weavers of the town and vicinity had formed clubs which assumed " an arbitrary power to ascertain their wages ", and committed outrages " not only on their masters but also on their fellow-labourers who refused to join with them in such their practices, by breaking into houses, spoiling of wool, and cutting and destroying the pieces in the looms and the utensils of trade : whereby several poor persons have been reduced to penury and want. And such offenders have not only insulted the civil magistrates, but also abused and threatened the con-stables and other peace officers who are thereby deterred from executing of justice on them " [1]. The ' poor oppressed weavers of Taunton ' responded with a counter-petition, in which they set forth "the great hardships they labour under from their masters by paying their wages in goods and setting extravagant prices on such goods " [2]. Parliament appointed a committee to hold an inquiry. One witness deposed that the weavers had many clubs in the West of England where they made by-laws constituting officers, arranging places of meeting at which ' ensigns and flags ' were openly displayed, fixing wages, and making allowances to unemployed work-men on travel. Another alleged that parties of weavers went round the weavers' homes demanding money for the support of those committed to prison in the recent riots ; and that any who did not pay their contributions, or worked at lower rates than others, were liable to have their looms ' cut ' and their work stolen. Testimony of the unruly character of the weavers was given in a description of a riot in which they forced their way into a court of justice, assaulted the magis-trate, and rescued the prisoners [3]. Rioting was a common practice on the part of textile workers in the eighteenth century for drawing attention to their wrongs ; and the

---

[1] *House of Commons Journals*, xx. 598.  Bristol, Exeter and Taunton presented similar petitions : *ibid.* xx. 598-599, 602.
[2] *Ibid.* xx. 627.                [3] *Ibid.* xx. 647-648.

wild passions of the West Country weavers and wool-combers easily flared up under the spur of their grievances [1].

As a result of the representations made by the employers, the parliamentary committee supported the proposal for legislation " to prevent unlawful combinations of workmen employed in the woollen manufactures " ; and a Bill based upon this recommendation passed into law in 1726. It forbade, under penalty of imprisonment, all combinations of weavers and wool-combers formed with the object of regulating the industry and improving the conditions of labour ; and breach of contract, quitting an employer's service before the expiration of the period for which the workman had been hired, was made a criminal offence [2]. The Act was intended by its authors to stifle the trade union movement at its birth, but one thing should be remembered. It was not a purely one-sided measure, for it also contained provisions for the ' better payment of wages '. While the State refused to recognize the right of workmen to combine together for the protection and advancement of their economic interests, it still accepted some responsibility for safeguarding those interests. This was demonstrated not long after (1727) when the weavers of Wiltshire and Somersetshire presented a petition to the King, complaining of the combinations of their masters, who had lengthened the warping bars and made illegal deductions from their wages ' upon pretence of damages ' in the cloth. The King referred the matter to a committee of the Privy Council, which after hearing evidence concluded that the clothiers had given grounds for the complaints of the weavers. As a result of its intervention the clothiers and weavers drew up articles of agreement, which not only fixed the size of the warping bars, but ordered all disputes between clothiers and weavers

*The Combination Act of 1726.*

---

[1] Several accounts of riots are given in Dunsford, *Historical Memoirs of Tiverton* (1790), 208-209, 226, 228, 230 seq. ; Smith, *Chronicon Rusticum-Commerciale* (ed. 1747), ii. 301 seq. ; *The Gentleman's Magazine*, viii. 658 ; ix. 213 ; xx. 41 ; xxii. 237. See also Lipson, *The History of the Woollen and Worsted Industries*, 122-124. For a riot among the Colchester weavers : *Victoria County History, Essex*, ii. 399.

[2] *Statutes at Large*, v. 435. While this Act was called forth by the combinations formed in the West Country, in the nineteenth century the industry was " entirely free from trade unionism " : Webb, *Industrial Democracy* (ed. 1913), 763, note.

" concerning wages, damages, stoppages, arrears of wages or
other disputes whatever any ways relating to the manufacturing woollen cloth " to be referred to two justices of the
peace, with the right of appeal from their decision to quarter
sessions.  On this occasion the Privy Council acted as a
court of conciliation, and the machinery which was set up
embodied the principle of arbitration.  The weavers, while
admonished not " to right themselves in an illegal manner "
by forming combinations, were at the same time recommended to lay their grievances ' in a regular way ' before the
King, who " would be always ready to grant them relief
suitable to the justice of their case " [1].  And the very next
year the justices of Gloucestershire revived the system of
wage-assessments [2].  This attitude affords a striking contrast
with the change of front at the beginning of the nineteenth
century, when the State stripped itself of the right to regulate
the industrial life of the community, without recognizing
that its abdication of authority involved the need for a fresh
orientation of policy towards the trade union movement [3].

*Employers'
combina-
tions.*
The real criticism against the Act of 1726 is that it did
not distribute justice with an even hand.  It left the employers free [3a] to exercise a right which was refused to working
men ; and, as Adam Smith expressly tells us [4], they entered
into combinations, " always conducted with the utmost
silence and secrecy ", in order to " sink the wages of labour ".
It was difficult to prove the existence of a secret association,
because the employers could have tacit understandings as to
the wages they would pay without attaching their signatures
to a single scrap of paper ; it was still more difficult to
obtain a verdict in a court of law, for the employers could
transfer the suit to the central courts, and involve their
opponents in legal expenses entirely beyond their capacity
to support.  In any case, however, the laws against combinations were powerless to check the development of

---

[1] *House of Commons Journals*, xx. 747.
[2] *Supra*, p. 266.                        [3] See *supra*, p. 324, note 5.
[3a] Until 1800 : *infra*, Appendix, p. 531, No. 3.
[4] *The Wealth of Nations* (ed. Cannan), i. 69.  There is mention of an
association formed by employers in Gloucestershire in 1728 : *House of
Commons Journals*, xxvii. 503.  For other references, see *The Gentleman's
Magazine*, ix. 9, 237 (1739) ; Kirby, *A Letter to a Member of Parliament*
(1787), 6.  Also see *supra*, pp. 266, 391.

trade unionism [1]. They could drive the movement underground ; they could awaken a sense of injustice in the hearts of those who considered themselves robbed of a natural instrument, by which to safeguard their interests ; but they could not uproot the irresistible instinct which prompts great bodies of men to associate together for the redress of their wrongs. In spite of common law and statute law trade unionism persisted throughout the eighteenth century, and bequeathed its traditions to the unions of the nineteenth century [2].

The wool-combers were the most highly organized body *Wool-* of textile workers. We get glimpses [3] of a seventeenth- *combers' unions.* century combers' union at Coggeshall in Essex, which was apparently an offshoot of a Company of Clothiers, Fullers, Baymakers and New Drapers. Originating in a movement to keep out ' intruders ' from their trade, it assumed the form of a friendly society " for the maintaining of those amongst them that fell into want, in imitation of their brethren at Colchester ". The ' Articles of the Combers' Purse ' (1688) stated that " being deeply sensible how incident we poor labouring men be to fall into decay through the many calamities, afflictions and troubles that do attend us, and thereby we stand in need of help from others : we have therefore concluded to maintain a purse for the relief of such of our trade as shall comply with us herein. Not that we do in the least contemn that excellent law of this land, whereby every parish is enjoined to provide for their own poor, nor do we slight the care and charity of our superiors ". Contributions were fixed at sixpence a month and a shilling on entrance ; if the fund fell short a special

---

[1] This does not mean that the Act was a dead letter. Two journeymen wool-combers were sent to prison at Norwich in 1747 for joining a union : *The Gentleman's Magazine*, xvii. 153.

[2] Gaskell, *Artisans and Machinery* (1836), 290, believed that handloom weavers " have rarely combined ", and he attributed this to the supposition that they were " a far more moral and conscientious body of people than the factory labourers ", and toiled on " nearly in silence "—a view hardly borne out by their early history. Poverty and isolation prevented the creation of strong and permanent unions among them : see *Report on the Handloom Weavers* (1834), x. 406, 419, 437, 453.

[3] *Hist. MSS. Comm. Various*, viii. 579 *seq.*

levy was to be imposed. The object of the fund was to ensure that when any member " or his charge be afflicted, he shall not sell, pawn or embezzle any of his goods or wearing clothes, nor run himself into debt, but to be in as good a condition when it shall please God to restore him as he was when he was first taken ". It was stipulated that no one who received parish relief should be entitled to draw benefit pay. The combers' friendly society was short-lived, and in 1690 the members " broke up their purse " owing to dissensions in their midst.

*Their organization.*   The combers' unions appear to have embraced in their ranks the vast majority of wool-combers : in the counties of Somerset and Devon it was said that not one comber in a hundred was outside a union [1]. The kingdom was mapped out into districts, each of which served as the province of an independent society ; and we are told that the members of the different societies refused to mix or work with one another, " so that a Yorkshire or Lancashire wool-comber could not obtain employment amongst the Midland wool-combers, whose chief society or club is held in Leicestershire " [2]. However this may be, the unions—which originated as benefit societies for the relief of the infirm and the unemployed [3]—developed into close corporations that tried to restrict their membership to the privileged few. The wool-combers were accustomed to take not more than two apprentices other than their eldest sons, and refused to instruct the apprentices and servants of their employers, in order to " prevent the trade being overstocked with hands ", and so maintain the standard of wages [4]. Their relations with their employers were in these circumstances far from harmonious. An anonymous pamphlet entitled *A Short Essay upon Trade in General : By a Lover of his Country* (1741), written by Thomas Cowper [5], contains an attack upon

---

[1] *House of Commons Journals*, xlix. 323 (1794).   [2] *Ibid.* 395 (1794).
[3] *Ibid.* 324 ; Dunsford, *Historical Memoirs of Tiverton* (1790), 205 ; Cowper, *A Short Essay upon Trade in General* (1741), 40 ; Alcock, *Observations on the Defects of the Poor Laws* (1752), 37.
[4] *House of Commons Journals*, xlix. 322, 395 ; *The Gentleman's Magazine*, xvii. 153.
[5] The authorship, hitherto unknown, is disclosed in *House of Commons Journals*, xxiv. 158.

the wool-combers whom it represents as wielding an absolute control over the industry, fixing the price of wool-combing, and allowing no one to employ a comber who was not a member of their union. " If he did, they agreed one and all not to work for him ; and if he had employed twenty, they all of them turned out, and often times were not satisfied with that but would abuse the honest man that would labour, and in a riotous manner beat him, break his comb-pots and destroy his working tools ". A worsted manufacturer of Nottinghamshire, William Toplis, who claimed to be the inventor of a combing machine, declared in 1794 that " the manufacturers are entirely at the mercy of their combers and must pay them whatever wages they demand, particularly when trade is in a flourishing state ; insomuch that if a manufacturer displeases one wool-comber, all the others either quit his service entirely or until he appeases the offended member, and no other wool-comber will work for him so long as he continues under the displeasure of any of the members of their society " [1]. The wool-combers were denounced as " a self-constituted corporation bound by laws of their own making ", whose members raised their wages at their own pleasure, and were in the habit of leaving their employers' service " in the most unwarrantable manner " : in short, " a set of men whom neither Law nor Morals have yet been able to restrain " [2].

The unions of cloth-workers or cloth-finishers first emerge into prominence at the end of the eighteenth century. An account of the Yorkshire union—the Croppers' Society, corresponding to the Cloth-Dressers' Society in the West of England—is given in the *Report on the State of the Woollen Manufacture* (1806). " It appears that there has existed for some time an Institution or society among the woollen manufacturers, consisting chiefly of cloth-workers. In each of the principal manufacturing towns there appears to be a *Cloth-finishers' unions.*

[1] *House of Commons Journals*, xlix. 395.
[2] *Ibid*. xlix. 546. For a striking episode in the history of the wool-combers of Tiverton, see Lipson, *The History of the Woollen and Worsted Industries*, 124. At Norwich in 1752 a strike of journeymen wool-combers lasted some weeks : *The Gentleman's Magazine*, xxii. 382, 476.

society composed of deputies chosen from the several shops of workmen, from each of which town-societies one or more deputies are chosen to form what is called the central committee, which meets as occasion requires at some place suitable to the local convenience of all parties. The powers of the central committee appear to pervade the whole Institution ; and any determination or measure which it may adopt may be communicated with ease throughout the whole body of manufacturers. Every workman on his becoming a member of the society receives a certain card or ticket on which is an emblematical engraving, the same—the committee are assured—both in the North and the West of England, that by producing his ticket he may at once show he belongs to the society. The same rules and regulations appear to be in force throughout the whole district ; and there is the utmost reason to believe that no cloth-worker would be suffered to carry on his trade, otherwise than in solitude, who should refuse to submit to the obligations and rules of the society. A stated weekly contribution, greater or less according to existing circumstances, is required from every member ; and . . . it also appears that from the same fund liberal weekly allowances have been made to whole shops of workmen who have turned out, as it is called—that is, who have illegally combined to quit the service of some particular master who had become obnoxious to them, and thereby to force him into a compliance with their terms " [1].

*Their objects.*   The members of the Croppers' Society were forbidden to work with non-unionists, and any cloth-worker who applied for work at one of the shops was required to show his ticket to the journeymen. If a dispute arose between a workman and his employer, and the union considered the workman in the right, all the men in the shop were called out, and during the strike no other member of the society was allowed to work for the master under penalty of ' disinheritance ' from the district. It was said that no Acts of Parliament availed against the will of the ' Institution '. " I believe ", said an employer, " they would obey the

[1] *Parliamentary Papers* (1806), iii. page 16 of the Report.

Institution of the workmen rather than obey the law of the land " [1]. The Yorkshire union seems to have comprised the bulk of the cloth-workers [2]. Its objects were to raise wages, to prescribe the age at which apprentices should be taken, and regulate their numbers in accordance with the number of journeymen, and to resist the introduction of machinery. And during the eighteenth century [3] the cloth-workers maintained their traditional practices in the face of the efforts of the capitalists to break loose from restrictions which obstructed the free development of their business.

The cotton industry was destined in the early decades of the nineteenth century to take the lead in the evolution of trade unionism, but the organization of cotton operatives had already begun by the middle of the eighteenth century, since it was expressly included in the Combination Act of 1749 [4]. The worsted smallware weavers were associated as early as 1747, when they framed rules governing apprenticeship ; and in 1756, a year of labour unrest due to the high price of corn, they held monthly meetings attended by a delegate from each ' shop '—a term which signified the group of workpeople employed by a manufacturer [5]. Three years later a notice in *The Manchester Mercury* [6] drew attention to " an unlawful combination among the worsted smallware weavers under the name of being members or being connected with or payers to a box ", and it gave warning " that all persons who are in any ways concerned in those unlawful combinations, or are in any ways aiding or assisting thereto, will be prosecuted to the utmost rigour of the law ; and that no weavers will be taken to work that are in any ways concerned in those unlawful combinations ". An indictment of the offenders was only withdrawn on their engaging to

*Cotton operatives' unions.*

[1] *Parliamentary Papers* (1806), iii. 178-179.     [2] *Ibid.* 231-232.
[3] And beyond. In 1834 the ' Croppers ' were described as " the most restless men in the cloth trade and the ringleaders in almost all strikes " : *Character, Object, and Effects of Trades' Unions* (1834), 58.
[4] *Infra*, pp. 407-408.
[5] Daniels, *The Early English Cotton Industry*, 40-44 ; Wadsworth and Mann, *The Cotton Trade*, 343. The smallware trade included laces, tapes, etc. ; the check trade included stuffs for aprons, gowns, shirts, etc. : Daniels, *op. cit.* 25-27.     [6] Quoted in Daniels, *op. cit.* 44.

" work for the prices already agreed upon with our respective masters, or such other wages as the circumstances of the trade make reasonable for the time being " ; and " never enter into, or promote, or encourage any combination whatsoever for the raising wages or any other unlawful purpose whatsoever ".

*Their activities.*    Combinations also existed among the check weavers who were at variance with their employers over the standard length of cloth, the price for weaving it, and the employment of ' illegal ' workmen [1]. These disputes provoked a strike in 1758 in Manchester and the neighbourhood lasting several weeks. At the assizes Lord Mansfield in his charge to the grand jury referred to " great disturbances in Lancashire, occasioned by several thousands having left their work and entered into combinations for raising their wages, and appointed meetings at stated times, formed themselves into a committee at such meetings, and established boxes, and fixed stewards in every township for collecting money for supporting such weavers as should by their committee be ordered to leave their masters, and made other dangerous and illegal regulations ; that they had insulted and abused several weavers who had refused to join in their schemes and continued to work ; and had dropped incendiary letters with threats to masters that had opposed their designs. His lordship . . . strongly urged to the jury the necessity of suppressing all such combinations and conspiracies on any pretence whatsoever ; gave them an account of all the attempts of the like nature that had been made at different times and in different parts of the kingdom ; and told them that an active and vigilant execution of the laws in being had always been sufficient to suppress such attempts " [2]. The strike collapsed and some of the weavers were brought to trial. A subsequent episode showed that the textile workers in the cotton industry did not abandon their organization, which in 1781 was strong enough to force the employers to enter into an agreement with them. The smallware weavers had threatened to withdraw from the service of their masters

---

[1] For the term ' illegal ', see *supra*, vol. ii. 41.
[2] Daniels, *op. cit.* 45-46 ; Wadsworth and Mann, *op. cit.* 362 *seq.*

unless their price-lists were accepted. On this occasion the employers did not have recourse to prosecution, but made proposals which appear to have compromised the dispute [1].

In the tailoring industry trade unionism made its appear- *Tailors'* ance early in the eighteenth century. The conditions here *unions.* were favourable to its rise. The industry was organized on a capitalist basis—some master tailors of London, whose number in the middle of the eighteenth century was estimated at one thousand, employed at certain periods of the year thirty or more working tailors, called journeymen tailors [2]. Among the latter, who were ' as numerous as locusts ' and generally ' as poor as rats ' [3], unrest was chronic, due to fluctuating wages and the debilitating nature of their work. Their normal rates of wages seemed high in comparison with those of textile workers in general, but their occupation being seasonal they were often out of work during several months in the year [4]. At 2s. 6d. a day the journeyman's wage was said to average throughout the year 9s. a week, while his expenses ' for himself only ' amounted to 8s. 6d. (without reckoning clothes, ' sickness and other incident charges ')[5].

| | | |
|---|---|---|
| " For breakfast, more than the master's allowance | 0 | 0½ |
| For meat, drink and bread for dinner | 0 | 6 |
| On the shopboard, in the afternoon, a pint of beer | 0 | 1½ |
| Bread, cheese and beer for supper | 0 | 3 |
| One day's expenses | 0 | 11 |
| Sunday's expense | 1 | 0 |
| The other five days' expense | 4 | 7 |
| Lodging for a week | 1 | 0 |
| Washing for a week | 0 | 8 |
| Shaving for a week | 0 | 4 |
| | 8 | 6 " |

Moreover the hours of work were long, and " by sitting so many hours in such a position, almost double on the shop-

---

[1] Daniels, *op. cit.* 53-54 ; Wadsworth and Mann, *op. cit.* 371 *seq.*
[2] Galton, *Select Documents* : *The Tailoring Trade*, 51, 54-55.
[3] Campbell, *The London Tradesman* (1747), 193.    [4] *Ibid.*
[5] Galton, *op. cit.* 53-54. For other budgets, see *infra*, Appendix, p. 531, No. 4.

board, with their legs under them and poring so long over their work by candle-light, their spirits are exhausted, nature is wearied out, and their health and sight are soon impaired"[1]. It is therefore not surprising that they began early to form combinations.

In 1721 the master tailors of London complained that their journeymen, " to the number of seven thousand and upwards, have lately entered into a combination to raise their wages and leave off working an hour sooner than they used to do ; and for the better carrying on their design have subscribed their respective names in books prepared for that purpose at the several houses of call or resort (being public houses in and about London and Westminster) where they use ; and collect several considerable sums of money to defend any prosecutions against them ". They insisted upon 12s. 9d. per week, instead of 10s. 9d. ' the usual wages ', and ceased work at eight o'clock at night instead of nine, ' their usual hour, time out of mind '[2]. The ' house of call ', alluded to in this petition, played an important rôle in the industry. It facilitated the formation of a trade union by providing a common meeting-place, where working tailors assembled and learnt to organize their forces ; and it also served the purpose of a labour exchange where masters made inquiries when they wanted hands. In addition " custom has established it into a kind of law that the house of call gives them credit for victuals and drink while they are unemployed ; this obliges the journeymen, on the other hand, to spend all the money they earn at this house alone. The landlord, when once he has got them in his debt, is sure to keep them so, and by that means binds the poor wretch to his house "[3]. The men, in their response to the masters' attack, urged that " to work fifteen hours per day [*i.e.* from 6 A.M. to 9 P.M.] is destructive to the men's health, and especially their sight, so that at forty years old a man is not capable by his work to get his bread. Therefore the journeymen are willing to work from six in the morning until eight

---

[1] Galton, *op. cit.* 52.

[2] *House of Commons Journals*, xix. 416, 424-425 ; Galton, *op. cit.* 1-4.

[3] Campbell, *The London Tradesman* (1747), 193.

at night, allowing half an hour for breakfast and an hour for dinner ". They further pointed out that "the masters are now subscribing and making purses of money to persecute the journeymen, as much as the journeymen are to defend themselves " [1]. As a result of the employers' representations Parliament passed an Act in 1721, which declared *The Act of 1721.* illegal all agreements between journeymen tailors "for advancing their wages or for lessening their usual hours of work ". Hours were fixed at six to eight [2]; and wages from March 25 to June 24 were to be " any sum not exceeding 2s. *per diem*, and for the rest of the year 1s. 8d. *per diem* ". The justices of the peace at their quarter sessions were empowered " to take into their consideration the plenty or scarcity of the time, and other circumstances necessarily to be considered, and to alter the wages and hours of work . . . upon application to be made to them for that purpose ". The Act laid penalties on masters who gave, and on journeymen who took, wages in excess of the authorized rates except when work was done overtime. It also provided that no unemployed journeyman " shall refuse to enter into work or employment after request made for that purpose by any master tailor ", under penalty of being " sent to the house of correction there to be kept to hard labour for any time not exceeding two months " [3].

The intervention of Parliament, if it did not stamp out *Later history of the* the movement among the working tailors of London, at *tailors'* least drove it underground. It emerged again into the light *unions.* of day in 1744, when the Privy Council was informed that " great numbers of journeymen (about 15,000) had entered into a combination, refusing to work for the wages established by law, and were supported in it by the keepers of the ale-houses where they resort ; that they threatened to fire the masters' houses, and abused those who in obedience to the laws continue to work " [4]. The next year the journeymen carried their case to the House of Commons, their main

---

[1] *An Abstract of the Master Taylors' Bill before the Honourable House of Commons, with the Journeymen's Observation on each Clause of the said Bill.*
[2] They had an hour for dinner, and an allowance of 1½d. for breakfast.
[3] *Statutes at Large,* v. 232-234.
[4] Galton, *op. cit.* p. xxx.

argument being that owing to irregularity of employment
the legal rate was insufficient. " Those poor laborious
tradesmen are rarely employed by the master tailors more
than one-half and never above two-third parts of the year,
which at a medium will reduce the statute wages not to
exceed fourteen pence *per diem* for the whole year ".
Nevertheless, in spite of their appeal to " their birth-right
secured to them by Magna Carta and the ancient constitution of this realm ", Parliament declined to take action [1]. A
few years later (1751) the justices of Middlesex increased the
wages of tailors to 2s. 6d. per day in summer and 2s. in winter.
Their order affected only the journeymen tailors of Westminster ; and those of the city of London applied to the
London quarter sessions, which fixed their wages at 2s. per
day for three-quarters of the year and 2s. 6d. for the remaining quarter, and at the same time reduced the hours of work
by one. Thereupon the journeymen tailors of Westminster
again approached the Middlesex magistrates with the demand
for a similar reduction of hours, which provoked the employers to appeal direct to the House of Commons [2]. The
control of the justices embraced only the area comprised
within the ' Weekly Bills of Mortality ' ; and it became the
practice for master tailors, who wished to evade the legal
restrictions and attract the best workmen, to carry " their
work and workmen out of the Bills of Mortality, by which
means . . . they give larger wages, and in times of hurry
can get journeymen from other masters " [3]. To check this
practice, the Act of 1768 established uniform rates of wages
in the city of London and five miles around ; at the same
time wages were raised to ' any sum not exceeding ' 2s. 7½d.
per day throughout the year, and the hours of work were
confirmed at six A.M. to seven P.M.[4]. The significance of this
legislation lies in the fact that, although it sought the repression of trade unionism, it did not leave the journeymen
unprotected since it provided machinery for the control of

---

[1] *House of Commons Journals*, xxiv. 733-734.
[2] *Ibid*. xxvi. 376-377.          [3] *Ibid*. xxxi. 535.
[4] *Statutes at Large*, viii. 57.  One hour was allowed for dinner.  In the
case of a general mourning the wage could be increased to 5s. 1½d.  The
daily wage was raised to 3s. 1½d. in 1772 :  Galton, *op. cit.* p. l.

wages. Actually the rates paid in the tailoring industry were in excess of statute wages, so that the Act in practice fixed the minimum and not the maximum [1]. Nor was the law against combinations among working tailors any more successful in its object. In the opening years of George III.'s reign a report made to the Home Office stated that the journeymen tailors ' within the Bills of Mortality ' had formed themselves into a kind of republic, holding illegal meetings at forty-two different public-houses, and appointing from each of these houses two persons to constitute the ' grand committee for the management of the town ', which framed rules and orders for the direction of the masters and journeymen [2]. Outside London evidence of concerted action appears among the journeymen tailors of several towns, including Sheffield (1720), Cambridge (1721), Liverpool (1756), and Birmingham (1777), where they opposed the introduction of piecework [3].

In other occupations we have information of trade union *Trade* activity, indicating the existence of strained relations between *unionism in other* capital and labour. One of the charges against the journey- *occupa-* men tailors of London in 1721 was that their combination *tions.* set a " very ill example to journeymen in all other trades ; as is sufficiently seen in the journeymen curriers, smiths, farriers, sail-makers, coach-makers, and artificers of divers other arts and misteries, who have actually entered into confederacies of the like nature ; and the journeymen carpenters, bricklayers and joiners have taken some steps for that purpose and only wait to see the event of others " [4]. In 1749 the Act against combinations in the woollen industry was extended to journeymen dyers, journeymen hot-pressers, and all other persons in the cloth manufacture who were not already included ; as well as to journeymen employed in the manufactures of silk, mohair, fur, hemp, flax, linen,

---

[1] In 1800 the master tailors petitioned to be protected from prosecutions for paying " greater wages than are allowed by law " : *House of Commons Journals*, lv. 922-923.

[2] *Home Office Papers*, 1760-1765, p. 429 (1764).

[3] Galton, *op. cit.* 23, 73 ; Lloyd, *The Cutlery Trades*, 237 ; Wadsworth and Mann, *The Cotton Trade*, 376-377.      [4] Galton, *op. cit.* 2-3.

cotton, fustian, iron, leather and hat-making [1]. Unrest among the workmen in the silk industry—manifested in rioting and the destruction of looms, the property of their employers—was responsible for the Act of 1773, which again forbade silk weavers to " enter into any combination to raise the wages " [2]. This Act also contained provisions for settling the rates of wages in the silk industry [3], so that it belongs to the same category as the Act of 1721 regulating the tailoring industry. Encouraged by the concession made to the silk weavers, the frame-work knitters in the Midland counties formed in 1777 a Stocking-Makers' Association for Mutual Protection, in order to press upon Parliament their demand for the legal regulation of wages. Bills were introduced in 1778 and 1779 but they failed to pass, and the disappointment of the artisans led to a riot at Nottingham where several hundred frames were broken. The interest of this episode is that it called forth a rival union of employers, who pledged themselves to resist the interference of the legislature as tending to drive the manufacture to France [4]. Among the Sheffield cutlers, filesmiths and grinders, benefit clubs came into existence during the first half of the eighteenth century. They doubtless intervened in industrial disputes, but a trade union movement among metal workers only became active in the last decade under the stimulus of rising prices [5]. Even in the paper-making industry, near the end of the eighteenth century, the workmen of a Hertfordshire parish were indicted for conspiring to compel

[1] *Statutes at Large*, vi. 430.
[2] *Ibid.* viii. 259. For the riots, see *The Gentleman's Magazine*, xxxiii. 514.
[3] *Supra*, p. 270. It was supplemented by later Acts extending its provisions to manufactures of silk mixed with other materials (1792), and to female workers in the silk trades (1811) : Brentano, *On the History and Development of Gilds*, p. clxxxix.
[4] Felkin, *A History of the Machine-Wrought Hosiery*, 115-117, 229.
[5] Lloyd, *The Cutlery Trades*, 239-249. The Saw Smiths' Society, founded in 1797, provided unemployment and superannuation benefits : *ibid.* 247. Nothing appears to be known of combinations among smelters, founders and forgemen before the nineteenth century : Ashton, *Iron and Steel in the Industrial Revolution*, 205-208. There were strikes among coal-miners (*supra*, vol. ii. 124, 126), but " no lasting combinations " in the eighteenth century : Webb, *The History of Trade Unionism* (ed. 1920), 44, note.

their employer to increase their wages by a shilling a week, and for threatening to quit his service if he refused to do so [1]. Combinations were not restricted to the workers in the productive industries. An organization existed among the corn porters in London, who numbered about eight hundred. Its management was entrusted to a committee of six ' rulers ' who fixed the price of labour ; and " if any of these porters work at an under-rate or defraud any man, they are immediately turned out of the Society " [1a]. It may be observed in conclusion that, while the conception of a class struggle was not fully developed until the nineteenth century, it was given intermittent expression at a much earlier period. The indictment of an offender in the reign of Charles II. for wishing that " all the gentry in the land would kill one another, so that the commonalty might live the better " [2], disclosed the latent feeling of class antagonism.

[1] *Hertford County Records*, ii. 167 (1790). A law against combinations in the paper manufacture was enacted in 1796 : *Statutes at Large*, xiii. 400.

[1a] A book was kept at Billingsgate, where every ' poor freeman ' could enter his name : Povey, *The Unhappiness of England as to its Trade* (1701), 46-47.

[2] *Middlesex County Records*, iii. 326 (1662). For an analysis of the causes of popular disturbances from 1660 to 1714, see Beloff, *Public Order and Popular Disturbances*.

# CHAPTER VI

## THE RELIEF OF THE POOR

*Increase of destitution.* THE creation of a national system of poor relief was the work of the sixteenth century. We have described elsewhere the factors responsible for the increase of destitution at this period—the development of sheep-farming at the expense of corn-growing, which involved the depopulation of villages; the growth of capitalism in industry and the expansion of foreign trade, which exposed the wage-earning community to the vicissitudes of an unstable commercial system; the changes in the currency, which effected a revolution in the general level of prices; and the dissolution of the monasteries, which aggravated all these evils by flinging upon the country-side the multitude of beggars whom in the past they had succoured [1]. Before the advancing tide of pauperism the religious and voluntary agencies which had served for the relief of the poor in the Middle Ages broke down completely, and the widening of the province of State action, hitherto confined to the regulation of begging and the repression of vagrancy [2], now became an imperative need.

*Municipal experiments.* The poor law of the sixteenth century, like the industrial code generally, was moulded to a large extent upon municipal practices. Although, as will be seen later [3], an Act of Parliament had sketched out a whole poor-law programme as early as 1536, it remained nothing more than a sketch for

[1] *Supra*, pp. 294 *seq.*; vol. i. 161, 167, 171, 474; vol. ii. 64, 184.
[2] The earliest poor law (1388) simply acknowledged the right of the impotent poor to beg: *Statutes*, ii. 58. For laws against vagrants, see *infra*, p. 422.
[3] *Infra*, p. 416.

several decades [1]. In the interim the towns provided the main, though not the only [2], field of administrative activity, and the experience which was gained as a result of their experiments furnished a solid basis, on which the legislature could construct a national system of poor relief. In its essentials the Elizabethan poor law was little more than the application, on a national scale, of principles which had already been worked out by the municipal authorities : and its importance lies less in the novelty of the organization which it created, than in its extension to the rural community at large.

London was the first in the field, and the successive London. stages in the evolution of its poor relief were reproduced with fidelity in the enactments of the legislature. The initial step was taken early in the reign of Henry VIII. when begging was put on an organized basis, and the right to ask for alms was restricted to the impotent, who were given a badge to show that they were licensed to beg. The next step foreshadowed the system of compulsory assessment : the municipal authorities in 1533 appointed persons to collect " the devotions of parishioners for the poor folk weekly, and to distribute them to the poor folk at the church doors " [3]. The third step was the institution of a compulsory poor rate in 1547—apparently the first of its kind [4]. After the dissolution of the monasteries the secular authorities were compelled to take over some of the old foundations in order to make provision for the sick and infirm : amongst them St. Bartholomew's Hospital was granted to the City by Henry VIII. and refounded under municipal control. But the attempt to provide for the maintenance of these establishments on a voluntary footing speedily broke down, and London was driven to adopt the principle which was destined to revolutionize the basis of poor relief, by substituting the principle of compulsory taxation—equal in its

[1] Until 1572–1576 : infra, p. 439.
[2] This is sometimes overlooked : cf. the activities of the Council of the North (infra, p. 428). For continental experiments, see Some Early Tracts on Poor Relief (ed. Salter).
[3] Leonard, The Early History of English Poor Relief, 26.
[4] The Order is printed in Tudor Economic Documents (ed. Tawney and Power), ii. 305.

incidence on all according to their means—for voluntary almsgiving, unequal alike in its incidence and distribution.

*Its organization of poor relief.*    London not only set the precedent for the first compulsory poor rate, but in other directions its organization of poor relief anticipated the main lines upon which subsequent legislation was destined to develop : the care of the fatherless, the relief of the sick and impotent, the provision of work for the willing, and the reform of the idle. This classification, and the methods of dealing with the different categories of the poor, give historic importance to the programme drawn up in 1552 when the citizens made suit to the Privy Council that the royal palace of Bridewell should be converted into a house of correction. Among the "needy and miserable persons", they explained [1], "we espied three sundry sorts which were diversely to be provided for : the succourless poor child, the sick and impotent, the sturdy vagabond or idle person. And first, we thought to begin with the poor child that he might be harboured, clothed, fed, taught and virtuously trained up, which thing we have (God be praised) already begun [2]. Next we thought to take up out of the streets the miserable aged, sore and sick persons (which also we have done) and the same to harbour, and by physic and surgery to cure and make whole [3]. Now resteth for the third sort an house of occupations to be erected : wherein as well the child, when he is brought up and grown to years and found unapt to learning, neither any honest person desireth or would have his service, may there be exercised and occupied, as also the sore and sick when they be cured. . . . And unto this shall be brought the sturdy and idle, and likewise such prisoners as are quit at the sessions, that there they may be set to labour. . . . The foundation shall be this. Certain godly and honest citizens will deliver matter in stock, whereof the idle shall be set on work—as wool, yarn, flax, wire, leather, etc. And when the same shall be wrought, to receive the same wrought wares in

---

[1] Bowen, *Extracts from the Records and Court Books of Bridewell Hospital* (1798), Appendix, No. ii.

[2] Christ's Hospital for children.

[3] St. Thomas's Hospital in Southwark for the aged and sick, together with St. Bartholomew's Hospital, refounded by Henry VIII.

satisfaction of the stock, allowing for the workmanship thereof, and always as the wares are wrought to renew the stock. And thus shall there never lack matter whereon the idle shall be occupied ".

The organization of poor relief in London thus con- *Influx of* sisted of three kinds of institutions : Christ's Hospital for *paupers into* children, St. Bartholomew's Hospital and St. Thomas's *London.* Hospital for the sick, and Bridewell for vagrants. These institutions could not cope with all the poor of London, and more were relieved outside than inside the hospitals [1] ; further, in addition to those who came under their special care, there was a class of ' decayed poor citizens ' who received outdoor relief in the shape of a weekly pension [2]. But the system when put into execution did not realize all the expectations formed by its authors ; and the Privy Council in 1589 admonished the lord mayor to take better care that " vagabond and idle persons that go up and down the streets a-begging might be restrained " [3]. The reason of its partial failure, apart from the negligence of the officials, provided the strongest argument in favour of a national system—London could relieve its own poor but it could not ' relieve England ' [4]. A ' great concourse of people of all sorts ' flocked to London from every part of the kingdom. It draweth unto it, wrote John Howes, youths ' which spend Michaelmas rent in Midsummer moon ', soldiers ' wanting wars to employ them ', masterless men, lusty rogues and common beggars [5]. When a search was made for ' rogues and masterless men ' in 1582, the recorder of the city wrote to Burghley : " I did note that we had not of London, Westminster, nor Southwark, nor yet Middlesex nor Surrey above twelve. . . . The residue for the most were of Wales, Shropshire, Chester, Somerset, Berkshire, Oxford and Essex " [6]. Newcomers were encouraged to settle in London by the facilities which existed for obtaining lodging there

---

[1] Howes, *A Ffamyliar and Frendly Discourse* (1587), ed. 1889, p. 42.
[2] *John Howes' MS. 1582* (ed. Lempriere), 15, 40.
[3] *Acts of the Privy Council*, 1589-1590, p. 266.
[4] Howes, *A Ffamyliar and Frendly Discourse* (1587), ed. 1889, p. 37.
[5] *Ibid.* 47.
[6] *Original Letters Illustrative of English History* (ed. Ellis), 1st ser. ii. 286.

owing to the 'miserable covetousness' of the landlords of
'alleys', who crowded tenants in their houses 'pestering three
or four inmates into one room ' [1]. The difficulties created
by the influx of paupers from other districts were largely
instrumental in developing the settlement regulations, which
became so prominent a feature of poor law administration [2].

*Norwich.* The system of poor relief in the metropolis had its counterpart in the provincial towns, of which Norwich may serve as
an example. In 1549, two years later than London, a compulsory assessment was sanctioned [3] and in 1570 a census of
the poor was taken, after which a Book of Orders was drawn
up. These Orders [4] laid down that none should be suffered to
beg on pain of whipping. The impotent poor were to receive
a weekly allowance, youths and maidens were to be put to
service, and the able-bodied but idle poor were to be committed to a bridewell, or house of correction, where the men
were to grind malt and the women to spin and card. The
inmates of the bridewell were to be kept as prisoners to work
for meat and drink for twenty-one days, or longer if necessary,
" and they shall not eat but as they can earn ". They were
to work from five to eight in summer and six to seven in
winter, with " one-half hour or more to eat and a quarter of
an hour to spend in prayer ". An ' officer surveyor ' was to
go daily about the city, arresting those who seemed ' apt for
bridewell' and bringing them before the mayor. Twelve
children were to be brought up in St. Giles Hospital, where
they were to be taught their ' letters and other exercises as
their capacities shall be able to attain '. In each parish
' select women' were to be appointed, whose duty was to
receive in their houses women, maidens and children, consigned to them by the authorities ' to work or learn letters '.
Lastly, those who had not lived three years in the city were to
be sent away with their families, and care was to be taken
that no more strangers should be " suffered here to inhabit
as be not able to live of themselves, or be like to be chargeable
to the city ". The effect of these Orders was to decrease the

[1] Howes, *A Ffamyliar and Frendly Discourse* (1587), ed. 1889, p. 40.
[2] *Infra*, pp. 457 *seq.*
[3] *Norwich Records* (ed. Tingey), ii. 126.
[4] *Ibid.* 339, 344 *seq.* The date of the Orders is 1571.

number of beggars ; and " these things being noised abroad
. . . was given unto the city great commendation ".

London and Norwich present examples of compulsory *Coventry*
assessments and the provision of work for the unemployed *and York.*
some years before they were embodied in a national system of
poor relief by Act of Parliament.   Coventry and York afford
other instances of municipalities which on their own initiative
assumed responsibility for the workless.   The aldermen of
Coventry in 1547 were instructed to take a census of the
inhabitants of their wards, and to find situations for those
out of work : idlers were to be punished, and if they did not
' amend ' they suffered the penalty of expulsion : the deserv-
ing poor were to be relieved ' by the common alms of the city
out of the common chest ' : and every alderman with the
constables " shall go every week once throughout his ward
and look upon the people what they do " [1].   At York it was
ordered in 1569 that the poor should be carried to St. George's
House, " where the city wool lieth, then and there to be
proved by the aldermen, wardens and twenty-four with the
advice of Roger Lighe, clothier, what they can do ; and such
of them as can do ought, or are meet to learn, to have wool
delivered them by discretion of such as have charge thereof
to work, and the said Roger to do his diligence to instruct
such of the said poor as he shall perceive not perfect ".   In
1587 the organization of relief was made more elaborate.
Those who were not born in the city were expelled and the
rest were arranged in three classes.   The aged and impotent
were given a minimum sum of three half-pence a day ' under
which sum a poor creature cannot live '.   Those able to work
were found employment by a novel arrangement in which
" the civic officials provided the work, the amount varying in
proportion to the provider's dignity ".   Each alderman had
to keep four men at work, the councillors two men, and ex-
occupants of the office of chamberlain one or two.   Those
who would not work were committed to the house of correction or banished the city, and in every street persons were
appointed to punish rogues and beggars [2].

[1] *Coventry Leet Book* (ed. Harris), 783-784.
[2] *Victoria County History, Yorkshire,* iii. 466-467.

*Features of the municipal system of relief.* Although municipal regulations for relief of the poor differed in details, they present the same general features—a census of the poor was instituted, and begging was either prohibited or restricted to those licensed for the purpose ; the impotent (where they were not allowed to beg) were supported by a weekly pension, and the sick provided for in hospitals which were sometimes mediaeval foundations reorganized under public management ; children were brought up in industrial schools ; the unemployed were found work ; and the idle and vagrant were committed to houses of correction. This municipal system was in marked contrast with the mediaeval. The relief was organized : it was in the hands of the secular authorities : it was based on compulsory taxation: it drew a distinction between the two classes of able-bodied poor, the willing and the idle, attempting in some cases to provide work for the former, and devising an entirely new method of dealing with the latter by the institution of houses of correction, for which there appears to be no mediaeval parallel in this country.

*The Act of 1536.* The national system of poor relief, embodied in a series of Statutes and supplemented by Orders of the Privy Council, proceeded on the same general lines. The first step was taken in the Act of 1531[1], which sought to put begging on an organized basis by licensing the aged and impotent poor to ask for alms. This was followed by the Act of 1536[2], which laid down in embryonic form all the fundamental principles of the Elizabethan poor law, with a single exception. These principles were as follows—the prohibition of begging ; the organized collection and distribution of alms amongst the aged and impotent ; the division of the able-bodied into two classes, those willing to work for whom work was to be provided, and those unwilling to work on whom punishment was to be inflicted ; and the apprenticing of pauper children. The Act provided that the authorities in towns, and the churchwardens or two others in every parish, were to collect

[1] *Statutes,* iii. 328-329. An earlier Act (1504) dealt with vagrancy : *infra,* p. 422.
[2] *Statutes,* iii. 558 *seq.*

voluntary alms every Sunday and holy day for the relief of the impotent poor, so that 'none of them be suffered to go openly in begging'; the able-bodied were to be 'kept to continual labour'; children between the ages of five and fourteen were to be placed out to service with 'masters of husbandry or other crafts'. The clergy were to exhort the people to give alms for relieving the impotent poor and setting on work 'sturdy vagabonds and valiant beggars'; and no one was to give alms to the poor except in the 'common box', under penalty of forfeiting ten times the amount.

The most important omission in the Act of 1536 was compulsory taxation. This omission was not repaired until 1572, and the interim was marked by tentative approaches to the principle of compulsion. In the first year of Edward VI. (1547) the curate was enjoined to "make, according to such talent as God hath given him, a godly and brief exhortation to his parishioners" to bestow alms on the poor [1]. A subsequent Act (1552) ordered that first the parish clergy should "gently exhort" those who did "obstinately and frowardly refuse to give towards the help of the poor", and then the bishop was to endeavour to persuade him and "according to his discretion to take order for the reformation thereof" [2]. Mary (1555) returned to the Act of 1531: where the poor were too numerous for relief, certain of them could be licensed to beg and to wear badges [3]. Elizabeth, following the precedent set by London in 1533, authorized the appointment of collectors of alms (1563), and for the first time the legislature admitted the principle of compulsion in the case of refractory individuals. Where the clergy failed the justices were to try their powers of persuasion, and "if he or she shall obstinately and wilfully stand in the same", then an assessment was to be made by the magistrates. When the poor were too numerous to be relieved by the parish, they could be licensed to beg within an appointed area [4]. In 1572 the voluntary system, which had been gradually undermined by the procedure laid down in

*Compulsory poor rate.*

---

[1] *Statutes*, iv. part i. 8.
[2] *Ibid.* iv. part i. 132.   Repeated in 1555: *ibid.* iv. part i. 280.
[3] *Ibid.* iv. part i. 281.       [4] *Ibid.* iv. part i. 411 *seq.*

earlier Acts, was discarded by the legislature, and a compulsory poor rate was assessed on all alike. The obligation was now laid upon the justices of the peace to assess the inhabitants of the parish, and appoint collectors and overseers [1]. Under the Act of 1598 the assessment was made by the overseers subject to the consent of the justices [2].

*Survival of private charity.* The Act of 1572 forbade begging in general and substituted compulsory assessments for almsgiving; but the parishes were often a law to themselves. Northampton in 1585 licensed twenty-one poor people to wear badges entitling them to ' beg the town ' [3]; and Dekker in 1621 lamented the fact that there had been no collection for the poor in many parishes, ' no, not these seven years ' [4]. Moreover there still survived the traditional channels of relief, for example, the succour of impoverished members by the gilds [5]; and there still existed opportunity for the display of private benevolence in the form of legacies bequeathed to the poor and in other ways [6]. In times of distress voluntary relief was still forthcoming in the shape of meals for the poor or the distribution of money [7]; and individuals, who had been afflicted with losses, were licensed to travel for a specified period ' to collect the charitable alms of well-disposed people ' [8]. On occasion, also, contributions to the fund for the poor were received from extraneous sources : thus the promoters of a London playhouse undertook to give ' a very liberal portion of money weekly ' towards the relief of the poor [9]. As late as 1693 the King appointed a week during which overseers in London were to

[1] *Statutes*, iv. part i. 593.
[2] *Ibid.* iv. part ii. 896. Non-resident occupiers of land were liable to rating : Cannan, *The History of Local Rates in England* (ed. 1927), 71 *seq.*
[3] *Northampton Records* (ed. Cox), ii. 179.
[4] Dekker, *Greevous Grones for the Poore* (1621), 14.
[5] *Hist. MSS. Comm. Beaufort*, 418 ; *ibid. Various*, i. 75. One of the charges of the yeomanry in the London Weavers' Company against the livery was that the latter " have not made that provision for the poor members of the Company as by their trust they ought to have done " (*c.* 1649) : Bland, Brown and Tawney, *English Economic History : Select Documents*, 311.
[6] For legacies to the poor, see *Norwich Records*, ii. pp. cix *seq.*
[7] Ricart, *The Maire of Bristowe is Kalendar* (ed. Toulmin Smith), 63.
[8] *Hist. MSS. Comm. Various*, ii. 95-96 (1576).
[9] *Tudor Economic Documents* (ed. Tawney and Power), ii. 369 (*c.* 1600).

' collect the benevolence of charitable people at their dwell- *Alms-houses.* ings ' for the succour of the poor [1]. Moreover the system of endowed charities survived the decay of the voluntary principle. Mediaeval almshouses or hospitals, for the reception of the aged and impotent, were often refounded under public management, and many new ones were built during the reigns of Elizabeth, James I. and Charles I.[2]. An example of private endowment is the erection of almshouses in Derby at the end of the sixteenth century by the Countess of Shrewsbury, the inmates being eight men and four women [3]. In some cases the almshouses were built by corporate bodies : thus the Merchant Adventurers of Bristol maintained an almshouse for ten poor sailors, and gave pensions to ' many decayed merchants and seamen's widows ' [4]. More rarely they were erected by the community : in one place the inhabitants built at their own expense an almshouse " to be for ever a habitation for poor people of the parish, many of whom are now enforced to dwell in barns, outhouses and other unwholesome places, and are often removed to their great discomfort " [5]. Although almshouses, taken in the aggregate, were numerous, they were limited to particular localities ; and Chief Justice Hale, writing about the middle of the seventeenth century, expressed the opinion that they did ' but little ' in the way of relief, since they " extend but to a few aged persons limited to some particular town " and were mainly voluntary [6].

Apart from those who were maintained in almshouses *Outdoor* the relief of the poor chiefly took the form, not of a work-*relief.* house, but of outdoor relief in the shape of a weekly pension, which was given to the aged and impotent, including disabled soldiers and sailors [7], to widows, and sometimes to

[1] *State Papers Domestic,* 1693, p. 424.
[2] Leonard, *The Early History of English Poor Relief,* 207, 210, 213.
[3] *Victoria County History, Derbyshire,* ii. 179.
[4] *State Papers Domestic,* 1638-1639, pp. 127-128.
[5] This was Keevil (Wiltshire) : *Hist. MSS. Comm. Various,* i. 95 (1625).
[6] Hale, *A Discourse touching Provision for the Poor* (1683), 2. Miss Leonard (*The Early History of English Poor Relief,* 211) holds that the almshouses of the period 1550-1650 " formed a very important part of the provision for the poor ".
[7] *Statutes,* iv. part ii. 847 (1593).

those with large families. To guard against the abuse of outdoor relief the Act of 1697, adopting a remedy already practised in some localities [1], went so far as to require the recipient of parish relief, and his wife and children living with him, to wear upon their shoulders as a badge 'a large Roman P, together with the first letter of the name of the parish' of his abode [2]. The penalty for refusal was the loss of part or the whole of the allowance, or commitment to the house of correction : and the penalty was being enforced as late as 1732 [3]. The amount paid in relief varied considerably. In 1639 East Barnet contained but one pauper, a widow, who was allowed two shillings a week [4]: in 1677 the overseers of a Lincolnshire parish were ordered by the justices to give five poor people twelvepence apiece weekly: in 1694, in another Lincolnshire parish, a widow with four children received eighteenpence a week [5]: and in London the weekly allowance in the reign of Charles II. appears to have been one, two or three shillings [6]. Relief was not confined to payments in money : it was frequently the practice to build or rent cottages for paupers who could not be accommodated in the homes of their relations, and to put their dwellings in repair [7]. Gifts in kind were made— food, coal, shoes, clothing [8] ; and medical relief was also provided. A town physician was sometimes appointed, as at Newcastle in the reign of Elizabeth, to attend on the poor ; while the corporation of Barnstaple engaged a 'learned physician' in 1629 to give free advice to the poor [9]. Nor was the public provision of medical relief always restricted to those actually destitute : one parish, for example,

[1] *Middlesex County Records : Sessions Books*, 1689–1709, p. 124 (1694). Also *supra*, pp. 417-418.

[2] *Statutes*, vii. 282.

[3] *Hertford County Records*, ii. 70.

[4] *Victoria County History, Hertfordshire*, iv. 218.

[5] *Ibid. Lincolnshire*, ii. 337.

[6] Firmin, *Some Proposals for the Imployment of the Poor* (1681), 14 ; *The Grand Concern of England explained in Several Proposals* (1673) 61.

[7] *Statutes*, iv. part ii. 897 ; *Victoria County History, Buckinghamshire*, ii. 78.

[8] Webb, *English Poor Law History*, i. 167. Also *infra*, Appendix, p. 532, No. 1.

[9] Leonard, *The Early History of English Poor Relief*, 201-202. For other examples, see Marshall, *The English Poor in the Eighteenth Century*, 121 ; Hine, *The History of Hitchin*, i. 263 *seq.*

paid the charges of a bone-setter among whose patients was the child of a miller [1].

We have dealt with the treatment of the aged and *Rogues and* impotent : we have now to trace the growth of a national *vagabonds.* policy with regard to the able-bodied, distinguishing between those who were idle by inclination—the ' rogues and vaga-bonds ' of the statute-book—and the industrious poor who were willing to work.    And first as to the rogues and vaga-bonds.    The term was elastic, and the legislature flung its net widely as will be seen from the following definition : scholars wandering about begging, sea-faring men pretending losses of their ships or goods, persons feigning knowledge in physiognomy and palmistry or telling fortunes, proctors, patent gatherers, collectors for prisons and hospitals, fencers, bearwards, unlicensed minstrels and players in interludes, jugglers, tinkers, pedlars and petty chapmen, labourers loitering and refusing to work for reasonable wages, persons pretending losses by fire or otherwise, or posing as Egyptians [2]. The charge against rogues and vagabonds was that they indulged in thievish practices and fomented disorder. " The wandering people ", wrote a magistrate to Burghley in 1596 [3], " are receivers of all stolen things that are portable —as namely, the tinker in his budget, the pedlar in his hamper, the glassman in his basket, and the lewd proctors which carry the broad seal and green seal in their bags, cover infinite numbers of felonies ".    Their chief victim was ' the poor husbandman '; and Burghley's correspondent protested : " I do not see how it is possible for the poor countryman to bear the burdens duly laid upon him and the rapines of the infinite numbers of the wicked, wandering, idle people of the land ; so as men are driven to watch their sheepfolds, their pastures, their woods, their cornfields. . . . Many wicked thieves escape, for most commonly the most simple countryman and woman, looking no further than to the loss of their own goods, are of opinion that they would not

---

[1] 1671 : *Victoria County History, Buckinghamshire,* ii. 79.   A municipal bone-setter was appointed at Norwich : *Norwich Records,* ii. 144 (1573).

[2] *Statutes,* iv. part i. 591 ; part ii. 899.

[3] Strype, *Annals of the Reformation* (ed. 1824), iv. 405-410.

procure any man's death for all the goods in the world ". But, he added, " the greatest fault is in the inferior ministers of justice, which should use more earnest endeavour to bring them to the seat of judgment and justice ". A generation earlier Harman in his *Caveat* (1567) had expressed a similar view. He urged the justices to be more vigilant to punish these malefactors, and constables more circumspect in executing the charge given them by the justices. Then, he promised, " will no more this rascal rabblement range about the country. Then greater relief may be showed to the poverty of each parish. Then shall we keep our horses in our pastures unstolen. Then our linen clothes shall and may lie safely on our hedges untouched. . . . Then shall we not have our houses broken up in the night. . . . Then shall we safely keep our pigs and poultry from pilfering. Then shall we surely pass by the highways leading to markets and fairs unharmed. Then shall our shops and booths be unpicked and spoiled " [1]. The apprehension aroused by the advent of a swarm of beggars is reflected in the nursery rhyme :

" Hark ! hark ! the dogs do bark ; the beggars are coming to town ".

And the sequel :

" Some gave them white bread, some gave them brown, And some gave them a good horse-whip, and sent them out of the town " [2].

*Laws against vagrancy.* Numerous enactments were passed in the sixteenth century for the suppression of vagrancy. The Act of 1504, like that of 1495, sought to soften the ' extreme rigour ' of earlier enactments, which condemned vagabonds to an indefinite term of imprisonment, by substituting the penalty of the stocks [3]. The Act of 1531 re-introduced a sterner

[1] Harman, *Caveat* (ed. Viles and Furnivall), 21. Ribton-Turner, *A History of Vagrants and Vagrancy*, 576 *seq.*, gives numerous extracts illustrating ' the habits and impostures ' of vagrants. See also Aydelotte, *Elizabethan Rogues and Vagabonds.*

[2] Ashley, *An Introduction to English Economic History and Theory* (ed. 1909), ii. 352.

[3] *Statutes*, ii. 33 (1383), 569 (1495), 656 (1504).

note when it ordered a vagrant to be whipped and sent to his place of birth, or where he last dwelt ' by the space of three years ', and ' there put himself to labour ' [1]. This was followed by the Act of 1547, a measure unique in the annals of the English poor law. A vagabond was to be branded on the breast with ' the mark of V ' and to serve as a slave for two years ; he was to be compelled to work " by beating, chaining or otherwise in such work and labour how vile soever it be as [his master] shall put him unto " ; if he ran away he was to be branded on the forehead or the cheek with ' the sign of an S ', and become the master's slave for ever ; a second time running away he was to be condemned to death as a felon [2]. Three years later this measure was repealed and the Act of 1531 restored [3]. A proposal made in 1559 to revive the enactment of 1547, by which vagrants were reduced to slavery, did not materialize [4]; but in 1572 it was ordered that vagabonds should be committed to prison [5].

After the first outburst of draconian severity a more *Houses of* humane method was adopted for the repression of vagrancy *correction.* by the institution of houses of correction. Thus in Suffolk men were appointed to ride about the country searching for vagrants, whom they were to carry before a justice for commitment to the house of correction [6]. The most famous was Bridewell [7], so that a house of correction was often called by the name of ' Bridewell '. The Act of 1576 ordered the erection of houses of correction in every county [8], but twenty years later it was stated that they had been " put down in most parts of England, the more pity " [9]. A writer in the reign of James I. lamented the fact that poor rogues and beggars should be punished for idleness, " when

---

[1] *Statutes*, iii. 329.                    [2] *Ibid*. iv. part i. 5.
[3] *Ibid*. iv. part i. 115.
[4] *Hist. MSS. Comm. Salisbury*, i. 162.
[5] *Statutes*, iv. part i. 590. The Acts of 1593 and 1598 revived the Act of 1531 for whipping : *ibid*. iv. part ii. 855, 899. In 1604 incorrigible rogues were ordered to be branded : *ibid*. iv. part ii. 1025. In 1662 they could be sentenced to transportation : *ibid*. v. 405. See *infra*, Appendix, p. 532, No. 2.
[6] Ribton-Turner, *A History of Vagrants and Vagrancy*, 116 (1589).
[7] *Supra*, p. 412.                    [8] *Statutes*, iv. part i. 611.
[9] Strype, *Annals of the Reformation* (ed. 1824), iv. 405 (1596).

no place is provided for them to set them to work "[1]. To revive the flagging energies of poor law administrators another Act was passed in 1610, which required 'one or more' houses to be set up in every county where one was not already established ; and they were to be equipped with "necessary implements to set the rogues or such other idle persons on work "[2]. The houses of correction were not moulded to a single pattern : they were sometimes workhouses in which innocent men without employment were set on work [3], but primarily they were penal establishments for 'rogues and idle persons'. "It was not meant", wrote John Howes in 1587, "that any honest soldier or serving man, having any good quality, should be brought to Bridewell ", and he declared that the very name of Bridewell was "odious in the ears of the people "[4].

*Two provincial establishments.* A description of two provincial establishments, one in York and the other in Winchester, will serve to supplement the account already given of the metropolitan institution. The York house of correction [5] at the end of the sixteenth century admitted not only vagrants but also 'common blasphemers, common drunkards, common railers or scolds'. On entrance the man or woman was whipped 'till his or her body be bloody', and the idle or refractory pauper was given the lash repeatedly. They were paid for their work, a deduction being made for maintenance. "The diet of the idle was bread and water, of those who were willing but unskilful coarse bread and small ale, but such as were willing and skilful were given pottage ". The inmates were kept at least twenty-one days unless they were taken into service ; and those who tried to run away were locked to a post by hand, foot or neck. The Winchester house of correction was set up about 1578. According to the articles drawn up for its management [6], the governor of the house was to provide work for eighty men and women, paying them at market

---

[1] *Stanleye's Remedy* in Eden, *The State of the Poor* (1797), i. 169.
[2] *Statutes*, iv. part ii. 1160.
[3] Webb, *English Poor Law History*, i. 83-84.
[4] Howes, *A Ffamyliar and Frendly Discourse* (1587), ed. 1889, pp. 47-48
[5] *Victoria County History, Yorkshire*, iii. 469.
[6] *Ibid. Hampshire*, v. 424.

rates, a trifling deduction being made for their lodging.
The occupations of the men included weaving, wool-combing,
dyeing, hatmaking and glove-making, and those of the
women spinning and knitting. This establishment was not
only a workhouse but an industrial school. Instructors were
provided for training unskilled workers, who were to be
" detained for at least five years, devoting three years to
learning the trade and two to working at it—in order to
repay the institution for their board, lodging and tuition ".
There was a considerable capital outlay for materials apart
from expenditure on furniture and equipment. The inmates
comprised persons committed to the house by the justices for
" pilfering, disorderly conduct or any offence which did not
rank as felony " ; and in addition, " parents or masters
might send their unruly children or lazy servants there for
correction by means of a justice's warrant, paying for their
lodging, and making whatever allowance they pleased for
food for the delinquents ". The impotent and the sick were
excluded, the house being managed on the principle that the
inmates should contribute by their work to the cost of their
maintenance. In some cases the keeper of the house of
correction received a stipend out of which he had to provide
stock, with which to set the inmates on work, at his own
cost [1] : in other cases the stock was provided by the authorities [2].

In their early days the houses of correction appear to *Effects*
have had a deterrent effect upon vagrants, who were said *produced
by houses of*
to prefer even gaol. An Elizabethan justice asserted that *correction.*
" at such time as our houses of correction were up . . . I
sent divers wandering suspicious persons to the house of
correction ; and all in general would beseech me with bitter
tears to send them rather to the gaol. And denying it them,
some confessed felony unto me, by which they hazarded their
lives, to the end they would not be sent to the house of
correction where they should be forced to work ". " And
in truth ", he declared, " work they will not ; neither can
they without most extreme pains by reason their sinews are

---

[1] *Hist. MSS. Comm. Various,* i. 93.
[2] *Hertford County Records,* i. 117.

so benumbed and stiff through idleness as their limbs, being
put to any hard labour, will grieve them above measure : so
as they will rather hazard their lives than work"[1]. Chief
Justice Coke spoke in high terms of the houses of correction :
" Few or none are committed to the common gaol amongst
so many malefactors but they come out worse than they
went in. And few are committed to the house of correction,
or working house, but they come out better "[2]. He predicted that if the justices " will erect more houses of correction . . . we shall have neither beggar . . . nor idle person
in the commonwealth " : but the course of events falsified
the prediction [3]. Roger North, writing towards the end
of the seventeenth century, declared that the houses of
correction were 'of little or no use'. They served as prisons :
" so doth the common gaol, but neither are famous for
increase of work, public stock or reformation of any note
there "[4]. Fielding, in the middle of the next century, wrote
in a similar strain : houses of correction were no other than
' schools of vice, seminaries of idleness ', and those who were
sent there were not put on work but ' confirmed in the
practice of iniquity'[5]. One reason for the failure of the
institution to fulfil the purpose, assigned to it by the legislature, was the uncertainty which existed as to what persons
the justices were authorized to send to it. The term ' idle
and disorderly persons ', as Chief Justice Hale pointed out[6],
left the justices either too great or too little power . Another
reason was the ' want of a convenient stock ' with which to
set the inmates on work [7] ; but it may be conjectured that
the fundamental cause lay in the new orientation of policy
for which the Civil War was responsible. During the
Great Rebellion the surplus population of the country was
largely absorbed in the ranks of the combatants, and there

[1] Strype, *Annals of the Reformation* (ed. 1824), iv. 405 (1596).
[2] Coke, *The Second Part of the Institutes* (ed. 1671), 728-729, 734.
[3] Coke, wrote Fielding, " was a much better lawyer than he was a
prophet " : *An Enquiry into the Causes of the late Increase of Robbers*
(2nd ed. 1751), 96.
[4] North, *A Discourse of the Poor* (ed. 1753), 18.
[5] Fielding, *An Enquiry into the Causes of the late Increase of Robbers*
(2nd ed. 1751), 96-97.
[6] Hale, *A Discourse touching Provision for the Poor* (1683), 4.
[7] *Ibid.*

was little if any need to provide work for the unemployed. Although the conclusion of peace was followed by a return to normal conditions, a breach had been made in the Elizabethan tradition. After the Restoration the poor were relieved as before, since in this direction there had been no breach of continuity in the organization of relief ; but the tradition of providing work for the able-bodied had to be recreated. When this was achieved the house of correction, discredited by its failure, was not utilized for the purpose, and a new institution was devised in the shape of the modern workhouse.

The establishment of houses of correction did not stamp out vagrancy : the love of ' delightful idleness and wandering '[1] was too deeply seated. After the Restoration the main concern of parochial officials was to get rid of vagrants as quickly as possible. They were whipped and passed on from place to place, until they arrived at the parish where they had a legal settlement[2]. When punishment had been inflicted a certificate, or pass, was issued to the delinquent ordering him to reach, within a given period, the place where he was legally settled, and requiring the constables of the parishes through which he passed to help him on the way[3]. The constables were allowed so much per head for lodging, relieving and conveying vagrants[4]. The cost of the removal of vagrants proved a heavy item, even though it was borne by the county. Early in the eighteenth century the matter attracted the attention of Parliament, and an Act was made in 1702 which required the justices in their quarter sessions to fix the charges for maintaining and conveying vagrants[5]. Nevertheless the cost still remained high, and a new arrangement was devised in some of the counties. The justices of Buckinghamshire discovered that the constable of a single parish was paid £140 in 1708 for conveying vagrants, while at

*Removal of vagrants.*

---

[1] *Hist. MSS. Comm. Salisbury*, vii. 118.
[2] *Ibid. Various*, ii. 384-385.
[3] For an example, see *Hertford County Records*, i. 266.
[4] *Ibid.* ii. 52-53.
[5] *Statutes*, viii. 181. The Act of 1699 had authorized individual justices to fix the amount : *ibid.* vii. 607-608. Webb, *English Poor Law History*, i. 379, assigns the fixing of rates by quarter sessions to the Act of 1699.

another parish the applications for the office " had been so numerous as to arouse the suspicions of the bench that the constables had made a considerable profit over this part of their duty ". They therefore adopted the plan of making contracts for the carriage of vagrants [1]. A similar arrangement was made in Hertfordshire where a contractor undertook to perform the work for two hundred pounds a year, by which the county was saved ' several thousand pounds ' [2].

*The industrious poor.*

We must now turn to the treatment of the industrious poor. To provide relief for the indigent has been, at all periods of its history, the *raison d'être* of the English poor law system. What was unique in its earlier stages was the effort of the public authorities to provide work for the unemployed. They assumed responsibility not only for the aged, the impotent and the vagrant, but also for the industrious poor who were unable to find work. The obligation to set the poor on work had been foreshadowed in the Act of 1536 [3] : the injunction, however, was couched in vague terms and forty years elapsed before the legislature issued precise instructions to the parochial authorities. In the interim the idea was not lost sight of, and one attempt at least was made to give effect to it outside the towns. The ' Articles ' framed by the Council of the North in 1557 are of peculiar interest, because their application was general throughout the area under its jurisdiction, and they show that the enterprise of the municipal authorities was not so exceptional as is sometimes represented [4]. The ' Articles' ordered the justices of the peace to appoint overseers in every parish ; and these overseers were to call before them the householders and others of the parish, and examine " what every of them have to occupy for maintenance or supportation of themselves and their families, either in husbandry or craft, or by other labour or industry, and what provision they make for setting to work

[1] *Victoria County History, Buckinghamshire*, ii. 81-82.
[2] *Hertford County Records*, ii. 76.    [3] *Supra*, p. 416.
[4] They also qualify the generalization in Miss Leonard's admirable monograph, *The Early History of English Poor Relief*, 65, that the organization for dealing with the poor " first grew up in order to lessen the number of vagabonds, and chiefly concerned beggars ".

themselves, their wives, children and families ". If the overseers found any man that " useth no trade whereby he may
attain his living in truth or to set his wife, children and
families to work, that then they persuade him or them . . .
not only thenceforthwith to give themselves to labour and
work for their living, but also to provide hemp, flax, wool or
some other thing for their wives, children and family to work
upon and to see them occupied continually therein, or to put
them to such other occupation or necessary labour as every
of them shall best be apt to take and use ". If anyone
practised husbandry or used some handicraft, yet not enough
to maintain himself and his family, he was to be persuaded
to make some further provision and "give himself to some
honest exercise to supply the want of his living "[1].

The problem of the industrious poor was first seriously *The Act*
attacked on national lines in 1576. The solution then *of 1576.*
adopted by Parliament was one of a group of measures,
enacted between the years 1572 and 1576, which together
provided the legal framework of a State organization of poor
relief, based on the maintenance of the aged and impotent by
means of a compulsory rate[2], the punishment of those unwilling to work by means of houses of correction[3], and the
provision of work for those willing to work. The Act of 1576
ordered that a ' stock of wool, hemp, flax, iron or other
stuff ' should be provided and entrusted to ' collectors and
governors of the poor ', who were to distribute it among the
poor ' to be wrought into yarn or other matter '. Payment
was to be made ' according to the desert of the work ', and
the finished product sold to furnish money for fresh supplies
of material. Anyone refusing to work was to be committed
to a house of correction. The authors of this important
measure hoped through its provisions to ensure that
" youth may be accustomed and brought up in labour and
work, and then not like to grow to be idle rogues " ; that
" such as be already grown up in idleness, and so rogues at
this present, may not have any just excuse in saying that
they cannot get any service or work " ; and that " other

---

[1] *Hist. MSS. Comm. Various*, ii. 89 *seq.*
[2] 1572 : *supra*, p. 417.          [3] 1576 : *supra*, p. 423.

poor and needy persons being willing to work may be set on work " [1].

*Provision of work for the unemployed.* In the main the authorities discharged their obligation to find work for the unemployed in one of four ways—exerting pressure on employers to keep their men at work during a trade depression ; assuming the rôle of employers in workhouses and houses of correction ; furnishing capital to individuals to start new enterprises ; and providing schools for technical instruction. The first two are considered elsewhere [2]: the third and fourth were closely connected and can best be treated together.

*Municipal enterprise.* The sixteenth century witnessed a series of attempts on the part of the corporate towns, whose prosperity was menaced by the competition of new industrial centres, to restore their decaying fortunes by attracting fresh blood into their midst. An example of municipal enterprise at Chester was the introduction of weavers from Shrewsbury in order to set up a new branch of the cloth trade [3]. At York the authorities contracted with a manufacturer of Hartlepool to introduce the making of fustians, and employ not less than fifty poor people in carding and spinning cotton wool [4] ; and in the reign of James I. a Norwich citizen was induced to settle in the northern capital and establish the manufacture of worsted cloth [5]. At Lincoln a committee was appointed to confer with an inhabitant of Boston, who offered to find work for four hundred poor people in Lincoln for five years, if the city would provide a convenient house and lend him three hundred pounds free of interest during the five years [6]. The scheme actually adopted assumed a character even more definitely eleemosynary. The city entered into an agreement with ' John Cheseman the knitter ' to start a knitting-school, Cheseman undertaking, " in consideration of six pounds being given him to discharge his debts, to set on work in his science all such as are willing to come to him or are sent by the aldermen, and to hide nothing from them that belongeth to

[1] *Statutes*, iv. part i. 611.　　　[2] *Supra*, pp. 303, 425.
[3] Morris, *Chester in the Plantagenet and Tudor Reigns*, 408 (1576).
[4] *Victoria County History, Yorkshire*, iii. 469 (1597).
[5] *Ibid.* 470 (1619).
[6] *Hist. MSS. Comm. Lincoln*, 74 (1591).

the knowledge of the said science ". Spinning wheels were provided together with forty stone of wool, the contractor receiving every week two stone and paying for the previous week's supply [1].

The ' stock ' or capital required to set the poor on work *Experiments at Lincoln.* was raised by assessing the community, utilizing legacies bequeathed for the use of the poor [2], and leasing town property [3]; and it was employed by the authorities directly—in a workhouse or in a house of correction, or on public works such as the repair of the highways [4]—or indirectly by placing it in the hands of clothiers, who agreed to find work for the poor in addition to those whom they already employed with their own capital [5], or who undertook to start new enterprises. Thus a freeman of Lincoln in 1624 contracted, " if he can have convenient stock, to take upon him to set all the poor of this city upon work to spin, knit stockings, weave garterings, make stuffs and other manufactures of wools. . . . And from Easter every citizen and other inhabitant of ability shall wear at least one suit of apparel and one pair of stockings of such cloth or stuff as shall be made in the city " [6]. Throughout the seventeenth century the corporation of Lincoln persisted in its efforts to furnish employment and training. In 1612 the mayor imported an inhabitant of Peterborough ' to set the poor on work to knit and spin ' : in 1615 a number of citizens combined to buy wool and employ the poor in a house rented for the purpose, while a marshal was appointed to go daily from parish to parish, and bring vagrants and beggars to the spinning school and the house of correction : in 1624, as we have seen, a freeman of the city undertook to find work for the poor in return for a loan of capital : and the records of the ' Jersey School ' for the employment of the poor in knitting and spinning extend from 1684 to 1718 [7].

Three other schemes may be briefly noticed. At Hatfield the Earl of Salisbury made a contract in 1608 with one,

---

[1] *Hist. MSS. Comm. Lincoln,* 17 (1591).
[2] *Ibid. Various,* iv. 222, 228 (Salisbury).
[3] *Ibid. Lincoln,* 285 (Grimsby : 1636).
[4] *Northampton Records,* ii. 180 (1647).
[5] *Hist. MSS. Comm. Various,* iv. 228 (Salisbury).
[6] *Ibid. Lincoln,* 97-99. The agreement terminated in 1629.
[7] *Ibid. Lincoln,* 18, 87, 91, 97.

Walter Morrall of Enfield, who agreed for the term of ten years to instruct in the art of cloth-making fifty persons chosen by the Earl, and to remunerate them for their work. The Earl undertook to provide a house rent-free, and to pay him a hundred pounds a year for ten years[1]. The novel element in the experiment at Plymouth was the agreement to feed the children as well as teach them. A serge-weaver was induced in 1597 to migrate from Exeter to Plymouth ; and the contract provided that he should maintain and ' instruct in his science ' twenty poor children, while the town, in addition to a loan, made a weekly allowance of twelvepence for the diet of every child and also furnished them with apparel[2]. The distinctive feature of the scheme at King's Lynn (1623) was making the contract, not with an individual as in most other places, but with a group of partners consisting of a dealer in raw material, a manufacturer and a London merchant—a kind of integration of industry on a small scale. The agreement stipulated that the contractors should supply raw material, and give instruction to children and employment to poor people, " paying those of them that are not mere learners fit wages for their work "[3]. The importance of these experiments in social amelioration lies in the cumulative evidence, which they afford, that the provision of employment and technical education was not an exceptional thing, but a widespread characteristic of the poor law system, in the Elizabethan and Early Stuart period[4].

Occasionally we meet with anticipations of the ' roundsman ' system, under which householders were required to find work for labourers wanting employment. At Bury St. Edmunds (1571) it was decided that " if any labourer shall

---

[1] *Victoria County History, Hertfordshire*, iv. 250.

[2] The exact terms of the contract were in dispute : *Hist. MSS. Comm.* ix. part i. 268-269. At Nottingham in 1636 a ropemaker was allowed by the town 12d. a week for each child whom he instructed, " towards their diet, and their parents to find them lodging " : *Nottingham Records*, v. 175.

[3] *Hist. MSS. Comm. King's Lynn*, 247.

[4] For the school at Norwich, see *supra*, p. 414. York had a knitting school near the end of the sixteenth century : *Victoria County History, Yorkshire*, iii. 468. For a spinning school at Dorchester, see Clark, *Working Life of Women in the Seventeenth Century*, 132-133.

not be provided of work on the Sunday for the week following, then the curate or constable to move the parish for work "[1]. In Cornwall (1597) the justices ordered "such poor as cannot provide work for themselves to present themselves in a convenient place in the church on the Sabbath Day a little before the ending of morning and evening prayer, and as soon as prayer is ended, order shall be taken to send them abroad among such householders as shall maintain them meat, work, and such wages as they can deserve for the week following "[2]. Locke, indeed, advocated a compulsory labour rate by which the inhabitants of a parish must in turn employ a poor man or pay his wages [3], but there was said to be a ' general averseness and abhorrence of the poor ' to ' work round the parish ' with ' lists ' of the inhabitants, and to render an account of the work which they had performed [4].

The treatment of children under the poor law raised *Parish* a problem of two categories : parish infants and parish *infants.* apprentices. In some towns orphanages were founded for the maintenance of poor children. The most famous was Christ's Hospital in London [5]: another, called Queen Elizabeth's Hospital, was erected at Bristol in 1590 [6]: and Shrewsbury possessed a foundling hospital which a traveller in 1766, impressed by the " healthy looks of five hundred children just sitting down to dinner in the open air on the finest natural terrace in England ", pronounced to be second only to the institution at London [7]. Sometimes children were ' billeted ' on parishioners [8] as a temporary expedient when distress was acute, but the most common method of disposing of poor children was to board them out with parish nurses in the town or country ; while after the Revolution, when numerous workhouses were established, they were also kept there. The

[1] *Hist. MSS. Comm. Lincoln*, 139.
[2] *Ibid. Salisbury*, vii. 160-162.
[3] Eden, *The State of the Poor* (1797), i. 245.
[4] Dunning, *Bread for the Poor* (1698) in *ibid.* 251, note.
[5] *Supra*, p. 413.
[6] John Carr, a merchant of Bristol, left lands for the purpose : Ricart, *The Maire of Bristowe is Kalendar* (ed. Toulmin Smith), 62.
[7] *Hist. MSS. Comm. Buckinghamshire*, 299-300.
[8] *State Papers Domestic*, 1631–1633, p. 16 (Devonshire).

appalling state of the infant poor in London in the eighteenth
century was brought to light by the investigations of parliamentary committees in 1716 and 1767 [1], and the conditions
which their reports disclosed probably existed in earlier times.
The report of 1767 stated that " the children are kept in the
several workhouses in town or in the hands of parish nurses
in town, only a small portion of them being sent into the
country to be nursed ; and the price of 3s. and 2s. 6d. per
week first paid is often reduced so low as 1s. 6d. and 1s. per
week that it cannot be presumed to be equal to the necessary
care of infants " [2]. The conduct of the parish nurses was
commented upon in the earlier report of 1716 in caustic
terms : " A great many poor infants and exposed children
are inhumanly suffered to die by the barbarity of nurses,
especially parish nurses, who are a sort of people void of
commiseration or religion, hired by the churchwardens to
take off a burthen from the parish at the cheapest and easiest
rates they can ; and these know the manner of doing it
effectually " [3]. It is therefore not surprising to learn that
" taking the children born in workhouses or parish houses, or
received of and under twelve months old, in the year 1763 and
following the same into 1764 and 1765, only seven in a hundred
appear to have survived this short period " [4]. In 1767 it was
enacted that the infant poor should be sent into the country
to be nursed, and that guardians should be appointed to
inspect the management and usage of the infants. For the
nursing and maintenance of each child, a sum not less than
2s. 6d. was to be paid weekly for the first six years of their
age and then not less than 2s. per week. In addition a nurse,
who took a child of or under nine months old, was to receive
not less than 10s. after the child had been under her care
twelve months, the child " being alive and having been
treated properly to the satisfaction of the guardians ".
Where nurses were not available children could be sent to the

---

[1] *House of Commons Journals*, xviii. 396 ; xxxi. 248.
[2] *Ibid.* xxxi. 248.　　　　　　　　　　[3] *Ibid.* xviii. 396.
[4] *Ibid.* xxxi. 248. " More young children die in England from the
birth to two years old than in any other country " : Tucker, *An Essay on
Trade* (ed. 1753), 90. See also Young, *The Farmer's Letters* (ed. 1768),
335-336.

Foundling Hospital[1]. The operation of this Act was limited to London but it saved the lives of thousands of children [2], and the greater care displayed in the preservation of infant life must be reckoned among the causes of the growth of population in the latter part of the eighteenth century.

The older children were placed out as apprentices, after they had received in some cases a preliminary training in industrial schools of which an account has already been given [3]. *Parish apprentices.* The system of parish apprenticeship became in the eighteenth and nineteenth centuries a byword, and the first Factory Act was passed expressly for the protection of its unfortunate victims. Our knowledge of its later history may easily colour our judgment of the institution in remoter times, and lead us to conclude that from its inception it was vicious in principle and inhuman in practice. But in the sixteenth century, when the system was inaugurated by the Act of 1536 [4], apprenticeship was compulsory on all who sought admission into industry or trade ; and, considered in the abstract, it offered the pauper child the best, indeed the only, opportunity of family life, social training and technical education [5]. The real criticism against the system lies elsewhere : it must be sought in the facility with which the institution lent itself to abuse. No legal safeguards could prevail against the indifference or greed of parish officers, whose limited vision and narrow conception of their duties betrayed in innumerable cases the interests of those committed to their charge.

Parish apprentices were either orphans maintained by public support, or the children of parents who received poor relief. They were frequently bound at the age of seven [6], and the term of servitude commonly expired at the age of

---

[1] *Statutes at Large*, viii. 18 *seq.*

[2] Eden, *The State of the Poor* (1797), i. 338.

[3] *Supra*, pp. 430 *seq.* These industrial schools admitted all poor children, and not only the orphaned and deserted.

[4] *Supra*, p. 416. As many as five hundred were apprenticed by the Norfolk justices upon the instructions of the judges : *Hist. MSS. Comm. Rye*, 463 (*temp.* James I.).

[5] Cf. *infra*, Appendix, p. 532, No. 3. For examples of indentures, see *Hertford County Records*, i. 90-91 (1647) ; Trotter, *Seventeenth Century Life in the Country Parish*, 81.

[6] *Hertford County Records*, ii. 125 ; *Parliamentary Papers* (1806), iii. 102. At 5½ years : *infra*, Appendix, p. 532, No. 4.

*Length of service and nature of occupation.*

twenty-four in the case of youths and twenty-one in the case of girls [1]. The result was to ' check marriage and discourage industry ', and a committee of the House of Commons recommended that " parish children should be placed out apprentice for a shorter time than is by law prescribed " [2]. The Act of 1767, accordingly, shortened the term of apprenticeship to seven years or until the apprentice became twenty-one [3]. This measure applied only to London, but in 1778 it was made general that the period of apprenticeship should terminate at the age of twenty-one [4]. The occupation of parish apprentices depended upon local circumstances. They were bound to a great variety of trades, though the most common were husbandry [5] and weaving—the latter had this advantage in the eyes of parish officers that children could be taken off their hands at an earlier age than in ' almost any other business ' [6]; while girls were apprenticed in ' house-wifery ' or husbandry [7], and probably in other occupations. Boys were also apprenticed to the sea, and the justices were empowered (1704) to apprentice poor boys of ten years or upwards to ' the sea service ' until they attained the age of twenty-one, the overseer paying the shipmaster fifty shillings to provide ' necessary clothing and bedding for sea service ' [8]. The statutory obligation to take parish apprentices sometimes conflicted with the limitations imposed by gild ordinances on the number of apprentices permitted to a master craftsman : and in such cases the result was to create for the parish apprentice an anomalous position when his term of servitude expired. The Cutlers' Company of Sheffield, for example, restricted its members to one apprentice and could refuse the freedom of the Com-

[1] *Statutes*, iv. part ii. 897 ; *State Papers Domestic*, 1633–1634, pp. 274, 534 ; *Parliamentary Papers* (1806), iii. 102.
[2] *House of Commons Journals*, xxxi. 249 (1767).
[3] *Statutes at Large*, viii. 20.
[4] *Ibid.* 592.
[5] *State Papers Domestic*, 1633–1634, p. 534 ; *Hertford County Records*, i. 435 ; Marshall, *The Rural Economy of the West of England* (1796), i. 110. Also *infra*, p. 438.
[6] *A State of the Case . . . relating to the . . . Rising of the Weavers in the County of Gloucester* (1757), 3.
[7] *Hist. MSS. Comm. Lothian*, 76 ; *State Papers Domestic*, 1633–1634, p. 534 ; and *infra*, p. 438.   [8] *Statutes*, viii. 258.

pany to any additional apprentice. The effect was to create for the masters a supply of cheap labour, debarred from the privileges of mastership and permanently condemned to an inferior status. In the case of the Cutlers the anomaly was not removed until 1801, when parish apprentices who had served their term were given a statutory right to their freedom in the Company [1].

The parish, when binding an apprentice, generally *Abuses of* though not invariably paid a premium, the amount of which *the system.* varied from place to place. In Hertfordshire £3 : 10s. was given with a child placed out by a parish in 1647 [2], but in London in the eighteenth century the apprenticeship fee was sometimes as low as twenty to forty shillings [3]. Parliament decided in 1767 that the London bounty was " by no means adequate to the procuring such masters and mistresses as are in general fit and proper ", and it required that the sum paid should be not less than £4 : 2s. [4]. It was obligatory in the eighteenth century for a parishioner to receive a parish child as an apprentice, but in the preceding century there was some legal uncertainty as to the powers of the parish officers to place out the children at their discretion. The Act of 1697 stated that the Elizabethan Statute for binding poor children had ' failed of its due execution ', owing to doubt " whether the persons to whom such children are to [be] bound are compellable to receive such children as apprentices ". It therefore ordered that refusal to receive and provide for parish children, ' according to the indenture signed and confirmed by two justices of the peace', should be punished with a penalty of ten pounds [5].

---

[1] Lloyd, *The Cutlery Trades*, 132-135.
[2] *Hertford County Records*, i. 90. In 1698 a boy was apprenticed to learn husbandry, forty shillings being allowed ' for clothing ' : *ibid.* i. 435. In 1773 some boys were ordered to be " bound apprentice to sea service or some other proper masters . . . with five pounds bounty money with each from the gift of the Earl of Salisbury". A subsequent order provided that a master receiving an apprentice should be paid three pounds to provide clothing : *ibid.* ii. 126.
[3] *House of Commons Journals*, xxxi. 249 (1767).
[4] *Statutes at Large*, viii. 20. Of this amount 42s. was to be paid after three years elapsed.
[5] *Statutes*, vii. 282-283. The justices of Suffolk were instructed (*temp.* James I.), " if any freeholder or other person sufficient to take an apprentice
[*contd.*]

The right to impose poor children upon parishioners often caused friction, and when the justices were armed with powers of compulsion the general discontent was intensified. A Derbyshire clergyman complained that some magistrates executed the Act "with that vigour as to force [parish children] upon the clergy : and particularly amongst others an apprentice girl is offered to be put upon me by an indenture . . . wherein I must covenant to teach her the art and mistery of husbandry. This has not been usually practised upon the clergy, as being unsuitable to their holy function and not agreeable to the nature and tenure of their church livings. Sir, we apprehend this to be a hardship upon us "[1]. Choice of a master was sometimes made by lot[2], but in innumerable cases the children were handed over at an early age to the tender mercies of those who were willing for a scanty premium to undertake an obligation, which they had neither the fitness nor the intention to discharge. Early in the seventeenth century the justices of the peace for Wiltshire charged the overseers with imposing apprentices out of malice 'upon such as are not of ability to keep them'[3]; and in the following century the evils of the system were the subject of caustic comment. 'Parish officers', said one writer (1728), place out orphans "so young with little money (two guineas a common price) to sorry masters that 'tis little better than murdering them"[4]: and another declared (1758)[5] that " few of these poor children now serve out their time[6], and many of them are driven by neglect or cruelty into such immoralities as too frequently render them the objects of public justice". The institution of parish apprenticeship survived into the nineteenth century, but its abuses[7] had long given it a distorted form in which the

be disobedient to our order, bind them over to appear before us " : *Hist. MSS. Comm. Rye*, 463. See *infra*, Appendix, p. 533, No. 1.

[1] *Hist. MSS. Comm. Cowper*, ii. 387 (1699).

[2] *Hertford County Records*, ii. 125.

[3] *State Papers Domestic*, 1633–1634, p. 273.

[4] *Some Few Letters selected from an Account of Workhouses and Charity Schools* (1728), 30.

[5] Hutchins and Harrison, *A History of Factory Legislation*, 6.

[6] They ran away from service : *Parliamentary Papers* (1802–3), vii. 283.

[7] For examples of the treatment of parish apprentices, see George, *London Life in the Eighteenth Century*, chapter v.

principle of public benevolence was utterly perverted in the interests of parish economy.

The history of poor relief has been treated hitherto from the standpoint of the relief of destitution. This is the key-note of the principal enactments which constituted the legal framework of the Elizabethan system of poor relief— namely, the Act of 1572 instituting a compulsory rate [1], and the Act of 1576 establishing houses of correction and making provision of work for the unemployed [2]. The different strands of poor law legislation were finally woven into a single texture in the Act of 1598 [3], a temporary measure continued with slight modifications in the Act of 1601 [4]: neither of these Acts, it should be observed, introduced any new principle [5]. There is, however, another side to the problem of relief, namely, the prevention of destitution. The problem of the poor involved, in fact, two distinct categories : the paupers or permanent poor, and the temporary victims of economic adversity. The former included the aged, the impotent and the idle ; the latter comprised those who were suddenly deprived of their earnings by a commercial crisis, or who found that their earnings had diminished in value owing to a rise in the cost of living. We have described the means adopted to cope with permanent destitution and with trade depressions [6]: it remains now to speak of the methods of handling the situation created by fluctuations in the general level of prices.

*Prevention of destitution.*

The two primary necessaries of the poor, in which a serious advance of prices easily assumed the proportions of a national catastrophe, were bread and fuel. These commodities differed in the respect that the supplies of coal were drawn mainly from one part of the kingdom [7], while corn was grown in every part and therefore seemed less exposed to monopolist influences. The difference, though real, must not be pressed since difficulties of communication often gave

*Bread and fuel.*

[1] *Supra*, p. 417.  [2] *Supra*, pp. 423, 429.
[3] *Statutes*, iv. part ii. 896 *seq.*  [4] *Ibid.* 962 *seq.*
[5] The Act of 1598 made a change in the method of assessment : *supra*, p. 418.  [6] *Supra*, pp. 300 *seq.*
[7] *I.e.* supplies for London and the home counties.

local producers a practical monopoly; and there were marked variations in the price of grain even in adjacent counties. Public opinion saw, indeed, no difference at all, and in each case a rise in price was attributed to the manipulations of middlemen. It is true that the quantity of corn available for consumption depended upon the state of the harvest, but the phenomena of a natural scarcity could be reproduced in the coal industry by limitation of output. The intervention of public authority was therefore frequent in the case of corn and coal alike : but here we are concerned only with the former [1].

*Methods of providing corn for the poor.* The methods of providing corn for the poor in times of scarcity were mainly three. The first was the purchase of grain by philanthropic individuals who sold it under market rates. At Bristol, for example, in 1594 an alderman of the city " did buy to the use of the commons of this city from Christmas till Michaelmas following twelve hundred pounds' worth of wheat and rye, and did bring . . . into the market every market day a quantity, and the other days did serve the commons of the city, to the great good of the whole commonalty "; and two years later when ' all manner of corn was dear ', another citizen bought from a London merchant three thousand quarters of Danzig rye for the benefit of the town [2]. This method of voluntary relief was encouraged by the Government, which exhorted the rich to raise a fund for the purchase of corn and its sale at moderate prices [3]. Sometimes, also, the owners agreed to sell a portion of their produce to the poor below market rates. Thus at Hertfordshire in 1630 " the farmers and corn-masters, to have the market free, agree to relieve the poor in their parishes with corn at home at 12d. or 18d. in a strike under the market price " [4]. The second method of supplying the markets was analogous in principle to the first, though the corn was purchased not by individuals but by the municipality. This practice was common in the

---

[1] For coal, see *supra*, vol. ii. 141 *seq.*
[2] Ricart, *The Maire of Bristowe is Kalendar* (ed. Toulmin Smith), 62-63.
[3] *Acts of the Privy Council*, 1595–1596, p. 26.
[4] *Hist. MSS. Comm. Buccleuch*, i. 272. Similarly : *ibid. Various*, i. 115

Middle Ages [1], and London in the sixteenth century reduced it to a system which ultimately became identified with the city companies [2]. The participation of the city companies in the provision of corn at first (1521) took the form of a contribution in money, but from 1578 down to the Fire of London, when the companies' mills and granaries were destroyed, they assumed direct responsibility [3]. The principle underlying these municipal arrangements was the conviction, expressed in a mandate of the Privy Council in 1613, that the market could not be ' so well provided for ' by the operation of economic forces ' as by providence and foresight ' on the part of the civic authorities [4]; and the mandate therefore enjoined the city companies, for ' keeping the prices at reasonable rates ', to make provision of " such quantities of wheat as are proportioned upon them severally . . . that out of that store the markets may be continually served " [5]. The third method of providing cheap bread for the poor involved the direct intervention of the State, and it wore the appearance of a tentative experiment in Socialism.

Precedents for the interference of the Privy Council during a bread famine existed in the first half of the sixteenth century : in 1544, for example, the justices of the peace were instructed to " search the houses, barns and yards of such persons as have been accustomed or used to sell corn ", and to command owners who had a surplus to bring it to market for sale [6]. Under Elizabeth [7] the system

[1] Supra, vol. i. 302. Fuel was sometimes sold by the municipality at reduced prices : Remembrancia of the City of London, 81, 84 (temp. James I.) ; Northampton Records, ii. 180 (1649). The London companies provided coal in 1665 : Jupp and Pocock, The Carpenters' Company, 498 ; supra, vol. ii. 142, note 6.
[2] For Norwich, see Norwich Records, ii. pp. xcvii, ci.
[3] Herbert, The History of The Twelve Great Livery Companies, i. 133, 145, 150. The Carpenters' Company discharged their obligation through a contractor : Jupp and Pocock, The Carpenters' Company, 414, 465. In 1632 the lord mayor committed to Newgate " divers of the wardens of those companies that have not laid in their proportion of corn " : State Papers Domestic, 1631–1633, p. 449. See also supra, vol. ii. 435.
[4] Acts of the Privy Council, 1613–1614, p. 207.
[5] Ibid. 207. State Papers Domestic, 1619–1623, p. 471 ; 1631–1633, p. 125.
[6] Schanz, Englische Handelspolitik, ii. 670 ; Tudor and Stuart Proclamations (ed. Steele), i. No. 265. At Coventry a corn census was taken in 1520 : Coventry Leet Book, 674-675.
[7] In 1573 commissioners were appointed to take measures for supplying the public markets with corn : State Papers Domestic, 1547–1580, p. 468.

*The Book of Orders.* was elaborated, and the scarcity of 1586 afforded the occasion for a detailed set of instructions, or ' Book of Orders '[1], that furnished the pattern on which subsequent policy was moulded. These Orders, issued in January 1587[2], laid down that the justices of the peace should group themselves into ' sundry parts ', and take into their charge different divisions of the county. In each division they were to summon before them ' the most honest and substantial inhabitants ', and arrange them into as many juries as they should think meet, excluding as far as possible those who were known to hold large stocks of corn. The juries were to ascertain " what number of persons every householder that hath corn in their barns, stacks or otherwhere . . . have in their houses . . . what number of acres they have certainly to be sown this year with any manner of grain ; what bargains they have made with any person for any kind of grain to be sold by or to them ", and the price and quantity. " Item, what number of badgers, kidders, broggers or carriers[3] of corn do inhabit within the parish, and whither they do use to carry their corn they buy, and where they do usually buy the same, and what their names be, and how long they have used that trade, and by whose licence, and to see the same licences of what tenor they are of. Item, what number of maltmakers, bakers, common brewers or tiplers[4] dwell within the parish, and who they are by name, and how long they have used that trade, and how much they bake or brew in the week. . . . Item, who within the same parish be the great buyers of corn or . . . have bought or sold any corn upon the ground ", and the particulars of the transactions. The justices were to summon before them all who appeared to enjoy a surplus, and after ' allowing to every householder for his expenses in his house ' and for seed, they were to bind them to offer for

---

[1] *Orders devised by the especiall commandement of the Queenes Maiestie for the reliefe and stay of the present dearth of Graine within the Realme* (1586).

[2] January 2, 1586–1587 : *Tudor and Stuart Proclamations* (ed. Steele), i. No. 791.

[3] For these terms, see *supra*, vol. ii. 421.

[4] Keepers of public-houses.

sale in open market whatever corn was not disposed of locally to the inhabitants of the parish. The transactions of the licensed dealers in grain were to be rigorously scrutinized. One justice at least was to be present at every market within each division of the county to see that the Orders were observed, and the poor ' served of corn at convenient and charitable prices ' [1]. There was to be no buying or bargaining for corn except in open market : the justices were to restrain the excessive use of malt by brewers : and they were to suppress unnecessary alehouses. Finally, the justices were instructed to see that the able-bodied were set on work, houses of correction provided, idle vagabonds punished, a ' convenient stock ' furnished, impotent persons relieved, and every month they were to certify their proceedings to the sheriff who was to make a report to the Privy Council.

We obtain glimpses of the operation of the system, and *Operation of the system.* its practical fruits, in the West of England. At Gloucester wheat was sold at 5s. 6d. the bushel, rye at 5s., beans at 3s. 8d., barley at 3s. 8d., and malt at 3s. These prices were communicated to the Privy Council, which sent letters to the local authorities in April 1586, giving instructions similar to those embodied a few months later in the Book of Orders [2]. A contemporary memorandum throws light upon the results achieved : " Mr. Mayor and the justices of peace by virtue of those letters did make search in the barns and garners of all farmers and corn breeders, and did bind by recognizance all persons having corn to serve and furnish the markets weekly. And the justices . . . did set down the prices and rates of corn, viz. wheat at 4s. 4d. the bushel, rye at 4s., beans at 3s. 4d., barley at 2s. 10d., and malt at 2s. 10d. Notwithstanding, in discretion the same was not thought good to be put in practice for fear the markets might be abridged, yet the justices of the city attending the markets abated the excessive prices required by the owners, and

[1] The personal attendance of J.P.'s at markets was frequently insisted upon : *Acts of the Privy Council*, 1596–1597, p. 82 ; *Hist. MSS. Comm. Various*, i. 87 (1614).

[2] *Hist. MSS. Comm. Beaufort*, 458 ; *Acts of the Privy Council*, 1586–1587, pp. 71-72.

kept the same about 5s. or 5s. 4d. the bushel till new corn came in. . . . During the most part of this summer corn continued at great and high prices, notwithstanding all the policy and consultation taken against the same. . . . The prices of all kinds of grain, even upon the inning of harvest in (1586), did abate very little from the former prices, but before Christmas following the same did arise to the full prices of the former year. Whereupon her majesty's most · honourable Privy Council devised sundry Orders for general searches . . . of every man's quantity of corn ", etc., " which Orders were contained in printed books thereof delivered into all places of the realm. The same Orders were diligently observed, but notwithstanding the prices did increase and so continued until the month of harvest happening this year (1587) sooner than in many years before, having little or no rain from Easter till the 13th of September. This year was as fruitful a year for corn as was seen by any man's memory, and commonly in every place harvest was inned by the middle of August. . . . This twenty-ninth year (1587) harvest being inned, the prices of corn fell and abated before the first of September so as then the best wheat was sold at 2s. 6d. the bushel " [1]. This account shows that though the justices had fixed a scale of prices, they did not venture to enforce it, and prices remained high until an abundant harvest in 1587 restored the equilibrium between production and consumption.

Re-issues of the Book of Orders.     The last decade of the sixteenth century was marked by a series of bad harvests : prices were doubled and even trebled [2]. The Book of Orders was re-issued (1594) [3] ; but the local authorities were reluctant to put it in operation, and Cecil was warned by correspondents that the poor were beginning to " murmur both at the want which they find in the markets and the great prices " [4]. The Government was anxious to avoid popular clamour at a time when foreign danger threatened, and it sternly reproved the justices for their neglect to carry out its instructions. It attributed the high

---

[1] *Hist. MSS. Comm. Beaufort*, 458-460.
[2] Rogers, *A History of Agriculture and Prices*, v. 268.
[3] *Acts of the Privy Council*, 1595–1596, pp. 8, 26.
[4] *Hist. MSS. Comm. Salisbury*, v. 418-419 ; vii. 118.

price of corn to hoarding, which made the scarcity worse than it really was, for the sake of ' excessive and ungodly lucre ', and also to the remissness of the justices, some of whom were themselves charged with being ' corn-masters ' [1]. In this, as in other directions, Tudor statesmen were hampered by the shortcomings of the administrative machinery : the progress of legislation outran executive efficiency, and many laws became a dead letter owing to the failure of the magistrates to enforce them. Pressure of the Privy Council alone kept the justices to their work ; and there was a marked contrast between the zeal displayed by the Privy Council and the lukewarmness of the justices [2]. The Book of Orders was re-issued under James I. in 1605, 1608 and 1622 [3], and ' revised and enlarged with some necessary additions ' by Charles I. in 1630 [4].

What was the effect of the intervention of the Privy *Effects of* Council in times of scarcity ? A contemporary view was *Government inter* that interference aggravated the distress it was designed to *vention.* alleviate : it raised the price of corn by disclosing the extent of the shortage and creating an apprehension of famine. Thus the justices in Hertfordshire reported in 1631 that " their strict looking to the markets is an occasion that *the markets are the smaller*, the corn dearer, and new shifts and devices found out to prevent doing of good, which they cannot suddenly meet withal " [5]. The mayor of Dover had a similar experience when he found that though the farmers were rated by the justices to bring into the Dover market every week twelve quarters of wheat, besides barley, they did not average four bushels [6]. It was also represented that the interests of the producer needed to be considered ; and a plea on behalf of the farmer was made in the report of the

[1] *Acts of the Privy Council*, 1596–1597, p. 95.
[2] See the letters in *Hist. MSS. Comm. Buccleuch*, i. 229 ; and *ibid. Somerset*, 20.
[3] 1605 : Webb, *English Poor Law History*, i. 60 (note), 73-74. 1608 : *Tudor and Stuart Proclamations* (ed. Steele), i. No. 1058. 1622 : *ibid*. i. No. 1344.
[4] Rymer, *Foedera*, xix. 195 ; *Orders for the preventing and remedying of the Dearth of Grain* (1630).
[5] *State Papers Domestic*, 1629–1631, p. 539.
[6] *Hist. MSS. Comm. Salisbury*, vii. 156-157 (1597).

Dorsetshire justices (1631), in which they pointed out that " corn was raised to so high price at the end of last year by the interference of the justices and the suspicion of want thereby excited. Best wheat is now at 5s. 6d. per bushel and barley at 3s. Beg them not to press too hard upon the poor husbandman, who toils and takes much pains, stands at high rents, buys all things at a dearer hand, almost by half than in former times, all foreign commodities, salt especially, being at such extraordinary prices. Great quantities of corn have been of late years gotten out of barren grounds by improvement of marl and lime, which is done with excessive charge "[1].

*A steadying influence on prices.* None the less we must not assume that the results of interference were in every case mischievous. Much depended upon the discretion and tact of the authorities ; but it is reasonable to suppose that the powers, with which the justices were armed, were instrumental in checking prices from reaching on occasion panic heights, and in mitigating the injurious effects of a local monopoly which were liable to be the more serious in the absence of an efficient system of transport [2]. The corn census, even if it did draw attention to the shortage, made hoarding more difficult since it forced owners to disclose concealed supplies, and in so far as the markets were kept more regularly furnished prices were kept more steady. The dealers naturally disliked these methods of control and were thus rendered more amenable to pressure, for they could always be warned that " if they raise the prices of their corn to excessive rates, it will be a means to cause the King to command the lords of his Council to stint them and to set rates upon their corn, which they would be unwilling to hear of "[3]. In this connexion the remarks of a sixteenth-century writer are noteworthy. He condemned the view that a " dearth of victual may be redressed by setting of prices upon victual ", because " it is not the setting of low prices that will anything amend the matter.

---

[1] *State Papers Domestic*, 1631–1633, p. 186.
[2] Prices sometimes fluctuated violently in a short period. Within the same year wheat in London sold at 3s. 6d. and 15s. a bushel, and barley at Northampton at 6d. and 5s. : Rogers, *A History of Agriculture and Prices*, v. 59.
[3] *Hist. MSS. Comm. Beaulieu*, 113 (1630).

But it must be the taking away of the occasion of the high prices ". Nevertheless he made a significant admission : " Yet I will not say nay but the rumour thereof, that such low prices should have been set at a certain day, would have done very well, for the doubt thereof would have caused many things to have fallen something of price "[1]. All things considered, the Book of Orders probably tended in years of scarcity to alleviate the distress caused by the shortage, in so far as it created an organization for the more regular and even distribution of supplies, and ensured in consequence a more moderate level of prices. And this view finds expression in the reports. The justices of Norfolk, for example, wrote that " throughout this shire by such order as we have taken with owners and farmers, and also badgers and buyers of corn and grain, the markets are by them plentifully served every market day with corn and the same sold at reasonable rates, viz. wheat at 22s. the quarter, rye at 16s., malt at 14s., and barley at 12s., of which kinds of corn the poorer sort are by persuasion served at meaner prices "[2].

The moral effects of intervention in preserving public order, and checking incipient agitation, must also be remembered. The Government was compelled to adopt measures, which on purely economic grounds might seem illadvised, in order to ' stay the fury of the inferior multitude '[3], whose standard of life must have been adversely affected by the failure of wages to keep pace with the rise in prices due to the influx of American silver[4]. A letter from the Privy Council, relating to the disturbances in Rutland in the year 1631, illustrates the connexion between efforts to relieve distress and the prevention of disorder. It states that information had been received of some speeches ' tending to the stirring up of the poor thereabout to a mutiny and insurrection ', and it quotes one speech as follows : " Hearest thou", saith a shoemaker of Uppingham to a poor man of

*Re-assures public opinion.*

---

[1] *Tudor Economic Documents* (ed. Tawney and Power), iii. 340 (1549).
[2] Leonard, *The Early History of English Poor Relief*, Appendix iv. (1586). Similarly, Suffolk : *ibid.* 195. For a list of ' certificates of corn to spare for market ', see Ashley, *The Bread of our Forefathers*, Appendix iv.
[3] *Hist. MSS. Comm. Somerset*, 20 (1596).
[4] See *supra*, vol. ii. 33.

Liddington, " if thou wilt be secret I will make a motion to thee". " What is your motion ? " saith the other. Then said the shoemaker : " The poor men of Oakham have sent to us poor men of Uppingham, and if you poor men of Liddington will join with us we will rise, and the poor of Oakham say they can have all the armour of the country in their power within half an hour, and (in faith saith he) we will rifle the churls". The letter orders the apprehension of the shoemaker but adds : " And likewise (which is indeed most considerable and the best means to prevent all disorders in this kind) that you deal effectually in causing the market to be well supplied with corn, and the poor to be served at reasonable prices and set on work by those of the richer sort, and by raising of stock to relieve and set them on work according to the laws " [1]. Yet other motives than the fear of popular outbreaks actuated the Government. There was not wanting a genuine desire to remove hardships and alleviate suffering—it showed itself in the policy of Wolsey who " favoured the people exceedingly and especially the poor " [2] ; in the instructions to the Council of the North to hear " the petition of the poorest man against the richest or against the greatest lord " [3] ; and in the intervention of the lords of the Privy Council on behalf of a maid-servant whose mistress was accused of ' hard dealings ' [4].

*Creation of new machinery.*    Apart from its effects in steadying prices and re-assuring public opinion, the Book of Orders influenced profoundly the development of the poor law system since it created machinery for coping with a national scarcity—a machinery of which the distinctive features were the assignment of particular areas to justices, and their meeting at stated intervals for the object of carrying out the instructions laid upon them ; the drawing up of reports indicating the measures taken to furnish the markets with corn ; and the direct interference of

[1] Printed in Leonard, *The Early History of English Poor Relief*, Appendix x.
[2] *State Papers Venetian*, 1509–1519, p. 560.
[3] Rymer, *Foedera*, xix. 425 (1633).
[4] *Acts of the Privy Council*, 1575–1577, p. 350. The Council also intervened on behalf of (1) a tenant threatened with expulsion ; (2) sailors' wives whose landlords turned them out of their houses " for want of payment of the rent at the time due " : *ibid.* 1580–1581, pp. 183, 365.

the Privy Council, which was kept in close touch with the situation in every part of the country by means of these reports on local conditions [1]. This procedure, devised for a particular purpose—the prevention of destitution as a result of exceptional stress—was extended in 1631 to the provision of relief in ordinary times : it was incorporated in the normal machinery of the poor law system, and utilized for wider purposes by administrators who had gained experience of its practical working in a more limited field [2]. The Book of Orders, intended for the provision of corn in years of scarcity, established the precedent for the Orders and Directions issued in 1631, which infused a new spirit into the organization created by the Elizabethan poor law. The personal government of Charles I. witnessed the adoption of an energetic policy in regard to the poor, and for a decade (1630–1640) the execution of the poor law was more vigorous than at any other period. The intervention of the Privy Council, hitherto restricted to special cases [3] or to emergencies such as a crisis in trade, the aftermath of a rebellion [4], or the failure of the harvest, now became part of the ordinary administration : it ceased to be spasmodic and intermittent, and became regular and continuous. This change of policy serves to give the government of Charles I. a distinctive place in the history of poor relief.

The intention to inaugurate a new departure was foreshadowed as early as 1629, when a proclamation deplored the neglect of the poor laws and urged the justices to take this ' into their most serious consideration ' [5]. Proposals began to be canvassed for a scheme to ' quicken ' the justices of the peace [6]. The social reformers in the Privy Council, at the head of whom were Strafford and Laud, had determined that it was " time for councillors to care for those things that concern government in these loose and dear

*Social policy of Charles I.*

---

[1] *E.g. State Papers Domestic,* 1581–1590, p. 333, etc.
[2] Cf. Leonard, *The Early History of English Poor Relief,* 91-92.
[3] *E.g. Acts of the Privy Council,* 1589–1590, p. 266.
[4] The rising of the Northern Earls in 1569 was followed by an active campaign for the repression of vagrancy.
[5] Rymer, *Foedera,* xix. 71-72.
[6] *Hist. MSS. Comm. Buccleuch,* i. 273.

times, lest mischief follow of it. The diligence of some
justices, and the good fruit of their pains, show that there
want no laws to reform all things but good executioners of
laws " [1]. Their zeal bore fruit in the appointment of a
large number of privy councillors, including Laud and
Wentworth, to act as commissioners for the execution of
the poor laws which, it was stated," in most places of this
kingdom are little regarded ". The commission [2], dated
January 1631, gave instructions for the issue of the necessary
Orders and Directions ; and for this purpose the whole
country was partitioned out among the commissioners.
The latter were divided into six groups, corresponding to the
six circuits : each group was to receive from the judges of
the circuit, at stated intervals, reports drawn up by the
justices of the peace in their several shires.

*The Orders and Directions.* The ' Orders ' were eight in number. Their general
tenor was to require the justices of the peace to " divide
themselves and allot amongst themselves what justices of
the peace and what hundreds shall attend monthly at some
certain places of the shire. And at this day and place the
high constables, petty constables, and churchwardens and
overseers for the poor of those hundreds shall attend the
justices ", and report on the administration of the poor law
in their districts : those who neglected their duty were to be
severely punished. The justices in their turn were to send
reports to the sheriff, and the sheriff to the judges of assize,
who were to transmit them to the commissioners [3]. The
judges were specially enjoined to make inquiry on their
circuits " what justices of the peace are careful and diligent
in execution of these laws and the directions given, and who
are negligent and remiss ". Two features in this procedure
call for comment. It imposed fresh responsibilities upon
the justices, who were required to meet at regular intervals
and to catechize the parish officers with regard to the performance of their duties ; and it made the judges of assize

---

[1] *Hist. MSS. Comm. Buccleuch,* i. 270-271.
[2] The commission will be found in the printed *Orders and Directions.*
See also Rymer, *Foedera,* xix. 231 ; *State Papers Domestic,* 1629–1631,
p. 474. The commissioners were given power to appoint deputies.
[3] Cf. *State Papers Domestic,* 1629–1631, p. 496.

intermediaries between the central and local government [1]
—in short, it established an administrative hierarchy.
The Orders were supplemented by twelve 'Directions'.
One instructed landowners to ensure that their tenants and
others were " relieved by work or otherwise at home, and
not suffered to straggle and beg up and down in their
parishes ". Another insisted upon the apprenticing of poor
children to 'husbandry and other handicrafts'. A third
ordered an increase in the 'weekly taxations' for the relief
of the poor 'in these times of scarcity'. A fourth required
that "the petty constables in all parishes be chosen of the
abler sort of parishioners, and the office not to be put upon
the poorer sort if it may be ". A fifth appointed "watches
in the night and warding by day in every town and village
for apprehension of rogues and vagabonds, and for safety
and good order ". A sixth laid down that "if in any parish
there be found any persons that live out of service or that
live idly, and will not work for reasonable wages or live to
spend all they have at the alehouse, those persons to be
brought by the high constables and petty constables to the
justices at their meetings, there to be ordered and punished
as shall be found fit ". Finally, houses of correction were
to be established " adjoining to the common prisons, and the
gaoler to be made governor of them that so he may employ
to work prisoners committed for small causes, and so they
may learn honestly by labour and not live idly and miserably
long in prison, whereby they are made worse when they
come out than they were when they went in " [2].

The Orders and Directions of 1631 were not suffered to re- *Vigour of*
main a dead letter. In all parts of the country the justices *the poor law ad-*
actively bestirred themselves, and they displayed a zeal *ministra-*
in the execution of their functions which gives these years *tion.*
a unique aspect. Among the state papers [3] are preserved
innumerable returns made by the justices in pursuance of

---

[1] The duty of receiving reports from the J.P.'s had been assigned to
the judges on previous occasions, *e.g.* in 1625 : *Hist. MSS. Comm. Various,*
i. 305.
[2] From the printed edition of 1631.
[3] *E.g. State Papers Domestic,* 1629–1631, pp. 533, 549, etc.; 1631–1633,
p. 65 ; 1634–1635, pp. 104, 440, etc.

the Orders, indicating the measures taken by them for relief
of the poor ; and they not only bear testimony to the un-
wonted vigour of the administration, but also throw light
upon the practical working of the poor law system at this
period. The conduct of the parish officers was scrutinized
with a minuteness which left no detail unobserved. Thus
in one of the Hampshire divisions the justices required the
' officers of every parish ' to furnish answers to over thirty
queries touching the performance of their duties[1]. Two
examples will indicate the nature of the reports made by
the local authorities. The lord mayor of London reported
(1632) that great sums of money were raised in the past
year for the relief of the poor and setting them to work ;
50 vagrants were bound apprentices to merchants to serve
in Barbados and Virginia ; 70 were taken as apprentices
into Bridewell ; 773 poor children were maintained by
Christ's Hospital ; 40 had been put apprentices to trades
since Easter last ; and 4000 and odd vagrants had been
' conveyed' according to the Statute[2]. The justices in
three Monmouthshire hundreds (1637) certified their conformity to the Book of Orders : they had set the poor on
work, relieved the aged and impotent, punished 83 vagrants,
and apprenticed 58 poor children[3].

*Activity of the Privy Council.* The activity of the Privy Council was maintained down
to the end of the personal government of Charles I. Thus in
1638, when the city of Gloucester was ' visited with plague ',
the justices of the county were admonished for their failure
to come to the assistance of the infected persons, and they
were ordered to levy " a weekly contribution, answerable to
their numbers and expectations, upon the county within
five miles of the city ", and to continue the contribution so
long as the contagion lasted[4]. The next year the municipal authorities of Exeter were instructed to confer with the
justices of Devon for the purpose of finding work for the
poor, "as they understand the trade of clothing is much

---

[1] The queries are printed in Leonard, *The Early History of English
Poor Relief*, Appendix xii.
[2] *State Papers Domestic*, 1631–1633, p. 433.
[3] *Ibid*. 1637, p. 275.  [4] *Hist. MSS. Comm. Beaufort*, 490.

decayed " [1]. The execution of the law for setting the poor on work remained, indeed, a constant preoccupation with the Government, and the duty of its observance was included in the charge delivered to the grand jury [2]. As late as 1640 it was the subject of a proclamation ordering a return to be made of the condition of the poor in each county, and of the steps taken to provide work for them, and enjoining the judges " in their several circuits to take an exact account how these things have been " observed [3].

The Interregnum was rich in political ideas and con-stitutional experiments, yet in the sphere of poor law administration it was, with a single exception, barren of constructive effort. The Commonwealth created nothing to set by the side of the Elizabethan Poor Law, the Stuart Orders and Directions, the Restoration Law of Settlement [4], or the Acts of the Revolution for erecting workhouses [5]. The Protector issued a proclamation (1655) for the enforce-ment of the poor law [6], but the only important measure of these years was due to the initiative of a body of London citizens, who petitioned Parliament for the establishment of a ' Corporation of the Poor ' [7]. As a result of their repre-sentations an Act was passed in 1647, which set up a Cor-poration of the Poor in the city of London consisting of a president (who was to be the lord mayor), deputy, treasurer and forty assistants. It was empowered to erect work-houses for relieving and setting the poor on work, and houses of correction for punishing rogues and vagabonds. It also authorized ' any county, corporation or boroughs ' to make choice of " able and sufficient persons for the like effectual relieving and regulating of the poor in their respective places " [8]. Two years later the constitution of the London Corporation was modified, the number of assistants being

*The Inter-regnum.*

---

[1] *Hist. MSS. Comm. Exeter,* 80.
[2] *Ibid. Verulam,* 195.
[3] Rymer, *Foedera,* xx. 407 ; *State Papers Domestic,* 1640, p. 184.
[4] *Infra,* p. 457. [5] *Infra,* p. 477.
[6] *Tudor and Stuart Proclamations* (ed. Steele), i. No. 3057.
[7] Bush, *The Poor Man's Friend* (1649).
[8] *Acts and Ordinances of the Interregnum,* i. 1042-1045.

raised to fifty-eight [1]. A poetical appeal of 'outcast children' made entreaty :

"Grave senators that sit on high,
Let not poor English children die " [2].

Although an attempt was made to put the scheme into operation, it was largely ineffective ; and the organization of poor relief in London continued to be based primarily upon the institutions created at the Reformation. The condition of these institutions in the reign of Charles II. is set forth in the " True Report of the great number of poor children and cther poor people maintained in the several hospitals under the pious care of the city of London the year last past. Christ's Hospital—children put forth apprentices and discharged out of Christ's Hospital 57, 15 whereof were placed apprentices to commanders of ships out of the Mathematical School founded by the King. . . . Children remaining in the care and charge of the Hospital in the house and divers places in London and the suburbs and at nurse in the country 530. . . . St. Bartholomew's Hospital—there have been cured at the charge of the said Hospital this last year 1703, many of whom have been relieved with moneys and other necessaries at their departure. . . . St. Thomas's Hospital—cured and discharged this last year 1331, many of whom have been relieved with moneys and other necessaries at their departure. . . . Bridewell Hospital—received this last year vagrants and other indigent and miserable people, many whereof had clothing and other necessary relief and were sent by passes to their native counties, 1124. Maintained therein and brought up in divers arts and trades 143 " [3].

*Effects of the Civil War.* The Civil War had profound effects upon the national organization of poor relief : it destroyed the control of the Privy Council, and led to the abandonment of the system of setting the poor on work. The two were closely interconnected, since the authority of the Privy Council had been

---

[1] *Acts and Ordinances of the Interregnum*, ii. 105. For its subsequent history, see *infra*, p. 476.
[2] Quoted in *Parliamentary Papers* (1851), xxvi. 432.
[3] *State Papers Domestic*, 1676–1677, p. 43.

most continuously exercised in the attempt to provide employment for the poor. We have now to follow the working out of these effects in their practical influence upon the administration of poor relief. The consequence of parochial independence was the restraints placed on mobility of labour[1]: the consequence of the failure to find work for the poor was the institution of the modern workhouse[2].

The system of control exercised by the Privy Council *Central* existed in its completest form, as we have seen, in the decade *control ended.* 1630 to 1640. It enabled the central government to make its supervision effective in every part of the kingdom : a chain was instituted which connected the lowest-placed official in the parish with the lords of the Privy Council at Westminster, the intermediate links being the judges of assize, the sheriffs and the justices of the peace. The need for this close surveillance is shown in one of the reports sent in by the justices (1631). It stated that when the constables and overseers were instructed to make presentments, ' for the most part ' they replied that " they have no poor that wanted work or relief ", and " no rogues but such as were punished ". The justices suspected the accuracy of this idyllic picture, and ascertained that the overseers had failed to summon meetings of the parish to consider means for the relief of the poor, that there were no ' stocks ' for setting the poor to work, and that some of the poor were ' in no small want '[3]. The result of the Civil War was to destroy the Stuart machinery of control. After the Restoration each parish was left to go its own way, and national uniformity, the ideal of the absolute monarchy, disappeared in a welter of parochialism. The justices still retained their statutory functions[4]: they appointed the overseers, sanctioned the assessments, examined the accounts, imposed contributions on the richer parishes in aid of the poorer ones, heard appeals in settlement cases, and administered the houses of correction for which they had the responsibility. But they were no longer subject to the strict supervision of the central government, and in turn their own

---

[1] *Infra*, pp. 457 *seq.*     [2] *Infra*, pp. 471 *seq.*
[3] Leonard, *The Early History of English Poor Relief*, 247. Cf. *Hist. MSS. Comm. Rye*, 439.
[4] *Statutes*, iv. part ii. 896-899.

surveillance, which they were intended to exercise over the parochial officials, also relaxed.

*The over-*
*seers.*
As a result the overseers, the actual administrators of poor relief, became the pivot of the poor law system. They consisted of the churchwardens of the parish and two to four ' substantial householders ' nominated by the justices of the peace [1]. They were required to meet together once every month ' at the least ' [2], and on their personal qualities largely depended the success or failure of the organization for relief. Unfortunately overseers were annually appointed, so that the office was held in rapid succession by a series of untrained and inexperienced householders—"all of them ", as might be expected, "wanting to get over the office with as little trouble to themselves as possible " [3]. Burn declared that in practice the office of an overseer " seems to be understood to be this: to keep an extraordinary look-out to prevent persons coming to inhabit without certificates . . . to maintain their poor as cheap as possibly they can . . . to bind out poor children apprentices, no matter to whom or to what trade, but to take especial care that the master live in another parish ; to move heaven and earth if any dispute happens about a settlement, and in that particular to invert the general rule and stick at no expense . . . to depopulate the parish in order to lessen the poor rate " [4]. The picture may have been overdrawn but it reflects, on the whole, the general contemptuous estimate [5] of the parochial officials, who in practice administered the poor laws without much interference or supervision on the part of the justices of the peace. One remedy for the situation thus created was to form the parishes into groups, and place each under a salaried superintendent whose function would be to control and direct the overseers. The adoption of this proposal [6] would have given

---

[1] *Statutes*, iv. part ii. 962.   [2] *Ibid.* 962.

[3] Burn, *The History of the Poor Laws* (1764), 211.

[4] *Ibid.* 211-212. For examples of negligent overseers, see *Hertford County Records*, i. 45, 405.

[5] Cf. Fielding, *An Enquiry into the Causes of the late Increase of Robbers* (2nd ed. 1751), 74.

[6] Burn (*Observations on the Bill intended to be offered to Parliament for the better Relief and Employment of the Poor*, 1776, pp. 36-37) assigns this proposal to Hale. But Hale spoke of a salaried workhouse-master under the
[*contd.*]

a new direction to the system of poor relief in this country. It would have mitigated the abuses inseparable from the employment of annual officers, required to give their service in a voluntary capacity ; and it would have created a staff of trained administrators, upon whose expert knowledge Parliament could have based legislative reforms. However it ran counter to the instinct of a nation in which the execution of public offices was considered, not the province of the salaried expert, but part of the normal obligations of citizenship.

In the absence of a system of poor relief based on a wider *The Law of Settlement (1662).* area than the parish, the settlement regulations assumed a disproportionate importance ; and it is significant that the question was taken up by Parliament shortly after the Restoration [1]. The Law of Settlement, passed in 1662, was destined to excite more controversy in the seventeenth and eighteenth centuries than any other part of the poor law system : it became the principal source of contention among neighbouring parishes, and exercised baneful effects upon the status and welfare of the working community. The Act empowered any two justices upon complaint made by the overseers, within forty days after any persons came to settle in any tenement under the yearly value of ten pounds, to convey them to the parish where they were last legally settled, unless they gave ' sufficient security for the discharge of the parish' from the obligation to support them [2]. As experience was gained in working the Law of Settlement, its provisions were supplemented by other enactments intended to remove loopholes for evasions or to define more precisely the conditions of acquiring a legal settlement. One method of evasion was for newcomers to conceal themselves until the forty days had elapsed—for example, a ' settled inhabitant ' in the parish of Aspeden in Hertfordshire migrated to Layston " where he obscured himself in a cottage about the space of three months unknown to the inhabitants, until exigency and

---

direction of the overseers : *A Discourse touching Provision for the Poor* (1683), chapter 3.

[1] A proclamation enforcing the laws relating to the poor was issued in 1661 : *Tudor and Stuart Proclamations* (ed. Steele), i. No. 3300.

[2] *Statutes*, v. 401.

necessity compelled him to crave their charity and relief to the burthening of the parish of Layston " [1]. On this occasion (1662) the justices decided that he should be conveyed back to Aspeden ; but there was evidently doubt as to the exact legal position of a pauper in these circumstances. Accordingly the Act of 1685 ordered that the period of forty days should be reckoned from the time notice was given in writing to one of the churchwardens or overseers [2]. The conditions of settlement were further defined in an Act of 1691 [3], by which anyone who ' executed any public annual office ' during a whole year, or ' paid his share towards the public taxes ', should be deemed to have a legal settlement. The privilege was also extended to unmarried persons hired for a year—a subsequent Act (1697) stipulated that they must remain in the same service one whole year [4]—and to apprentices bound by indenture [5], subject to the proviso laid down in 1712 that the master must have a legal settlement in the parish, otherwise his apprentice did not gain a settlement there ' by reason of such apprenticeship ' [6].

*Early restraints on settlements in towns.*
The principle of the Restoration Law of Settlement was not new. As far back as the fourteenth century the impotent poor had been required, in certain circumstances, to remove to the place of their birth [7] ; and in the sixteenth century they were bidden to reside either in the place of their birth, or where they had " last made their abode by the space of three years " [8]. Both Edward VI. and Elizabeth expressly authorized the removal of the aged and impotent poor, who had not been born in the parish nor resided there for three years [9]. The policy of expelling newcomers, who might become chargeable on the rates, was frequently put into operation by the local authorities during the late sixteenth and early seventeenth centuries. The ' Orders for the Poor ', drawn up at Norwich in 1571, insisted that " such as have not remained three years in the city . . . to be presently sent away with their families " [10]. In London (1576) the constables, beadles

---

[1] *Hertford County Records*, i. 149.  [2] *Statutes*, vi. 19.
[3] *Ibid.* vi. 314.     [4] *Ibid.* vii. 282.     [5] *Ibid.* vi. 314 (1691).
[6] *Ibid.* ix. 797.     [7] 1388 : *ibid.* ii. 58.     [8] 1504 : *ibid.* ii. 656.
[9] *Ibid.* iv. part i. 7-8 (1547), 116 (1550), 593-594 (1572).
[10] *Norwich Records*, ii. 353.

and churchwardens were charged to inspect the houses of the poor every fortnight, and to banish new arrivals who could not support themselves [1]. At Warwick (1586) the authorities held a census of paupers, and drove away from the town several families which were not born there [2]. At Basingstoke (1587) it was ordered that those who had not " remained here by the space of three years last past (according to the Statute) are to be removed " [3]. In the West Riding of Yorkshire some were sent away who had been domiciled for twenty years, and it was therefore laid down (1598) that a residence of three years should confer a right to relief [4]. In other cases a shorter period of domicile was required [4a]. The ' opinion of the court ' of quarter sessions held in Somersetshire in 1616 was that " when a man hath been in covenant or settled a year from the place of his birth, and if there he hath any mishap and then become maimed, he shall then be relieved and not sent to the place of his birth " [5]. The stringency of the settlement regulations becomes more comprehensible, when viewed in the light of the municipal attitude towards strangers in general : for it is evident that a system, which confined the right to carry on trade to the freemen of a borough, served as a practical bar to settlement in the borough. The inter-connexion of the one with the other was clearly shown in a letter written by the mayor and jurats of Rye in 1651 [6], which incidentally throws light upon the effects of the Civil War. " Upon several complaints of the poor tradesmen of this town unto us made, that many of the disbanded soldiers and other strangers did set up and exercise public trades and callings, to their great prejudice and apparent ruin, and desiring redress therein, and withal being acquainted that divers of the said disbanded soldiers and strangers had wives and children which are like to be a sudden and great charge to this place, which is already so poor that the inhabitants are

---

[1] Leonard, *The Early History of English Poor Relief*, 98.

[2] *Victoria County History, Warwickshire*, ii. 169.

[3] Baigent and Millard, *A History of Basingstoke*, 351, 353.

[4] *West Riding Sessions Rolls* in *The Yorkshire Archæological and Topographical Association*, Record Series, iii. 85.

[4a] See *infra*, Appendix, p. 533, No. 2.

[5] *Quarter Sessions Records for the County of Somerset*, i. 192.

[6] *Hist. MSS. Comm. Rye*, 217.

very much oppressed in bearing the charge thereof. . . . For remedy whereunto we did proceed, according to law and the privileges of this corporation, for our own conservation that we fall not into an irrecoverable mischief ". They permitted soldiers who were natives of the town, or had married wives of the place, to set up in trade ; and some other categories were allowed to continue in service as journeymen. As to the rest, " we gave them timely warning to desist the public exercise of their callings, and depart this place and go to their several places of birth or last abode " [1].

*And in the country.* These early restraints on settlement were enforced not only in towns but also in the country. Cases are recorded which show that the hardships, associated with the Settlement Law of 1662, were experienced long before its enactment. In one case (1618), which came before the justices of Worcestershire, permission to settle in a parish was sought by an applicant who stated that he worked in Stockton where he was born, but when he " fortuned to marry with an honest young woman " the parish was " not willing I should bring her in the parish, saying we would breed a charge amongst them. Then I took a house in Bewdley and there my wife doth yet dwell, and I myself do work in Stockton . . . and now the parish of Bewdley will not suffer her to dwell there for doubt of further charge " [2]. In another case (1631) a labourer complained to the justices of Somersetshire that he had lived five years in his parish, but after his marriage " some of the parish hath forbidden him to remain there any longer, and threateneth him and those that would set or let him any house to impose great pains on them . . . whereby he is enforced to travel from place to place with his wife and children, and thereby doubteth that he shall in the end be taken as a vagrant " [3].

The Statute of Charles II. appeared on the surface the logical outcome of a system which entitled the poor to re-

---

[1] This proposal to expel persons, who were neither impotent nor chargeable, shows that the Act of 1662 did not introduce ' a new and perfectly unprecedented system ' as stated in Coode, *The Report on the Law of Settlement and Removal*, 14, in *Parliamentary Papers* (1851), xxvi.

[2] *Hist. MSS. Comm. Various*, i. 298.

[3] *Quarter Sessions Records for the County of Somerset*, ii. 139. Other examples : *infra*, Appendix, p. 533, No. 3.

ceive relief in the parish where they happened to be. The treatment of the poor was not everywhere the same, for some overseers were more generous than others ; and the poor were naturally attracted to the places ' where they could find best accommodation ' [1]. The consequence was, as Fielding observed, that " the poor of one parish began to bring a charge on another " [2]. There was only one possible remedy for this situation : the substitution of a group of parishes in place of a single parish as the unit of the poor law system. The poor would then have been relieved in the locality where they resided, but the burden of their support would have been distributed over a wider area. Instead of adopting this solution the Restoration Parliament adhered to the principle that a parish was to be responsible for maintaining its own poor [3], and established its legal right to expel newcomers likely to become chargeable. The definite embodiment of this right in an Act of Parliament caused the question of settlement to assume the proportions of a national problem, which set parish against parish [4], gave rise to endless litigation, hampered the free flow of labour, and poisoned the fount of organized charity [5]. In one respect the provisions of 1662 might seem more liberal than earlier settlement regulations. In the sixteenth century, as we have seen [6], a domicile of three years was usually necessary in order to acquire a right of settlement ; and a letter of the Privy Council (1598) describes how in London ' certain persons of wealth ' had converted mansions into tenements and filled them with poor people, " and though those poor folks are set at great rents yet they make shifts to pay the same, knowing if they can but hold out for three years, then the parish where they remain are tied to find and relieve them ever after" [7]. Actu-

---

[1] A Digest of the Poor Laws (1768), p. xiv.
[2] Fielding, An Enquiry into the Causes of the late Increase of Robbers (2nd ed. 1751), 132-133.
[3] Child called this ' the radical error ' : A New Discourse of Trade (4th ed.), 92.
[4] " Every parish is, in fact, in a state of war . . . with every other parish throughout the kingdom " : Tucker, The Manifold Causes of the Increase of the Poor (1760), 6.
[5] " Every parish . . . regards the poor of all other places as aliens " ; Annals of Agriculture, xvii. 80.          [6] Supra, p. 458.
[7] Acts of the Privy Council, 1597-1598, pp. 435-436.

ally the Restoration enactment was more severe, because although it only required a domicile of forty days to establish a right of settlement, it empowered parish officers to remove newcomers within the period of forty days whether or not they had become 'chargeable'. Yet apparently one of the principles on which the Statute of 1662 was based—namely, that a person who was not removed on some pretext or other, within a very short period, obtained a settlement—was not unknown to law. In 1633 the question was put to Chief Justice Heath: "What is accounted a lawful settling in a parish, and what not?" And his answer was: "This is too general a question to receive a perfect answer to every particular case which may happen. But generally this is to be observed—that the law unsettleth none who are lawfully settled, nor permits it to be done by a practice or compulsion; and everyone who is settled as a native householder, sojourner, an apprentice or servant for a month at the least, without a just complaint made to remove him or her, shall be held to be settled"[1]. Heath's statement was considered the expression of a private opinion, but presumably it had some foundation. And even the right, which the Restoration Parliament now sanctioned, to expel newcomers before they had become 'chargeable', was sometimes practised before 1662, as we have shown[2].

*Execution of the law haphazard.* The execution of the law was haphazard and casual. Child vividly describes the practical working of the system in London[3]: "A poor idle person that will not work, or that nobody will employ in the country, comes up to London to set up the trade of begging. Such a person probably may beg up and down the streets seven years, it may be seven-and-twenty, before anybody asks why she does so, and if at length she has the ill-hap in some parish to meet with a more vigilant beadle than one of twenty of them are, all he does is but to lead her the length of five or six houses into another

---

[1] Dalton, *The Country Justice* (ed. 1705), 166.
[2] *Supra*, p. 460, note 1. The opinion of Sir John Popham (chief justice 1592–1607) was that "none ought to be sent to the places of their birth or habitations but such only as are vagrant or wandering": *Hist. MSS. Comm. Lothian*, 76. See also *infra*, Appendix, p. 534, No. 1.
[3] Child, *A New Discourse of Trade* (4th ed.), 93-94.

parish, and then concludes, as his masters the parishioners do, that he has done the part of a most diligent officer. But suppose he should yet go further to the end of his line, which is the end of the law and the perfect execution of his office, that is, suppose he should carry this poor wretch to a justice of the peace, and he should order the delinquent to be whipped and sent from parish to parish to the place of her birth or last abode, which not one justice in twenty through pity or other cause will do : even this is a great charge upon the country, and yet the business of the nation itself wholly undone. For no sooner does the delinquent arrive at the place assigned, but for shame or idleness she presently deserts it and wanders directly back, or some other way, hoping for better fortune, whilst the parish to which she is sent, knowing her a lazy and perhaps a worse qualited person, is as willing to be rid of her as she is to be gone from thence ".

The settlement regulations were productive of infinite evils. " To enumerate all the mischiefs of settlements in particular", exclaimed a writer in 1768, "would be endless "[1]. In the first place, the system lent itself readily to chicanery and trickery. A settlement could be gained by birth, parentage, marriage, service, apprenticeship, purchase of a house, and payment of ten pounds a year rent [1a]. The qualification for settlement by service was a year's contract as well as a year's service : to evade this it was common to hire servants on short contracts, " by which astute contrivance a servant will gain no settlement though he continues in the same service for many years "[2]. In the case of apprenticeship a pauper was often bound to a master in another parish, expressly in order to transfer the settlement from his native parish. To acquire settlement by purchase the fraudulent practice was adopted of buying a house in another parish, residing in it not less than forty days, and then selling it again. Finally, paupers were imposed upon other parishes by the simple expedient of renting houses on their behalf. In short the energies of parish officers were consumed in the effort, not to maintain their poor, but to

*Evils of the settlement system :*

*(i.) Chicanery.*

---

[1] *A Digest of the Poor Laws* (1768), p. xv.
[1a] *Infra*, Appendix, p. 534, No. 2.
[2] *A Digest of the Poor Laws* (1768), p. xvi.

get rid of them [1]. The poor were sometimes given sums of money on condition that they transferred themselves elsewhere. An example is recorded in 1672, when a woman complained to the justices of Hertfordshire that she was removed by an order of sessions from Hertford to Hartingfordbury, and that there she and her children suffered much want through the cruelty and injustice of the overseers, who deducted a shilling from her weekly allowance and offered that " if the petitioner would by stealth and privately creep into the parish of All Saints, Hertford, again, or into any other parish ", they would give her five pounds [2].

(ii.) *Litigation.*    In the second place, the system involved the parishes in costly litigation, in which they squandered resources that could have been expended more profitably on behalf of the poor. There was, at the outset, the trouble and expense of attending at a private session and securing an order of removal, since statute law required the consent of two justices and the court of King's Bench required them to be present together [3]. There was, next, the expense of removing the pauper, perhaps with wife and children, sometimes to a distant county, sometimes even from one end of the kingdom to the other. The removal was often ineffectual because a wealthy parish would appeal to quarter sessions to have the order reversed : and " as the appeal is almost certain to be brought if an attorney lives in the neighbourhood, so is it almost as sure to succeed if a justice lives in the parish " [4]. There was, lastly, the possibility of an appeal to the court of King's Bench ; and the net result might be " the poor returned upon you, with costs of suit to pay over and above all your own charges of journeys, attorneys, counsel, carrying up witnesses, etc." [5]. It is therefore not surprising that the law was ' very imperfectly

---

[1] *A Digest of the Poor Laws* (1768), p. xv.
[2] *Hertford County Records*, i. 231.
[3] " Though they seldom are so ", comments Fielding : *An Enquiry into the Causes of the late Increase of Robbers* (2nd ed. 1751), 135.
[4] *Ibid.* 135. In 1697 it was enacted that " for the more effectual preventing of vexatious removals and frivolous appeals " concerning settlements, the justices were to award costs to the party in whose favour the appeal should be determined : *Statutes*, vii. 282.
[5] Alcock, *Observations on the Defects of the Poor Laws* (1752), 18.

executed ', or that the remedy was often considered worse than the disease [1]. Many cases, moreover, involved technical and intricate points, which no Act could cover in their entirety, and which could only be determined by the judges at Westminster [2]. The delay and expense of working the system were thus bound to be considerable in any case, but they were greatly intensified by the acrimonious relations existing between neighbouring parishes, since the main disputes arose from the movements of labourers within the confines of the same hundred [3]. Sometimes years elapsed while a lawsuit was being fought out in the courts [4]; and meanwhile the poor were ' tossed from justice to justice, and from pillar to post ' [5]. A committee of the House of Commons expressed the prevailing sentiment in a resolution, which declared (1759) that " the controversies and lawsuits concerning the settlements of poor persons occasion a very great, and in general an useless, expense to the public to the amount of many thousand pounds per annum, and that often more money is expended in ascertaining such settlements by each of the contending parishes than would maintain the paupers " [6]. And Dean Tucker concluded that the settlement laws brought benefit to none but lawyers [7].

In the third place, the settlement system was gravely (iii.) *Social* injurious in its social and economic effects : it degraded the *and economic* status of the working population, and in so far as it was *effects.* in operation it hindered the free mobility of labour. It discouraged workmen from migrating to the places where they were most wanted, and where they could find the best employment for their support. " If a Cornish man comes into Norfolk ", exclaimed Roger North, " he hath a hard journey back again with a whip at his tail ". He wrote :

[1] Fielding, *An Enquiry into the Causes of the late Increase of Robbers* (2nd ed. 1751), 134-135.
[2] For examples of legal problems connected with settlement, see *Hertford County Records*, i. 285 ; *Victoria County History, Warwickshire*, ii. 170. Also see *infra*, Appendix, p. 534, No. 3.
[3] Alcock, *Observations on the Defects of the Poor Laws* (1752), 65.
[4] *A Digest of the Poor Laws* (1768), p. xvii.
[5] *Britannia Languens* (1680), 155 (in sect. vii.).
[6] *House of Commons Journals*, xxviii. 599. A similar resolution was passed in 1751 : *ibid.* xxvi. 289.
[7] Tucker, *Instructions* (ed. 1757), 34.

" The poor are imprisoned in their towns and chained down
to their wants, so that they are deprived of means to mend
their condition . . . by removing to places more proper for
them. . . . If any chance to move for an experiment, then
are they sent back and tossed from pillar to post in carts
till they return to their old settled misery again. No town
willingly receives a poor man though they want poor people
to do the ordinary works of husbandry, because they say
his family may become a charge to the parish ". In short
" men want the work and the work men, and are by laws
kept from accommodating each other " [1]. Even when a
newcomer was left undisturbed—and this was no doubt
frequently the case, since a great many overseers would be
anxious to avoid the trouble and expense attending his
removal [2]—the uncertainty of his position robbed him of all
sense of security. It was the peculiar vice of the system
that the industrious poor suffered most. Anyone who
showed dexterity in his calling was sure to awaken the
jealousy of his rivals in the trade, and he was then liable to
be driven away with his family, " especially if the overseer
or any of his relations should be of the same occupation " ;
but the idle poor, who competed with none, were left alone
until they became actually chargeable [3]. Nor was the
mischief of the settlement laws confined to workmen, in
depressing their wages and impairing their prospects of
advancement. They must be counted among the factors
which retarded the progress of the ancient corporate boroughs,
once the principal seats of industry and trade. " Almost
in every town in England where trade flourishes greatly ",
remarked a writer in 1779, " they never ask whether a
man has served his apprenticeship or where his settlement
is, by which means you see Leeds, Manchester, Halifax,

[1] North, *A Discourse of the Poor* (ed. 1753), 35, 62, 76. Similarly : *A Digest of the Poor Laws* (1768), p. xiv.
[2] Adam Smith exaggerated when he remarked — " There is scarce a poor man in England of forty years of age, I will venture to say, who has not in some part of his life felt himself most cruelly oppressed by this ill-contrived law of settlements " : *The Wealth of Nations* (ed. Cannan), i. 142. Cf. Eden, *The State of the Poor* (1797), i. 297-298 ; Webb, *English Poor Law History*, i. 334 *seq.*
[3] Fielding, *An Enquiry into the Causes of the late Increase of Robbers* (2nd ed. 1751), 136.

Birmingham, etc., rise on the ruins of these places " [1]. A petition presented to Parliament on behalf of the iron-master, Wilkinson, reflects the difficulties to which the settlement laws gave rise : it asked that his men " might be deemed extra-parochial in order to avoid their removal to their respective settlements " [2].

Even in the seventeenth century restraints on the liberty of workmen were condemned by those who recognized the importance of the free movement of labour. Critics of the settlement system fastened upon the argument that mobility of labour would " balance the work of the nation and bring prices to a standard with respect to all circumstances of living " ; and would " mightily help the sort of men we call Undertakers [3], who are very instrumental in the public by advancing manufactures " [4]. And Child wrote : " The resort of poor to a city or nation well-managed is in effect the conflux of riches to that city or nation " [5]. In order to alleviate, partially at any rate, the evils of the Restoration Law of Settlement an important modification was introduced, which left untouched its basic principle that a parish was responsible only for its own poor, but relaxed its rigid provisions in the direction of some degree of mobility. *Contemporary criticisms.*

The first measure, which afforded the labourer an opportunity to move from his locality, was the clause inserted in the Restoration Statute itself, giving liberty to the poor to go to any place for harvest or other work without being deemed to gain a settlement there, provided they obtained a certificate from the minister of the parish, one of the churchwardens and one of the overseers, and returned as soon as their work was done [6]. At the Revolution a further concession was made when the obligation to return was no longer imposed. The Act of 1697—after explaining that many poor people were compelled to live in their own parishes, " and not permitted to inhabit elsewhere though their labour is wanted in many *The certificate system.*

---

[1] *Victoria County History, Yorkshire*, iii. 453.
[2] Eden, *The State of the Poor* (1797), i. 395 (*c.* 1788).
[3] *I.e.* entrepreneurs.
[4] North, *A Discourse of the Poor* (ed. 1753), 62.
[5] Child, *A New Discourse of Trade* (4th ed.), 95.
[6] *Statutes*, v. 401.

other places where the increase of manufactures would
employ more hands "—laid down that if a person brought
a certificate from the parish where he was legally settled
acknowledging responsibility for him, he might live in another
parish without being removed until he became actually
' chargeable '[1]. Even then, instead of taking back emigrants
who had become ' chargeable ', the parish, where they had
their legal settlement, often arranged that they should
receive a regular allowance in the place where they resided [2].
A person thus permitted to dwell in another parish on the
strength of a certificate did not gain a legal right of settlement
there, unless he rented a tenement of the yearly value of ten
pounds or held office in the parish [3].

*Its in-
adequacy.*    In practice these concessions only partially achieved their
object.  As the law required the parish, which gave the
certificate, to reimburse all the expenses that the pauper
might occasion to the parish which received him, parishes in
general were said to be ' extremely tender ' about giving
certificates, and some ' wholly refuse them '[4].  The difficulty
of obtaining a certificate was greatest when the applicant was
proposing to remove to a distant place [5].  The law remained,
therefore, to some extent a dead letter ; and in 1759 a committee of the House of Commons recommended that parish
officers should be compelled to grant certificates to the poor
as " a means of preventing the hardships they now suffer in
being debarred gaining their livelihood where they can do it
most usefully to themselves and the public "[6].  Moreover

[1] *Statutes*, vii. 281-282.  He then became chargeable in the parish where
the certificate was given.  The system was in operation before 1697.  *E.g.*
in 1682 the parish of Wigginton gave a certificate that it would at any
time take back a certain bricklayer and his family who wished to remove
to another parish :  *Hertford County Records*, i. 321.
[2] Ashby, *One Hundred Years of Poor Law Administration in a Warwickshire Village*, 74.
[3] *Statutes*, vii. 365.
[4] *A Digest of the Poor Laws* (1768), p. xiii.  " Grant a certificate !
Never will we do that.  Let marrying alone, and live where you are.  But
if you come here with your wife—you know what lodging we have for you ;
our houses are full already " :  Young, *The Farmer's Letters* (ed. 1768), 289.
[5] *Annals of Agriculture*, ix. 660.
[6] *House of Commons Journals*, xxviii. 599-600.  But the author of
*Considerations on Several Proposals lately made for the Better Maintenance
of the Poor* (1752), 9, claimed that a certificate was " seldom denied now to
any industrious person who applies for it upon good reasons ".  Cf. also
[contd.]

the issue of a certificate was attended with certain disadvantages to the recipient. With two exceptions—renting a tenement of ten pounds a year and holding office in the parish —he was precluded from all the means of gaining a settlement by which others were enabled to acquire it, for example, a year's service. Again, the posterity of a ' certificate person ' were also considered ' certificate persons ' : " and many instances have happened of numerous families being sent back at the distance of many years, with their children and grandchildren, to the place from whence their ancestor came by certificate " [1]. These defects of the certificate system reinforced the criticisms directed against the settlement regulations as a whole : nevertheless reform did not come until the close of the eighteenth century, when in 1795 Parliament enacted that " no poor person shall be removed . . . to the place of his or her last legal settlement until such person shall have become actually chargeable to the parish " [2]. This marked the end of one phase of the problem of pauperism—its epitaph had already been written by a committee of the House of Commons in 1735, when it pronounced the settlement laws to be " very difficult to be executed and chargeable in their execution ; vexatious to the poor and of little advantage to the public ; and ineffectual to promote the good ends for which they were intended " [3].

The effects of the Civil War may now be studied in another direction. After the Great Rebellion a single note permeates the literature of poor relief—its burden is that the poor are not employed [4]. The poor law, as we have seen [5], enjoined the local authorities to raise a ' stock ' and set the unemployed on work ; and the reign of Charles I. had been conspicuous for the attempts made to enforce this provision.

*Complaints of the failure to employ the poor.*

---

the evidence cited in Marshall, *The English Poor in the Eighteenth Century*, 179.

[1] *A Digest of the Poor Laws* (1768), p. xiii.

[2] *Statutes at Large*, xiii. 181.

[3] *House of Commons Journals*, xxii. 483.

[4] Occasionally attempts were made to provide work for the poor, *e.g.* *Hist. MSS. Comm. Various*, iv. 311 (1662) ; vii. 75 (1683). A spinning school was established at Hitchin, as late as 1761 : Hine, *The History of Hitchin*, 248. Other examples : *infra*, Appendix, p. 535, No. 1.

[5] *Supra*, p. 429.

But the fall of the absolute monarchy relaxed the control of
the central over the local government ; and the parishes, left
to their own devices, allowed one half of the poor law to fall
into neglect. This was the half which, in the opinion of
contemporaries, was the more important. Chief Justice
Hale, for example, based his famous *Discourse touching
Provision for the Poor* on the principle that the relief of the
impotent poor might seem ' a charity of more immediate
exigence ', yet the employment of the poor was ' a charity of
greater extent ', which affected more nearly the peace and
welfare of the nation and the benefit of the poor themselves.
He complained that the former alone now absorbed the
attention of parish officers. " Let any man look over most
of the populous parishes in England. Indeed, there are
rates made for the relief of the impotent poor. . . . But it is
rare to see any provision of a stock in any parish for the relief
of the poor ". He proceeds to give the reasons for this
neglect. First : " the generality of the people that are able
are yet unwilling to exceed the present necessary charge . . .
although possibly trebling their exhibition in one gross sum
at the beginning of the year, to raise a stock, might in all
probability render their future yearly payments for seven
years together less by half or two-thirds ". Secondly :
" those places, where there are most poor, consist for the most
part of tradesmen whose estates lie principally in their stocks,
which they will not endure to be searched into to make them
contributory to raise any considerable stock for the poor, nor
indeed so much as to the ordinary contributions ; but they
lay all the rates to the poor upon the rents of lands and
houses, which alone without the help of the stocks are not
able to raise a stock for the poor, although it is very plain
that stocks are as well by law rateable as lands ". Thirdly :
" because the churchwardens and overseers, to whom this
power is given, are inhabitants óf the same parish, and are
either unwilling to charge themselves or displease their
neighbours in charging more than they needs must towards
the poor ". Finally : there were defects in the law itself,
" which are these—no power in the justices of the peace or
some superintendent power to compel the raising of a stock

where the churchwardens and overseers neglect it ; the Act chargeth every parish apart where it may be they are able to do little towards it, neither would it be so effectual as if three, four, five or more contiguous parishes did contribute towards the raising of a stock proportionable to their poor respectively; there is no power for hiring or erecting a common house or place for their common workhouse " [1]. Hale's indictment was re-echoed by other critics. Roger North asserted that the poor law had failed in both its objects : it had not ' hindered or reformed the trade of common begging ', nor had it found work for the able-bodied. " Who, by these laws, are supplied with work ? " he asked. " What country parishes have raised stocks of hemp, flax, etc., and kept the same going as the law requires, whereby the poor may have a constant employment ? " The munificence of individuals had in some places provided stocks and even workhouses, but " you will find even those stocks wasted and slunk into private purses " [2]. Another writer succinctly observed that the Elizabethan poor law, " although the law of the land, is not the practice of the land " [3].

These criticisms created the atmosphere in which the modern workhouse system took shape and form. The favourite argument, advanced as early as 1673, was that the money raised for the relief of the poor, being " employed only to maintain idle persons, doth great hurt rather than good, makes a world of poor, more than otherwise there would be, prevents industry and laboriousness, men and women growing so idle and proud that they will not work, but lie upon the parish wherein they dwell for maintenance, applying themselves to nothing but begging or pilfering, and breeding up their children accordingly. . . . But if instead of giving them weekly allowances for maintaining them in their idleness, the money collected were employed to set all of them, that are able, at work to some kind of employment or other suitable to their capacities, it would be of infinite use and advantage to the nation " [4]. This was the keynote

*Proposals for the establishment of workhouses.*

---

[1] Hale, *A Discourse touching Provision for the Poor* (1683), 3, 7 *seq.*
[2] North, *A Discourse of the Poor* (ed. 1753), 14-17.
[3] *Annals of Agriculture*, xviii. 212.
[4] *The Grand Concern of England explained in Several Proposals* (1673), 60.

of Child's proposal that the whole of London should form one area under the authority of a corporate body to be known as the ' Fathers of the Poor ', who were to erect workhouses, hospitals and houses of correction, and " exercise all other powers relating to the poor that . . . justices of the peace now may do " [1]. There was a consensus of opinion, to which a series of parliamentary reports in the eighteenth century gave authoritative expression, that the existing " method of regulating the poor by annual parochial officers in separate parishes and townships [was], in general, ineffectual for their proper relief and employment " [2]. It imposed heavy burdens on the ratepayers, yet rendered the poor ' miserable in themselves and useless to the community ' [3], because it produced the demoralization reflected in their maxim—

" Hang Sorrow, cast away Care,
The Parish is bound to find us " [4].

These reports, in harmony with many writers on the problem of pauperism, concurred in recommending that public work-houses should be established in each county, and that all the poor should be consigned to them. The workhouse became the Mecca of poor-law reformers, who promised themselves that the assemblage of the poor within its walls, without distinction of age or sex, would be the most effectual method of relieving the aged and impotent, employing the able and industrious, reforming the idle and profligate, and educating the young in religion and industry. One report (1735) is noteworthy since it contemplated the segregation of the poor in different kinds of institutions—the workhouse for the industrious ; the hospital for children and the impotent and infirm ; and the house of correction where idle and disorderly persons, vagrants, ' and such other criminals as shall be thought proper ', should be confined to hard labour [5].

Individual enterprise pointed the way ; and the private

---

[1] Child, *A New Discourse of Trade* (4th ed.), 96 *seq.*
[2] *House of Commons Journals*, xxx. 38.
[3] *Ibid.* xxviii. 599.
[4] *The Gentleman's Magazine*, ix. 206.
[5] *House of Commons Journals*, xxii. 483-484.

workhouse foreshadowed the advent of the public workhouse *Thomas* though the latter was constituted on different lines. The *Firmin's institution.* original impulse came from the desire to promote a native linen manufacture. This inspired a proposal in 1677 for the erection of a ' working almshouse ' in every county, where the poor could be employed and maintained, and beggars and vagrants kept in restraint [1]; and a beginning was made when Thomas Firmin, a well-known philanthropist, erected a workhouse in London for the employment of the poor in the linen industry [2]—an experiment which attracted wide attention [3]. But Firmin's establishment, though called a workhouse, differed in a material respect from the public workhouse, because it was intended to house children only and was more in the nature of a technical school, of which there were many examples in pre-Restoration days [4]. Adults were given work to do in their own homes, for Firmin condemned the idea " which some of late have proposed " of bringing the poor to a public workhouse, on the ground that it would never effect the end desired since " not one person of many will endure the thoughts of going to a public work-house ". The latter was necessary for vagrants and sturdy beggars who had no habitation and would not work, but others should have work found for them which they could carry to their homes, " which though never so mean and homely are more desirable than any other place " [5]. Firmin's own project thus contemplated technical schools for the instruction of young children, part of the day being set aside for reading ; the provision of work in their homes for adults ; public workhouses for the idle ; and almshouses for the aged [6]. The interesting feature of this scheme was the proposal to

[1] Haines, *Proposals for building in every county a Working Almshouse or Hospital* (1677) in *Harleian Miscellany* (ed. Malham), viii. 120.
[2] Firmin, *Some Proposals for the imployment of the Poor* (1681).
[3] Houghton, *Husbandry and Trade Improv'd* (ed. 1728), iv. 116, wrote in 1682 : "Mr. Firmin here at London hath done mighty things; he hath built a workhouse . . . taught the children and others gratis . . . and for their encouragement—besides better wages than the thing will bear— gives them a good part of their manufacture back, when wove and whited to make them sheets (etc.)".
[4] *Supra*, pp. 430 *seq.*
[5] Firmin, *Some Proposals for the imployment of the Poor* (1681), 11.
[6] *Ibid.* 8, 30, 37.

keep the different categories of the poor entirely apart. Another plan (1691), which enjoyed official recognition, was the creation of a joint-stock company with a capital of £300,000 to erect workhouses for the employment of the poor. The company was to provide work for the poor and to pay wages not exceeding three-fourths of the market rate ; and it was to receive from the parishes an amount equal to the poor rate [1]. The Owenite communities of the early nineteenth century were foreshadowed in Bellers, *Proposals for raising a Colledge of Industry* (1696). He wished to provide for the poor by establishing a self-sufficing community, which would educate the children and make labour the standard of value [2].

*The Bristol work-house.* In the erection of public workhouses the initiative was taken by the towns, whose experiments at the end of the seventeenth century inaugurated new methods of relief second in importance only to their experiments in the sixteenth century. The first modern workhouse was established in Bristol shortly after the Revolution [2a]. The enterprise attracted general attention and was followed by the widespread adoption of the workhouse system in other parts of the country. The starting point was an Act of Parliament [3] which set up at Bristol, in 1696, a corporation consisting of the mayor, aldermen and forty-eight other persons chosen by the wards. These 'Guardians of the Poor' were given power to erect hospitals and workhouses; to compel applicants for relief to enter them and do the work for which they were fitted ; to detain poor children in their service until the age of sixteen, after which they were to be bound apprentices ; to apprehend rogues and vagabonds and put them on work in the workhouses for the space of three years. Two committees were set up : one for the poor, the other for the workhouse [4]. The former endea-

---

[1] *State Papers Domestic*, 1690–1691, pp. 369, 422 ; Davenant, *Works*, (ed. 1771), ii. 206 *seq.* See also Brewster, *Essays on Trade and Navigation* (1695), 61 *seq.*
[2] Page 3. Cf. Owen's " Report to the County of Lanark " in *The Life of Robert Owen* (1858), supplementary vol. i. A, 261 *seq.*
[2a] But see *infra*, Appendix, p. 535, No. 2.
[3] Cary, *An Essay towards Regulating the Trade* (ed. 1719), 125 *seq.* See *infra*, Appendix, p. 536, No. 1.    [4] Cary, *op. cit.* 148.

voured to provide for the poor according to their needs.
" To such as were sick ", wrote John Cary, " we gave
warrants to our physician to visit them : such as wanted the
assistance of our surgeons were directed to them : and all
were relieved till they were able to work : by which means
the poor, having been well attended, were set at work again,
who by neglect might with their families have been chargeable to the corporation. For some we provided clothes, for
others work. Where we found people careful but wanted a
stock to employ themselves and their children, we either
lent or gave it : where they wanted houses, we either paid
the rent or became security for it : where we found them
oppressed, we stood by them : where differences arose, we
endeavoured to compose them : so that in a little time all
the complaints of the poor came to this committee . . . and
care was taken that none went away unheard"[1]. The
committee for the workhouse furnished it for the reception
of a hundred girls [2]. " We appointed them set hours for
working, eating and playing, and gave them leave to walk
on the hills with their tutresses when their work was over . . .
by which means we won them into civility and a love to
their labour. . . . But we soon found that the great cause of
begging did proceed from the low wages for labour, for after
about eight months' time our children could not get half so
much as we expended in their provisions. The manufacturers who employed us were always complaining the
yarn was spun coarse, but would not advance above eightpence per pound for spinning "[3]. Another house was
fitted up for ' ancient people, boys and young children ',
the boys being employed at spinning cotton wool and weaving fustians. " The boys are kept at a distance from the
ancient people, who do also lodge in distinct apartments,
the men in several chambers on one floor and the women on
another : all do something though perhaps some of their
labours comes to little, yet it keeps them from idleness "[4].
Cary claimed that " the success hath answered our expectation. We are freed from beggars : our old people are com-

---

[1] Cary, *An Essay towards Regulating the Trade* (ed. 1719), 150-151.
[2] *Ibid.* 152.  [3] *Ibid.* 153-155.  [4] *Ibid.* 157-158.

fortably provided for : our boys and girls are educated to
sobriety and brought up to delight in labour : our young
children are well looked after and not spoiled by the neglect
of ill nurses : and the face of our city is changed already " [1].

*London work- houses.*   Priority in the erection of a public workhouse is claimed
by Bristol, but the metropolis preceded Bristol in the con-
ception of its scheme. We have seen that a Corporation of
the Poor was set up in the city of London, as early as 1647,
with power to establish workhouses [2]. This Corporation was
in existence at the Restoration, when its work in employing and relieving the poor received recognition from the
King, who " desired the city to continue their care of this
institution " [3]. There was evidently some doubt as to the
legal position of the Corporation which had been created
during the Interregnum, and in 1662 its constitution and
powers were defined by Act of Parliament [4]. According to
a circumstantial account written in the early years of the
eighteenth century, the Corporation did not erect a workhouse until after the Revolution. In 1699, with the aid of
a grant from the common council, it fitted up a house in
Bishopsgate to serve as a workhouse, and received children
who were a burden upon the parishes. The parishes paid
a weekly allowance towards the maintenance of the children
whom they sent to the workhouse, and in addition every
benefactor, who subscribed to the upkeep of the establishment, was allowed to recommend a child. The children
were kept on ' the steward's side ' ; they were employed in
spinning wool or flax, or in sewing and knitting ; they were
also taught to read, write and ' cast accompts ', to qualify
them for service and ' honest ways of livelihood ' [5]. Then

---

[1] Cary, *An Essay towards Regulating the Trade* (ed. 1719), 161. See
also *Bristol Corporation of the Poor : Selected Records, 1696–1834* (ed.
Butcher).

[2] *Supra*, p. 453.

[3] *Remembrancia of the City of London*, 364 (1660).

[4] *Statutes*, v. 401 (also *ibid.* v. 732). In their valuable *English Poor
Law History*, i. 118 (note), S. and B. Webb state that they " are not aware
that any other Corporations [besides the Corporation of the city of London]
were formed either in Westminster or elsewhere under this Statute [of 1662]".
Attention may therefore be drawn to the fact that a Corporation of Westminster and a Corporation of Middlesex are referred to in *Hist. MSS.
Comm.* ix. part ii. 15, and in *Middlesex County Records*, iii. 331, 337.

[5] The history of the Corporation is obscure. I have followed the
version given in *An Account of Several Workhouses* (ed. 1732), 1-5.

in 1700 the authorities began to receive on 'the keeper's side' vagabonds, sturdy beggars and disorderly persons to whom was assigned 'such relief as is proper for them'; and they were employed in beating hemp and in other occupations[1]. Between 1701 and 1731 over two thousand children were educated and placed out as apprentices 'to officers of ships, to trades, and to service in good families'; and more than fifteen thousand vagabonds and beggars were received and discharged. In addition to the workhouse in Bishopsgate, other parishes in London erected workhouses in the early part of the eighteenth century[2].

Shortly after the Bristol workhouse was established Colchester, Crediton, Exeter, Hereford, Hull, Shaftesbury and Tiverton (1698) were empowered by private Acts of Parliament to erect workhouses; and their example was followed by King's Lynn and Sudbury (1700), Gloucester (1702), Worcester (1704), Plymouth (1708) and Norwich (1712)[3]. The coincidence of a large number of workhouses springing into existence about the same time was not accidental. The workhouse system was one of the fruits of the long war with France, which extended England's colonial empire abroad while at home the price was paid in the increase of destitution as a result of the decay of trade and consequent unemployment[4]. The Acts for the erection of workhouses expressly stated that "the numbers of poor people have of late years very much increased throughout this kingdom of England"[5], and they followed a stereotyped form in empowering the municipal authorities to compel 'idle or poor people begging or seeking relief', or already in receipt of alms, 'to inhabit or to work' in the public workhouse[6]—in other words, they established the workhouse test. Although in the cases enumerated above the workhouse was a municipal institution, its sphere em-

*Provincial workhouses.*

---

[1] *An Account of Several Workhouses* (ed. 1732), 2-3.
[2] *Ibid.* 5 *seq.*
[3] Eden, *The State of the Poor* (1797), i. 257; Webb, *English Poor Law History*, i. 120.
[4] Cf. the petition from Norwich in *House of Commons Journals*, xvii. 9 (1711).
[5] *Statutes* ,viii. 262.　　　　　　　　[6] *Ibid.* viii. 265; ix. 585.

braced the whole county since the authorities could contract
with any parish to receive its poor and put them on work [1].

*The Act of 1723.* The history of the poor law in the sixteenth century now
repeated itself in the eighteenth century : the policy of the
State once more moulded itself upon the example set by the
towns. The recommendation of a parliamentary committee
in 1699, that any one or more parishes should be allowed to
' incorporate themselves ' in order to erect workhouses [2], had
been still-born ; but the success which appeared to attend
the municipal experiments led to the passing of the Act of
1723 [3], in which it was sought to make the system of workhouses general throughout the country. The Act empowered
the churchwardens and overseers in any parish, with the
consent of the major part of the parishioners, to purchase or
hire houses, and contract with any person for lodging, maintaining and employing the poor ; and any one who refused to
enter the workhouse should not be entitled to receive relief.
Where a parish was too small to purchase or hire a house, two
or more parishes could unite for the purpose [4]. This enactment gave a stimulus to the erection of workhouses in many
parts of England ; and within a few years it was claimed that
" this method of maintaining the poor has met with approba-
tion and success throughout the kingdom " [5]. The rapid
progress of the movement is shown in a list printed in 1732 :
it enumerates nearly fifty workhouses in the metropolis and
nearly sixty in the provinces [6]. Numerous advantages were
said to have accrued from the adoption of the Act. The poor
were relieved in a more economical manner and there was a

---

[1] *Statutes*, viii. 268.
[2] *House of Commons Journals*, xii. 534, 583.
[3] *Statutes at Large*, v. 308.
[4] The statement in Webb, *English Poor Law History*, i. 121, that the
Act of 1723 gave " no power to parishes to combine for the purpose " of
hiring or purchasing premises, appears to overlook this clause.
[5] *An Account of Several Workhouses* (ed. 1732), p. iii.
[6] *Ibid.* 186 *seq.* The list is not complete, *e.g.* it omits Exeter, etc. ;
and some of the establishments were ' working charity-schools '. For
rural unions, see Webb, *English Poor Law History*, i. 125 *seq.* Also *ibid.*
221 *seq.* for a valuable discussion of the various uses of the workhouse
" as a device for organizing employment, correcting idleness and disorder,
deterring applicants for relief, maintaining the orphans, the sick and the
aged, or treating, with a view to their improvement, special classes of the
community ".

consequent saving in poor rates : children were taught habits of industry and " put in a way of being a blessing instead of a burden to their country " :  the poor were better provided for " than when they lived on common begging or in a miserable ruinous cottage " :  and finally, " no vagabond poor dare come into or stay long in a parish where such a house is erected " [1].  In short the advocates of the workhouse system, in their optimistic enumeration of its benefits, saw in these establishments potential ' nurseries of religion, virtue and industry '.  Any reluctance of the poor to enter the workhouse was dismissed with the rebuke that it was " a sin for them to murmur and complain or to refuse to work " ;  they must be " content and thankful and do their duty, that is, all they can do, in that state of life wherein it has pleased God to place them ", remembering that they received food and raiment, that their dwelling was ' warm, sweet and cleanly ', and that they were not kept closer nor longer to their work than the industrious poor without doors [2].  Perhaps some of the enthusiasm, which was displayed at this period for the erection of workhouses, was generated less by the conviction that they could be made ' nurseries of religion, virtue and industry ', than by the discovery, of which Oxford affords an example, that the poor rate in one parish fell by one-half, " and in some it is entirely taken away " owing to the refusal of the poor to enter ' these confinements ' [3].

After its rapid progress at the beginning of the eighteenth century the movement inevitably slackened its course ; and by the middle of the century complaints that the poor were not set on work were once more repeated.  The House of Commons passed a resolution in 1751, which declared that " the provision for the poor of England and Wales is become a very great, and is at present an increasing, charge on the real and personal estates of the subjects ", one reason being

*Administrative difficulties in working the Act of 1723.*

---

[1] *Some Few Letters selected from an Account of Workhouses and Charity-Schools* (1728), pp. x-xii.

[2] *An Account of Several Workhouses* (ed. 1732), p. iii.  The hours of labour in the Holborn workhouse were from 6 A.M. to 6 P.M. in summer, and 7 A.M. to 5 P.M. in winter, 1½ hours being allowed for meals : *ibid.* 18-19.

[3] *Ibid.* 157-158.

that the money is in general expended on maintenance only,
" and very little or no care taken to provide for their employment " or to train the children of the poor in habits of industry [1]. Many parishes were too small to raise a separate
stock sufficient to employ the poor to any advantage, still less
could they afford to defray the expense of erecting workhouses and providing proper persons to superintend them.
The Act of 1723 had sought to meet this difficulty by encouraging incorporation, but the powers which it gave to
parishes to unite were said to be ' too limited and defective
for the purpose [2]. It provided no means for overcoming the
inertia or recalcitrance of parishes which were reluctant to
combine with other parishes ; and in the absence of any strong
inducement or compulsion it was difficult to secure agreement as to the place where the workhouse should be erected,
and the amount which each parish should contribute towards
its erection and maintenance [3]. It was doubtless for these
reasons that the House of Commons proposed in 1751 that a
common fund should be established in every county for the
employment and support of the poor [4]. Yet apart from
administrative difficulties there were other causes for the
*Change in* change in public opinion as regards the workhouse. For one
*the public* thing, it was natural that the enthusiasm which marked the
*attitude*
*towards* early stages of the movement should gradually evaporate, but
*work-* experience also showed that the institution of workhouses did
*houses.* not bring in their train all the benefits so confidently predicted.
They were condemned on the ground that they were un-
healthy for children [5] ; they separated members of the same
family ; and, as Defoe remarked, they mixed the good and
the bad, and too often made reprobates of all alike [6]. The
evils of the workhouse system were accentuated when the
workhouse was ' farmed out ' to a contractor [7]. It is not
unlikely, also, that the sufferings of those who shrank from

---

[1] *House of Commons Journals*, xxvi. 289.
[2] *A Digest of the Poor Laws* (1768), pp. xiv-xv.
[3] Tucker, *The Manifold Causes of the Increase of the Poor* (1760), 5.
[4] *House of Commons Journals*, xxvi. 289.
[5] Burn, *The History of the Poor Laws* (1764), 226.
[6] *Parochial Tyranny* (?1727), written under the pseudonym of A. Moreton.
[7] Burn, *The History of the Poor Laws* (1764), 211. Sometimes a contractor ' farmed ' the entire poor of a parish. Eden, who considered this
[contd.]

entering the ' parish prison ' caused some revulsion of feeling. But the main reason for the change was the discovery that the economies anticipated from the institution of workhouses —and which had been the most important argument in promoting their establishment—did not always materialize. It was asserted that workhouses were seldom properly managed [1]; and in any case they involved an initial outlay in building as well as the running charges of removing the poor to them. The conclusion was therefore reached that it was more economical to relieve the poor in their own dwellings than to erect workhouses. The gradual adoption of this point of view opened up a new chapter in the history of poor relief.

We now reach a fresh stage in the evolution of the poor *The allowance system.* law system, in which ' the workhouse test ' was discarded in many districts, and relief was given to the able-bodied poor without requiring them to enter the workhouse. This was the distinctive feature of what is known as the ' Speenhamland System ' inaugurated by the Berkshire magistrates in 1795, though the action of these magistrates was new neither in point of law nor of administration. A century before Roger North had described the methods of the Colchester bay-makers who were ' the chiefs in the town ' : " At all assessments they rule the roast, and they give the poor starving wages for their work as fourpence per day, and make them amends in collections out of which they allow sixpence per day. And so the charge of the bay-making falls upon the owners and general inhabitants, whereof the gains fall in their purses " [2]. The influence of the allowance system in depressing wages was well understood a hundred years before the Poor Law Inquiry Commissioners framed the famous Report of 1834. The Earl of Egmont wrote in his *Diary* (1730) : " One of [Lord Townshend's] notions . . .

---

an improvement upon direct management by overseers, gives numerous examples, *e.g.* St. Albans and Leicester : *The State of the Poor* (1797), i. p. v ; ii. 272, 386.
[1] *An Inquiry into the Management of the Poor* (1767), 75. For the financial failure of the workhouse, see Webb, *English Poor Law History*, i. 233 *seq.*
[2] North, *A Discourse of the Poor* (ed. 1753), 75.

which I could not but relish is that the poor's tax, notwithstanding a heavy one, is extremely beneficial to trade, as it is a sort of bounty or premium on the manufacturer, and consequently makes sundry sorts of our work cheap by beating down the price of labour, for we all know that as heavy as the poor tax is, the poor are not entirely supported by it, but they are only helped a little, which small help, together with their own industry in knitting or spinning (to apply this to the woollen manufacture) enables them to live ; but were it not for what they receive out of the tax abovementioned, they would not knit or spin for so small wages as they receive for that work, because they would starve by it " [1]. Arthur Young relates that previous to the year 1727 the rates at Norwich were " immoderately burdened with weekly allowances to the poor, of 1s. 6d., 2s., 2s. 6d., or 3s. a family, in which manner £1200 a year was given. A resolution was taken in that year to strike them all off : it was accordingly done, and nothing ensued but murmuring : no ill consequence at all " [2]. A parliamentary committee in 1759 condemned the practice " of giving money out of the parochial rates to persons capable of labour, in order to prevent such persons claiming an entire subsistence for themselves and their families from the parishes, [as] contrary to the spirit and intention of the laws for relief of the poor, a dangerous power in the hands of parochial officers, a misapplication of the public money, and a great encouragement to idleness and intemperance " [3]. In spite of these animadversions upon the system, Parliament in 1782 enacted *Gilbert's Act* (1782). the measure known as Gilbert's Act, which authorized the granting of allowances in aid of wages. It recited [4] that inasmuch as the Act of 1723, from want of proper management of the workhouses and control over the contractors, had not had the desired effect, no person was to be sent to

---

[1] *Hist. MSS. Comm. Egmont (Diary)*, i. 91.
[2] Young, *Tour through the East* (ed. 1771), ii. 76.
[3] *House of Commons Journals*, xxviii. 599. On the Isle of Wight wages were supplemented by parish allowances under a regulation of the Corporation of the Poor erected in 1771 : Eden, *The State of the Poor* (1797), ii. 235.
[4] *Statutes at Large*, ix. 268 *seq.* Another Act enabling the overseers to relieve persons in their own homes was passed at the end of 1795 : *ibid.* xiii. 282.

the workhouse except the aged, sick and infirm, and orphan
children consigned there by order of the guardians of the
poor. And " where there shall be in any parish " any poor
person " able and willing to work but who cannot get employment ", the guardian of the poor was required " to agree
for the labour of such poor person at any work or employment suited to his or her strength and capacity in any parish,
township or place near the place of his or her residence, and
to maintain or cause such person to be properly maintained,
lodged and provided for, until such employment shall be
procured and during the time of such work, and to receive
the money to be earned by such work or labour, and apply
it in such maintenance as far as the same will go, *and make
up the deficiency if any*".

Gilbert's Act thus legalized the allowance system under *The Speen-*
which the parish supplemented the wages of labourers ; and *hamland scale.*
on the basis of this Act the Berkshire magistrates framed
their famous resolutions at a meeting held in 1795 at the
Pelican Inn in Speenhamland : " That it is not expedient
for the magistrates to grant assistance by regulating the
wages of day labourers, according to the directions of the
Statutes of the 5th Elizabeth and 1st James. But the magistrates very earnestly recommend to the farmers and others
throughout the county to increase the pay of their labourers
in proportion to the present price of provisions ; and agreeable thereto, the magistrates now present have unanimously
resolved that they will, in their several divisions, make the
following calculations and allowances for relief of all poor
and industrious men and their families, who to the satisfaction of the justices of their parish shall endeavour (as far as
they can) for their own support and maintenance. That is
to say : When the gallon loaf of second flour, weighing
8 lb. 11 oz., shall cost 1s. then every poor and industrious
man shall have for his own support 3s. weekly, either produced by his own or his family's labour, or an allowance
from the poor rates, and for the support of his wife and every
other of his family 1s. 6d. When the gallon loaf shall cost
1s. 4d. then every poor and industrious man shall have 4s.
weekly for his own, and 1s. 10d. for the support of every

other of his family. And so in proportion, as the price of bread rise or falls (that is to say) 3d. to the man, and 1d. to every other of the family on every 1d. which the loaf rise above 1s." [1]. The wide application of the ' Speenhamland System ', and the effects which it produced, belong to the history of the nineteenth century.

*Estimates of the amount of the poor rates.*  One of the principal themes in the literature of poor relief was the burden of the poor rates [2]. It was assumed as an axiom that the burden had increased, was increasing, and ought to be diminished. " They rise ", complained Arthur Young, "without a shadow of reason" [3]. Roger Coke, writing in 1671, declared that " the charge of maintaining poor people in very many places is six, seven, eight, nine-fold more than before " [4]. Nearly a century later the House of Commons resolved " that the provision for the poor of England and Wales is become a very great, and is at present an increasing, charge on the real and personal estates of the subjects " [5]. The earlier estimates of the amount of the rates were nothing more than mere guesses, which possess value only in so far as they may have influenced public policy. A writer in 1641, for example, expressed the opinion that " the fourth part of the inhabitants of most of the parishes of England are miserable poor people, and (harvest time excepted) without any subsistence " [6]. Another writer (1673) calculated that " the money yearly paid by the subjects for the relief of the poor is nigh as much as an assessment of £70,000 a month to the King " (*i.e.* £840,000 a year) [7]. Shortly afterwards (1677) Yarranton

[1] Eden, *The State of the Poor* (1797), i. 577 ; Bland, Brown and Tawney, *English Economic History : Select Documents*, 656.
[2] The poor relief accounts of two rural parishes in Bedfordshire, 1563–1598, are given by F. G. Emmison in *The Economic History Review*, iii. No. 1. For the assessments of a Bristol parish, 1656–1698, see Wilkins, *Transcription of the Poor Book of the Tithings of Westbury-on-Trym, Stoke Bishop and Shirehampton*.
[3] Young, *Political Arithmetick* (1779), part ii. 17.
[4] Coke, *Treatise* (1671), i. 74.
[5] *House of Commons Journals*, xxvi. 289 (1751).
[6] *Considerations Touching Trade, with the Advance of the King's Revenue* (1641), 15.
[7] *The Grand Concern of England explained in Several Proposals* (1673), 60.

postulated that there were in England and Wales a hundred thousand unemployed, " and each one costs the public fourpence the day in food "[1]. The author of *Britannia Languens* (1680) mentions an estimate of £400,000 [2]. Davenant cites an estimate made towards the end of Charles II.'s reign that the poor rates for one year amounted to £665,362, and he adds : " We have reason to think it is now [1695] much higher because of the great decay in our foreign trade and home manufacture. Besides which sum there is yearly given a vast deal to their relief in voluntary charity and contributions ; so that in time of peace we may pay near as much to the poor as to the maintenance of the Government and for our protection "[3]. The estimates for the eighteenth century, while less hypothetical, are unsatisfactory because their basis is unreliable. Alcock stated in 1752 that in certain years the poor rates amounted in some parishes to five and six shillings in the pound, while " the whole sum laid out on the poor-account in South Britain for four years last past amounted at a medium to near three million yearly, according to the accounts given into Parliament last session, which is equal to a land tax of six shillings in the pound "[4]. Yet the returns made to Parliament in 1776 by the parish authorities gave the ' net expense ' of maintaining the poor at approximately £1,530,000 [5]. These returns, which were also made in 1786 when the average was about £2,000,000, should provide us with a solid basis for our calculations, but there is reason to believe that they were sometimes erroneously compiled [6].

It is evident that the opinions of writers on the burden of

[1] Yarranton, *England's Improvement* (1677), 61.
[2] *Britannia Languens* (1680), 132 (in sect. viii.).
[3] Davenant, *Works* (ed. 1771), i. Table facing p. 39, 41, 72.
[4] Alcock, *Observations on the Defects of the Poor Laws* (1752), 4, 17. See also Alcock, *Remarks on Two Bills for the Better Maintenance of the Poor* (1753). Decker reckoned it at about two millions : *Essay on the Causes of the Decline of the Foreign Trade* (ed. 1744), 20.
[5] Eden, *The State of the Poor* (1797), i. 383 ; *Annals of Agriculture*, ix. 225.
[6] For a striking example, see Howlett, *Examination of Mr. Pitt's Speech* in Eden, *The State of the Poor* (1797), i. 394, note. The amount of the poor rates was swollen by the inclusion of other expenses : *Annals of Agriculture*, xxv. 389 *seq.*

*Causes of the increase in the poor rates.* the poor rates were based on estimates which were either purely hypothetical or erroneously calculated. There was unquestionably an increase in the amount of the poor rates in the course of the seventeenth and eighteenth centuries, but we must take into account the growth of population, the advance in wealth, and the rise in prices. The increase was most marked in periods of scarcity, and also in time of war when the decay of trade and the obligation to provide for disabled soldiers and sailors, and probably also for the families of those on active service, swelled the normal volume of the rates. On these occasions criticism more easily made itself heard, and the blame was laid upon the shoulders of the overseers whose lax administration was held responsible for the rise in the poor rates. Parliament shared this view, for in 1691 it sought to provide a remedy by transferring to the justices of the peace the duty of accepting or rejecting applications for relief [1]. The effect of this enactment was apparently the reverse of what its authors intended. It became common for a justice to order relief without consulting the overseers, and the division of authority tended to produce friction rather than economy [2]. The root of the trouble, it may be conjectured, was not in normal times the actual burden of the assessment, but the widespread belief that the relief of the able-bodied was an incentive to idleness. Roger Coke expressed a general view in his assertion that the Elizabethan Act was " a discouragement to all industrious and labouring people, when lazy and idle people shall be maintained in their idleness from the fruits of their labour and industry ", and that " in making provision for such who will neither serve nor labour " it was " the principal, if not the only, reason of the excessive wages of servants as well as labourers " [3]. Davenant even declared that the poor law was " the true bane and destruction to all the English manufactures " [4]. This explains the

---

[1] *Statutes*, vi. 315.
[2] As a remedy, it was provided that J.P.'s were not to order relief until the overseers had been consulted : *Statutes at Large*, v. 307 (1723).
[3] Coke, *Treatise* (1671), i. 74-75. Some, probably more correctly, believed that the poor law system depressed wages : see *supra*, p. 481.
[4] Davenant, *Works* (ed. 1771), i. 100.

perpetually recurring demand that the poor should be set to *Causes of the failure to provide work for the unemployed.* work : a demand which was reinforced by the conviction that there was an actual shortage of hands in industry. Yet the overseers, as we have seen [1], showed marked disinclination to provide ' stocks ' for the purpose, and though the explanation may simply be that they disliked the trouble of finding work for the poor, they may well have concluded that this method of relief was more costly than a small weekly pension which the recipient could eke out in various ways. Moreover some of the early economists were apprehensive lest schemes for providing work for the unemployed might create unemployment for those already in work. " 'Twere better ", said Petty, " the public should keep the beggars though they earned nothing ", for " if there be but a certain proportion of work to be done, and the same be already done by the non-beggars, then to employ the beggars about it will but transfer the want from one hand to another ; nor can a learner work so cheap as a skilful practised artist can " [2]. Defoe gave expression to similar ideas in an influential pamphlet entitled *Giving Alms No Charity*. The erection of parochial manufactures, he affirmed, would turn ' thousands of families ' out of their employment. " If they will employ the poor in some manufacture which was not made in England before, or not bought with some manufacture made here before, then they offer at something extraordinary. But to set poor people at work on the same thing which other poor people were employed on before, and at the same time not increase the consumption, is giving to one what you take away from another " [3]. Thus the problem of finding work for the unemployed, without producing adverse reactions upon the economic system as a whole, is one which has been the subject of repeated experiments and incessant discussions : and it is one of the cardinal problems that confront our own generation.

---

[1] *Supra*, p. 470.
[2] Petty, *Economic Writings*, ii. 353-354.
[3] *Giving Alms No Charity* (1704) in *The Works of Daniel Defoe* (ed. 1869), 544-545.

# APPENDIX

## (1) *Page* 1, *note* 3

Mr. E. Heckscher [1] interprets economic self-sufficiency as follows—to " limit or entirely abolish all trade relations with other communities, and not imports alone ", that is, to abolish exports as well as imports. People, he observes, did not realize that exports as well as imports forged links with other countries. " So long as the ultimate goal of Mercantilism was to export as much as possible . . . it was far removed from any real aspiration towards " self-sufficiency. In common usage the conception of self-sufficiency scarcely implies economic isolation, that is, the complete severance of all economic ties with other countries. The mercantilist ideal was that a nation should rely upon its native resources, agricultural and industrial, essential for its existence—so far as it was able to do so—and utilize commercial relationships with other countries to supply its deficiencies in return for the export of its surplus products. In contrast, the system of free trade was held to sacrifice a balanced national economy for a lop-sided development of certain industries, certain branches of agriculture, certain forms of trade, combined with a preference for capital investment overseas in return for a greater command over the products of the whole world. A country which aims at self-sufficiency does not exclude either imports or exports; but the former are intended to supply deficiencies which cannot be made good at home, and the latter consist of particular kinds of commodities (other than raw materials) offered in exchange for particular kinds of imports (raw materials, precious metals, etc.). This is not a fallacious economic view. It is a deliberate preference for security

[1] Heckscher, *Mercantilism* (revised ed. 1935), ii. 130-131.

in place of a higher (though possibly less stable) standard of life. If the Mercantilists chose the ideal of self-sufficiency, as interpreted in the above sense, there is no reason to infer that they were unable to grasp elementary economic principles, as some of their critics have implied. Life is not governed purely by economic considerations, nor can the complex factors which mould the evolution of society be explained solely in terms of economic analysis.

### (1) *Page* 3, *note* 3 (*and page* 65, *note* 3)

To give an example. The author of *An Enquiry into the Causes of the Present High Price of Provisions* (1767) [1] wrote that the first general cause of high prices in this country was " the wealth of it or the great quantity of money accumulated in it ". Yet on the next page he is careful to explain that money is " representation merely and a conventional contrivance for the easier exchange of goods ".

The term money, like the term wealth, was also a source of ambiguity. Writers sometimes used ' money ' as a synonym of ' capital '. Thus E. Philips (*An Appeal to Common Sense*, 1720) [2] in one place used money in its proper sense of an instrument of exchange : " Money is only valuable according to the proportion it bears against other commodities ". Elsewhere he presumably means capital : " Plenty of money reduces the interest of money ". The ambiguity of mercantilist phraseology is no less marked than that of the classical economists, as may be seen from J. S. Mill's varying—and inconsistent—definitions of the term wealth.

[1] Part i. 1-2.    [2] Pages 12-13.

### (2) *Page* 4, *note* 3

A sea-captain, " who discoursed well of the good effects in some kind of a Dutch war ", remarked to Pepys : " The trade of the world is too little for us two, therefore one must down " [1].

[1] *The Diary of Samuel Pepys* (ed. Wheatley), iv. 31 (1664) ; Williamson, *The Ocean in English History*, 179.

## (1) *Page 4, note 4*

Sir W. Holdsworth rightly stresses the fact that England did make great commercial and industrial strides during the Age of Mercantilism [1]. The question how far this advance was due to mercantilist legislation is discussed above [2].

[1] See the section on " Commerce and Industry " in Holdsworth, *A History of English Law* (ed. 1938), vol. xi.
[2] Introduction (*supra*, vol. ii. pp. xcvi. *seq.*).

## (2) *Page 5, note 5*

The view that private interests coincided with public interests was expressed even as early as 1623 by Misselden [1]: " Is it not lawful for merchants to seek their *privatum commodum* in the exercise of their calling? Is not gain the end of trade? Is not the public involved in the private, and the private in the public? What else makes a commonwealth but the private wealth, if I may so say, of the members thereof in the exercise of commerce amongst themselves and with foreign nations? "

[1] Misselden, *The Circle of Commerce* (1623), 17.

## (3) *Page 7, note 4*

In giving evidence before a Committee on the Decay of Trade in 1669, Child observed that " labourers' wages are the test of a nation's wealth " [1].

[1] *Hist. MSS. Comm.* viii. part i. 134.

## (4) *Page 8, note* 8A

Internal tolls levied by towns on the goods of strangers had not entirely disappeared in the seventeenth century. In 1689 Lancaster " had a contest with Liverpool about the toll of goods we had from them ; our town alleging that their charter exempted them from passage-toll all over this nation and Ireland ; but for refusing it our goods were taken and kept ". In a lawsuit " some hundred pounds [were] spent on each side without being determined. Our town, being tired with the suit, let it drop, upon which Liverpool vaunted that [whoever] had the better cause, they had the better purse ". London cheesemongers also had their goods seized by Liverpool and went to law, " and cleared themselves from toll there " [1].

[1] *Autobiography of William Stout of Lancaster* (ed. 1851), 27. On the subject of tolls, see *supra*, vol. i. 279 *seq.*

## (1) *Page* 9, *note* 1 (*and page* 66, *note* 3)

Spain, it was said in 1621, " for his gold is rich but consumes many men in fetching it home ; none are set on work but his coiners ; it hires men unto the wars but maketh not his country populous " [1].

[1] *Commons Debates*, 1621 (ed. Notestein, Relf, and Simpson), vii. 251-252.

## (2) *Page* 10, *note* 1

The list of references given above on the causes assigned for the prosperity of Holland can be supplemented [1]. Other reasons were the Dutch " fidelity in their seal " (*i.e.* on their products [2]) and their possession of colonies. The absence of restrictions in internal trade [3] refers particularly to the easy admission of burghers [4]. The predominant influence of mercantile law in Holland is reflected in the negotiable character of bills [5] and the swift determination of mercantile suits [6].

[1] *The Advocate* (1651) ;  *Hist. MSS. Comm.* viii. part i. 133 (1669).
[2] Cf. *supra*, p. 337.  [3] *Supra*, p. 10.
[4] Cf. *supra*, p. 347.  [5] *Supra*, p. 221.
[6] *Supra*, p. 10.

## (3) *Page* 15, *note* 2

A speaker in the House of Commons in 1621 put the case for protection in a nutshell, when he criticized the importation of grain, which " makes the price too low for the husbandman to live, it being against all policy of State that foreign commodities should be brought in till our own be spent " [1].

[1] *Commons Debates*, 1621 (ed. Notestein, Relf, and Simpson), iv. 105. Cf. *supra*, vol. ii. 461.

## (1) *Page* 16, *note* 3

North's doctrine did not fall on stony soil. J. Vanderlint in 1734 repeated it in the words : " All nations of the world should be regarded as one body of tradesmen, exercising their various occupations for the mutual benefit and advantage of each other ". He also wrote that prohibitions " cut off so much trade and employment from mankind as these mutual prohibitions can affect " [1].

[1] Vanderlint, *Money answers all Things* (1734), 42-3.

## (2) *Page* 16, *note* 5

That imports paid for exports was recognized in the instructions given to the Committee on Trade set up in 1622 [1]. In order to enable English merchants to export cloth, the Committee was instructed to " take into your consideration by what means to enlarge their returns " [2]. Similarly, it was said in Parliament in 1621 : " To restrain the merchant for importing of corn is the way to restrain the exporting of our cloth " [3].

J. Vanderlint (1734) called this " an invincible argument for a free and unrestrained trade "—" If any nation makes goods for us, we must be making others for them or some other nation, and so mutually for each other " [4].

[1] *Supra*, p. 310, note 3.  [2] Rymer, *Foedera*. xvii, 414.
[3] *Commons Debates*, 1621 (ed. Notestein, Relf, and Simpson), ii. 178. Cf. *supra*, vol. ii. 462.
[4] Vanderlint, *Money answers all Things* (1734), 78.

## (3) *Page* 19, *note* 1

Similarly J. Vanderlint wrote (1734) : " No inconvenience can arise by an unrestrained trade, but very great advantage " [1].

[1] Vanderlint, *Money answers all Things* (1734), 43.

## (4) *Page* 21, *note* 6

Bounties were also paid on the export of British-made gunpowder (1731) and of British calicoes and cottons (1781) [1].

[1] *Statutes at Large*, v. 579 ; ix. 153.

(1) *Page 23, note 4*

The Company of the Merchants of the Staple survived into the twentieth century [1]. It is of interest to observe that the present century has witnessed the nominal survival of one of the two oldest English trading companies and the active survival of one of the two youngest (the Hudson's Bay Company) [2].

[1] *The Ordinance Book of the Merchants of the Staple* (ed. Rich), 3.
[2] *Supra*, vol. ii. 362.

(2) *Page 28, note 2A*

" The landed and trading interests are eternally jarring, and jealous of each other's advantages " [1].

[1] *An Enquiry into the Causes of the Present High Price of Provisions* (1767), part i. 22, note 1.

(3) *Page 29, note 4*

" Our wool doth help all nations in making of cloth ", ran the argument in favour of a Bill (1621) for prohibiting the export of wool [1].

[1] *Commons Debates*, 1621 (ed. Notestein, Relf, and Simpson), vii. 251.

(4) *Page 31, note 8*

In *The Marchants Humble Petition and Remonstrance to his late Highnesse* (1659) [1], it was stated that imported Spanish wool was " of important concernment ".

[1] Page 3.

(5) *Page 38, note 8*

Miege wrote in 1691 : " So hard it is sometimes to know a tradesman's wife from a lady, or the maid from the mistress " [1].

[1] Miege, *The New State of England* (1691), 39.

(6) *Page 46, note 4*

It was also proposed in the House of Commons to tax women who wore hoods instead of hats made of wool [1].

[1] *State Papers Domestic*, 1698, p. 188.

## (1) *Page* 48, *note* 3

In 1625 the Privy Council was informed that a Frenchman had come over " to seduce beyond the seas the workmen in his majesty's furnaces for making of iron ordnance " [1].

[1] *Acts of the Privy Council*, 1623–1625, p. 492.

## (2) *Page* 48, *note* 4

The Spanish ambassador in London was sent orders to entice British artisans, woollen workers and shipwrights, to Spain in the reign of George II [1].

[1] McLachlan, *Trade and Peace with Old Spain*, 143-144, 215-217.

## (3) *Page* 51, *note* 1

The railway employed in the sixteenth century for the conveyance of coal from the pits was an English invention [1]. It was introduced into the Ruhr district at the end of the eighteenth century as an " englischer Kohlenweg " [2].

[1] *Supra*, vol. ii. 152.
[2] Nef, *The Rise of the British Coal Industry*, i. 245.

## (4) *Page* 63, *note* 3

The Quantity Theory is implied in the statement made in 1621 that " since the treasure of the Indies was found, when we had plenty of silver come home, the price of things did arise " [1]. A clear exposition was given in 1720 by E. Philips, *An Appeal to Common Sense* [2]—" Money is only valuable according to the proportion it bears against other commodities ; plenty of money always occasions the rise of the value of other things, as scarcity of money brings it down, provided the commodity is not scarce too, and then the demand for that commodity makes it rise in proportion to the necessity of the purchaser ". He also touched upon an aspect rarely mentioned, the velocity of circulation— " The same money may serve by circulation the purposes of twenty people " [3].

[1] *Commons Debates*, 1621 (ed. Notestein, Relf, and Simpson), ii. 29.
[2] Philips, *An Appeal to Common Sense* (1720), 12. See also Philips, *The State of the Nation* (ed. 1726), 7 ; Vanderlint, *Money answers all Things* (1734), 112.
[3] Philips, *An Appeal to Common Sense* (1720), 16.

(1) *Page* 65, *note* 1

Davenant's contention that paper money performed ' all the offices of money ' was in substance anticipated by R. Murray twenty-two years previously (1676) : " Money being no more than a deposit given for such commodities as men part withal, if in lieu thereof a credit be raised upon a substantial fund, it will in all respects answer the use of money " [1].

[1] Murray, *A Proposal for the Advancement of Trade* (1676), 4.

(2) *Page* 65, *note* 3

J. Vanderlint explained that the functions of money were to serve as a medium of exchange and a standard of value. He expressly dissociated himself from the notion that money constituted wealth—" Gold and silver are of little use besides procuring the necessaries and conveniences of life, which alone are real riches, and for which gold and silver are now universally exchanged " [1].

[1] Vanderlint, *Money answers all Things* (1734), 53 (also pp. 2-3). See also *supra*, p. 495, No. 4.

(3) *Page* 65, *note* 7

That the promotion of industry—and not the accumulation of money—was the kernel of Mercantilism, is demonstrated in the following passage. " Our wool if it be clothed at home . . . breedeth men for the king's service, it maketh the kingdom populous, it makes rich subjects, a much respected and honourable State, . . . an invincible monarchy " [1].

[1] *Commons Debates*, 1621 (ed. Notestein, Relf, and Simpson), vii. 252.

(4) *Page* 65, *note* 8

Similarly E. Philips wrote—" The riches of a nation consists of numbers of industrious inhabitants " [1].

[1] Philips, *An Appeal to Common Sense* (1720), 18.

(5) *Page* 67, *note* 5

The use of money as an instrument of war was stressed by Whiston—" Since the introduction of the new artillery of powder, guns, etc. . . . . war is become rather an expense of money than men, and success attends those that can most and longest spend money "[1].

[1] Whiston, *The Causes of our present Calamities in reference to the Trade of the Nation fully Discovered* (1696), 2.

## (1) *Page* 67, *note* 7

While importance was attached to money for war purposes, we need not infer that English mercantilist writers had in mind the hoarding of gold by the State. They apparently wanted an abundance of precious metals within a country upon which the Government could draw by taxation or loans—just as to-day the Government may take possession of foreign credits owned by subjects.

## (2) *Page* 68, *note* 7

A document drawn up by merchants in 1621 declared that " money is the life of all trade and commerce ", and that " as a body cannot move without sinews, so a realm cannot prosper or maintain itself without money "[1].

[1] *Commons Debates*, 1621 (ed. Notestein, Relf, and Simpson), vii. 583, 585.

## (3) *Page* 69, *note* 3

Hume apparently had in mind the words of J. Vanderlint (1734)—" It is of no consequence whether any nation hath a vast deal of gold and silver or but very little money amongst them "[1].

[1] Vanderlint, *Money answers all Things* (1734), 55.

## (4) *Page* 69, *note* 5

Although the export of gold and silver from Spain was prohibited, there existed at Cadiz an organized corps of bullion smugglers. British merchants employed the royal packet boats to carry their silver, and British consuls resisted Spanish claims to search these boats since they were not ordinary merchant vessels[1].

[1] McLachlan, *Trade and Peace with Old Spain*, 14.

(1) *Page 70, note 2*

In the Parliament of 1621 some speakers were aware that scarcity of money was due to the absence of demand. " The want of money is because trade is sick ; and as long as trade is sick, we shall be in want of money "[1]. And again—" I heard it debated at the Council Board that there were two causes that pulled down the price of wool—first, want of buyers of wool ; secondly, want of buyers of cloth " (that is, absence of demand, not an alleged scarcity of coin) [2].

[1] *Commons Debates*, 1621 (ed. Notestein, Relf, and Simpson), vi. 296.
[2] *Ibid.* ii. 77.

(2) *Page 74, note 1*

The absence of bullion restrictions doubtless facilitated the development of a bullion market in London [1].

[1] On the growth of London as a bullion market, see Sutherland, *A London Merchant*, 19-23.

(3) *Page 78, note 5B*

A contemporary account states that the old money, coined before the Restoration, " was called ' hammered money ', which had the king's reign and year of coinage, etc., stamped in a ring on each side on the outward, but in much of that money the ring was cut away, which at least was one-third of the weight of 6d. 1s. or half or whole crown it was cut from. . . . And as to the money coined after the restoration of King Charles II. called ' milled money ', which was lettered on the edge, there was scarce any of it to be seen, and [it was] supposed to be melted down or . . . clipped. . . . The diminishing of our old silver coin increased and made great confusion in trade ; people being cautious in setting a price on their goods without knowing in what money they would be paid. . . . It was feared the distraction about the coin would be more fatal than the war with France ". In London guineas were advanced to 28s. or 30s. apiece ; in a provincial town (Lancaster) to 22s. or 23s. apiece ; " and all goods in the market advanced accordingly "[1].

[1] *Autobiography of William Stout of Lancaster* (ed. 1851), 36-41.

## (1) *Page* 80, *note* 4

" Exchange is a way of paying the debts reciprocally due between two cities of the same or different countries, without transmitting any money from the one to the other, and only by changing the debtors of one city into the debtors of the other. . . . As long as the total sums due from each city to the other are equal, the whole may be discharged by bills of exchange without transmitting a single farthing from or to either of the cities " [1].

[1] *The Course of Exchange between London and Paris before the Revolution* (1713), 2.

## (2) *Page* 89, *note* 2

It is possible that mercantilist writers sometimes used the term money to mean capital [1]. In that case the importance which they attached to foreign trade can be explained by their belief that a favourable balance increased a nation's capital by augmenting its resources and so decreased the rate of interest [2].

[1] See *supra*, p. 490, No. 1.
[2] *E.g.* Philips, *An Appeal to Common Sense* (1720), 13.

## (3) *Page* 89, *note* 5

Hume shared the mercantilist view in dwelling upon the " advantage of foreign commerce in augmenting the power of the State. . . . A kingdom that has a large import and export must abound more with industry . . . than a kingdom which rests contented with its native commodities. It is therefore more powerful as well as richer and happier " [1]. J. Vanderlint wrote : " Affluence and strength are so connected with the maritime trade of a nation that they must increase or diminish together " [2].

[1] Hume, *Essays* (ed. Green and Grose), i. 295.
[2] Vanderlint, *Money answers all Things* (1734), 80.

## (4) *Page* 90, *note* 1

Mr. E. A. J. Johnson in his *Predecessors of Adam Smith* [1] dissents from my description of *The British Merchant* as " the most unimpeachable exposition of mercantilist thought ". He appears to read into the phrase more than was intended. It meant that this group of authors belonged unquestionably to the mercantilist school ; but it did not imply that the set of economic ideas which they propounded was either complete or fundamental. Mr. Johnson elsewhere concedes that the standpoint embodied in *The British Merchant* " formed an integral part of the fabric of British economic thought before Adam Smith " ; that in it " protection emerges as a fundamental creed " ; and that its " economic doctrines had a profound effect " and " enjoyed ' unique authority ' " [2]. With this view of *The British Merchant* I am in agreement.

It may be added that, though the motives which led *The British Merchant* to rank domestic above foreign trade [3] may have differed from those which influenced Adam Smith [4], this does not invalidate the statement that both reached a similar conclusion. From the point of view of formulating a national policy the preference for domestic trade, expressed by influential writers, was of greater significance than the particular lines of reasoning which prompted it.

[1] Johnson, *op. cit.* 7, 157, 383-384.     [2] *Ibid.* 141, 147.
[3] *Supra*, p. 89.     [4] Johnson, *op. cit.* 383-384.

### (1) Page 91, note 3

" *Trading is dead* is every man's complaint " [1].

[1] G. M. " The Citizens Complaint for Want of Trade " (1663), in *Fugitive Tracts*, second series (1875), 3.

### (2) Page 93, note 1

William Culliford was appointed in 1696 to be inspector-general of exports and imports at a salary of £500 per annum, with a staff of three, " in order to make a balance of the trade between this kingdom and any other part of the world " [1]. This appointment was perhaps the most useful outcome of the controversy over the balance of trade, since it led to the accumulation of valuable statistical data, which in 1776 were published by Sir C. Whitworth under the title *State of the Trade of Great Britain*.

¹ *Calendar of Treasury Books*, xi. 264.

### (1) *Page* 95, *note* 1A

Another ' invisible export ' is referred to by a writer in 1767. " It often happens that money is spent in a kingdom, which has not been acquired there "—by foreigners, by natives whose riches have been gained abroad (*e.g.* 'nabobs'), by colonists who flock to the mother country [1].

[1] *An Enquiry into the Causes of the Present High Price of Provisions* (1767), part i. 26.

### (2) *Page* 97, *note* 4A

Hume was not the first to expound this view. Thus in 1734 J. Vanderlint pointed out that if the money of a nation be decreased by an unrestrained trade " which prohibitions are designed to prevent, those nations that get the cash will certainly find everything advance in price ", and then the money will flow out again to countries where prices are lower. He instanced Spain as " the conduit-pipes to disperse the gold and silver over the world, which other nations, by making goods cheaper than they can do, are fetching from them " [1].

The fundamentals of the theory of the international distribution of specie had been enunciated in the speech attributed by Lord Herbert (whose *History* was published in 1649) to Sir Thomas More (1523) [2].

[1] See Vanderlint, *Money answers all Things* (1734), 43-46, 54, 170.
[2] Introduction (*supra*, vol. ii. p. lxxviii.).

### (3) *Page* 98, *note* 2A

In commenting on the view advanced in the text that the Mercantilists were concerned primarily with ' the short run ', Mr. J. Viner [1] concedes that the mercantilist position is not indefensible " if appraised " from ' the short run ' point of view. But he avers that " they were ordinarily not aware of any distinction between what was desirable monetary or trade practice, to meet a temporary situation, on the one hand, and as permanent policy on the other ". The reply may be fairly described as irrelevant. The Mercantilists were perpetually exercised about the balance of trade inasmuch as it was impossible to ascertain the true balance[2]; hence they were not induced to carry their analysis beyond ' the short run '. And Great Britain's departure from free trade in 1931, due to the exigencies of ' a temporary situation ', affords convincing proof that even at the present day ' monetary or trade practice ' is still governed primarily by ' short run ' considerations. In this respect the mercantilist standpoint does not differ essentially from the modern attitude towards economic problems, in which ' long run ' considerations are usually relegated to the province of economic science. It may be added that the Mercantilists' continued preoccupation with the problem of money was also due to the fact that currency difficulties were always cropping up [3].

[1] Viner, *Studies in the Theory of International Trade*, 111.
[2] *Supra*, p. 92.        [3] See Introduction (*supra*, vol. ii. p. lxxxii.).

## (1) *Page* 100, *note* 6

Four years before Fortrey wrote, the adverse balance was estimated at one million pounds, which agrees with the amount stated in ' A Scheme of the Trade ', 1674 [1]. The nation, it was claimed, was " very much impoverished by the present French trade, which doth exceedingly drain us ; for that thereby our national stock is diminished—and the French stock increased—a million of pounds sterling *per annum* " [2].

[1] *Supra*, p. 101.
[2] *The Marchants Humble Petition and Remonstrance to his late Highnesse* (1659), 13.

## (2) *Page* 112, *note* 7

The career of William Braund (1695–1774) shows the business activities of a merchant in the Portugal trade, first in the export of cloth and subsequently in the import of gold bullion [1].

[1] See Sutherland, *A London Merchant, passim.*

## (3) *Page* 116, *note* 1A

As early as 1734 a writer expressed the view that imports should be discouraged " not by Acts of Parliament which

can never do any good to trade, but by raising such goods
ourselves [cheaper]. This is the only natural and effectual
prohibition " [1].

[1] Vanderlint, *Money answers all Things* (1734), 54.

## (1)  *Page* 116, *note* 2A

Sir W. Holdsworth, after quoting the passage in the
text, comments : " The truth of this is clear from the way
in which Pitt stated his case " [1].

[1] *A History of English Law* (ed. 1938), xi. 394, note 3.

## (2)  *Page* 131, *note* 6

In his valuable study of *The English Navigation Laws*
(1939), Mr. L. A. Harper defends the navigation policy,
though he acknowledges that " from year to year I changed
my mind as to whether the laws were beneficial, merely
ineffectual or positively harmful " [1]. He contends [2] that
after the Restoration English shipping developed more
rapidly than did the growth of commerce — but the
statistical data are admittedly insufficient [3]. He also
alludes [4] to the argument in the text [5] that the difficulties
confronting English shipping were only temporary and
" would have adjusted themselves without legislation ". He
proceeds [6] : " Our researches do not show that the laws
materially affected England's maritime relations with Asia
and Africa, but they . . . definitely benefited English shipping in America ". As to their influence on European commerce " English vessels fared worst in trades like those with
Denmark and Norway . . . and best with Russia and the
Mediterranean ". He disputes [7] Coke's view that the Navigation Acts were responsible for the loss of the Baltic trade,
and in this he is in agreement with Brewster [8]. Yet in
1671—when Coke issued the first two parts of his *Treatise*—
only 106 English ships entered the Sound, as compared with
173 in 1641. The Sound Toll Accounts have been printed
by N. E. Bang (*Tabeller over Skibsfart og Varetransport
gennem Øresund*). They furnish evidence of very considerable variations in the numbers of ships entering the
Sound during the first half of the seventeenth century.

Thus in 1606 there were 985 Dutch and 109 English ; in 1623—1074 Dutch and 159 English; in 1641—771 Dutch and 173 English[9] ; but the Dutch always greatly outnumbered the English. It must be remembered, however, that the navigation policy was in operation before 1651[10] ; and the failure of English shippers to contest successfully Dutch supremacy in the Baltic, in spite of the expansion of trade after the Restoration, may be reasonably attributed to the combination of factors enumerated in the text. The Sound Toll Accounts show that the exclusion from English ports of Dutch vessels engaged in the Baltic trade benefited Scandinavian shipping. Between 1601 and 1650 the percentage of Dutch ships leaving England for the Sound was 11·36, and of Scandinavian ships 4·90 ; between 1661 and 1700 the corresponding figures were 0·67 and 12·27[11].

[1] Page ix.    [2] Pages 342-343.    [3] Page 368.    [4] Page 349.
[5] *Supra*, pp. 129-130.    [6] Harper, *op. cit.* 365.    [7] *Ibid.* 314.
[8] See *supra*, p. 130, note 5.    [9] Bang, *op. cit.* i. 190, 258, 322.
[10] Cf. *supra*, vol. ii. 321 ; iii. 120.    [11] Harper, *op. cit.* 316, note.

### (1) *Page* 141, *note* 4

In 1661 Parliament made a grant, assigning in advance to each county and borough a specified sum as its contribution to the grant. Commissioners, nominated for each county and borough, assessed the proportions of this sum to be charged on each district in their area ; and they appointed assessors who determined the amount to be paid by individual payers within that district[1]. In 1663 Parliament levied a national pound rate, and no fixed quotas were specified either for the kingdom as a whole or for each county and borough[2]. In 1664, 1665 and 1666 it revived the method adopted in 1661[3]. In 1671 it reverted to the method of 1663[4]. In 1672, 1677, 1678 and 1679 it returned to the method of 1661[5], and again in the first session of 1689[6] ; but in the second session of 1689 it reverted to 1663[7]. In 1690 and 1691 it returned to 1661[8]. In 1692, 1693, 1694, 1696 and 1697 it reverted to 1663[9]. In 1698 it again adopted the method of a fixed sum for each county and borough, but it now laid down the principle that the proportions assessed in the several districts (hundreds and other divisions) were to be those of 1692 [10], which had been made on the basis of a national pound rate. This was repeated in 1701 [11] and in the next reign. Contrast the statement [12] that whenever after 1665 Parliament voted an aid or direct subsidy it " steadily refused to assess rates on particular counties".

Actually, as we have shown, Parliament alternated down to 1698 between the two methods of assigning the total amount to be paid by each county or imposing a national pound rate for the entire kingdom. After 1698, instead of a national pound rate equitably distributed over the whole country, the sum to be raised by taxation was henceforth partitioned out in stereotyped proportions. Thus it was in 1698 that the ' land tax ' of the eighteenth century originated.

[1] *Statutes*, v. 325. An Act of 1660 made a grant with the same proportions and the same commissioners as were specified in an Ordinance enacted before Charles II.'s return : *ibid.* v. 250, 252.

[2] *Ibid.* v. 453.    [3] *Ibid.* v. 525, 570, 616.
[4] *Ibid.* v. 693.    [5] *Ibid.* v. 752, 802, 867, 897.
[6] *Ibid.* vi. 24.    [7] *Ibid.* vi. 104.
[8] *Ibid.* vi. 180, 259.    [9] *Ibid.* vi. 323, 426, 510 ; vii. 8, 166.
[10] *Ibid.* vii. 484. Under the Act of 1698 personal estates were to pay 3s. in the pound, but land was to be " charged with as much equality . . . as is possible " by a pound-rate : *ibid.* vii. 473. Similarly in the reign of Queen Anne personal estates paid a fixed pound rate, but land was to be charged as equally as possible.
[11] *Ibid.* vii. 648.
[12] Hughes, *Studies in Administration and Finance*, 169.

### (1) *Page 142, note* 6

Farming was abandoned in the customs from 1643 to 1662 and revived in 1662–1671. It was finally abandoned in 1671 in the customs, in 1683 in the excise, and in 1684 in hearth money [1].

[1] Hoon, *The Organization of the English Customs System*, 1696–1786, pp. 6-7 ; Hughes, *Studies in Administration and Finance*, 138, 154-155. On the scope of the farm of the customs, see Dietz, *English Public Finance*, 1558–1641, pp. 337 *seq.* Various ' petty farms ' of the minor branches of revenue survived : see Harper, *The English Navigation Laws*, 83.

### (2) *Page 142, note* 8

The ' artisan ', who figures in Massie's calculations, is " a manufacturer of woollen cloth, stuffs, etc. in the country ".

## (1) Page 144, note 1

The system of free ports was advocated in a pamphlet entitled *Free Ports* (1652). The writer remarked that " Dover, after the composition trade was settled there (that made it in some kind a free port), did within ten years' time arise from nothing to have near two hundred sail of pretty great shipping " [1]. The ' composition trade ', by which Dover was made a free port for the transhipment of goods, was established under Charles I., and again after the Restoration [2].

[1] *Free Ports* (1652), 4.
[2] Ogg, *England in the Reign of Charles II.*, i. 234-235 ; Harper, *The English Navigation Laws*, 70.

## (2) Page 146, note 2

A contemporary, William Stout, relates in his *Autobiography* [1] that the proposed excise on wine and tobacco " was approved of by the majority of the Parliament and by most prudent and impartial people ; but it gave a great deal of alarm to the clandestine dealers in wine and tobacco ; and the Jacobites and disaffected to the Government took in with them, and petitions [were] sent from all parts of the kingdom against it. They represented it to the people as if they were about to excise all eatables and clothes. They were so offended that the mayor of London, aldermen and common council and others to the number of 800 went to the Parliament in 200 coaches with a petition against it, which much astonished the Parliament that they should bring their petition in such a tumultuous or riotous manner, and [the House] unanimously voted it as seditious and a slight of their authority. Upon a vote it was carried for an excise . . . but, considering what a ferment the nation was in about it, they thought fit to drop or postpone it ".

[1] *Autobiography of William Stout of Lancaster* (ed. 1851), 122.

## (3) Page 146, note 3

A writer in 1652 alleged that " the trade we now drive [is] very little of foreign commodities that is re-transported upon the present encouragement or settled rate of half

custom " [1].  A broadsheet dated 10th September, 1694—
entitled *Whiston's Merchants Weekly Remembrance of the
Present Money Prices of their goods ashore in London*—shows
the prices of imports (*e.g.* drugs, dyeing, fruits, rice, raw
silk, spices, sugar, tobacco), and whether rising or falling,
as well as customs duties and the drawbacks laid upon
re-exportation.

[1] *Free Ports* (1652), 5.

### (1) *Page 148, note 3*

The Venetian ambassador in France referred in 1664
to the " well-known and habitual quarrels " between the
English and Dutch " over the injuries received from the
usurped fisheries " [1].

[1] *State Papers Venetian*, 1664–1666, p. 2.

### (2) *Page 156, note 4*

A memorial from the Treasury (1763) stated that the
revenue arising from the duties imposed in America and the
West Indies " is very small . . . and is not yet sufficient to
defray a fourth part of the expense necessary for collecting
it . . . through neglect, connivance and fraud " [1].  The
benefit derived by the mother country from the colonies
came not from revenue but from trade.  The Elder Pitt
declared in 1766 : " I will be bold to affirm that the profits
to Great Britain from the trade of the colonies through all
its branches is two millions a year. . . . This is the price
that America pays you for her protection " [2].

[1] *Acts of the Privy Council*, Colonial Series, 1745–1766, p. 569.
[2] *The Parliamentary History of England*, xvi. 105-106.

### (3) *Page 161, note 4*

Sir Thomas Dale, governor of Virginia, proposed in 1611
that all offenders condemned to death should be sent for
three years to the colony : he had taken out with him 300
' disorderly persons ' [1].  Oxfordshire prisoners were transported overseas in 1617 [2].  In 1619 the Privy Council laid
down the policy of transporting offenders condemned to
death provided they were able-bodied and were not convicted for murder and other specified crimes [3].  In 1620 it

ordered the transportation of certain reprieved offenders [4]—
in 1621 a reprieved prisoner returned from the plantations
owing to sickness [5]. In 1622 there is an allusion to a commission for reprieving criminals and sending them to the
plantations [6]. In 1622 a horse-stealer petitioned to be
transported to Virginia ; in 1623 it was represented that the
prisons might be emptied, and much blood saved, by sending
offenders to the plantations ; and in 1638 a woman petitioned
to be transported to Virginia [7].

[1] *State Papers Colonial*, 1574–1660, p. 12.
[2] Gretton, *Oxfordshir Justices of the Peace in the Seventeenth Century*,
p. xciii.
[3] *Acts of the Privy Council*, 1619–1621, pp. 53, 101, 175.
[4] *Ibid.* 1619–1621, p. 175.
[5] *Ibid.* 1621–1623, p. 39.
[6] *Ibid.* 1621–1623, p. 294.
[7] *State Papers Colonial*, 1574–1660, pp. 33, 50, 281.

### (1) *Page 163, note 4*

The register, in which were entered the names of servants
legally bound who left Bristol for the plantations, has been
preserved. It is known as the *Servants to Foreign Plantations*, and frequently records the place of origin, occupation,
age and sex of the servant, the master, and the place of
destination [1].

[1] MacInnes, *A Gateway of Empire*, 161.

### (2) *Page 163, note 5*

A proclamation in 1682, after alluding to the malpractices of ' spirits ', stated that many voluntarily enlisted
for the plantations, and afterwards procured their friends
to prosecute the merchants. It therefore ordered servants
to be taken by indenture, which was to be executed in the
presence of a magistrate [1].

[1] Bodleian Library—Ashmole 1681 (138).

### (3) *Page 165, note 6*

There are some early estimates of the population of
England (and also of London) before and after the Reformation [1].

[1] See *A Discourse of the Growth of England in Populousness and Trade*
(1689), 111 *seq.*

## (1) *Page 167, note* 3

In a famous dictum Seeley observed : " We seem, as it were, to have conquered and peopled half the world in a fit of absence of mind " [1]. Mr. J. A. Williamson, however, has pointed out : " The British Empire, indeed, was not founded in a fit of absent-mindedness. . . . Its planning occupied the best brains of thinkers and masters of action " [2].

[1] Seeley, *The Expansion of England* (ed. 1883), 8.
[2] Williamson, *The Ocean in English History*, 85.

## (2) *Page 170, note* 3

Light is thrown on tobacco-growing in England by the petition of a London capitalist to the Privy Council in 1622. He had planted 100 acres of ground with tobacco at ' a very high ' rent of £7 and £8 an acre, involving an outlay of £5000, whereof £1400 were disbursed in wages. He was now faced with ruin by the restraint laid on the planting of tobacco in England [1].

[1] *Acts of the Privy Council*, 1621–1623, pp. 347, 463.

## (3) *Page 171, note* 4

A petition of Giles Dowle in 1696, showing that he had a commission to prosecute planters of tobacco at a stipend of £80 a year, carries the history of tobacco-planting in England to the year 1696 [1].

[1] *Calendar of Treasury Books*, xi. 146.

## (4) *Page 187, note* 4

It is significant that Thomas Jefferson, the author of the Declaration of American Independence, did not favour the development of manufactures in America. He wrote : " The political economists of Europe have established it as a principle that every State should endeavour to manufacture for itself ; and this principle, like many others, we transfer to America without calculating the difference of circumstance. . . . In Europe the lands are either cultivated or locked up against the cultivator. Manufacture must therefore be resorted to of necessity, not of choice, to support the surplus of their people. But we have an immensity of land courting the industry of the husbandman. . . . For the general operations of manufacture, let our workshops remain in Europe " [1].

[1] *The Writings of Thomas Jefferson* (ed. Washington), viii. 405-406 (*circa* 1781).

## (1) *Page* 191, *note* 3

At the time of the American Revolution the colonies contained more blast furnaces and forges than did England and Wales, and they were as large in size. The Act of 1750, which did not apply to iron works already in existence, was disregarded [1].

[1] Bining, *British Regulation of the Colonial Iron Industry*, 24, 27, 30-31, 70-72, 86, 92.

## (2) *Page* 193, *note* 2

On numerous occasions the Privy Council disallowed Acts passed by colonial legislatures laying duties upon British manufactures as " not being consonant to reason and repugnant to the laws of England " [1]. In 1731 the Board of Trade was directed to prepare instructions for colonial governors prohibiting them from giving assent to any laws " where the inhabitants of the colonies are put on a more advantageous footing than those of Great Britain ", or from passing " any laws by which the trade or navigation of this kingdom may be any ways affected " [2]. In 1775 the Privy Council approved the principle that " all laws enacted by the legislatures " in the colonies imposing duties upon the ships and manufactures of this kingdom " are not warranted by the constitution " [3].

[1] *Acts of the Privy Council*, Colonial Series, 1680–1720, p. 740 (1718). Similarly *ibid.* 1720–1745, pp. 63-64, 70, 162.
[2] *Ibid.* 1720–1745, p. 348. [3] *Ibid.* 1766–1783, p. 408.

## (3) *Page* 194, *note* 1

T. Pownall wrote (1765)—" Nothing does at present, with that active and acute people [*sc.* Americans], prevent their going into manufactures except the proportionate dearness of labour " [1]. Franklin observed (1768) that the reports of colonial governors " are all much in the same strain,

that there are no manufactures of any consequence. . . .
All speak of the dearness of labour that makes manufactures
impracticable " [2].

[1] Pownall, *The Administration of the Colonies* (1765), 199.
[2] Franklin, *Works* (ed. 1887), iv. 132.

## (1) *Page* 194, *note* 5

Among the grievances of the colonies one related to the
shortage of currency. England did not allow the establishment of separate colonial mints, and refused to sanction
colonial legislation against the export of specie on the ground
that it would stop the flow of coin to the mother country [1].

[1] Nettels, " British Policy and Colonial Money Supply ", in *The
Economic History Review*, iii. No. 2, 230, 244.

## (2) *Page* 195, *note* 3

The Act of 1696 " gave parliamentary recognition to
the admiralty courts in the colonies, and enlarged and
defined their jurisdiction ", but it " did not institute these
courts ". Between 1660 and 1696 cases were occasionally
tried in what were called admiralty courts. Following the
Act of 1696 a dozen vice-admiralty courts were set up in
the colonies. Their powers were extended in 1764 and
1768 [1].

[1] See Andrews, *The Colonial Period of American History*, iv. chapter
viii. ; Andrews, " The Acts of Trade ", in *The Cambridge History of the
British Empire*, i. 295-299 ; Crump, *Colonial Admiralty Jurisdiction in the
Seventeenth Century, passim* ; Holdsworth, *A History of English Law* (ed.
1938), xi. 60-61.

## (3) *Page* 196, *note* 1

Agreement with the views contained in the text [1] is
expressed by the eminent American historian, C. M.
Andrews, who quotes this passage *in extenso* [2].

[1] *Supra*, pp. 194 *seq.*
[2] Andrews, *The Colonial Period of American History*, iv. 425 *seq.*

## (4) *Page* 200, *note* 6

The Irish Parliament legislated in 1522 against the export
of Irish wool on the ground that it injured the native cloth

manufacture. The prohibition was evaded by the issue of licences to export [1].

[1] Longfield, *Anglo-Irish Trade in the Sixteenth Century*, 77-78.

### (1) *Page* 209, *note* 1

Capitalism has denoted different things at different periods; and the lucid analysis contained in N. S. B. Gras's Essay, " Types of Capitalism " [1], serves to disentangle the complex phenomena comprised in a historical category.

[1] In *Facts and Factors in Economic History*.

### (2) *Page* 212, *note* 4

Contrast also the statements—(1) " The Mercantilists did not have in mind the possibility that a country may make investments abroad or may borrow from abroad " [1]; and (2) " Deposits abroad are a result of economic developments since the Age of Mercantilism " [2].

[1] Viner, *Studies in the Theory of International Trade*, 16.
[2] Heckscher, *Mercantilism* (revised ed. 1935), ii. 213.

### (3) *Page* 213, *note* 3

In a statement laid before Parliament by merchants in 1621, it was represented that : " In former times [strangers], being not able to make above 5 or 6 per cent. in foreign parts, brought their money hither and had 10 per cent. ; and yet the debtor by employment thereof made 30 or 40 per cent." [1]

[1] *Commons Debates*, 1621 (ed. Notestein, Relf, and Simpson), vii. 581.

### (4) *Page* 213, *note* 9

Foreigners purchased English stock because they were attracted by the rate of interest and had confidence in ' our parliamentary securities ' [1]. The Dutch were large proprietors of the stock of the Bank of England and the East India Company, and the stock quotations on the Amsterdam Bourse (1758) included both these and the South Sea Company. The Swedish ambassador in London wrote in 1735 : " The world knows that a great part, perhaps a third, of the capital of the English East India Company belongs to the Dutch and other foreigners ". In 1773 foreigners held £940,227 East India stock (out of £3,200,000), that is, nearly one-third [2].

[1] Vanderlint, *Money answers all Things* (1734), 51.
[2] DuBois, *The English Business Company after the Bubble Act*, 283, 308. Cf. also, *An Enquiry into the Causes of the Present High Price of Provisions* (1767), part i. 32.

### (1) *Page 214, note 2*

English capital was also invested in water and canal enterprises in France. Boulton and Watt frequently received payment for engines sold abroad in the form of shares in foreign companies [1]. It is significant that in 1722 British subjects were forbidden to subscribe to the stock of the Ostend East India Company—another indication of English investments abroad [2]. Cf. also the project for an international pooling of capital [3].

[1] DuBois, *The English Business Company after the Bubble Act*, 283, 308.
[2] *Supra*, vol. ii. 313.  [3] *Supra*, vol. ii. 305.

### (2) *Page 215, note 7*

The Coles of Northumbria provide an example of enterprising men who pushed themselves up from the ranks [1].

[1] Nef, *The Rise of the British Coal Industry*, ii. 40-41 ; and *supra*, vol. ii. Introduction, p. xi.

### (3) *Page 216, note 5. (Cf. vol. ii. 6, note 1)*

The London Mercers' Company carried on corporate trading [1].

[1] *Acts of Court of the Mercers' Company* (ed. Lyell), pp. x, 178. For the Eastland Company, see *supra*, vol. ii. Appendix, p. 499, No. 2.

### (4) *Page 218, note 1*

In an interesting study of the effects of the ' Bubble Act ' Mr. DuBois [1] points out that it decreased the number of incorporated companies, and so " ensured England the benefits of experimentation " with the joint-stock association which had no formal act of incorporation, and thereby it ensured a " variety of financial devices. . . . But the

unexpected freedom, resulting paradoxically from prohibition, . . . had its penalties ". The profit-making motive
in joint-stock enterprise enjoyed freer scope in the unin-
corporated association. " Therefore to the extent that the
' Bubble Act ' prevented the early introduction in England
of a carefully planned system for the regulation by governmental control of joint-stock business organization . . . it
had an unfortunate influence ". It eliminated the possi-
bilities of intelligent official control. Furthermore, owing
to the ambiguity of its wording and the severity of its
penalties, it created for counsel " a new and great role in
the shaping of big business. This was the first step by
which the lawyer came into his own as the originator of
business practices that were to be crystallized into the
company laws of the future. ' On advice of counsel ' was
to be the keynote of the developments in the realm of
business organization ".

[1] DuBois, *The English Business Company after the Bubble Act*, 3, 13,
24, 40, 437.

### (1) *Page* 219, *note* 1

In addition the shopkeepers bought goods on credit [1].

[1] See *supra*, vol. ii. Appendix, p. 479, No. 1.

### (2) *Page* 219, *note* 4

A Lancashire firm of calico printers failed in 1788 for—
it was reported—nearly a million and a half pounds [1].

[1] Wadsworth and Mann, *The Cotton Trade*, 307.

### (3) *Page* 220, *note* 5

In 1659 it was stated that " the English trade with
Spain is driven and upheld in a circular motion, as well by
credits as by the real stock [*i.e.* coin] of the nation " [1].

[1] *The Marchants Humble Petition and Remonstrance to his late Highnesse* (1659), 2.

### (4) *Page* 242, *note* 1

The statement [1]—that after the South Sea Bubble [2] the
policy of financing the State by corporations was discredited
—needs to be modified. Both the Bank of England and

the East India Company made loans to the Government
after 1720 [3].

[1] Hargreaves, *The National Debt*, 10.
[2] *Supra*, vol. ii. 369.
[3] *Supra*, vol. ii. 311, note 5 ; vol. iii. 242, note 1.

## (1) *Page* 244, *note* 6

In the latter part of the seventeenth century the credit
of a Lancaster grocer and ironmonger " was so much that
any who had money lodged it with him to put out to interest
or make use of " [1].

[1] *Autobiography of William Stout of Lancaster* (ed. 1851), 8.

## (2) *Page* 248, *note* 4

Legislation on the subject of bankruptcy showed, as
Sir W. Holdsworth observes, that " the bankrupt had
ceased to be regarded as necessarily a criminal ". An Act
of 1705 laid down that a bankrupt who made over his
property to his creditors was entitled to his discharge.
Lord Hardwicke, in 1744, declared that this provision was
unique, that it was " temporary at first and never intended
to be a perpetual law, but was made in consideration of two
long wars which had been very detrimental to traders, and
rendered them incapable of paying their creditors " [1].

[1] Quoted in Holdsworth, *A History of English Law* (ed. 1938), xi. 445.

## (3) *Page* 256, *note* 1—*s.v.* 1563 (Kent)

A recent study [1]—in which are listed numerous wage
assessments printed since the first edition of this work (1931)
—has omitted to notice that the Kent assessment (1563)
and the Maidstone assessment (1563), which are cited as
two separate assessments, are identical. The heading reads :
" Rates of wages set forth by the Queen's proclamation . . .
and proclaimed at the town of Maidstone " [2]. (The list omits
the assessment of 1673 appointed for the hundred of Blackburn at the sessions held in Preston [3].)

[1] Kelsall, *Wage Regulation under the Statute of Artificers* (1938),
Appendix I.
[2] *Archæologia Cantiana*, xxii. 316.
[3] Hardwick, *History of Preston*, 405-406.

## (1) Page 256, note 1

Our statement that other wage assessments " will doubt-less come to light " [1] has been amply confirmed. It is now possible to supplement the lists given above [2]—1563 (Holland) [3] ; 1570 (Chester) [4] ; 1597 (Chester) [5]. Wage assessments were continued in operation at St. Albans in 1587 and 1588 [6].

[1] *Supra*, p. 262.         [2] *Supra*, pp. 256-263.
[3] Kelsall, *Wage Regulation under the Statute of Artificers*, Appendix I.
[4] Morris, *Chester*, 367-368.         [5] *Ibid.*
[6] Gibbs, *The Corporation Records of St. Albans*, 17, 25.

## (2) Page 257, note 5

Additional wage assessments are recorded—1612 (Essex)[1]; 1621 (Faversham) [2] ; 1634 (Norwich) [3] ; 1640 (Norwich) [4] ; 1641 (Staffordshire) [5] ; 1642 (Portsmouth) [6]. Wage assessments were continued in operation in Wiltshire in 1629 and 1630 [7].

[1] Kelsall, *l.c.*     [2] *Ibid.*     [3] *Ibid.*     [4] *Ibid.*     [5] *Ibid.*
[6] *Ibid.*     [7] *Records of the County of Wiltshire* (ed. Cunnington), 93-94.

## (3) Page 260, note 4

Additional wage assessments are recorded—1647 (Somer-set) [1] ; 1648 (Somerset) [2] ; 1648 or 1649 (Staffordshire) [3] ; 1650 (Norwich) [4] ; 1650 (Somerset) [5] ; 1651 (Somerset) [6] ; 1652 (Somerset) [7] ; 1653 (Somerset) [8] ; 1654 (Somerset) [9] ; 1655 (Somerset) [10] ; 1655 (Gloucester) [11] ; 1656 (Stafford-shire) [12] ; 1657 (Warwickshire) [13] ; 1657 (Norwich) [14].

[1] *Quarter Sessions Records for the County of Somerset*, iii. 40.
[2] *Ibid.* iii. 67.         [3] Kelsall, *l.c.*         [4] Kelsall, *l.c.*
[5] *Quarter Sessions Records for the County of Somerset*, iii. 121.
[6] *Ibid.* iii. 151.         [7] *Ibid.* iii. 177.         [8] *Ibid.* iii. 211.
[9] *Ibid.* iii. 236.         [10] *Ibid.* iii. 263.
[11] Rogers, *A History of Agriculture and Prices*, vi. 694.         [12] Kelsall, *l.c.*
[13] Ashby, *One Hundred Years of Poor Law*, 170.         [14] Kelsall, *l.c.*

## (4) Page 262, note 1

Additional wage assessments are recorded—1661 (Nor-folk) [1] ; 1662 (Norfolk) [2] ; 1666 (Somerset) [3] ; 1668 (Somer-set) [4] ; 1669 (Somerset) [5] ; 1669 (East Riding of Yorkshire) [6]; 1669 (Hull) [7] ; 1669 (Lindsey) [8] ; 1671 (Somerset) [9] ; 1672

(Warwickshire) [10]; 1672 (Somerset) [11]; 1673 (Somerset) [12]; 1673 (Blackburn) [13]; 1676 (Somerset) [14]; 1676 (Holland) [15]; 1677 (Somerset) [16]; 1677 (Bury St. Edmunds) [17]; 1679 (East Riding of Yorkshire) [18]; 1684 (West Riding of Yorkshire) [19]; 1687 (Buckinghamshire) [20]; 1687 (Hertfordshire) [21]; 1687 (Oxfordshire) [22]; 1688 (Buckinghamshire) [23]; 1690 (Buckinghamshire) [24]; 1690 (Kesteven) [25]; 1693 (Hertfordshire) [26]; 1695 (West Riding of Yorkshire) [27]; 1697 (Buckinghamshire) [28].

Rates of wages were fixed without change in Somersetshire in 1670, 1674 and 1675 [29]. Wage assessments were 'continued' or 'confirmed' or 'agreed upon' in Buckinghamshire from 1679 to 1684 [30]. (The reference to an assessment of 1673 [31] may be a misprint or clerical error.) Wage assessments "as they were last year" were continued in Nottinghamshire in 1678 and 1686, while in 1694 the clerk was instructed to procure the rates of wages and deliver them to the constables [32]. Wage assessments were reissued without changes in Buckinghamshire from 1691 to 1696, and from 1698 to 1700 [33]. The Herefordshire Sessions Records are said to contain " practically a complete set " of wage assessments from 1666 to 1762—" The assessed wages were altered in some respect on 20 occasions, the old rates were reissued without alteration 59 times, and for only 18 years out of the 97 have we no information at all " [34].

[1] Kelsall, l.c.     [2] Ibid.
[3] Quarter Sessions Records for the County of Somerset, iv. 13.
[4] Ibid. iv. 43.     [5] Ibid. iv. 61.
[6] Kelsall, l.c.     [7] Ibid.     [8] Ibid.
[9] Quarter Sessions Records for the County of Somerset, iv. 99.
[10] Ashby, One Hundred Years of Poor Law, 172.
[11] Quarter Sessions Records for the County of Somerset, iv. 116.
[12] Ibid. iv. 134.
[13] Hardwick, History of Preston, 405-406.
[14] Quarter Sessions Records for the County of Somerset, iv. 202.
[15] Kelsall, l.c.
[16] Quarter Sessions Records for the County of Somerset, iv. 224.
[17] Kelsall, l.c.     [18] Ibid.     [19] Ibid.
[20] Buckinghamshire Sessions Records, i. 227.     [21] Kelsall, l.c.
[22] Gretton, Oxfordshire Justices of the Peace in the Seventeenth Century, p. lxiii.
[23] Buckinghamshire Sessions Records, i. 262.     [24] Ibid. i. 337.
[25] Minutes of Proceedings in Quarter Sessions held for the Parts of Kesteven in the County of Lincoln (ed. Peyton), ii. 364, 376.

[contd.]

[26] Kelsall, *l.c.*                                              [27] *Ibid.*
[28] *Buckinghamshire Sessions Records*, ii. 125.
[29] *Quarter Sessions Records for the County of Somerset*, iv. 84, 159, 173.
[30] *Buckinghamshire Sessions Records*, i. 29, 52, 71, 95, 121, 149.
[31] *Ibid.* i. 149-150.
[32] *Nottinghamshire County Records* (ed. Copnall), 65.
[33] *Buckinghamshire Sessions Records*, i. 386, 425, 465, 504; ii. 44, 87, 173, 204, 247.
[34] Kelsall, " A Century of Wage Assessment in Herefordshire ", in *The English Historical Review*, lvii. 115 *seq.*

### (1) *Page 262, note* 1A

It has been pointed out [1] that " the original order [of a schedule of assessed wages] should have been filed by the clerk of the peace with other county records, though not of necessity enrolled among quarter sessions' orders, non-appreciation of this difference leading at one time to the belief that the seventeenth-century justices failed to exercise their powers concerning wages ". When the actual schedules are not forthcoming, proof that assessments were made and enforced is provided by presentments of offenders for refusal to work at the official rates or for paying excessive wages [2].

[1] *Minutes of Proceedings in Quarter Sessions held for the Parts of Kesteven in the County of Lincoln* (ed. Peyton), i. p. cxi.
[2] See *infra*, p. 521, No. 3.

### (2) *Page 262, note* 2

The reason advanced by the Worcestershire grand jury for the assessment of wages may be compared with the preamble to a wage assessment in Lancashire (the hundred of Blackburn) in 1673 : " To the end that masters and mistresses of families shall not so frequently tempt a good servant to leave his service by offering more or greater wages than the law permits " [1].

[1] Hardwick, *History of Preston*, 405.

### (3) *Page 263, note* 4

Additional wage assessments are recorded—1701 (Devonshire) [1]; 1701 (Oxfordshire) [2]; 1708 (Hertfordshire) [3]; 1714 (Holland) [4]; 1719 (Kendal) [5]; 1721 (Hull) [6]; 1722 (East Riding of Yorkshire) [7]; 1723 (Nottinghamshire) [8];

1724 (Suffolk) [9] ; 1730 (Warwickshire) [10] ; 1731 (Holland) [11] ; 1732 (Devonshire) [12] ; 1738 (Warwickshire) [13] ; 1750 (Devonshire) [14] ; 1778 (Devonshire) [15]. The wage assessment of 1723 was regularly confirmed for ten years in Nottinghamshire [16]. The assessment of 1738 held good in Warwickshire until 1773 [17]. In Devonshire wage assessments have been found for the years 1700–1704, 1712, 1716–1722, 1724–1726, 1728–1733, 1740–1741, 1750, 1752–1753, 1778. Except for 1701, 1732, 1750 and 1778, they were reissues without changes in the rates [18]. In Buckinghamshire there were reissues without change from 1701 to 1710 [19].

[1] Gilboy, *Wages in Eighteenth-Century England*, 88.
[2] Gilboy, *op. cit.* 89.   [3] Kelsall, *l.c.*   [4] *Ibid.*
[5] *Ibid.*   [6] *Ibid.*   [7] *Ibid.*
[8] Chambers, *Nottinghamshire in the Eighteenth Century*, 281.
[9] Kelsall, *l.c.*   [10] Ashby, *One Hundred Years of Poor Law*, 174.
[11] Kelsall, *l.c.*   [12] Gilboy, *op. cit.* 88.   [13] Ashby, *op. cit.* 175.
[14] Gilboy, *op. cit.* 88.   [15] *Ibid.*   [16] Chambers, *op. cit.* 281.
[17] Ashby, *op. cit.* 176.   [18] Gilboy, *op. cit.* 88.
[19] *Buckinghamshire Sessions Records*, ii. 288, 325, 383, 422 ; iii. 11, 51, 94, 132, 165, 216.

## (1) *Page 263, note 7*

The Courts (1685 and 1691) held that the Statute of Apprentices applied only to servants hired by the year[1]. " This decision ruled out most of the workmen who were employed by the capitalist manufacturer by the week or by the day " [2].

[1] See *supra*, p. 301.
[2] Holdsworth, *A History of English Law* (ed. 1938), xi. 468.

## (2) *Page 264, note 5*

J. Vanderlint wrote in 1734 : " As is notoriously known, the dearness of labour hath been found so burthensome to our farmers that the gentry and justices of the peace in their open quarter sessions have lately, in several places in the kingdom, attempted to redress this evil by regulating the rates of servants' wages ". He stigmatized this attempt as " unnatural and impossible to answer the end " [1].

As late as 1787 the employers of the wool-sorters in

ECONOMIC HISTORY

Exeter applied to the justices to assess the wages of their journeymen according to the Act of 1563 [2].

[1] Vanderlint, *Money answers all Things* (1734), 148.
[2] Hoskins, *Industry, Trade and People in Exeter*, 54.


## (1) *Page 271, note 1*

It has been said that the Mercantilist State " everywhere exerted its influence on the side of low wages " [1]. Evidence is given in the text suggesting a different conclusion [2]. And the advocacy in the early nineteenth century of low wages for the sake of the export trade shows that the notion that " a country might become rich through the poverty of its people " was not confined to certain mercantilist writers [3].

[1] Heckscher, *Mercantilism* (revised ed. 1935), ii. 167, 171.
[2] *Supra*, pp. 254-259, 266, 274, 395. See also *infra*, No. 3.
[3] Some mercantilist writers considered high wages a sign of national prosperity : see *supra*, pp. 273-274.


## (2) *Page 272, note 1A*

The principle of a sliding scale, in which wages were regulated by the cost of living, was adopted by the London (Quaker) Lead Company. At first wages were related to the price of lead. Then at the end of the eighteenth century a monthly estimate of the cost of food was made and wages were adjusted accordingly [1].

[1] Raistrick, *Two Centuries of Industrial Welfare*, 36.


## (3) *Page 273, note 1A*

It might appear that writers who advocated a reduction of wages wanted to lower the workers' standard of living. This was not necessarily the case. For example, J. Vanderlint argued that money wages were too high, but he did not approve of " making the poor fare harder or consume less than their reasonable wants in that station require ; for they being the bulk of mankind would in this case affect the consumption of things in general so mightily that there would be a want of trade and business amongst the other part of the people ", and this would " affect the rents ".

He added : " If it was unreasonable to muzzle the ox that trod out the corn, what name shall I give the measures that render it so difficult for the bulk of mankind " to raise families? He believed that " when the necessaries of life were rendered so much cheaper ", the value of the reduced money wages would be greater, *i.e.* real wages would rise [1].

[1] Vanderlint, *Money answers all Things* (1734), 61, 87-88.

### (1) *Page 275, note 1*

In 1611 the duke of Rutland paid his chief hop-grower £6 : 13 : 4, while the highest wage in the assessment of 1610 in Rutland was £2 : 12s. [1]

[1] Chambers, *Nottinghamshire in the Eighteenth Century*, 279.

### (2) *Page 275, note 1A*

The payment of ' Statute wages ' in a particular locality might also be evaded by moving to other districts where the same rates did not apply. Thus master tailors in the City of London sometimes set up in the suburbs with the express purpose of paying *higher* wages and attracting the best workmen [1]. Again, the migration of the silk industry from London and Middlesex was stimulated by the motive of paying *lower* wages than those fixed by law for the metropolis and adjoining areas [2].

[1] *Supra*, p. 406.          [2] *Supra*, p. 270.

### (3) *Page 275, note 5*

The reluctance to accept ' Statute wages ' is shown in the indictment of labourers for their refusal to work according to the rates fixed by the justices of the peace [1].

[1] See *supra*, pp. 253 (note 3), 257 (note 5), 260 (note 4), 262 (note 1) ; and *Minutes of Proceedings in Quarter Sessions held for the Parts of Kesteven in the County of Lincoln* (ed. Peyton), i. 35, 86, 93 (1676, 1678-1679).

### (4) *Page 276, note 2*

There are numerous other examples of the reissue of wage assessments without changes in the rates [1]. The formal entry " that rates of servants' wages do stand as they were at the last general quarter sessions " was inserted almost every year from 1610 to 1725 in the Middlesex sessions register [2].

[1] Buckinghamshire (*Buckinghamshire Sessions Records*, i. 29, 52, 71, 95, 121, 149-150, 386, 425, 465, 504 ; ii. 44, 87, 173, 204, 247, 288, 325, 383, 422 ; iii. 11, 51, 94, 132, 165, 216) ; Devonshire (Gilboy, *Wages in Eighteenth-Century England*, 88) ; Herefordshire (*The English Historical Review*, lvii. 115 *seq.*) ; Nottinghamshire (*Nottinghamshire County Records*, ed. Copnall, 65 ; Chambers, *Nottinghamshire in the Eighteenth Century*, 281) ; Somersetshire (*Quarter Sessions Records for the County of Somerset*, iv. 84, 159, 173) ; Warwickshire (Ashby, *One Hundred Years of Poor Law*, 176) ; Wiltshire (*Records of the County of Wiltshire*, ed. Cunnington, 93-94).

[2] Dowdell, *A Hundred Years of Quarter Sessions*, 149.

### (1) *Page 277, note 2*

The author of *An Enquiry into the Causes of the Present High Price of Provisions* (1767) [1] dissented from this view. " We have been told that the poor have been found to live better in years of scarcity and dearness than when provisions have been more plentiful and cheap. I cannot but question the truth of this fact. . . . It is, I must say, totally contrary to all my observation ". He also questioned the truth of the statement that when workmen can earn as much in two days as in three, they would only work two days.

[1] Part i. 59, 61.

### (2) *Page 277, note 2A*

*The Spectator* wrote (1711) : " The poor, which are the bulk of a nation, work only that they may live " [1]. But J. Vanderlint believed that the workers would work harder if real wages were higher and there was ' plenty of everything ' [2].

[1] *The Spectator*, No. 200 (1711).
[2] Vanderlint, *Money answers all Things* (1734), 122, 124.

### (3) *Page 279, note 1*

A recent Essay [1] analyses some of the forces behind the introduction of the Acts for the enforcement of apprenticeship, and examines the prosecutions under the Acts.

[1] M. R. Gay, " Aspects of Elizabethan Apprenticeship ", in *Facts and Factors in Economic History*.

## (1) *Page* 279, *note* 2

The statement made by a recent historian, that the period of apprenticeship was often extended beyond " the legally prescribed seven years ", overlooks the fact that the Act of 1563 laid down the term of seven years ' at the least ' as the *legal minimum*.

## (2) *Page* 279, *note* 3

The Witney Blanket Weavers limited their members to one apprentice at a time [1].

[1] Plummer, *The Witney Blanket Industry*, 127 (1711).

## (3) *Page* 280, *note* 1

An Act of 1777 required hatters to employ one journeyman for every apprentice [1].

[1] *Statutes at Large*, viii. 550.

## (4) *Page* 281, *note* 5

The indictment of a shoemaker in a Nottinghamshire village in 1737—who was charged with exercising the trade of a shoemaker, without having served an apprenticeship to it—was quashed on the ground that the offence was " done in a country village ", and that the Act of 1563 did not extend to trades carried on in such places [1].

In 1763 " all the judges of England at a meeting lately resolved that if any man as a master had exercised and followed any trade as a master without interruption or impediment for the term of seven years, he was not liable to be sued or prosecuted upon the Statute of the 5th of Elizabeth " [2].

[1] *Nottinghamshire County Records* (ed. Copnall), 13.
[2] Quoted Holdsworth, *A History of English Law* (ed. 1938), xi. 420.

## (5) *Page* 284, *note* 2

In a debate in Parliament in 1621 it was said : " The abuse and vexation of these men is very great, for when they come to a town they warn thirty or forty to come before them. If they sell anything, be it but a pound of candles besides the trade he was bound apprentice unto, they must come to London or else give £4 or £5 for a composition " [1].

[1] *Commons Debates*, 1621 (ed. Notestein, Relf, and Simpson), ii. 125.

### (1) *Page 289, note* 5

The register of Surrey apprenticeships states the premiums paid with apprentices. A ' merchant of London ' received £500 (1722) ; a ' cloth-worker and merchant, free of trading to the Levant ' £800 (1713) ; a merchant of the Staple £90 with one apprentice (1717), £10 with another (1717), and £10 with a third (1724) ; another merchant of the Staple was paid £118 : 5s. (1712) [1].

William Stout was apprenticed in 1681 at the age of sixteen to a grocer and ironmonger for seven years. His father agreed to pay £20 and to find clothes [2]. Stout received with his own apprentice £20, " I to find him maintenance and his mother clothes all the term " [3]. When his apprentice was ' loose ', Stout sold him his goods and shop equipment to be paid for by instalments [4].

[1] *Surrey Apprenticeships*, 1711–1731 (Surrey Record Society), 8, 11, 14, 107, 118, 166.
[2] *Autobiography of William Stout of Lancaster* (ed. 1851), 7-8.
[3] *Ibid.* 29.                                    [4] *Ibid.* 45.

### (2) *Page* 290, *note* 1

The Act of 1710, levying a duty on premiums, was the origin of a series of registers of apprentices—now in the Public Record Office [1].

[1] Some are printed in *Surrey Apprenticeships*, 1711–1731 (Surrey Record Society).

### (3) *Page* 296, *note* 1A

It was observed in *The Spectator* that " if the profit and loss by wars could be justly balanced, it would be rarely found that the Conquest is sufficient to repay the Cost " [1]. J. Vanderlint (1734) described war as " one of the greatest calamities . . . the end of which none can well foresee, and the burthens of which [public debts and taxes] are seldom discharged in one generation ". He pointed out that it

" commonly ruins . . . such nations as are vanquished, as we know the late war did France, and what we who conquered got by it the taxes . . . will amply testify ". He concluded that " ordinary causes, *viz.* extending dominion or trade, will not justify it " [2].

[1] *The Spectator*, No. 200 (1711).
[2] Vanderlint, *Money answers all Things* (1734), 57, 125-126. For Thomas Paine's eloquent indictment, see *The Rights of Man*.

### (1) *Page 302, note 6*

Though the Yearly Bond—by which miners bound themselves to give a year's service [1]—doubtless contributed to making employment less irregular, the volume of employment was seriously affected by the fact that coal-mining was a seasonal occupation. Sea-borne trade was largely suspended in the winter months, and there were also interruptions due to wars and privateers [2]. The prevalence of unemployment is shown by the institution of a provident fund for distressed keelmen [3]; and in 1666 the coalowners set up a temporary unemployment fund for colliery workers [4]. Though some miners combined their occupation with farming pursuits [5], this was only occasional. Hence, unless their families had by-occupations (*e.g.* spinning), irregularity of employment must have greatly diminished the income enjoyed by the mining population. In any event the daily wage of a miner affords a very imperfect guide to the actual amount of his annual earnings.

[1] *Supra*, vol. ii. 124.  [2] *Supra*, vol. ii. 154.
[3] *Supra*, vol. ii. 127.  [4] *Supra*, vol. ii. 133.
[5] *Supra*, vol. ii. 127.

### (2) *Page 309, note 2*

In the course of a debate on trade in 1621 a member of the House of Commons observed : " I doubt you meet not with the right causes of the decay of clothing, which I conceive to be two—(1) that unhappy project of dyeing and dressing; (2) the peace of other nations that hath set them awork " [1].

[1] *Commons Debates*, 1621 (ed. Notestein, Relf, and Simpson), iv. 150-151.

## (1) *Page* 317, *note* 5

In 1662 the Venetian resident reported that " many are firmly of the opinion " that the friction between England and Holland would end in a rupture. " The merchants desire this beyond expression, and not without cause, seeing that the Dutch are cleverly drawing to themselves a great part of the trade of this country " [1].

[1] *State Papers Venetian*, 1661–1664, pp. 137-138.

## (2) *Page* 329, *note* 4

Parliament was informed in 1621 that " the overseers in the county, who are trusted by the statute to measure and size the cloths in the water and to note the faults upon the seals, made a common matter of it to set their seals to cloth which they never measured, yea to sell their seals to the clothier and suffer him to put them on his cloth, being never visited " [1].

[1] *Commons Debates*, 1621 (ed. Notestein, Relf, and Simpson), vii. 235. For the abuses of searchers and measurers of cloth, see also Smith, *An Essay for Recovery of Trade* (1661), 7 *seq.*

## (3) *Page* 331, *note* 1

A by-law of the Witney Blanket Weavers laid down that no one other than those admitted to the Company might exercise the mistery of a blanket weaver in Witney or within twenty miles thereof [1].

[1] Plummer, *The Witney Blanket Industry*, 128 (1719).

## (4) *Page* 331, *note* 4

The London Dyers' Company had sought further powers for preventing false and deceitful work in 1703 [1]. In 1783 it was ' empowered and required ' by an Act of Parliament to appoint searchers to inspect shops, warehouses, workhouses, etc., while outside London searchers were to be appointed by the justices of the peace [2].

[1] *State Papers Domestic*, 1703–1704, p. 358.
[2] *Statutes at Large*, ix. 290-291.

## (1) *Page* 335, *note* 6

In 1702 a royal warrant was issued to prepare a bill for incorporating the Tanners of London as a company " for the better regulation of the trade " [1]. The Witney Blanket Weavers were incorporated in 1711 to remedy the " many frauds and abuses of late practised in the deceitful working up of blankets . . . which for want of some established government amongst them they are not able to prevent " [2].

[1] *State Papers Domestic*, 1702–1703, pp. 444, 608.
[2] The charter, oaths, by-laws, court books and accounts are printed in Plummer, *The Witney Blanket Industry*, 114 seq.

## (2) *Page* 336, *note* 1

In 1727 an Act for " the better regulation of the woollen manufacture " expressly reserved the " powers formerly given by charter or Act of Parliament to the corporation of clothiers in the city of Worcester " [1].

[1] *Statutes at Large*, v. 450.

## (3) *Page* 336, *note* 5

After the Restoration a proposal was made that " the whole body of clothing throughout England and Ireland may be brought under one uniform regulation and government by incorporating the same . . . and that halls may be established " for the inspection of cloth [1].

[1] Smith, *An Essay for Recovery of Trade* (1661), 19.

## (4) *Page* 337, *note* 5

Colchester had both an English and a Dutch Company engaged in making bays and says, and there was conflict between them [1].

[1] *Acts of the Privy Council*, 1623–1625, p. 179.

## (5) *Page* 338, *note* 5

Bradford's reputation for fraudulent work may be gauged from a verse in a Methodist hymn :

" On Bradford likewise look Thou down
Where Satan keeps his seat ".

And a verse of the *Beggars' Litany* ran :

" From Hell, Hull and Halifax,
Good Lord, deliver us ! " [1]

[1] Defoe, *Tour of Great Britain* (ed. 1727), iii. 111 ; Heaton, *The Yorkshire Woollen and Worsted Industries*, 273, 394.

### (1) *Page* 340, *note* 4

A petition of the London Grocers' Company laid before Parliament in 1621 represented that " there is a special custom in London confirmed by sundry Parliaments that all freemen of the City may use any trade whatsoever (not being a manual trade) ".  From this it followed that " none of the chief companies in London stand by professing that art or mistery whereof they bear a name, but is mixed of men of several arts and families " [1].

[1] *Commons Debates*, 1621 (ed. Notestein, Relf, and Simpson), vii. 84.

### (2) *Page* 341, *note* 1A

Another example of the support given by the Government to ' handicraft ' companies, in their efforts to make membership compulsory on all who practised their trades, is shown by the order of the Privy Council requiring " all artisan cloth-workers, of what company soever they be free ", to be subject to the control of the Company of Cloth-workers " for so much as concerneth their trade only " [1].

[1] *Acts of the Privy Council*, 1619–1621, p. 39 (1619).

### (3) *Page* 343, *note* 1A

The London Pewterers' Company was confirmed in 1702 in its powers of supervision " for correcting all false and deceitful workers and sellers of defective pewter " [1].

[1] *State Papers Domestic*, 1702–1703, p. 238.

### (4) *Page* 346, *note* 1A

Quakers at first were apparently unable to become freemen because of their inability to take an oath.  At Lancaster a grocer and ironmonger " although a freeman's son and had also served an apprenticeship to a freeman, yet could not be admitted a freeman without an oath which he would not in conscience make " [1].

When the Witney Blanket Weavers were incorporated in 1711, two members were " admitted into this Company. But being both Quakers they made the solemn affirmation or declaration pursuant to the Act of Parliament in that behalf ". So runs an entry in the Company's court books [2].

[1] *Autobiography of William Stout of Lancaster* (ed. 1851), 7, 27 (*temp.* Charles II.). [2] Plummer, *The Witney Blanket Industry*, 132.

#### (1) *Page* 350, *note* 3

This action was taken by the city of Winchester against the defendant for exercising a trade without being brought up an apprentice to it within the city. Chief Justice Holt, who tried the case, observed : " All people are at liberty to live in Winchester, and how can they be restrained from using the lawful means of living there ? . . . Such a custom is an injury to the party and a prejudice to the public " [1].

[1] *A Report of all the Cases determined by Sir John Holt* (1738), 187-188.

#### (2) *Page* 353, *note* 7

In 1620 a patent granted for the making of steel stipulated that only coal should be used—" he will waste no wood "—and there was no bar on importation. Thus it sought to encourage a new process which would dispense with wood, while avoiding the creation of a monopoly [1].

[1] *Acts of the Privy Council*, 1619–1621, p. 319.

#### (3) *Page* 354, *note* 2A

In a project laid before James I. for raising money by the sale of pardons for breaches of penal laws, twenty-eight economic practices were not to be pardoned, *e.g.* forestalling, regrating and engrossing, enclosures, etc.[1]

[1] Robertson, *Aspects of the Rise of Economic Individualism*, 62.

#### (4) *Page* 363, *note* 2A

Bristol soapmakers were rationed on the basis of 600 tons annually, which were allocated among them [1].

[1] *The Company of Soapmakers*, 1562–1642 (ed. Matthews), 6, 199 (1634).

## (1) *Page* 372, *note* 1

Mention is made in 1346 of ' alym de Wyght ', presumably alum from the Isle of Wight [1].

[1] Salzman, *English Industries of the Middle Ages* (ed. 1923), 208.

## (2) *Page* 372, *note* 3

It has been recently pointed out that " it is uncertain whether the Exchequer gained or lost by acquiring the alum rights from the first patentees. . . . The estimates of loss were . . . unreliable. . . . For many years the Crown was decidedly out of pocket, but from 1617 onward a steady flow into the Exchequer resulted, which must have almost, if not quite, wiped out the debit balance " [1].

[1] Turton, *The Alum Farm*, 194.

## (3) *Page* 373, *note* 1

In spite of the misfortunes of the early patentees, the alum industry survived. The port books show that production was carried on in the alum works on the northeast coast during the seventeenth century [1].

[1] Nef, *The Rise of the British Coal Industry*, i. 185.

## (4) *Page* 381, *note* 3

It was stated in Parliament in 1621 that the Merchant Adventurers paid £60,000 for the renewal of their charter [1].

[1] *Commons Debates*, 1621 (ed. Notestein, Relf, and Simpson), iv. 50; v. 457.

## (5) *Page* 382, *note* 7

The Merchant Adventurers in 1621 stated that their trade had " fallen to be scarcely half so much in the quantity of cloth as formerly it was ". The first reason which they assigned was " the great increase of cloth made in the Netherlands caused by the provocation of the late project of dyeing and dressing ". But they also alluded to " the wars in Germany " and " the daily falsification of the coins in those parts " [1].

[1] *Commons Debates*, 1621 (ed. Notestein, Relf, and Simpson), vii. 233. See also *supra*, p. 308.

## (1) *Page* 392, *note* 3

The miners of Alston Moor had a friendly society. Their rules are dated 1755 [1].

[1] Printed in Raistrick, *Two Centuries of Industrial Welfare*, 42 *seq*.

## (2) *Page* 392, *note* 4

For Sir W. Holdsworth's comment on the view expressed in the text, see *A History of English Law* [1].

[1] (Ed. 1938), xi. 492-494.

## (3) *Page* 396, *note* 3A

Combinations among masters were made illegal in 1800 [1].

[1] *Statutes at Large*, xiv. 468.

## (4) *Page* 403, *note* 5

Budgets of agricultural labourers are noticed above [1]. J. Vanderlint (1734) gives " an estimate of the necessary charge of a labouring man and his family in London, consisting of a man and his wife and four children, which I take to be a middling family ". The ' yearly expense ' amounted to £54, 10s. 4d. The weekly items include " rent of two rooms, which is as little as such a family can or ought to shift with " (1s. 6d.) ; " schooling for the children " (9d.) ; bread (2s. 7½d.) ; butter (10½d.) ; milk (5¼d.) ; coal (1s. 2d.) ; candles (5¼d.). He declared that " whatever wage a working man may sometimes earn, 10s. or 12s. per week ", when deductions are made for loss of time due to want of work or illness, his yearly income amounted only to £26 or £30—half of what he considered the minimum expenditure.

He also gives an estimated budget for a family (man, wife, four children and a maidservant) " in the middling station of life ". The annual total, £390, includes £75 put by for his wife and children after his death, and also business expenses. Among other items are the following—" schooling for four children " £8 ; clothes £16 (man), £16 (wife), £28 (children) ; maid's wages ' may be ' £4, 10s. ; coal (between 4 and 5 London chaldrons a year) 2s. 6d. weekly ; tea and

sugar 4s. 1d. weekly.   One item is ' Christmas-box-money ',
of which the amount is not specified [2].

[1] *Supra*, vol. ii. 392.
[2] Vanderlint, *Money answers all Things* (1734), 75, 77, 141-142.

### (1) *Page* 420, *note* 8

The practice of making gifts in kind lent itself to abuse.
In 1702 the Derbyshire justices issued an order putting an
end to the system by which " the overseers of the poor of
divers parishes . . . do instead of giving weekly allowances
in money to the poor people of such parishes . . . force
them to take weekly the same in bread, meal, corn and other
victuals, and thereby make a gain to themselves by selling
such commodities to them at much dearer rates ".   Accordingly they ordered that relief to the poor should be given
" in ready money in specie " only [1].

[1] Cox, *Three Centuries of Derbyshire Annals*, ii. 167.   A long list of
weekly payments made to the poor in 1683 is printed in *ibid*. ii. 165.

### (2) *Page* 423, *note* 5

Legislation relating to vagrants was also enacted in the
eighteenth century [1].

[1] See Holdsworth, *A History of English Law* (ed. 1938), x. 178-179.

### (3) *Page* 435, *note* 5

In 1706 William Stout, a Quaker shopkeeper at Lancaster,
" had a parish apprentice put upon me, about ten years of
age.   I sent him to the free school for at least four years,
and he learned well to the entering into Greek, and could
write well.   I bound him an apprentice to a worsted weaver ;
gave £4 with him and found him clothes. . . .   He cost me
at least £40 " [1].

[1] *Autobiography of William Stout of Lancaster* (ed. 1851), 75.

### (4) *Page* 435, *note* 6

In 1718 the justices of Middlesex discharged a boy
apprenticed by St. Martin's-in-the-Fields to a chimney-
sweep at the age of five and a half [1].

[1] Dowdell, *A Hundred Years of Quarter Sessions*, 57, note 2.

## (1) *Page* 437, *note* 5

The difficulties experienced in administering the system of parish apprenticeship are illustrated by the following example.  In 1675 a parish complained that the leader in refusing to take a parish apprentice was the rector.  Encouraged by his example eleven parishioners had declined to accept the child placed with them [1].

[1] Furley, *Quarter Sessions Government in Hampshire in the Seventeenth Century*, 28.

## (2) *Page* 459, *note* 4A

A shorter period of domicile was specified in the case of vagrants by the Acts of 1598 and 1604.  The former required them to be sent to their birthplace, and if unknown to the place where they last dwelt for ' one whole year '.  The latter ordered ' incorrigible rogues ' to be sent to the place where they last dwelt ' by the space of a year ', and if not known then to the place of birth [1].

[1] *Statutes*, iv. part ii. 899, 1025.

## (3) *Page* 460, *note* 3

Other examples of the removal of persons prior to the Act of Settlement may be noticed.  In Northamptonshire, in 1630, " a settled inhabitant with his family for the space of two years last past and upwards " was sent to another village " upon pretence that he was there born ".  The court of quarter sessions, however, adjudged this " to be altogether unlawful, he being no rogue.  It is thereupon ordered that he be forthwith sent back again " [1].  In 1657 complaint was made of a man and his wife residing in a village where they had not gained a legal settlement, " and in respect of their poverty are like to bring a sudden charge if they should there abide ".  In this case it was ordered that they should be removed [2].  In Derbyshire, in 1649, the justices ordered the removal of a man and his family to another parish [3].  In Surrey, in 1659, certain persons " are lately come into the parish and are likely to prove a charge and burthen ", and they were therefore to be " immediately removed " to another parish [4].

[1] *Quarter Sessions Records of the County of Northampton* (ed. Wake), 94.
[2] *Ibid.* 189.  [3] Cox, *Three Centuries of Derbyshire Annals*, ii. 146.
[4] *Surrey Quarter Sessions Records*, 1659–1661 (Surrey Record Society), 14.

### (1) *Page 462, note* 2

In connexion with the earlier usage regarding settlement, see a review by the present writer of *Minutes of Proceedings in Quarter Sessions held for the Parts of Kesteven in the County of Lincoln* [1].

[1] *The Economic History Review*, iv. No. 4, 504.

### (2) *Page 463, note* 1A

A table has been compiled showing the methods of acquiring a settlement—birth, parentage, marriage, service, apprenticeship, etc.—and the origin (whether by statute or interpretation) [1].

[1] See Holdsworth, *A History of English Law* (ed. 1938), x. 259.

### (3) *Page 465, note* 2

The intricacies of the Law of Settlement are illustrated in the following catch, in which a case (1723) affecting a settlement acquired by marriage was reported [1]:

> " A woman having a settlement
> Married a man with none :
> The question was, he being dead,
> If that she had, was gone ?
> Quoth Sir John Pratt—Her settlement
> Suspended did remain,
> Living the husband ; But, him dead,
> It doth revive again.
>
> *Chorus of Puisne Judges*
> Living the husband ; But, him dead,
> It doth revive again ".

Another case in 1815 was held to determine whether a pauper was " settled in parish A or B.  The house he occupied was in both parishes, and models of both of the house and of the bed in which the pauper slept were laid before the court that it might ascertain how much of his body lay in each parish. The court held the pauper to be settled where his head (being the nobler part) lay, though one of his legs at least, and great part of his body, lay out of that parish " [2].

[1] Quoted in Holdsworth, *A History of English Law* (ed. 1938), x. 261, note.
[2] Henry Crabb Robinson, *Diary*, cited Webb, *English Poor Law History*, i. 347, note 2.

## (1) *Page 469, note 4*

There is other evidence to show that the practice of providing a parish stock for employment of the poor did not completely lapse. The overseers of the poor in Surrey were instructed in 1663 to give in " their accounts of their receipts and payments as well of stock as money for the poor " [1]; and in many Nottinghamshire parishes the custom of finding employment survived during the greater part of the eighteenth century [2].

[1] *Surrey Quarter Sessions Records*, 1663–1666 (Surrey Record Society), 4.
[2] Chambers, *Nottinghamshire in the Eighteenth Century*, 233-234.

## (2) *Page 474, note 2A*

Although the first modern workhouse is associated with Bristol, a public workhouse was established at Preston in 1675. A contemporary account (*circa* 1686) states that there " is lately raised a public workhouse to employ the poorer sort of people, especially women and children, in a worsted trade of yarn, thereby better to maintain their family from begging ". The workhouse was set up by the corporation, and the overseers of the poor were instructed to present the names of all the poor people in the town " that thereout may be choice made who of them shall be set on work ", and " not suffered to beg or wander abroad ". In particular " all young children and other persons who are not mothers of families " were " to go and work at the said workhouse " in carding and spinning wool. They were remunerated for their work, since it was laid down that

" the wages of such as shall be employed in the workhouse
[shall] be weekly paid unto every person working or unto
their parents " [1].

[1] Hardwick, *History of Preston*, 212, 281-282 ; Hewitson, *Preston Court
Leet Records*, 187-188.


## (1) *Page* 474, *note* 3

Two proposals at Bristol prior to 1696 may be noticed.
One (1653), for " setting the poor on work ", included a
proviso that " all such parish poor which cannot . . . come
to work at the workhouses, they shall have work delivered
them to their particular dwellings ", namely, spinning of
yarn, knitting of stockings " and other manufactures " ; and
their services were to be remunerated.   Another (1679) contemplated erecting " a linen manufactory " in a workhouse [1].

[1] *Bristol Corporation of the Poor : Selected Records*, 1696–1834 (ed.
Butcher), 2, 39-40.

# AUTHORITIES

Abram, W. A.   *A History of Blackburn.*
*Acts and Ordinances of the Eastland Company*, ed. M. Sellers.
*Acts and Ordinances of the Interregnum*, ed. C. H. Firth and R. S. Rait.
*Acts of the Privy Council.*
*Acts of the Privy Council*, Colonial Series.
Addy, S. O.   *Church and Manor.*
Aikin, J.   *A Description of the Country . . . round Manchester* (1795).
Albion, R. G.   *Forests and Sea Power.*
Alcock, T.   *Observations on the Defects of the Poor Laws* (1752).
  *Remarks on Two Bills for the Better Maintenance of the Poor.*
*All the Year Round*, ed. C. Dickens.
Anderson, A.   *The Origin of Commerce* (ed. 1764).
Anderson, J.   *Report . . . on Shetland Wool* (1790).
Andréadès, A.   *History of the Bank of England* (ed. 1909).
Andrews, C. M.   *British Committees, Commissions, and Councils of Trade
    and Plantations, 1622–1675.*
  *The Acts of Trade*, in *The Cambridge History of the British Empire*,
    vol. i.
  *The Colonial Background of the American Revolution.*
*Angliæ Tutamen* (1695).
*Annals of Agriculture*, ed. A. Young.
*Annual Register.*
Anonymous : see end of Authorities.
Anstie, J.   *A General View of the Bill . . . for preventing the Illicit Ex-
    portation of British Wool* (1787).
  *A Letter to the Secretary of the Bath Agriculture Society* (1791).
*Archæologia.*
*Archæologia Cantiana.*
Asgill, J.   *A Brief Answer to A Brief State of the Question* (1719).
Ashby, A. W.   *One Hundred Years of Poor Law Administration in a
    Warwickshire Village.*
Ashley, W. J.   *An Introduction to English Economic History and Theory*
    (ed. 1909).
  *Surveys Historic and Economic.*
  *The Bread of our Forefathers.*
  *The Economic Organization of England.*
Ashton, T. S.   *Iron and Steel in the Industrial Revolution.*
Ashton, T. S., and Sykes, J.   *The Coal Industry of the Eighteenth Century.*
Atton, H., and Holland, H. H.   *The King's Customs.*
*Autobiography of Arthur Young*, ed. M. Betham-Edwards.
Aydelotte, F.   *Elizabethan Rogues and Vagabonds.*

Bacon, F.   *Essays.*
  *The Letters and the Life of Francis Bacon*, ed. J. Spedding.
  *Works*, ed. J. Spedding, R. L. Ellis and D. D. Heath.

Baigent, F. J., and Millard, J. E. *A History of Basingstoke.*
Bailey, J., and Culley, G. *Agriculture of Cumberland* (1794).
Baines, E. *History of the Cotton Manufacture.*
Baines, T. *Yorkshire Past and Present.*
Baker : see *Nottingham.*
Bakewell, R. *Observations on the Influence of Soil and Climate upon Wool* (1808).
Bamford, S. *The Dialect of South Lancashire.*
Barbon, N. *A Discourse concerning coining the New Money lighter* (1696). *A Discourse of Trade* (1690).
Barbour, V. *Dutch and English Merchant Shipping in the Seventeenth Century,* in *The Economic History Review,* vol. ii. No. 2.
Barnes, D. G. *A History of the English Corn Laws.*
Basye, A. H. *The Lords Commissioners of Trade and Plantations, 1748-1782.*
Beckmann, J. *A History of Inventions* (ed. 1846).
*Bedfordshire County Records.*
Beer, G. L. *British Colonial Policy, 1754-1765.*
  *The Commercial Policy of England towards the American Colonies.*
  *The Old Colonial System.*
  *The Origins of the British Colonial System.*
Bell, B. *Essays on Agriculture* (1802).
Bellers, J. *Proposals for raising a Colledge of Industry* (1696).
Benbrigge, J. *Usura Accommodata* (1646).
Bennett (Mr.). *Two Letters and Several Calculations on the Sugar Colonies and Trade* (1738).
Best : see *Rural.*
Betham-Edwards : see *Autobiography.*
*Bibliotheca Gloucestrensis,* ed. J. Washbourn.
Bidwell, W. H. *Annals of an East Anglian Bank.*
Bieber, R. P. *The Lords of Trade and Plantations, 1675-1696.*
Birdwood : see *First Letter Book.*
Bischoff, J. *History of the Woollen and Worsted Manufactures.*
Bishop, J. L. *A History of American Manufactures.*
Bisschop, W. R. *The Rise of the London Money Market.*
Blackstone, W. *Commentaries on the Laws of England* (ed. 1765).
Bland, A. E., Brown, P. A., and Tawney, R. H. *English Economic History : Select Documents.*
Bland, J. *Trade Revived* (1659).
Blith, W. *The English Improver* (1649).
*Book of John Fisher,* ed. T. Kemp.
*Book of John Rowe,* ed. W. H. Godfrey.
*Book of Orders* (1586).
Boroughs, J. *The Sovereignty of the British Seas* (1633 : ed. 1920).
Bowden, W. *Industrial Society in England towards the End of the Eighteenth Century.*
Bowen, T. *Extracts from the Records and Court Books of Bridewell Hospital* (1798).
Bowley, A. L. *England's Foreign Trade in the Nineteenth Century* (ed. 1922).
Boyce, G. *Historical Memoirs of Tiverton.*
Boyle : see *Newcastle.*
Boys, J. *Agriculture of Kent* (1796).
Brand, J. *The History and Antiquities of Newcastle-upon-Tyne* (1789).
Brentano, L. *Eine Geschichte der wirtschaftlichen Entwicklung Englands.*
Brewster, F. *Essays on Trade and Navigation* (1695).
Brinkmann, C. *England and the Hanse under Charles II.,* in *The English Historical Review,* vol. xxiii.
*British Merchant* (1713 : ed. C. King, 1721).

*British Merchant : Or A Review of the Trade of Great Britain* (1719).

Brown, A.   *The Genesis of the United States.*

Brown, R.   *Agriculture of the West Riding* (1799).

Brown, T.   *Miscellanea Aulica : Or A Collection of State Treatises* (1702).

Brownlee, J.   *The History of the Birth and Death Rates in England and Wales taken as a whole, from 1570 to the present time,* in *Public Health,* vol. xxix., June and July, 1916.

Bruce, J.   *Annals of the East India Company.*

Bruce, P. A.   *Economic History of Virginia in the Seventeenth Century.*
*Social Life of Virginia in the Seventeenth Century.*

Brugis, T.   *The Discovery of a Projector* (1641).

Bryce, G.   *History of the Hudson's Bay Company.*

Buer, M. C.   *Health, Wealth and Population in the Early Days of the Industrial Revolution.*

Burgon, J. W.   *The Life and Times of Sir Thomas Gresham.*

Burke, E.   *Observations on a Late State of the Nation* (ed. 1769).
*Thoughts and Details on Scarcity* (ed. 1800).
*Two Letters . . . on the Proposals for Peace with the Regicide Directory of France* (1796).

Burn, J. S.   *The History of the French, Walloon, Dutch, and Other Foreign Protestant Refugees.*

Burn, R.   *Observations on the Bill intended to be offered to Parliament for the better Relief and Employment of the Poor* (1776).
*The History of the Poor Laws* (1764).

Burnley, J.   *The History of Wool and Wool-combing.*

Bush, R.   *The Poor Man's Friend* (1649).


C. J.   *The Compleat Collier* (1708 : ed. 1845).

C. J.: see Collinges.

*Cambridge History of the British Empire.*

Camden, W.   *Britannia* (ed. 1586).

  „     (ed. 1607).

  „     ed. E. Gibson (1695).

  „     ed. R. Gough (1806).

Campbell, R.   *The London Tradesman* (1747).

Cannan, E.   *The History of Local Rates in England* (ed. 1927).   See also Smith.

Carr, C. T.   *Select Charters of Trading Companies.*

Carte, T.   *The Life of James, Duke of Ormond* (ed. 1851).

Carter, W.   *An Abstract of Proceedings to prevent Exportation of Wool Unmanufactured* (1689).
*A Brief Advertisement to the Merchant and Clothier* (1672).
*England's Interest by Trade Asserted* (1671).
*England's Interest asserted in the Improvement of its Native Commodities* (1669).
*The Proverb Crossed* (1677).

Cartwright, J. J.   *Chapters in the History of Yorkshire.*

Cary, J.   *An Essay on the State of England in Relation to its Trade* (1695).
*An Essay towards Regulating the Trade* (ed. 1719).
*A Reply to a Paper entituled The Linnen Drapers' Answer.*

*Catalogue of the Cotton MSS.* (1802).

Cave, C. H.   *A History of Banking in Bristol.*

Cawston, G., and Keane, A. H.   *The Early Chartered Companies.*

Chalmers, G.   *An Estimate of the Comparative Strength of Britain* (ed. 1782).

Chamberlayne, E.   *Angliæ Notitia* (ed. 1700).

Chambers, R.   *Book of Days.*

Channing, E.   *A History of the United States.*

Chapman, S. J.　*The Lancashire Cotton Industry.*
Chappel, S.　*A Diamond or Rich Jewel presented to the Commonwealth of England* (1650).
*Charters of the Clothworkers' Company.*
Child, J.　*A Discourse about Trade* (1690).
　*A New Discourse of Trade* (4th ed.).
　*Brief Observations concerning Trade and Interest of Money* (1668).
Child, R.　*A Large Letter concerning the Defects and Remedies of English Husbandry* (1651).
*Chronicon Walteri de Hemingburgh* (ed. 1848).
Churchill, A. and J.　*A Collection of Voyages and Travels* (1704).
Clapham, J. H.　*An Economic History of Modern Britain.*
　*Industrial Organization in the Woollen and Worsted Industries of Yorkshire,* in *The Economic Journal* (1906).
　*The Spitalfields Acts,* in *The Economic Journal* (1916).
Clarendon, Lord.　*The History of the Rebellion* (ed. 1888).
　*The Life of Edward, Earl of Clarendon* (ed. 1827).
Clark, A.　*Working Life of Women in the Seventeenth Century.*
Clark, D. M.　*British Opinion and the American Revolution.*
Clark, G. N.　*The Dutch Alliance and the War against French Trade, 1688–1697.*
　*War Trade and Trade War, 1701–1713,* in *The Economic History Review,* vol. i. No. 2.
Clark, J.　*Agriculture of Herefordshire* (1794).
Clode, C. M.　*Early History of the Guild of Merchant Taylors.*
Coates, C.　*The History and Antiquities of Reading* (1802).
Cobbett, W.　*Parliamentary History.*
Coffler, D.　*Dissertatio juridica de Lana et Lanificis* (1682).
Coke, E.　*His Speech and Charge* (1607).
　*The Second Part of the Institutes* (ed. 1671).
Coke, R.　*A Detection of the Court and State of England* (ed. 1718).
　*A Treatise [Wherein is demonstrated that the Church and State of England are in Equal Danger with the Trade of it],* Parts i. and ii. (1671), Parts iii. and iv. (1675).
Collinges, J.　*The Weaver's Pocket Book or Weaving Spiritualized* (1675).
Collingwood, W. G.　*Elizabethan Keswick.*
Collins, J.　*A Plea for the bringing in of Irish Cattle* (1680).
　*Salt and Fishery* (1682).
Collinson, J.　*History of the County of Somerset* (1791).
*Commune Concilium tentum in Camera Guildhald* (1623).
Coode, G.　*The Report on the Law of Settlement and Removal,* in *Parliamentary Papers* (1851), xxvi.
Cooke, J.　*Unum Necessarium* (1648).
Cooke Taylor, W.　*Notes of a Tour in Lancashire* (1842).
Cooper, W. D.　*Smuggling in Sussex,* in *Sussex Archæological Collections,* vol. x.
Corbet, J.　*An Historical Relation of the Military Government of Gloucester* (1645).
*Court Minutes of the East India Company,* ed. H. Stevens and E. B. Sainsbury.
*Court Rolls of the Manor of Wimbledon.*
Cox : see *Northampton.*
*Coventry Leet Book,* ed. M. D. Harris.
Cowper, J.　*An Essay proving that Inclosing Commons and Common Field Lands is contrary to the Interest of the Nation* (1732).
*Cowper, T.　*A Short Essay upon Trade in General* (1741).

---

* See vol. iii. 398.

Cradocke, F.  *Wealth Discovered* (1661).
Cromwell, T.  *History of Colchester* (1825).
Crowley, A. and J.  *The Law Book* (British Museum :  Additional MS. 34555).
Crowley, R.  *Epigrammes.*
Cunningham, W.  *Alien Immigrants.*
   *The Growth of English Industry and Commerce :  Modern Times* (Part i., ed. 1907 ; Part ii., ed. 1912).
Curtler, W. H. R.  *The Enclosure and Redistribution of our Land.*

Dale, H. B.  *The Fellowship of Woodmongers.*
Dalton, M.  *The Country Justice* (ed. 1705).
Daniels, G. W.  *The Early English Cotton Industry.*
Darell, J.  *Mr Courtens Catastrophe* (1652).
   *Strange News from th'Indies* (1652).
Davenant, C.  *Works* (ed. 1771).
Davies, D.  *The Case of Labourers in Husbandry* (1795).
Davies, E.  *The Small Landowner, 1780–1832,* in *The Economic History Review,* vol. i. No. 1.
Davis, R.  *Agriculture of Oxfordshire* (1794).
Davis, T.  *Agriculture of Wiltshire* (1794).
Decker, M.  *An Essay on the Causes of the Decline of the Foreign Trade* (ed. 1744).
Defoe, D.  *A Plan of the English Commerce* (ed. 1728).
   *A True Collection of the Writings* (ed. 1703).
   *An Essay upon Projects* (1697).
   *Giving Alms No Charity* (1704).
   *Parochial Tyranny* (? 1727).
   *The Complete English Tradesman* (ed. 1727).
   „        „        „        „        (ed. 1732).
   *The Freeholders' Plea against Stock-jobbing Elections of Parliament Men* (1701).
   *The Villany of Stock-Jobbers Detected* (1701).
   *Tour of Great Britain* (ed. 1724).
   „        „        „        (ed. 1725).
   „        „        „        (ed. 1727).
   *Works* (ed. 1869).
Dekker, T.  *Greevous Grones for the Poore* (1621).
Dendy : see *Newcastle,* and *Records.*
D'Ewes, S.  *The Journals of all the Parliaments during the Reign of Queen Elizabeth* (1682).
De Witt, J.  *The True Interest of Holland* (ed. 1746).
Dickens : see *All.*
*Dictionary of National Biography.*
*Dictionary of Political Economy.*
Digges, D.  *The Defence of Trade* (1615).
Dionysius Periegetes.  *The Survey of the World* (ed. 1572).
*Discourse of the Common Weal of this Realm of England,* ed. E. Lamond.
*Documents relative to the Colonial History of the State of New York.*
Dowell, S.  *A History of Taxation* (ed. 1888).
Drayton, M.  *Polyolbion* (1613).
Dryden, J.  *Tragedy of Amboyna.*
Dudley, D.  *Mettallum Martis* (1665).
Dugdale, W.  *The History of Imbanking and Drayning of Divers Fens and Marshes* (1662).
Duncan, J.  *Essays on the Art of Weaving* (1808).
Dunlop, J.  *English Apprenticeship.*

Dunn, M. *View of the Coal Trade* (1844).
Dunning, R. *Bread for the Poor* (1698).
Dunsford, M. *Historical Memoirs of Tiverton* (1790).
Dyer, J. *The Fleece* (1757).

*Early Voyages and Travels to Russia and Persia* (Hakluyt Society Publications).
Easton, H. T. *The History of a Banking House (Smith, Payne and Smiths)*.
*Economic History Review*.
*Economic Journal*.
Eden, F. M. *The State of the Poor* (1797).
Ehrenberg, R. *Hamburg und England im Zeitalter der Königin Elisabeth*.
    *Capital and Finance in the Age of the Renaissance*.
Elder, J. R. *The Royal Fishery Companies of the Seventeenth Century*.
Ellis, H. *Original Letters Illustrative of English History*.
Emmison, F. G. *Poor Relief Accounts of Two Rural Parishes in Bedford-shire, 1563–1598*, in *The Economic History Review*, vol. iii. No. 1.
*English Factories in India, 1618–1621*, ed. W. Foster.
*English Garner*, ed. A. Lang.
*English Historical Review*.
*English Reports*.
Epstein, M. *The Early History of the Levant Company*.
Ernle, Lord. *English Farming Past and Present*.
Espinasse, F. *Lancashire Worthies*.
Evelyn, J. *Diary*, ed. A. Dobson.
    *Navigation and Commerce* (1674).

Fabyan, R. *The New Chronicles of England and France* (ed. 1811).
Felkin, W. *A History of the Machine-Wrought Hosiery*.
Fell, A. *The Early Iron Industry of Furness*.
Fielding, H. *An Enquiry into the Causes of the late Increase of Robbers* (2nd ed. 1751).
Fiennes, C. *Through England on a Side Saddle*.
Firmin, T. *Some Proposals for the Imployment of the Poor* (1681).
*First Letter Book of the East India Company*, ed. G. Birdwood.
*First Report on Factories* (1833).
*First Report of the Commissioners appointed to inquire into the Municipal Corporations* (1835).
*First Report of the Commissioners for Inquiring into the State of Large Towns* (1844), xvii.
Firth : see *Acts*.
Fitzherbert, Master. *The Book of Husbandry* (ed. W. W. Skeat).
Fitzmaurice, Lord. *The Life of Sir William Petty*.
Fleming, A. P. M., and Brocklehurst, H. J. *A History of Engineering*.
Fletcher, I. *The Archæology of the West Cumberland Coal Trade*, in *Transactions of the Cumberland and Westmorland Antiquarian and Archæological Society*, vol. iii.
Fortrey, S. *England's Interest and Improvement* (1663).
Foster : see *English*, and *Letters*.
Fox Bourne, H. R. *English Merchants*.
French, G. J. *The Life and Times of Samuel Crompton* (ed. 1859).
Friis, A. *Alderman Cockayne's Project*.
Fuller, T. *The History of the Worthies of England* (ed. 1662).
        ,,          ,,          ,,      (ed. 1840).
    *The Holy State* (ed. 1642).
Furniss, E. S. *The Position of the Laborer in a System of Nationalism*.
Furnivall : see Harman, and Harrison.

AUTHORITIES 543

Galloway, R. L.   *Annals of Coal Mining.*
Galpin, W. F.   *The Grain Supply of England during the Napoleonic Period.*
Galton, F. W.   *Select Documents : The Tailoring Trade.*
Gardiner, R.   *England's Grievance Discovered, 1655* (ed. 1796).
Gardiner, S. R.   *History of England* (ed. 1883).
Gaskell, P.   *Artisans and Machinery* (1836).
Gatford, L.   *Publick Good without Private Interest* (1657).
Gay, E. F.   *The Midland Revolt,* in *Transactions of the Royal Historical Society,* N.S., vol. xviii.
Gee, J.   *The Trade and Navigation of Great Britain* (ed. 1730).
Gentleman, Tobias.   *England's Way to Win Wealth* (1614).
*Gentleman's Magazine.*
George, M. D.   *London Life in the Eighteenth Century.*
Gibbs, A. E.   *The Corporation Records of St. Albans.*
Giesecke, A. A.   *American Commercial Legislation before 1789.*
Gilbart, J. W.   *The History, Principles and Practice of Banking* (ed. 1882).
Gill, C.   *The Rise of the Irish Linen Industry.*
Glyde, J.   *The New Suffolk Garland* (1866).
Godfrey, M.   *A Short Account of the Bank of England.*
Godfrey : see *Book.*
Goldsmith, O.   *The Deserted Village.*
Gonner, E. C. K.   *Common Land and Inclosure.*
Googe, B.   *Foure Bookes of Husbandry* (1577).
Gorges, A.   *The Publicke Register for Generall Commerce* (1611).
Gower, J.   *Mirour de l'Omme,* ed. G. C. Macaulay.
Graham, W.   *The One Pound Note.*
Gras, N. S. B.   *The Early English Customs System.*
*The Evolution of the English Corn Market.*
See also Szelagowski.
Gray, A.   *A Treatise on Spinning Machinery* (1819).
Gray, W.   *Chorographia* (1649).
Green, V.   *The History and Antiquities of Worcester* (1796).
Griffith, G. T.   *Population Problems of the Age of Malthus.*
Gross, C.   *The Gild Merchant.*
Guest, R.   *A Compendious History of the Cotton Manufacture* (1823).
Guilford : see *Nottingham.*


Haines, R.   *Proposals for building in every county a Working Almshouse or Hospital* (1677).
Hakluyt, R.   *The Principal Navigations, Voyages, Traffiques and Discoveries of the English Nation* (ed. 1903-5).
Hale, M.   *A Discourse Touching Provision for the Poor* (1683).
Halhead, H.   *Inclosure Thrown Open* (1650).
Halifax, Marquess of.   *An Essay upon Taxes* (1693).
Hall, E.   *Chronicle* (ed. 1809).
Hall, H.   *A History of the Custom-Revenue in England* (ed. 1892).
*Society in the Elizabethan Age.*
Halliwell, J. O.   *The Norfolk Anthology* (1852).
Hamilton, A. H. A.   *Quarter Sessions from Queen Elizabeth to Queen Anne.*
Hamilton, H.   *The English Brass and Copper Industries to 1800.*
Hammond, J. L. and B.   *The Skilled Labourer.*
*The Village Labourer.*
Hansard.   *The Parliamentary Debates.*
Hardres, T.   *Reports of Cases adjudged in the Court of Exchequer* (1693).
Harford, W.   *Proposals for . . . A Working Almshouse* (1677).
*Harleian Miscellany,* ed. J. Malham.

Harlow, V. T.  *A History of Barbados, 1625–1685.*
Harman, T.  *Caveat, 1567*, ed. E. Viles and F. J. Furnivall.
Harris : see *Coventry.*
Harrison, W.  *Description of England*, ed. F. J. Furnivall.
Harte, W.  *Essays on Husbandry* (1764).
Hartlib, S.  *His Legacy of Husbandry* (1655).
   *The Complete Husbandman* (1659).
Hasbach, W.  *A History of the English Agricultural Labourer.*
Haskins, C.  *The Ancient Trade Guilds and Companies of Salisbury.*
Haslam, J.  *The Hand-loom Weaver's Daughter.*
Hasted, E.  *The History and Topographical Survey of the County of Kent*
   (1778).
Hawkins, R.  *A Discourse of the Nationall Excellencies of England* (1658).
*Hawkins' Voyages* (Hakluyt Society Publications).
Haynes, J.  *A View of the Present State of the Clothing Trade in England*
   (1706).
Hazlitt, W. C.  *The Livery Companies.*
Heaton, H.  *The Yorkshire Woollen and Worsted Industries.*  See *Letter*
   *Books.*
Herbert, W.  *The History of the Twelve Great Livery Companies.*
*Heresbach :* see Googe.
*Hertford County Records.*
Hertz, G. B.  *England and the Ostend Company*, in *The English Historical*
   *Review*, vol. xxii.
   *The English Silk Industry in the Eighteenth Century*, in *The English*
   *Historical Review*, vol. xxiv.
Hewins, W. A. S.  *English Trade and Finance.*
Hewitt, J.  *A Treatise upon Money, Coins and Exchange* (1740).
Hibbert, F. A.  *The Influence and Development of English Gilds.*
Hilton Price, F. G.  *A Handbook of London Bankers* (ed. 1891).
Hine, R. L.  *The History of Hitchin.*
Hirst, W.  *History of the Woollen Trade for the last Sixty Years* (1844).
*His Majesties Speach in the Starre-Chamber* (1616).
*Historiæ Anglicanæ Scriptores Quinque* (ed. 1687).
*Historical Manuscripts Commission Reports* (vols. **i.-ix.**): *Abergavenny,*
   *Ancaster, Bath, Beaufort, Beaulieu, Buccleuch, Buckinghamshire, Bury*
   *St. Edmunds, Carlisle, Charlemont, Cowper, Dartmouth, Denbigh,*
   *Downshire, Eglinton, Egmont, Egmont (Diary), Exeter, Finch, For-*
   *tescue, Franciscan, Gloucestershire, Grimsby, Hodgkin, Kenyon, Kings*
   *Lynn, Leeds, Le Fleming, Leyborne-Popham, Lincoln, Lonsdale, Lord*
   *de L'Isle and Dudley, Lothian, Middleton, Ormonde, Pepys, Polwarth,*
   *Portland, Rutland, Rye, Salisbury, Shrewsbury, Skrine, Somerset,*
   *Southampton, Stopford-Sackville, Stuart, Various* (vols. i.-viii.), *Veru-*
   *lam, Westmorland.*
\*Hitchcock, R.  *A Brief Note of the benefits that grow to this realm by the*
   *Observation of Fish Days* (1594).
   *A Pollitique Platt* (1580).
Hoare, C. M.  *The History of an East Anglian Soke.*
Holdsworth, W. S.  *A History of English Law.*
Holinshed, R.  *Chronicles* (ed. 1808).
*Home Office Papers (Calendars of).*
Homer, H.  *An Essay on . . . the Inclosure of Common Fields* (2nd ed.).
   *An Enquiry into the Means of Preserving and Improving the Publick*
   *Roads of this Kingdom* (1767).
Hostmen : see *Records.*

---

* See vol. iii. 118, note 4.

Houghton, J. *A Collection of Letters for the Improvement of Husbandry and Trade* (1682).

*England's Great Happiness: or a Dialogue between Content and Complaint* (1677).

*Husbandry and Trade Improved* (ed. 1727-1728).

*House of Commons Journals.*

*House of Lords Journals.*

*House of Lords MSS.*

Howes', John, *MS. 1582*, ed. W. Lempriere.

Howes, J. *A Ffamyliar and Frendly Discourse* (1587: ed. 1889).

Hughes, J. *Liverpool Banks and Bankers.*

Hull: see Petty.

Hume, D. *Essays*, ed. T. H. Green and T. H. Grose.

Hunter, J. *The History and Topography of Sheffield* (ed. 1819).

Hunter, W. W. *A History of British India.*

Hustler, J. *Observations upon the Bill for preventing the Exportation of Wool* (1787).

Hutchins, B. L., and Harrison, A. *A History of Factory Legislation.*

Illingworth, W. *An Inquiry into . . . Forestalling, Regrating, and Ingrossing* (1800).

ΙΧΘΥΟΘΗΡΑ, or *The Royal Trade of Fishing* (1662).

J. C. : see C.

Jackman, W. T. *The Development of Transportation in Modern England.*

James, J. *History of the Worsted Manufacture.*

James, M. *Social Problems and Policy during the Puritan Revolution.*

Jars, G. *Voyages métallurgiques* (1774).

Jenner, T. *London's Blame, if not its Shame* (1651).

Jessopp: see North.

Johnson, A. H. *The Disappearance of the Small Landowner.*

*The History of the Worshipful Company of the Drapers of London.*

Johnson, E. R. *History of Domestic and Foreign Commerce of the United States* (ed. 1922).

Johnson, T. *A Plea for Free-Men's Liberties or the Monopoly of the Eastland Merchants Anatomized* (1646).

*Journal of George Fox* (ed. 1852).

*Journal of the Derbyshire Archæological and Natural History Society.*

*Journal of the Statistical Society.*

Jupp, F. B., and Pocock, W. W., *The Worshipful Company of Carpenters.*

Justice, A. *A General Discourse of Commerce* (1707).

*A General Treatise of Monies and Exchanges* (1707).

†Kayll, R. *The Trades Increase* (1615).

Keith, T. *Commercial Relations of England and Scotland.*

Kennedy, W. *English Taxation, 1640-1799.*

Kent, N. *Agriculture of Norfolk* (1796).

*Hints to Gentlemen of Landed Property* (1775).

Keymor, J. *Observation made upon the Dutch Fishing about the year 1601.*

Khan, S. A. *The East India Trade in the Seventeenth Century.*

King, G. *Natural and Political Observations and Conclusions upon the State and Condition of England, 1696*, ed. G. Chalmers.

King: see *British Merchant.*

Kirby, J. *A Letter to a Member of Parliament* (1787).

Knowler, W. *The Earl of Strafforde's Letters and Despatches* (ed. 1739).

---

\* See vol. ii. 396, note 6.

† See vol. ii. 279.

*Knox, W.  Helps to a Right Decision upon the Merits of the late Treaty of Commerce with France (1787).
Korthals-Altes, J.  Sir Cornelius Vermuyden.
Kramer, S.  The English Craft Gilds.

Lambard, W.  A Perambulation of Kent (1576).
Lambe, S.  Seasonable Observations humbly offered to his Highness the Lord Protector (1657).
Lambert, J. M.  Two Thousand Years of Guild Life.
Lamond : see Discourse.
Lappenberg, J. M.  Urkundliche Geschichte des Hansischen Stahlhofes zu London.
Latimer, H.  Sermons (ed. 1844).
Latimer, J.  Merchant Venturers of Bristol.
Laurence, E.  The Duty of a Steward to his Lord (1727).
Laurence, J.  A New System of Agriculture (1726).
Law Quarterly Review.
Lawes, Customes and Ordinances of the Fellowshippe of Merchantes Adventurers, ed. W. E. Lingelbach.
Lee, J.  A Vindication of a Regulated Inclosure (1656).
Leland, J.  Itinerary, ed. L. T. Toulmin Smith.
Lempriere : see Howes.
Lennard, R.  Rural Northamptonshire under the Commonwealth.
Leonard, E. M.  The Early History of English Poor Relief.
    The Enclosure of Common Fields in the Seventeenth Century, in Transactions of the Royal Historical Society, N.S. vol. xix.
Letter Books of the City of London, ed. R. R. Sharpe.
Letter Books of Joseph Holroyd and Sam Hill, ed. H. Heaton.
Letters and Papers, Foreign and Domestic, of Henry VIII.
Letters received by the East India Company from its Servants in the East, ed. W. Foster.
Levi, L.  History of British Commerce (ed. 1872).
Levy, H.  Large and Small Holdings.
    Monopoly and Competition.
Lewis, G. R.  The Stannaries.
Liber Custumarum, ed. H. T. Riley.
Lingelbach : see Lawes.
Liverpool Municipal Records, ed. J. A. Picton.
Lipson, E.  The History of the Woollen and Worsted Industries.
    The Elections to the Exclusion Parliaments, in The English Historical Review (1913).
Lloyd, G. I. H.  The Cutlery Trades.
Lloyd, S.  The Lloyds of Birmingham (3rd ed.).
Locke, J.  Works (ed. 1801).
Lodge, E. C.  The Account Book of a Kentish Estate.
London Journal, The (1719).
Lord, E.  Industrial Experiments in the British Colonies of North America.
Lowndes, W.  An Essay for the Amendment of the Silver Coins (1695).
Luccock, J.  Wool (1805).

M. S. : see S.
Macaulay, T. B.  The History of England (ed. 1906).
McCulloch, J. R.  A Dictionary of Commerce (ed. 1882).
    Early English Tracts on Commerce.
    The Literature of Political Economy.
Mace, T.  Discourse concerning the Highways of England (1675).

---

* See vol. iii, 116, note 1.

MacInnes, C. M.   *The Early English Tobacco Trade.*
Macpherson, D.   *Annals of Commerce* (1806).
Maddison, R.   *England's Looking In and Out* (1640).
Malham : see *Harleian.*
Malynes, G. de.   *A Treatise of the Canker of England's Commonwealth* (1601).
    *Consuetudo vel Lex Mercatoria* (1622)
    *Saint George for England* (1601).
    *The Maintenance of Free Trade* (1622).
Man, J.   *The History of Reading.*
Manley, T.   *A Discourse shewing that the Exportation of Wool is Destructive to this Kingdom* (1677).
Mantoux, P.   *La Révolution industrielle.*
*Manufacturer, The* (1719).
Marius, J.   *Advice Concerning Bills of Exchange* (ed. 1655).
Markham, G.   *The English Husbandman* (1613).
Marshall, A.   *Industry and Trade* (ed. 1920).
    *Principles of Economics* (7th ed.).
Marshall, D.   *The English Poor in the Eighteenth Century.*
Marshall, T. H.   *Jethro Tull and the New Husbandry,* in *The Economic History Review,* vol. ii. No. 1.
Marshall, W.   *The Rural Economy of the West of England* (1796).
Martin, E. C.   *The English Establishments on the Gold Coast in the Second Half of the Eighteenth Century,* in *Transactions of the Royal Historical Society,* 4th ser. v. 167 *seq.*
Martin, J. B.   *" The Grasshopper " in Lombard Street.*
Marx, K.   *Capital.*
Matthew, F.   *A Mediterranean Passage by Water* (1670).
    *Of the Opening of Rivers for Navigation* (1656).
Matthews, P. W., and Tuke, A. W.   *History of Barclays Bank Limited.*
May, J.   *A Declaration of the Estate of Clothing* (1613).
Melville, L.   *The South Sea Bubble.*
*Merchants New Royal Exchange. A Law Book for English Merchants* (1604).
*Mercurius Publicus.*
Meteyard, E.   *The Life of Josiah Wedgwood.*
*Middlesex County Records,* vols. i.-iv.
*Middlesex County Records : Sessions Books, 1689–1709.*
Middleton, J.   *Agriculture of Middlesex* (1798).
Mill, J.   *The History of British India* (ed. 1858).
Mill, J. S.   *Principles of Political Economy,* ed. W. J. Ashley.
Milles, T.   *The Customers Replie* (1604).
Misselden, E.   *Free Trade* (1622).
    *The Circle of Commerce* (1623)
Moens, W. J. C.   *The Walloons and their Church at Norwich.*
Monson, W.   *Naval Tracts.*
Moore, A.   *Bread for the Poore* (1653).
Moore, J.   *A Target for Tillage* (1612).
Moore, J.   *The Crying Sin of England, of not Caring for the Poor* (1653).
    *A Reply to a Pamphlet intituled Considerations concerning Common Fields and Inclosures* (1653).
Morison, S. E.   *The Maritime History of Massachusetts.*
Morris, R. H.   *Chester in the Plantagenet and Tudor Reigns.*
Morse, H. B.   *The Chronicles of the East India Company Trading to China.*
Mortimer, J.   *Every Man his Own Broker* (ed. 1762).
Mun, T.   *A Discourse of Trade from England unto the East Indies* (1621).
    *England's Treasure by Forraign Trade* (1664).

Murdin, W.  *A Collection of State Papers relating to Affairs in the Reign of Queen Elizabeth* (1759).
Murray, A. E.  *A History of the Commercial and Financial Relations between England and Ireland.*

*Narratives of Voyages towards the North-West* (Hakluyt Society Publications).
Newbury, N.  *The Yeoman's Prerogative* (1652).
*Newcastle Merchant Adventurers*, ed. J. R. Boyle and F. W. Dendy.
Nicholls, H. G.  *Iron Making in the Forest of Dean.*
Nicolas, N. H.  *Memoirs of the Life and Times of Sir Christopher Hatton* (1847).
Noake, J.  *Worcester in Olden Times.*
Norden, J.  *The Surveyors Dialogue* (1607).
North, D.  *Discourses upon Trade* (1691).
North, R.  *A Discourse of the Poor* (ed. 1753).
    *The Lives of the Norths*, ed. A. Jessopp.
*Northampton Records*, vol. ii., ed. J. C. Cox.
Norton, G.  *Commentaries on the City of London* (1829).
*Nottingham Records*, ed. W. H. Stevenson, W. T. Baker, E. L. Guilford.
*Norwich Records*, vol. ii., ed. J. C. Tingey.
Noy, W.  *Reports and Cases* (1669).

O'Brien, G.  *The Economic History of Ireland in the Seventeenth Century.*
Ogden, J.  *A Description of Manchester* (1783).
*Orders set down for Blackwell Hall.*  2 James I.  By the Mayor.
*Orders for the Reliefe of the Poore* (1630).
*Orders and Directions* (January 163$\frac{9}{0}$).
*Orders devised by the especiall commandement of the Queenes Maiestie for the reliefe and stay of the present dearth of Graine within the Realme* (1586).
*Orders for the preventing and remedying of the Dearth of Grain* (1630).
*Ordinance for the Cutting and Selling of Wood* (1643).
*Ordinances of the Clothworkers' Company.*
*Original Letters Illustrative of English History*, ed. H. Ellis.
Owen, R.  *Report to the County of Lanark*, in *The Life of Robert Owen* (1858), supplementary vol. i. A.
    *The Life of Robert Owen.*  By Himself (ed. 1857–1858).
*Oxford Records*, ed. W. H. Turner.

Pamphlets : see end of Authorities.
Parker, H.  *Of a Free Trade* (1648).
*Parliamentary Papers.*
    (1802–3), v. : *Report from the Select Committee on the Petition of persons concerned in the Woollen Trade and Manufactures in the counties of Somerset, Wilts, and Gloucester.*
    (1802–3), v. : *Report from the Select Committee on the Petitions of Merchants and Manufacturers concerned in the Woollen Manufacture in the county of York and town of Halifax (York).*
    (1802–3), vii. : *Minutes of Evidence taken before the Select Committee on the Bill respecting the Laws relating to the Woollen Trade.*
    (1806), iii. : *Report on the State of the Woollen Manufacture of England.*
    (1871), xviii. : *Report on the Coal Trade*, iii.
Parry, C. H.  *The Practicability of producing in the British Isles Clothing Wool equal to that of Spain* (1800).
Penketham, J.  *Artachthos, A New Booke declaring the Assise or Weight of Bread* (1638).
Pennant, T.  *A Tour in Scotland and Voyage to the Hebrides, 1772* (ed. 1774).
    *Of London* (1790).

Penney, N.  *The Household Account Book of Sarah Fell.*
Pepys, S.  *Diary*, ed. H. B. Wheatley.
Petty, W.  *Economic Writings*, ed. C. H. Hull.
*Phœnix, The.*
Phillips, M.  *A History of Banks, Bankers and Banking in Northumberland, Durham and North Yorkshire.*
Picton : see *Liverpool.*
Plat, H.  *The Jewel House of Art and Nature* (1653).
Plattes, G.  *Practicall Husbandry Improved* (ed. 1656).
Plot, R.  *The Natural History of Staffordshire* (1686).
Pollexfen, J.  *England and East India inconsistent in their Manufactures* (1697).
Polwhele, R.  *History of Cornwall* (1803).
Porter, G. R.  *The Progress of the Nation* (ed. 1847).
Postan, M.  *Credit in Mediæval Trade* in *The Economic History Review,* vol. i. No. 2.
    *Private Financial Instruments in Mediæval England* in *Vierteljahrsschrift für Sozial- und Wirtschaftsgeschichte,* xxiii.
Postlethwayt, M.  *Dictionary of Trade and Commerce.*
Potter, W.  *The Trades-Man's Jewel* (1650).
Powel, J.  *The Assize of Bread* (ed. 1661).
Powell, R.  *Depopulation Arraigned* (1636).
Power, E. : see *Tudor.*
Pownall, T.  *Live and Let Live* (1787).
    *On the Bread Assize,* in *Annals of Agriculture,* vol. ix.
Pratt, E. A.  *A History of Inland Transport and Communication in England.*
*Premiums offered by the Society for the Encouragement of Arts, Manufactures and Commerce.*
Price, W. H.  *The English Patents of Monopoly.*
Price : see Hilton.
Primatt, S.  *The City and Country : Purchaser and Builder* (1667).
*Proceedings of the Society of Antiquaries of Scotland.*
*Proceedings of the Suffolk Institute of Archæology.*
*Public Health.*
Puckle, J.  *England's Path to Wealth and Honour* (1700).
Purchas, S.  *His Pilgrimes* (ed. 1905).
Pym, J.  *The Kingdome's Manifestation* (1643).

*Quarter Sessions Records for the County of Somerset.*
*Quarter Sessions Records* (The North Riding Record Society).
*Quarterly Journal of Economics.*
*Quarterly Review.*

Radcliffe, W.  *Origin of Power-loom Weaving* (1828).
Rae, J.  *Life of Adam Smith.*
Raines, F. R., and Sutton, C. W.  *Life of Humphrey Chetham.*
Rait : see *Acts.*
Raleigh, W.  *Works* (ed. 1829).
*Rates of Marchandizes as they are set downe in the Booke of Rates.*
Rathbone, H. M.  *Memoirs of R. Reynolds.*
*Reading Records,* ed. J. M. Guilding.
*Records of the Hostmen,* ed. F. W. Dendy.
Redhead, Laing, Marshall.  *Observations on the different Breeds of Sheep* (1792).
Rees, J. F.  *Mercantilism and the Colonies,* in *The Cambridge History of the British Empire,* vol. i.
*Remembrancia of the City of London.*

*Reports from the Committees of the House of Commons.*
*Report on the Hand-loom Weavers* (1834).
*Reports on the Hand-loom Weavers* (1840).
*Report on the Hand-loom Weavers* (1841).
*Report on the Coal Trade*, iii., in *Parliamentary Papers* (1871), xviii.
*Report on the State of the British Wool Trade*, in *Reports from Committees* (1828).
*Report on the State of the Woollen Manufacture of England*, in *Parliamentary Papers* (1806), iii.
*Report of the Earl of Sheffield to the Meeting at Lewes Wool Fair* (1816).
Reports : see *First*, and *Historical*, and *Second*.
Rey, C.   *Observations on Mr. Asgill's Brief Answer* (1719).
    *The Weavers' True Case, Or the Wearing of Printed Callicoes and Linen destructive to the Woollen and Silk Manufactures* (1719).
Reyce, R.   *Breviary of Suffolk* (1618: ed. 1902).
Ribton-Turner, C. J.   *A History of Vagrants and Vagrancy.*
Ricardo, J. L.   *The Anatomy of the Navigation Laws* (1847).
Ricart, R.   *The Maire of Bristowe is Kalendar*, ed. L. T. Toulmin Smith.
Richards, R. D.   *The Early History of Banking in England.*
Rickman, J.   *Comparative Account of the Population of Great Britain.*
Risdon, T.   *The Chorographical Description of Devon* (ed. 1811).
Roberts, G.   *Social History of the Southern Counties.*
Roberts, L.   *The Merchants Mappe of Commerce* (ed. 1638).
    *The Treasure of Traffike* (1641).
Robinson, H.   *Certain Proposals* (1652).
    *England's Safety in Trades Encrease* (1641).
Robinson : see *Rural.*
Roe, T.   *Journal of His Voyage to India.*
    *Sir Thomas Roe's Speech* (1641), in *Harleian Miscellany.*
Rogers, J. E. T.   *A History of Agriculture and Prices.*
    *Oxford City Documents.*
    *Six Centuries of Work and Wages* (ed. 1912).
    *The First Nine Years of the Bank of England.*
Rose, J. H.   *William Pitt and National Revival.*
*Rotuli Parliamentorum* (Record Commission, 1767).
Rovenzon, J.   *A Treatise of Mettallica* (1613).
Rowland, A. L., and Manhart, G. B.   *English Commerce and Exploration in the Reign of Elizabeth.*
Rozer, E.   *Reasons showing the desires of the Clothiers against ingrossing* (1648).
Ruding, R.   *Annals of the Coinage* (ed. 1840).
*Rural Economy in Yorkshire in 1641, being the Farming and Account Books of Henry Best*, ed. C. B. Robinson.
Rushworth, J.   *Historical Collections* (1721).
*Russia at the Close of the Sixteenth Century* (Hakluyt Society Publications).
Rye, W. B.   *England as seen by Foreigners.*
Rymer, T.   *Foedera.*


S. M.   *A Memoir of Edmund Cartwright.*
S. W., Gent.   *The Golden Fleece* (1656).
Sainsbury : see *Court.*
Salter : see *Some Early Tracts.*
Salzman, L. F.   *English Industries of the Middle Ages.*
Samuel, A. M.   *The Herring.*
Savine, A.   *English Monasteries on the Eve of Dissolution.*
Scarlett, J.   *The Stile of Exchanges* (1682).
Schanz, G.   *Englische Handelspolitik.*

Scott, W. R.   *Joint-Stock Companies.*
  *Records of a Scottish Cloth Manufactory at New Mills.*
Scrivenor, H.   *History of the Iron Trade* (ed. 1841).
*Second Report of the Commissioners appointed to inquire into the Municipal Corporations* (1837).
Sée, H.   *Modern Capitalism.*
Selden : See *Table Talk.*
Sellers : see *Acts,* and *York.*
Seyer, S.   *Memoirs of Bristol.*
Shakespeare, W.   *King Henry VIII.*
Sharpe : see *Letter.*
Shaw, W. A.   *The History of Currency* (2nd ed.).
  *Writers on English Monetary History.*
Sheffield, Earl of.   *Observations on the Manufactures, Trade and Present State of Ireland* (ed. 1785).
  *Observations on the Objections made to the Export of Wool from Great Britain to Ireland* (1800).
  See *Report.*
Sheppard, W.   *Of Corporations, Fraternities and Guilds* (1659).
  *Of the Office of the Clerk of the Market* (1665).
Shillington, V. M., and Chapman, A. B. W.   *The Commercial Relations of England and Portugal.*
Simon, J.   *English Sanitary Institutions.*
Sinclair, J.   *The History of the Public Revenue* (ed. 1801–1804).
Skeat : see Fitzherbert.
Skeel, C. A. J.   *The Canary Company,* in *The English Historical Review,* vol. xxxi.
Slater, G.   *The English Peasantry and the Enclosure of Common Fields.*
Smiles, S.   *The Huguenots.*
  *Men of Invention and Industry* (ed. 1884).
Smith, A.   *The Wealth of Nations,* ed. E. Cannan.
Smith, C.   *Three Tracts on the Corn Trade and Corn Laws* (ed. 1766).
Smith, J.   *Chronicon Rusticum-Commerciale* (ed. 1747).
Smith, S.   *A True Narration of the Royall Fishings of Great Britain and Ireland* (1641).
Smith, T.   *De Republica Anglorum,* ed. L. Alston.
*Some Early Tracts on Poor Relief,* ed. F. R. Salter.
Somers, Lord.   *Tracts* (ed. 1809–1815).
*Somersetshire Archæological and Natural History Society's Proceedings.*
Spedding : see Bacon.
*Speech of Randle Jackson on behalf of the Cloth-workers* (1806).
Standish, A.   *The Commons' Complaint* (1611).
  *New Directions for the Planting of Timber* (1613).
*Stanleye's Remedy.*
*State Papers America and West Indies.*
*State Papers Colonial.*
*State Papers Domestic.*
*State Papers East Indies.*
*State Papers Foreign.*
*State Papers Ireland.*
*State Papers Rome.*
*State Papers Spanish.*
*State Papers Thurloe.*
*State Papers Venetian.*
*Statutes at Large,* ed. C. Runnington (1786).
*Statutes [of the Realm]*—Record Commission, 1810.
*Statutes of the United Kingdom,* ed. T. E. Tomlins.

Steele, R.   *The Spinster : In Defence of the Woollen Manufactures* (1719).
Steele: see *Tudor.*
Stevens : see *Court.*
Stevenson: see *Nottingham.*
Stow, J.   *A Survey of London,* ed. C. L. Kingsford.
   *Annales* (ed. 1631).
*Stowe MSS.* (British Museum).
Stringer, M.   *Opera Mineralia Explicata* (1713).
Strype, J.   *Annals of the Reformation* (ed. 1824).
   *Ecclesiastical Memorials* (ed. 1822).
Sturtevant, S.   *Metallica, 1612* (ed. 1854).
*Sussex Archæological Collections.*
Szelagowski, A., and Gras, N. S. B.   *The Eastland Company in Prussia,*
   *1579–1585,* in *Transactions of the Royal Historical Society,* 3rd ser. vi.

*Table Talk of John Selden,* ed. F. Pollock.
Tawney, R. H.   *Religion and the Rise of Capitalism.*
   See *Tudor,* and Wilson.
Taylor, J.   *The Carriers' Cosmography* (1637).
Taylor, W. C. : see Cooke.
Temple, Sir R.   *Some Short Remarks upon Mr. Locke's Book* (1696), in
   Somers, *Tracts.*
Temple, W.   *A Refutation of Mr. Smith's Memoirs of Wool* (1750).
Tench, N.   *Reasons humbly Offered by the . . . . Eastland Merchants against*
   *the giving of a general Liberty to all persons whatsoever to export the*
   *English woollen manufacture whither they please* (1689).
*Tenth Report on Trades Unions* (1868).
Thomas, D.   *An Historical Account of the Rise and Growth of the West-*
   *India Colonies* (1690), in *Harleian Miscellany.*
Thomas, P. J.   *Mercantilism and the East India Trade.*
*Thoresby Society Publications.*
Thoresby, R.   *Topography of Leeds* (1715).
Thornton, H.   *An Enquiry into the Nature and Effects of the Paper Credit*
   *of Great Britain* (1802).
Timmins, S.   *Industrial History of Birmingham and the Midland Hardware*
   *District.*
Tingey : see Norwich.
Tooke, T.   *A History of Prices* (ed. 1857).
Toynbee, A.   *The Industrial Revolution.*
*Transactions of the Cumberland and Westmorland Antiquarian and Archæo-*
   *logical Society.*
*Transactions of the Devonshire Association.*
*Transactions of the Gaelic Society of Inverness.*
*Transactions of the Royal Historical Society.*
*Treasury Books (Calendar of ).*
Trevers, J.   *An Essay to the Restoring of our Decayed Trade* (1675).
Trigge, F.   *The Humble Petition* (1604).
Trotter, E.   *Seventeenth Century Life in the Country Parish.*
Tucker, J.   *An Essay on Trade* (1753) [*A Brief Essay on the advantages and*
   *disadvantages of Trade*].
   *Instructions* (ed. 1757).
   *The Manifold Causes of the Increase of the Poor* (1760).
*Tudor Economic Documents,* ed. R. H. Tawney and E. Power.
*Tudor and Stuart Proclamations,* ed. R. Steele.
Tuke, J.   *Agriculture of the North Riding of Yorkshire* (1800).
Tupling, G. H.   *The Economic History of Rossendale.*
Turnor, T.   *The Case of the Bankers and their Creditors* (ed. 1675).

*Ulster Journal of Archæology.*
Unwin, G.  *The Gilds and Companies of London.*
  *Industrial Organization.*
Unwin, G.  *Studies in Economic History.*
Unwin, G., Hulme, A., and Taylor, G.  *Samuel Oldknow and the Arkwrights.*

Vaughan, R.  *Most Approved and Long Experienced Water-Workes* (1610).
*\*Veneris* (1662).
Vermuyden, C.  *A Discourse touching the Drayning the Great Fennes* (1642). See also Korthals-Altes.
*Victoria County Histories* : *Bedfordshire, Berkshire, Buckinghamshire, Cumberland, Derbyshire, Durham, Essex, Gloucestershire, Hampshire, Hertfordshire, Lincolnshire, Middlesex, Nottinghamshire, Oxfordshire, Suffolk, Surrey, Sussex, Warwickshire, Worcestershire, Yorkshire.*
*Vierteljahrsschrift für Sozial- und Wirtschaftsgeschichte.*
Vinogradoff, P.  *The Collected Papers of Paul Vinogradoff.*
Violet, T.  *A True Discovery* (1650).
  *An Humble Declaration* (1643).
  *Humble Proposal against Transporting of Gold and Silver out of the Kingdom* (1661).
  *The Advancement of Merchandize* (1651).
*Voyage of Captain John Saris to Japan* (Hakluyt Society Publications).

W. S. : see S.
Walford, C.  *Gilds* (ed. 1888).
Walker, T.  *Original.*
Warner, R.  *History of Bath* (1801).
Washbourn : see *Bibliotheca.*
Watson, J.  *History of Halifax* (1775).
*Weaver, The* (1719).
Webb, S. and B.  *English Poor Law History.*
  *History of Trade Unionism* (ed. 1920).
  *Industrial Democracy* (ed. 1913).
  *The Parish and the County.*
  *The Assize of Bread,* in *The Economic Journal,* vol. xiv.
  *The King's Highway.*
Webber, S.  *A Short Account of the State of our Woollen Manufactures* (1739).
Weeden, W. B.  *Economic and Social History of New England.*
*Weekly Review.*
Welbourne, E.  *The Miners' Unions of Northumberland and Durham*
Welford, R.  *History of Newcastle.*
Westcote, T.  *A View of Devonshire in 1630* (ed. 1845).
Westerfield, R. B.  *Middlemen in English Business.*
Weston, R.  *A Discours of Husbandrie* (ed. 1652).
Wheatley : see Pepys.
Wheeler, J.  *A Treatise of Commerce* (1601).
Whitelock, B.  *Memorials of the English Affairs* (ed. 1853).
Whitelocke, B.  *A Proposal for preventing effectually the Exportation of Wool* (1695).
Whitworth, C.  *State of the Trade of Great Britain* (1776).
Wilkins, R.  *The Sope-Patentees of Londons Petition Opened and Explained* (1646).
  *A Looking-Glasse for Sope-Patentees* (1646).
Wilkins, H. J.  *Transcription of the Poor Book of the Tithings of Westbury-on-Trym, Stoke Bishop and Shirehampton.*

---

\* See vol. ii. 229, note 3.

Williams, W. M.  *The Founders' Company.*
Willsford, T.  *The Scales of Commerce* (1660).
Willson, B.  *The Great Company.*
Wilson, F. P.  *The Plague in Shakespeare's London.*
Wilson, T.  *A Discourse upon Usury*, ed. R. H. Tawney.
*Wiltshire Archæological and Natural History Magazine.*
Winstanley, J.  *An Appeal to the House of Commons* (1649).
  *A Letter to the Lord Fairfax* (1649).
  *A New-Yeers Gift for the Parliament and Armie* (1650).
Wood, A. C.  *The English Embassy at Constantinople, 1660-1762*, in *The English Historical Review*, vol. xl.
Wood, W.  *A Survey of Trade* (1718).
Woodcroft, B.  *Brief Biographies of Inventors.*
Woodford, W.  *A Representation of Great Evils arising by the Exportation of Wool.*
Worcester, Marquess of.  *A Century of Inventions* (1663).
Worlidge, J.  *Systema Agriculturae* (1669).
Wright, T.  *A History of Domestic Manners* (ed. 1871).
  *Queen Elizabeth and Her Times* (1838).


Yarranton, A.  *England's Improvement* (1677).
*York Merchant Adventurers*, ed. M. Sellers.
*Yorkshire Archæological and Topographical Association* (Record Series).
Young, A.  *Autobiography*, ed. M. Betham-Edwards.
  *Political Arithmetick* (1779).
  *The Farmer's Letters* (ed. 1768).
  *The Question of Wool Truly Stated* (1788).
  *Tour through the East* (ed. 1771).
  *Tour through the North* (ed. 1771).
  *Tour through the Southern Counties* (ed. 1772).
  *Travels in France*, ed. C. Maxwell.
  See also *Annals of Agriculture.*

## ANONYMOUS PAMPHLETS *

*A Brief Account of the Woollen Manufactory of England* (1708).
*A Brief History of Trade in England* (1702).
*A Brief State of the Question between the Printed and Painted Calicoes, and the Woollen and Silk Manufacture* (1719).
*A Dialogue or accidental discourse betwixt Mr. Alderman Abell & Richard Kilvert* (1641).
*A Digest of the Poor Laws* (1768).
*A Discourse concerning the East India Trade*, in Somers, *Tracts.*
*A Discourse consisting of Motives for the Enlargement and Freedom of Trade* (1645).
*A Further Examination of the Weavers' Pretences* (1719).
*A Letter from a Gentleman in Ireland to his Brother in England* (1677).
*A Letter from a Merchant . . . The Case of the British and Irish Manufacture of Linen* (1738).
*A Letter to a Friend concerning the East India Trade* (1696).
*A Petition presented unto His Majestie . . . By High Sheriffe of the County of Gloucester* (1643).
*A Proposal for Regulating and Advancing the Woollen Manufacture.*

---

* Pamphlets in the British Museum, in the Bodleian Library, Oxford, in the Cambridge University Library, and in the Goldsmiths' Library, London University.

*A Proposal Humbly Offered to the King and Parliament for raising a Considerable Sum of Money yearly to His Majesty.*

*A Record of some Worthie Proceedings in 1611* (1641).

*A Reply to a Pamphlet intituled Considerations concerning Common Fields and Inclosures* (1653).

*A Representation of the State of Trade of Ireland* (1750).

*A Second Humble Address from the Poor Weavers and Manufacturers to the Ladies.*

*A Short Account of the Present State of New England* (1690).

*A Short and True Relation concerning the Soap-business* (1641).

*A State of the Case . . . relating to the Rising . . . of the Weavers in the County of Gloucester* (1757).

*A Supplement* (1689) *to a former Treatise concerning the East India Trade,* printed 1681.

*A Treatise of Wool and the Manufacture of it* (1685).

*A Treatise wherein is Demonstrated that the East India Trade is the most national of all Foreign Trades.* By Φιλοπάτρις (1681).

*A True Discovery of the Projectors of the Wine Project* (1641).

*A True and Impartial Account of the South Sea Company* (1743).

*A True Relation of the Rise and Progress of the East India Company.*

*A Vindication of the Considerations concerning Common Fields and Inclosures* (1656).

*Abbreviate of the Weavers' Business* (1648).

*Aggravii Venetiani* (1697).

*An Abstract of the Master Taylors' Bill before the Honourable House of Commons, with the Journeymen's Observation on each Clause of the said Bill.*

*An Account of Several Workhouses* (ed. 1732).

*An Account of the French Usurpation upon the Trade of England.* By J. B. (1679).

*An Account of the Proceedings of the Merchants, Manufacturers and others concerned in the Wool and Woollen Trade of Great Britain* (1800).

*An Account of the late Design of buying up the Wool of Ireland in Company* (1674).

*An Alarum to England to prevent its Destruction by the loss of Trade and Navigation.* By W. C. (1700).

*An Answer to Two Letters concerning the East India Company* (1676).

*An Essay on the Improvement of the Woollen Manufacture.* By a Merchant (1741).

*An Essay on the Treaty of Commerce with France* (1713).

*An Essay on Wool and Woollen Manufacture for the Improvement of Trade* (1693).

*An Estimate of the Manners and Principles of the Times* (1757).

*An Humble Petition and Remonstrance concerning the insupportable grievance of the Transportation of Leather* (1641).

*An Inquiry into the Management of the Poor* (1767).

*An Olde Thrift Newly Revived.* By R. C. (1612).

*Anglia Restaurata.* By the Cheshire Weaver (1727).

*Angliæ Tutamen* (1695).

*Britain's Buss.* By E. S. (1615).

*Britannia Languens* (1680).

*Calculations of Taxes for a Family of each . . . Class for one year* (1756).

*Character, Object and Effects of Trades Unions* (1834).

*Considerations concerning Common Fields and Inclosures.* By Pseudomisus (1654).

*Considerations on the Propriety of imposing Taxes in the British Colonies* (1766).

*Considerations on Several Proposals for Preventing the Exportation of Wool* (1741).

*Considerations on Several Proposals lately made for the Better Maintenance of the Poor* (1752).

*Considerations on the East-India Trade* (1701).

*Considerations on Taxes as they are supposed to affect the Price of Labour* (1765).

*Considerations Touching Trade, with the Advance of the King's Revenue* (1641).

*Considerations upon a Bill for repealing the Code of Laws respecting the Woollen Manufacture* (1803).

*East India Trade : A True Narration* (? 1641).

*England's Wants ; Or Several Proposals probably Beneficial for England.* By a True Lover of His Country (1667).

*Essays on Several Subjects* (1769).

*Excidium Anglicae, or a View of the Fatal Consequences attending the Smuggling of Wool.* By a Cheshire Weaver (1727).

*Five Queries Humbly Tender'd Relating to the Bill for the Prohibiting the Consumption of the East-India Silks.*

*Leather : A Discourse tendered to the High Court of Parliament* (1629).

*Letters to the Lincolnshire Graziers.*

*Miscellaneous Reflections upon the Peace and its Consequences* (1749).

*News from Newcastle* (1651).

*Prince Butler's Tale : Representing the State of the Wool-Case, or the East-India Case truly Stated* (1699).

*Proposals and Reasons for Constituting a Council of Trade* (1701).

*Propositions for Improving the Manufactures . . . of Great Britain* (1763).

*Prospects on the Rubicon* (1787).

*Reasons against the Prohibiting the Wearing of East India and Persia Wrought Silks.*

*Reasons for a limited exportation of Wool* (1677).

*Reasons humbly offered by the Card-Makers and Wier-Drawers of Froome-Selwood.*

*Reasons for Preserving the Public Market of Blackwell Hall.*

*Reasons for restraining the Factors of Blackwell Hall from dealing in Spanish and English Wool.*

*Reasons humbly offered for excepting the Rivers of Elbe, Weser and Eyder out of the Bill for a General Liberty of Exporting the Woollen Manufactures of this Kingdom.*

*Reasons Humbly Offered for Restraining the Wearing of Wrought Silks, etc.*

*Reasons humbly shewing that . . . an exception of the Rivers Elbe, Weser and Eyder will make the Bill of no effect.*

*Reasons of the Decay of the Clothing Trade.* By a Wellwisher (1691).

*Reasons Presented to the Parliament for a more strict Prohibition of the Transportation of Wool.*

*Remarks on the . . . Necessity of preventing the Irish Wool being run* (1730).

*Remarks upon Mr. Webber's Scheme* (1741).

*Sea-coale, Char-coale, and Small-coale* (1643).

*Seasonable Observations on the Present Fatal Declension of the General Commerce of England* (1737).

*Serious considerations on the several High Duties* (1743).

*Short Notes and Observations drawn from the present decaying condition of this Kingdom in point of Trade* (1662).

*Some Considerations for Employing the Poor of this Kingdom.* By a Member of the House of Commons (1737).

*Some Few Letters selected from an Account of Workhouses and Charity Schools* (1728).

*Some Impartial Thoughts on the Woollen Manufacturies* (1742).

*Some Observations on the Petitions now before the House of Commons.*
*Some Thoughts on the Bill, etc.* (1698).
*Some Thoughts on the Woollen Manufactures of England* (1731).
*Subtilty and Cruelty ; or A True Relation of Sr Sackvile Crow* (? 1648).
*The Advantages of the Kingdom . . . under . . . the Merchant Adventurers of England.*
*The Argument against the Bill for Regulating the Stuffs in Norfolk and Norwich.*
*The Beaux Merchant : A Comedy.* By a Clothier (1714).
*The Belgicke Pismire* (1622).
*The Blackwell Hall Factors Case.*
*The Case between the Clothiers and Weavers.*
*The Case of the British and Irish Manufacture of Linen* (1738).
*The Case of the British Woollen Manufacturies.*
*The Case of the Commonalty of the Corporation of Weavers of London truly Stated.*
*The Case of His Majesty's Sugar Plantations.*
*The Case of the Linen Drapers and other Dealers in Printed Calicoes and Linen.*
*The Case of the Merchants and Clothiers . . . concerned in the free exportation of the woollen manufacture of England.*
*The Case of the Printing of Linen in Great Britain.*
*The Case of the Printers of Callicoes and Linens.*
*The Case of Several Thousand Poor of the Wool Manufacture.*
*The Case of the Weavers of the City of London.*
*The Cities Advocate* (1629).
*The Clothiers' Complaint* (1692).
*The Clothiers' Reason against . . . prohibiting . . . foreign Wool Cards.*
*The Commercial Restraints of Ireland Considered in a Series of Letters* (1780).
*The Consequences of Trade as to the Wealth and Strength of any Nation.* By A Draper of London (1740).
*The Contrast, or a Comparison between Our Woollen, Linen and Silk Manufactures.*
*The Declaration of Thomas Lord Fairfax and the rest of . . . York* (1645).
*The Deplorable Case of the Chief and other Agents or Officers . . . concerned in tho Preventing . . . the Exportation of the Wool.*
*The Drayner Confirmed* (1647).
*The East India Trade a most profitable Trade to the Kingdom* (1677).
*The Female Manufacturers' Complaint* (1720).
*The Firste Parte of Churchyardes Chippes* (1575).
*The Golden Fleece* (1739).
*The Grand Concern of England explained in Several Proposals* (1673).
*The Grasier's Complaint.* By A Lincolnshire Grasier (1726).
*The Groans of the Plantations* (1689).
*The Humble Petition of the Clothiers . . . of Suffolk and . . . Essex* (1642).
*The Humble Petition of the Poor Spinners* (1788).
*The Importance of the Ostend Company Consider'd* (1726).
*The Interest of England . . . considered in a Dialogue between Sir T. Flourishing, a Merchant, and T. Castdown, a Clothier* (1701).
*The Interest of England Considered in an Essay upon Wool* (1694).
*The Interest of England Consider'd with respect to the Woollen Manufactures* (1731).
*The Interest of Great Britain in Supplying Herself with Iron Impartially Considered.*
*The Just Complaints of the Poor Weavers Truly Represented* (1719).
*The Languishing State of our Woollen Manufacture, humbly represented to the Parliament.*
*The Last Discourse betwixt Master Abel & Master Kilvert* (1641).

*The Linen Drapers' Answer to . . . Mr. Cary his Essay on Trade.*
*The Merchants Avizo.* By J. B. (1607).
*The Merchants' Remonstrance.* By J. B. (1644).
*The Mystery of the New Fashioned Goldsmiths or Bankers* (1676).
*The Petition and Remonstrance of the . . . Merchants of London trading*
    *to the East Indies* (1628).
*The Petty Navy Royal.*
*The present Case of our English Wool.*
*The Present Interest of England Stated.* By a Lover of His Country (1671).
*The Present State of the British Empire* (1768).
*The Prevention of Poverty.* By R. H. (1674).
*The Prevention of Poverty ; or, New Proposals* (1677).
*The Regulations lately made concerning the Colonies* (1765).
*The Reply of the Card-Makers and English Wool-Clothiers to the Observations*
    *of the Spanish Wool-Clothiers.*
*The State of the Difference between the Clothiers and the City of London.*
    By D. S.
*The Stuff Weavers' Case against Printing Callicoes Examined.*
*The Substance of the Arguments for and against the Bill* (1698).
*The Trade of England Revived* (1681).
*The Trade with France, Italy, Spain and Portugal Considered* (1713).
*The Triumphant Weaver* (1682).
*The Use and Abuses of Money* (1671).
*The Valiant Weaver* (1685).
*The Vintners' Answer* (1642).
*The Wealth and Commerce of Great Britain considered* (1728).
*The Weavers' Garland.*
*The Weavers' Pretences Examined.* By a Merchant (1719).
*The Woodmongers Remonstrance.* By W. L. (1649).
*The World's Mistake in Oliver Cromwell* (1668).
*Two Letters and Several Calculations on the Sugar Colonies and Trade* (1738).
*Wool Encouraged without Exportation.* By a Wiltshire Clothier (1791).

# SUPPLEMENT TO THE AUTHORITIES

*A Discourse of the Growth of England in Populousness and Trade* (1689).
*Acts of Court of the Mercers' Company,* ed. L. Lyell.
*Acts of the Parliaments of Scotland* (ed. 1816).
*Advocate, The* (1651).
Allen : see Raistrick.
Ambrose, G.    *English Traders at Aleppo, 1658–1756,* in *The Economic History Review,* vol. iii. No. 2.
*An Enquiry into the Causes of the Present High Price of Provisions* (1767).
Andrews, C. M.    *The Colonial Period of American History.*
Ashton, T. S.    *An Eighteenth-Century Industrialist.*
*Autobiography of William Stout of Lancaster,* ed. J. Harland (1851).

Balderston : see *Thraliana.*
Bang, N. E., and Korst, K.    *Tabeller over Skibsfart og Varetransport gennem Øresund.*
Battie, J.    *The Merchants Remonstrance* (1644).
Baxter : see *Reliquiæ.*
Beloff, M.    *Public Order and Popular Disturbances.*
Bining, A. C.    *British Regulation of the Colonial Iron Industry.*
Birch, T.    *The History of the Royal Society* (1756).
Brassey, T.    *Work and Wages* (1872).
*Bristol Corporation of the Poor : Selected Records, 1696–1834,* ed. E. E. Butcher.
*Buckinghamshire Sessions Records,* ed. W. Le Hardy and G. L. Reckitt.
Butcher : see *Bristol.*

Chambers, J. D.    *Nottinghamshire in the Eighteenth Century.*
Clutterbuck, R.    *The History and Antiquities of the County of Hertford.*
Coate, M.    *Cornwall in the Great Civil War and Interregnum.*
*Commons Debates, 1621,* ed. W. Notestein, F. H. Relf, and H. Simpson.
*Company of Soapmakers, 1562–1642,* ed. H. E. Matthews.
Copnall, H. H.    *Nottinghamshire County Records.*
*Course of Exchange :* see *The Course.*
Cox, J. C.    *Three Centuries of Derbyshire Annals.*
Crump, H.    *Colonial Admiralty Jurisdiction in the Seventeenth Century.*
Cunnington : see *Records.*

Davies, D. S.    *The Records of the Mines Royal and the Mineral and Battery Works,* in *The Economic History Review,* vol. vi. No. 2.
Dean, F. M.    *Scottish Spinning Schools.*
Dechesne, L.    *L'Évolution Économique et Sociale de l'Industrie de la Laine en Angleterre.*
Dietz, F. C.    *English Public Finance, 1558–1641.*
*Discourse :* see *A Discourse.*

Dodd, A. H.   *The Story of an Elizabethan Monopoly*, in *Economica* (1929 : No. 26).
Dowdell, E. G.   *A Hundred Years of Quarter Sessions.*
DuBois, A. B.   *The English Business Company after the Bubble Act.*

*Economica.*
*Encyclopaedia of the Social Sciences.*
Engels, F.   *Die Lage der arbeitenden Klasse in England* (1845).
*Enquiry* : see *An Enquiry.*

*Facts and Factors in Economic History* [Presented to E. F. Gay].
Feavearyear, A. E.   *The Pound Sterling.*
Foster : see *Travels.*
Franklin, B.   *Works* (ed. 1887).
*Free Ports* (1652).
Furley, J. S.   *Quarter Sessions Government in Hampshire in the Seventeenth Century.*

G. M.   *The Citizens Complaint for Want of Trade* (1663) in *Fugitive Tracts*, second series (1875).
Gay, M. R.   *Aspects of Elizabethan Apprenticeship*, in *Facts and Factors in Economic History.*
Gilboy, E. W.   *Labour at Thornborough* in *The Economic History Review*, vol. iii. No. 3.
   *Wages in Eighteenth-Century England.*
Gonner, E. C. K.   *The Population of England in the Eighteenth Century*, in *Journal of the Royal Statistical Society*, new series, vol. lxxvi. part iii.
Gough, J. W.   *Mendip Mining Laws* (Somerset Record Society, vol. xlv.)
   *The Mines of Mendip.*
Gras, N. S. B.   *Types of Capitalism*, in *Facts and Factors in Economic History.*
Gretton, M. S.   *Oxfordshire Justices of the Peace in the Seventeenth Century.*

Hall, E.   *The Triumphaunt Reigne of Kyng Henry the VIII.* (ed. 1548).
Hardwick, C.   *History of Preston* (1857).
Hardy : see *Buckinghamshire.*
Hargreaves, E. L.   *The National Debt.*
Harland : see *Autobiography.*
Harper, L. A.   *The English Navigation Laws.*
Hartshorne, A.   *Old English Glasses.*
Heckscher, E. F.   *Mercantilism* (revised English edition, 1935).
Held, A.   *Zwei Bücher zur Socialen Geschichte Englands.*
Herbert, Lord E.   *The Life and Raigne of King Henry the Eighth* (1649).
Hewitson, A.   *Preston Court Leet Records.*
Holt : see *Report.*
Hoon, E. E.   *The Organization of the English Customs System, 1696–1786.*
Hoskins, W. G.   *Industry, Trade and People in Exeter, 1688–1800.*
Hughes, E.   *Studies in Administration and Finance.*
Humpherus, H.   *History of the Company of Watermen and Lightermen.*
Hutton, W.   *The History of Derby* (1791).

Jefferson, Thomas.   *The Writings*, ed. P. L. Ford.
   *The Writings*, ed. H. A. Washington.
Jenckes, A. L.   *The Origin, the Organization and the Location of the Staple of England.*

Jenkinson :  see *Surrey.*
Johnson, E. A. J.  *Predecessors of Adam Smith.*
Jones, P. E., and Judges, A. V.  *London Population in the Late Seventeenth Century,* in *The Economic History Review,* vol. vi. No. 1.
*Journal of the Royal Statistical Society.*
Judges :  see Jones.

Kelsall, R. K.  *A Century of Wage Assessment in Herefordshire,* in *The English Historical Review,* vol. lvii.
  *Wage Regulation under the Statute of Artificers.*
Keynes, J. M.  *A Treatise on Money.*
Korst :  see Bang.

Lennard, R.  *English Agriculture under Charles II :  The Evidence of the Royal Society's 'Enquiries',* in *The Economic History Review,* vol. iv. No. 1.
Longfield, A.  *Anglo-Irish Trade in the Sixteenth Century.*
  *Anglo-Irish Trade in the Sixteenth Century,* in *Proceedings of the Royal Irish Academy,* xxxvi., section C.
Lyell :  see *Acts.*

MacInnes, C. M.  *A Gateway of Empire.*
McLachlan, J. O.  *Trade and Peace with Old Spain, 1667–1750.*
Mann :  see Wadsworth.
*Marchants Humble Petition :*  see *The Marchants.*
Marsden, R. G.  *English Ships in the Reign of James I,* in *Transactions of the Royal Historical Society,* N.S., vol. xix.
Massie, J.  *Brief Observations and Calculations on the present high Prices of Provisions* (1765).
  *Calculations of Taxes for a Family of each Rank, Degree or Class for one year* (1756).
  *Observations on the New Cyder-Tax* (1764).
  *Ways and Means* (1757).
Matthews :  see *Company.*
Miege, G.  *The New State of England* (1691).
*Minutes of Proceedings in Quarter Sessions held for the Parts of Kesteven in the County of Lincoln,* ed. S. A. Peyton.
Moller, A.  *Coal-Mining in the Seventeenth Century,* in *Transactions of the Royal Historical Society,* 4th series, vol. viii.
Morant, P.  *The History and Antiquities of Colchester* (1748).
Murray, R.  *A Proposal for the Advancement of Trade* (1676).

Naumann, F.  *Central Europe.*
Nef, J. U.  *The Rise of the British Coal Industry.*
Nettels, C.  *British Policy and Colonial Money Supply,* in *The Economic History Review,* vol. iii. No. 2.
Notestein :  see *Commons.*

Ogg, D.  *England in the Reign of Charles II.*
*Ordinance Book of the Merchants of the Staple,* ed. E. E. Rich.
Owen, G.  *The Description of Pembrokeshire* (1603), ed. H. Owen.

Peyton :  see *Minutes.*
Philips, E.  *An Appeal to Common Sense* (1720).
  *The State of the Nation* (ed. 1726).
Pinchbeck, I.  *Women Workers and the Industrial Revolution.*

Plummer, A.　*The Witney Blanket Industry.*
Postlethwayt, M.　*Britain's Commercial Interest* (1757).
Povey, C.　*The Unhappiness of England as to its Trade* (1701).
Powell : see *Surrey.*
Pownall, T.　*The Administration of the Colonies* (1765).
*Proceedings of the Archæological Institute (Memoirs of Northumberland).*
*Proceedings of the Royal Irish Academy.*

*Quarter Sessions Records of the County of Northampton,* ed. J. Wake.

Raistrick, A.　*Two Centuries of Industrial Welfare.*
Raistrick, A., and Allen, E.　*The South Yorkshire Ironmasters,* in *The Economic History Review,* vol. ix. No. 2.
Ravenhill, W.　*The Case of the Company of Grocers Stated* (1682).
Read, C.　*Profits on the Recoinage of 1560–1561,* in *The Economic History Review,* vol. vi. No. 2.
Reckitt : see *Buckinghamshire.*
*Records of the County of Wiltshire,* ed. B. H. Cunnington.
Relf : see *Commons.*
*Reliquiæ Baxterianæ,* ed. M. Sylvester (1696).
*Report of all the Cases determined by Sir John Holt* (1738).
*Report of the Balfour Committee on Industry and Trade.*
Rich : see *Ordinance Book.*
Robertson, H. M.　*Aspects of the Rise of Economic Individualism.*

Sanderson : see *Travels.*
Schlatter, R. B.　*The Social Ideas of Religious Leaders, 1660–1688.*
Seeley, J. R.　*The Expansion of England* (ed. 1883).
Simpson : see *Commons.*
Smith, W.　*An Essay for Recovery of Trade* (1661).
*Some Memorials of the Controversie with the Woodmongers or Traders in Fuel from the year 1664 to this time* (1680).
*Some Thoughts concerning the better security of our Trade and Navigation* (1695).
*Somerset Record Society Publications.*
*Spectator, The.*
Sprat, T.　*The History of the Royal Society* (1667).
Stout : see *Autobiography.*
*Surrey Apprenticeships, 1711–1731,* ed. H. Jenkinson.
*Surrey Quarter Sessions Records,* ed. D. L. Powell and H. Jenkinson.
*Surrey Record Society Publications.*
Sutherland, L.　*A London Merchant.*
Sylvester : see *Reliquiæ.*

Taylor, E. G. R.　*Late Tudor and Early Stuart Geography.*
Taylor, T. J.　*The Archæology of the Coal Trade,* in *Proceedings of the Archæological Institute (Memoirs of Northumberland),* vol. i. (1852).
*The Course of Exchange between London and Paris before the Revolution* (1713).
*The Marchants Humble Petition and Remonstrance to his late Highnesse* (1659).
Thornton, G. A.　*A History of Clare, Suffolk.*
Thoroton, R.　*The Antiquities of Nottinghamshire* (1677).
*Thraliana,* ed. K. C. Balderston.
*Transactions of the Newcomen Society.*

*Travels of John Sanderson in the Levant,* ed. W. Foster.
Turton, R. B.    *The Alum Farm.*

Vanderlint, J.    *Money answers all Things* (1734).
Viner, J.    *Studies in the Theory of International Trade.*
Voltaire, F. M. A. de.    *Letters concerning the English Nation* (ed. 1733).
  *Le Siècle de Louis XIV* (ed. 1753).

Wadsworth, A. P., and Mann, J. de L.    *The Cotton Trade.*
Wagner, D. O.    *Coke and the Rise of Economic Liberalism,* in *The Economic
  History Review,* vol. vi. No. 1.
  *The Common Law and Free Enterprise,* in *The Economic History
  Review,* vol. vii. No. 2.
Wake : see *Quarter Sessions.*
Whiston, J.    *The Causes of our present Calamities in reference to the Trade
  of the Nation fully Discovered* (1696).
*Whiston's Merchants Weekly Remembrance of the Present Money Prices of
  their goods ashore* (1694).
Willan, T. S.    *River Navigation in England, 1600–1750.*
  *The English Coasting Trade.*
Williams, W. P.    *Reports of Cases in Chancery* (1826).
Williamson, J. A.    *The Ocean in English History.*
Wood, A. C.    *A History of the Levant Company.*

Young, W. A.    *Works Organization in the Seventeenth Century,* in *Transactions of the Newcomen Society,* vol. iv.

# INDEX

THE END

Printed in Great Britain by R. & R. CLARK, LIMITED, Edinburgh.